*Germany
and the American Revolution*
1770–1800

C'était comme la voix de Jean criant du fond du
désert que de nouveaux temps étaient proches.
—Alexis de Tocqueville, 1856

Die Deutschen haben in der Politik gedacht, was
die anderen Völker getan haben.
—Karl Marx, 1843/44

Germany
and the American Revolution
1770–1800

by HORST DIPPEL

A Sociohistorical Investigation of
Late Eighteenth-Century Political Thinking

Translated by BERNHARD A. UHLENDORF
With a Foreword by R. R. PALMER

Published for the
Institute of Early American History and Culture
Williamsburg, Virginia
by The University of North Carolina Press
Chapel Hill

The endpapers are a line photograph of an engraving by Johann Gottfried Abraham Frenzel: "Mt. Vernon in Virginia, Residence of the great George Washington, Commander of the armies of the U. States in the Revolutionary war" (n.p., n.d.). The wording of the caption suggests that the illustration was done before Washington's death, although evidence from Frenzel's biography would indicate that it was done in the early nineteenth century.
    Courtesy Universitätsbibliothek, Karl Marx University, Leipzig

The Institute of Early American History and Culture
is sponsored jointly by
The College of William and Mary
and The Colonial Williamsburg Foundation.

Copyright © 1977 by The University of North Carolina Press
All rights reserved
Manufactured in the United States of America
ISBN 0-8078-1301-X
Library of Congress Catalog Card Number 77-367

Library of Congress Cataloging in Publication Data

Dippel, Horst, 1942–
  Germany and the American Revolution, 1770–1800.

  Translation of Deutschland und die amerikanische
Revolution.
  Bibliography: p.
  Includes index.
  1. United States—History—Revolution, 1775–1783—
Influence. 2. United States—History—Revolution,
1775–1783—Foreign public opinion, German.
3. Germany—Intellectual life. 4. France—History—
Revolution, 1789–1799—Influence. 5. Public opinion—
Germany. I. Institute of Early American History and
Culture, Williamsburg, Va. II. Title.

E209.D5713   301.15'43'9733   77-367
ISBN 0-8078-1301-X

To GUDRUN, NICOLETTE, *and* ISABEL

Contents

Illustrations

Foreword

This is surely one of the most important books ever written on the impact in Europe of the American Revolution. Appearing in 1977, though representing the labors of many years, it will long stand as a constructive and influential contribution to the bicentennial observance of that event. It is welcome evidence of the vitality of American studies in Germany and could only have been written by a German scholar, for Horst Dippel, while fully at home with the American Revolution, tells us much about eighteenth-century Germany as well.

The author's work has changed my own thinking, persuading me that an "American dream" existed in Germany as much as in France, for which it has been more fully studied. To use the title of Durand Echeverria's work on the impact of the American Revolution in France, there was a "mirage in the West." The amount and variety of Mr. Dippel's evidence hardly leave the reader any other conclusion. But it is a merit of his work that he puts the "mirage" in context with other perceptions. In Germany there was more variety of opinion than in France. Partly because the electorate of Hanover, with its very active University of Göttingen, was still associated with the British crown, there were intelligent Germans who took the official British side in discussing the affairs of America. And besides the partisans, there were others of more scientific bent who had a hard-headed and informed knowledge of the United States. Mr. Dippel's book is among other things a study in the sociology of knowledge. He asks not only what certain people thought and why, but also what it was possible for them to know. He describes the difficulties in international communication, the role of the press and other "media," such as traveler's reports, and the timing and dissemination of news, trying thus to assess subjective opinion against objective standards.

While expanding and refreshing our understanding, the book also confirms ideas that have been held before and gives us added reason to believe what we suspected already. For example: That the revolt of the British North American colonies produced an immediate outburst of interest in Europe to an almost incredible degree. That this outburst was a step in the development of European political thinking and public opinion. That the Germans, excited though they were, were less interested than the French in the actual political and constitutional questions raised in the United States. That the idea of America was changed by the French Revolution: having seen how really violent and sweeping revolution might be, there were some who wondered whether revolution was a good thing or bad and so raised the question, still often asked, of whether the American Revolution was a revolution at all, and, if so, in what sense. That America nevertheless remained the haven of liberty and equality, the land of the common man. That the American Revolution was of universal significance, having a mission or message to the world. Indeed, Mr. Dippel supplements the conclusion reached by another German historian, Otto Vossler, fifty years ago. Vossler held that the idea of an American mission resulted more from the French Revolution than from the American. We can now feel that the American "mission" developed and grew in Germany as well.

These favorable conceptions of the United States and its revolutionary origins are seen by Mr. Dippel as "bourgeois," that is, most characteristically entertained by the German middle classes. The book is primarily a study of bourgeois ideas, not surprisingly, since the world of periodicals and books was a middle-class world into which members of the subliterate laboring classes and the leisured aristocracy only occasionally ventured. We do learn of the views of some noblemen, liberal or conservative, and what the diplomats were reporting to German princes from their stations in London, Paris, and The Hague. On the ideas of the subordinate classes there is less evidence, but thousands of ordinary Germans from Hesse and other principalities served the British in the War of Independence, and Mr. Dippel has examined the letters that some of them wrote home. Many of these Germans remained in America after the war, but most returned to their homeland. Going beyond written documents and attempting a rough quantitative study, the author finds a spurt of emigration to America in the 1780s from those regions of Germany where returned veterans spread their impressions of the new country across the sea. America thus seems to have attracted the working poor, whose ideas came by word of mouth. We are confirmed again in what we thought before, that already in the 1780s, as throughout the nineteenth century, it was generally the unprivileged classes in Europe, and not merely the bourgeoisie, who looked favorably on the United States, while the privileged classes were more skeptical or downright hostile.

The author's researches have been enormous, both in Germany and in the United States, and carried on in all kinds of sources, printed and unprinted, public and private. He has unearthed much that no student of the subject has found before, and he can offer an almost bewildering array of examples for any point. Since even the bibliography appended to the present volume cannot do justice to his findings, Mr. Dippel has published a separate *Americana Germanica*, which lists almost one thousand extant German titles on the subject, year by year, from 1770 to 1800.*

It is a pleasure to wish a happy reception to this truly distinguished work.

R. R. Palmer

*Horst Dippel, *Americana Germanica 1770–1800. Bibliographie deutscher Amerika-literatur* (Stuttgart, 1976).

Preface

Libri sui fati habent. The present study developed out of a doctoral dissertation accepted in February 1970 by the University of Cologne. A generous grant from the Institut für Europäische Geschichte in Mainz—for which I desire to thank the director of its Department of Universal History, Professor Karl Otmar Freiherr von Aretin—has allowed me to rework the entire text. However, to prepare an English version on this basis proved to be more difficult than anticipated, and as time went on I was able to incorporate important recent publications only to about 1973.

It would have been impossible for me to complete this study without the advice and support of all those who generously gave their help during the past years. My special gratitude goes to those archivists and librarians who so often made valuable material accessible to me and listened patiently to even my most exorbitant demands, and to the staff of the Cologne Stadt- und Universitätsbibliothek, without whose assistance it would have been impossible for me to find and use such an amount of widely scattered printed material. The financial support granted by the University of Cologne, the German Academic Exchange Service, and the German Association for American Studies enabled me to evaluate in situ material that would not otherwise have been available.

For valuable suggestions and criticisms which greatly improved this study I am especially obliged to: Erich Angermann; Freiherr von Aretin; Bernard Bailyn; Joachim Fischer; Ulrich Im Hof; Georg G. Iggers; Günter Kahle; Günter Moltmann; Richard B. Morris; Robert R. Palmer; Claus Scharf; Gerald Stourzh; and Rudolf Vierhaus. Helpful as they all were, the remaining errors are, of course, always mine. I am also grateful to my editors, James H. Hutson, Norman S. Fiering, David Ammerman, and Freiherr von Aretin, for considering this investigation worthy of incorporation into the outstanding publication series of the Institute of Early American History and Culture at Williamsburg, Virginia, and of the Institut für Europäische Geschichte in Mainz. My special thanks go to Bernhard Uhlendorf, Norman Fiering, and the editorial staff of the Institute, who did their very best to transform the text into readable and intelligible English. This work would never have been completed without the encouragement, patience, and support of my dear wife.

A note on the text: Direct quotations from contemporary European sources have been translated into English in the text, and repeated in the original language in the footnotes. German and French spelling was adapted to modern usage.

Introduction

More than a hundred years ago Leopold von Ranke remarked that the American Revolution "exceeded in importance all earlier revolutions" because it was "a complete turnover in principle" of the basis of political power: the king, appointed by the grace of God, was replaced by a sovereign people.[1] Ranke thus put his finger on the one decisive distinction between the states of absolutist Europe at the end of the eighteenth century and the young republic in the New World. But if the difference between the two forms of statehood was truly so fundamental, we are confronted with an important question: Did contemporary Europeans, and especially those in Germany, who in various ways learned of events in the Western Hemisphere, recognize the difference clearly? And, more generally, what was the European reaction to the American Revolution as a contemporary event of worldwide political significance?

To be sure, these questions are not new; historians and social scientists have asked them frequently ever since Karl Biedermann introduced the problem at about the same time that Ranke made his observation.[2] In order to show the prevailing state of opinion in late eighteenth-century German intellectual life, Biedermann simply selected well-known public statements by outstanding figures. Most of his successors chose the same method, but they also tried to draw on the increasing amount of printed source materials to reinforce their line of argument. At the same time, however, they limited their frame of reference. For instance, Gerhard Desczyk, Paul C. Weber, Henry S. King, Ursula Wertheim, and Harold Jantz, as Germanists, stressed mainly what could be gleaned from contemporary belles lettres. Scholars like Herbert P. Gallinger, Guy S. Ford, and John A. Walz confined their investigations primarily to the field of journalism. Eugene E. Doll, who set himself the task of analyzing the attitudes of German historians contemporary with the American Revolution, was the only one to draw on

1. Ranke, *Über die Epochen der neueren Geschichte* (1854), ed. Theodor Schieder and Helmut Berding, in Ranke, *Aus Werk und Nachlaß*, ed. Walther Peter Fuchs and Theodor Schieder, II (Munich, 1971), 417.
2. Biedermann, "Die nordamerikanische und die französische Revolution in ihren Rückwirkungen auf Deutschland," *Zeitschrift für deutsche Kulturgeschichte*, III (1858), 483–495, 562–576, 654–668, 723–727.

a limited amount of manuscript sources and unpublished archival material. Finally, Elisha P. Douglass, one of the more recent investigators, has tried to expand the basis of study along Biedermann's line, laboring with that highly amorphous term *intellectual*.³

This is not the proper place to criticize such studies in detail. Most of these scholars produced valuable results that have led to better understanding of certain aspects of their respective fields of interest. But they did not succeed in plumbing the depths of the questions they asked, and, having only a limited knowledge of the sources, they could not always come up with acceptable answers. Moreover, these investigations had a common methodological characteristic: most of them were written by Americans whose paramount interest, for obvious reasons, was in compiling the largest possible number of individual opinions on the American Revolution and the new republic.

The present study unquestionably follows in the historiographical tradition characterized above. However, by employing a different method, it goes beyond the old framework to open up a wider prospect. I do not confine my analysis to the thoughts of outstanding late eighteenth-century German cultural figures. If we were only to investigate the opinions of men like Friedrich Gottlieb Klopstock, Johann Gottfried Herder, or Friedrich von Gentz, we would still have little idea of the impact of the American Revolution in Germany. Moreover, we would repeat a mistake often made

3. Desczyk, "Amerika in der Phantasie deutscher Dichter," *Deutsch-Amerikanische Geschichtsblätter*, XXIV–XXV (1925), 7–142; Weber, *America in Imaginative German Literature in the First Half of the Nineteenth Century* (New York, 1926) (refers also to the late 18th century); King, "Echoes of the American Revolution in German Literature," University of California, *Publications in Modern Philology* (hereafter cited as *PMP*), XIV (1930), 23–193; Wertheim, "Der amerikanische Unabhängigkeitskampf im Spiegel der zeitgenössischen deutschen Literatur," *Weimarer Beiträge*, III (1957), 429–470; Jantz, "Amerika im deutschen Dichten und Denken," in Wolfgang Stammler, ed., *Deutsche Philologie im Aufriß*, 2d ed., III (Berlin, 1962), 309–372; Gallinger, "Die Haltung der deutschen Publizistik zu dem amerikanischen Unabhängigkeitskriege, 1775–1783" (publ. Ph.D. diss., University of Leipzig, 1900); Ford, "Two German Publicists on the American Revolution," *Journal of English and Germanic Philology* (hereafter cited as *JEGP*), VIII (1909), 144–176; Walz, "The American Revolution and German Literature," *Modern Language Notes* (hereafter cited as *MLN*), XVI (1901), 336–351, 411–418, 449–462; Walz, "Three Swabian Journalists and the American Revolution," *Americana Germanica* (hereafter cited as *AG*), IV (1902), 95–129, 267–291, *German American Annals* (hereafter cited as *GAA*), N.S., I (1903), 209–224, 257–274, 347–356, 406–419, 593–600; Doll, "American History as Interpreted by German Historians from 1770 to 1815," American Philosophical Society, *Transactions* (hereafter cited as *APST*), N.S., XXXVIII (1948), 421–534; Douglass, "German Intellectuals and the American Revolution," *William and Mary Quarterly* (hereafter cited as *WMQ*), 3d Ser., XVII (1960), 200–218. Those studies cited so far are among the most important with regard to our questions. Further works, among them those by Constantin Breffka, Julius Goebel, James Taft Hatfield and Elfrieda Hochbaum, and Walter Wehe, will be referred to in the following pages.

in the eighteenth century, namely, trying to interpret this event merely as "an intellectual and philosophic phenomenon of the first magnitude."[4]

This study does not concentrate on the personal views of individuals, but rather on the problem of discovering the intellectual presuppositions, the epistemological limits, and the guiding interests behind the acquisition of political knowledge by social groups. The starting point of this investigation is the conviction that the late eighteenth-century German population consisted of groups, strata, orders, and estates, each of which held various and manifold views and ideas of its own. Dealing, as we are, with a heterogeneous society incorporating widely divergent and often contradictory interests, we cannot view the comments apart from the commentators and their social groups, especially in the case of an event as politically incisive as the American Revolution. This study will not, however, give equal consideration to the opinions of all social strata but will stress the bourgeoisie, although such an emphasis will necessitate frequent comparison with the opinions of the nobility and, whenever source material permits, with those of the petite bourgeoisie and the lower social strata.

Régine Robin has defined in detail what the term *bourgeoisie* meant, in a socioeconomic sense, in Europe before 1789:

Within the framework of the *ancien régime*, the bourgeoisie would be the class whose legal status was that of commoner and which encompassed everybody in the cities and in the country who was economically and socially in a dominant position in a capitalistic situation; . . . its members opposed those who were privileged and not part of their own social milieu, and they demanded, consciously or unconsciously, a different governmental structure, and, in the long run, a different social and economic organization of production. Nevertheless, its members could be incorporated into the seigniorial system by leaving their own sphere and entering the nobility as a rentier, by way of office or as a seignior, going through a more or less complicated *cursus honorum*.[5]

As we cannot speak in late eighteenth-century Germany of a firmly formed bourgeois class in any modern sense, the term *bourgeoisie* (*Bürgertum*) will be used more in a descriptive than an analytical way. Indeed, in Germany at the time, the term *Bürger* still waited for an accepted definition comparable to the French *bourgeois*.[6] Taking into account these problems, our investi-

---

4. Otto Vossler, *Die amerikanischen Revolutionsideale in ihrem Verhältnis zu den europäischen. Untersucht an Thomas Jefferson* (Munich, 1929), 8.

5. Robin, "Idéologies et bourgeoisie avant 1789," *La nouvelle critique*, N.S., XXXII (Mar. 1970), 48.

6. See Manfred Riedel, "Bürger, Staatsbürger, Bürgertum," in Otto Brunner, Werner Conze, and Reinhart Koselleck, eds., *Geschichtliche Grundbegriffe. Historisches Lexikon zur politisch-sozialen Sprache in Deutschland* (Stuttgart, 1972–), I, 683–702; for France com-

gation will center on contrasting the objective facts in America with the subjective opinions of German contemporaries. Thus, it will pose the question of whether the interpretation of an event generally believed to be of extreme importance (even though it happened at a vast distance from the observer) was really dependent on problems of communication and information or on the interests and the overall political or intellectual outlook of its observers. Was it the amount of information that cast the balance, or was this information preformed by the ultimate criteria of the interests and ideas of the onlookers?

These questions touch on what Jürgen Habermas has called the problem of "knowledge and interest," which requires that we take into account the degree of critical self-reflection practiced by those observing and judging events, for "the process of research is itself part of the objective context to be studied."[7] This problem must, of course, be discussed again and again in individual cases. Our example is the American Revolution. If there is indeed a connection between knowledge and interest, then examination of the way in which the German bourgeoisie debated some aspects of the American Revolution and ignored others, the way in which they interpreted and judged events, will provide information about their own political views. An analysis of the German bourgeoisie's confrontation with the American Revolution is, in the end, an exposition of its political consciousness, because, as Theodor W. Adorno argues convincingly, "Society becomes . . . a problem [for study or investigation] only to him who can imagine it to be different from what it is; only through recognition of its nonexistent qualities will society reveal itself for what it is."[8]

Mindful of such aims, this study will attempt to make a contribution to German social history and especially to a *histoire des mentalités* of Germany on the eve of and during the French Revolution. My intention is to arrive at a critical understanding of the political thinking of the German bourgeoisie during the last third of the eighteenth century. At the same time, I will of necessity place strong emphasis on the question of the impact of the American Revolution. Only when we are cognizant of the impression made in Europe by the actions of the American patriots and their opponents, and by

pare Régine Pernoud, *Histoire de la bourgeoisie en France*, Vol. II, *Les temps modernes* (Paris, 1962), 200–284, 607–611.

7. Habermas, "Analytische Wissenschaftstheorie und Dialektik," in Theodor W. Adorno *et al.*, *Der Positivismusstreit in der deutschen Soziologie*, 3d ed. (Neuwied and Berlin, 1971), 156. See also Habermas, "Erkenntnis und Interesse," in his *Technik und Wissenschaft als "Ideologie*," 4th ed. (Frankfurt, 1970), 164 and *passim*, and his *Erkenntnis und Interesse* (Frankfurt, 1968), 84 and *passim*.

8. Adorno, "Zur Logik der Sozialwissenschaften," in Adorno *et al.*, *Positivismusstreit*, 142.

the young republic, will we be able to appreciate the extent of the moral as well as material support that the colonies and states found in Europe during those years. Concerning the question of the repercussions of the American Revolution, which leaders in America at the time thought to be of great importance, this investigation will give an answer for a limited part of the Old World.

Although I speak of the American "Revolution" in this connection, I am fully aware of the continuing and often futile debate over whether the events that occurred in America between 1763 and 1787 can really be interpreted as a revolution. Certainly they did not constitute a social revolution in the latter-day sense of the word—as is demonstrated by the existence of Negro slavery into the second half of the nineteenth century—so that from today's point of view we are inclined to characterize it as a middle-of-the-road, if not conservative, event. The reason for this scholarly controversy is not solely the ambiguity of events in America; it also involves the absence of a conclusive definition of what constitutes a revolution and what must be considered its indispensable characteristics.[9] I do not intend to try to define the term in detail, but I think there are several factors that allow events in America during the years in question to be interpreted as a revolution in the true sense of the word.[10] The declaration of the natural rights of man and of popular sovereignty as fundamental constitutional principles; the establishment of the right to resist unlawful government as a basic legal principle; and the implementation of a republican and altogether new federal political structure—all of these innovations made the American Revolution a tremendously significant contribution to the development of modern constitutionalism, actively creating something new, even when compared with the situation in the colonies before 1776. I am of the opinion, therefore, that even with all the indicated reservations we may indeed speak of an American "revolution."

There may, in addition, be even more important grounds for using the term *revolution* in this context. It corresponds to contemporary usage before as well as during the French Revolution.[11] Since we are inquiring into

9. Compare among others Thomas C. Barrow's attempt to reach a definition, "The American Revolution as a Colonial War for Independence," *WMQ*, 3d Ser., XXV (1968), esp. 453.

10. See also Ernst Bloch, *Naturrecht und menschliche Würde* (Frankfurt, 1961), 194–200.

11. See, however, the errant opinion of Eugen Rosenstock, "Revolution als politischer Begriff in der Neuzeit," in *Festgabe für Paul Heilborn zum 70. Geburtstag* (Breslau, 1931), 113, that only after 1789 was it possible to describe the War of Independence as a "revolution," and that this term did not in fact appear until the beginning of the 19th century. On the impact of the American Revolution on the term *revolution* see Dippel, "The American Revolution and the Modern Concept of 'Revolution,'" in Erich Angermann *et al.*, eds., *New Wine in Old Skins: A Comparative View of Socio-Political Structures and Values Affecting the American Revolution* (Stuttgart, 1976), 115–134.

eighteenth-century comments and self-understanding, we are, I think, sufficiently justified in speaking of a revolution, even if it must be left to detailed analysis to show just what, according to the convictions of contemporaries, constituted the revolutionary character of American events.

One more term needs explanation, namely, the word *Germany*. For the eighteenth century the use of this name suggests two verses from Goethe and Schiller's set of epigrams, "Xenien":

> Germany? Tell me, where is it? For I do not know how to find it.
> Where culture begins, politics end.[12]

At that time there was no Germany, politically speaking. I do not use the word in a political sense but merely for the sake of convenience, to designate the German-speaking countries. I have included the German-speaking part of Switzerland simply because at the end of the eighteenth century, owing to similar socioeconomic conditions, there was a lively exchange of ideas between this region and the rest of the German-language area, as is illustrated by the careers of men like Albrecht von Haller, Johann Georg Sulzer, Johann Georg Zimmermann, and Johannes von Müller.

The temporal scope of this investigation is limited roughly to the years between 1770 and 1800. In 1770 the situation in America was critically exacerbated, and the events of this year were close enough to the war that they had some influence on the opinions of the German bourgeoisie about the American Revolution. Moreover, this year is often mentioned by historians as the beginning of a new phase in the development of political consciousness in Germany. The year 1800, which saw Thomas Jefferson's election as president, introduced a new stage in American history. In this year, too, Europe became aware of the death of Washington, the great military hero of the Revolutionary period. Moreover, German discussion relative to the formation of political parties in America reached its first climax, and for the first time a political *Amerikabild* developed, one independent of attitudes toward the Revolution. And then, in 1800, Friedrich von Gentz published the last great work comparing the American and the French revolutions, putting an end to the intellectual developments in this field for the time being.

There are several reasons for expanding the scope of this treatise beyond the years of the War of Independence or the period up to the federal Constitution. If the American Revolution had any influence on Germany at all, that influence most certainly did not suddenly end in 1783 or 1787, but continued to be effective through the period of the French Revolution. Our understanding of the influence of the American Revolution on the German bourgeoisie's

12. Schiller, *Werke*, National ed. (Weimar, 1943–), I, 320.

political consciousness will be more complete if we take into account how the events of the French Revolution affected its continued development. We all know how gigantic an impression the French Revolution left on European thinking. This study cannot bypass that fact; but we will have to see whether, in view of these occurrences, the German bourgeoisie thought about the American Revolution at all as a political matter in these later years. And while discussing the American Revolution, we will have to answer such questions as: What were the basic political opinions held by the German bourgeoisie in 1789? Did the French Revolution shed a different light on the events in America? Was the German experience of the American Revolution just a fleeting one, or did it have lasting effects?

To answer these questions, as well as a multitude of others, I have expanded considerably the number of primary and secondary sources consulted as compared with earlier analyses. I do not claim to have employed all available sources; the quantity of material alone forbade that. Only in the field of printed monographic literature have I tried to use as many works as possible. Since the total number of books about America that were printed in Germany during this period far exceeds that given in previous bibliographies, I have published separately a special bibliography of my own.[13] Furthermore, I have tried to evaluate as many newspapers, periodicals, letters, diaries, memoirs, and other printed source materials as my topic seemed to justify. Finally, I have searched the more important archives and libraries in the German-speaking countries, the United States, and London for manuscript material, public as well as private, and I am happy to report that I have succeeded in unearthing valuable material hitherto unknown to earlier scholars working in this field. Only the course of the investigation can prove to what extent these new materials are apt to broaden our knowledge of German political consciousness and the American Revolution.

13. Dippel, *Americana Germanica 1770–1800. Bibliographie deutscher Amerikaliteratur* (Stuttgart, 1976). The bibliography includes the complete titles of almost 1,000 books bearing on the territory that was in 1783 proclaimed the "United States of America," that is, it excludes books on California and Florida. Only those books are listed that contain at least one coherent passage (and not just scattered remarks) on America, the length varying according to the size of the publication. Included are all works of at least eight octavo pages published in German, and all foreign-language publications that were edited in the German-speaking part of Europe. The bibliography is based only on books still extant in a library in the United States or Europe; however, further editions mentioned in previous bibliographies have been added even when they could not be located in any library.

Abbreviations

REPOSITORIES

AAW	Archiv der Akademie der Wissenschaften, Göttingen
APSA	American Philosophical Society Archives, Philadelphia
APSL	American Philosophical Society Library, Philadelphia
DZA	Deutsches Zentralarchiv, Merseburg
GH	Gleimhaus, Halberstadt
GLA	Generallandesarchiv, Karlsruhe
GSA	Goethe- und Schiller-Archiv, Weimar
GStA	Geheimes Staatsarchiv, Munich
HHStA	Haus-, Hof- und Staatsarchiv, Vienna
HptStA	Hauptstaatsarchiv
	Hanover, Stuttgart, Wiesbaden
HVMF	Historischer Verein für Mittelfranken, Ansbach
KA	Kriegsarchiv
	Munich, Vienna
KB	Kantonsbibliothek, Aarau
LB	Landesbibliothek
	Gotha, Hanover, Karlsruhe, Kiel, Stuttgart
LC	Library of Congress, Washington, D.C.
MB	Murhardsche Bibliothek, Kassel
MHi	Massachusetts Historical Society, Boston
NA	National Archives, Washington, D.C.
NB	Nationalbibliothek, Vienna
NYPL	New York Public Library, New York
PHi	Pennsylvania Historical Society, Philadelphia
PRO	Public Record Office, London
StA	Staatsarchiv
	Aarau, Basel, Bern, Breslau, Coburg, Darmstadt, Dresden, Hamburg, Koblenz, Ludwigsburg, Marburg, Münster, Nuremberg, Oldenburg, Sigmaringen, Speyer, Wolfenbüttel, Würzburg
StadtA	Stadtarchiv
	Ansbach, Brunswick, Frankfurt, Korbach, Mainz
StadtB	Stadtbibliothek, Schaffhausen

SuUB	Staats- und Universitätsbibliothek Göttingen, Hamburg
UB	Universitätsbibliothek Freiburg, Kiel, Tübingen, Würzburg
YUL	Yale University Library
ZB	Zentralbibliothek, Zurich

PERIODICALS

AG	*Americana Germanica*
AGAO	*Archiv für Geschichte und Altertumskunde von Oberfranken*
AHR	*American Historical Review*
ALG	*Archiv für Literaturgeschichte*
APSP	American Philosophical Society, *Proceedings*
APST	American Philosophical Society, *Transactions*
FRA	*Fontes Rerum Austriacarum*
GAA	*German American Annals*
HZ	*Historische Zeitschrift*
JEGP	*Journal of English and Germanic Philology*
MLN	*Modern Language Notes*
PMHB	*Pennsylvania Magazine of History and Biography*
PMP	University of California, *Publications in Modern Philology*
WMQ	*William and Mary Quarterly*

PART I

The Interest
of the German Bourgeoisie
in the American Revolution

1. *The German Bourgeoisie Discover North America*

The View of America around 1770

Let us imagine that we are back in the year 1770 and that we ask a member of the German bourgeoisie to describe the New World. The likely answer would be: America is a land of savages. However startling, this would not be the singular view of an individual; on the contrary, contemporaries could refer to a considerable amount of earlier as well as current literature in support of this statement.[1] The entire Western Hemisphere tended to appear to the European onlooker as a still intact ethnological entity. Americans, as the Indians were called, lived everywhere on the continent; in comparison, the settlements of European colonists seemed to be a *quantité négligeable*. This view was confirmed by the opinion that the entire continent was most easily divided according to the living areas of the several major Indian nations.

Thinking of the historic civilizations of America, we remember the names of the Incas, Mayas, Aztecs, Toltecs, and others, that is, the representatives of the highly developed Indian cultures, whose former grandeur still amazes us. Late eighteenth-century Europeans, however, had different interests. All those who equated a simple and primitive way of life with the

---

1. See, e.g., [Georg Adam Dillinger], *Nach dem jetzigen Staat eingerichtete Bilder-Geographie* . . . (Nuremberg, 1770). Much the same may be said of the following works from the succeeding years: André Guillaume Contant d'Orville, *Geschichte der verschiedenen Völker des Erdbodens* . . ., 6 vols. (Hof and Leipzig, 1773–1778); [François Marie de Marsy and Adrien Richer], *Neuere Geschichte der Chineser, Japaner, Indianer, Persianer, Türken, Russen und Amerikaner etc.*, XIX–XXVI (Berlin, 1775–1777); Ludwig Adolph Baumann, *Abriß der Staatsverfassung der vornehmsten Länder in Amerika* (Brandenburg, 1776); [Johann Georg Purmann], *Sitten und Meinungen der Wilden in America*, 4 vols. (Frankfurt, 1777–1781); [Johann Gottlieb Lindemann], *Geschichte der Meinungen älterer und neuerer Völker*, 7 vols. (Stendal, 1784–1795); Friedrich Christian Franz, *Ueber die Kultur der Amerikaner* (Stuttgart, 1788); Philipp Wilhelm Gottlieb Hausleutner, *Gallerie der Nationen*, 4 vols. (Stuttgart and Ulm, [1792–1800]). The work by Dillinger saw two further editions, in 1773 and 1781; Marsy and Richer, Purmann, and Lindemann either appeared in reprint or went into a second edition.

lost paradise or the golden age of the past found their most persuasive example in the New World. At the same time, the imaginary "state of nature," as it had been glorified particularly by Rousseau, could best be illustrated by the example of America—an opinion shared by his supporters and opponents alike. But man's state of nature could not be exemplified by the civilized and culturally high-ranking inhabitants of the Mexican and Peruvian highlands of the time before the Spanish Conquest. Only the more primitive Indians of the eastern North and South American lowlands between Labrador and the La Plata area served this purpose. As in the first half of the sixteenth century, these were the tribes that fired the imagination of the European bourgeoisie of the late eighteenth century.[2]

The followers of Rousseau were not alone in believing that their views were confirmed in America. Rousseau's opponents also found proof in the New World for their arguments. The French count Georges Louis Leclerc de Buffon and the Dutch canon Corneille de Pauw obviously deserve to be mentioned here. Whereas the natural scientist Buffon at the beginning of the 1760s had stated very cautiously his hypothesis that the unhealthy climate of America would cause animal forms of life there to degenerate, the popular philosopher de Pauw succeeded around 1770 in formulating Buffon's thesis much more generally and efficaciously. In the New World, the alleged exemplary land of the state of nature, all life, according to de Pauw, was exposed to deterioration. Even man, including the European settler, would degenerate irresistibly. The conception of the ideal character of the state of nature was therefore nothing but an empty myth; only Europe, its culture and its luxury, embodied the desirable aims of mankind.[3]

2. In addition to the works already quoted see Preston A. Barba, "The American Indian in German Fiction," *GAA*, N.S., XI (1913), 143–174; also Friedrich Wilhelm Sixel, *Die deutsche Vorstellung vom Indianer in der ersten Hälfte des 16. Jahrhunderts* (Vatican City, 1966), 182–183, 206–216.

3. The works by Buffon, *Histoire naturelle générale et particulière*, and by de Pauw, *Recherches philosophiques sur les Américains*, as well as their refutations by Pernety, *Dissertation sur l'Amérique et les Américains*, and by Pazzi de Bonneville, *De l'Amérique et des Américains*, saw numerous editions in Germany in the 1770s. Among those disparaging de Pauw's views, see in particular Moses Mendelssohn to Johann David Michaelis, Apr. 10, 1771, in Michaelis, *Literarischer Briefwechsel*, ed. Johann Gottlieb Buhle, II (Leipzig, 1795), 546–547. Discussion of the whole controversy, and especially of de Pauw, can be found in: Bernard Fay, *L'Esprit révolutionnaire en France et aux États-Unis à la fin du XVIIIᵉ siècle* (Paris, 1925), 14; Gisbert Beyerhaus, "Abbé de Pauw und Friedrich der Große, eine Abrechnung mit Voltaire," *Historische Zeitschrift* (hereafter cited as *HZ*), CXXXIV (1926), 465–493; Henry Ward Church, "Corneille de Pauw, and the Controversy over his *Recherches Philosophiques sur les Américains*," Modern Language Association, *Publications*, LI (1936), 178–206; Gilbert Chinard, "Eighteenth-Century Theories on America as a Human Habitat," American Philosophical Society, *Proceedings* (hereafter cited as *APSP*), N.S., XCI (1947), 27–57; An-

This attack on the idealized American state of nature was aimed primarily, though indirectly, at a widespread European cultural fatigue and was inevitably bound to provoke contradictions, the echoes of which could be heard well into the nineteenth century.[4] However, Buffon's and de Pauw's theory of degeneration embraced a second view, namely, that it was not Europe but the uncivilized savage that exemplified decadence. Inevitably, this assertion also met widespread resistance, for it stood in sharp contradiction to the popular conception of the noble savage. The idol of natural man, untouched by civilization and its rules of behavior, typified the thinking of the late eighteenth century just as much as it had in the first half of the sixteenth century.[5] Up to the end of the eighteenth century, poems and other forms of literary expression reflecting this image continued to appear: in the work of Christian Friedrich Daniel Schubart or, later, in Schiller's "Nadowessische Totenklage," and in Johann Gottfried Seume's famous exclamation, "See, we savages are better men after all!"[6]

These opinions show that from the German point of view at the beginning of the 1770s, America was still a distant, strange land, about which very little was known. This situation favored the poet or novelist, since it enabled him to transfer to the New World idealized actions that would have seemed incredible in a European environment; characters from America could be made to turn up suddenly in Europe, or Europeans might vanish conveniently in the New World. What may have been an advantage to an author, however, was a disadvantage to the majority of his fellow citizens; even after the continent was no longer regarded exclusively as the land of the Indians, ignorance about America abounded.

Thus, had we limited our initial fictitious question to the northern part of the hemisphere, we might have received the following answer: America is divided into Canada and Florida, which in turn may be subdivided into

---

tonello Gerbi, *La Disputa del Nuevo Mundo. Historia de una polémica 1750–1900*, trans. from the Italian by Antonio Alatorre (Mexico City and Buenos Aires, 1960), 29, 93; Lewis Hanke, *Aristotle and the American Indian: A Study of Race Prejudice in the Modern World* (Chicago, 1959), 92–93.

4. Durand Echeverria, *Mirage in the West: A History of the French Image of American Society to 1815* (1957; repr. Princeton, N.J., 1968), 4, 8–13, 29–30. Jefferson also criticized Buffon seriously in the years following 1783; see, e.g., Julian P. Boyd *et al.*, eds., *The Papers of Thomas Jefferson* (Princeton, N.J., 1950–), VI, *passim*.

5. On the discrepancy between the European ideal and the American reality see Bernard W. Sheehan, "Paradise and the Noble Savage in Jeffersonian Thought," *WMQ*, 3d Ser., XXVI (1969), esp. 342–343. In addition to Sixel's *Deutsche Vorstellung vom Indianer*, see Lee E. Huddleston, *Origins of the American Indians: European Concepts, 1492–1729* (Austin, Tex., 1967), for a discussion of earlier views.

6. Seume, "Der Wilde," in his *Sämmtliche Werke*, 4th ed., VII (Leipzig, 1839), 75.

English, Spanish, and French possessions.[7] This statement does represent distinct progress beyond the antiquated conception that America was almost solely a land of the Indians. It must amaze us, however, that in 1770 it was still possible to write of, for example, French Canada, completely disregarding the changes brought about by the Seven Years' War (known in the American colonies as the French and Indian War) and the events of subsequent years. German contemporaries, however, had reason enough to be thankful if their children studied school books whose information was not outdated by decades.[8]

These examples show how limited was general knowledge of North America around 1770 and how little of what was known corresponded to fact. About the political and geographical structure of the continent, which must be the basis for any further and detailed understanding, the German bourgeoisie had very little information. Nor was knowledge significantly greater within those circles that had contact with emigrants in North America. We find, for instance, a notation in a Württemberg record that many subjects had "emigrated to the American Island Pen-Sylvania."[9] This example reveals, to be sure, a level of information that did permit acquaintance with a few outstanding names, but not enough to integrate these names into an adequate picture of the context.

7. German geographies of the period include: Johann Heinrich Zopf, *Neueste Geographie nach allen vier Theilen der Welt . . .*, new ed., 2 vols. (Leipzig, 1770); [Anton Michael Zeplichal], *Neueste Geographie zum Gebrauche der Jugend*, 2 vols. (Breslau, 1774); Johann Gottfried Schenk, *Geographische Tabellen zum Gebrauche der Anfänger*, 2d ed. (Dresden and Leipzig, [1775]); [Georg Friedrich Sebaldt], *Kurzes Lehrbuch der Historie und Geographie, zum nützlichen Gebrauch niederer Schulen für die allerersten Anfänger auf die leichteste Art entworfen* (Nuremberg, 1775); [Daniel Vogel], *Neues Geographisches Handbuch zum Unterricht der Jugend eingerichtet* (Breslau, 1775); [Lorenz von Westenrieder], *Erdbeschreibung für die churbaierischen Realschulen* (Munich, 1776); Johann Georg Bayer, *Die Geographie im Kleinen, in deutsche Verse gebracht* (Breslau, 1777).

8. See among others *Kurze Vorstellung der ganzen Welt, oder Atlas cosmographiae portatilis. Zum Unterricht der Jugend in ein und dreyßig Landkarten beschrieben* (Nuremberg, 1780); Johann Gottlieb Volkelt, *Kurze Erdbeschreibung zum Gebrauch der Landcharten für die Jugend . . .*, 2d ed. (Breslau, 1791); Christian Benedikt Milke, *Geographie, tabellarisch eingekleidet zum Schul-Gebrauch* (Leipzig and Altona, 1792).

9. "in die Americanische Insul Pen-Sylvanien emigriret": Abzug nach Pennsylvanien 1770 (Staatsarchiv [hereafter cited as StA], Ludwigsburg).

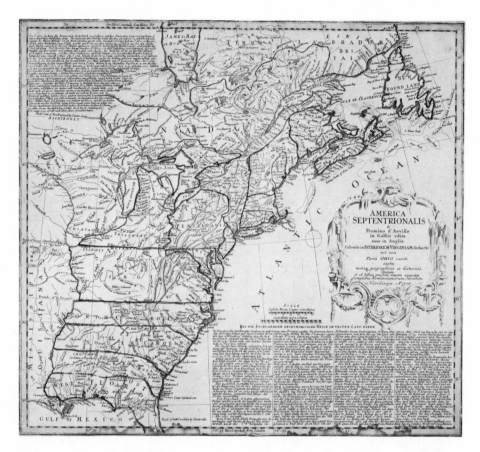

Figure 1. Jean Baptiste Bourguignon d'Anville, Map of North America. Published in Nuremberg in 1777, with accompanying text on the English possessions in North America.

Courtesy John Carter Brown Library, Brown University, Providence, R.I.

The Development of Interest in America
from 1770 to the Outbreak of the War

In general, German contemporaries in 1770 knew little about the America of their time. The entire continent was still widely regarded as a vague entity whose focal point, if any, was to be seen in its southern half, that is, in Latin America. For many, America was still a land of savages. However, the events of the preceding fifteen years began to have enduring effects on this conception, and the years after 1770 proved to be a significant turning point.

The Seven Years' War was not altogether without consequences in this respect.[10] The northeastern part of the American continent began to emerge from the whole and to gain importance in European eyes. But events during the late 1760s barely accelerated this process. The impulse, which necessarily had to come from America itself, was received too weakly in Germany. It cannot be assumed that the process of emergence took place within a few years, but the long-term development was beginning to take its course by 1770. Just before 1775 more news from the English colonies in North America began to come in. Even so, the circle of interested observers grew only slightly.

The situation changed abruptly with the outbreak of open conflict in America and the recruiting of troops in various parts of Germany. Now, suddenly, were "the eyes of almost all directed to this war."[11] Virtually overnight it had become an event "in which almost the whole of Europe took part in one way or another."[12] Speaking with greater breadth of experience, an observer later recalled: "The revolution in America became the affair of the civilized world. Every European citizen believed himself to be directly concerned with the outcome of this event."[13] What had been

10. The American theater of war naturally drew less attention than the battles in Germany. Thus, there is no account of a war in America in Johann Wilhelm von Archenholtz's *Geschichte des siebenjährigen Krieges in Deutschland von 1750 bis 1763*, repr. in 2 vols. (Berlin, 1793 [orig. publ. Mannheim, 1788]), the outstanding contemporary German work on the Seven Years' War that was reprinted for almost 150 years.

11. "fast aller Augen auf den Krieg hingerichtet": Johann Zinner, *Merkwürdige Briefe und Schriften der berühmtesten Generäle in Amerika...* (Augsburg, 1782), [3].

12. "an welchem beinahe das ganze Europa auf eine oder die andere Art teil[nahm]": German editor's preface to William Russell, *Geschichte des Ursprunges und des Fortganges des gegenwärtigen Streites zwischen England und seinen Colonien*, trans. from the English (Leipzig, 1780), iii. For similar statements see *Wienerisches Diarium*, Apr. 2, 1774; Jakob Rieger to Benjamin Franklin, Oct. 10, 1778 (Franklin Papers, XII, 40, American Philosophical Society Library [hereafter cited as APSL], Philadelphia).

13. "Die Revolution von Amerika wurde die Sache der zivilisierten Welt. Jeder Bürger

almost completely outside the contemporary European's field of vision suddenly moved into the center of the scene.

The neglect of the past years became acutely apparent. Information about the part of the continent affected by these happenings lagged hopelessly behind as interest rose by leaps and bounds. Who in German bourgeois circles, let alone in the lower strata of the population, was well informed about North America at the outbreak of the war, about the English colonies in the northeast, about their political and social structure and their economic situation?

The extent of ignorance among the rural population, which supplied by far the greatest number of auxiliary troops, cannot be overemphasized. Even the long and dangerous voyage across the Atlantic was often insufficient to instill a sense of the geographical location of the New World. The regimental surgeon Julius Friedrich Wasmus, encamped in Canada with Brunswick troops, reported that "the Spanish possessions in South America are called New Spain; our people often talk about this part of the world and firmly believe that Spain borders America, confusing the European and American Spain and assuming that it is possible to come by land from Spain to France and thence to Germany."[14] Desertions based on such geographical misinterpretations usually came to a sudden and tragic end at the St. Lawrence River. Thus, Johann Jakob Meyen hardly exaggerated when he later sang of the German auxiliary troops:

> Hired for pay, they came to a war they did not know;
> They did not know the climate, the Northern Sea
> And they hardly knew the name of this continent.[15]

To Hector Saint John de Crèvecoeur it was an established fact that German soldiers "had almost no knowledge of America."[16]

There is nothing to indicate that the majority of the urban bourgeoisie

---

von Europa glaubte sich unmittelbar beim Ausgange dieser Begebenheit interessiert": Friedrich Gentz, in his *Historisches Journal* (Berlin), I, no. 1 (1799), 286–287.

14. "Die spanischen Besitzungen in Südamerika werden Neuspanien genannt; unsere Leute unterhalten sich öfters miteinander von diesem Weltteile und glauben fest, daß Spanien an Amerika grenzt, irren sich aber in den europäischen und amerikanischen Spanien, glauben aber doch, daß es möglich sei, aus Spanien nach Frankreich und so weiter zu Lande nach Deutschland zu kommen": Aufzeichnungen des Feldschers Julius Friedrich Wasmus, II, 36, entry from July 27, 1776 (StA, Wolfenbüttel).

15. "Kamen um Lohn gedungen zum Kriege, den sie nicht kannten; / Das Klima kannten sie nicht, das Nordmeer nicht und dieses Weltteils / Namen kannten sie kaum": Meyen, *Franklin der Philosoph und Staatsmann. In fünf Gesängen* (Alt-Stettin, 1787), 87.

16. [Crèvecoeur], *Briefe eines Amerikanischen Landmanns an den Ritter W. S. in den Jahren 1770 bis 1781*, trans. from the English by Johann August Ephraim Goeze, 3 vols. (Leipzig, 1788–1789), III, 154.

in the mid-1770s were any better informed about America than their rural compatriots. An order from legal authorities in the Palatinate to an heir living in North America, summoning him to come to Horchheim within a period of nine months to take possession of a ridiculously small inheritance, shows what little understanding there was of geographic realities. Aware of the widespread ignorance of North America and its distance from Europe, August Ludwig Schlözer, a professor of history at the University of Göttingen, concluded that there was "an urgent need, not only for the German reader of newspapers but also for the German courts of law, to have available a geography of North America, so that nobody would imagine it to be something like North Holland or Northern Ditmarschen" (the western part of the former duchy of Holstein).[17] Schlözer's demand was entirely justified; the vast majority of the population, with their strictly limited mobility, were completely incapable of imagining the great distance to America. Indeed, the distance of anything beyond the familiar home and village was spatially incomprehensible to them, be it only "out there behind the hedge."[18]

The Period of the American War of Independence, 1775–1783

Considering the ignorance of the vast majority of the German bourgeoisie about even the simplest geographic facts concerning North America, we can imagine how little was known about the issues raised by the conflict between England and its American colonies. It was natural, therefore, that the suddenly awakened interest coincided with a general demand for information. Since America had become "such an important part of the world

17. "So ein dringendes Bedürfnis für den deutschen Zeitungsleser nicht nur, sondern auch für deutsche Justizhöfe ist eine Erdbeschreibung von Amerika, damit sich niemand unter Nordamerika so etwas wie Nordholland oder Norder-Ditmarsen denke": Schlözer, in his *Briefwechsel meist historischen und politischen Inhalts*, II, no. 8 (1777), 112. A similar case occurred nine years later; cf. Rosenthal to the government at Kassel, Zwesten, Aug. 2, 1786 (17 b Gef. 97ª, no. 6, fols. 425r–v, StA, Marburg).

18. Johann Christoph Krauseneck, *Die Werbung für England* (Bayreuth, 1776), 24. See also Friedrich Nicolai, ed., *Allgemeine deutsche Bibliothek* (Berlin and Stettin), XXI (1777), 497. Ignorance of geography, especially among the rural population, is discussed in Irene Jentsch, "Zur Geschichte des Zeitungslesens in Deutschland am Ende des 18. Jahrhunderts. Mit besonderer Berücksichtigung der gesellschaftlichen Formen des Zeitungslesens" (publ. Ph.D. diss., University of Leipzig, 1937), 12, and in Ludwig Maenner, *Bayern vor und in der Französischen Revolution* (Stuttgart, 1927), 45–48.

now,"[19] "everybody [was] extremely eager for reliable news from this distant part of the world."[20] For some, interest probably grew from a sense that the American Revolution presaged the future. According to Anton Friedrich Büsching's *Wöchentliche Nachrichten*, "everybody wants to learn all he can about the future republic of the united North American provinces right now, and therefore any publication that promises such knowledge is welcome."[21] Georg Christoph Lichtenberg, a professor at Göttingen, spoke for many when he expressed his eagerness for American news.[22] The Vienna court physician Jan Ingenhousz waited with similar impatience for any report from his friend Benjamin Franklin about the latest events.[23] Never before had there been such a close connection between the two continents; the latest European affairs were incomprehensible without knowledge of America. Schlözer's conception of the need sounds very modern: "Statesmen, scholars, and merchants, all must be at home in America, each for his different purpose."[24]

In the mid-1770s German politicians and statesmen were no more familiar with American affairs than scholars and merchants. However, after 1775 the governments of the larger German territories observed the conflict between England and its colonies with an interest at least as great as that in bourgeois circles. Early in 1775 the Bavarian minister Joseph Franz Maria Ignaz Graf (count) von Seinsheim remarked that in his circles America increasingly occupied everyone's mind. [25] In the following year his

19. "jetzt ein so wichtiger Weltteil": Christian Garve to Christian Felix Weiße, Mar. 11, 1775, in Garve, *Briefe von Christian Garve an Christian Felix Weiße und einige andere Freunde*, 2 vols. (Breslau, 1803), I, 119.

20. "jedermann nach zuverlässigen Nachrichten von diesem entfernten Weltteil äußerst begierig": [Johann Nikolaus Karl Buchenröder], *Gesammlete Nachrichten von den Englischen Kolonien in Nord-Amerika bis auf jetzige Zeiten* (Hamburg and Schwerin, 1776), iii.

21. "Freilich will jetzt jedermann die künftige Republik der vereinigten nordamerikanischen Provinzen zum voraus kennenlernen, und also ist eine jede Schrift, die dergleichen Kenntnis verspricht, willkommen": Anton Friedrich Büsching, ed., *Wöchentliche Nachrichten* (Berlin), Feb. 22, 1776, 70.

22. "Ich bin nunmehr sehr begierig auf amerikanische Nachrichten": Lichtenberg to Johann Andreas Schernhagen, Aug. 29, 1776, in Lichtenberg, *Briefe*, ed. Albert Leitzmann and Carl Schüddekopf, 3 vols. (Leipzig, 1901–1904), I, 261.

23. For similar remarks see his letters to Franklin, Dec. 5, 1780, Feb. 7, 1781 (Franklin Papers, XX, 106, XXI, 51, APSL, Philadelphia). Albrecht von Haller saluted a German translation of the *History of the Dominions in North America*: "Ein bei den jetzigen Vorfällen in Nordamerika willkommenes Werk" (*Göttingische Anzeigen von gelehrten Sachen*, Nov. 11, 1775 [no. 135], 1158).

24. "Staatsmänner, Gelehrte und Kaufleute, alle müssen, jeder nach verschiedenen Zwecken, in Amerika zu Hause sein": Schlözer's preface to his edition of [Daniel Fenning], *Neue Erdbeschreibung von ganz Amerika*, trans. from the English (not by Schlözer), 6 vols. (Göttingen and Leipzig, 1777), I, [1–2].

25. Seinsheim to Joseph Xaver Graf von Haslang, Jan. 22, Apr. 30, Oct. 1, 1775 (Bayerische Gesandtschaft, London, no. 253, Geheimes Staatsarchiv [hereafter cited as GStA], Munich).

colleague, Heinrich Anton Freiherr (baron) von Beckers von Wetterstetten of the Palatinate, observed: "Everywhere one speaks only about American affairs."[26]

The events in the New World aroused great interest not only in Munich and Mannheim (at this time the capital of the Palatinate); almost as much attention was paid to them at the other important German courts. As early as the spring of 1775 the Prussian foreign ministry expressed its keen interest in American developments.[27] And Frederick II of Prussia repeatedly asked his ambassadors in Western European countries to report about events in America.[28] He was especially eager for information from Friedrich Wilhelm von Thulemeyer, his ambassador at The Hague. Whereas the king had originally expressed a general interest in other news from the West as well, he told Thulemeyer in November 1775 to make it "his specific business to learn what is happening in the English colonies in America."[29]

A comparable degree of interest is revealed in the instructions of the Saxon minister, Heinrich Gottlieb von Stutterheim, to his Paris envoy, Johann Hilmar Adolph von Schönfeld. Stutterheim asked, rather harshly, why he should have to learn of the English surrender at Yorktown from the *Leipziger Zeitung*, which referred to Versailles sources, while the Saxon legation at Versailles obviously had no knowledge of the surrender at the time and reported it only several days later in their dispatches.[30]

The desire for news was equally intense among the bourgeoisie, but the sources of information generally available before 1775 proved totally inadequate to satisfy their demand for knowledge. William Robertson's deci-

26. "On ne parle partout que des affaires de l'Amérique": Beckers von Wetterstetten to Haslang, Sept. 14, 1776 (*ibid.*, no. 254).

27. Auswärtiges Departement to Joachim Karl Graf von Maltzahn, Mar. 18, 1775, and to Bernhard Wilhelm Freiherr von der Goltz, June 13, 1775 (Rep. XI. 73, conv. 129A, fol. 34, and Rep. XI. 89, fasc. 244, fol. 119, Deutsches Zentralarchiv [hereafter cited as DZA], Merseburg).

28. Royal instructions to the Prussian ambassador at The Hague, Friedrich Wilhelm von Thulemeyer, Sept. 7, Nov. 2, 20, 23, 1775, Apr. 21, 1777, Feb. 16, 1778, and to the minister at London, Spiridion Graf von Lusi, Aug. 22, 1781, in Gustav Berthold Volz, ed., *Politische Correspondenz Friedrichs des Grossen*, XXV–XLVI (Berlin, 1902–1939), XXXVII, 197, 315. For the unpublished dispatches see Rep. 96. 41B, vol. 14, fols. 252, 268; 41D, vol. 16, fol. 105; 41E, vol. 17, fol. 38; 36A, vol. 1, fol. 107, DZA, Merseburg. Further proof of the king's interest can be found in his marginal note to a letter telling of Arthur Lee's offer to supply him with information on events in America: "J'apprendrai volontiers de leurs nouvelles, surtout si elle leur sont favorables" (Friedrich Wilhelm Graf von der Schulenburg-Kehnert to Frederick II, July 6, 1777, in Volz, XXXIX, 248n).

29. "principalement à apprendre ce qui se passe dans les colonies anglaises d'Amérique": royal instruction to Thulemeyer, Nov. 9, 1775, in Volz, ed., *Politische Correspondenz Friedrichs des Grossen*, XXXVII, 290.

30. Stutterheim to Schönfeld, Dec. 23, 1781 (Loc. 2748, conv. 26, fols. 384r–v, StA, Dresden).

sion to postpone adding a description of the eighteenth-century English colonies in North America to his widely known *History of America* until after the present disturbances were over was generally regretted.[31] His neglect was the prime reason for the publication of a German edition of William Russell's *History of America*, the fourth volume of which was available separately under the title *Geschichte des Ursprunges und des Fortganges des gegenwärtigen Streites zwischen England und seinen Colonien*.

Numerous publications sought to supply the prevailing deficiency. In 1777 the historian Matthias Christian Sprengel gave as the reason for the publication of his *Briefe den gegenwärtigen Zustand von Nord America betreffend*: "These letters go to the public, for whom North American affairs are becoming increasingly interesting, in the hope that they contain some things that will make the conflict between Great Britain and its colonies easier to understand."[32] Two years later Johann Georg Meusel urged that this publication be continued, "since its subject occupies the general attention more than ever."[33] Even at the time of the Paris peace treaty, August Friedrich Wilhelm Crome wrote to Franklin, "Doubtless, Europe wishes nothing more than to acquire an exact knowledge of a country that people are hurrying to and that draws the attention of all merchants."[34] Crome began his book, which was published that same year, with the declaration, "Hardly any state has deserved so much attention at the time

31. Robertson, *Geschichte von Amerika*, trans. from the English by Johann Friedrich Schiller, 2 vols. (Leipzig, 1777), I, [9]. Similarly, see the German editor's preface to Russell, *Geschichte von Amerika*, trans. from the English, 4 vols. (Leipzig, 1779–1780), I, iii–iv; the translator's note to [Edmund Burke], *Beschreibung der Europäischen Kolonien in Amerika*, I (Leipzig, 1778), iv–v; Johann Heinrich Schinz to Johann Jakob Bodmer, Nov. 13, 1777 (MS. Bodmer, VIII, 485, Zentralbibliothek [hereafter cited as ZB], Zurich); and Johann Georg Meusel, ed., *Neueste Litteratur der Geschichtkunde*, I, no. 1 (1778), 15–18.

32. "Diese Briefe wagen sich mit der Hoffnung ins Publikum, daß sie vielleicht einiges enthalten, was deutschen Lesern, denen die nordamerikanischen Angelegenheiten immer interessanter werden, die Kenntnis der Kolonien und ihrer Streitigkeiten mit Großbritannien erleichtern möchte": [Sprengel], *Briefe den gegenwärtigen Zustand von Nord America betreffend* (Göttingen, 1777), [3–4]. See also Johann Christoph Gatterer, ed., *Historisches Journal* (Göttingen), VII (1776), 62; *Über den Aufstand der englischen Colonien in Amerika* (Frankfurt and Leipzig, 1776), 6.

33. "da ihr Gegenstand die allgemeine Aufmerksamkeit mehr als jemals beschäftigt": Meusel, ed., *Neueste Litteratur*, I, no. 2 (1779), 96. See also Christian Wilhelm Dohm, *Materialien für die Statistick und neuere Staatengeschichte*, 5 vols. (Lemgo, 1777–1785), I, [9], and the German publisher's preface to [Adrien Richer], *Neuere Geschichte von Amerika*, trans. from the French [by Friedrich Wilhelm Zachariä], 8 vols. (Berlin, 1778), I, [4].

34. "Sans doute que l'Europe ne souhaite rien tant que d'acquérir une connaissance exacte d'un pays où l'on se presse de se rendre, et qui attire l'attention de tous les commerçants": Mar. 4, 1783 (Franklin Papers, XXVII, 164, APSL, Philadelphia).

of its foundation and opened greater prospects to the entire civilized world than the republic of the united provinces in North America."[35]

Comparing the war years with the period before 1775, we find that America, at the perimeter of German interest during the first half of the 1770s, had become the topic of the day by the second half. Even though the extent of the interest that the German bourgeoisie had in American events cannot be measured in absolute figures, it is reflected in the quantity of related publications. Between 1770 and 1775 there appeared hardly more than twelve works per year in Germany and the German-speaking area of Europe that partially or totally concerned North America. But the number increased so abruptly that Andreas Friedrich Loewe could write on February 28, 1777: "Since the beginning of the present war an amazing number [of books] written in German or translated from the English language, big and little, good and bad, has been published."[36] More than forty publications appeared in both 1776 and 1777. Although by 1779 this number had decreased by more than half, it reached a new climax in 1783. Looking to the end of the century, we find that such a climax was reached only once more, in 1793. However, the number of publications never again decreased to the pre-1776 level.

These figures indicate not only a considerable increase in German interest in North America and the United States after 1775, but also a general increase in the production of books. If we compare the trend with the overall growth in the annual total of books published on all subjects in Germany at the semiannual book fairs during the same period, the years 1776–1777, 1783, and 1793 also come out slightly above the average. On the whole, both lines seem comparable. The total production of books in Germany increased rapidly during these years, more than doubling. Taking the average figure for literature on America published during the periods 1770 to 1775, 1776 to 1783, 1784 to 1788, and 1789 to 1800, we see a trend that corresponds roughly to the increase in total production. Although the percentage of Americana in the total production thus remains about the same, the war years nevertheless show a distinct deviation from the general

35. "Schwerlich hat irgend je ein Staat bei seiner Gründung so viel Aufmerksamkeit verdient und der ganzen kultivierten Welt größere Aussichten eröffnet als der Freistaat der vereinigten Provinzen in Nordamerika": Crome, *Über die Größe, Volksmenge, Clima und Fruchtbarkeit des Nordamerikanischen Freystaats* (Dessau and Leipzig, 1783), 1.

36. "Seit dem Anfange des jetzigen Krieges ist freilich eine erstaunliche Menge teutsch geschriebener und aus dem Engländischen übersetzter, großer und kleiner, guter und schlechter [Bücher] herausgekommen": [Loewe], *Historische und geographische Beschreibung der zwölf Vereinigten Kolonien von Nord-Amerika* (Bunzlau, 1777), [1].

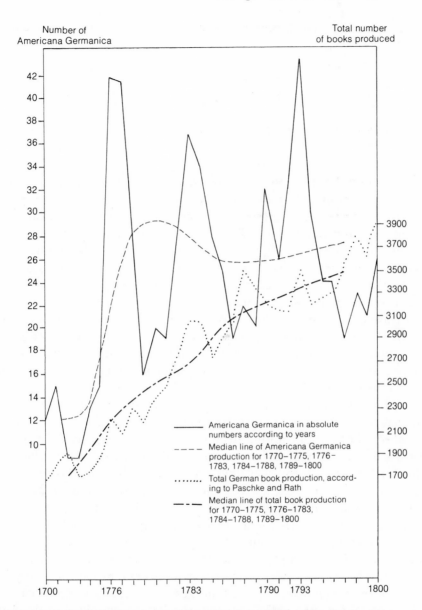

Chart 1. Number of Americana Germanica published in Germany as compared to total German book production, 1770–1800. Data on total book production is from Max Paschke and Philipp Rath, *Lehrbuch des Deutschen Buchhandels*, 5th ed., I (Leipzig, 1920), 68.

trend, confirming that the climax in interest was reached during the second half of the 1770s.[37]

Means of Communication

Despite the demand for knowledge, it was often difficult to obtain precise information. After all, America was faraway, and the road from the scene of action to the interested German onlooker was a long one. News therefore usually came indirectly. None of the German newspapers that I have examined had a permanent correspondent in North America during the war. To be sure, firsthand reports about America could occasionally be found in newspapers as well as in magazines; they probably came either from members of the German auxiliary troops or from emigrants (later, also from travelers), if indeed they had not simply been copied from another paper.[38] Government sources of information were not much better, since no German state had either official or unofficial representatives in North America at this time. Only rarely did publications by American authors reach Germany directly.

Today we have difficulty forming an adequate notion of the problems that plagued eighteenth-century communications. Reports, either written or oral—and often transmitted from person to person several times—were forwarded from the place of action to one of the harbors from which ships sailed for Europe. But this was only a first step in the transmission process, for not all problems were solved when the ship arrived at its destination after a long and often dangerous voyage across the Atlantic.

Because direct contact with the German capitals was seldom possible, the principal means of communication was via what we may call the news exchanges of Western Europe. News from America was received in London, Paris, and The Hague and passed on in newspapers, broadsides, or government reports. It is no coincidence that these three capitals in particular had such a central function. All three countries became involved in the American conflict in the course of time, and events there were of vital importance

37. Information on the number of books published annually for the book fairs is found in Max Paschke and Philipp Rath, *Lehrbuch des Deutschen Buchhandels*, 5th ed., I (Leipzig, 1920), 68.

38. See the avowal of the publisher of the Zurich *Freytags-Zeitung*, Dec. 19, 1783, regarding his practice of copying news from other newspapers.

to their governments. In addition, relatively liberal censorship legislation in England and the Netherlands favored the emergence of news and made the withholding of unwelcome facts difficult. The significance of these three cities as sources of information about America was further enhanced by the many works on America that were published there and then translated into German. The London news market, with its court newspaper as well as opposition papers, held the first rank among the three cities, particularly in view of the direct link between England and the rebellious colonies. But both the French capital and the Dutch gained in influence during the course of the war.

These three news exchanges were of decisive importance, not only answering the bourgeoisie's need for information, but also enabling the envoys of the governments of the larger German territories to gain a deeper insight into events. Because heads of states and their ministers were dependent on such reports, we understand why Frederick insisted on information from his envoy at The Hague and why Stutterheim censured his Paris chief of mission for failing to make better use of the sources available in the French capital.

The usual path of news from the American scene to Germany can be essentially reconstructed. Usually it came as third-, fourth-, or fifth-hand information and took weeks, or even months, to get there.[39] As a rule, four to six weeks passed before a message reached London, Paris, or The Hague. Obviously, it first reached northern or western Germany on its way east and south. In the meantime, however, it had become one or two weeks older. The transmission to the south or to the east took correspondingly longer; a report in a Hamburg newspaper might be read in a Zurich paper two weeks later. Even under the most favorable conditions, an American event could be known in Germany only about six weeks after its occurrence. News of the British surrender at Saratoga or at Yorktown (on October 17, 1777, and October 19, 1781, respectively) did not spread east of the Rhine until early December. In the case of Yorktown, news arrived in the north of Germany extraordinarily early, in the last days of November. If the event was less spectacular and the general situation more unfavorable, a greater delay could easily occur.

The distance between America and Germany added another disadvantage. A large proportion of the news coming into German-speaking countries was inaccurate, incomplete, or simply the propagation of a rumor that had arisen elsewhere. Final confirmation or denial entailed further delay, and even if it arrived quickly, the confusion of the observer was com-

39. For a similar observation with regard to France see Echeverria, *Mirage in the West,* 43.

pounded. Small details were too often neglected in view of the possible unreliability of the information, thus increasing interest in the general and the spectacular. While this situation favored the reporting of military events scattered over a vast territory, it afforded little opportunity for detailed analysis of day-to-day political and constitutional debates. Reconstruction of the political and social context of the Revolution was left instead to the reader.

2. *The Sources of Information*

Public Information

Germany as a Recipient of News

There were several means of transmitting reports from America to the contemporary German. Neglecting oral transmission and confining our attention to printed materials that were generally available, at least theoretically, we find a great number of newspapers, periodicals, and books that could serve the interested citizen as sources of information. Within certain limits, which will be discussed in detail, they were suited in form and content to their function of providing information. Since "at the end of the eighteenth century an increased interest in reading can be detected in all estates,"[1] we can assume a certain readiness to give attention to such news and reports.

However, there were important differences in the sources of information that were theoretically available to all. Among educated Germans, French was so widely known that it was not unusual for many to read French periodicals and books. Many works in French, including some on America, were published in Germany, some of them without an appearance in a German edition.[2] Thus, the educated had access to information within Germany itself that was not available to the less educated. The ability to draw on French-language sources gains additional importance in the German-speaking part of Switzerland, where knowledge of French was even more widespread than in the remainder of the German-language area.[3]

English was less widely read in Germany, even though there were certainly exceptions in those circles of Hanover, northwestern Germany, and

1. Jentsch, "Zeitungslesen in Deutschland," 14.
2. E.g., Guillaume-Thomas-François Raynal, *Considérations sur la paix de 1783* (Berlin, 1783); Gabriel Bonnot de Mably, *Observations sur le gouvernement des États-Unis d'Amérique* (Hamburg, 1784); Thomas Cooper, *Renseignemens sur l'Amérique* (Hamburg, 1795).
3. Dippel, *Americana Germanica*. As it was, only about 4% of all Americana was published by publishers whose central office was in the German part of Switzerland; of the Americana appearing in French, however, Swiss publications made up almost 20%. More than a quarter of all the Americana Germanica published in Switzerland appeared in French.

Switzerland that were oriented toward England. The number of works published in English in German-speaking areas was much smaller than the number published in French. Not one important book on America seems to have been published in Germany solely in an English version.[4]

The person who knew French or English obviously had much greater access to information than the monolingual reader, especially when sources from France and England, or even America itself, were available to him. This point must not be overlooked, even though it is rarely possible to demonstrate in individual cases the direct influence of sources of information from outside the German-speaking area. Certainly, the close ties of the Swiss bourgeoisie with French culture must have been a significant factor in shaping opinion.

We face a completely different set of problems when we turn to the lower classes. Their access to information was naturally limited. Moreover, their material and mental readiness to buy a newspaper, a periodical, or a book was probably far less than that of the upper classes. Still another obstacle made the acquisition of knowledge difficult for the lower classes. It is estimated that at the end of the eighteenth century 50 percent of the German population were illiterate. This figure was probably lower in the cities and in northern and central Germany than, for example, among the Bavarian rural population.[5] The illiterate had to depend on oral information alone; and if they had any comprehension of America at all, it was, to be sure, not very well grounded.

Neither the level of education nor the readiness to buy printed material was necessarily decisive, however. An aid for the expansion of the citizen's mental horizon that should not be underestimated was provided by the so-called readers' societies. Formed by the hundreds in German towns in the last three decades of the eighteenth century, they were a first stage in the development of the later rental libraries, and a small fee brought membership. As a rule, these *Lesegesellschaften* subscribed to the most important newspapers and periodicals and bought books that were of general interest, thus making available to the middle strata—sometimes including master artisans and retailers—far more information than an individual could have gathered on his own.[6]

Even the rural population and illiterates, in the end, did not entirely lack sources of information. In the late eighteenth century the village tavern

4. Only the small pamphlet *Some Short and Impartial Enquiries into the Propriety and Equity of the Present War in America* (Göttingen, 1778) seems to have been published in Germany solely in an English edition during these years.
5. Jentsch, "Zeitungslesen in Deutschland," 10.
6. *Ibid.*, 33.

served an important public function. In almost all taverns newspapers were read aloud to those present, and the contents could be discussed among the listeners. The information thus obtained may not have been very rich in content, but it was above the level that ordinarily would correspond to the education and financial situation of the less educated.[7] Institutions such as readers' societies and village taverns remind us that the distribution figures of a publication tell us little about the actual dissemination of its contents.[8]

Newspapers

Five political newspapers published in different German-speaking regions from 1770 through 1783 were chosen for this study. Each was of more than local importance and so provided information to a large number of citizens. From north to south they are: the *Hamburgischer Correspondent*, particularly in the 1790s, "undeniably the most read paper in Europe, 'an international paper', so to speak"[9]; the *Leipziger Zeitung*,[10] with its five issues per week; the *Frankfurter Oberpostamtszeitung*,[11] which, like the Hamburg paper, was published four times a week; the *Wienerische Diarium*,[12] which appeared twice a week; and the Zurich *Freytags-Zeitung*, as

7. *Ibid.*, 114–118.

8. *Ibid.*, 16–20, 28–84; Jürgen Habermas, *Strukturwandel der Öffentlichkeit. Untersuchungen zu einer Kategorie der bürgerlichen Gesellschaft*, 4th ed. (Neuwied, 1969), 84–85. See also Klaus Gerteis, "Bildung und Revolution: Die deutschen Lesegesellschaften am Ende des 18. Jahrhunderts," *Archiv für Kulturgeschichte*, LIII (1971), 127–139.

9. Ernst Baasch, *Geschichte des Hamburgischen Zeitungswesens von den Anfängen bis 1914* (Hamburg, 1930), 7. Frederick Hertz, *The Development of the German Public Mind: A Social History of German Political Sentiments, Aspirations and Ideas*, II (London, 1962), 402, maintains that the *Hamburgischer Correspondent* was printed in 1780 in 30,000 copies; see also Ludwig Salomon, *Geschichte des deutschen Zeitungswesens, von den ersten Anfängen bis zur Wiederaufrichtung des Deutschen Reiches*, 2d ed., I (Oldenburg and Leipzig, 1906), 141–142.

10. The acting editor of the *Leipziger Zeitung* during these years was Johann Christoph Adelung. See Cäsar Dietrich von Witzleben, *Geschichte der Leipziger Zeitung. Zur Erinnerung an das zweihundertjährige Bestehen der Zeitung* (Leipzig, 1860), esp. 47–59; Margot Lindemann, *Deutsche Presse bis 1815. Geschichte der deutschen Presse*, I (Berlin, 1969), 146–148; and, more recently, Gerhard Hense, "Leipziger Zeitung (1665–1918)," in Heinz-Dietrich Fischer, ed., *Deutsche Zeitungen des 17. bis 20. Jahrhunderts* (Pullach, 1972), esp. 82–83. Alfred Kröger, *Geburt der USA: German Newspaper Accounts of the American Revolution 1763–1783* (Madison, Wis., 1962), has cataloged the articles in this newspaper pertaining to the American Revolution.

11. See Salomon, *Deutsches Zeitungswesen*, I, 133–134. According to Otto Groth, *Die Zeitung. Ein System der Zeitungskunde (Journalistik)*, I (Mannheim, 1928), 243–244, the *Frankfurter Oberpostamtszeitung* reached a circulation of 5,543 copies in 1807.

12. In 1780 the name of the newspaper was changed to *Wiener Zeitung*; see Ernst Victor Zenker, *Geschichte der Wiener Journalistik von den Anfängen bis zum Jahre 1848. Ein Bei-*

important to German-speaking Switzerland as the Vienna newspaper was to the area south of the Main River, even though it appeared only once a week.[13]

The importance of these five newspapers must be understood relative to their time. A difference more decisive than frequency of appearance that distinguishes these eighteenth-century publications from comparable modern daily papers is that the political newspaper in Germany during that period still restricted itself to the simple transmission of news, without analysis or commentary. These newspapers were "institutions of news, but not yet institutions of public opinion."[14] In addition to the political newspapers, there were a limited number of *Intelligenzblätter* (newspapers containing mostly official announcements) and scholarly periodicals. Although unsuited by their very nature to transmit information concerning America, their occasional reports about the New World indicate the great interest that existed.[15]

The political newspapers, Johann Heinrich Voss tells us, were "full of America."[16] My sampling of newspapers confirms this; but the statement is not valid for the entire period under discussion. Until the late summer of 1770 there are repeated references to the unrest and tensions between England and its American possessions. In the subsequent months and years, however, the time intervals between reports become greater, until, especially in 1771 and 1772, America is sometimes almost completely out of the picture. Then, in May 1773, at about the time of Parliament's ratification of the Tea Act, the amount of news begins to increase, slowly at first, and then steadily increases during the following months. By the end of 1774, at the latest, America had become the most important topic in the German politi-

---

trag zur deutschen Culturgeschichte. Mit einem bibliographischen Anhang (Vienna and Leipzig, 1892), 31–32.

13. See Adolf Jacob, "Die Zürcherische Presse bis zur Helvetik," in *Beiträge zur Geschichte des Zürcherischen Zeitungswesens* (Zurich, 1908), 20–32. From 1784 to 1799 the *Freytags-Zeitung* was published under the name *Zürcher Zeitung*. With reference to its publisher, it is also called the *Bürkli-Zeitung*, in order to distinguish it from the *Zürcher Zeitung* published after 1780 by Robert Elsasser, which has appeared since 1821 under the title of *Neue Zürcher Zeitung*. See Fritz Blaser, ed., *Bibliographie der Schweizer Presse, mit Einschluß des Fürstentums Lichtensteins*, II (Basel, 1958), 742–743.

14. Franz Schneider, *Pressefreiheit und politische Öffentlichkeit. Studien zur politischen Geschichte Deutschlands bis 1848* (Neuwied, 1966), 77.

15. E.g., "Merkwürdigkeiten von Pensylvanien," *Wiener Realzeitung*, June 18, 25, 1776, and "Eine kurze Nachricht von Nord-Amerika. Aus des Major Roggers Beschreibung desselben. Ausgezogen durch B.," *Westphälische Beyträge* to the *Osnabrückische Intelligenzblätter*, Sept. 2, 9, 16, 1780, cols. 281–304.

16. "voll von Amerika": Johann Heinrich Voss, "Des Bräutigams Besuch. An F. H. Jacobi," in Voss and Leopold Friedrich Günter von Goeckingk, eds., *Musenalmanach für 1783* (Hamburg, 1782), 19.

cal newspapers. This rank was essentially maintained until 1783. Only the Bavarian War of Succession and France's entry into the American war made the New World, for a time, move a little into the background and leave the scene to European conflicts.

But what was the content of the reports that figured so prominently in the newspapers? During the first half of the 1770s the center of the news was occupied by actions of the Americans and reactions of the English government, including occasional reports of the political opposition in Great Britain. But a thorough airing of the arguments on both sides and of their political and juridical basis was missing. Instead, the papers usually reported, in a rather superficial manner, the most outstanding events, such as the disagreement on tea and its taxation, without examining the reasons in depth.[17] In subsequent years, under the impact of military events, the interest of the press shifted clearly to the war.

As in the period before 1775, the newspapers generally avoided taking a clear position in favor of one or the other of the disputing parties, since "the advantages that each party pretends to have gained over the other must be reported with impartiality."[18] This statement expressed not only a renunciation of editorial opinion but also a skepticism toward the reliability of the news received. In the effort to maintain balanced reporting, pro-American and pro-English passages were often placed side by side, as in the case of the *Hamburgischer Correspondent* and the *Frankfurter Oberpostamtszeitung*. But the other three newspapers appear to have received their news from a source in London that was closer to the Rockingham Whigs than to the court and government.[19]

The informational value of the newspapers as a whole must be judged on the basis of how much space they gave to social, political, and constitutional questions, for the events in America were more than a military conflict. However, only occasionally do we find news about the internal development of the emerging republic. Even such basic documents as the Declaration of Independence and the Articles of Confederation were printed only sporadically, and usually in excerpts.

17. E.g., the reports of the American refusal to import English goods in the *Hamburgischer Correspondent*, June 29, 1770, and in the *Wienerisches Diarium*, July 7, 1770, and, later, the reports on the Boston Tea Party in the *Freytags-Zeitung*, Feb. 4, 1774.

18. "Mit Unparteilichkeit müssen die Vorteile angezeigt werden, die jede Partei über die andere erhalten zu haben vorgibt": *Frankfurter Oberpostamtszeitung*, Jan. 21, 1777.

19. E.g., the *Freytags-Zeitung*, Apr. 12, 1782, reported great pleasure in England over the change of the cabinet and the rise to power of the Whigs. On the other hand, see the polemical generalization in the pro-English booklet *Über den Aufstand der englischen Colonien* (pp. 6–7): "Zeitungsschreiber und Zeitungsleser werden nicht müde, den Engländern den Untergang und den Amerikanern die Freiheit zu prophezeien. Diese Parteilichkeit hat mich bewogen, gegenwärtige Schrift zu entwerfen."

Thus, it is not the frequency but rather the content of the German newspaper reports that shows the inadequate coverage afforded the motives, aims, and effects of the American Revolution. The political newspapers were unable to satisfy the desire of many Germans to become acquainted with a new republic in the very hour of its birth. Conscious of this shortcoming, Jakob Mauvillon wrote: "He who knows what our newspapers deal with will have to admit that a public which is satisfied with that must be completely indifferent to the reason and context of political events in the world."[20] The relatively large circulation of a few newspapers did not change the fact that "the influence of the press on the formation of opinion among the population was quite limited."[21] The press had not yet begun to exert itself in the formation of opinion; moreover, the information it propagated was totally insufficient for a basic understanding of the American Revolution.

Periodicals

Were the large gaps in German newspaper reporting on America filled by the periodicals, or did the periodicals provide a similar coverage? Using a definition of *periodical* no longer wholly acceptable, Joachim Kirchner reckoned that from 1770 to 1790 more than nineteen hundred new periodicals appeared in German-speaking Europe.[22] Taking into consideration those periodicals established before 1770 and still published during this period, as well as those originating during the years 1790 to 1800, we can estimate that the total number of periodicals published during these three decades may have approached three thousand.

20. "Wer da weiß, was unsre Zeitungen liefern, der wird gestehen müssen, daß ein Publikum, welches sich damit begnügt, eine ganz vollkommene Gleichgültigkeit gegen den Grund und den Zusammenhang der politischen Weltbegebenheiten haben muß": Jakob Mauvillon, *Sammlung von Aufsätzen über Gegenstände aus der Staatskunst, Staatswirtschaft und Neuesten Staaten Geschichte* (Leipzig, 1776–1777), I, [11]. Buchenröder, *Nachrichten von den Englischen Kolonien*, iv, agreed that even a regular reader of the newspapers "aus Mangel der hierzu nötigen Kenntnis" could not form an adequate idea of the nature of the present conflict. The statements by Weber, *America in Imaginative German Literature*, 5, and Robert R. Palmer, "Der Einfluß der amerikanischen Revolution auf Europa," in Golo Mann *et al.*, eds., *Propyläen-Weltgeschichte*, VIII (Berlin, 1960), 37, on the remarkable value of newspapers and periodicals in providing information in Germany seem be be convincing only for the periodicals.

21. Fritz Valjavec, *Die Entstehung der politischen Strömungen in Deutschland, 1770–1815* (Munich, 1951), 95. See also Schneider, *Pressefreiheit*, 81.

22. Joachim Kirchner, *Das deutsche Zeitschriftenwesen, seine Geschichte und seine Probleme*, 2d ed., I (Wiesbaden, 1958), 115. Cf. Kirchner, *Die Grundlagen des deutschen*

The great majority of these journals were extremely short-lived, served only local needs, or had no notable importance for our purposes. I have restricted my research to about fifty periodicals, trying to select representative ones, including those of foremost cultural significance. My choices are therefore somewhat arbitrary. Historical-political journals and literary magazines stand side by side; reviews, as well as Johann Georg Jacobi's women's magazine *Iris* (Düsseldorf), have been examined; August Ludwig Schlözer's journals were included, as was the Dresden weekly *Nichts Neues, aber doch manches Brauchbare*.[23] Christian Friedrich Daniel Schubart's *Chronik* (Stuttgart), published several times weekly, must be included, and also the quarterlies. The very fact that the selection has not been confined to sharply delineated categories may help us to arrive at a sounder and more general judgment of the information on the American Revolution found in German periodicals. The discussion that follows, which covers the period up to 1800, will necessarily abstract and generalize from the individual periodicals studied.

As Kirchner's figures indicate, periodical publication underwent a great expansion in the last third of the eighteenth century, an expansion that should be viewed as directly related to the increased interest in reading observed by Irene Jentsch. The difference from preceding years and decades was not only in quantity; the character of the periodicals themselves began to change. Besides scholarly journals of all kinds, the most numerous type of publication earlier in the century had been the moralizing weekly. Modeled after the English *Spectator*, the main function of this type of publication was the general propagation of the ideas of the Enlightenment.[24]

In the last three decades of the eighteenth century, however, a new form of periodical journalism made its appearance in Germany: the political review. We meet it for the first time in 1773, with the establishment of Christoph Martin Wieland's *Teutscher Merkur* (Weimar). Its new and still unusual function, namely, to report and comment on events and situations in public affairs and politics, soon found followers and emulators. Schubart's journal appeared the very next year, and Schlözer's and Wilhelm Ludwig Wekhrlin's journals soon followed. They all picked up the example set by Wieland, and some of them adhered to it exclusively; the *Teutscher*

Zeitschriftenwesens. Mit einer Gesamtbibliographie der deutschen Zeitschriften bis zum Jahre 1790, Vol. II, *Bibliographie* (Leipzig, 1931).

23. The Dresden weekly was published for barely two years (1778–1779) and obviously saw only a strictly local distribution.

24. Salomon, *Deutsches Zeitungswesen*, I, 99–112; Hertz, *German Public Mind*, II, 236–240.

Merkur itself, however, continued to deal with literary questions as well.[25] This new orientation allowed the periodical to achieve a position in public life unknown to it in the past, with Schlözer's journals at the apex of this new prominence.[26]

Not surprisingly, the increased esteem had its effects on circulation. While the old type of journal retreated into the background, the new ones were able to achieve unprecedented circulation. Wieland's *Teutscher Merkur* varied between twelve hundred and twenty-five hundred copies up to 1800.[27] Schubart's journal reached a circulation of sixteen hundred copies in 1775, twenty-four hundred in 1789, and almost four thousand in 1791.[28] Schlözer's journals eventually reached an occasional circulation as high as forty-four hundred copies.[29] By comparison, Heinrich Christian Boie's *Deutsches Museum* (Leipzig), which to a lesser extent covered the field of political affairs, experienced a peak circulation of one thousand copies in the year of its inception, 1776, but never reached it again.[30] Though these figures are helpful, it should be remembered that because these well-known journals were probably acquired by most readers' societies, their actual readership is largely a matter of guesswork.

To what degree were the events in the New World reflected in these journals? America was a topic in almost all the journals under discussion.

25. See Hubert Max, *Wesen und Gestalt der politischen Zeitschrift. Ein Beitrag zur Geschichte des politischen Erziehungsprozesses des deutschen Volkes bis zu den Karlsbader Beschlüssen* (Essen, 1942), 85–89, 91, 106; Erich Schairer, "Christian Friedrich Daniel Schubart als politischer Journalist" (publ. Ph.D. diss., University of Tübingen, 1914), 15–17; Valjavec, *Politische Strömungen*, 96; Ulrich Im Hof, *Isaak Iselin und die Spätaufklärung* (Bern, 1967), 63–68.

26. According to rumor, even Maria Theresa was afraid of Schlözer's pen; see Christian von Schlözer, *August Ludwig von Schlözer. Öffentliches und Privatleben aus Originalurkunden und mit wörtlicher Beifügung mehrer dieser letzteren*, 2 vols. (Leipzig, 1828), I, 275; also Salomon, *Deutsches Zeitungswesen*, I, 230; Hertz, *German Public Mind*, II, 411. On Schlözer's periodicals see Robert von Mohl, *Geschichte und Literatur der Staatswissenschaften*, II (Erlangen, 1856), 443; Friedrich Christoph Schlosser, *Geschichte des achtzehnten Jahrhunderts und des neunzehnten bis zum Sturz des französischen Kaiserreichs mit besonderer Rücksicht auf geistige Bildung*, 5th ed., 8 vols. (Heidelberg, 1864–1866), IV, 243; Salomon, I, 224; Friederike Fürst, *August Ludwig von Schlözer, ein deutscher Aufklärer im 18. Jahrhundert* (Heidelberg, 1928), 82; Lindemann, *Deutsche Presse*, 199–200.

27. Hans Wahl, *Geschichte des Teutschen Merkur. Ein Beitrag zur Geschichte des Journalismus im achtzehnten Jahrhundert* (Berlin, 1914), 24; Max, *Politische Zeitschrift*, 88; Walter H. Bruford, *Culture and Society in Classical Weimar 1775–1806* (Cambridge, 1962), 42.

28. Horst Adamietz, "Christian Friedrich Daniel Schubarts Volksblatt *Deutsche Chronik*" (publ. Ph.D. diss., University of Berlin, 1941), 32–33; Max, *Politische Zeitschrift*, 90; Kirchner, *Deutsche Zeitschriftenwesen*, I, 132–133.

29. Max, *Politische Zeitschrift*, 96; Hertz, *German Public Mind*, II, 411.

30. Walther Hofstaetter, *Das "Deutsche Museum" (1776–1788) und das "Neue Deutsche Museum" (1789–1791). Ein Beitrag zur Geschichte der deutschen Zeitschriften im 18. Jahrhundert* (Leipzig, 1908), 83.

This applies to the political journals as well as to the topically restricted publications of Heinrich Freiherr von Bibra, Boie, and Jacobi.[31] The pervasive echo of American events in German periodicals is amazing at first glance. But if we use Otto Groth's definition of a journal (which has better balance than earlier definitions), we must note that in Germany, unlike France, there was no journal devoted exclusively to the study of the American Revolution and of the United States.[32]

Roughly subdividing our selection of periodicals into groups and viewing each separately, we find first of all the old and familiar type of scholarly journal that dealt here and there with economic, geographic, and ethnological questions, but not with questions that were political in a narrow sense.[33] A second, related group consists of the reviews, including those mainly scholarly publications that found room for the review of books on America.[34] In the case of the *Göttingische Anzeigen von gelehrten Sachen*, it is worth remarking that reviews of controversial literature concerning America were

31. On Bibra and his journal see Max Braubach, "Die kirchliche Aufklärung im katholischen Deutschland im Spiegel des *Journal von und für Deutschland* (1784–1792)," *Historisches Jahrbuch*, LIV (1934), 1–63, 178–220, and Juliane Breunig, "Das *Journal von und für Deutschland* 1784–1792. Eine deutsche Zeitenwende im Spiegel einer deutschen Zeitung" (publ. Ph.D. diss., University of Munich, 1941). For Boie see Karl Weinhold, *Heinrich Christian Boie. Beitrag zur Geschichte der deutschen Literatur im achtzehnten Jahrhundert* (Halle, 1868). On Dohm's contribution to the *Deutsches Museum* see Ilsegret Dambacher, "Christian Wilhelm von Dohm. Ein Beitrag zur Geschichte des preußschen aufgeklärten Beamtentums und seiner Reformbestrebungen am Ausgang des 18. Jahrhunderts" (unpubl. Ph.D. diss., University of Munich, 1956).

32. Otto Groth, *Die unerkannte Kulturmacht. Grundlegung der Zeitungswissenschaft (Periodik)*, 6 vols. (Berlin, 1960–1966), I, esp. 425–426, 621, II, 6; Günter Kieslich, "Zur Definition der Zeitschrift," *Publizistik*, X (1965), 314–319; Kieslich, "Die Zeitschrift: Begriff," in Emil Dovifat, ed., *Handbuch der Publizistik*, III (Berlin, 1969), 370–383, with reference to the earlier literature. See also Wilmot Haacke, *Die politische Zeitschrift 1665–1965*, I (Stuttgart, 1968), 116–121. Kirchner lists Ebeling's *Amerikanische Bibliothek* and Remer's *Amerikanisches Archiv* in his bibliography of periodicals. Modern definitions preclude such a classification, which would also twist the intentions of the editors themselves, who wanted their publications to be understood as collections and not, Ebeling emphasized, as periodicals. Cf. Ebeling, *Amerikanische Bibliothek*, I (Leipzig, 1777), and Remer, *Amerikanisches Archiv*, 3 vols. (Brunswick, 1777–1778), I, the prefaces by the editors.

33. E.g., *Göttingisches Magazin der Wissenschaften und Litteratur* (1780–1785); *Göttingisches historisches Magazin* (1787–1794); Anton Friedrich Büsching, ed., *Magazin für die neue Historie und Geographie* (Halle, 1770–1788); and Büsching, ed., *Wöchentliche Nachrichten* (Berlin, 1773–1787).

34. Nicolai, ed., *Allgemeine deutsche Bibliothek* (Berlin and Stettin, 1770–1800); *Göttingische Anzeigen von gelehrten Sachen* (1770–1800); Gatterer, ed., *Historisches Journal* (Göttingen, 1772–1781); *Frankfurter gelehrte Anzeigen* (1774–1784); Johann Georg Meusel, ed., *Historische Litteratur* (Erlangen, 1781–1784). Schiller called Nicolai "gleichsam der Souverain der Litteratur" (Friedrich to Christophine Schiller, Nov. 6, 1782, in Schiller, *Werke*, National ed., XXIII, 49). Meusel also printed some articles on America. Some other periodicals contained book reviews, too.

almost totally absent during the war, a fact that probably cannot be attributed solely to the death of Albrecht von Haller.[35]

Third, looking at journals dealing specifically with historical and political questions, we detect certain differences among them, though of course there is much overlapping. Included in this group are numerous journals that had almost exclusively local distribution, as well as supra-regional journals. The local journals usually could not afford large editorial staffs and were therefore dependent on easily available news. Consequently, it is not surprising that their reports were often quite similar in content to those of the newspapers.[36]

The direction taken by Wieland's, Schubart's, and Wekhrlin's journals is more important for our discussion. They were less restricted in their choice of topics and tried to analyze and comment on the news in order to clarify the meaning of certain events. Schubart's skillful quill, as well as the satires and glosses in Wekhrlin's journals, greatly contributed to this objective.[37]

The Leipzig monthly *Englische allgemeine Bibliothek* differs from these journals in approach and content. In its first six issues, without comment and without taking sides, it reprinted a great number of pamphlets, among them Edmund Burke's *Speech on American Taxation*, Samuel Johnson's *Taxation no Tyranny* (with almost half a dozen retorts), and other important polemical treatises.[38] This documentary emphasis is also a trait—at least as far as America is concerned—of Schlözer's important journals, the two *Briefwechsel* and the *Stats-Anzeigen*.[39] However, after open conflict began in America the differentiation between the journal of political commentary and the archival journal effectively disappeared as the independent essay came to the forefront. At the same time, the mere reprinting of pamphlets and documents faded away.

35. In the *Göttingische Anzeigen von gelehrten Sachen*, books on America were mainly reviewed by Albrecht von Haller until his death (see Haller's personal copy in the Stadt- und Universitätsbibliothek, Bern). After the war Sprengel presumably took Haller's place (see Sprengel to Heyne in Briefe an Heyne zur Zeit seiner Redaktion, 1770–1812, Scient. 47, 3, Archiv der Akademie der Wissenschaften [hereafter cited as AAW], Göttingen).

36. E.g., *Neueste Geschichte der Welt* (Ulm and Augsburg, 1774–1777); Friedrich Schiller, ed., *Nachrichten zum Nuzen und Vergnügen* (Stuttgart, 1781); *Bunzlauische Monatsschrift* (1774–1784); Heinrich Martin Gottfried Köster, ed., *Neueste Staatsbegebenheiten* (Frankfurt and Mainz, 1776–1783).

37. Wieland, ed., *Teutscher Merkur* (Weimar, 1773–1800); Schubart, ed., *Chronik* (Stuttgart, 1774–1791), with interruptions and slightly varying name; Wekhrlin, ed., *Chronologen* (Frankfurt, 1779–1781), *Das graue Ungeheuer* (Nuremberg, 1784–1787), and *Hyperboreische Briefe* (Nuremberg, 1788–1790). See also Jacobi, ed., *Iris* (Düsseldorf, 1775–1776), and Isaak Iselin, ed., *Ephemeriden der Menschheit* (Basel, 1776–1782).

38. *Englische allgemeine Bibliothek* (1775).

39. Schlözer, ed., *Briefwechsel meist statistischen Inhalts* (1775), *Briefwechsel meist historischen und politischen Inhalts* (1777–1782), *Stats-Anzeigen* (1782–1793), all published in Göttingen.

The political journals seldom published debates about the American Revolution based on arguments put forward by both parties. There is, however, some compensation in the form of an occasional essay or letter from America on some aspect of domestic matters, especially finance, economics, and foreign affairs. But these articles, as well as the controversies that sometimes accompanied them, were not always written with well-grounded knowledge. This will become clear when we discuss in detail some German conceptions of America from the late 1790s.[40]

In another serious omission, the political journals rarely reprinted even those documents that were basic to an understanding of the United States. Isaak Iselin was probably the first, and perhaps the only, journalist to publish a complete German translation of the Declaration of Independence, and he failed to do justice to its full import in the accompanying commentary.[41] Other relevant texts were similarly neglected. Only in the journals of Johann Wilhelm von Archenholtz was there a translation of the federal Constitution of 1787 and of Franklin's famous speech before its ratification by the Constitutional Convention.[42] Washington's Farewell Address, however, received more widespread attention.[43]

In sum, the informational value of periodicals was generally limited. Their practice of commenting on and analyzing the news certainly made them a valuable source of information, but they did not satisfactorily fill all the gaps left by the newspapers. Although their scope was indeed much broader than that of the newspapers, they too failed to deal with the basic nature of the American Revolution and the new nation, with the issues raised by the American structure of government and its safeguards, or with

40. See, e.g., Gottlob Benedikt von Schirach, ed., *Politisches Journal* (Hamburg, 1781–1800); August Hennings, ed., *Genius der Zeit* (Altona, 1794–1800); Ernst Ludwig Posselt, ed., *Europäische Annalen* (Tübingen, 1795–1800); Karl Ludwig Woltmann, ed., *Geschichte und Politik* (Berlin, 1800). See also F. von Kleist *et al.*, eds., *Deutsche Monatsschrift* (Berlin, 1790–1799), and Friedrich Gedike and Johann Erich Biester, eds., *Berlinische Monatsschrift* (1783–1796). On the latter see Max, *Politische Zeitschrift*, 103–104; Ludwig Geiger, *Berlin 1688–1840. Geschichte des geistigen Lebens der preußischen Hauptstadt*, 2 vols. (Berlin, 1892), I, 341, 426–427; Joseph Hay, "Staat, Volk und Weltbürgertum in der *Berlinischen Monatsschrift* von Friedrich Gedike und Johann Erich Biester" (publ. Ph.D. diss., University of Breslau, 1913), 7, 17.

41. *Ephemeriden der Menschheit*, Oct. 1776, 96–106.

42. *English Lyceum* (Hamburg), Oct., Dec. 1787, 1–13, 229–310, 1788, 265–267; *Neue Litteratur und Völkerkunde* (Dessau and Leipzig), 1788, 3–31 (the federal Constitution only).

43. Posselt, ed., *Europäische Annalen*, Nov. 1796, 156–180; and Archenholtz, ed., *Minerva* (Berlin), Dec. 1796, 489–525, and *Deutsches Magazin* (Hamburg), Feb. 1797, 174–206. Information on the *Minerva* can be found in Friedrich Ruof, *Johann Wilhelm von Archenholtz. Ein deutscher Schriftsteller zur Zeit der Französische Revolution und Napoleons (1741–1812)* (Berlin, 1915), 129, and in Max, *Politische Zeitschrift*, 111–115. John Quincy Adams remarked that the Farewell Address "has been republished, translated, and admired

the mechanisms of political decision-making. Instead, they all too often became entangled in questions of second- and third-rate importance.

Books

We now turn to books, that is, the "Americana Germanica" from 1770 to 1800. This term refers to those publications that in at least one continuous passage of at least half a book page in length (rather than in scattered remarks throughout the text) dealt with the area that was declared the territory of the United States in 1783. The various aspects of America treated in these books are unimportant here. To qualify as a book, according to my definition, the publication must have at least eight pages. Folio sheets, even when they corresponded to about eight octavo pages, were taken into consideration only in exceptional cases and only when they had been published in the German-speaking area. Works published in the German-speaking language area by an author known to be a North American were included regardless of whether they related to America or not. All available works published in the German language (or in any other language, if the book was published in the German cultural area) that fulfill the criteria of a book related to America have been drawn upon. In total, about 780 books were used for this study.

This number does not correspond to the actual total published, however. Numerous additional publications noted in previous bibliographies could not be located in any library; thus the sum total of all Americana Germanica may actually have been well above 1,000. But since total German book production between 1770 and 1800 came to more than 86,000 titles, and possibly even 150,000,[44] the share of Americana Germanica publications was hardly 1 percent. If we consider only our 780 publications and subtract about 50 titles that were published in German in America, the figure still amounts to about ½ percent. These figures seem small, but they are still remarkable, given the restricted nature of the topic.

The 780 books before us can, with a few exceptions, be divided into

---

all over Europe": to Abigail Adams, Feb. 8, 1797, in Worthington C. Ford, ed., *The Writings of John Quincy Adams*, 7 vols. (New York, 1913–1917), II, 109.

44. All in all, about 86,000 books were published for the two book fairs held annually at Frankfurt and Leipzig from 1770 through 1800; cf. Paschke and Rath, *Lehrbuch des Deutschen Buchhandels*, I, 68. But not all books were published for the fairs. Goldfriedrich, *Geschichte des deutschen Buchhandels vom Beginn der klassischen Litteraturperiode bis zum Beginn der Fremdherrschaft (1740–1804)*, III (Leipzig, 1909), 247–249, assumed an annual average of about 5,000 titles, which would come to an overall sum of more than 150,000 for these years.

three groups. The largest is that of the German-language originals, amounting to about two-thirds of the total. The ratio of this figure to the entire German book production of the period seems clearly to have been below average. That is, for any given subject area, the percentage of German-language originals ordinarily would be higher. In the second category, books published in a modern foreign language, there was no deviation from the average. The share of about 8 percent in the field of the Americana Germanica lies exactly between the general figures given for this time by Johann Goldfriedrich.[45]

But a significant difference is found in the category of translations. Goldfriedrich arrived at the conclusion that the percentage of translations produced for the book fairs did not even equal that of the works published for the fairs in a modern foreign language.[46] Since the basis for his analysis was the book fair catalogs, with their often inaccurate specifications, the actual percentage of translations may have been higher, perhaps close to today's figure of about 11 percent.[47] However, in the field of Americana, translations amounted to almost 30 percent of the total and were thus obviously far more common than was usual for other fields. Works concerning North America that were originally published in England or France became available to the German contemporary in greater percentage than foreign-language publications in general. It is quite understandable that the translator of Burke's *Account of the European Settlements in America* expressed amazement that this work so far had "escaped the attention of our busy translators" even though it had already gone through six editions in England.[48]

If we try to separate the books used for this study roughly on the basis of the kinds of information about America that they offered, we can ignore the approximately one-quarter that conveyed hardly any information. This group includes German-language works published in America itself, which, it is safe to assume, did not find a considerable distribution in Germany. Theological works, medical-scientific treatises, encyclopedias, novels, dra-

45. Of the books published for the Easter fairs of 1775, 1785, and 1795, 10.6%, 5.1%, and 6.7%, respectively, were written in a modern foreign language; see Goldfriedrich, *Geschichte des deutschen Buchhandels*, III, 305.

46. According to Goldfriedrich, *ibid.*, 7.1%, 6.8%, and 4.8% of the works published for the Easter fairs of 1775, 1785, and 1795, respectively, were translations from modern foreign languages.

47. Börsenverein des deutschen Buchhandels, *Buch und Buchhandel in Zahlen* (Frankfurt, 1964), 73; 1965 ed., p. 91; 1966 ed., p. 94; 1967 ed., p. 19; 1968 ed., pp. 20–21; 1969 ed., p. 20; 1970 ed., pp. 19–20 (for 1969 and 1970 the respective percentages were between 9 and 10).

48. "unsern geschäftigen Übersetzern entgangen": Burke, *Europäischen Kolonien in Amerika*, I, iii–iv (note of the translator).

mas, and poems also belong to this group, as well as general military studies that did not specifically discuss the American War of Independence. A reader would hardly turn to such works for general information about the Revolution and the new state; they served different and much more specific interests.

For more general information it was necessary to search among the other three-quarters of the literature on America. The dominant categories here were the purely historical, political-historical, geographical, and popular philosophical treatises, as well as travel descriptions. Yet about two-thirds of these approximately 580 titles, out of the total 780, deal with America only as one small subject among several others. In a description of overseas trade or in a book on universal geography, the paragraphs about that part of the American continent that was declared the territory of the United States in 1783 could be very small and offer very little information. But the reverse also occurred: America might have above-average importance within the entire presentation. Viewed as a source of knowledge about the northeastern part of the continent, this group is extremely heterogeneous. It embraces useless geographical tables like those of Johann Gottfried Schenk, as well as Julius August Remer's well-grounded historical descriptions, which appeared at the end of the century.[49]

About 190 works, or a quarter of the entire Americana Germanica, are devoted more or less exclusively to the questions of interest to us. Investigating further, we find that the greatest number of these are political-historical works, including presentations of the American Revolution and descriptions of travels. Some of these, such as the travel accounts of Jacques Pierre Brissot de Warville and Isaac Weld, went through numerous editions, thus increasing the total number of such works.[50] The various treatises on the American Revolution, in fact all of the political-historical works, will be examined more closely as to number, content, and origin.

Leaving aside all works in a foreign language and all reprints of books

49. Schenk, *Geographische Tabellen*; Remer, *Handbuch der neuern Geschichte*, (Brunswick, 1799) (3d ed. of Vol. III of *Handbuch der allgemeinen Geschichte*); Remer, *Handbuch der Geschichte unsrer Zeiten vom Jahre 1740 bis zum Jahre 1799* (Brunswick, 1799); and Remer, *Lehrbuch der algemeinen Geschichte* (Halle, 1800). See also Remer's publications of the preceding 30 years.

50. Brissot de Warville, *Neue Reise durch die vereinigten Staaten von Nordamerika in dem Jahr 1788*, trans. from the French [by Johann Reinhold Forster] (Berlin, 1792); Weld, *Reisen durch die Staaten von Nordamerika, und die Provinzen Ober- und Nieder-Canada, während den Jahren 1795, 1796 und 1797*, trans. from the English (Berlin, 1800). Brissot de Warville's account appeared in at least nine different German editions between 1792 and 1797. In 1800 alone, three Berlin publishers produced five different editions of Weld's book.

already published in Germany, we find in the first half of the 1770s only a single thin volume that offered a little information about the political situation in the colonies before the outbreak of the war.[51] In the following years, that is, up to 1780, eight other works attempted to provide information about the outbreak of the war and the first years of the Revolution.[52] Between 1778 and 1783 six publications, half of them translations, offered comprehensive accounts of the Revolution up to the dates of their publication.[53] After the Peace of Versailles there appeared five works, among them two German originals, that attempted to arrive at a synthesis of the American Revolution.[54] Six additional works published after 1776 centered on the

51. *Nachricht von der Provinz Virginien in Nord-America, nebst ausführlichen Beschreibungen der entsetzlichen Wasser-Fluth so gedachte Provinz im Jahre 1771. Monaths May erlitten. Als auch Beschreibung von der Schlacht und gänzlichen Ausrottung der Regulatoren in Nord-Carolina in America. Deme annoch beygefüget eine ausführliche und accurate Geographische Beschreibung der Provinz Pennsylvanien in Nord-America* (Frankfurt, 1772). The booklet contained no more than 16 pages.

52. *Über den Aufstand der englischen Colonien; Briefe über die jetzige Uneinigkeit zwischen den Amerikanischen Colonien und dem Englischen Parlament*, trans. from the English (Hanover, 1776); Buchenröder, *Nachrichten von den Englischen Kolonien; Gedanken über den Aufstand der englischen Colonien in dem nördlichen Amerika* (Göttingen, 1776); [Gottlob Benedikt von Schirach], *Historisch-statistische Notiz der Großbritannischen Colonien in America* (Frankfurt and Leipzig, 1776); *Bericht eines Englischen Amerikaners von Philadephia an seinen Freund in Engelland über den dermahligen Krieg Groß-Brittaniens mit seinen Amerikanischen Colonien vom 15 December 1776*, trans. from the English (Frankfurt and Leipzig, 1777); [William Barron], *Geschichte der Kolonisirung der freien Staaten des Alterthums, angewandt auf den gegenwärtigen Streit zwischen Großbritannien und seinen amerikanischen Kolonien*, trans. from the English (Leipzig, 1778); Joseph Galloway, *Briefe . . . über den in den Mittlern Colonien in America geführten Krieg*, trans. from the English (Hamburg, 1780).

53. Sprengel, *Briefe den gegenwärtigen Zustand von Nord America betreffend*; Christian Leiste, *Beschreibung des Brittischen Amerika* (Wolfenbüttel, 1778); [Pierre Ulric Du Buisson], *Historischer Abriß der in Nord-Amerika vorgefallenen Staats-Veränderung*, trans. from the French (Bern, 1779); Guillaume-Thomas-François Raynal, *Staatsveränderung von Amerika*, trans. from the French (Frankfurt and Leipzig, 1782); [Johann Christian Schmohl], *Über Nordamerika und Demokratie* (Copenhagen [i.e., Königsberg], 1782); Michel René Hilliard d'Auberteuil, *Historischer und politischer Versuch über die Anglo-Amerikaner und die Staats-Veränderung in Nord-Amerika*, trans. from the French [by Albrecht Wittenberg] (Hamburg and Kiel, 1783).

54. *Beschreibung der dreizehn unabhängigen Nordamerikanischen Staaten*, trans. from the French (Cologne, 1783); Matthias Christian Sprengel, *Allgemeines historisches Taschenbuch oder Abriß der merkwürdigsten neuen Welt-Begebenheiten enthaltend für 1784 die Geschichte der Revolution von Nord-America* (Berlin, 1783); Johann Jakob Moser, *Nord-America nach den Friedensschlüssen vom Jahre 1783* (Leipzig, 1784–1785); Honoré Gabriel Riquetti, comte de Mirabeau, *Sammlung einiger philosophischen und politischen Schriften, die vereinigten Staaten von Nordamerika betreffend*, trans. from the French (Berlin and Libau, 1787); François Soulès, *Vollständige Geschichte der Revolution in Nord-Amerika*, trans. from the French (Zurich, 1788).

events of the war,[55] and another seven books from the 1790s, among them five translations, dealt with the American Revolution.[56]

Valuable supplements to these relatively helpful works were Christoph Daniel Ebeling's *Amerikanische Bibliothek* (1777), Julius August Remer's *Amerikanisches Archiv* (1777–1778), and, with certain limitations, Christian Wilhelm Dohm's *Materialien für die Statistick* (1777–1785). All of them attempted to fill numerous gaps in the knowledge of German contemporaries by reprinting individual pamphlets, including Paine's *Common Sense* and some rebuttals to it.[57] The *Amerikanisches Magazin*, published by Dietrich Hermann Hegewisch and Ebeling during the 1790s, served a similar purpose with its various treatises, analyses, and comments.[58]

This survey leads to the conclusion that in this period only about half of all German first editions of political-historical works about America related directly to the American Revolution, and, with few more than ten publications, the percentage of German originals in this group is far below half. The picture shifts favorably only when reprints of books by German authors are taken into consideration. However, in relation to the total 780 Americana Germanica, the percentage of German originals pertaining to the Revolution remains extremely small.

Furthermore, it would be a mistake to assume that even these books

55. [Christoph Heinrich Korn], *Geschichte der Kriege in und ausser Europa Vom Anfange des Aufstandes der Brittischen Kolonien in Nordamerika an* (Nuremberg, 1776–1784); [Korn], *Kurzgefaßte Geschichte des englisch-französisch-spanischen Krieges* (Salzburg, 1780); [Julius August Remer], *Geschichte des Krieges zwischen Großbritannien und den vereinigten Bourbonischen Mächten und Nordamerikanischen Kolonien* (Leipzig, 1780); Matthias Christian Sprengel, *Über den jetzigen Nordamerikanischen Krieg und dessen Folgen für England und Frankreich* (Leipzig, 1782); Zinner, *Merkwürdige Briefe und Schriften*; Adam Friedrich Geisler, *Geschichte und Zustand der Königlich Grosbrittannischen Kriegsmacht zu Wasser und zu Lande . . . Nebst einem Abris des lezten amerikanischen Krieges . . .* (Dessau and Leipzig, 1784).

56. Thomas Paine, *Gesunder Menschenverstand*, trans. from the English (Copenhagen, 1794); Paine, *Sammlung verschiedener Schriften über Politik und Gesetzgebung*, trans. from the English (Copenhagen, 1794); David Ramsay, *Geschichte der Amerikanischen Revolution*, trans. from the English (Berlin, 1794–1795); Charles Stedman, *Geschichte des Ursprungs, des Fortgangs und der Beendigung des Americanischen Kriegs*, trans. from the English by Julius August Remer (Berlin, 1795); Eberhard August Wilhelm Zimmermann, *Frankreich und die Freistaaten von Nordamerika. Vergleichung beider Länder*, 2 vols. (Berlin, 1795–1799); George Washington, *Officielle und eigenhändige Briefe und Berichte, welche er während des ganzen Krieges . . . an den Congreß geschrieben*, trans. from the English (Leipzig, 1796–1797); Friederike Charlotte Luise Riedesel, *Die Berufs-Reise nach America* (Berlin, 1800).

57. Dohm, *Materialien für die Statistick*, I. The first German edition of *Common Sense* was published in Philadelphia in 1776 under the title *Gesunde Vernunft*; a separate German translation first appeared in Europe in 1794 (see n. 56).

58. Hegewisch and Ebeling, eds., *Amerikanisches Magazin*, 4 vols. (Hamburg, 1795–1797).

reported the essential aspects of the Revolution, though they are comparatively the most informative. John Adams's judgment on such books in 1782, in a comment to the French publicist Gabriel Bonnot de Mably, is worth remembering: "Monuments of the complete ignorance of the writers of their subject."[59] To be sure, Adams was thinking only of English and French authors; but there is no reason to assume that the average treatises by Germans were above the level of other European publications on America. Adams would no doubt have included these German works in his judgment if he had known them. Convinced of the shortcomings of discussions about the American Revolution, he told Jefferson in 1817 that he had given up reading them, for "the Truth is lost, in adulatory Panegyricks, and in vituperary Insolence."[60] One may not agree with the harshness of Adams's judgment, but reading the German works in question leads to the opinion that he did not exaggerate very much.

Two spheres of Americana Germanica that are of decisive importance for our study have not yet been discussed. The first consists of publications of documents (including political and constitutional works); the second is made up of books like travel accounts that deal with political, social, and economic aspects of the United States or parts of it in the period after the Revolution but that cannot be included in other categories. These two areas point to the most noticeable gaps in the German record. Even if interpreted generously, they constitute not even 2 percent of all Americana Germanica, amounting to hardly a dozen of the 190 books that meet our more strictly defined criteria.

Looking closer at these works, one is struck by the paucity of American documents published for the German book market—disregarding those that were scattered about in a few books.[61] The only separate publications of individual documents are the translations of the *Articles of War* of June 30,

59. Charles Francis Adams, ed., *The Works of John Adams*, 10 vols. (Boston, 1851–1856), V, 494.

60. May 18, 1817, in Lester J. Cappon, ed., *The Adams-Jefferson Letters: The Complete Correspondence Between Thomas Jefferson and Abigail and John Adams*, 2 vols. (Chapel Hill, N.C., 1959), II, 516.

61. The federal Constitution of 1787 was reprinted in [Filippo Mazzei], *Geschichte und Staatsverfassung der vereinigten Staaten von Nordamerika*, trans. from the French, 2 vols. (Leipzig, 1789), II, 266–287 (the Declaration of Independence and the Virginia Bill of Rights were also included: I, 315–321, 152–157); Georg Friedrich von Martens, *Receuil des principaux traités d'Alliance* . . . (Göttingen, 1791–1801), III, 76–95 (also the Declaration of Independence, the Articles of Confederation, and other documents and treaties); Cooper, *Renseignemens sur l'Amérique*, appendix, 1–34. Furthermore, the Declaration of Independence was completely reprinted in Hilliard d'Auberteuil, *Versuch über die Anglo-Amerikaner*, I, pt. i, 175–185; *Geschichte der zweyten Decade der Regierung Georgs des Dritten* . . . , trans. from the English by Albrecht Wittenberg (Hamburg, 1784), 427–434.

1775;[62] the *Declaration of the Causes and Necessity of Taking Up Arms* of July 6, 1775; and the *Public Laws of the Thirteen American States*, which had been prepared by Franklin and was published with great hopes by a Dessau publishing house.[63] The latter contained the constitutions of the thirteen individual states, the Declaration of Independence, the Articles of Confederation, and the American treaties with France, the Netherlands, and Sweden. Other political or constitutional works that included some documents are a French-language edition of de Mably's *Observations sur le gouvernement des États-Unis d'Amérique*[64] and an abridged German translation of two volumes of Filippo Mazzei's four-volume *Recherches historiques et politiques sur les États-Unis de l'Amérique Septentrionale*;[65] the second volume of that translation was also sold separately under a meaningless title.[66] As the last work of this kind, the transläsion of Jacques Vincent Delacroix's *Constitutions des principaux États de l'Europe et des États-Unis d'Amérique* should be mentioned, even though it deals with the United States only partially and therefore does not really belong to this category.[67]

The situation does not improve when we consider descriptive works on the new republic. Of the five pertinent publications, three thin books relate to the German emigration to North America.[68] Another work, by Thomas Cooper, existed only in a French-language edition.[69] The one substantial and general source of information was Dietrich Heinrich Freiherr von Bülow's *Freistaat von Nordamerika in seinem neuesten Zustand*.[70]

62. *Erklärung der Repräsentanten der vereinigten Colonien in Nord-Amerika*, trans. from the English (Frankfurt and Leipzig, 1775).

63. *Staatsgesetze der dreyzehn vereinigten amerikanischen Staaten*, trans. from the French (Dessau and Leipzig, 1785). "Wir gedenken auf d[er] O[ster-]M[e]sse eine Übersetzung der Gesetze, welche Franklin für die Staaten von Amerika verfertiget hat, zu liefern. Ob sie Glück machen werde, kann ich nicht wissen. H. hofft viel davon": Ernst Wolfgang Behrisch to Friedrich Johann Justin Bertuch, Jan. 3, 1785 (Nachlaß Bertuch, I, 172, Goethe- und Schiller-Archiv [hereafter cited as GSA], Weimar).

64. (Hamburg, 1784).

65. *Geschichte und Staatsverfassung* (see n. 61).

66. *Amerikanische Anekdoten aus den neuesten Zeiten* (Leipzig, 1789).

67. Jacques Vincent Delacroix, *Verfassung der vornehmsten europäischen und der vereinigten amerikanischen Staaten*, trans. from the French, 6 vol. (Leipzig, 1792–1803).

68. Benjamin Franklin, *Bericht für diejenigen, welche nach Nord-Amerika sich begeben, und alldort ansiedeln wollen*, trans. from the English [by Jean Rodolphe Vautravers] (Hamburg, 1786); *Berichte über den Genesee-Distrikt in dem Staate von Neu-York der vereinigten Staaten von Nord-Amerika . . .*, trans. from the English (n.p., 1791); Gotthilf Nicolas Lutyens, *Etwas über den gegenwärtigen Zustand der Auswanderungen und Ansiedlungen im Staate von Pennsylvanien in Nord-Amerika, besonders in Ansehung der Deutschen* (Hamburg, 1796).

69. Cooper, *Renseignemens sur l'Amérique* (1795).

70. (Berlin, 1797).

Even if we include the translations from English or French, the overall picture is not very encouraging. Works like John Adams's *Defense of the Constitutions* or *The Federalist* remained completely unknown in Germany, though by no means in France.[71]

That Americana rarely went through more than one edition in Germany —contrary to the publishing history of such works in other Western European countries—must have had an effect on the general level of information. Moreover, the editions do not seem to have been very large, for some of these books are hard to find today. Exceptions, so far as any exist, are found mostly in the field of travel and description. By comparison, it was not unusual for books on universal history or cosmography to go through several editions, sometimes more than ten.

The diversified character of German literature relating to America makes it quite difficult to sum up its informational value in a few words. A few works satisfactorily met the contemporary demand for information, but the majority failed to meet this demand at all or did so only inadequately. Considering their number and diversity, the books were better suited to inform the German reader about North America than either newspapers or magazines. But book publication, too, left large gaps that had important consequences for the nature of political discussion in Germany. Most important was the general neglect of the American domestic scene and of the constitutional development of the United States.

Other Sources of Information

Reports of the Legations

In addition to the sources of information theoretically available to all are those that were available only to certain groups or individuals. Only in special cases can we determine which of these two different channels was the most important. But we can safely assume that governments were strongly influenced by the private reports sent to them by legations.

It is virtually impossible to discuss the hundreds of German petty states that did not have a diplomatic service. Our analysis therefore must be limited to the larger territories, and it can take into account only the reports of

71. Weber, *America in Imaginative German Literature*, 25–26, evaluates the amount and the content of the translated literature too optimistically.

their Western European legations. I have examined the reports for the years 1770 to 1783 from the Austrian envoys in London, Paris, The Hague, Madrid, and Lisbon; the Prussian and Saxon diplomats in London, Paris, and The Hague; the Palatinate-Bavarian, the Hesse-Kassel, and the Württemberg legations in London and Paris; and the Baden legations in Paris and The Hague.[72] With the help of this diplomatic correspondence I have attempted to determine whether and to what extent the general level of information possessed by governments differed from that of the average citizen.

The legation reports reveal immediately a high degree of interest in America. They are similar to the political newspapers as far as the course and intensity of reports about America are concerned, though during the first half of the 1770s they gave somewhat more attention to America than did the newspapers. Paris and The Hague were more important as sources of information for legation reports than for newspapers, although London ranked first as a diplomatic source, just as it did for newspaper stories. The immense number of incoming reports conveys the impression that, from the mid-1770s at the latest, German governments regarded the events in the English colonies of North America as the most important happenings outside of Germany. Only during the War of the Bavarian Succession (1778–1779) did interest in America lag behind that in domestic complications.[73]

Nevertheless, in the diplomatic dispatches no less than in the newspaper reports one looks in vain for a thorough discussion of fundamental political and constitutional questions. Before the outbreak of the war, reports dealt only with the most outstanding issues; during the subsequent years, military events stood in the foreground. In contrast with the newspapers, diplomats often made preliminary efforts to comment on the news received and forwarded. For example, Florimond Claude, comte Mercy d'Argenteau, the Austrian envoy in Paris, referred constantly to information received by Charles Gravier, comte de Vergennes. But overall, diplomatic messages mainly offered narrative accounts of the American situation as it appeared at the moment, rather than deeper analyses of the underlying significance of the events and their possible consequences. Without following a fixed line, the reports differed according to the location and the personality of the envoy but corresponded to the generally neutral attitude of the governments.

This waiting-and-watching neutrality, which Arthur Lee once bitingly

72. The margravate of Baden had no diplomatic representative in Great Britain during the last third of the 18th century; see Otto Friedrich Winter, ed., *Repertorium der diplomatischen Vertreter aller Länder*, III (Graz and Cologne, 1965), 10–14.

73. The War of the Bavarian Succession "empêchera l'Allemagne de porter ses regards et son attention vers l'Amérique": Matthäus Graf von Vieregg to Joseph Franz Xaver Freiherr von Haslang, July 15, 1778 (Kasten schwarz 15380, GstA, Munich).

called "froideur allemande,"[74] may be explained by the state interests of the German governments. The war in America, like the preceding tensions in East Europe and on the Iberian peninsula, occupied German ministries primarily because of its possible effects on the European constellation of powers.[75] The diplomatic correspondence shows that political, social, and constitutional events in America received little attention in proportion to the question of their implications for German foreign policy. There was no tendency to take sides, since German interests were not directly concerned. Moreover, because of the unsolved question of the Bavarian succession, the political situation in Germany itself was unstable until the Peace of Teschen (1779). In short, diplomatic interest was directed toward the war in America, but not toward the Revolution.

Despite the high respect in which Benjamin Franklin was held in Germany, his presence in Paris could neither change this detachment nor contribute decisively to the supply of better information to the governments east of the Rhine.[76] In any case, German diplomats accredited in the French capital had almost no contact with Franklin before 1782, owing to the policy of neutrality practiced by their governments.[77]

Other forms of communication open to the German governments counted for little in this one-sided picture that was oriented heavily toward the big powers. Even the sporadic appearance of American negotiators in Berlin and Vienna does not seem to have had any noteworthy influence. Aside from the six states that furnished auxiliary forces to Great Britain, no government had its own liaison in America during the war. Berlin had to

74. "There is a cold tranquillity here, that bodes us no good. On ne peut pas echauffer le froideur allemagne [*sic*]": Lee, from Vienna, to the commissioners at Paris, May 27, 1777, in Lee, Letters to the Continental Congress 1776–1780 (M 247, R11, National Archives [hereafter cited as NA], Washington, D. C.). Francis Wharton, ed., *The Revolutionary Diplomatic Correspondence of the United States* (Washington, D. C., 1889), II, 327, translated from the French as follows: "It is not possible to quicken this German indifference."

75. See also the obviously similar interests of Catherine II of Russia: Frank A. Golder, "Catherine II and the American Revolution," *American Historical Review* (hereafter cited as *AHR*), XXI (1915–1916), 92.

76. Franklin's collection of documents did not appear in Germany until 1785 and obviously saw much more limited distribution there than in France; see Albert H. Smyth, ed., *The Writings of Benjamin Franklin*, 10 vols. (New York, 1905–1907), IX, 131–132, and Echeverria, *Mirage in the West*, 71.

77. Ewald Friedrich Graf von Hertzberg, on June 2, and Frederick II, on June 3, 1778, forbade Goltz any official contact with Franklin (Rep. XI. 89, fasc. 253, fols. 166r–v, DZA, Merseburg; Volz, ed., *Politische Correspondenz Friedrichs des Grossen*, XLI, 131–132). Goltz, like his Saxon colleague Schönfeld, had no official contact with Franklin until 1782–1783 (Rep. 96. 29E, vol. 20, fols. 169v–169a, 192r–v, DZA, Merseburg; Smyth, ed., *Writings of Franklin*, IX, 67). See also Freiherr von Boden, from Paris, to the landgrave of Hesse-Kassel, Mar. 24, 1779 (4 f Frankreich, no. 1718, fols. 82r–v, StA, Marburg).

ask its London envoy to issue a public denial concerning a rumor of official Prussian contacts in America.[78] The official distance maintained toward the Americans was also observed generally toward Great Britain. None of the more important German governments had a pronounced hostile attitude toward any of the quarreling parties,[79] excluding, of course, Hanover, with its dynastic links to the English crown, and the six states with treaties involving subsidies from Britain and the supply of troops to the war in America.

The interests of their governments necessarily affected the reports that diplomats transmitted home. Though we have noted that legation reports did not differ greatly in quality from those of the newspapers, they reflect a decided difference between the interests of the governments and those of the bourgeoisie. Whereas the journals and books concerned themselves only slightly with the American war and its meaning for the European structure of power and dwelled on the Revolution instead, the reverse was true of the reporting in government circles. Consequently, the American Revolution was discussed in the legation reports as inadequately as in the newspapers. In other words, despite the availability of diplomatic dispatches, the German governments were no better informed concerning the American Revolution than interested circles of the bourgeoisie.

Private Sources of Information

The variety of other ways in which news and facts about America could be obtained can be shown only by examples. Those Americans who traveled through Germany in the late eighteenth century—including Benjamin Franklin (who had some personal relationships with Germans during his stay in France),[80] Arthur and William Lee,[81] John Quincy Adams,[82] John

78. Auswärtiges Departement to Lusi, May 22, 1781 (Rep. XI. 73, conv. 140A, fol. 105, DZA, Merseburg).

79. However, George Cressener, the English envoy in Bonn, observed that the prince-bishop of Würzburg "is almost the only catholic prince that wishes success to His Majesty's arms": to Thomas Howard, earl of Suffolk, Apr. 14, 1777 (S.P. 81/155, Public Record Office [hereafter cited as PRO], London).

80. The details of Franklin's journey through Germany are still not entirely known. While at Göttingen, he was elected to membership in the Royal Academy of Sciences: Beatrice Marguerite Victory, *Benjamin Franklin and Germany* (New York, 1915), 48–56; Hans Walz, "Benjamin Franklin in Hannover 1766," *Hannoversche Geschichtsblätter*, N.S., XXI (1967), 59–65; Leonard W. Labaree *et al.*, eds., *The Papers of Benjamin Franklin* (New Haven, Conn., 1959–), XIII, 314–316, 383–384, 429. On Franklin's stay at Göttingen, and especially on his discussions with Gottfried Achenwall, see Günther Meinhardt's "Gottfried

Trumbull,[83] Thomas Jefferson,[84] and Gouverneur Morris,[85] to name only a few[86]—certainly played an important role.

Achenwall und Benjamin Franklin. Beziehungen des Elbinger Gelehrten zu dem amerikanischen Staatsmann," *Westpreußen-Jahrbuch*, XXII (1972), 83–86. Among those who met Franklin, Georg Forster saw him at Passy in 1777: Forster, *Tagebücher*, ed. Paul Zincke and Albert Leitzmann (Berlin, 1914), 25–26; Robert L. Kahn, "George Forster and Benjamin Franklin," *APSP*, N.S., CII (1958), 1–6. In 1785 Johann Heinrich Landolt traveled from Zurich to see him: Kahn, "Franklin, Grimm, and J. H. Landolt," *ibid.*, N.S., XCIX (1955), 401–404. On Friedrich Freiherr von der Trenck's acquaintance with Franklin see Trenck, *Merkwürdige Lebensgeschichte* (Stuttgart, 1883), 278. The plans made by Emperor Joseph II to see Franklin in 1777 during his journey to France were obviously never realized: see Jan Ingenhousz to Franklin, Jan. 4, June 28, 1777 (Franklin Papers, V, 2, VI, 83, APSL, Philadelphia), and Victory, 26–28. Information on others who made Franklin's acquaintance during his journey through Germany can be found in: Christine Margarete Häberlin (née Luther) to Franklin, Dec. 4, 1784 (Franklin Papers, XXXII, 192, APSL, Philadelphia); Johann David Michaelis, *Lebensbeschreibung* (Rinteln and Leipzig, 1793), 110–111; Michaelis to Jean Le Rond d'Alembert, June 17, 1780 (Cod. MS. Michaelis, vol. CCCXX, fol. 21v, Staats- und Universitätsbibliothek [hereafter cited as SuUB], Göttingen); Johann Stephan Pütter, *Selbstbiographie*, II (Göttingen, 1798), 490–491; Gottfried Achenwall, *Einige Anmerkungen über Nord-Amerika ... Aus mündlichen Nachrichten des Herrn D. Franklins verfaßt*, 2d ed. (Helmstedt, 1777). The first edition of Achenwall's book appeared in 1769; it had been published two years before as an article in the *Hannoverisches Magazin*.

81. For the German travels of Arthur and William Lee, William Carmichael, and Francis Dana during the American war see Wharton, ed., *Revolutionary Diplomatic Correspondence*, II, 185, 319, 321, 327, 330, 363, 369, 714–715, 787–789, III, 66–67, 346–349, 495, IV, 610–613, 679–681.

82. On the journeys of John Quincy Adams through Germany and his tenure as U.S. minister at Berlin (1797–1801) see his *Memoirs* and *Writings*. His years at Berlin have been treated almost exclusively from the point of view of American foreign policy; see Samuel F. Bemis, *John Quincy Adams and the Foundation of American Foreign Policy* (New York, 1949), 86–110, and George A. Lipsky, *John Quincy Adams* (New York, 1950), 12.

83. In 1786 Trumbull toured the Rhineland, and in 1795 and 1797 he visited the Stuttgart engraver Johann Gotthard Müller. Cf. Trumbull, *Autobiography*, (New York, 1841), 122–141, 179–180, 219, and Trumbull to Jefferson, Oct. 9, 1786, in Boyd *et al.*, eds., *Jefferson Papers*, X, 438–441.

84. Jefferson toured the Rhineland in 1788, followed in the same year by John Rutledge, Jr., the son of the governor of South Carolina, and by Thomas Lee Shippen, the son of the physician. All three saw Jefferson's friend Friedrich Wilhelm Freiherr von Geismar at Hanau. Cf. Boyd *et al.*, eds., *Jefferson Papers*, VIII, 10–11, XII, 680, 691–692, and *passim*, XIII, 444–449, 454, 527.

85. Gouverneur Morris stayed in Germany for a total of almost three years, 1794–1795 and 1796–1798. Cf. Anne C. Morris, ed., *The Diary and Letters of Gouverneur Morris*, II (New York, 1888), 74–90, 170–374; Jared Sparks, *The Life of Gouverneur Morris*, III (Boston, 1832), 51–52, 83–113; and, more recently, Max M. Mintz, *Gouverneur Morris and the American Revolution* (Norman, Okla., 1970), 226–228.

86. Other American travelers included Francis Kinloch, who was befriended by Johannes von Müller; see Kinloch's *Letters from Geneva and France* (Boston, 1819). See also the entries of July 1786 in the Basler Fremden-Buch, fols. 284v–285 (Universitätsbibliothek [hereafter cited as UB], Basel), for a loyalist American named [John?] Montrésor (cf. *Dictionary of American Biography*, s.v. "Montrésor") and for a Mr. Norris and a Mr. Fox, both identified

The approximately thirty thousand German soldiers who went to America in the English service were another invaluable source of information. Their letters and private diaries gave information particularly to the lower social classes, and the oral reminiscences of returning soldiers could complement what had been reported in writing.[87] German officers and soldiers serving on the American side played a similar role. Their number was much smaller, but their acquaintance with the land and its inhabitants was often superior.[88] A small number of individuals who had lived in America before as well as after the war later returned to Germany, where they exerted a considerable influence on the formation of opinion.[89] Finally, there were several former German officers and men in the British army who settled in America and later returned to their old homes in Germany to visit.[90]

as "Citoyen des Etats-Unis de l'Amérique." In 1789 Benjamin Smith Barton received his Ph.D. from the University of Göttingen (Cod. MS. Hist. lit. 108, p. iv, SuUB, Göttingen).

87. See Weber, *America in Imaginative German Literature*, 5–6. Numerous letters and diaries are still scattered in various libraries and archives. Some of them have appeared in print in Germany or America, but a considerable number, no doubt, are still in private hands. I should like here to give my sincere thanks to Mrs. Juliana Gräfin von Gatterburg-Stockhausen of Eberstadt, and to Mr. Fritz Koch of Kassel, for their generous permission to look through the letters of August Du Roi to his sister Cornelia, 1776–1782, and through the war diary of Barthold Koch.

88. There was no recruiting in Germany for American service. Many officers and nobles, however, expressed to Franklin their wish to fight alongside the Americans; but Franklin was unable to accept their offers. Cf. Isaac Minis Hays, ed., *Calendar of the Papers of Benjamin Franklin*, 5 vols. (Philadelphia, 1908), esp. I and II.

89. This was especially true for Peter Hasenclever, who failed as a merchant-manufacturer in America in the 1760s only partly through his own fault. In the late 1770s and the 1780s he gave advice to the Prussian government on matters of American trade. Cf. the biographical studies: [Christian Gottlieb Glauber], *Peter Hasenclever* (Landeshut, 1794); *Zum Laufen hilft nicht schnell seyn oder ... Lebensgeschichte des Kaufmanns Hasenclever ... nebst dessen Bemerkungen über den Handel von Nordamerika* (Hamburg, 1796); and, more recently, Hermann Kellenbenz, "Peter Hasenclever (1716–1793)," in *Rheinische Lebensbilder*, IV (Düsseldorf, 1970), 79–99. There was also the physician Johann David Schoepf, who went with the Ansbach troops to America and who toured the United States after the end of the war. His *Reise durch einige der mittleren und südlichen vereinigten nordamerikanischen Staaten* (Erlangen, 1788) is the most important—and almost the only—American travel account by a German author. See also his further books on America from the 1780s. Johann Ferdinand Heinrich von Autenrieth, who later became chancellor of the University of Tübingen, traveled to the United States at the beginning of the 1790s. He published a small account of this journey in Hegewisch and Ebeling, eds., *Amerikanisches Magazin*, I (1795), 131–159. A further result of this tour was his translation of Benjamin Rush's *Beschreibung des gelben Fiebers ...* (Tübingen, 1796). Lastly, I should refer once more to Bülow's influential work, *Der Freistaat von Nordamerika* (1797).

90. See among others the letters by A. von Bardeleben, Murrarius (later Murray), and Justus Hartmann Scheuber to Friedrich von der Malsburg between 1788 and 1802 (340 v. d. Malsburg, Escheberg, StA, Marburg). I gladly acknowledge my indebtedness to Dr. Joachim Fischer, Frankfurt, for calling these letters to my attention.

In individual cases useful information could come from still another source. For instance, General Lord Cornwallis, who surrendered at Yorktown in 1781, stayed in Germany for a time in the mid-1780s.[91] Of much greater importance in every way was Lafayette's journey to Kassel, Berlin, and Vienna in 1785. The bright and youthful hero's tour through Germany resembled above all a triumphal march, during which he frequently played the role of an advocate for America.[92]

When there was no direct personal contact with former or present participants, the existing positive inclination toward France or England, present in the higher classes, was itself likely to be fruitful. The *Gazette de Leyde* (Leyden), the *Mercure de France* (Paris), and other literary journals were not unknown east of the Rhine.[93] Books ordered from Great Britain were another source of information.[94] A journey to the British Isles during the time of the conflict with the colonies could also contribute to a more sophisticated understanding.[95]

Jan Ingenhousz, who reported at the Vienna court both orally and in writing about the events in North America, derived his information from his correspondence with Franklin.[96] The Prussian general and minister, Hein-

91. Louis Gottschalk, *Lafayette between the American and the French Revolution (1783–1789)* (Chicago, 1950), 186.

92. *Ibid.*, 181–201; Lafayette to John Jay, Feb. 11, 1786, in Lafayette, *Mémoires, correspondance et manuscrits du général Lafayette*, II (Paris, 1837), 144; Louis Gottschalk, ed., *Letters of Lafayette to Washington 1777–1799* (New York, 1944), 303–305. The general admiration for Lafayette was reversed by the events of the French Revolution and Lafayette's imprisonment in Germany; cf. Friedrich Leopold zu Stolberg to his brother Christian, Nov. 1, 1797, in F. L. zu Stolberg, *Briefe*, ed. Jürgen Behrens (Neumünster, 1966), 345–346. In Berlin Lafayette met the American William S. Smith; see Gottschalk, *Lafayette between the Revolutions*, 195, and *DAB*, s.v. "Smith, William Stephen."

93. The *Mercure de France* inspired Wieland to name his periodical *Teutscher Merkur*; see Wahl, *Geschichte des Teutschen Merkur*, 39–42, and Max, *Politische Zeitschrift*, 88. Karl Graf von Zinzendorf first read the Declaration of Independence in the *Gazette de Leyde* (entry of Sept. 14, 1776, in his Tagebuch, XXI, fol. 154v [Nachlaß Zinzendorf, Haus-, Hof- und Staatsarchiv (hereafter cited as HHStA), Vienna]).

94. See, e.g., Mauvillon, *Sammlung von Aufsätzen*, I, [11].

95. See Robert Elsasser, *Über die politischen Bildungsreisen der Deutschen nach England (vom achtzehnten Jahrhundert bis 1815)* (Heidelberg, 1917); John A. Kelly, *England and the Englishman in German Literature of the Eighteenth Century* (New York, 1921), 144; P. E. Matheson, *German Visitors to England 1770–1795, and Their Impressions* (Oxford, 1930). Georg Christoph Lichtenberg traveled to England in 1774–1775 and returned with a copy of the pro-American resolution of the Rockingham Whigs of Feb. 7, 1775, and with a publisher's advertisement for Edmund Burke's *Speech on American Taxation* (Anhang III, 4, and XIIa, Cod. MS. Lichtenberg, SuUB, Göttingen).

96. Ingenhousz and Franklin presumably became acquainted in England between 1765 and 1767. The Viennese court physician was Franklin's only real friend in Germany, and their correspondence, now scattered, continued until Franklin's death. See Labaree *et al.*, eds., *Franklin Papers*, IV, 127, VIII, 358, XIV, 4, 165; Hays, ed., *Calendar of the Franklin Papers*, *passim*; also Boyd *et al.*, eds., *Jefferson Papers*, XIII, 261–262, and *passim*.

rich Adrian Graf von Borcke, garnered much pertinent information from Hamburg and Amsterdam commercial houses.[97] A short time before his death Albrecht von Haller was able to obtain special news about America through his son-in-law, Louis Braun, who was secretary to the English legation in Bern.[98] Sophie von La Roche's acquaintance with the new republic also came by way of relatives, and she used their information in her writings.[99]

Some church groups like the Moravian Brothers (Herrnhuters), the Halle Pietists, and the Helmstedt theologians had special means of obtaining information, that is, through their organizational links with their brethren in North America. They either handed on this information to the members of their congregations or gave it to the public in printed form.[100]

But not only the educated classes had access to such incidental means of information. In large parts of Germany the lower classes of the population directly confronted the war in America. Six states had concluded treaties with Great Britain, and the troops recruited according to these treaties drew added attention to the events in the New World. Although the information about actual happenings in the Western Hemisphere thus gained was virtually negligible, the recruiting of the auxiliary troops probably was an incentive to learn more about these events.

What is true for the recruiting of troops is equally true for the recruiting

97. See, e.g., the letters of Theophile Cazenove, especially those of the 1770s, from Amsterdam. In the 1780s and 1790s Cazenove was active in land speculation in the state of New York; see David M. Ellis *et al.*, *A History of New York State*, 2d ed. (Ithaca, N.Y., 1967), 154, and *DAB*, s.v. "Cazenove," which, however, contains no reference to his connections with von Borcke. See also Peter Boué and sons, from Hamburg, to von Borcke (Rep. 92 v. Borcke III, esp. no. 53, vols. II–IX, DZA, Merseburg).

98. Haller to Gemmingen, Nov. 5, 1777, in Haller, *Briefwechsel zwischen Albrecht von Haller und Eberhard Friedrich von Gemmingen. Nebst dem Briefwechsel zwischen Gemmingen und Bodmer*, ed. Hermann Fischer (Tübingen, 1899), 138. Haller was wrong when he identified Braun as the chargé d'affaires. Actually, Braun occupied this position only between 1783 and 1792; see Ernest Giddey, "Quelques aspects des relations anglo-suisses à la fin du XVIIIᵉ siècle: Louis Braun et Hugh Cleghorn," *Zeitschrift für Schweizerische Geschichte*, XXIX (1949), 47–48.

99. La Roche, *Erscheinungen am See Oneida* (Leipzig, 1798). In a letter of Apr. 29, 1795, Christoph Martin Wieland mentioned Fritz von La Roche, Sophie's eldest son, who was then in America: Wieland, *Briefe an Sophie von La Roche*, ed. Franz Horn (Berlin, 1920), 312. This connection was unknown to Gabriele von Koenig-Warthausen, "Sophie von La Roche," in *Lebensbilder aus Schwaben und Franken*, X (Stuttgart, 1966), 101–125. In this author's less likely opinion, Sophie received her information and inspiration in the 1780s from Fritz's Dutch wife. Fritz had been active during the Revolution on the American side.

100. E.g., Nachrichten von den Unruhen in N. Amerika, 1764–1781 (Rubrik 14.A, no. 46, Archiv der Unitäts-Ältesten-Conferenz, Archiv der Brüder-Unität, Herrnhut; copy in the Library of Congress [hereafter cited as LC], Washington, D.C.); see also theological publications from Halle and Helmstedt, especially those by Velthusen.

of emigrants. Although civilian recruitment did not, during the last third of the eighteenth century, reach the proportions of the recruiting of soldiers, it did result in the spread of some information to the regions where emigrants were enlisted. This knowledge was supplemented by letters from emigrants to their friends and relatives at home and by emigration pamphlets, several of which were widely distributed.[101]

This short summary is meant solely to hint at the potential diversity of sources of information; one cannot generalize about their importance. Only in exceptional cases might it be possible to judge the relative impact of private sources of information as compared with news generally received. The effects of knowledge transmitted to a few persons may have been decisive in some instances; in others, very slight.

101. Franklin's booklet for emigrants to America, first published in Germany in 1786, appeared once more in 1791 in a heavily abridged form: *Auszug der Anmerkungen zum Unterricht derjenigen Europäer, die sich in Amerika niederzulassen gesonnen sind* (n.p., [1791]). The brochure by Lutyens, *Zustand der Auswanderungen*, appeared in 1796 in Hegewisch and Ebeling, eds., *Amerikanisches Magazin*, II, 25–40, as well as in a separate printing, also in 1796. Further pamphlets were published in connection with the recruiting of emigrants in 1791–1792.

3. The Process of Reception

The receptiveness of the bourgeoisie to news and information about America cannot be separated from the question of their political and economic interests.[1] Interest, both objective and material, is the incentive that must exist before the potentiality of information can be converted into real knowledge. The first step toward this conversion, the beginning of the interaction, was the demand for information that became manifest around 1776, a demand that originated with the bourgeoisie's assumption that the events in America could have some real significance for their own situation.

There can be no doubt that there was a ready market for information about America. The number of political newspapers and journals containing news about America increased constantly.[2] In the last decades of the century numerous books dealt with the events of the 1770s and 1780s, as well as with the new republic. The need for information must have been intense, judging from the number of editions that Johann Nikolaus Karl Buchenröder's and Matthias Christian Sprengel's publications went through within a relatively short time.[3] Also, the several editions of many of the travel accounts, such as Brissot de Warville's, indicate a wide distribution. Suffice it to say that there was a general readiness for and interest in gaining accurate information about American events.

Members of the aristocracy and the educated strata of the bourgeoisie were the first to move from mere detached interest to the active acquisition of knowledge. Financial means, the necessary leisure, and intellectual concern were more often found in combination among them than among other groups in the population. It is therefore not surprising that important libraries such as those in Göttingen and Dresden began in the late eighteenth century to acquire many books on North America and on the events taking

1. Basic to these questions are two works by Habermas, *Technik und Wissenschaft als "Ideologie,"* 146–168, and *Erkenntnis und Interesse*, esp. 59–87.

2. See Schneider, *Pressefreiheit*, 85.

3. Sprengel's *Kurze Schilderung der Grosbrittannischen Kolonien in Nord-America*, first published in Göttingen in 1776, was reprinted in 1777 and saw a second edition later in that same year; his *Geschichte der Revolution von Nord-America* appeared in five editions between 1783 and 1788. Buchenröder's *Nachrichten von den Englischen Kolonien* was published in three editions between 1776 and 1778; his four-volume *Nord-Amerika Historisch und Geographisch beschrieben* saw two editions in 1777 and 1778.

place there.[4] As has already been mentioned, Jakob Mauvillon procured books directly from England. Friedrich Leopold Graf zu Stolberg, whom Henry S. King assumed had no interest in America,[5] tells us in a letter written after the outbreak of the war that his reading was confined solely to pamphlets about this conflict, preferably those that defended the actions of the rebellious Americans.[6] A year earlier, in 1775, Johann Jakob Bodmer informed Hans Heinrich Schinz, pastor of Alstetten, that he had read the pamphlets in the *Englische allgemeine Bibliothek* and assumed that Schinz had also read them.[7] Finally, to cite an example from Vienna, the diary of Karl Graf von Zinzendorf contains numerous entries on readings and discussions about America.[8]

It is much more difficult to verify the process of reception among the lower strata of the population. Schubart's journal, *Chronik*, seems to have been well received by the petty bourgeoisie of southwestern Germany,[9] while Buchenröder's publications probably appealed to the same classes in the northwestern German area.[10] No doubt, the emigration pamphlets were addressed to related parts of the population. An Ansbach ordinance of December 21, 1781, gives us an intriguing hint of the means by which news was received and digested among the lower social classes. After it became known in Germany that the Ansbach auxiliary troops had been taken prisoner at Yorktown, the inhabitants of the margravate were ordered "to abstain henceforth from all judging and reasoning about that event and everything pertaining thereto at the threat of monetary or bodily penalty or

4. E.g., the library of the University of Göttingen charged Ebeling with the purchase of books relating to America; see Ebeling to Charles Ghequiere, Dec. 9, 1791 (Lea and Febiger Collection, Historical Society of Pennsylvania [hereafter cited as PHi], Philadelphia), and Ebeling to Jeremias David Reuß, Oct. 1, 1801 (Nachlaß Reuß, I, 483, SuUB, Göttingen). The Saxon Landesbibliothek at Dresden still possesses one of the most eminent collections of 18th-century Americana.

5. King, "Echoes of the American Revolution," *PMP*, XIV (1930), 32.

6. Stolberg, *Briefe*, ed. Behrens, 84, 86, 99 (letters of Sept. 25, Oct. 22, 1776, and Dec. 23, 1777).

7. Bodmer to Schinz, Oct. 16, 1775 (MS. Bodmer 14, no. 355, ZB, Zurich).

8. The diary is deposited in the Nachlaß Zinzendorf, Haus-, Hof- und Staatsarchiv, Vienna. Vols. XV–XLV pertain to the years 1770–1800.

9. Adamietz, "Schubarts *Chronik*," 46–50; Valjavec, *Politische Strömungen*, 96.

10. Since we seldom have subscription lists, little can be said about the readers of certain books. It is noteworthy that Buchenröder's books, though they saw several editions, are found today in only a few libraries. The following sentences from his *Nord-Amerika* may help to underline our assumption: "Mit gegenwärtigem Werke hoffe ich verschiedenen Lesern, welche sich um wahre Kenntnis dieses Weltteils bemühen, einen Dienst getan zu haben, besonders da anitzt so viele aus Pflicht Deutschland verlassen müssen, um Englands Rechte auf dieses Land zu verteidigen. Viele hingegen warten mit Sehnsucht auf den Frieden, um nach diesem Weltteil hinschiffen zu können und sich allda ein erträglicheres Leben zu verschaffen" (III, vii).

imprisonment in a penitentiary."[11] This is assuredly an isolated case, but it is unlikely that only in Ansbach-Bayreuth did people inform one another about events in America and discuss them with their neighbors.

Yet it would be wrong to assume that everyone read books or pamphlets about the former British colonies or discussed the events there with friends. Several important exceptions help to keep the situation in proper perspective. Two of the most significant will be briefly dealt with here. One of them is Goethe, whose often-quoted words, "Amerika, du hast es besser," stem only from the year 1827, when his interest in America, which belongs essentially to the nineteenth century, reached a climax. Goethe paid little attention to America before 1807, when Alexander von Humboldt visited him upon returning from a journey to the New World. Goethe's interest was aroused again around 1817 by the visits of numerous Americans, among them Joseph Green Cogswell, Edward Everett, and George Ticknor —all three of whom studied for two years at the University of Göttingen. The decisive stimulus was given by Prince Bernhard's journey to America in 1825.[12] (Prince Bernhard was the young son of the grand duke Karl August, Goethe's patron.) Prior to these events was a long period of indifference toward the American Revolution and the young state, as Goethe himself later admitted: "I participated in all those events only in so far as they interested the majority of society; I myself and the circle of my closer friends did not concern ourselves with newspapers and news; we wanted to study man; men as such we left alone."[13] Goethe's allusions to America

---

11. "sich von nun an alles Urteilens und Räsonierens über jenen Vorfall und die dahin einschlagende Angelegenheiten bei zu befahren habender Geld-, Leibes- oder Zuchthausstrafe zu enthalten": Soldaten Marsch- und Quartiersachen 1675–1783 (Stadtarchiv [hereafter cited as StadtA], Ansbach).

12. From the voluminous literature on Goethe see among others Paul Carus, "Goethe on America," *Open Court*, XXIII (1909), 502; Victory, *Franklin and Germany*, 109–110; Julius Zeitler, ed., *Goethe-Handbuch*, I (Stuttgart, 1916), 37–38. On numerous points I do not agree with Frank H. Reinsch, "Goethe's Political Interest Prior to 1787," *PMP*, X (1923), 199, 244, 260, 274, 275–276. See also Walter Wadepuhl, "Goethe and America," *Deutsch-Amerikanische Geschichtsblätter*, XXII/XXIII (1924), 77–79, 81; Wadepuhl, *Goethe's Interest in the New World* (Jena, 1934), 8–9, 14–15, 17–18; Anna Hellersberg-Wendriner, "America in the World View of the Aged Goethe," *Germanic Review*, XIV (1939), 270, 276; Friedrich C. Sell, "American Influences upon Goethe," *American-German Review*, IX, no. 4 (1943), 15; Harry W. Pfund, "'Amerika, du hast es besser': The Main Aspects of Goethe's Interest in America," German Society of Pennsylvania, *Yearbook*, I (1950), 35–36, 40; Ernst Beutler, "Von der Ilm zum Susquehanna. Goethe und Amerika in ihren Wechselbeziehungen," in Beutler, *Essays um Goethe*, 5th ed. (Bremen, 1957), 581–582, 584, 594–595, 603–604; Johannes Urzidil, *Das Glück der Gegenwart. Goethes Amerikabild* (Zurich and Stuttgart, 1958); Robert R. Palmer, *The Age of the Democratic Revolution: A Political History of Europe and America, 1760–1800*, 2 vols. (Princeton, N.J., 1959–1964), I, 257.

13. "An allen diesen Ereignissen nahm ich jedoch nur in so fern teil, als sie die größere Gesellschaft interessierten, ich selbst und mein engerer Kreis befaßten uns nicht mit Zeitungen

before 1800 do not seriously contradict this testimony. On the contrary, during the 1790s he summed up, with unmistakable clarity, his rejection of the general interest in America and the illusions associated with it: "Here or nowhere is America!"[14]

The circle of friends of which Goethe spoke must have been a close one. As far as we know, neither Johann Gottfried Herder,[15] nor Christoph Martin Wieland, nor Friedrich Johann Justin Bertuch belonged to it. However, Friedrich Schiller, the author of *Abfall der Niederlande* and of *Wilhelm Tell*, was a friend of Goethe's and perhaps shared his indifference to America. One would have expected Schiller to have had a lively interest in the ideas of the American Revolution, which in some ways were not very different from his own views.[16] But precise statements or opinions have not come down to us; at best, we can find only casual remarks made here and there.[17] Schiller did read Jonathan Carver's *Travels through North America*, but only for the purpose of using the material for his poem "Nadowessische Totenklage."[18] He asked Johann Wilhelm von Archenholtz to write a history of the American Revolution,[19] but when his publisher, Johann Friedrich Cotta, had earlier sent him a biography of Franklin, Schiller had replied with nothing more than a meager thanks.[20] As far as we know, Schiller neither bought books about America nor borrowed any from the Weimar library.[21]

---

und Neuigkeiten; uns war darum zu tun, den Menschen kennen zu lernen; die Menschen überhaupt ließen wir gern gewähren": Goethe, "Dichtung und Wahrheit," bk. XVII, in Goethe, *Werke*, Weimar ed., 143 vols. (Weimar, 1887–1912), I/XXIX, 69.

14. "Hier, oder nirgend ist Amerika": Goethe, "Wilhelm Meisters Lehrjahre," bk. VII, chap. 3, *ibid.*, I/XXIII, 20.

15. Marion D. Learned, "Herder and America," *GAA*, N.S., II (1904), 551–555; Albert R. Schmitt, *Herder und Amerika* (The Hague and Paris, 1967).

16. W. W. Florer, "Schiller's Conception of Liberty and the Spirit of '76," *GAA*, N.S., IV (1906), 111–113.

17. Julius Goebel, "Amerika in der deutschen Dichtung," in *Forschungen der deutschen Philologie. Festgabe für Rudolf Hildebrand* (Leipzig, 1894), 113; J. A. Walz, "American Revolution and German Literature," *MLN*, XVI (1901), 341–342; Walz, "Three Swabian Journalists," *AG*, IV (1902), 99; William H. Carruth, "Schiller and America: An Address at the Schillerfeier of the University of Wisconsin, May 9, 1905," *GAA*, N.S., IV (1906), 139, 141, 145; King, "Echoes of the American Revolution," *PMP*, XIV (1930), 79, 82; Reinhard Buchwald, *Schiller*, 2d ed., I (Wiesbaden, 1953), 256; Ernst Fraenkel, *Amerika im Spiegel des deutschen politischen Denkens. Äußerungen deutscher Staatsmänner und Staatsdenker über Staat und Gesellschaft in den Vereinigten Staaten* (Cologne and Opladen, 1959), 18.

18. To Goethe, June 30, 1797, in Schiller, *Briefe. Kritische Gesamtausgabe*, ed. Fritz Jonas, 7 vols. (Stuttgart, 1892), V, 212.

19. To and from Archenholtz, July 10, 28, 1795, in Schiller, *Werke*, National ed., XXVIII, 8, XXXV, 267.

20. From and to Cotta, Nov. 24, Dec. 9, 1794, *ibid.*, XXXV, 95, XXVII, 101.

21. "Schillers Bibliothek," in *Zum 9. Mai 1905. Schiller-Ausstellung im Goethe- und*

During the last two years of his life, however, Schiller possessed a print of the Battle of Bunker Hill, which today decorates the Schiller house in Weimar.[22] This copper engraving was made by Johann Gotthard Müller of Stuttgart after a painting by John Trumbull. Trumbull had commissioned Müller in 1789 to make the engraving and visited him several times during the following years, the last time being in 1797, when he came to pick up the just-finished plate and his original painting.[23] At the end of August, immediately before Trumbull's last visit, Goethe was staying in Stuttgart and visited Müller. Later, he wrote to Schiller about the painting and about the master's work.[24] When Müller was himself in Weimar in 1801, he called on Schiller, and they obviously discussed, among other things, the Bunker Hill engraving. At any rate, at the end of the year Müller sent a copy of the engraving to Schiller as a present, which clearly gave the poet great pleasure.[25]

But here we come to the end of Schiller's interest in America, at least as far as it can be documented. The Enlightenment and Classicism probably occupied him much more than immediate political events. The same inclinations that led him to refuse to take sides openly during the French Revolution apparently governed his thinking in the earlier years. When he wanted to express his ideal of freedom poetically, he had other topics available that were, from his point of view, more timeless.

The Reception and Transmission of Knowledge

During the last third of the eighteenth century numerous scholars and publicists endeavored to raise the general level of knowledge about North America.[26] Their essays and articles and their historical, political-historical, and geographical publications seem to have satisfied, at least

---

Schiller-Archiv (Weimar, 1905), 47–83 (the list, however, is incomplete); Paul Ortlepp, "Schillers Bibliothek," in *Zuwachs der Grossherzoglichen Bibliothek zu Weimar in den Jahren 1911 bis 1913* (Weimar, 1914), ix–lxxvi. Ortlepp also lists those books that Schiller is known to have borrowed from the Weimar library.

22. Gerhard Hendel, *Das Schillerhaus in Weimar*, 4th ed. (Weimar, 1966), 46.

23. [John Trumbull], Memorandum of Agreement with Johann Gotthard von Müller for Plate of Bunker Hill, August 9, 1789 (Gratz Collection, PHi, Philadelphia); Trumbull, *Autobiography*, 179–180, 219, 221; Theodore Sizer, *The Works of Colonel John Trumbull*, 2d ed. (New Haven, Conn., 1967), table 145.

24. Aug. 30, 1797, in Goethe, *Werke*, Weimar ed., 4/XII, 278–279.

25. Schiller to Müller, Jan. 3, 1802, in Schiller, *Briefe*, ed. Jonas, VI, 327–328.

26. Among the editors of periodicals, university professors loomed largest; see Max, *Politische Zeitschrift*, 278–281.

partially, the widespread need for information. The list of those who hoped to contribute something is remarkably long. It contains such well-known names as Johann Jakob Moser,[27] and obscure names that have long been forgotten. All of these contributors provide evidence of the steps by which mere interest was transformed into the actual acquisition of knowledge. By revealing to us the points of emphasis within the given framework and telling us about them, they convey to us an idea of what the receiving population learned.

The author was a mediator, no matter whether he was well known or obscure. Some men became well known in the contemporary German intellectual life on the basis of their expertise about America. The demand for information in the mid-1770s was the cornerstone for the rise of the "American expert" in the 1780s. Just as Friedrich Nicolai was considered the dean among German literary critics of his time, so Sprengel and Ebeling were the authorities on American studies in Germany during the 1780s and 1790s, respectively. What they said was accepted as definitive, not only because of their personal authority, but also because they satisfied a desire for believable descriptions of the land beyond the sea. The desire was especially great during the last two decades of the century because of the uncertainty and contradictions in the news, the specific historical situation after the peace of 1783, and the changed circumstances in the world after the French Revolution.

Nobody was able to assume a position of authority during the American Revolution, neither Schlözer, who largely abstained from expressing his own opinion, nor Buchenröder, who published much between 1776 and 1778 but never overcame anonymity and obscurity. Julius August Remer failed as well to make the grade, in part because he lived in Brunswick, one of the states that furnished auxiliary troops.

Matthias Christian Sprengel was more fortunate. Born in Rostock in 1745,[28] he attended the University of Göttingen during the 1770s. There he was a student of Schlözer's, with whom he also had a close personal relationship, and there his interest in America was awakened. As early as 1776 he published a short survey of the rebelling colonies, which sold well even though it appeared anonymously.[29] His *Briefe den gegenwärtigen Zustand von Nord Amerika betreffend* was very likely published at about the same

27. Moser, *Nord-America nach den Friedensschlüssen.*

28. Bruno Felix Hänsch, "Matthias Christian Sprengel, ein geographischer Publizist am Ausgange des 18. Jahrhunderts"(publ. Ph.D. diss., University of Leipzig, 1902), 14, proves with the Rostock parish registers that Sprengel was born in 1745 and not in 1746 as hitherto assumed.

29. *Kurze Schilderung der Grosbrittannischen Kolonien.* Both a reprint and a second edition were published at Göttingen in 1777.

time.[30] About a year later, probably in 1778, he was appointed associate professor of history at Göttingen, and his first academic lecture dealt with "the history and present situation of the British colonies in America."[31]

In the following year Sprengel moved to Halle to accept the post of full professor of history; his inaugural address was "On the Origin of the Negro Slave Trade" and again concerned North America.[32] He soon won new friends in the Prussian university town, among them the scientist Johann Reinhold Forster, later his father-in-law. Their common interest in the Anglo-Saxon and non-European world was an added bond of friendship. In Halle, too, Sprengel gave public lectures on the American colonies, the War of Independence, the treaties of 1763 and 1783, and numerous other topics.[33] His favorite study continued to be America, to which he devoted two more publications in the fall of 1782, the first to appear with his full name as author.[34]

Sprengel had succeeded in gaining a reputation as an authority on America among both academicians and the educated bourgeoisie. In doing so, he prepared the way for the success of his history of the American Revolution. Published as a volume of the *Allgemeines historisches Taschenbuch* by the renowned Berlin firm of Haude and Spener immediately after the Treaty of Paris, it was the first comprehensive German study of the subject. The investigation, which has some similarities to Guillaume-Thomas-François Raynal's *Révolution de l'Amérique*,[35] emphasized the revolutionary character of the events in America and the beneficial changes resulting from them. It quickly gained popularity. No more than a year after its publication a contemporary historian remarked that the book "is in everybody's hands, or, at least, should be."[36] Going through five editions between 1783 and 1788, it was not only the most successful book by a German author of the late

30. According to the catalogs of the book fairs, both the *Kurze Schilderung* and the *Briefe* were published for the 1776 fall fair.

31. Hänsch, "Sprengel," 15.

32. Sprengel, *Vom Ursprung des Negerhandels. Ein Antrittsprogramm* (Halle, 1779).

33. Hänsch, "Sprengel," 17. See also Sprengel's letter to Christian Gottlob Heyne, June 22, 1782, in which he asked for new books on the American Revolution for reviewing (Scient. 47, 3, vol. II, no. 335, AAW, Göttingen).

34. *Geschichte der Europäer in Nordamerika*, I (Leipzig, 1782); *Über den jetzigen Nordamericanischen Krieg und dessen Folgen für England und Frankreich* (Leipzig, 1782). Both appeared at the fall fair.

35. Interestingly, Sprengel failed to list Raynal's book in his bibliography, though it was published in a German translation (*Staatsveränderung von Amerika*) in 1782, i.e., at the very time that Sprengel was looking around for new items on the American Revolution. Raynal was too famous an author in his day for it to be probable that Sprengel missed this publication.

36. "in jedermanns Händen ist oder doch wenigstens sein muß": Johann Friedrich Poppe, *Geschichte der Europäischen Staaten*, 2 vols. (Halle, 1783–1784), II, 360. The *Taschenbuch* was published at Berlin in 1784 in a reprint; the other reprints appeared at Speyer in 1785 and

eighteenth century dealing specifically with North America, but it was also an authoritative presentation of events.

Until his death in 1803 Sprengel's main interest continued to be the United States, but in his last years he limited his activities primarily to the publication of sets of volumes containing, among other items, treatises on America by other authors.[37] This later period already belonged to someone whose erudition and knowledge were superior to Sprengel's: Christoph Daniel Ebeling, the most important European Americanist of his time.

Ebeling was born in 1741 in Garmissen, near Hildesheim, the son of a later Lüneburg superintendent. From 1763 to 1767 he studied theology at Göttingen and afterward was employed as a private tutor in Leipzig. Two years later he moved to Hamburg, where he was a teacher and then, together with Johann Georg Büsch, became director of the Handlungsakademie. In 1784 the city of Hamburg appointed him professor of history and Greek at the Akademische Gymnasium, and fifteen years later he was also appointed city librarian, an office he held until his death in 1817.[38]

Ebeling's first article touching on America appeared in 1765 in the *Hannoverisches Magazin.*[39] With the outbreak of the American war and the increased demand for information, Ebeling came out with a translation of Andrew Burnaby's *Travels through the middle settlements in North-America,* in the preface to which he announced his intention to publish further on American events.[40] The next year brought his *Amerikanische Bibliothek,* and in 1780 he published a German translation of Jonathan Carver's *Travels* with his own foreword.[41]

---

at Frankenthal in 1785 and 1788 under its real title, *Geschichte der Revolution von Nord-America.* See also Doll, "American History," *APST,* N.S., XXXVIII (1948), 461.

37. See especially the articles on America in Johann Reinhold Forster and Sprengel, eds., *Beiträge zur Völker und Länderkunde,* 14 vols. (Leipzig, 1781–1790); Sprengel and Georg Forster, eds., *Neue Beiträge zur Völker- und Länderkunde,* 13 vols. (Leipzig, 1790–1793); Sprengel, ed., *Auswahl der besten ausländischen geographischen und statistischen Nachrichten zur Aufklärung der Völker und Länderkunde,* 14 vols. (Halle, 1794–1800).

38. See two brief biographies: Charles I. Landis, *Charles [i.e., Christoph] Daniel Ebeling, Who from 1793 to 1816 Published in Germany a Geography and History of the United States in Seven Volumes* (Lancaster, Pa., 1929); Hermann Tiemann, "Christoph Daniel Ebeling. Hamburger Amerikanist, Bibliothekar und Herausgeber Klopstocks," *Zeitschrift des Vereins für Hamburgische Geschichte,* XLI (1951), 352–374.

39. Christoph Daniel Ebeling, "Fragen, welche erst nach einigen Jahrhunderten können aufgelöst werden," *Hannoverisches Magazin,* Nov. 15, 1765, cols. 1441–1448.

40. Ebeling's preface to his translation of Burnaby, *Reisen durch die mittlern Kolonien der Engländer in Nord-Amerika, nebst Anmerkungen über den Zustand der Kolonien* (Hamburg and Kiel, 1776), [6].

41. Jonathan Carver, *Reisen durch die innern Gegenden von Nord-Amerika in den Jahren 1766, 1767 und 1768, mit einer Landkarte,* trans. from the English (Hamburg, 1780). The translation was not by Ebeling.

In 1793 the first volume of Ebeling's promised work was published. It evaluated American sources and literature methodically and thoroughly— for the first time in Germany, and without parallel in eighteenth-century Europe. With his voluminous correspondence with leading representatives of American intellectual life and with his private library that housed a singular collection of Americana, Ebeling became for Germans the personification of all that could be known about America. His uncompleted seven-volume *Erdbeschreibung und Geschichte von Amerika* is a lasting expression of a lifetime of study. Five volumes of it appeared in quick succession before the end of the century, plus a substantially enlarged second edition of the first volume.[42] Proceeding from north to south, state by state, until the discussion breaks off with Virginia, Ebeling pictured in several thousand pages the land of his dreams, a land which enjoyed the contentment and happiness of liberty and the blessings of a wise republican constitution, while Europe was plagued by the excesses of revolutions and wars.

As early as the 1790s Ebeling had an enormous reputation because of this monumental work. The leading representatives of Hamburg society, men like Georg Heinrich Sieveking and Friedrich Gottlieb Klopstock, were among his friends, and only the least educated did not know his name, so famous was the man and so respected his work.[43] Because he was an outstanding

42. Christoph Daniel Ebeling, *Erdbeschreibung und Geschichte von Amerika. Die vereinten Staaten von Nordamerika* (Hamburg, 1793–1816): Vol. I, *New Hampshire, Massachusetts* (1793); Vol. II, *Rhode Island, Connecticut, Vermont, New York* (1794); Vol. III, *New York, New Jersey* (1796); Vols. IV and VI, *Pennsylvania* (1797, 1803); Vol. V, *Delaware, Maryland* (1799); Vol. VII, *Virginia* (1816). In a uniform scheme of 21 sections each, Ebeling tried to describe all aspects of the history and life of each state. The volumes each contain 800 to 1200 pages. Vol. I appeared in a second edition, revised and much enlarged, in 1800. Vols. I–V were first published as Pt. XIII of Büsching's *Erdbeschreibung*, a multivolume universal history and geography.

43. On Ebeling's outstanding esteem among his contemporaries see among others: Joel Barlow to Ezra Stiles, May 27, 1794, Massachusetts Historical Society, *Collections*, 2d Ser., VIII (1826), 269; Friedrich von Matthisson to Carl Victor Freiherr von Bonstetten, June 1794, in Matthisson, *Erinnerungen*, 3 vols. (Zurich, 1810–1816), II, 152; Günther Karl Friedrich Seidel, in his translation of David Ramsay, *Geschichte der Amerikanischen Revolution aus den Acten des Congresses der vereinigten Staaten . . .*, 4 vols. (Berlin, 1794–1795), IV, iv; Friedrich Gentz, in *Neue Deutsche Monatsschrift*, July 1795, 244n. Others were not as taken with Ebeling. Johann Wilhelm Ludwig Gleim wrote sarcastically about the people of Hamburg in a letter to Archenholtz, Mar. 2, 1797: "Ebeling ist ihnen ein unbekannter Name; sie haben keine Seelen, sie bestehen aus Zunge nur und Magen" (MSS collection, N, no. 8, Gleimhaus [hereafter cited as GH], Halberstadt). (I gratefully acknowledge the kind assistance of Mrs. Gerlinde Wappler, manuscript librarian at the Gleimhaus, in the gathering of information from this and other letters housed in the Gleim collection.) For 20th-century evaluations of Ebeling see: Bruno Albin Müller, *Hamburger Beiträge zur Amerikanistik. Beschreibung und Würdigung ausgewählter Schaustücke aus der zum 24. Internationalen Amerikanisten-Kongreß in Hamburg von der Staats- und Universitäts-Bibliothek veranstalteten Ausstellung* (Hamburg, 1933), 9–11; Michael Kraus, "Literary Relations Between Europe

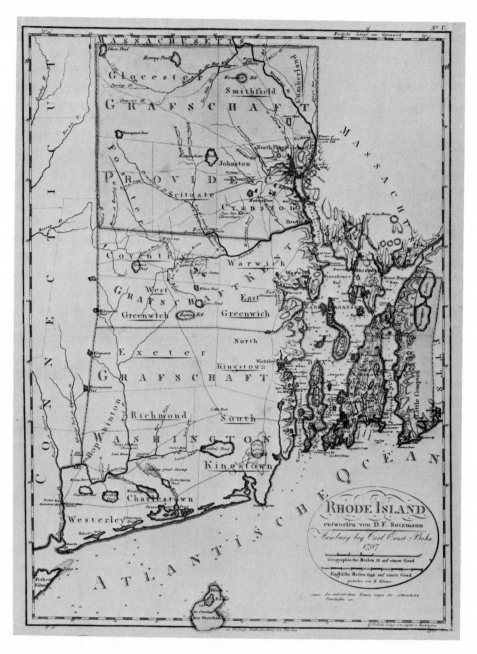

Figure 2. Daniel Friedrich Sotzmann, Map of Rhode Island. Published in Hamburg in 1797 to accompany Vol. II of Christoph Daniel Ebeling's *Erdbeschreibung und Geschichte von Amerika* (Hamburg, 1794).

Courtesy John Carter Brown Library, Brown University, Providence, R.I.

member of the so-called republic of letters and because his authoritative work was on a subject that had great appeal, Ebeling became his own legend in the 1790s, the father of German scientific research on North America. But in spite of its thoroughness, Ebeling's presentation was by no means complete. A discussion of the American Revolution was lacking, since he had planned to add it only after completing his description of the individual states.[44] Besides, Ebeling's influence on the general level of German understanding of America was probably not very great; it cannot be assumed that even among his most enthusiastic followers the thousands of pages of his work were read with the necessary thoroughness.[45] His fame was more likely founded on his extensive erudition than on the factual knowledge that his contemporaries obtained from his books.

Neither Sprengel's nor Ebeling's treatises were comprehensive. Notwithstanding their dedicated scholarship, serious gaps remained. No one in the circle of those Germans who tried to bring North America closer to their contemporaries, and perhaps throw some light on phases hitherto neglected, succeeded in achieving the needed authority. Sufficient opportunity remained for others to collect, compile, and publish additional material that would contribute to public understanding of American events.

Another intellectually outstanding figure, and, as far as we are concerned, the most controversial one, was the Göttingen historian August Ludwig Schlözer. Born in 1735 in Württemberg, Schlözer spent long years in an influential position in Russia, coming to Göttingen at the end of the 1760s. Eventually becoming a Königlich grossbrittanischer Hofrat, he paid close attention to the course of the American Revolution but was reserved in uttering his own opinions. Consequently, we know him mainly as the editor of Daniel Fenning's geography of America, A New System of Geography,[46] and of letters of German officers in the War of Independence.[47] His greatest influence, however, was exerted through his periodicals, in which he published soldiers' letters and other material on the American Revolution.

The numerous reports about events in North America that appeared in Schlözer's periodicals came, as a rule, from British sources or from German officers in the English army. The reports had, therefore, a generally friendly

---

and America in the Eighteenth Century," WMQ, 3d Ser., I (1944), 218; Doll, "American History," APST, N.S., XXXVIII (1948), 474.

44. Ebeling, Erdbeschreibung, I, xi.

45. See Gotthold Ephraim Lessing, Werke, ed. Herbert G. Göpfert (Munich, 1970–), I, 9: "Wir wollen weniger erhoben und fleissiger gelesen sein."

46. Fenning, Neue Erdbeschreibung. A reprint of the Göttingen and Leipzig first edition of 1777 appeared in Bern that same year. The translation is not by Schlözer.

47. August Ludwig Schlözer, Vertrauliche Briefe aus Kanada und Neu-England vom J. 1777 und 1778 (Göttingen, 1779).

tone toward England. But on the whole, Schlözer's productions cannot justifiably be labeled as anti-American, as has occasionally been done.[48] Schlözer
published commentaries on a variety of topics, always keeping an eye, however, on the censorship policy of his government. The danger of censorship
may have been an important reason for his reluctance to take sides. Nevertheless, it was possible for him to add measurably to his fellow citizens'
knowledge of North America and of what was happening there, for his voice
carried weight in Germany.

A personality of quite a different kind was the historian Julius August
Remer, who was born in 1738 in Brunswick, became a professor there in
1770 and in Helmstedt in 1787, and who died, like Sprengel, in 1803. His
interests were directed mainly to what we might today call contemporary
history. Thus oriented, he devoted his energy to a lifelong study of the
American Revolution and the United States. Although there were only hints
of this in his first historical compendium,[49] his unusual interest in events of
the Western Hemisphere is documented by the *Amerikanisches Archiv*,
which he edited during the first years of the war, as well as by his anonymous *Geschichte des Krieges zwischen Großbritannien und den vereinigten
Bourbonischen Mächten und Nordamerikanische Kolonien*,[50] of which
only the first volume, ending in 1778, was published. During the subsequent
two decades he did not write again specifically on America. As far as is
known, Remer's only pertinent contribution of this time was a translation of
Charles Stedman's *History of the Origin, Progress, and Termination of the
American War*, which was published with his critical notes as *Geschichte des
Ursprungs, des Fortgangs und der Beendigung des Americanischen Krieges*.[51]
But in the 1780s and 1790s Remer brought out a series of historical trea-
tises, usually handbooks concerning recent history,[52] that duly considered

48. E.g., Gallinger, "Haltung der deutschen Publizistik," 49–50, and, not wholly convincing, Renate Zelger, "Der Historisch-Politische Briefwechsel und die Staatsanzeigen August Ludwig von Schlözers als Zeitschrift und Zeitbild" (unpubl. Ph.D. diss., University of
Munich, 1953), 171–172. More balanced are Theodor Zermelo, "August Ludwig Schlözer,
ein Publizist im alten Reich," in *Jahresbericht über die Friedrichs-Werdersche Gewerbeschule
in Berlin* (Berlin, 1875), 18, and Ford, "Two German Publicists," *JEGP*, VIII (1909), 155,
164.
49. Remer, *Handbuch der Geschichte neuerer Zeiten von der grossen Völkerwanderung
bis auf den Hubertusburger-Frieden* (Brunswick, 1771).
50. (Leipzig, 1780).
51. (Berlin, 1795).
52. Remer, *Handbuch der allgemeinen Geschichte*, 3 vols. (Brunswick, 1783–1784). Part
III, the important one in our context, appeared in a third edition in 1799 as *Handbuch der
neuern Geschichte*. See also Remer's *Darstellung der Gestalt der historischen Welt in jedem
Zeitraume* (Berlin and Stettin, 1794), reprinted at Frankfurt and Leipzig in 1794, and his
Handbuch der Geschichte unsrer Zeiten (1799) and *Lehrbuch der allgemeinen Geschichte*
(1800).

contemporary American history. These works, which, in view of the many editions and reprints, were probably widely read, are testimony to an amazing insight into current events and to a remarkable knowledge of North America. They were in their time a valuable supplement to Sprengel's and Ebeling's works.

Historians were not the only commentators on the American scene. During the 1790s a noteworthy contribution was made by the Brunswick botanist Eberhard August Wilhelm Zimmermann (not to be confused with the Hanover physician Johann Georg Zimmermann, whose interest in America will be discussed later). Like those scholars mentioned above, E.A.W. Zimmermann was born between 1735 and 1745, specifically, in 1743 in Uelzen. He too was a student for a time at the University of Göttingen, and like Ebeling, Schlözer, and Remer, he was the son of a Protestant minister. Although he had expressed a certain interest in America during the War of Independence,[53] Zimmermann did not reveal a deeply felt interest until the 1790s, when he published his translations of travel descriptions by John Long, Edward Umfreville, William Bartram, and Gilbert Imlay, as well as a medical treatise by Benjamin Smith Barton, with some annotations of a general character.[54] Together with Paul Jakob Bruns, he edited a collection of geographical material in three volumes, which dealt in part with North America.[55] Zimmermann had several direct connections with America, and he was a member of the American Philosophical Society.[56] Also during these years, which were devoted primarily to gathering material, he prepared his great work comparing the American and the French

53. See his *Geographische Geschichte des Menschen und der allgemein verbreiteten vierfüßigen Thiere nebst einer hierher gehörigen Weltcharte*, 3 vols. (Leipzig, 1778–1783).

54. Long, *Westindischen Dollmetschers und Kaufmanns See- und Land-Reisen, enthaltend: eine Beschreibung der Sitten und Gewohnheiten der Nordamerikanischen Wilden . . .*, trans. from the English (Hamburg, 1791); Umfreville, *Über den gegenwärtigen Zustand der Hudsonsbay, der dortigen Etablissements und ihres Handels, nebst einer Beschreibung des Innern von Neu Wallis, und einer Reise von Montreal nach Neu York*, trans. from the English (Helmstedt, 1791); Bartram, *Reisen durch Nord- und Süd-Karolina, Georgien, Ost- und West-Florida . . .*, trans. from the English (Berlin, 1793); Imlay, *Nachrichten von dem westlichen Lande der Nordamerikanischen Freistaaten . . .*, trans. from the English (Berlin, 1793); Barton, *Abhandlung über die vermeinte Zauberkraft der Klapperschlange und anderer amerikanischen Schlangen . . .*, trans. from the English (Leipzig, 1798).

55. Bruns and E.A.W. Zimmermann, eds., *Repositorium für die neueste Geographie, Statistik und Geschichte*, 3 vols. (Tübingen, 1792–1793).

56. A few letters from Zimmermann to David Rittenhouse and to Mathew Carey are in the American Philosophical Society Archives and in the Lea and Febiger Collection, Historical Society of Pennsylvania, both at Philadelphia. See Gilbert Chinard, "The American Philosophical Society and the World of Science (1768–1800)," *APSP*, LXXXVII (1943–1944), 2–5.

revolutions, the first volume of which was published in 1795.[57] At the request of "many experts here,"[58] Zimmermann published a French translation of the first volume before the second and final one was issued.[59]

Other Americanists, none of whom attained a level of importance equivalent to the foregoing, included: the Kassel and later Brunswick professor Jakob Mauvillon, a friend of Mirabeau's who made American affairs his "favorite study" around the mid-1770s,[60] although he produced only a translation of Raynal and a collection of essays that did not deal exclusively with North America;[61] Johann Reinhold Forster and Georg Forster, who during the 1790s made many contributions toward a better understanding of America;[62] and the Berlin professor Günther Karl Friedrich Seidel, who published translations and some works of his won.[63] However, the influ-

57. *Frankreich und die Freistaaten von Nordamerika*.
58. "von vielen hiesigen Kennern": E.A.W. Zimmermann to Bertuch, Oct. 4, 1795 (Nachlaß Bertuch I, 3813, GSA, Weimar).
59. *Essai de Comparaison entre la France et les Etats-Unis*, trans. by the author, 2 vols. (Leipzig, 1797).
60. "Lieblingsstudium": Mauvillon's preface to his translation of [Guillaume-Thomas-François Raynal], *Philosophische und politische Geschichte der Besitzungen und des Handels der Europäer in beiden Indien*, 7 vols. (Hanover, 1774–1778), VI (1777), [3].
61. Mauvillon, *Sammlung von Aufsätzen* (1776–1777).
62. While in England, J. R. Forster had edited several works on North America as early as 1770. In the 1780s, in Germany, he and Sprengel edited the already-mentioned *Beiträge zur Völker und Länderkunde*, which Forster's son Georg continued at the beginning of the 1790s, also with Sprengel. In the 1790s the elder Forster edited the much esteemed series, *Magazin von merkwürdigen neuen Reisebeschreibungen*, which included translations from several works on America, e.g., his own translation of Jacques Pierre Brissot de Warville, *Neue Reise durch die Nordamerikanischen Freistaaten im Jahre 1788* (Berlin, 1792), and Georg's translation of Thomas Anburey, *Reisen im Innern von Nordamerika* (Berlin, 1792). Furthermore, the elder Forster wrote the preface to the German edition of *La Fayette als Staatsmann als Krieger und als Mensch*, trans. from the French [by Heinrich Julius Ludwig von Rohr] (Magdeburg, 1794). To Georg Forster we also owe several works which bear, at least in part, on Franklin and on America: *Kleine Schriften. Ein Beytrag zur Völker- und Länderkunde, Naturgeschichte und Philosophie des Lebens*, 6 vols. (Leipzig and Berlin, 1789–1797); *Erinnerungen aus dem Jahr 1790 in historischen Gemälden und Bildnissen von D. Chodowiecki, D. Berger, Cl. Kohl, J. F. Bolt und J. S. Ringck* (Berlin, 1793); *Geschichte der Reisen, die seit Cook an der Nordwest- und Nordost-Küste von Amerika und in dem nördlichsten Amerika selbst . . .*, 3 vols. (Berlin, 1791). The third volume of the latter work appeared once more as *Nathaniel Portlocks und Georg Mortimers Reisen an die Nordwestküste von Amerika . . .* (Berlin, 1796). Both this and the original publication are mainly annotated translations, and both contain Long's travel account, which Georg also translated and published separately as *Reisen eines Amerikanischen Dolmetschers und Pelzhändlers . . .* (Berlin, 1792). The younger Forster's plans to translate Ramsay's *History of the American Revolution* failed for political reasons, leaving that project for Günther Karl Friedrich Seidel; see Georg Forster, *Briefe an Christian Friedrich Voß*, ed. Paul Zincke (Dortmund, 1915), 15, 134 (letters of Dec. 18, 1790, Mar. 27, 1792).
63. Seidel's translation appeared as Ramsay, *Amerikanische Revolution* (1794–1795), the fourth volume of which is largely by Seidel himself. Furthermore, he wrote the *Neueste*

ence of these men on the formation of opinion was much more limited than that of their predecessors, Sprengel and Remer, who published more.

Limits to the Acquisition of Knowledge

Judged quantitatively, the material about America at the disposal of the interested German contemporary was remarkably manifold. But how did he make use of it, what did he retain, and, finally, how much did he know measured against today's knowledge? This problem leads back to the quality of the information at his disposal. Where were the points of emphasis in the average presentation and in what light were the facts presented? Of equal importance is the determination of what aspects of American events were more or less neglected. Constant shortcomings in the quality of available information could not fail to have had a decisive influence on the final judgment.

It is evident that these first questions can be discussed only in a few representative instances by selecting certain personalities, in this case members of the top national and social strata, since their interest and level of knowledge would eventually have political consequences. Information about the average member of the middle class and his general knowledge may be drawn from an examination of the number, content, and limitations of the sources generally available to him.

Government circles deserve special attention because their view of events was so markedly dictated by political and other interests. As will be shown, the total content of the generally available sources of information was less important for them than for the bourgeoisie, not because they had access also to the reports of their legations, but because they selected from the news only that which could be related to their own immediate interests. The politics of their governments determined what they picked out and paid attention to, especially since the events took place at such a great distance and seemed to concern them only tangentially or not at all. Their degree of knowledge about events in North America was therefore mainly

---

Geschichte von Europa seit dem Ende des siebenjährigen Krieges, 2 vols. (Berlin, 1798–1799), which is mainly a history of North America, especially in the 1760s, and which appeared as Vols. XIII and XIV of William Russell, *Geschichte des heutigen Europa*. Seidel's early death cut off the *Neueste Geschichte* with the second volume.

the result of a narrow selection from the abundance of information, dictated by state interests.

More than pure curiosity about events in the Western Hemisphere motivated the interest of a man like Frederick II of Prussia.[64] He had been following events in the New World closely since at least the mid-1770s, all the time taking no note whatsoever of the domestic development of America. For him, world politics and the question of possible consequences for Prussia were clearly of uppermost concern. The problem of how far the war would spread and whether it might extend to France and Spain confronted him very early.[65] He also asked himself whether the recent events permitted the conclusion that Great Britain's power had passed its zenith,[66] a prospect that would not have met his dislike. Also affecting his interest in American events was his determination to keep the American market open, no matter how the conflict might end.[67] In the meantime, he intended to pursue a policy that was least harmful to the commercial interests of his state, and, if at all possible, to make the war useful in this respect.[68] "Without shocking anyone," Frederick's main purpose was "to profit quietly from whatever opportunity is offered."[69]

The interests of the Prussian monarch were doubtlessly one-sided, and he was unable to do justice to the importance of the American Revolution. If one contemplates his policies and his pertinent statements, one may possibly gain the impression that he was aware of the immanent contrast of American ideals and the European *ancien régime*. However, he apparently did not attribute to these ideals a direct political meaning as far as Germany was concerned.

64. Richard Konetzke, "Zwischen Berlin und Madrid," in *Festschrift Peter Rassow* (Wiesbaden, 1961), 163, generalizes, for example, from a single very specific remark by the king to Bernhard Wilhelm Freiherr von der Goltz, Mar. 20, 1779 (Volz, ed., *Politische Correspondenz Friedrichs des Grossen*, XLII, 481), when Frederick wrote from Breslau at a time when the War of the Bavarian Succession was not yet over and the Peace of Teschen (May 13, 1779) was not yet concluded. The priorities of Prussian foreign policy in a situation like that are obvious.

65. To Joachim Karl Graf von Maltzahn, Mar. 25, 1776, in Volz, ed., *Politische Correspondenz Friedrichs des Grossen*, XXXVII, 552.

66. To Prince Heinrich, Jan. 16, 1776, *ibid.*, 418.

67. Cabinet order to Karl Wilhelm Graf Finck von Finckenstein, June 20, 1777, *ibid.*, XXXIX, 228.

68. To Prince Heinrich, June 17, July 2, and to Goltz, Aug. 31, 1777, *ibid.*, 225, 243, 307; Schulenburg to A. Lee, June 26, 1777, in Wharton, ed., *Revolutionary Diplomatic Correspondence*, II, 350–351.

69. "Sans choquer personne, nous profitons sans bruit de l'occasion qui s'offre à nous": to Prince Heinrich, June 25, 1777, in Volz, ed., *Politische Correspondenz Friedrichs des Grossen*, XXXIX, 233–234. On the interweaving of Prussia's English and American policy with its commercial interests see Horst Dippel, "Prussia's English Policy after the Seven Years' War," *Central European History*, IV (1971), esp. 206–212.

Frederick's views correspond to those of Emperor Joseph II. At the Vienna court, events in the West were followed with interest. But here too there was no inclination to take sides openly. The Austrians moved in the tracks of European power politics just as did their Prussian antagonists.[70] Little significance, therefore, should be given to Joseph's desire to meet Franklin during his journey to France in 1777. Nothing in official Vienna policy hints that such a meeting—which in the end did not take place—would have been more than a *rencontre* between two exponents of the Enlightenment.[71]

Vienna, however, was much better informed about American events than the court of the Prussian king, owing to the presence of court physician Jan Ingenhousz, a personal friend of Franklin's. Ingenhousz handed on his superior knowledge in reports to Maria Theresa and to other court and government figures.[72] Graf von Zinzendorf noted in his diary in October 1775: "I talked with Ingenhousz about the colonies. He explained the origin of the controversies to me."[73] And Zinzendorf continued to be interested in America, just as he took a vivid interest in the French Revolution in later years.[74] Highly esteemed at court, Ingenhousz must have exerted considerable influence on the judgment of others concerning conditions and events in America.

In spite of all this, Joseph II was not cognizant of the revolutionary character of American ideas and of their antimonarchical trend. It sounds very improbable that, in 1777 in France, when asked his opinion on Ameri-

70. See among others Hans-Otto Kleinmann, "Die Politik des Wiener Hofes gegenüber der Spanischen Monarchie unter Karl III. 1759–1788" (publ. Ph.D. diss., University of Cologne, 1967), 281–318. Also, the remarks of Maria Theresa and Florimond Claude, comte Mercy d'Argenteau, on the attitude of Joseph II from the years 1779–1780, in Alfred Ritter von Arneth and M. A. Geffroy, eds., *Correspondance secrète entre Marie-Thérèse et le Cte de Mercy-Argenteau*, III (Paris, 1875), 334–335, 453, 480. Arthur Lee (to the commissioners, May 27, 1777) and William Lee (to the Committee of Foreign Affairs, Sept. 28, 1779) had the same impression; see Wharton, ed., *Revolutionary Diplomatic Correspondence*, II, 327, III, 348. See also Charles Guillaume Frédéric Dumas to A. Lee, June 1778 (Arthur Lee Papers, IV, 149, Harvard University Library, Cambridge, Mass.).

71. See Ingenhousz to Franklin, Jan. 4 and June 28, 1777 (Franklin Papers, V, 2, VI, 83, APSL, Philadelphia). Ingenhousz did not accompany Joseph on his journey to France. The second letter, written from Swabia, shows that he believed the encounter actually to have taken place. Victory, *Franklin and Germany*, 26, however, very convincingly argues that the meeting, scheduled for May 28, 1777, never took place.

72. These reports, among them a French translation of Benjamin Franklin's *Comparison of Great Britain and the United States in Regard to the Basis of Credit in the Two Countries* from 1777, are today housed in the Nationalbibliothek and the Haus-, Hof- und Staatsarchiv, both in Vienna.

73. "Je causais avec Ingenhousz sur les Colonies. Il m'explique l'origine des querelles": entry of Oct. 3, 1775, in Karl Graf von Zinzendorf, Tagebuch (XX, fol. 131, HHStA, Vienna).

74. Cf. the volumes of his diary for the 1790s.

can events, he answered, "I am a royalist by trade."[75] This kind of interpretation of the American Revolution was much more characteristic of the period of the French Revolution. It is therefore not surprising that the remark is handed down to us only from the second half of the 1790s,[76] rather than from the earlier period of his interest in the fate of the "poor Americans."[77]

On the other hand, Joseph's brother, the Tuscan grand duke and later emperor, Leopold II, had a noteworthy interest in American domestic events, the effects of which were reflected in the Tuscan constitutional project of 1779–1782. The Pennsylvania constitution of 1776, which exerted a decisive influence on these plans, was not completely unknown in Europe—Isaak Iselin, for instance, had reprinted it in his *Ephemeriden der Menschheit*[78] —but it received little attention in Germany. Some of Leopold's advisors (among them, Filippo Mazzei of Florence, a friend of Jefferson's) had direct contacts with America, and some knew the land from personal experience. Such men probably provided the main impetus behind Leopold's involvement with the constitutional project.[79] Unfortunately, however, this early and encouraging promise of modern constitutionalism on the European continent never became a reality.

Leopold's Tuscan constitutional project shows that interest in American ideas could sometimes run along unpredictable paths, making it difficult to trace them back. There is, for example, in the literary bequest of Goswin Anton von Spiegel a French text of the Declaration of Independence, the provenance of which is not known.[80] And around the mid-1780s, a certain Georg Septimus Andreas von Praun compiled a list of German works on North America and the Revolution that contains well over two hundred

75. "Moi, je suis royaliste par métier": Francis Cunningham to Johann Kaspar Lavater (MS. 506, no. 33, Familienarchiv Lavater, ZB, Zurich). The letter is undated, however, probably from c. 1795.
76. The answer to the same question is in the *Examen impartial de la vie privée et publique de Louis XVI* (Hamburg and Paris, 1797), 70: "Quant à moi, mon métier est d'être royaliste." The only difference in Cunningham's version is that Joseph was not asked by somebody unknown and inferior, but by Louis XVI.
77. "pauvres Américains": to Catherine II, Jan. 10, 1781, in Alfred Ritter von Arneth, ed., *Joseph II. und Katharina von Russland. Ihr Briefwechsel* (Vienna, 1869), 34. It may be questioned, however, whether we can attribute to Joseph any sympathy for the Americans, as John Adams did in his letter to the President of Congress, Aug. 3, 1781, in Wharton, ed., *Revolutionary Diplomatic Correspondence*, IV, 620.
78. *Ephemeriden der Menschheit*, II (1777), no. 1, pp. 101–119; see also no. 4, pp. 82–84. For the Delaware constitution see *ibid.*, no. 4, pp. 119–124.
79. Adam Wandruszka, *Leopold II., Erzherzog von Österreich, Großherzog von Toskana, König von Ungarn und Böhmen, Römischer Kaiser*, 2 vols. (Vienna and Munich, 1963), I, 372–373.
80. Goswin Anton von Spiegel, Nachlaß, no. 32 (StA, Münster).

titles.[81] To these two examples numerous others could be added, which, however, would only serve to emphasize that special interest in America was sometimes translated into surprising kinds of knowledge. Clear differences in the level of knowledge of individuals were by no means unusual, and undoubtedly there were occasional individuals who possessed a remarkable grasp of details.

Most of the bourgeoisie, however, were content with what was supplied by the generally available sources of information, which formed the framework within which the process of reception took place. Such sources had some serious shortcomings. Their presentations were often too short and frequently reported inaccurate or incomplete information. These shortcomings necessarily affected the judgment of contemporary readers. It is therefore essential to say something about the gaps and oversights of the generally available sources before discussing contemporary opinions about America.

In the field of geography the popular encyclopedia of Johann Hübner (of which many editions appeared over a period of more than two generations) was obsolete in the 1770s and 1780s.[82] Not until 1795, however, was it thoroughly revised by the inclusion of large amounts of material from Wolfgang Jäger's much more modern and detailed encyclopedia, the second edition of which had been published in the meantime.[83] Leaving aside Ebeling's unsurpassed work, there were other geographies, some of them short but well grounded, such as those by Johann Ernst Fabri[84] and by Adam Christian Gaspari,[85] as well as Christian Carl André's detailed continua-

81. Praun, "Literarische Geschichte der Engl. Colonien in Nord-America u. des Kriegs zwischen Engelland u. demselben," in his manuscript "Materialien zur außerdeutschen Geschichte" (StA, Wolfenbüttel).

82. Hübner, *Reales Staats- Zeitungs- und Conversations-Lexicon . . .*, first published early in the 18th century. I drew upon the Leipzig editions of 1777, 1782, 1789, and 1795, and the Vienna edition of 1780.

83. Jäger, *Geographisch-Historisch-Statistisches Zeitungs-Lexicon*, 2 vols. (Nuremberg, 1782–1784), 2d ed. (1791–1793). In addition, I used Johann Jakob Volkmann, *Neues geographisches Handlexicon* (Leipzig, 1778), the *Neues geographisches Zeitungslexicon* (Augsburg, 1790), and the *Deutsche Encyclopädie* (Frankfurt, 1778–1804). Edited by Heinrich Martin Gottfried Köster and Johann Friedrich Roos, the 23 volumes of the *Deutsche Encyclopädie* run only through the letters *Ky* and contain few articles on American subjects. Biographical information on American authors is to be found only in Jeremias David Reuss, *Das Gelehrte England oder Lexikon der jeztlebenden Schriftsteller in Grosbritannian, Irland und Nord-Amerika . . .* (Berlin and Stettin, 1791). Friedrich Nicolai suggested this title in analogy to the famous multivolume publication by Johann Georg Meusel, *Das gelehrte Teutschland*: Nicolai to Reuss, Mar. 29, 1791 (Nachlaß Reuß, V, 25, SuUB, Göttingen).

84. Esp. Fabri, *Handbuch der neuesten Geographie für Akademien und Gymnasien* (Halle, 1784–1785). The *Handbuch* appeared through 1800 in seven different editions and contained extensive bibliographies.

85. Gaspari, *Lehrbuch der Erdbeschreibung*, 2 vols. (Weimar, 1792–1793). The fourth edition appeared from 1799 to 1801.

tion of Georg Christian Raff's *Geographie für Kinder*.[86] Johann Christoph Gatterer's *Geographie*,[87] the fourth edition of Daniel Vogel's *Neues geographisches Handbuch*,[88] and the anonymous *Lehrbuch der neuesten Erdbeschreibung*[89] were also very useful, specifically the parts concerning North America.

Generally speaking, the works mentioned were most accurate and comprehensive for Pennsylvania, the center of German settlement in America. Information about the northeastern states, and, above all, the southern states, was less extensive. But the ignorance about the territory acquired in 1783 between the Alleghenies and the Mississippi could hardly be more astounding, particularly since the works of Thomas Anburey, Jonathan Carver, and Gilbert Imlay were available, some even in several translations. The Northwest Ordinance of 1787, printed in 1791 in Georg Friedrich von Martens's collection of treaties,[90] was completely disregarded. While Tennesee remained almost entirely unknown, a dim light was shed on Kentucky by the widely read adventures of Daniel Boone.[91] The name "Ohio" enjoyed a real popularity.[92] But even the leading German geographers did not know the location of all of these states or how they fitted into the totality of the western territories.

The works mentioned so far were the best of their kind and stemmed from the period between 1785 and 1800, mainly from the 1790s. They were much better than their predecessors, many of which still continued in use as

86. Raff, *Geographie für Kinder*, 3 vols. (Göttingen, 1786–1791). Vol. I is by Raff himself, and this was its fifth edition. The other two volumes are by André and appeared from 1792 to 1794 in a second edition.

87. Gatterer, *Kurzer Begriff der Geographie*, 2 vols. (Göttingen, 1789), 2d ed. (1793). The book is a wholly revised edition of his *Abriß der Geographie* (Göttingen, 1775 [i.e., 1778]).

88. Vogel, *Neues geographisches Handbuch zum Unterricht der Jugend*, 4th ed. (Breslau, 1792). The first, rather poor, edition appeared in 1775.

89. *Lehrbuch der neuesten Erdbeschreibung für öffentliche und Privat-Schulen . . .*, 3 vols. (Berlin, 1794–1796).

90. Martens, *Receuil des traités*, III, 68–71.

91. In John Filson, *Reise nach Kentucke und Nachrichten von dieser neu angebaueten Landschaft in Nordamerika*, trans. from the English (Leipzig, 1790), and in several periodicals.

92. As part of his "Abschied eines Teutschen von seiner Geliebten, beym Feldzug nach Amerika," Johann Christoph Krauseneck wrote in 1777: "Traurig wirst du harren, meine Liebe! / Viele bange Monden harren mein; / Sei es! Ist uns jede Sonne trübe, / Bin ich am Ohio dennoch dein!" (Krauseneck, *Gedichte*, 2 vols. [Bayreuth, 1776–1783], II, 102). See also *Gedancken eines Land-Geistlichen über eine an dem Ohio-Fluß in America entdeckte Juden-Kolonie* (Frankfurt and Leipzig, 1774), of which Georg Christoph Lichtenberg made a note; cf. Lichtenberg, *Gedanken, Satiren, Fragmente*, ed. Wilhelm Herzog, I (Jena, 1907), 133.

textbooks. The new books were thus an expression of a desire to make up for past neglects and a sign of distinct qualitative improvement.

What has been said about geographies applies as well to historical works because of the close connection between geography and history at the time.[93] There are a few outstanding works, among them a translation of the *History of the British Dominions of North America*.[94] Remer's studies on more recent American history were among the most useful ones available. But not until shortly before the end of the century did a German historian attempt to present a detailed history of the United States.[95] Among the contemporary historical works, as among the geographies, many poor and worthless books were published along with the few useful ones. That in 1776 John Oldmixon's *Britisches Reich in Amerika* was reprinted without change—though it had first appeared in German more than thirty years before—reveals how difficult it was to make use of the best current literature available in England or America.[96]

The point of emphasis in all of these works was clearly the Revolutionary War and its immediate prehistory, which was often presented with many gaps. Colonial history, the importance of which is today undisputed for an understanding of the American Revolution, was not considered a worthy field of study and so remained, like the western territories, terra incognita.[97] During the Revolution several German historians had focused on the most recent American past, but by the later years of the century no one was undertaking any original investigation of this crucial period. Just as historians had assigned the colonial past to oblivion, so too they failed to produce a well-founded study of the beginnings of the new republic.

The most serious shortcoming of the usual presentation was the complete neglect of the loyalist problem. This failing was, of course, not universal. Wilhelm Ernst Christiani recorded the presence of patriots, moderates,

93. On history as a science in the late 18th century, see Josef Engel, "Die deutschen Universitäten und die Geschichtswissenschaft," *HZ*, CLXXXIX (1959), 280–281.

94. *Geschichte der Englischen Kolonien in Nord-Amerika, von der ersten Entdeckung dieser Länder durch Sebastian Cabot bis auf den Frieden 1763*, trans. from the English, 2 vols. (Leipzig, 1775–1776), 2d ed. (1777). The story is brought up only to 1763.

95. [Joseph Milbiller], *Allgemeine Geschichte der berühmtesten Königreiche und Freistaaten in und ausserhalb Europa*, Pt. II, *Die vereinigten nordamerikanischen Provinzen*, 2 vols. (Leipzig, 1798–1799).

96. [John Oldmixon], *Das Britische Reich in America Worinnen enthalten Die Geschichte der Entdeckung, der Aufrichtung, des Anwachses und Zustandes der Englischen Colonien . . .*, 2 vols. (Lemgo, 1776). This is a reprint of the first German edition of 1744, which was a translation of the English edition of 1741.

97. Colonial history was almost completely overlooked before the outbreak of the war; see, e.g., the popular work by Johann Georg Essich, *Einleitung zu der allgemeinen und besonderen Welthistorie*, 10th ed., ed. Johann Christian Volz (Stuttgart, 1773). The same is true of Remer's *Handbuch der Geschichte neuerer Zeiten* (1771).

and loyalists in the American colonies during the conflict with England.[98] The editor of the *Correspondance du Lord G. Germain* went so far as to state that the loyalists outnumbered the patriots,[99] a fact that Joseph Galloway had already endorsed when he said that the patriots would not even amount to 10 percent of the total population.[100] More examples could be given,[101] but as a rule the problem of the loyalists, if it was touched upon at all, was dealt with in cursory statements.

Only attentive observers among the auxiliary troops had more precise information, although even informed comments were sometimes inaccurate. Friedrich Christian Cleve gained the impression that "the majority of the English inhabitants are wicked rebels." But he was of the opinion that the loyalists were in the majority in the state of New York, even though the presence of American troops forced them to keep in the background or else to flee.[102] A letter printed by Schlözer stated that two out of three inhabitants of New Hampshire were patriots, while about 15 percent were loyalists, who were treated "harshly and cruelly" by the rebels.[103] In the *Historisches Portefeuille* it was reported that the "new republicans" had "a deadly hatred of the loyalists," that "cruelty" was their policy toward them, and that loyalist "leaders [were] generally condemned to be hanged without a trial."[104]

It is remarkable that nobody seems to have noted that the loyalists were expelled to Canada by the thousands.[105] This expulsion from "home and

98. Wilhelm Ernst Christiani, *Geschichte der neuesten Weltbegebenheiten*, 3 vols. (Leipzig, 1788–1793), II, 563–564.

99. George Sackville, Lord Germain, *Correspondance du Lord G. Germain, avec Les Generaux Clinton, Cornwallis & les Amiraux dans la station de l'Amérique . . .*, trans. from the English (Bern, 1782), xii.

100. Galloway, *Briefe*, 38.

101. See among others Joseph von Sartori, "Bemerkungen der englischen Staatsfehler vom Jahr 1712 bis 1782" (c. 1783), (Collectio manuscriptorum: Anglia, IV, fol. 48, NB, Vienna); Barthold Koch, "Kurze Kriegsgeschichte," 133 (privately owned by Mr. Fritz Koch, Kassel).

102. "Der größeste Teil der englischen Einwohner sind arge Rebellen": Friedrich Christian Cleve, "Tagebuch über den Feldzug in Amerika," 198–199, entry of Nov. 26, 1778 (StadtA, Brunswick). See also the entry of Johann Ernst Prechtel in his diary, June 21, 1778, p. 151 (Kriegsarchiv [hereafter cited as KA], Munich). Contrary to the generally accepted interpretation, Herbert Aptheker, *The American Revolution 1763–1783*, Vol. II, *A History of the American People: An Interpretation* (London, 1960), 52–59, believes that the large majority of the population backed the policy of the patriots.

103. "hart und grausam": Schlözer, ed., *Briefwechsel*, III (1778), no. 17, 278.

104. "neuen Republikaner . . . einen tödlichen Haß auf die Loyalisten . . . Grausamkeiten . . . Anführer gemeinhin ohne Untersuchung zum Strange verdammt": Karl Renatus Hausen, ed., *Historisches Portefeuille*, Dec. 1783, 777–778, June 1783, 852–853.

105. E.g., Journal von Lotheissen, fol. 45v, entry of Aug. 12/13, 1783 (StA, Marburg); "Feldzug der Hessen nach Amerika," in J. F. Engelschall, ed., *Ephemeriden über Aufklärung, Litterartur und Kunst*, II (1785), 56. According to George Bancroft (Hessian Mss., no. 5, New York Public Library [hereafter cited as NYPL], New York), Johann Ewald was the

farm" nearly always meant the loss of the property left behind. An appreciation of this fact and its consequences required a degree of knowledge and deliberation that could be mustered by very few.[106] There was almost complete ignorance of the fate of the American loyalists, even though their expulsion meant the loss of at least 2.4 percent of the total population—the corresponding figure in France was only 0.5 percent[107]—and the confiscation of much property.[108] Although this problem was also ignored in other European countries, the complete disregard of the American loyalists was to become indirectly an important fact in German comparisons of the American and the French revolutions, to the advantage of the former.

American constitutional developments, study of which is essential for an understanding of the Revolution and the United States, were similarly slighted. Before 1783 there were, no doubt, some promising beginnings toward an intellectual comprehension of the young state, but no breakthrough to a direct influence on the formation of opinion in larger circles of the population took place. As a rule, the few texts available on the German market did not give the needed incentives for further investigation in this area. An indication of the problems involved in comprehending American political developments is provided by Gabriel Bonnot de Mably's characterization of the right of free assembly guaranteed in Pennsylvania's 1776 constitution as institutionalized anarchy.[109] If so distorted an analogy could be

---

author of the article. Governments may have had slightly better information on the loyalists; see the dispatchs by Christian Moritz Freiherr von Kutzleben, July 4, Aug. 29, 1783 (300 Philippsruhe E 11/6, VIII, fols. 74r–v, 96, StA, Marburg), and Sigismund Graf von Haslang to Vieregg, Aug. 18, 1786 (Kasten schwarz 15387, GStA, Munich).

106. "von Haus and Hof": diary of Karl Bauer, 392–393, entry of Nov. 8, 1783 (StA, Marburg). To my knowledge, this is the only diary by a German war participant that contains some reflections on the matter. See also *Historisches Portefeuille*, June 1784, 789.

107. Palmer, *Age of the Democratic Revolution*, I, 188–189.

108. A definitive study of the loyalists is still wanting. Wallace Brown, *The King's Friends: The Composition and Motives of the American Loyalist Claimants* (Providence, R.I., 1965), 249–251, assumed their portion of the whole population to have been between 6.4% and 15.3%; see also Brown's *The Good Americans: The Loyalists in the American Revolution* (New York, 1969), 227. Claude H. Van Tyne, *The Loyalists in the American Revolution* (New York, 1929), 299, counted about 85,000 emigrants, which would have been about 3.5% of the population. Mary Beth Norton, *The British-Americans: The Loyalist Exiles in England 1774–1789* (Boston, 1972), esp. 36–37, counted about 7,000 loyalists taking refuge in England. Paul H. Smith, "The American Loyalists: Notes on Their Organization and Numerical Strength," *WMQ*, 3d Ser., XXV (1968), 267, found 19,000 American loyalists fighting in the British army. As the first exact census dates from 1790, we can only estimate about the development of population during these years; see Evarts B. Greene and Virginia D. Harrington, *American Population before the Federal Census of 1790* (New York, 1932), 6–8, and J. Potter, "The Growth of Population in America, 1700–1860," in D. V. Glass and D.E.C. Eversley, eds. *Population in History* (London, 1965), 638–639.

109. Mably, *Observations*, 45–47; cf. the constitution of Pennsylvania, Declaration of

drawn in a detailed study of the American constitutional system, how much more difficult must it have been for the average German observer to understand the two structural principles of the federal Constitution: the separation of powers and the system of checks and balances.

From the time of the war, when names like John Hancock and Henry Laurens were on many lips, people knew that there was a president at the head of the Congress. But subsequent changes, including those brought about by the new Constitution, were generally ignored. Such basic innovations as the division of government into an executive, a legislative, and a judicial branch, and the restructuring of both the Congress and the office of the president, took place unnoticed by the majority of the German bourgeoisie. Jean Rodolphe Vautravers of Biel, who had been interested in America since the outbreak of the War of Independence, spoke for many when he addressed Washington as "President of the United States in Congress" and described Henry Laurens as "your unfortunate Predecessor in the Presidency of your States in Congress."[110]

The individual states were an implicit part of the constitutional system of checks and balances. This federal structure and its complement, the territorial domain, as well as their relations to each other and to the federal government after 1787, represented new problems for German contemporaries. Johann Ernst Fabri tried to bring his geographical knowledge up to date with each new edition of his excellent handbook. But he did not know that the Articles of Confederation had in the meantime been replaced by a new constitution, nor did he know the precise number of individual states at any one time, a dilemma he solved in the fourth edition (1793) with the trick of writing "13 (15–16)."[111]

Two examples will illustrate how the world of the *ancien régime* determined the thought processes of those of its inhabitants who attempted to make America's political and social ideas intelligible. When the assemblies of the individual states were spoken of as "Stände" (estates),[112] a freeholder as

Rights, Art. XVI, in Francis N. Thorpe, ed., *The Federal and State Constitutions*, V (Washington, D.C., 1909), 3084.

110. Vautravers to Washington, June 6, 1792 (Washington Papers, LC, Washington, D.C.). For similar examples see Karl von Zinzendorf in Eduard Gaston Graf von Pettenegg, ed., *Ludwig und Karl Grafen und Herren von Zinzendorf: Ihre Selbstbiographien* (Vienna, 1879), 244; Joseph Wilhelm Bayer, *Historisch-summarische Darstellung der vorzüglichsten Staatsveränderungen* (Vienna, 1796), 73–74.

111. Fabri, *Handbuch der neuesten Geographie*, 4th ed. (Halle, 1793), 462. Although Tennessee was admitted as the sixteenth state in 1796, Fabri's knowledge of these matters improved slightly only with the seventh edition in 1800 (pp. 591–602).

112. "Stände": Mercy d'Argenteau to Prince Wenzel Kaunitz, Feb. 16, 1779, and Josef Graf von Kaunitz-Rietberg to Prince Kaunitz, July 4, 1782 (Staatskanzlei, Staatenabteilung: Frankreich, K. 160, fol. 51, and Spanien, K. 144, fol. 1v, HHStA, Vienna).

"völliger Eigentumsherr eines Allodialgutes" (absolute proprietor of a private feudal estate),[113] or as "Freilehnbesitzer" (proprietor of a free feudal tenure),[114] the inherently different political and social forms of the United States had been translated into a feudal system of coordinates that could not comprehend those forms. In such a case the depth of the gap between the Old World and the New begins to show. At best, knowledge of America in German-speaking Europe only touched on the difference in the political and social reality. The inadequacies of the available information had its consequences. Certainly, "the names of Franklin and Washington began to shine and sparkle on the political and military horizons,"[115] and the names of Hancock, Laurens, and Adams had a familiar sound, though there was some confusion between John Adams and his cousin Samuel. But such important personalities as Jefferson and Hamilton remained almost completely unknown—and what was true for them applies also to the political directions they represented.

All these shortcomings, of which only the most conspicuous have been mentioned, necessarily entailed consequences for the German understanding of America. Inadequate information and vague conceptions thus assumed decisive importance in the discussion of the American Revolution by German contemporaries.

113. "völliger Eigentumsherr eines Allodialgutes": *Entwurf der neuesten Culturgeschichte seit der Ideenwanderung über Freiheit und Rechte der Menschheit* (Leipzig, 1800), 19.

114. "Freilehnbesitzer": Burke, *Europäischen Kolonien in Amerika*, II, 163.

115. "Die Namen Franklin und Washington fingen an, am politischen und kriegerischen Himmel zu glänzen und zu funkeln": Goethe, "Dichtung und Wahrheit," bk. XVII, in his *Werke*, Weimar ed., 1/XXIX, 68.

PART II *Confrontation with the American Revolution in the 1770s and 1780s*

4. *The War of Independence*

The famous shots that reverberated even through Europe were fired on April 19, 1775, in Lexington and Concord. Thus began the armed confrontation between Great Britain and its North American colonies that in the course of the following years would affect the interests of all the great powers of Europe in one way or another. It was evident that although Europeans might see things differently from their American contemporaries, the significance of this war would transcend the borders of America. What was taking place in the Western Hemisphere was more than a replay of the Seven Years' War; the problems touched upon were not the problems of an ordinary war. A number of questions about the German understanding of the war and the German response to it immediately come to mind. Was the outbreak of the war in and over America foreseen by German observers, or did it come as a surprise? What were assumed to be the fundamental causes of the conflict and what its more superficial pretexts? How did Germans respond to the legal issues, the question of who was in the right, and to the idea of independence? And lastly, how did the contemporary German judge the events of the war itself?

Causes and Origins

We shall see that a discussion of these questions is closely related to another problem more intimately connected with the phenomenon we call the American Revolution: that of the German grasp of the fundamental principles at stake. For even German contemporaries saw very quickly that the events taking place in America were more than a conventional war. Georg Christoph Lichtenberg, when talking about another case, said in April 1778: "I see that this dispute will develop like the American one: it will start over tea and will end as a dispute over kingdoms."[1]

1. "Ich merke wohl, es wird in diesem Streit gehen wie in Amerika, er fängt mit Tee an und endigt in Königreichen": to Johann Andreas Schernhagen, Apr. 12, 1778, in Albert

Figure 3. Stamp Act Crisis. "The Americans oppose the Stamp Act and burn stamped paper sent from England to America, at Boston, August 1764." Obviously meant to illustrate the Boston Stamp Act riots of August 1765. (Figures 3–14 were illustrations by Daniel Chodowiecki for Matthias Christian Sprengel's *Allgemeines historisches Taschenbuch . . . enthaltend für 1784 die Geschichte der Revolution von Nord-America* [Berlin, 1783].)

Courtesy John Carter Brown Library, Brown University, Providence, R.I.

In the first half of the 1770s many Germans held the opinion that the happenings in the West had reached the stage of a serious crisis.[2] At the beginning of the decade we already find some hints that developments could lead to an Anglo-American war.[3] Despite the relative quiet during the ensuing months, it was soon recognized that "the flame was by no means extinguished but only fluttering less brightly,"[4] a flame that flared up much more dangerously late in 1773. The opinion that the vaguely known developments in the Western Hemisphere might lead to war gained more and more followers, especially in government and newspaper circles.[5] What happened in the following months did nothing to dispel that opinion. On the contrary, diplomats and journalists detected an increasing number of omens of war, and in February and March 1775 the opinion was voiced that, in view of the rigid attitudes of both sides, war could hardly be avoided.[6] Some later commentators saw this very intransigence and the lack of mutual understanding between the American patriots and the British government to be the true cause of the armed conflict.[7]

Although there were repeated premonitions of war during the first half of the 1770s, they never led to a major effort by German students of the subject to explain to contemporaries what was really happening. Up to the mid-1770s only government officials and journalists, especially in the larger German territories, attended to the problem at all. But journalists and diplomats alike were capable of only meager reports based on what they had heard about the disputes over taxation and the Tea Act and their consequences. They did talk about the American refusal to buy British goods, about aspects of trade, and even about smuggling. But it was obviously very difficult to get a clear picture of what was happening. Nobody succeeded in grasping the

---

Leitzmann, ed., "Neues von Lichtenberg," *Zeitschrift für Bücherfreunde*, N.S., IV, no. 1 (1912), 84.

2. See, e.g., *Wienerisches Diarium*, Apr. 7, Sept. 26, 1770, or Jean Palairet's reports from London to Duke Frederick III at Gotha, May 22, July 20, 31, 1770 (Chart. A 1052, fols. 455, 461, 463v, Landesbibliothek [hereafter cited as LB], Gotha).

3. *Hamburgischer Correspondent*, Nov. 27, 1771.

4. "eine nicht ganz ausgelöschte, sondern nur eingeschläferte Flamme": Karl Ludwig Graf von Barbiano und Belgiojoso to Prince Wenzel Kaunitz, Feb. 13, 1774 (Staatskanzlei, Staatenabteilung: England, K. 117, fol. 40v, HHStA, Vienna).

5. On the whole, this is seen in newspaper reports and in diplomatic dispatches on Britain's conflict with its colonies; the opinion becomes more common after 1773.

6. *Wienerisches Diarium*, Feb. 11, 1775; Gottlieb Heinrich von Treuer to Karl Friedrich, margrave of Baden, Mar. 14, 1775 (Abt. 48, no. 2186, Generallandesarchiv [hereafter cited as GLA], Karlsruhe).

7. Karl Hammerdörfer and Christian Traugott Kosche, *Amerika ein geographisch-historisches Lesebuch zum Nutzen der Jugend und ihrer Erzieher*, 2 vols. (Leipzig, 1788), I, 462–463. For a similar view from a modern historian see Esmond Wright, *Fabric of Freedom 1763–1800* (New York, 1961), 100–105.

true import of the individual problems, in working out the principles involved in the disputes (especially those motivating the Americans' actions), or in clarifying the complexity of developments. Since, moreover, the course of events had not yet aroused an abiding interest among the bourgeoisie, there was no demand for clarifying discussion. During the winter of 1773–1774 there was almost complete concentration on the spectacular conflicts about tea,[8] to the neglect of other relevant events.

In spite of the several premonitions of future developments, few persons were sufficiently informed about the issues at the outbreak of the war. The large majority of German contemporaries seem to have been highly confused about what was really happening. Even in the middle of 1775, most had no idea of the probable outcome of the confrontation, nor had they decided which side deserved their approbation.[9] "The affairs of this country are today of such extent and so involved and the events so varied and numerous that our whole journal would not suffice to discuss them all. We have to be content to present the state of affairs at the moment of going to press."[10] Thus Wieland's *Teutscher Merkur* avoided the task of making clear to its readers the most essential points in the dispute between England and its colonies. The inability of the German bourgeoisie to form an accurate idea of the origins of the American War of Independence resulted from the failure of both newspapers and books to impress the German public with the importance of the stream of news coming from America in the years preceding the outbreak of war. It was so difficult to distinguish the causes from the mere pretexts that only weak efforts were made to do so.[11] An Ansbach soldier,

8. See, e.g., *Hamburgischer Correspondent*, Feb. 1, 1774; *Freytags-Zeitung*, Feb. 4, 1774; Belgiojoso to Prince Kaunitz, Mar. 1, 1774 (Staatskanzlei, Staatenabteilung: England, K. 117, fols. 46–50, HHStA, Vienna); Hans Moritz Graf von Brühl zu Martinskirch to Sacken, Dec. 24, 31, 1773 (Locat 2685, conv. X, fols. 6v–7, 9, StA, Dresden); Joachim Karl Graf von Maltzahn to Frederick II, Dec. 31, 1773, Jan. 28, 1774 (Rep. 96, 34H, vol. VIII, fol. 374v; 35A, vol. IX, fol. 33v, DZA, Merseburg).

9. Generally this holds true for the diplomatic dispatches and for the newspapers through mid-1775. Cf. especially the *Hamburgischer Correspondent* and the *Wienerisches Diarium*, both Feb. 1, 1775.

10. "Die Angelegenheiten dieses Landes sind jetzt von solchem Umfange und so verwickelt, die Begebenheiten so abwechselnd und so zahlreich, daß unser ganzes Journal nicht zureichen würde, sie alle aufzufassen. Wir müssen uns damit begnügen, bloß anzuzeigen, wie die Lage der Sache ist in dem Augenblick, da wir schreiben": *Teutscher Merkur*, Mar. 1773, 288.

11. See Adolf Hasenclever, ed., *Peter Hasenclever aus Remscheid-Ehringhausen ein deutscher Kaufmann des 18. Jahrhunderts. Seine Biographie, Briefe und Denkschriften* (Gotha, 1922), 131 (letter of Dec. 1768); Olof Torén, *Reise nach Surate* (Leipzig, 1772), 208; Theophil Cazenove to Heinrich Adrian Graf von Borcke, Nov. 29, 1774, June 16, 1775 (Rep. 92 v. Borcke III, no. 53, vol. II, fol. 297, vol. III, fol. 62, DZA, Merseburg); Sprengel, *Kurze Schilderung der Grosbrittannischen Kolonien* (1776); Sprengel, *Briefe*, 2–3; *Bericht eines*

Johann Konrad Döhla, a member of the lower middle class by virtue of his social and economic status and his profession as an artisan in later years,[12] explained the conflict as follows: the British Parliament had asked for more "tribute and work" from the colonists. "Moreover, they sent them some very expensive tea to buy, in order to gain more profit and income from this country. Since there is no lack of the very best tea in America, everyone having all he wants, they refused to accept this tea from England."[13]

During the first years of the war an effort was made to identify the reasons and events that had led to the outbreak of military violence. These retrospective observations did come to grips with some of the essential problems and merited attention even after the end of the war. Some noteworthy statements suggest that a few individuals had a better overall view. Thus, Gebhard Friedrich August Wendeborn, a preacher who had lived in London for a long time, thought the "true causes" to be: 1) the British policy of commerce, including the Navigation Acts; 2) the taxation and customs policy; 3) the licentious measures taken by some governors, some of whom had come from England; and 4) "the secret efforts made by the Anglican Church and its bishops, who had the support of the government, to introduce bishops in the colonies as well."[14] Wendeborn touched some, though not all, of the essential problem complexes, most of which had not been recognized in this form by his German contemporaries. He came very close to a reasonably accurate analysis of the immense complexity of events.[15] In later years, another anonymous author reduced that complexity to the formula of a "burden that oppressed the whole." This burden he thought to be the cause

Englischen Amerikaners, 22–23, 37–38; Hübner, *Lexikon* (Vienna, 1780), 322; Jäger, *Zeitungs-Lexicon*, I (1782), 91b–92a, II (1784), 338.

12. Cf. Helmut Möller, *Die kleinbürgerliche Familie im 18. Jahrhundert* (Berlin, 1969), 2–8.

13. "Abgaben und Travaillien. . . . Zudem schickten sie ihnen auch Tee zu, welchen sie kaufen sollten und sehr teuer, um desto mehr Nutzen und Einkünfte aus diesem Land zu ziehen. Da nun in Amerika selbst genug und der beste Tee wächst, daß die Einwohner dessen reichlich haben, so weigerten sie sich, auch diesen Tee von England anzunehmen": Döhla, "Tagebuch eines Bayreuther Soldaten aus dem Nordamerikanischen Freiheitskrieg 1777–1783," *Archiv für Geschichte und Altertumskunde von Oberfranken* (hereafter cited as *AGAO*), XXV, no. 1 (1912), 109 (entry of June 4, 1777, the day after his arrival in America).

14. "wahren Ursachen . . . die heimlichen Bemühungen der englischen Kirche und ihrer Bischöfe, die von der Regierung unterstützt wurden, in den Kolonien ebenfalls Bischöfe einzuführen": Wendeborn, *Der Zustand des Staats, der Religion, der Gelehrsamkeit und der Kunst in Grosbritannien gegen das Ende des achtzehnten Jahrhunderts*, 4 vols. (Berlin, 1785–1788), I, 285–286.

15. Cf. the fairly useful compilation by Esmond Wright, ed., *Causes and Consequences of the American Revolution* (Chicago, 1966), esp. 65–229; also, Richard B. Morris, *The American Revolution Reconsidered* (New York, 1967), 84.

of American resistance against British policy, since the colonists refused to submit to any kind of coercion.[16]

During the war the German spectator tended to see these questions in a different light. His horizon was usually too limited to allow him to recognize the variety and complexity of the problems. He was therefore inclined to select one factor as the determining one, leaving the others practically out of consideration. If he was interested in the problem at all, and if he differentiated between causes and origins, he generally picked out economic factors as the driving force. America's adversaries were especially inclined to see the limitations of trade imposed on the American colonists as the decisive reason for the dispute.[17] Perhaps the whole thing had been started by smugglers like Hancock?[18] It was not by accident, of course, that comments like these from anti-American circles largely reflected the arguments of the British Tories. Such opinions, however, overlooked the split between the American merchants and the patriots in the years after the Stamp Act crisis. Alterations in the economic and political situation caused the merchants gradually to desert the patriots, so that by the mid-1770s they maintained a neutral or pro-British attitude.[19]

A similar emphasis on economic factors is revealed by a member of the Hessian auxiliary troops who sent his analysis of the reasons for the American Revolution from Rhode Island. He thought it sad to see a wonderful, rich, and fertile country like America inhabited by men "whose lust and luxury have blinded them to what they have started, and who have nothing to blame for their fall but their own arrogance. Every man who takes their side at home . . . would soon change his mind and agree with me that it is not

16. "Last, die das Ganze drückte": *Reise von Hamburg nach Philadelphia* (Hanover, 1800), 92.

17. Tagebuch eines Teilnehmers am Feldzug des General Bourgoyne in Albany 1776, p. 1 (Museumsverein [hereafter cited as MV], Lüneburg); Frederick Hervey, *Geschichte der Schiffahrt und Seemacht Groß-Britanniens*, trans. from the English, 3 vols. (Leipzig, 1779–1781), III, 689, 691; *Politisches Journal*, 1783, I, 111 (by Peter Hasenclever; see also 1781, I, 51); Raynal, *Considérations*, 3; Wilhelm Friedrich Gercken, *Periodisch-synchronistische Tabellen zur Universal-Geschichte* (Hamburg, 1792), 35, 56. See also Johann Matthias Schroeckh, *Allgemeine Weltgeschichte für Kinder*, 4 vols. (Leipzig, 1779–1784), IV, pt. 2, 248–249.

18. Sprengel, *Briefe*, 4–9, 21–24, 27–28; *Nichts Neues, aber doch manches Brauchbare*, Sept. 25, 1778, 171–172. See also Ludwig Timotheus Spittler, "Geschichte der Friedensschlüsse und der Hauptrevolutionen des 16.–18. Jahrhunderts" (notes on a course held at the University of Göttingen during the winter semester, 1782–1783), p. 441 (Universitätsbibliothek [hereafter cited as UB], Kiel).

19. Arthur M. Schlesinger, Sr., *The Colonial Merchants and the American Revolution 1763–1776* (1918; repr. New York, 1957), 591–592; Oliver M. Dickerson, *The Navigation Acts and the American Revolution* (Philadelphia, 1951), 290–300; and, more recently, Marc Egnal and Joseph A. Ernst, "An Economic Interpretation of the American Revolution," *WMQ*, 3d Ser., XXIX (1972), 3–32.

want but wantonness and lust that are the cause of the whole rebellion."[20]
He was right insofar as American farmers and tradesmen as a rule enjoyed a
higher standard of living than did the bourgeoisie and especially the lower
middle classes in Germany.[21] But to identify the mere desire for economic
well-being as the cause of political opposition to an established order does
not vouch for a high degree of political sophistication on the part of these
observers.

There were numerous spectators in faraway Germany, however, who
viewed American events from a different perspective. They too thought that
economic factors were important, but in the foreground they saw the legal
and constitutional questions that were evoked by the attempt of the British
government to tax the colonies at will.[22] The German adherents of London
considered this imperial policy to be a just one, and they rejected the American opposition as groundless.[23] The Stamp Act of 1765 was often mentioned
in this context as the original cause of the war, since its introduction had
triggered the American revolt against the laws and statutes of the British
government and Parliament.[24] Thus, a student of the history lectures of the
Göttingen professor Ludwig Timotheus Spittler noted in the winter term of
1782–1783: "The Stamp Act spoiled everything."[25] Already at the beginning
of the war Ingenhousz believed the Stamp Act to be the "source of discord
and of this insurrection."[26] These statements show that a number of commentators grasped the eminent importance of the Stamp Act crisis as a pre-
lude to the Revolution, a view also held by modern American historians.[27]

20. "die für Wollust und Üppigkeit nicht gewußt, was sie haben anfangen wollen, und
daher auch nichts anderem als ihren Hochmut ihren Fall zu danken haben. Jeder, der bei uns
ihre Partei nimmt, . . . der würde gewiß bald aus einem andern Tone sprechen, und mit mir
einsehen, daß nicht der Not, wohl aber der Frevel und Wollust die Ursache der ganzen Rebellion sei": Schlözer, ed., *Briefwechsel*, III, no. 13 (1778), 32–33.
    21. Arthur M. Schlesinger, Sr., *The Birth of the Nation: A Portrait of the American People
on the Eve of Independence* (New York, 1968), 215–225.
    22. Zinzendorf, Tagebuch, entry of Oct. 3, 1775 (XX, fol. 131, HHStA, Vienna); *Briefe
über die jetzige Uneinigkeit*, 41; *Bericht eines Englischen Amerikaners*, 5–6.
    23. Gatterer, ed., *Historisches Journal*, VII (1776), 82–83; Korn, *Geschichte der Kriege*,
II (1776), 67–68; Sprengel, *Briefe*, 7–8; Leiste, *Beschreibung des Brittischen Amerika*, 151.
    24. Achenwall, *Anmerkungen über Nordamerika* (1769), 89–90, 93, 2d ed. (1777), 52,
53–54; Christophe Guillaume Koch, *Abrégé de l'Histoire des traités de paix entre les puissances de l'Europe depuis la paix de Westphalie*, 4 vols. (Basel, Paris, Strasbourg, and Leipzig,
1796–1797), II, 159.
    25. "Die Stempelakte verdarb alles": Spittler, "Geschichte der Friedensschlüsse," 438
(UB, Kiel).
    26. "source de la discorde et de cette insurrection": Ingenhousz, "Remarques sur les af-
faires presente de l'Amerique septentrionale" (Aug./Sept. 1777), p. 5 (HHStA, Vienna).
    27. Edmund S. and Helen M. Morgan, *The Stamp Act Crisis: Prologue to Revolution*,
new rev. ed. (New York, 1963), 369–370. See also Bernhard Knollenberg, *Origin of the
American Revolution: 1759–1766* (New York, 1960).

Insofar as the bourgeois partisans of the American cause reflected on the matter at all and did not simply take over the arguments offered by others, they were convinced that the decisive causes of the Revolution were of a political and juristic nature. In this, their convictions reflected the viewpoint of the American patriots. The British government had launched a frontal attack on the rights and privileges of the free Americans. London had not only violated the fundamental principles of the British constitution but had also attempted to deny Americans the most important rights of British citizenship by taxing them without their consent. This not only deprived the Americans of their due rights as British subjects but also threatened their property and, most important, their liberties.[28]

Until the war began, this argument had been only sporadically and casually presented in newspapers. Thus, the *Hamburgische Correspondent* stated early in 1773 that the inhabitants of the American colonies were "extremely worried about their liberty."[29] A year later the Zurich *Freytags-Zeitung* spoke of the "spirit of liberty inspiring the Americans."[30] Not until 1775 do we find in Germany an awareness that American patriots were resolved "to defend their liberty with their lives."[31] This idea spread rapidly during the following months;[32] by 1776 it had taken hold to such an extent that it was considered the characteristic mark of events in America and was ever present in discussions of the Revolution by German bourgeoisie.

Concerning the question of the origins of the Revolution, there was a remarkable measure of agreement by the end of the war. The starting point was thought to have been the tea problem and the destruction of a cargo of tea in Boston harbor in 1773, the so-called Boston Tea Party. There was

28. See, e.g., Jacobi, ed., *Iris*, Mar. 1775, pp. 154–155; Ingenhousz, "Remarques," 5 (HHStA, Vienna); *Bericht eines Englischen Amerikaners*, 5–6; *Vorläufige Nachricht und Beschreibung von dem großen siebenjährigen Kalbskopf*, trans. from the English (n.p., 1783), 1–3; [Friedrich Ludwig Walther], *Neueste Erdkunde welche Asien, Afrika, Europa, Amerika . . . enthält* (Nuremberg and Altdorf, 1785), 249–250; Mazzei, *Geschichte und Staatsverfassung*, I, 131; Ramsay, *Amerikanische Revolution*, I, 246–247; "Anleitung zur Geschichte der Friedensschlüsse" (1797), fol. 153 (LB, Karlsruhe); Seidel, *Neueste Geschichte von Europa*, II, 88.

29. "wegen ihrer Freiheit äußerst besorgt": Feb. 23, 1773.

30. "Geist der Freiheit, welcher die Amerikaner belebet": Feb. 18, 1774. See also Schubart, ed., *Deutsche Chronik*, Sept. 12, 1774, 377–378; Isaak Iselin to Jean Rodolphe Frey, May 19, 1775 (Nachlaß Iselin, LV, StA, Basel); Jacobi, ed., *Iris*, Sept. 1775, 180–181.

31. "die Freiheit mit ihrem Blute zu verteidigen": *Freytags-Zeitung*, Apr. 28, 1775.

32. See, e.g., Iselin's entry in his diary, Jan. 27, 1776 (Nachlaß Iselin, XV, 23–24, StA, Basel); *Leipziger Zeitung*, May 1, 1776; *Freytags-Zeitung*, May 3, 1776; Schirach, *Notiz der Großbrittannischen Colonien*, 96-page ed., 64–65; Korn, *Geschichte der Kriege*, II, 64; Buchenröder, *Nachrichten von den Englischen Kolonien*, xxxiv–xxxv; *Briefe über die jetzige Uneinigkeit*, 90; Christian Friedrich Daniel Schubart, "Freiheitslied eines Kolonisten" (1776), in his *Gesammelte Schriften und Schicksale*, 8 vols. (Stuttgart, 1839–1840), IV, 286–287.

some disagreement only on the question of how closely these events were associated with the immediate causes. Were the Tea Act of 1773 and the Boston Tea Party only milestones on the way to armed conflict? Were they a mere pretext for an intensification of the dispute after a relatively quiet period? Or was the refusal of the Americans to buy the East India Company's tea a major cause of the American Revolution? To take the latter viewpoint would be to inflate the tea incidents.[33] But even those observers who thought of the event as more of a starting point than a cause tended to overrate this truly spectacular development.[34] They saw the Boston Tea Party more and more as a real signal of the war.[35]

The Question of Legality

The German bourgeoisie, while largely at sea as to the causes and origins of the American Revolution, seemed to think another question easier to answer: In terms of legality, which side had the best of the argument? But we are not only interested in the different arguments. We shall also have to see what was thought to be the legal basis of the dispute between England and its colonies.

If we examine the remarks of American patriots during the years before the war, when they staked out their position toward the English government, we see that they always went back to the English constitution. It supplied the arguments on which they based their resistance to the measures of London. At the same time, the English government used the ancient constitution as the legal justification of its own policy. Thus, there was no agreement on the

33. Benjamin Woods Labaree, *The Boston Tea Party* (New York, 1964), 256–264, regards the event as catalytic; quite similar is Lawrence H. Gipson, *The Coming of the Revolution 1763–1775* (New York, 1954), 222.

34. Döhla, "Tagebuch," *AGAO*, XXV, no. 1 (1912), 109–110, 160 (entries of June 4, 1777, and Nov. 30, 1778); Johannes von Müller, "De l'Empire Britannique considéré dans son origine et sa constitution jusqu' au moment de la guerre actuelle" (c. 1780), 34 (Msc. Mü. 51/6, Stadtbibliothek [hereafter cited as StadtB], Schaffhausen).

35. See among others von Langenschwarz, "Meine militär Laufbahn," I, 51 (Murhardsche Bibliothek [hereafter cited as MB], Kassel); Leiste, *Beschreibung des Brittischen Amerika*, 154–155; Hübner, *Lexikon* (Vienna, 1780), 196; Jäger, *Zeitungs-Lexicon*, I (1782), 246b–247a, 397a; *Vorläufige Nachricht und Beschreibung*, 2–3; Sprengel, *Allgemeines historisches Taschenbuch*, 74; *Geschichte der zweyten Decade*, 215; Christiani, *Geschichte der neuesten Weltbegebenheiten*, II, 542; Friedrich Georg August Lobethan, *Schauplatz der merkwürdigsten Kriege und der übrigen politischen Hauptbegebenheiten des achzehnten Jahrhunderts . . .*, 4 vols. (Leipzig, 1793–1796), II, 347.

Figure 4. Boston Tea Party, December 16, 1773. "The inhabitants of Boston throw English-East Indian tea into the sea, December 18, 1773." (Chodowiecki, for Sprengel, *Allgemeines historisches Taschenbuch.*)

Courtesy John Carter Brown Library, Brown University, Providence, R.I.

meaning of the English constitution, and the interpretation that the leaders of the American Revolution put on it was quite different from that of Lord North and the Tories, which in turn differed substantially from that of the parliamentary opposition.

In 1775–1776, however, a basic change occurred in the legal discussion. The Americans, rather than continuing to base their arguments primarily on real and imagined rights derived from the English constitution (with natural rights mentioned only occasionally), reversed themselves and made natural rights and the right to resist the main basis of their defense.[36] The best-known expression of this change is the Declaration of Independence. This document gave legal justification to their policy while bringing the leaders of the American Revolution to break with the parliamentary opposition in England. The Whig opposition, in spite of its hostility to government policies, was not willing to abandon its ideological grounding in the English constitution.[37]

Did German contemporaries, if indeed they followed the events at all, grasp the juristic difference in viewpoints and the change in the argumentation of the American patriots? If they did not keep pace with the course of events, what was the legal basis for their opinions? If not in 1776, then when, where, and to what extent did emphasis on natural rights and the right to resist turn up in German public discussion of the American Revolution?

Even a quick look at contemporary commentaries shows that the German bourgeoisie were only hazily aware of these problems. Julius August Remer was almost the only observer who approached a true analysis of the problems when he wrote, with an accuracy astonishing for his time: "The dispute between the two nations can be settled by two courts of law: that of natural rights and that of English law. Having it settled by the latter alone, . . . means choosing a judge whom the Americans will never recognize as competent."[38] In this statement Remer pointed clearly to natural rights and their

36. Charles H. McIlwain, *The American Revolution: A Constitutional Interpretation* (1923; repr. Ithaca, N.Y., 1958), 190–192; Lawrence H. Gipson, *The British Empire before the American Revolution*, XIII (New York, 1967), 213; Gerald Stourzh, *Alexander Hamilton and the Idea of Republican Government* (Stanford, Calif., 1970), 11–17.

37. J. C. Long, *Mr. Pitt and America's Birthright* (New York, 1940), 510–511, 535; see also the works of Richard W. Van Alstyne, especially his "Europe, the Rockingham Whigs, and the War for American Independence," and "Parliamentary Supremacy versus Independence," both *Huntington Library Quarterly*, XXV (1961–1962), 1–28, XXVI (1962–1963), 201–233.

38. "Die Streitfrage zwischen den beiden Nationen kann vor einem doppelten Forum entschieden werden: nämlich vor den Gerichten des Rechts der Natur und des englischen Staatsrechts. Sie allein durch das letzte entscheiden zu lassen, . . . heißt einen Richter erwählen, den die Amerikaner nie für kompetent erkennen werden": Remer, *Amerikanisches Archiv*, III (1778), [4]. See also his preface to his translation of Stedman, *Americanischer Krieg*, I, [1–2].

importance for arriving at a realistic judgment of the conflict. Yet even he could not bring himself to analyze the situation from the standpoint of natural rights. And hardly anyone else availed himself of this starting point in the times that followed.

It would be wrong to assume that the use of the word *rebel* to denote an American is a clue to the legal interpretation of the user. As it happens, Americans were never widely called rebels in Germany. And even when the word was introduced it did not always reflect the viewpoint of the British court and government, which had declared North America to be in a state of open rebellion.[39] Some individuals, of course, did use this catchword.[40] But the only group among whom the term *rebel* did take hold and was in widespread use was the German auxiliary forces. "That the Americans are called rebels and treated as such can be readily excused by the fact that they were declared to be such by the English government at the time, thus causing the whole army to call them by the same name."[41]

The propaganda purpose of those responsible for this policy is obvious. But the simple use of a word is not the same as a political credo. The word *rebel* was used with thoughtlessness bordering on the ludicrous. Crèvecoeur probably exaggerated but little when he remarked on this mixture of ignorance and innocence: "The Hessians, as is well known, knew next to nothing about America, believing for a long time that the term rebels really was the name for the inhabitants of this country. Consequently, those who were surprised by General Washington at Trenton said quite innocently 'gentle-

39. Royal proclamation, Aug. 23, 1775, and royal address to Parliament, Oct. 26, 1775, in David C. Douglas, ed., *English Historical Documents*, Vol. IX, *American Colonial Documents to 1776*, ed. Merrill Jensen (London, 1955), 850–851, 851–852.

40. See, e.g., Schirach, *Notiz de Großbrittannischen Colonien*, 96-page ed., 42–43.

41. "Daß übrigens die Amerikaner als Rebellen geschildert und behandelt werden, ist dadurch leicht zu entschulden, daß sie zu damaliger Zeit von England als Rebellen erkläret, mithin von der ganzen Armee mit diesem Namen belegt waren": [Christian Friedrich von Bartholomäi], *Die Eroberung von Charlestown* (n.p., 1785), 6. See also the entry in the diary of August Wilhelm Du Roi of 1776, p. 1 (StadtA, Brunswick); Barthold Koch's diary for 1782, pp. 132–133 (privately owned by Fritz Koch, Kassel); Bernhard A. Uhlendorf, ed., *The Siege of Charleston* (Ann Arbor, Mich., 1938), 320–322; [von Heeringen], *Auszug eines Schreibens aus Amerika* ([Darmstadt?], 1776); *Fortgesetztes Schreiben eines Hessischen Officiers aus Amerika* (n.p., 1776), 6–7; Friedrich Valentin Melzheimer, *Tagebuch von der Reise der Braunschweigischen Auxiliär Truppen von Wolfenbüttel nach Quebec*, 3 pts. (Frankfurt and Leipzig, 1776), I, 7, II, 22, 31, III, 18, 28, 33; also "Fragment eines Tagebuchs," "Tagebuch von A.A.H. Du Roi," and "Amerikanische Briefe an den Erbprinzen" (all StA, Wolfenbüttel); "Tagebuch eines Teilnehmers am Bourgoyne-Feldzug" (MV, Lüneburg); "Tagebuch von G. A. Stang" (Historischer Verein für Mittelfranken [hereafter cited as HVMF], Ansbach). Döhla wrote in his diary, June 4, 1777: "Es sind 13 Provinzen, die sich verbunden haben, von der Krone England abzufallen und jetzt rebellieren" (Döhla, "Tagebuch," *AGAO*, XXV, no. 1 [1912], 104).

men rebels, please spare our lives.'"[42] The more alert, "for reasons of courtesy," no longer called the Americans rebels while imprisoned by them.[43]

Most informed Germans, when dealing with the question of legality, were content to refer to the principles of the English constitution as understood since the days of Montesquieu and Voltaire. According to the supporters of British government policy, these principles settled the dispute quite clearly:

> You say you wage a righteous war:
> It's nothing but sedition.
> At heart you're just another boar,
> A slave to opposition.[44]

This far from subtle characterization does more than express a basic aversion to all sorts of political opposition. The stanza quoted is merely one among numerous other utterances that demonstrate the widespread unawareness of the differences between the political aims of the American patriots and those of the Rockingham Whigs. But if what was happening in the colonies was a rebellion, then England's cause was necessarily just; time and again the Göttingen professor Georg Christoph Lichtenberg enjoyed being able to follow "each step of justice" in detail on his wall chart.[45]

America's adversaries generally invoked the English constitution as a basis for defending the British legal position. They believed that the central question of the right of taxation must be answered in favor of the mother country. In defending this conviction they frequently displayed extraordinary ignorance of the issues, and, instead of presenting genuine proof, they

42. "Die Hessen, die bekanntermaßen fast gar keine Kenntnis von Amerika hatten, glaubten lange Zeit, daß der Name Rebellen wirklich der Name der Einwohner des Landes sei. Daher sagten die, welche der General Washington zu Trenton überfiel, mit aller Treuherzigkeit: 'Ihr Herren Rebellen schenkt uns doch das Leben'": Crèvecoeur, *Briefe eines Amerikanischen Landmanns*, III, 154–155.
43. "der Politesse wegen": Capt. O'Connel to Schrader, Nov. 13, 1777 (No. 3152, Landschaftliche Bibliothek, Brunswick, at StA, Wolfenbüttel).
44. "Nenn'immer deinen Krieg gerecht,/Er bleibt Rebellion:/Und du bist selbst im Grund ein Knecht/Der Opposition": Bartholomäi, *Eroberung von Charlestown*, 68. See also Helferich Peter Sturz, *Schriften* (Leipzig, 1779–1782), II, 357–358; Schirach, *Notiz der Großbrittannischen Colonien*, 88–89; *Geographische Belustigungen zur Erläuterung der neuesten Weltgeschichte*, 2 vols. (Leipzig, 1776), 58; Leiste, *Beschreibung des Brittischen Amerika*, 148–149; also the diary of Duke Ludwig Ernst of Brunswick for Nov. 25 and Dec. 14, 1774 (1 Alt 22, no. 871, fols. 112, 120v, StA, Wolfenbüttel); and generally the diplomatic dispatches for the years 1775–1777.
45. "alle Schritte der Gerechtigkeit": to Schernhagen, Jan. 16, 1777, in Lichtenberg, *Briefe*, ed. Leitzmann and Schüddekopf, I, 274. See also his letters to Schernhagen, Nov. 22, 1779, and to Friedrich August Lichtenberg, Mar. 29, 1783, *ibid.*, I, 335, II, 73.

were often content to justify English actions summarily.[46] Thus, Christoph Heinrich Korn of Stuttgart merely stated: "The British government, far from transgressing the boundaries of law in proceeding against the colonies, stayed well within them."[47] The well-known Wittenberg historian, Johann Matthias Schroeckh, was also convinced that the "more tenable law" was on England's side, for "like any other mother country, it had the right to keep its colonies dependent and constrained to some degree, having sacrificed for them much treasure and many armies."[48] According to the ideas common to this group of people, England had made sacrifices in the defense of its American subjects in the Seven Years' War, and it was only just and fair to have the colonies pay their share of the debts.

When Germans tried to develop more elaborate defenses of British policy they often lost themselves in queer lines of reasoning. One anonymous author, moving away from the shelter of the British constitution, used in its place a "sovereign's prerogative," which he supposed to be superior to the constitution. As he saw it, the rights of the English king, such as the right of taxation, were restricted at a time when his realm was still limited to the British Isles. However, this restriction of the king's sovereign rights did not apply to later additions to the kingdom. Here the king was free to exercise fully his rights under the prerogative of sovereigns. Thus, in taxing the Americans the English monarch did not intend to enslave them; he was merely making use of his legitimate rights. Consequently, American actions had to be regarded as highly illegal.[49]

On the one hand, such statements are permeated by the monarchical principle of sovereignty as it was justified by Roman law and the political ideas of the age of absolutism. On the other hand, feudal law principles—the belief that laws evolve in cooperation between the sovereign and the estates of the realm and that they are applicable only in the territories embodied by the estates—dominated this author's thinking. Ideas of the latter sort were to

46. Cf. Gatterer, ed., *Historisches Journal*, VII (1776), 82–83; *Über den Aufstand der englischen Colonien*, 14–15, 20, 24; Leiste, *Beschreibung des Brittischen Amerika*, 140–141, 151, 526.

47. "Die britannische Regierung, weit entfernt die Grenzen ihres Rechts gegen die Kolonien zu überschreiten, ist weit innerhalb denselben geblieben": Korn, *Geschichte der Kriege*, II, 76.

48. "das strengere Recht. . . . Es war, wie jedes andere Mutterland, berechtigt, seine Kolonien, für welche es auch große Schätze und Kriegsheere aufgeopfert hatte, in einer gewissen Abhängigkeit und Einschränkung zu erhalten": Schroeckh, *Allgemeine Weltgeschichte*, IV, pt. 2 (1783), 249–250.

49. *Gedanken über den Aufstand der englischen Colonien*, 32–37; see also *Über den Aufstand der englischen Colonien*, 12–20.

be met with in England as well as, to some extent, in America at this time.[50] But as regards the principle of sovereign prerogative, the author overlooked completely the two revolutions that England had gone through in order to avoid continental absolutism. Such an uncritical defense of official English policy, marked by questionable and contradictory ideas, could hardly be convincing.[51]

Most opponents of the American patriots, being ignorant of the necessary facts, made use of the familiar moral criteria of the times to sum up their discussion of the legal question. Of course, they did not analyze the English constitution or the colonial charters, of which they probably had no knowledge anyway. Instead, they made use of the slogan, "ungrateful children have risen against their gentle mother,"[52] which by itself seemed to justify England's response. America's actions against Great Britain and its lawful king were ungrateful and provocative, and no formality of law could excuse them.[53] And if there was no justification for the colonial position, there was no excuse for such turmoil. Had Americans, or at least interested groups of Americans, precipitated the war under false pretexts and with little reason?[54]

The distance between the adversaries of the American Revolution and those who wavered and were undecided was relatively small. The latter also adhered to the English constitution, but they were unable to arrive at a determination of who was right.[55] When they became convinced that the constitu-

50. Cf. Erich Angermann, "Ständische Rechtstraditionen in der amerikanischen Unabhängigkeitserklärung," *HZ*, CC (1965), esp. 79.

51. The reviewer in the *Allgemeine deutsche Bibliothek*, XXXV, no. 2 (1778), 527, reserved as he was, thought the booklet unconvincing. Though grotesquely distorted, the ideas presented in the *Gedanken über den Aufstand* can be understood as foreshadowing the "monarchical principle" worked out at the beginning of the 19th century. See Franz Schnabel, *Deutsche Geschichte im 19. Jahrhundert*, 2d ed., II (Freiburg, 1949), 83; Otto Brunner, "Vom Gottesgnadentum zum monarchischen Prinzip," in Theodor Mayer, ed., *Das Königtum: Seine geistigen und rechtlichen Grundlagen. Vorträge und Forschungen*, III (1956; repr. Darmstadt, 1963), 301–302.

52. "undankbare Kinder gegen ihre zärtliche Mutter": Karl Gotthelf Lessing, *Die Mätresse* (1780; repr. Heilbronn, 1887), 34.

53. Schirach, *Notiz der Großbrittannischen Colonien*, 73, 92–93; Sturz, "Über den amerikanischen Krieg" (1776), in his *Schriften*, II, 353–357; Stedman, *Americanischer Krieg*, I, 37–38, 41–42.

54. Cf. Schirach, *Notiz der Großbrittannischen Colonien*, 96-page ed., 44–45; Sturz, *Schriften*, II, 356–357; Johann Heinrichs, "Extracts from the Letter-Book, 1778–1780," *Pennsylvania Magazine of History and Biography* (hereafter cited as *PMHB*), XXII (1898), 137 (letter of Jan. 18, 1778); Hammerdörfer's preface to Soulès, *Revolution in Nord-Amerika*, I, iv; Stedman, *Americanischer Krieg*, I, 3.

55. Cf. Johann Heinrich Meister to Johann Jakob Bodmer, June 15, Aug. 1, 1777 (Ms. Bodmer X, 338, 343, ZB, Zurich); Lessing, *Mätresse*, 33–34.

Figure 5. Battle of Lexington April 19, 1775. "The first blood of citizens spilled for the foundation of American liberty at Lexington, April 19, 1774." (Chodowiecki, for Sprengel, *Allgemeines historisches Taschenbuch*.)

Courtesy John Carter Brown Library, Brown University, Providence, R.I.

tion gave no clear legal answer to the problem, they tried to solve it on the basis of equity, and, depending upon personal inclination, sided with either the Americans[56] or the English.[57] Like the opponents of the Revolution, they also ignored the importance of natural law in attempting to form an accurate judgment of arguments and events.

Did the advocates of the American Revolution succeed in doing what its adversaries and the skeptics could not? Did they argue from the same standpoint that was used by the leaders of the Revolution after 1775? The most important work in this regard is undoubtedly Bengt Lidner's dissertation at the University of Greifswald, *De Iure revolutionis Americanorum* (1777).[58] This Swedish doctoral candidate vehemently defended his conviction that the Americans were thoroughly justified by law in revolting and that they deserved the applause of all humanity. But instead of presenting the concepts of the American patriots themselves, and the legal arguments for natural rights and the right to resist, Lidner developed his thesis exclusively on the basis of the English constitution, just as was done earlier by the author of the *Briefe über die jetzige Uneinigkeit zwischen den Amerikanischen Colonien und dem Englischen Parlament*,[59] a work he used as a model. Both studies tried to prove from the English constitution that American conduct was legally justified, while the British government's actions ran contrary to the constitution. Lidner never realized that his model had adopted that viewpoint of the Whig opposition, and that as a consequence his own interpretation reflected that viewpoint far more than it did the ideas of his friends in America.

Judging from the available material, it seems permissible to assume that the majority of the German bourgeoisie who followed the events were fully convinced of the legality of the American revolt. As they saw it, the Americans were not insurgents; they were merely resisting a wanton and fundamental interference with their rights and liberties, which, as Jefferson put it in the Declaration of Independence, was intended "to reduce them under

56. Burnaby, *Reisen durch die mittlern Kolonien*, 12–16; Russell, *Geschichte*, IV, 14, 20–21; Sprengel, *Allgemeines historisches Taschenbuch*, 59; Christiani, *Geschichte der neuesten Weltbegebenheiten*, II, 104, 106.

57. Cf. *Über den Aufstand der englischen Colonien*, 16–17; Korn, *Geschichte der Kriege*, II, 74; *Some Short and Impartial Inquiries*, 30; Sprengel, *Briefe*, 27. All of these authors agree in condemning the politics of the American patriots.

58. On its academic history see Harald Elovson, *Bengt Lidners Greifswalder Dissertation "De iure revolutionis Americanorum"* (Jena, 1928). History professor Johann Georg Möller happened to be anti-American and declined acceptance of the dissertation; it was then accepted by the professor of logic and metaphysics, Peter Ahlwardt.

59. (Hanover, 1776).

absolute despotism."[60] Statements to that effect were not always so clear-cut, yet they showed the general view that the principles of the English constitution alone were sufficient to justify American resistance.[61] It was of course true that the patriots, many of whom were lawyers deeply rooted in British legal tradition and completely averse to breaking with it, stressed English legal thought and the juristic principles derived from it. They quoted William Blackstone, the great commentator on English law, as one of their star witnesses in the dispute with London. Anglo-Saxon common and constitutional law were essential parts of American life before and during the Revolution.[62] Thus, it was by no means wrong to speak of English law in connection with the former colonies. But the German defense of the American legal standpoint still resembled much more the argumentation of the English parliamentary opposition (in simplified form) than that of the leaders of the Revolution.

The legal basis on which most German sympathizers and adversaries alike judged the American Revolution remained too narrow. The one notable exception was Johann Christian Schmohl. We know only a little about him. He was born in 1756 in Anhalt-Zerbst, probably studied in Wittenberg, lived in Switzerland for a brief time, and is known to have lived in Halle before 1782. In that year his important book, *Über Nordamerika und Demokratie,*

60. See, e.g., Mauvillon, *Sammlung von Aufsätzen,* I, 77–78, 89–94, 149–150, 152, 167, II, 12–13; Ingenhousz, "Remarques," 5–7 (HHStA, Vienna); [Jacques Accarias de Sérionne], *Situation politique actuelle de l'Europe* (Augsburg, 1781), 74, 98–99; Wendeborn, *Grosbritannien,* I, 283–284; Soulès, *Revolution in Nord-Amerika,* I, v; Friedrich Gentz, "Der Ursprung und die Grundsätze der Amerikanischen Revoluzion, verglichen mit . . . der Französischen," Gentz, ed., *Historisches Journal,* II, no. 2 (1800), 48, 64–65; see also Peter Force, ed., *American Archives* (Washington, D.C., 1837–1853), 4th Ser., II, 10 (Mar. 1, 1775).

61. Cf. Achenwall, *Anmerkungen über Nordamerika* (1769), 88; Schubart, ed., *Deutsche Chronik,* Aug. 4, 1774, 292; Wieland, ed., *Teutscher Merkur,* Nov. 1775, 189; Schubart, ed., *Neueste Geschichte der Welt,* I (1776), 81; Zinzendorf, Tagebuch, Feb. 1, 1776, XXI, 17 (HHStA, Vienna); [Philip Francis], *Briefe über den jetzigen Zustand von Großbrittannien. Erster Band welcher die Briefe des Junius enthält,* trans. from the English (Leipzig, 1776), 223–224; *Geographische Belustigungen,* 57–59; Ebeling, ed., *Amerikanische Bibliothek,* 52; Loewe, *Beschreibung von Nord-Amerika,* 140; [Karl August Struensee], *Kurzgefaßte Beschreibung der Handlung der vornehmsten europäischen Staaten* (Liegnitz and Leipzig, 1778–1779), I, 169; Accarias de Sérionne, *Situation politique,* 101–102, 113; James Adair, *Geschichte der Amerikanischen Indianer,* trans. from the English by Hermann Ewald Schatz (Breslau, 1782), 397–398; Zinner, *Merkwürdige Briefe und Schriften,* 46; Ambroise Marie Arnould, *System der Seehandlung und Politik der Europäer,* trans. from the French by J. Dominikus (Erfurt, 1798), 365, 376.

62. Lawrence H. Leder, *Liberty and Authority: Early American Political Ideology, 1689–1763* (Chicago, 1968), 93, 95–130; Clinton Rossiter, *Seedtime of the Republic: The Origins of the American Tradition of Political Liberty* (New York, 1953), 326; Daniel J. Boorstin, *The Genius of American Politics* (Chicago, 1953), 98.

was issued by a Königsberg publisher.[63] He then left Germany for North America but was drowned near the Bermudas while crossing.[64] Schmohl's knowledge about and admiration of America was presumably derived from an acquaintance with several Americans, among them perhaps Henry Laurens, or John Adams, whom Johann Georg Hamann believed to be Schmohl's idol.[65] With these sources, Schmohl produced what was by far the most radical publication about the American Revolution to appear in Germany in the closing years of the eighteenth century.[66]

In defending the American Revolution, Schmohl came closer to assimilating the ideas of its leaders than any other German writer, although his presentation was not always accurate. It seems that his original convictions were influenced to a substantial degree by another source, namely, the modern European law of nations as taught by Emer de Vattel, who, after all, was highly esteemed in the American colonies as well.[67] Schmohl was probably following Vattel when he defended American actions with the words: "The colonies, acting as a legislative body, openly proclaimed their disobedience toward the British crown because of its attacks on natural and civil rights; the king and Parliament would not allow them to make their own laws and tax themselves, or to have a parliament of their own; and according to the crown and Parliament, the Americans should be governed and taxed at foreign discretion and should not enjoy the rights of English citizenship nor those of settlers in another part of the world."[68] The reasoning corresponds to that given in a more general vein by Vattel in 1758 in his book, *Droit des*

63. The book appeared anonymously with the false publication place of Copenhagen; actually it was published at Königsberg by the firm of Wagner.

64. The most informative study is still Philip Merlan's "Parva Hamanniana (II): Hamann and Schmohl," *Journal of the History of Ideas*, X (1949), 567–574; see also Johann Georg Hamann, *Briefwechsel*, ed. Walther Ziesemer and Arthur Henkel (Frankfurt, 1955–), esp. Vols. IV and V.

65. Hamann to Johann Gottfried Herder, July 7, 1782, in Hamann, *Briefwechsel*, ed. Ziesemer and Henkel, IV, 399.

66. Douglass, "German Intellectuals," *WMQ*, 3d Ser., XVII (1960), 212.

67. Rossiter, *Seedtime of the Republic*, 141, 359; Bernard Bailyn, *The Ideological Origins of the American Revolution* (Cambridge, Mass., 1967), 27, 178; see also Thomas to John Garland Jefferson, June 11, 1790, in Boyd *et al.*, eds., *Jefferson Papers*, XVI, 481.

68. "Die Kolonien kündigten der Krone Großbritannien weltkündig den Gehorsam auf wegen der letzteren ihrer kriegerischen Angriffe auf derselben natürliche und bürgerliche Rechte, besonders als gesetzgebende Staatskörper, weil ihnen der König und das Parlament nicht das Recht, sich selbst Gesetze zu geben und zu besteuern, ein eigenes Parlament zu haben, zugestehen wollte, weil sie sich sollten von fremder Willkür gubernieren und besteuern lassen, und in Amerika nicht sollten der Rechte Engländischer Bürger oder der ihnen als Anbauren in einem andern Weltteil gehörenden, genießen": Schmohl, *Über Nordamerika und Demokratie*, 7, also pp. 50, 67–68, 96–99, 208.

gens: "Only a denial of rights or the delaying tactics of a sovereign may excuse and even justify the revolt of an oppressed people, and then, only if the misdeeds are unbearable and the oppression patent and gross."[69] Schmohl's ideas on colonial status and uncodified law,[70] though they may have originated elsewhere, also sound very much like those of Vattel.[71]

Thus far I have tried to show that the majority among the interested German bourgeoisie were convinced of the righteousness of American resistance but that both defenders and adversaries of the American cause were generally unable to put forth decisive arguments in defense of their ideas. The central theme of the Revolution as announced by the Declaration of Independence was the conception of natural rights and the right to resist. Yet there was no well-founded inquiry into the nature of these rights and the questions raised by them.

This may seem amazing, since the right to resist had been mentioned long before the American Revolution; it had been practiced, for example, in the Netherlands in the sixteenth century and in England in the seventeenth. The theory of the monarchomachic movement had been greatly influenced by it,[72] as had the French Huguenots[73] and British political theorists at the time of the Stuarts.[74] In the eighteenth century there were also some advocates of these ideas.[75] Vattel was not the only one to deal in detail with the right to resist, for Christian Wolff had propounded similar ideas in Germany at an earlier time.[76] Yet the ideas resulting from natural rights theory never

---

69. Emer de Vattel, *Le Droit des gens*, trans. from the French (Tübingen, 1959), 515 (bk. III, chap. 18, § 290).

70. Schmohl, *Über Nordamerika und Demokratie*, 12–16, 25, 47.

71. Vattel, *Droit des gens*, 26, 142 (introduction, § 25; bk. I, chap. 19, § 210).

72. Kurt Wolzendorff, *Staatsrecht und Naturrecht in der Lehre vom Widerstandsrecht des Volkes gegen rechtswidrige Ausübung der Staatsgewalt. Zugleich ein Beitrag zur Entwicklungsgeschichte des modernen Staatsgedankens* (1916; repr. Aalen, 1961), 95–123. On the early natural law theorist Johannes Althusius see Erik Wolf, *Große Rechtsdenker der deutschen Geistesgeschichte*, 4th ed. (Tübingen, 1963), 193–194, and Otto von Gierke, *Johannes Althusius und die Entwicklung der naturrechtlichen Staatstheorie. Zugleich ein Beitrag zur Geschichte der Rechtssystematik*, 5th ed. (Aalen, 1958).

73. Wolzendorff, *Staatsrecht und Naturrecht*, 292–308; Erich Haase, *Einführung in die Literatur des Refuge. Der Beitrag der französischen Protestanten zur Entwicklung analytischer Denkformen am Ende des 17. Jahrhunderts* (Berlin, 1959), 136–138, 307–309; also George H. Sabine, *A History of Political Theory*, 3d ed. (New York, 1961), 375–377.

74. Perez Zagorin, *A History of Political Thought in the English Revolution* (London, 1954), 9, 15–16, 24, 84, 86, 114, 153–154, 184–185; Sabine, *Political Theory*, 509–510, 535–536; Peter Cornelius Mayer-Tasch, *Thomas Hobbes und das Widerstandsrecht* (Tübingen, 1965), 63–65, 74–76, 83–118.

75. Wolzendorff, *Staatsrecht und Naturrecht*, 326–350.

76. Vattel, *Droit des gens*, 51–53, 55 (bk. I, chap. 4, § 51, 54); Christian Wolff, *Ius naturae methodo scientifica pertractatum* (Halle, 1740–1748), reprinted in his *Gesammelte*

gained a firm foothold among the German bourgeoisie. In the 1770s and 1780s the right to resist was mentioned only sporadically and vaguely, without any specific reference to the American Revolution.[77] However, we do find that Woldemar Friedrich Graf von Schmettau, a staunch adversary of the Americans, refuted categorically in a few sentences the notion of a right to resist based on natural rights, and so rejected any justification of the American patriots.[78]

One of the most prominent contemporary German advocates of the right to resist was August Ludwig Schlözer, the eminent historian from Göttingen whom we have met several times before. His political views, as revealed in his periodicals, prove him to be the "father of German liberalism,"[79] with his ideal of liberty oriented toward the British constitution.[80] It has been assumed that just because Schlözer sympathized with British constitutionalism he was also an opponent of the American Revolution, as appears to be indicated in his periodicals.[81] This theory is hardly more than a gross generalization, even though Friedrich Nicolai in 1777 reproached Schlözer and offered to "quarrel" with him because Schlözer so "fiercely defended" Britain's war against the Americans.[82]

Schlözer's reply to Nicolai remains unknown (Schlözer used to write "to be burnt" [*verbrennen*] on letters of his that contained critical remarks). Some idea of what it might have contained is conveyed in an often-overlooked

---

Werke, 2/XVII–XXIV (Hildesheim, 1968–1972), esp. VIII, 827 (§ 1054): "Si Principes, qui sub populo sunt, in leges fundamentales et Remp. peccant; populus iisdem vi resistere potest."

77. See, e.g., Christoph Martin Wieland, *Werke*, ed. Gustav Hempel, XXXV (Berlin, 1879), 384 (on Algernon Sidney, 1778); [J.B.K. von Schönebeck], *Das Gesetzbuch der reinen Vernunft* (Bonn, 1787), reprinted in Joseph Hansen, ed., *Quellen zur Geschichte des Rheinlandes im Zeitalter der Französischen Revolution 1780–1801*, 4 vols. (Bonn, 1931–1938), I, esp. 195, 198–199.

78. Schmettau, "Brutus: Freyheit und Schwärmerey" (1784), in his *Kleine Schriften*, 2 vols. (Altona, 1795), I, 219; cf. King, "Echoes of the American Revolution," *PMP*, XIV (1930), 104. See also *Gedanken über den Aufstand der englischen Colonien*, 30–31.

79. Valjavec, *Politische Strömungen*, 99.

80. Gallinger, "Haltung der deutschen Publizistik," 25; Arnold Berney, "August Ludwig von Schlözers Staatsauffassung," *HZ*, CXXXII (1925), 51; Douglass, "German Intellectuals," *WMQ*, 3d Ser., XVII (1960), 204.

81. Gallinger, "Haltung der deutschen Publizistik," 46–47; Berney, "Schlözers Staatsauffassung," *HZ*, CXXXII (1925), 56–57; Zelger, "Schlözers Briefwechsel und Staatsanzeigen," 171–172; Palmer, *Age of the Democratic Revolution*, I, 248; Douglass, "German Intellectuals," *WMQ*, 3d Ser., XVII (1960), 209; Gerhard Schilfert, "August Ludwig von Schlözer," in Joachim Streisand, ed., *Die deutsche Geschichtswissenschaft vom Beginn des 19. Jahrhunderts bis zur Reichseinigung von oben* (Berlin, 1963), 91. More cautious evaluations are Zermelo, "Schlözer," in *Jahresbericht über die Friedrichs-Werdersche Gewerbeschule*, 18, and Ford, "Two German Publicists," *JEGP*, VIII (1909), 155, 164.

82. "zanken . . . so heftig verteidigen": Nicolai to Schlözer, Oct. 13, 1777 (Nachlaß Nicolai, LXVII/54, Staatsbibliothek der Stiftung Preussischer Kulturbesitz, Berlin).

public response that Schlözer made to the same accusation from Christian Wilhelm Dohm in the *Deutsches Museum*.[83] In his *Briefwechsel* Schlözer rejected the accusation, though cautiously (as was his custom in public statements): "I try to inform others about this great development as a cosmopolitan and contemporary, collecting data and handing them down to my readers. I leave judgment entirely to them, without anticipating it in any way."[84] He continued his refutation by listing four points concerning the American Revolution that seemed to him to be crucial for judging it. First, he condemned the Boston Tea Party. Second, he denied that England had a right to tax the colonies. Third, he could not decide whether Parliament really had intended to tax the colonies. Finally, he considered the most important problem to be "whether the colonies are morally obligated to contribute their share toward the upkeep of the whole monarchy, the royal court, the land and sea power, and the payment of interest and repayments on debts incurred mostly on their behalf."[85] He admitted that he was unable to answer that question, and he was therefore content to state the opposing ideas of the two sides.

Such remarks from Schlözer, and the ambiguous tenor of his periodicals, seem to make it worthwhile to determine whether Jakob Mauvillon was not right in his observation that "a Göttingen professor cannot write in favor of the colonies."[86] Mauvillon maintained that Schlözer, in his various defenses of the British government, intentionally and very subtly selected only reports whose argumentation was completely nonsensical and ridiculous, so that they would create just the opposite impression from what they appeared to be on the surface. When reading those pamphlets, one could be consoled by the thought "that Herr Schlözer is a secret friend of liberty and the Americans."[87]

Mauvillon may have had a special purpose of his own in mind when he wrote that. Nevertheless, it is difficult to believe that Schlözer was a true opponent of the American Revolution. Such an assumption would run contrary not only to the comments already quoted but also to his concept of the

---

83. *Deutsches Museum*, Sept. 1776, 835–851.

84. "Ich suche von dieser großen Begebenheit als Weltbürger und Zeitgenosse zu unterrichten, sammle Facta und teile das Gesammlete meinen Lesern mit. Das Urteil überlasse ich ihnen, ohne ihnen darin vorzugreifen": Schlözer, ed., *Briefwechsel*, I, no. 5 (1777), 316.

85. "ob die Kolonien die Pflicht haben, etwas zum Unterhalt der ganzen Monarchie, des königl. Hofs, der Land- und Seemacht und zur Verzinsung und Abbezahlung der großenteils für sie gemachten englischen Staatsschulden beizutragen": *ibid.*, 318.

86. "daß ein Göttingischer Professor nicht für die Kolonien schreiben kann": Mauvillon, *Sammlung von Aufsätzen*, I, 142.

87. "daß Herr Schlözer ein heimlicher Freund der Freiheit und mithin der Amerikaner ist": *ibid.*, 143.

right to resist, which makes him an adherent of the old tradition of natural rights, which he often developed in his well-known, and sometimes notorious, lectures.[88] To many, the professor must have seemed to be a revolutionary when he praised democracy as the "most natural" form of government[89] and proclaimed that "state and government do not exist of themselves; but are established by man."[90]

In an age of absolutism and anointed kings these words had significant impact, even though Schlözer also spoke of a constitutional and parliamentary monarchy as the ideal form of government.[91] Schlözer's belief in the human foundation of all government was a transition to his conception, "not yet advanced in any reasoned treatise on governmental law,"[92] that it was right to depose a sovereign "where there are sufficient reasons."[93] He did not consider either a change of religion or a mentally and physically weak or disabled monarch to be sufficient reasons. "The only reason is tyranny."[94]

Of course, this reasoning embodied elements from the old concept of natural law, but it also expressed precisely the reproach of the American patriots against George III, as Schlözer doubtlessly knew, though he chose not to mention it. Significantly, he never tried to rebut the grave accusations made by the Americans against this monarch. Circumventing this most recent example, still vivid in the minds of his listeners, he was content to search far back into history to support his statements. In view of the interest displayed in his periodicals and his position as one of the most eminent intellectuals of his day, it is hardly conceivable that his failure to make any mention of American affairs was purely accidental. As Königlich grossbritannischer Hofrat, he probably had weighty reasons constraining him from discussing George III in this context.

88. Walter Habenicht, *Georg Friedrich von Martens. Professor des Natur- und Völkerrechts in Göttingen. Eine biographische und völkerrechtliche Studie* (Göttingen, 1934), 98–99. On Schlözer's idea of a right of resistance see Ford, "Two German Publicists," *JEGP,* VIII (1909), 155, and Berney, "Schlözers Staatsauffassung," *HZ,* CXXXII (1925), 45, 51–52.

89. "natürlichste": Schlözer, "Vorlesungen über die Regierungsformen" (notes on a course at the University of Göttingen during the winter semester 1787), 11, 14, also 15 (Kantonsbibliothek [hereafter cited as KB], Aarau).

90. "Staat u. Regierung existieren nicht von sich selbst, sondern sind durch den Menschen gesetzt": Schlözer, "Vorlesungen über die Politik" (notes on a course at the University of Göttingen during the winter semester 1787), 6 (KB, Aarau).

91. Schlözer, "Regierungsformen," 71 (*ibid.*).

92. "noch in keinem vernünftigen Kompend. übers Staatsrecht aufgeworfen worden": Schlözer, "Politik," 114 (*ibid.*).

93. "wenn hinreichende Gründe vorhanden sind": *ibid.,* 115.

94. "Die einzige Ursache ist Tyrannei": *ibid.,* 136.

Figure 6. Battle of Bunker Hill, June 17, 1775. "The first formal action of Americans and Englishmen at Bunker Hill, June 17, 1774." (Chodowiecki, for Sprengel, *Allgemeines historisches Taschenbuch.*)

Courtesy John Carter Brown Library, Brown University, Providence, R.I.

The Problem of Independence

The question of American independence and its official announce-ment opens a whole new vista of topics. The idea of American separation from the mother country was not entirely new to Europeans around 1776. Peter Kalm had mentioned it in his influential book of travels: "I have been told by Englishmen, and not only such as were born in America but also by those who came from Europe, that the English colonies in North America, in the space of thirty or fifty years, would be able to form a state by themselves entirely independent of Old England."[95] And no less a scholar than Ebeling (though he was unknown at the time) contradicted Kalm indirectly in the mid-1760s when he voiced the opinion that several centuries would pass before "the inhabitants of the newer worlds could tear away from domina-tion by Europeans."[96] Both examples show that the question of American independence had turned up in Germany before 1775–1776, although only peripherally. But no other subject shows better the lack of clarity as to the reasons and aims of the Americans that prevailed among the German bour-geoisie before the outbreak of the war.

During the fifteen years preceding the war there was a fundamental change in the notions of the American patriots about authority. Looking back, John Adams thought this decisive but slow process to be the revolution proper.[97] Serious consideration of independence was a relatively late pro-duct of this change. The same applies to the change from predominantly constitutional argumentation to arguments based more and more on natural law. It was not until the end of 1775 that the call for independence became an open political demand. Before that time, even unbending fighters for the American cause like Samuel Adams, Richard Henry Lee, and Patrick Henry[98]

95. Peter Kalm, *The America of 1750: Peter Kalm's Travels in North America; The En-glish Version of 1770* [by Johann Reinhold Forster], trans. Edith M. L. Carlborg and Adolph B. Benson, ed. Benson, 2 vols. (1937; repr. New York, 1966), I, 139–140 (entry of Nov. 2, 1748).

96. "die Einwohner der neuern Welten sich von der Herrschaft der Europäer losreißen": Ebeling, "Fragen, welche erst nach einigen Jahrhunderten können aufgelöset werden," *Han-noverisches Magazin*, Nov. 15, 1765, 1448.

97. Adams to Jefferson, Aug. 24, 1815, in Cappon, ed., *Adams-Jefferson Letters*, II, 455; Bailyn, *Ideological Origins*, 301–319.

98. Since George Bancroft's *History of the United States of America, From the Discovery of the Continent*, III (New York, 1883), 306, it has always been maintained that Samuel Adams postulated independence as early as 1768; cf. John C. Miller, *Sam Adams: Pioneer in Propaganda* (1936; repr. Stanford, Calif., 1960), 229, and, similarly, E. Wright, *Fabric of Freedom*, 97. However, Stewart Beach, *Samuel Adams: The Fateful Years, 1764–1776* (New York, 1965), 177–178, has proved conclusively that this assumption can no longer be sup-

had not openly postulated independence,[99] a point often missed by German contemporaries.

In addition to the fundamental economic, political, and, of course, military reasons behind this new demand, two occurrences affected the timing of the promotion of the idea of separation from Britain. First of all, at the end of 1775 it became known in America that George III had denied royal protection to his rebellious subjects in a speech made on October 26. Second, in the first days of the new year there appeared Thomas Paine's pamphlet *Common Sense*, which called for independence in hitherto unheard-of radical, determined, and uncompromising terms. The quick and immense popularity of this pamphlet resulted in the spread of the catchword *independence* all over the country in a very short time. Dohm overrated Paine's influence, however, when he said, "The pamphlet *Common Sense* . . . probably has caused Congress's Declaration of Independence."[100]

The desire for independence was not the decisive reason for the dispute with the mother country. Rather, it was only one aspect of the quarrel; it turned up relatively late in the discussion but gained increasingly in importance. This belated verbal controversy about the pros and cons of American independence culminated in the Declaration of Independence of July 4, 1776. The character of this document is ambivalent in a remarkable way. On the one hand, it is a justification of the Americans' political actions in the dispute with Great Britain; on the other, it is a fundamental declaration of those

---

ported. See also the resolution of the first session of the Boston Committee of Correspondence, Nov. 20, 1772 (Boston Committee of Correspondence, General Correspondence, Case 4, Box I, 1, 61–62, NYPL, New York); S. Adams to Darius Sessions, Jan. 2, 1773, and to Christopher Gadsden, July 18, 1774, in Harry Alonzo Cushing, ed., *The Writings of Samuel Adams*, 4 vols. (1904–1908; repr. New York, 1968), II, 395–401, III, 141–143; S. Langdon to S. Adams, Feb. 5, 1776 (Samel Adams Papers, Case 5, NYPL, New York). Though the tone of these letters and their postulations are generally radical, the idea of independence appears only in the last one. For Richard Henry Lee see Oliver P. Chitwood, *Richard Henry Lee: Statesman of the Revolution* (Morgantown, W. Va., 1967), 92. Cf. R. H. Lee to Patrick Henry, Apr. 20, 1776, in James Curtis Ballagh, ed. and comp., *The Letters of Richard Henry Lee*, 2 vols. (New York, 1911–1914), I, 178–179. On Patrick Henry see George F. Willison, *Patrick Henry and His World* (Garden City, N.Y., 1969), 303–305, and Robert D. Meade, *Patrick Henry: Practical Revolutionary* (Philadelphia and New York, 1969), 99–102.

99. See, e.g., Herbert Friedenwald, *The Declaration of Independence: An Interpretation and an Analysis* (New York, 1904), 50–76; John H. Hazelton, *The Declaration of Independence: Its History* (New York, 1906), 13; Julian P. Boyd, *The Declaration of Independence: The Evolution of the Text . . .* (Princeton, N.J., 1945), 5–6; Edward Dumbauld, *The Declaration of Independence and What it Means Today* (1950; repr. Norman, Okla., 1968), 11–12; Bernard Mason, *The Road to Independence: The Revolutionary Movement in New York 1773–1777* (Lexington, Ky., 1966), 134–177; and, less satisfactory, John M. Head, *A Time to Rend: An Essay on the Decision for American Independence* (Madison, Wis., 1968).

100. "Das Pamphlet: The Common Sense . . . hat wahrscheinlich die Independenzerklärung des Kongresses veranlaßt": Dohm, ed., *Materialien für die Statistick*, I, [9].

principles that, according to the ideas of the leaders of the American Revolution, should and must support a commonwealth. Thus, it is at the same time an ad hoc political pamphlet and a fundamental state document laying claim to universal validity.

Thomas Jefferson was able to unite convincingly in one continuous statement these manifold viewpoints. If the Declaration of Independence was to justify its function, it would have to summarize the previous years' political discussions rather than evolve new theories. Jefferson himself stated that the purpose of the Declaration was "not to find out new principles, or new arguments, never before thought of, not merely to say things which had never been said before; but to place before mankind the common sense of the subject, in terms so plain and firm as to command their assent, to justify ourselves in the independent stand we are compelled to take. Neither aiming at originality of principle or sentiment, nor yet copied from any particular and previous writing, it was intended to be an expression of the American mind."[101] In fulfilling this purpose, the Declaration of Independence was very well suited to explain the American patriots' point of view to their European contemporaries. For it not only gave reasons for their most recent political actions, it also dealt with questions of principle: the rights of the individual and of society, the inalienable rights of man, and the right of resistance—the indispensable foundations of every state.[102]

Questions of legality and independence were closely associated, even though, chronologically, the idea of independence became most real for the colonists at the very moment when the discussion of legal standpoints became irrelevant because of the outbreak of the war. But the German bourgeoisie were bound to see things very differently. Up to the mid-1770s newspapers constituted virtually the only source of information. Reports were meager, and there were no thorough investigations and analyses of the continuously changing scene in the British possessions. Developments in America were alien to Germans, and the American patriots' motives remained inscrutable, despite repeated hints of what was coming. Peter Kalm, whose work was published in an English translation by Johann Reinhold Forster at the beginning of the decade, had considerable influence on newspaper stories coming

101. Jefferson to H. Lee, May 8, 1825, H. A. Washington, ed., *The Writings of Thomas Jefferson*, 9 vols. (New York, 1854–1856), VII, 407; see also letter to James Madison, Aug. 30, 1823, *ibid.*, 305. In addition, see Carl L. Becker, *The Declaration of Independence: A Study in the History of Political Ideas*, 2d ed. (1922; repr. New York, 1956), 72–73; Wilbur S. Howell, "The Declaration of Independence and Eighteenth-Century Logic," *WMQ*, 3d Ser., XVIII (1961), 465–482; James Sullivan, "The Antecedents of the Declaration of Independence," American Historical Association, *Annual Report for the Year 1902* (New York, 1903), I, 66–85.

102. Cf. Boyd, *Declaration of Independence*, 3.

from London, and these reported again and again that sooner or later independence would become an issue. Some went a step further, declaring that the colonists were striving for separation from Great Britain.[103] Reports from envoys in London presented a similar picture.[104]

Before 1776, however, speculations such as these fell largely on deaf ears. There were no discussions in Germany about the advantages and disadvantages of possible independence for the English colonies, especially since there were no comparable examples in recent history that could have furnished food for thought. If an opinion was expressed at all at this time, it was usually more in favor of continuing dependence on Great Britain than of separation, thus tending to reaffirm the status quo.[105]

During the second half of 1776 the situation changed quickly. In early summer there were already some reports that Congress was on the "path toward independence"[106] and that it would soon be announced officially.[107] A confirmation of these reports reached Germany in the last days of August. In a few cases the text of the Declaration of Independence was transmitted, usually in an abbreviated form.[108] A German translation of the whole text appeared probably for the first time in October,[109] but there was little noticeable interest. Matthias Christian Sprengel professed amazement at not being able to find an unabridged German version, but contented himself with reproducing only the catalog of grievances, the portion of the document that seemed to him to be of special importance.[110] In doing so, however, he misinterpreted the import of the Declaration, giving the British government as its addressee, whereas the Americans quite intentionally had directed their reproaches to the king personally.[111]

103. Cf. *Wienerisches Diarium*, esp. May 19, 1770, July 21, 1773, Mar. 30, 1774, Apr. 22, 1775; *Leipziger Zeitung*, Feb. 6, 1773, Feb. 22, Dec. 15, 1774. Also, the German translator's preface to *Geschichte der Englischen Kolonien*, I, [2].

104. See, e.g., Belgiojoso to Kaunitz, Aug. 25, 1775 (Staatskanzlei, Staatenabteilung: England, K. 117, fol. 19, HHStA, Vienna); Maltzahn to Frederick II, Feb. 20, 1776 (Rep. 96. 35C, vol. XI, fols. 32r–v, DZA, Merseburg).

105. Cf. *Teutscher Merkur*, Mar. 1773, 279; Raynal, *Europäer in beiden Indien*, ed. Mauvillon, VI, 217, 485–486, 545; *Geschichte der Englischen Kolonien*, I, [2–3].

106. "Weg der Unabhängigkeit": *Freytags-Zeitung*, June 14, 1776; cf. *Hamburgischer Correspondent*, June 1, 1776.

107. Johann Adolf Graf von Loss to Sacken, July 26, 1776 (Locat 2747, conv. XXI, fol. 250, StA, Dresden).

108. Cf. *Oberpostamtszeitung*, Aug. 23, 1776; *Hamburgischer Correspondent*, Aug. 24, 1776; Joseph Franz Xaver Freiherr von Haslang to Beckers von Wetterstetten and to Seinsheim, Aug. 20, 1776 (Bayer. Gesandtschaft, London, no. 254, GStA, Munich).

109. Iselin, ed., *Ephemeriden der Menschheit*, Oct. 1776, 96–106.

110. Sprengel, *Briefe*, 47–54.

111. Angermann, "Ständische Rechtstraditionen," *HZ*, CC (1965), 65–66, 76–80.

Few German contemporaries paid adequate attention to the Declaration of Independence, and insufficient knowledge plagued those who attempted an evaluation of it. A report from London by the Württemberg envoy, Wilhelm Römer, shows the extent of misunderstanding. He told his government at the end of August 1776 that the general part of the Declaration of Independence, the remarks about the origin of governments, the people's right to resist, and the natural right of independence, contained nothing that had not been known for a long time, just "some well-known general principles," as he put it.[112] This interpretation failed to differentiate between a merely theoretical treatise and a program for political action.

Interest in the Declaration of Independence did not grow in the German-speaking regions during the following years as it did in England and France.[113] It is consequently not surprising that the "Register of the Most Important Developments in America since the Beginning of the Unrest," published at the end of 1781 by the *Leipziger Zeitung*, did not mention the Declaration of Independence, the Articles of Confederation, or the new state constitutions.[114]

The question of independence, however, was treated differently during the second half of the 1770s. Ironically, it was of greater concern to the opponents of America than to its supporters, for the former could make good use of the proclaimed independence to establish what they believed were long-standing American aims. In announcing independence, the American patriots themselves handed men like Johann Matthias Schroeckh, Gottlob Benedikt von Schirach, and Christoph Heinrich Korn an argument most easily and convincingly turned against the patriot cause. The announcement at last laid bare the real reason for the conflict, all other reasons vanishing into thin air or being reduced to their true value. "We do not deny that the colonies in general and some especially may have well-founded reasons for complaint. . . . But they have never made any argument that was not tied to independence."[115]

Such was the typical conclusion of those who rejected and condemned the American Revolution. They believed that the striving for independence,

112. "quelques principes généraux assez connûs": dispatch by Wilhelm Römer, Aug. 20, 1776 (A 74, Bü. 178, Hauptstaatsarchiv [hereafter cited as HptStA], Stuttgart).
113. Cf. John Warder to his parents, Sept. 18, Oct. 13, 1776 (Letterbook, 1776–1778, fols. 20v, 20 1/2v, PHi, Philadelphia). Warder, a loyalist, was in England at this time. Fay, *L'Esprit révolutionnaire*, 56–57.
114. *Leipziger Zeitung*, Nov. 28, 1781.
115. "Man leugnet nicht, daß die Kolonien überhaupt, oder einige insbesondere, gegründete Beschwerden haben können. . . . Aber nie haben sie eine Vorstellung getan, die nicht auf Unabhängigkeit zielte": *Über den Aufstand der englischen Kolonien*, 16–17. Also in Korn, *Geschichte der Kriege*, II (1776), 74; cf. *ibid.*, XXI (1780), 12.

which Kalm had already commented on and which had seemingly manifested itself after the end of the Seven Years' War at the latest, represented the Americans' true intentions. Everything else was simply veiling tactics, pretexts, and collusion; all the American complaints against England were, with a few exceptions, completely unfounded. It became evident in the end that American actions against the mother country were insidious, hypocritical, and morally despicable.[116] The Declaration showed quite clearly how closely "rebellion and insolence [were] connected" in America,[117] and that the Americans were nothing but "a people with a propensity for unrestrained insolence."[118]

The adversaries of the American patriots thought it superfluous to examine the Declaration for elements of truth or to attempt to disprove the complaints raised in it point by point. The document condemned itself, and they were content with this summary judgment. They did not hesitate to agitate against the "insulting" character of its baseless complaints.[119] The mere existence of this phony creation was enough to label it "a true violation of all religious, moral, and social duties."[120]

The longer the war lasted and the more independence became a quasi-established fact, the less the Declaration was condemned, especially since it was by no means obvious that an independent America would be to England's detriment.[121] To be sure, some people would not accept the colonies' separation from the mother country; Georg Christoph Lichtenberg, the physicist and satirist from Göttingen who had many connections to the Anglo-Saxon world, was one of them. But the denunciations by these diehards were hardly more than final attempts to defy immutable facts.[122] The majority of the ad-

116. Schroeckh, *Lehrbuch der allgemeinen Weltgeschichte zum Gebrauche bey dem ersten Unterrichte der Jugend* (Berlin and Stettin, 1774), 452; Schroeckh, *Allgemeine Weltgeschichte*, IV, pt. 2, 250, 252; *ibid.*, 2d ed. (1799); Schroeckh, *Histoire universelle à l'usage de la jeunesse*, trans. from the German, 4 vols. (Leipzig, 1784–1791), IV, pt. 2 (1790), 156, 158; *Auszug der allgemeinen Weltgeschichte . . .*, 3 vols. (Amberg, 1776), III, 66–67; Schirach, *Notiz der Großbrittannischen Colonien*, 90–91; Russell, *Geschichte von Amerika*, IV, 37.

117. "Aufruhr und Frechheit verbunden": Johann Heinrich Schinz to Bodmer, Oct. 20, 1775 (Ms. Bodmer, VII, 358, ZB, Zurich).

118. "zu einer zügellosen Frechheit geneigtes Volk": Korn, *Kurzgefaßte Geschichte des Krieges*, 23.

119. "beleidigenden": *ibid.*, 28. Similarly, Sprengel, *Briefe*, 54.

120. "eine wahre Verletzung aller Pflichten der Religion, der Sittenlehre und der bürgerlichen Gesellschaft": Struensee, *Beschreibung der Handlung*, I, 172.

121. Adam Smith, *Untersuchung der Natur und Ursachen von Nationalreichthümern*, trans. from the English [by Johann Friedrich Schiller], 2 vols. (Leipzig, 1776–1778), II, 284–285; Struensee, *Beschreibung der Handlung*, I, 174–175; *Politisches Journal* (1781), I, 29–30.

122. Cf. Lichtenberg to Schernhagen, July 6, 1778, Nov. 8, 1779, in Lichtenberg, *Briefe*, I, 299, 332; see also his letters in Leitzmann, ed., "Neues von Lichtenberg," *Zeitschrift für*

versaries of independence, so vociferous in 1776, had gradually become silent. The public, whether it approved of the separation or not, had already turned away from these problems and concentrated on others that seemed more important.

Independence, we find, was not the central question for the majority of German contemporaries, especially when we concentrate on those who sympathized with the American Revolution. A genuine interest in the causes of independence would surely have dictated a careful study of the history and founding of the colonies.[123] Many of the first settlers had, after all, turned their backs on the mother country out of discontent with prevailing conditions. This absence of any serious inquiry into colonial origins was one indication of the secondary importance of the problem of independence.

The defenders of the American Revolution hardly went any deeper into the problem of independence than their opponents. Yet their views, also formed mostly after the outbreak of war, were a closer approximation to the facts. Kalm could not influence their thinking. To them the actions of the Americans were the resistance "of virtuous, faithful, and devoted people" who had had no design to separate from the mother country.[124] What had caused a shift in American opinion was not France's disappearance from the North American continent but the malevolent and unjust treatment of the colonists by the government and Parliament in London. "This shows that the Declaration of Independence was merely a consequence of the ministers' obstinacy."[125] Today's historians are also inclined to believe that the decision in favor of full independence was made only reluctantly and against sizable resistance within patriotic ranks.[126]

Bücherfreunde, N.S., IV, no. 1 (1912), 75–77, 91; King, "Echoes of the American Revolution," *PMP*, XIV (1930), 51. Also, *Some Short and Impartial Inquiries*, 14–15, 30; J.C.J. Dehn to Ehrhard Dehn, Apr. 13, 1781 (StadtA, Brunswick); Anburey, *Reisen*, 203. Dehn and Anburey fought the Americans during the war.

123. There were some attempts in this direction: *Geographische Belustigungen*, 53–54, and Köster and Roos, eds., *Deutsche Encyclopädie*, VI (1782), 76a.

124. "eines tugendhaften, treuen und ergebenen Volks": Buchenröder, *Nord-Amerika*, II, 185; see also I, 95, 102–103, and II, 182–185.

125. "Man kann hieraus sehen, daß die Unabhängigkeitserklärung bloß eine Folge von der Hartnäckigkeit der Minister war": Soulès, *Revolution in Nord-Amerika*, I, 40. Similarly, Ingenhousz, "Remarques," 3–4 (HHStA, Vienna), and Johann Leonhard Neusinger, *Kurze Geschichte von der Erschaffung der Welt bis auf unsre Zeiten für die Jugend*, 4 vols. (Nuremberg, 1786–1788), IV, 249–250.

126. E.g., E. Wright, *Fabric of Freedom*, 96; William Allen Benton, *Whig-Loyalism: An Aspect of Political Ideology in the American Revolutionary Era* (Rutherford, N.J., 1969), 155–189; Leopold S. Launitz-Schürer, Jr., "Whig-Loyalists: The De Lanceys of New York," *New-York Historical Society Quarterly*, LVI (1972), 179–198. Another example of the numerous Americans who parted with the Revolution at this point is the "Diary of James Allen, Esq., of Philadelphia, Counsellor-at-Law, 1770–1778," *PMHB*, IX (1885), 186–191.

We cannot determine whether America's advocates were indeed better informed than its opponents, or whether the argument they adopted happened coincidentally to be a better representation of actual developments. However, some of those who voiced approval of American independence based their opinions on broad, general considerations. Followers of the Enlightenment, for example, disapproved of colonialism and welcomed the independence of the British colonies because it coincided with what they thought to be the natural order of things.[127] In announcing the right "to assume among the Powers of the earth, the separate and equal station to which the laws of Nature and of Nature's God entitle them," the Declaration of Independence voiced not only a political claim against Great Britain but also the credo of all physiocrats and anticolonialists.

Of all German writers of the 1770s, the municipal secretary and popular philosopher from Basel, Isaak Iselin, probably best expressed these convictions in his numerous publications, such as his periodical *Ephemeriden der Menschheit* and his popular *Geschichte der Menschheit*. Always ready to accept reforms in all walks of human life, Iselin frankly approved of America's fight for freedom. His sympathies for the Revolution easily overcame questions of objective law, which he left for others to resolve. "After all, the emancipation of individuals and states must take its course."[128] However, being a legitimist and anti-Rousseauist, and deeply rooted in the tenets of moral philosophy, he could not help but make one complaint against the Americans on account of the Declaration of Independence, and that on moral grounds: "In this declaration we miss the respect that children owe to their parents and peoples owe to their kings, even after they have freed themselves of the latters' authority."[129]

Jakob Mauvillon, a professor at Kassel and later at the Collegium Carolinum of Brunswick, held similar views, though he was a convinced "friend of liberty" and sympathized with the rebellious Americans.[130] He thoroughly

---

127. Cf. *Briefe über den gegenwärtigen Zustand von England*, trans. from the English (Leipzig, 1777), [I], 69–70, and [Justin Girod-Chantrans], *Reisen eines Schweizers in verschiedene Kolonien von Amerika während dem letztern Krieg*, trans. from the French (Leipzig, 1786), 293, 295. See also Philippe Sagnac, *La Fin de l'Ancien Régime et la révolution américaine (1763–1789)*, 3d ed. (Paris, 1952), 10–11.

128. "Allein zuletzt muß doch die Emanzipation der Menschen und Staaten einmal vor sich gehen": *Ephemeriden der Menschheit*, Mar. 1776, 117. Cf. Iselin's entry in his diary, Aug. 4, 1779, and Iselin to Frey, Aug. 23, 1779 (Nachlaß Iselin, XV, 117, LVI, 240, StA, Basel).

129. "Wir vermissen in dieser Erklärung gar sehr die Ehrerbietungen, die Kinder ihren Eltern und Völker ihren Königen schuldig sind, auch nachdem sie sich von ihrer Gewalt befreit haben": *Ephemeriden der Menschheit*, Oct. 1776, 106; cf. Iselin, *Über die Geschichte der Menschheit*, 4th ed., 2 vols. (Basel, 1779), II, 475–477; also Gallinger, "Haltung der deutschen Publizistik," 23, 25; Im Hof, *Iselin und die Spätaufklärung*, 143–144.

130. Ebeling to Bentley, Mar. 13, 1799, in William Coolidge Lane, ed., *Letters of Chri-*

disapproved of the Declaration of Independence; he thought it to be "unnecessary." While the patriots' determined resistance seemed to him to be fully justified, because they had been driven into it by an unscrupulous policy, he nevertheless felt that "severing the bond of duty" at the same time exceeded the limits of excusable action.[131]

We gain the impression that, faced with the problems of independence, and especially with the Declaration of Independence, most of the German bourgeoisie were rather helpless. Even Schmohl, that great apologist of the American Revolution who used keener logic and understanding in defending his views than the majority of his contemporaries, cannot rid us of this impression. As he saw it, Britain's efforts to enslave the colonies drove them to war, thus compelling the Americans to declare themselves independent in order to come under international law. Only as a nation could they effectively wage war and conclude alliances. Thus, the Declaration of Independence was a necessary step according to international law—this shows again the influence of Vattel and of legal considerations upon Schmohl[132]—to enable the Americans to meet England on the level that had been forced upon them.[133] He believed that American independence would be sustained, although there had been some doubts about it at the beginning of the war.[134] Since all European powers were equally, directly, and vitally interested in America's rich natural resources, the wealth of the land, according to Schmohl, was the best guarantee of the new nation's continued independence.[135] At this time probably no one else in Germany used similarly cogent arguments to support his views.

Military Aspects: The War Scene

Military events were much more intriguing to Germans than the question of independence. Even the smallest skirmishes were reported by the newspapers. Thus, the news of the outbreak of war and of the first shots fired

---

stoph Daniel Ebeling to Rev. Dr. William Bentley of Salem, Mass., and to other American Correspondents (Worcester, Mass., 1926), 58. Cf. Alfred Stern, "Jakob Mauvillon als Dichter und Publizist," *Preußische Jahrbücher*, CCXXX (1932), 239, 248.

131. "unnötig. . . das Band ihrer Verpflichtung aufzuheben": Mauvillon, *Sammlung von Aufsätzen*, II, 8; cf. 10–11.

132. Vattel, *Droit des gens*, 255–256 (bk. II, chap. 12, § 152–154).

133. Schmohl, *Über Nordamerika und Demokratie*, 26.

134. See, e.g., Thomas Boone to Johannes von Müller, May 29, 1778 (Msc. Mü. LXXXI, 10, StadtB, Schaffhausen).

135. Schmohl, *Über Nordamerika und Demokratie*, 93.

Figure 7. Declaration of Independence, July 2, 1776. "Congress declares the thirteen united states of North America to be independent, July 4, 1776." (Chodowiecki, for Sprengel, *Allgemeines historisches Taschenbuch*.)

Courtesy John Carter Brown Library, Brown University, Providence, R.I.

at Lexington and Concord spread in relatively short time. One aspect of the newspaper accounts that surely influenced the formation of opinion in Germany was the almost invariable report that the British had indisputably opened fire.[136] This interpretative slant occurred even though most newspaper accounts came from London.[137] In embassy circles there seems to have been some difference of opinion on this point,[138] but among the bourgeoisie the idea was quickly formed that the British commanders had fired the first shots at Lexington.[139] Astonishingly, this interpretation of the outbreak of the war was almost never disputed in Germany.[140] At the time of the French Revolution it was said to be an established fact that at Lexington the British caused "the first civilian blood to be spilled."[141]

At first the adherents of British policy were very optimistic, always inclined to believe that "the colonists will not hold out for long."[142] Although some doubts might have crept in, the supporters were still convinced that American resistance would be beaten down in one or two dashing campaigns.[143] But the longer the struggle lasted, the more thoughtful they be-

---

136. *Oberpostamtszeitung*, June 9, 1775; *Wienerisches Diarium*, June 14, 1775; *Freytags-Zeitung*, June 23, 1775.

137. Cf. the contradictory reports in Jensen, ed., *American Colonial Documents*, 828–832.

138. Cf., e.g., Brühl to Sacken, June 13, 1775 (Locat 2685, conv. XI, fol. 218, StA, Dresden).

139. Cf. Döhla, "Tagebuch," *AGAO*, XXV, no. 1 (1912), 110 (entry of June 4, 1777); Buchenröder, *Nord-Amerika*, II, 167–168; Du Buisson, *Historischer Abriß*, 99; Jäger, *Zeitungs-Lexicon*, I (1782), 397a; Sprengel, *Allgemeines historisches Taschenbuch*, 85; Soulès, *Revolution in Nord-Amerika*, I, 90–91; Mazzei, *Geschichte und Staatsverfassung*, II, 5.

140. Cf., however, Hammerdörfer and Kosche, *Amerika*, I, 451–452.

141. "das erste Bürgerblut": Christiani, *Geschichte der neuesten Weltbegebenheiten*, II, 663. Leonhard Meister, *Vermischte historische Unterhaltungen über Europens Umbildung während der letzten Hälfte des XVIII.ten Jahrhunderts* (St. Gallen, 1790), 216, and Lobethan, *Schauplatz der Kriege*, II, 352, used the same phrasing.

142. "die Kolonisten nicht lange machen": Jakob Michael Reinhold Lenz to Lindau(?), Mar. 1776, in Lenz, *Briefe von und an J.M.R. Lenz*, ed. Karl Freye and Wolfgang Stammler, 2 vols. (Leipzig, 1918), I, 202. See also Belgiojoso to Kaunitz, Mar. 11, May 24, 1774, Mar. 31, 1775 (Staatskanzlei, Staatenabteilung: England, K. 117, fols. 67, 25, 31v, HHStA, Vienna); Seinsheim to Haslang, Feb. 12, 1775 (Bayer. Gesandtschaft, London, no. 253, GStA, Munich); Mercy d'Argenteau to Kaunitz, Nov. 15, 1775 (Staatskanzlei, Staatenabteilung: Frankreich, K. 155, fol. 169, HHStA, Vienna); Thulemeyer to Frederick II, Jan. 2, 1776 (Rep. 96. 41C, vol. XV, fols. 2r–v, DZA, Merseburg); Mr. S. to Haenichen, Feb. 18, 1776 (1 Alt 22, no. 1505, StA, Wolfenbüttel); Rochus Friedrich Graf von Lynar to Zacharießen, Feb. 19, 1776 (Nachlaß Lynar, XXIV, 508, StA, Oldenburg).

143. Cf. Beckers von Wetterstetten to Haslang, Apr. 13, June 15, 1776 (Bayer. Gesandtschaft, London, no. 254, GStA, Munich); Mr. S. to Haenichen, Aug. 22, 1776, June 1, Aug. 21, 24, 1777 (1 Alt 22, nos. 1505, 1506, StA, Wolfenbüttel); dispatch by Freiherr von Thun, Aug. 26, 1776 (A 74, Bü. 130, HptStA, Stuttgart); Haller to Gemmingen, Nov. 5, 1777,

came. Obviously, the Americans, though a motley crew arrayed before the British regulars, were not as easy to subdue as had been assumed. The news from America caused increasing disquiet and consternation.[144]

This apprehension was augmented by doubts about Britain's inner strength, doubts that had been rife for some time. The dispute between government and opposition was strongly condemned, and the prevailing party spirit provoked disgust. The eighteenth century did not recognize parties as necessary carriers of political will,[145] and it was widely believed, especially among German supporters of the British, that internal political conflict was responsible for England's military inadequacies. Instead of cowing the rebellious Americans for their atrocious deeds, England was dissipating its energies through internal discord.[146]

If contemporary German statements about the political and military strength of England seem vague to us, discussions of the American situation were practically nonexistent. From a modern perspective, most of the statements about the colonists were either casual remarks or related to individual cases. There was almost nothing from which one could draw generalizations. Assessments varied widely: the military situation of the American troops was said to be good,[147] or regrettable;[148] the troops were said to be inferior to the European units,[149] or at the end of their fighting strength.[150] They were con-

in Haller, *Briefwechsel mit Gemmingen*, ed. Fischer, 138–139; Johann Peter Isaak Dubois to Stutterheim, Nov. 11, 1777 (Locat 2862, vol. XXXIV, StA, Dresden).

144. Johann Georg Zimmermann to Johann Georg Sulzer, May 26, 1776, in Zimmermann, *Sein Leben und bisher ungedruckte Briefe an denselben*, ed. Eduard Bodemann (Hanover, 1878), 253; Mercy d'Argenteau to Kaunitz, Mar. 5, 12, 1777 (Staatskanzlei, Staatenabteilung: Frankreich, K. 157, fols. 82v, 84v, HHStA, Vienna); Mr. S. to Haenichen, Mar. 9, May 18, 1777 (1 Alt 22, no. 1506, StA, Wolfenbüttel); Lynar to Zacharießen, Mar. 15, Apr. 26, 1777 (Nachlaß Lynar, XXV, 539, 546, StA, Oldenburg); Peter Boué and sons to Borcke, Mar. 25, 1777 (Rep. 92 v. Borcke III, no. 53, vol. V, fol. 52, DZA, Merseburg); Dubois to Stutterheim, Aug. 1, 1777 (Locat 2862, vol. XXXIV, StA, Dresden).

145. See Madison's eloquent warning against factionalism in Federalist No. 10: Alexander Hamilton, John Jay, and James Madison, *The Federalist*, ed. Jacob E. Cooke (Middletown, Conn., 1961), 56–58.

146. Cf. *Bunzlauische Monatsschrift*, Apr. 1775, 123–124; dispatch by Thun, Nov. 6, 1775 (A 74, Bü. 129, HptStA, Stuttgart); *Freytags-Zeitung*, Feb. 16, 1776; Korn, *Geschichte der Kriege*, II, 77, 81, III, 59; J. G. Zimmermann to Schmid, May 29, 1780, in Zimmermann, *Briefe an einige seiner Freunde in der Schweiz*, ed. Albrecht Rengger (Aarau, 1830), 269.

147. Mercy d'Argenteau to Kaunitz, May 28, 1777 (Staatskanzlei, Staatenabteilung: Frankreich, K. 157, fol. 75, HHStA, Vienna).

148. Mr. S. to Haenichen, Dec. 31, 1779 (1 Alt 22, no. 1508, StA, Wolfenbüttel).

149. Friedrich Ferdinand Drück, "Vorlesungsmanuskripte, III" (1780), fol. 6a v (LB, Stuttgart).

150. Belgiojoso to Kaunitz, Oct. 20, 1780 (Staatskanzlei, Staatenabteilung: England, K. 120, fols. 39r–v, HHStA, Vienna).

sidered well equipped,[151] disunited and quarreling with one another,[152] poor fighters,[153] or terrible enemies.[154] More penetrating thinking was rare. Before the outbreak of the war there was little speculation on the question of whether the colonists were really prepared to fight. But the indecisive campaigns of 1775–1776 had shown that it would not be an easy war for England.[155] Then an increasing number of observers said openly what was more or less clear to others, "that the North American colonies might well be lost forever to Great Britain."[156] In mid-1775 the Württemberg envoy in Paris told his government in plain words: "If the London court does not grant them acceptable conditions, there will result a cruel war, followed by the independence of the colonies."[157] Others also concluded that England could not win the war.[158]

Such statements confidently anticipating a final victory for the Americans were often supported by other than military reasons. The colonists had the advantage not only because they were led by George Washington, the idol of the age, but because they fought for liberty. Believing that there was "no better soldier than a liberty enthusiast,"[159] publisher Johann Georg Jacobi,

151. Goltz to Frederick II, Jan. 21, 1776 (Rep. 96. 28C, vol. IXᵃ, fol. 20, DZA, Merseburg).

152. Christian Moritz Freiherr von Kutzleben to the landgrave of Hesse-Kassel, July 9, 1776 (300 Philippsruhe E 11/6, vol. II, fol. 23, StA, Marburg); *Oberpostamtszeitung*, Jan. 8, 1780.

153. Cazenove to Borcke, Dec. 6, 1776 (Rep. 92 v. Borcke III, no. 53, vol. IV, fol. 119, DZA, Merseburg).

154. Buchenröder, *Nachrichten von den Englischen Kolonien*, vi–vii, and his *Kurzgefaßte Historisch-geographische Nachrichten von den Englischen Kolonien in Nord-Amerika bis auf jetzige Zeiten*, 2d ed. (Hamburg, 1778), 4.

155. Cf. three works by Buchenröder: *Nachrichten von den Englischen Kolonien*, v–vi; *Kurzgefaßte Nachrichten*, 3–4; and *Grundriß von Nordamerika* (Hamburg, 1778), xxxv. Also, Thulemeyer to Frederick II, Feb. 14, 1777 (Rep. 96. 41D, vol. XVI, fol. 38v, DZA, Merseburg), and *Frankfurter Oberpostamtszeitung*, Feb. 21, 1777.

156. "daß die nordamerikanischen Kolonien wohl auf immer für Großbritannien verloren sein möchten": *Nichts Neues, aber doch manches Brauchbare*, Mar. 26, 1779, 184. Cf. Buchenröder, *Grundriß von Nordamerika*, xxxviii, and his *Nord-Amerika*, 2d ed., I (1778), xxxviii; also Frank Arthur Mumby, *George III. and the American Revolution* (London, 1924), 382.

157. "Si la cour de Londres ne leur accorde pas des conditions acceptables, il en resultera une guerre cruelle, suivie de l'indépendance des colonies": dispatch by Thun, June 30, 1775 (A 74, Bü. 129, HptStA, Stuttgart).

158. Cf. "Auszüge aus dem Tagebuche . . . von Heister," *Zeitschrift für Kunst, Wissenschaft und Geschichte des Krieges*, XII, no. 3 (1828), 236 (entry of Sept./Oct. 1776). See also a dispatch by Römer, Aug. 6, 1776 (A 74, Bü. 178, HptStA, Stuttgart); Mercy d'Argenteau to Kaunitz, Aug. 17, 1776 (Staatskanzlei, Staatenabteilung: Frankreich, K. 155, fols. 5v–6, HHStA, Vienna); Ingenhousz, "Remarques," 12 (HHStA, Vienna); Mr. S. to Haenichen, Apr. 16, 1778 (1 Alt 22, no. 1507, StA, Wolfenbüttel).

159. "kein besserer Soldat sei als der Enthusiast der Freiheit": Jacobi, ed., *Iris*, June 1775, 161.

for one, was convinced of England's defeat even at the beginning of the war. Christian Friedrich Daniel Schubart said with absolute certainty: "Our enemies believe that we lack good leaders; but where the fight is for liberty, everyone is a hero."[160] From this point of view, purely military factors were of secondary importance. Victory would not be decided by the supposed advantage of Britain's professional army in its contest with inadequately trained and equipped troops, nor was the success of the rebellious colonists dependent on foreign support, military or otherwise. "Fear not for the people whose arm carries the shield provided by liberty and the fatherland."[161]

One consequence of such sentiment was that numerous Germans, officers and members of the nobility among them, turned to Franklin with the request that they be permitted to participate in the fight for liberty.[162] Since there was insufficient demand for European officers, their wishes remained largely unfulfilled. Some of them, however, were taken into the insurgents' forces, Steuben being the best-known, though not the most typical, example. But there were also those who wanted to fight in America merely for the sake of adventure. August von Hennings, a writer and an official in the Danish service, put it this way: "How often have I heard people ask, where in this world are great things to be done? Then they mention Corsica and America and wish they were there."[163] The desire for adventure was probably the decisive stimulus for many of those who wished to participate in the war.[164]

All of this shows that German contemporaries, in spite of their interest

160. "Unsere Feinde glauben, daß es uns an guten Anführern fehle; aber wo man vor die Freiheit ficht, da ist jeder ein Held": *Deutsche Chronik*, Jan. 11, 1776, 31.
161. "Fürchte nicht für das Volk, dem Freiheit und Vaterland das Schild um den Arm gehängt hat": [Johann Jakob Bodmer], *Die Cherusken. Ein politisches Schauspiel* (Augsburg, 1778), 14. See also *Neueste Mannigfaltigkeiten* (1778), I, 347–348; [Joseph Milbiller], *Allgemeine Geschichte der berühmtesten Königreiche und Freistaaten in und außerhalb Europa*, Sect. 1: *Engelland* (Leipzig, 1797–1798), III, 358–359.
162. Cf., e.g., the letters to Franklin by P. P. Burdett, Apr. 5, 1777, Lt. Wommrad, July 28, 1777, Friedrich Barnzen, Aug. 29, 1777, Nikolaus Jakob Holtermann, Sept. 1, 1777, Karl Freiherr von Emerich, Dec. 4, 1777, and Franz Anton Freiherr von Seyffertitz, Sept. 13, 1778 (Franklin Papers, V, 138, VI, 146, LIX, 27, LXII, 58, LIX, 83, XI, 135, APSL, Philadelphia).
163. "Wie oft habe ich nicht fragen hören, wo ist eine Bahn für edle Taten, wo ist in der Welt etwas Großes zu machen? Dann nannte man Korsika, Amerika und wünschte sich hinüber": Hennings to Emilie Gräfin von Schimmelmann, Nov. 18, 1779 (Nachlaß Hennings, XLIII, fol. 72v, SuUB, Hamburg).
164. Cf., e.g., the cases of Friedrich Maximilian Klinger and J.M.R. Lenz in: King, "Echoes of the American Revolution" *PMP*, XIV (1930), 58; Walz, "American Revolution and German Literature," *MLN*, XVI (1901), 415. A different ideal, however, motivated the former Brunswick officer and later American colonel, Heinrich Emanuel Lutterloh; cf. his letters to Franklin and to the American commissioners at Paris (Franklin Papers, APSL, Philadelphia); also Friedrich Adolf Riedesel to Duke Ferdinand of Brunswick, May 9, 1778, in Max von Eelking, *Leben und Wirken des Herzoglichen Braunschweig'schen General-Lieutenants Friedrich Adolf Riedesel Freiherrn zu Eisenbach . . .* , 3 vols. (Leipzig, 1856), III, 226.

in the progress of the war, made little effort to study the military problems systematically. Among the auxiliary troops in America there was a more careful assessment. Some of them observed that Great Britain had undertaken a very difficult military task, attempting to conquer and control a gigantic enemy country while grappling with a practically unmanageable logistical problem at the same time. The interior of the country was almost inaccessible, making it difficult, if not impossible, to move large armies about. Besides, the enemy only rarely fought in closed formation, often sending the militia into the fray. This made the war not only much more harassing than any European campaign, it also placed completely new demands on military theory.[165] "We have to attack, storm, and occupy post after post, redoubt after redoubt, garrison after garrison. Even with the best of luck we have losses in each encounter. Before we have conquered we shall be completely exhausted. What use will it be to England if America is devastated and ruined? Conquest will ruin us, and we are not at all assured of it."[166] This comment came from one of the few contemporaries who thought about the matter at all. By and large, the bourgeoisie did not bother with these military problems. The Steuben myth, that Prussian discipline was needed to win the war, does not belong to this time.[167] On the contrary, the former Prussian officer remained as little esteemed as most of his American colleagues—with the exception of Washington, to be sure.

165. Cf. Ernst Philipp Theobald, "Diarium," entry of Mar. 23, 1776, fol. 2 (MB, Kassel); Lt. Sarorius, entry in his diary, June 20, 1777 (Verschiedene Berichte über den Feldzug der Hessen in Amerika, II, 129–130, *ibid.*); Friedrich to Wilhelm von Münchhausen, Sept. 1, 1777 (Diarium-Briefe von F. v. Münchhausen, I, 27v–28, HptStA, Hanover); Riedesel to hereditary prince of Brunswick, June 1, 1777 (38 B Alt 236, fol. 89v, StA, Wolfenbüttel); Bartholomäi, *Eroberung von Charlestown,* 56; also Johann von Ewald's book based on his American experiences, *Abhandlung über den kleinen Krieg* (Kassel, 1785). For the results of modern research see Eric Robson, *The American Revolution in its Political and Military Aspects, 1763–1783* (London, 1955), 93–122; Piers Mackesy, *The War for America 1775–1783* (London, 1964), 510–516; also the interesting remarks by Palmer, *Age of the Democratic Revolution,* I, 209–210.

166. "Wir haben Posten für Posten, eine Schanze nach der anderen, Garnison für Garnison anzugreifen, zu stürmen und einzunehmen. Man habe auch alles mögliche Glück bei jedem Vorfall, so müssen wir Leute verlieren. Bevor wir es bald erobert, werden wir gänzlich erschöpft sein. Wenn Amerika verwüstet und zu Grunde gerichtet, was wächst Engelland dadurch zu? Eroberung richtet uns zu Grund, und wir sind der Eroberungen keineswegs versicheret": *Freytags-Zeitung,* Aug. 2, 1776; quite similar is Remer in his translation of Stedman, *Americanischer Krieg,* I, [3–4], 154n.

167. The myth grew lavishly in later years. For an early, though still scholarly, example see Friedrich Kapp, *Leben des Amerikanischen Generals Friedrich Wilhelm von Steuben* (Berlin, 1858), esp. 611–612. Extremely curious offsprings of this myth appeared in the Nazi period; cf., e.g., such a title as Karl Hermann Böhmer's *Preußengeist befreit Amerika. General Steuben, der Stratege Washingtons, siegt im amerikanischen Freiheitskampf gegen England. Tatsachenbericht* (Essen, 1939) (see Hans Hainebach, *German Publications on the United States 1933 to 1945* [New York, 1948]).

Leaving aside day-to-day events, let us examine the German reaction to decisive military developments. A good example is General John Burgoyne's surrender to Horatio Gates at Saratoga in October 1777. Of course, Germans took it differently according to their predilection, pro-American or pro-British. The former celebrated it as "great news,"[168] while the latter considered it "grievous news"[169] and blamed it all on Burgoyne.[170] For pro-American Germans the British defeat merely confirmed their long-held conviction that a final American victory was inevitable. To be sure, they honored Gates as a hero during those weeks, but they were far too sure of America's final victory to make much of the individual steps toward this end. Saratoga thus passed without having a lasting impact on their minds. Several years later they had almost forgotten Gates's name:

> Of all those generals you too were one,
> Yet no one knows what you have done.[171]

It was not as easy for America's adversaries to gloss over the event. Strangely enough, they reacted to it more strongly than did the sympathizers. North German poet Heinrich Christian Boie was compelled to think of the surrender as a rather "sad" affair.[172] Johann Georg Zimmermann, the Hanoverian physician, was even more deeply affected by the news; Burgoyne's misfortune made him ill.[173] Defenders of British policy became more thoughtful after hearing the news about Saratoga. Obviously, British victory

168. "grande nouvelle": Zinzendorf, Tagebuch, XXII, entry of Dec. 21, 1777 (HHStA, Vienna). See also François-Alexandre-Frédéric, duc de La Rochefoucauld Liancourt, *Reisen in den Jahren 1795, 1796 und 1797 durch alle an der See belegenen Staaten der Nordamerikanischen Republik . . .*, trans. from the French, 3 vols. (Hamburg, 1799), II, 73.

169. "facheuse nouvelle": Brühl to Stutterheim, Dec. 5, 1777 (Locat 2685, conv. XV, fol. 349, StA, Dresden). See also Belgiojoso to Kaunitz, Dec. 5, 1777 (Staatskanzlei, Staatenabteilung: England, K. 118, fol. 12, HHStA, Vienna); dispatch by Römer, Dec. 5, 1777 (A 74, Bü. 178, HptStA, Stuttgart); Maltzahn to Thulemeyer, Dec. 9, 1777 (Rep. 92 Thulemeier, no. 10, vol. VI, DZA, Merseburg); Mr. S. to Haenichen, Dec. 14, 1777 (1 Alt 22, no. 1506, StA, Wolfenbüttel); Dubois to Stutterheim, Jan. 6, 1778 (Locat 2862, vol. XXXV, StA, Dresden).

170. Korn, *Geschichte der Kriege*, XXI (1780), 10–11. See also the anti-Burgoyne booklet, *Betrachtungen über den Feldzug des Generals Bourgoyne in Canada und Neu-York*, trans. from the English (Brunswick, 1780).

171. "Unter Generalen warst du auch einer. / Was du verrichtet hast, weiß keiner": *Das graue Ungeheuer*, III (1784), 269 (according to the table of contents, not by editor Wekhrlin himself).

172. "traurige": to Louise Mejer, Dec. 24, 1777. Cf. also his letter to her, Dec. 18, 1777 (MSS in SuUB, Göttingen; abridged version in Heinrich Christian Boie, *Ich war wohl klug, dass ich dich fand: Heinrich Christian Boies Briefwechsel mit Luise Mejer 1777–85*, ed. Ilse Schreiber [Munich, 1961], 26, 22).

173. Cf. Zimmermann to Jean André de Luc, Nov. 7, 1777, Jan. 27, 1778 (StA, Aarau). Zimmermann, of course, could have had no news of Saratoga by Nov. 7. From hearsay, however, he was sure of Burgoyne's decisive defeat in September.

was by no means a sure thing. The American success seemed to confirm what others had predicted a considerable time before, and it could win new friends for the patriots.[174] Voices urging a settlement increased in number. England was advised to stop rigidly pursuing the war and to come to an agreement with the Americans to bring it to an end.[175] Indeed, London did take some hesitant steps in that direction.[176] The self-assuredness of Britain's friends had been shaken by the surrender, even though they would not admit it in public. Only a few dared to dispute that England had received a severe blow; more thought of the lost troops it would now have to replace.[177]

Such opinions may have reflected the growing expectation that France would soon intervene and that an Anglo-French war was unavoidable and to be expected at any time.[178] The French-American alliance and the declaration of war in early 1778 were no surprise to most educated Germans. As early as December 1774 Schubart had reported: "It is feared that France will side with the Bostonians."[179] During the following years rumor was rife that the Bourbon courts of France and Spain were secretly supporting the Americans and arming against Britain. After all, Franklin had been in France for

174. E.g., Sprengel was strictly anti-American in his *Briefe* (1777). However, during the later years of the war he became carefully neutral, and by 1783, in his *Allgemeines historisches Taschenbuch*, he proved openly pro-American. For another example, Ebeling admitted in his *Erdbeschreibung*, I (1793), ii, that during the war he changed from opposition to sympathy with the American Revolution, though we have no precise information on when this change occurred.

175. See Belgiojoso to Kaunitz, Dec. 12, 1777 (Staatskanzlei, Staatenabteilung: England, K. 118, fol. 27, HHStA, Vienna); Mr. S. to Haenichen, Jan. 15, Feb. 19, 1778 (1 Alt 22, no. 1507, StA, Wolfenbüttel); Georg Friedrich Brandes to Christian Gottlob Heyne, Jan. 30, 1778 (Cod. MS Heyne, CXXVII, fol. 8v, SuUB, Göttingen); P. Nettelbeck to Gottfried August Bürger, Feb. 7, 1778, in Bürger, *Briefe von und an Gottfried August Bürger. Ein Beitrag zur Literaturgeschichte seiner Zeit*, ed. Adolf Strodtmann, 4 vols. (Berlin, 1874), II, 229; Korn, *Geschichte der Kriege*, X, 66–67. The Palatinate-Bavarian ministers Beckers von Wetterstetten and Seinsheim, especially, did not cease to plead for a compromise in the earlier years; cf. Beckers von Wetterstetten to Haslang, Feb. 19, Nov. 12, 1774, and Seinsheim to Haslang, Jan. 22, Feb. 19, Dec. 24, 1775 (Bayer. Gesandtschaft, London, nos. 252, 253, 254, GStA, Munich).

176. Robson, *American Revolution*, 175–199.

177. Cf. Boie to Mejer, Dec. 18, 1777, in Boie, *Ich war wohl klug* ed. Schreiber, 22; Prince Peter Friedrich Ludwig to Duke Friedrich August, Dec. 23, 1777, and the duke to the prince, Dec. 29, 1777 (StA, Oldenburg).

178. Mercy d'Argenteau to Kaunitz, Jan. 17, Mar. 20, 1778 (Staatskanzlei, Staatenabteilung: Frankreich, K. 158, fols. 10v, 117v, HHStA, Vienna); Brühl to Stutterheim, Jan. 30, 1778 (Locat 2686, conv. XIV, fol. 35, StA, Dresden); Mr. S. to Haenichen, Feb. 26, Mar. 22, 1778 (1 Alt 22, no. 1507, StA, Wolfenbüttel); Goltz to Frederick II, Mar. 19, 1778, and Daniel Alfons von Sandoz-Rollin to Frederick II, Mar. 22, 1778 (Rep. 96. 28E, vol. XI, fols. 92, 97, DZA, Merseburg).

179. "Man fürchtet, Frankreich werde sich der Bostonier annehmen": *Deutsche Chronik*, Dec. 1, 1774, 56.

some time, and Lafayette and other French officers were in America.[180] Remarkably, however, Germans did not think that French participation would in any way be decisive, although many believed that France was taking this opportunity to seek revenge against Great Britain for its defeat in the Seven Years' War.[181] Most of the German bourgeoisie were by then completely convinced of the Americans' military strength, and of their victory.

Even America's most enthusiastic adherents, however, were not altogether overjoyed to learn of France's entry into the war. The expanding conflict increasingly represented a definite threat to peace in Europe, and especially in Germany. The ghost of the Seven Years' War appeared over the horizon, a war that had also started in the Western Hemisphere and was eventually fought largely on German soil. Of course, there was no lack of apologists of war as an instrument of national politics, men who could see nothing horrifying or detestable in it.[182] But the majority of the bourgeoisie and of the lower strata of the population abhorred war and saw nothing but catastrophe and death as a result of it; they could wail with Matthias Claudius:

> It is war! It is war! . . .
> It is war, alas—I only desire
> That none of the blame is mine.[183]

They fervently hoped for a quick end to the fighting—with victory to the party they favored—and to see the danger of war averted from their own country before it was too late.[184]

180. Cf. Mercy d'Argenteau to Kaunitz, Dec. 18, 1776, Nov. 19, 1777 (Staatskanzlei, Staatenabteilung: Frankreich, K. 155, fols. 123r–v, K. 157, fol. 120v, HHStA, Vienna); Mr. S. to Haenichen, Jan. 30, 1777 (1 Alt 22, no. 1506, StA, Wolfenbüttel); Boden and Treuer to Karl Friedrich, Apr. 3, July 25, 1777 (Abt. 48, nos. 1966, 2188, GLA, Karlsruhe); dispatch by Thun, Aug. 11, 1777 (A 74, Bü. 131, HptStA, Stuttgart); Cazenove to Borcke, July 10, 1781 (Rep. 92 v. Borcke III, no. 53, vol. IX, fol. 41, DZA, Merseburg); S. Stürler von Altenberg to Johannes von Müller, c. end of 1790 (Msc. Mü. CXLVIII, StadtB, Schaffhausen).

181. Cf. dispatch by Thun, May 29, 1775 (A 74, Bü. 129, HptStA, Stuttgart); Goltz to Frederick II, Apr. 14, 1776 (Rep. 96. 28C, vol. IX^a, fol. 91v, DZA, Merseburg); Brühl to Sacken, July 9, 1776 (Locat 2685, conv. XII, fol. 262, StA, Dresden); dispatch by Römer, Aug. 13, 1776 (A 74, Bü. 178, HptStA, Stuttgart). According to modern research, however, the French-American alliance was of substantial military and political importance, as the American contemporaries realized at once; cf. William C. Stinchcombe, *The American Revolution and the French Alliance* (Syracuse, N.Y., 1969), 14–31, 152.

182. Cf., e.g., the booklet by [Friedrich Samuel Gottfried Sack], *Briefe über den Krieg* (Berlin, 1778).

183. "'s ist Krieg! 's ist Krieg! . . . / 's leider Krieg—und ich begehre / Nicht schuld daran zu sein": Matthias Claudius, *Werke. Asmus omnia sua secum portans oder Sämtliche Werke des Wandsbecker Boten*, 6th ed. (Stuttgart, 1965), 290 (from 1782).

184. Cf. Mercy d'Argenteau to Kaunitz, Sept. 18, 1775 (Staatskanzlei, Staatenabteilung: Frankreich, K. 155, fols. 99–100, HHStA, Vienna); Mr. S. to Haenichen, Oct. 17, 1776 (1 Alt

The war continued but did not spread to Germany; the Bavarian War of Succession was only an isolated interlude. The continued fighting did not seem to be to the advantage of Great Britain, whose governmental views were echoed only by an ever-shrinking number of followers, excluding the German emissaries in London. But even the ministers were unable to report favorably on the remainder of the war, except in a few isolated cases. They spoke with increasing frequency of England's steadily worsening military situation; there was no longer any hope that it might win the war.[185] Even the treason of General Benedict Arnold could not allay their fears—if they thought the incident important at all.[186]

Thus, the news that the British army under Lord Cornwallis had surrendered at Yorktown in October 1781 did not have much effect even on the German supporters of British policy. Only a few thought the event to be a "catastrophe,"[187] and still fewer thought that England should fight on for

---

22, no. 1505, StA, Wolfenbüttel); Köster, ed., *Neueste Staatsbegebenheiten*, Jan. 1777, 93; Thulemeyer to Frederick II, Mar. 7, 1777 (Rep. 96. 41D, vol. XVI, fol. 57v, DZA, Merseburg); Friedrich to Wilhelm von Münchhausen, Apr. 16, 1777 (Diarium-Briefe von F. v. Münchhausen, I, 5v, HptStA, Hanover); Lichtenberg to Schernhagen, Jan. 5, Oct. 8, 1778 (SuUB, Göttingen); J. G. Zimmermann to Albrecht Rengger, Jan. 15, 1778, in Zimmermann, *Briefe*, ed. Rengger, 32; J. G. Zimmermann to Sulzer, Mar. 8, 1778, in Zimmermann, *Leben und Briefe*, ed. Bodemann, 277; J. G. Zimmermann to de Luc, Mar. 10, 1778 (StA, Aarau); Iselin to Frey, Oct. 4, Dec. 19, 1778 (Nachlaß Iselin, LVI, 172, 186, StA, Basel). Whereas Lichtenberg and Zimmermann hoped for an English victory, Iselin wished for an American success.

185. Thulemeyer to Frederick II, Jan. 16, 1778, and Lusi to Frederick II, Aug. 7, 1781 (Rep. 96. 41E, vol. XVII, fol. 8, and 36A, vol. I, fols. 100r–v, DZA, Merseburg); Akim Grigoriewich Lisakewitz to Hennings, Jan. 28, 1778 (Nachlaß Hennings, IX, 32r–v, SuUB, Hamburg); Vieregg to Haslang, July 15, 1778, Seinsheim to Haslang, Apr. 18, 1779, and Haslang to Vieregg, Mar. 31, June 27, 1780 (Kasten schwarz 15380; Bayer. Gesandtschaft, London, no. 434; Kasten schwarz 15382, GStA, Munich); Mr. S. to Haenichen, Oct. 4, 1778 (1 Alt 22, no. 1507, StA, Wolfenbüttel); Mercy d'Argenteau to Kaunitz, Oct. 28, 1778, Nov. 29, 1780, Oct. 16, 1781, Josef Graf von Kaunitz-Rietberg to Prince Kaunitz, May 20, 1780, Jan. 12, 1781, Belgiojoso to Kaunitz, Apr. 3, 1781, and Adam Ritter von Lebzeltern to Kaunitz, Dec. 5, 1781 (Staatskanzlei, Staatenabteilung: Frankreich, K. 158, fol. 159, K. 162, fol. 40v, K. 165, fols. 75r–v; Spanien, K. 141, fols. 99r–v, K. 143, fols. 38v–39; England, K. 120, fol. 2; Portugal, K. 22, fols. 178r–v, HHStA, Vienna); Schönfeld to Stutterheim, Dec. 18, 1778, Mar. 10, 1780, and Brühl to Stutterheim, Sept. 24, 1779 (Locat 2747, conv. XXIV, fol. 5, conv. XXV, fols. 95r–v; Locat 2686, conv. XV, fol. 280, StA, Dresden); von Dincklage, "Tagebuch," 232, entry of mid-Oct. 1779 (MB, Kassel); Peter Boué and sons to Borcke, Nov. 2, 1779, Cazenove to Borcke, July 31, 1781 (Rep. 92 v. Borcke III, no. 53, vol. VII, fol. 152v, vol. IX, fol. 59, DZA, Merseburg); Schlözer, ed., *Briefwechsel*, IV, no. 35 (1780), 300; J. G. Zimmermann to Johann Kaspar Hirzel, May 29, 1780 (Nachlaß Hirzel, CCXL, 19, ZB, Zurich); Lichtenberg to Schernhagen, June 1, 1780 (SuUB, Göttingen).

186. Cf. Stang, "Tagebuch," 43 (HVMF, Ansbach); Vieregg to Haslang, Nov. 26, 1780 (Kasten schwarz 15382, GStA, Munich); Korn, *Geschichte der Kriege*, XXII (1781), 47.

187. "catastrophe": Thulemeyer to Frederick II, Nov. 30, Dec. 4, 7, 1781 (Rep. 96. 41I, 2, vol. XXI^b, pp. 135, 145–146, 156, DZA, Merseburg); Belgiojoso to Kaunitz, Nov. 27,

victory.[188] The majority of contemporaries, and surely also a respectable number of anglophiles, looked upon Yorktown as the second great victory for America and the conclusive defeat for Great Britain, for "England cannot make up by itself a loss of seven thousand battle-hardened and acclimated veterans."[189] It was correctly assumed by many that the surrender at Yorktown had decided the war.[190]

Even before the decision at Yorktown, diplomatic circles in London talked openly about the imminent loss of North America.[191] After the defeat the Austrian envoy, Karl Ludwig Graf von Barbiano und Belgiojoso, one of America's most determined adversaries among the diplomats of German-speaking countries, concluded that "it was impossible to subdue the colonies or prevent their independence." Three months later he stated that "the war against the colonies in America is as good as over."[192] Thus, the war ended with the confirmation of American independence that had been foreseen early on and that surprised no one.[193] News of the conclusion of peace at Versailles in the autumn of 1783 was received in the same spirit. "For the

---

1781 (Staatskanzlei, Staatenabteilung: England, K. 120, fol. 25, HHStA, Vienna); Brühl to Stutterheim, Nov. 30, 1781 (Locat 2686, conv. XVIII, fol. 4, StA, Dresden); Korn, *Geschichte der Kriege*, XXV, 44–45.

188. Brandes to Heyne, Dec. 3, 1781 (Cod. MS Heyne CXXVIII, fol. 173, SuUB, Göttingen); dispatches by Treuer, Jan. 15, 1782 (Abt. 48, no. 2192, GLA, Karlsruhe), and by Römer, Nov. 19, 1782 (A 74, Bü. 130, HptStA, Stuttgart). They all believed that the war would be continued. Eberhard Hehl later reproached England for having given up prematurely; cf. the entry in his diary for Oct. 19, 1784 (UB, Tübingen).

189. "L'Angleterre ne peut plus réparer par elle même une perte de 7/m. vétérans aguerris et acclimatés": Jean Baptiste Rivière to Stutterheim, Nov. 26, 1781 (Locat 2748, conv. XXVI, fols. 378r–v, StA, Dresden).

190. Finckenstein and Hertzberg to Lusi, Nov. 24, 1781 (Rep. XI. 73, conv. 140A, fol. 187, DZA, Merseburg); Vieregg to Haslang, Dec. 5, 1781 (Bayer, Gesandtschaft, London, no. 259, GStA, Munich); *Politisches Journal*, 1781, II, 471. From a retrospective view: Sprengel, *Allgemeines historisches Taschenbuch*, 138; Lobethan, *Schauplatz der Kriege*, II, 394.

191. E.g., Lusi to Frederick II, Nov. 6, 1781 (Rep. 96. 36A, vol. I, fol. 168, DZA, Merseburg).

192. "von der Unmöglichkeit, die Kolonien zu bezwingen oder ihre Unabhängigkeit zu verhindern . . .": to Kaunitz, Nov. 30, 1781. "daß der Krieg in Amerika gegen die Kolonien so viel als geendigt sei": to Kaunitz, Mar. 1, 1782 (both Staatskanzlei, Staatenabteilung: England, K. 120, fol. 34v, K. 121, fol. 33, HHStA, Vienna).

193. Cf. Brühl to Stutterheim, Dec. 7, 1779, May 7, 1782, and Schönfeld to Stutterheim, June 24, July 12, 1782 (Locat 2686, conv. XVI, fol. 15, conv. XVIII, fol. 172; Locat 2748, conv. XXVII, fols. 188v–189, 204, StA, Dresden); Köster, ed., *Neueste Staatsbegebenheiten*, 1782, 9; Schlözer, ed., *Stats-Anzeigen*, II, no. 5 (1782), 6; Riedesel to duke of Brunswick, Sept. 8, 1782 (237 N 49, fol. 136, StA, Wolfenbüttel); Sprengel to Heyne, c. end of 1782 (Scient. 47, 3, vol. II, 337, AAW, Göttingen); Ignaz Josef Doringer to Kaunitz, Dec. 10, 1782 (Staatskanzlei, Staatenabteilung: Holland, K. 72, fol. 163v, HHStA, Vienna); Brandes to Heyne, Dec. 20, 1782, Jan. 31, 1783 (Cod. MS Heyne CXXIX, fols. 105v, 118v, SuUB, Göttingen).

newspapers of Europe have acquainted everyone with the articles of peace, and all of Germany rejoices."[194]

The German Auxiliary Troops

The participation of German auxiliary troops in the American war significantly influenced the formation of opinion among a broad strata of German contemporaries. But before going into this, let us turn briefly to the participation of the troop units from Zweibrücken and Hanover, which were not part of the auxiliary forces. When France entered the conflict, it sent an army under comte de Rochambeau to North America. Almost one-third of that army was a 2,500-man unit from Zweibrücken, led by Wilhelm and Christian Grafen von Forbach. This was the Royal Deuxponts regiment that was in continuous service for France.[195] Despite the friendly relations between the Zweibrücken court and Benjamin Franklin,[196] this regiment was not sent as direct aid from the duchy to the Americans. The unit remained in French service, not American, even during engagements.[197]

A battalion from Trier, which also had formerly served in France, was a part of this or another regiment of Rochambeau's army.[198] The elector of Trier, who had not assembled the unit for the specific purpose of sending it to America, leaned heavily toward French policy and was not very friendly

194. "Denn die Friedensartikel sind durch alle Zeitungen von Europa bekannt gemacht worden, darüber ganz Deutschland sich erfreuet": an East-Frisian Mennonite to H. Dulheuer, Dec. 2, 1783 (Papers of the Continental Congress, 18, VIII, 80, NA, Washington, D.C.). I gratefully thank Dr. Gerhard Kollmann, Cologne, for bringing this quotation to my attention.

195. Cf. Ernst Drumm, *Das Regiment Royal Deuxponts. Deutsches Blut auf fürstlichen Befehl in fremden Dienst und Sold* (Zweibrücken, 1936).

196. Cf. Hays, ed., *Calendar of the Franklin Papers*, I–IV, *passim*.

197. Cf. Karl Theodor von Heigel, "Die Beteiligung des Hauses Zweibrücken am nordamerikanischen Befreiungskrieg," Bayerische Akademie der Wissenschaften, Philosophisch-philologische und historische Klasse, *Sitzungsberichte*, VI (Munich, 1912); also the diaries of Wilhelm Graf von Forbach, *My Campaigns in America: A Journal kept by Count William de Deux-Ponts, 1780–81*, trans. and ed. Samuel Abbott Green (Boston, 1868), and Ludwig Freiherr von Closen, *The Revolutionary Journal of Baron Ludwig von Closen*, trans. and ed. Evelyn M. Acomb (Chapel Hill, N.C., 1958).

198. Cf. Evelyn M. Acomb, "The Journal of Baron Von Closen," *WMQ*, 3d Ser., X (1953), 200. According to her estimate, the Germans and Swiss amounted to one-third of Rochambeau's army at Yorktown. See also the not always accurate investigation by Heinrich Neu, "Die rheinische Auswanderung nach Amerika bis zum Beginn des 19. Jahrhunderts," *Annalen des Historischen Vereins für den Niederrhein*, CXLIV/CXLV (1946–1947), 136.

toward Britain.[199] This was probably why he had allowed some of his subjects, such as Friedrich von Brahm of Koblenz, to join the Americans even before 1778.[200]

In the electorate of Hanover, which in personal union was ruled by King George III, the situation was different. There England could have had a reservoir of additional soldiers for the war in America. Yet, for military and political reasons, the British government did not draw any large body of troops from Hanover, in order not to weaken the country and so risk a renewed attack from France, as during the Seven Years' War. Thus, apart from a few individuals, only five battalions from Hanover took part in the war. These were sent not to America but to Gibraltar and Minorca.[201]

Of greater importance for our purposes were the subsidiary treaties concluded between Great Britain and six German principalities: Brunswick, Hesse-Kassel, Hesse-Hanau, Waldeck, Ansbach-Bayreuth, and Anhalt-Zerbst. As a result of these treaties, about thirty thousand Germans joined the English troops to suppress the rebels in North America. German reasons for concluding these treaties were neither directly political nor ideological, and the treaties themselves did not document open opposition to the American Revolution and its ideals. The arrangements were primarily economic and financial in nature. From the viewpoint of the rulers it was a means of conveniently adding to their virtually empty treasuries, thus glossing over their own financial mismanagement.[202] Hesse-Kassel and Ansbach especially,

199. Helmut Göring, *Die auswärtige Politik des Kurfürstentums Trier im 18. Jahrhundert* (Heidelberg, 1922), 61–70. On the elector's coldness toward England see George Cressener to Thomas Howard, earl of Suffolk, Apr. 14, 1777 (S.P. 81/155, PRO, London); cf. Albert Schulte, *Ein englischer Gesandter am Rhein: Georg Cressener als Bevollmächtiger Gesandter an den Höfen der geistlichen Kurfürsten und beim Niederrheinisch-Westfälischen Kreis 1763–1781* (Bonn, 1971), esp. 178–184.

200. Franz von Brahm to Franklin, Apr. 20, 1777 (Franklin Papers, V, 159, APSL, Philadelphia). Franz's son Friedrich later was a member of the American Philosophical Society; cf. Chinard, "American Philosophical Society," *APSP*, N.S., LXXXVII (1943–1944), 3.

201. Cf. Friedrich Kapp, *Der Soldatenhandel deutscher Fürsten nach Amerika. Ein Beitrag zur Kulturgeschichte des achtzehnten Jahrhunderts*, 2d ed. (Berlin, 1874), 29–31.

202. In addition to Kapp, studies on the German subsidy troops include: Philipp Losch, *Soldatenhandel. Mit einem Verzeichnis der Hessen-Kasselischen Subsidienverträge und einer Bibliographie* (Kassel, 1933); Karl Ehlers, "Der Soldatenhandel Karl Wilhelm Ferdinands von Braunschweig während des nordamerikanischen Freiheitskrieges," *Niedersachsen*, XXXI (1926), 601–604; Erhard Städtler, "Die Ansbach-Bayreuther Truppen im Amerikanischen Unabhängigkeitskrieg, 1777–1783" (publ. Ph.D. diss., University of Erlangen, 1955); Ernst Kipping, *Die Truppen von Hessen-Kassel im amerikanischen Unabhängigkeitskrieg 1776–1783* (Darmstadt, 1965). The treaties are printed in Frances Gardiner Davenport, ed., *European Treaties bearing on the History of the United States and its Dependencies*, Vol. IV, *1716–1815*, ed. Charles Oscar Paullin (Washington, D.C., 1937), 112–134, 142–144; see also the contemporary edition in English and German of the three treaties with Brunswick, Kassel, and Hanau, *Die drey vollständigen Subsidien-Tractaten . . .* (Frankfurt and Leipzig, 1776).

having a steady eye for such opportunities, had repeatedly offered troops to the English government.[203] Thus, George III was able to tell both houses of Parliament as early as October 26, 1775: "I have also the satisfaction to inform you that I have received the most friendly offers of foreign assistance."[204] Once the business of hiring German subjects was in full swing, other German rulers, like the prince of Saxe-Hildburghausen or the prince-bishop of Würzburg, tried to get their share of British gold.[205] It is a matter of debate whether the initiative toward the desired treaties always came from the German sovereigns concerned, but it is known that they were generally only too willing to sign them.

The recruiting of these thirty thousand men, of which Hesse-Kassel furnished more than half, was certainly not a local affair. Volunteers were called for by means of "posters hanging in all public houses and on town gates all over Hesse."[206] But that alone would not suffice to raise the contingent promised to England. Of necessity, this "Recruiting for England"—the title of a popular comedy[207]—had to go beyond the borders of the six states, undermining more or less the established principle of volunteer enlistments. Frensdorff, the minister of the small principality of Waldeck, announced that the usual practice had been followed of sending many officers and subalterns "into foreign countries to raise recruits with much money" and that doubtless "enough foreigners could be assembled." It was only as a safeguard

203. Cf. the dispatches of the minister of Hesse-Kassel at London, especially for the year 1775 (300 Philippsruhe E 11/6, vol. I, StA, Marburg); Karl Friedrich Reinhard Freiherr von Gemmingen to Karl Sigismund Freiherr von Seckendorff, Nov. 9, 1776 (Hessian MSS, no. 47, Anspach Papers, vol. I, pt. 1, MS 1a, NYPL, New York).

204. Jensen, ed., *American Colonial Documents*, 852. Kutzleben mailed a copy to Kassel (vol. I, fol. 84, StA, Marburg).

205. Robert Murray Keith to Suffolk, Apr. 9, 1777, Cressener to Suffolk, Apr. 14, 1777 (S.P. 80/219, 81/155, PRO, London). For some time the duke of Württemberg was also interested in a treaty; Thun reported to Stuttgart on alleged plans of the duke of Zweibrücken, Apr. 15, 1776 (A 74, Bü. 130, HptStA, Stuttgart); cf. also Donathien Le Ray de Chaumont to Franklin, Jan. 27, 1780 (Franklin Papers, IV, 12, University of Pennsylvania Library, Philadelphia).

206. "in allen Wirtshäusern und an die Stadttore im Hessenlande Plakate angeschlagen": Johann Ernst Grassmeder, "Chronik der Stadt Cassel, 1734–1779," 56 (MB, Kassel).

207. Johann Christoph Krauseneck, *Die Werbung für England. Ein ländliches Lustspiel in einem Aufzuge* (Bayreuth, 1776). After a performance at the Electoral Theater at Munich, a reprint of the play was published at Augsburg in 1777. For comments on the play see Philipp Franz Freiherr von Gudenus to Samuel Wilhelm Oetter, Feb. 20, July 3, 1777 (Nachlaß Oetter, K. 3, fols. 195r–v, 154v, Germanisches Nationalmuseum, Nuremberg); *Allgemeine deutsche Bibliothek*, XXXI (1777), 497. Wilhelm Georg Neukam, "Brandenburgisch-Ansbachisch-Bayreuthische Kriegsdichtung aus den Jahren 1776–1783. Zugleich ein Beitrag der Beziehungen Frankens zu Nordamerika im 18. Jahrhundert," *Fränkisches Land*, I (1953–1954), 70, is wrong when he contradicts Krauseneck's statement that the comedy did not play in his native Franconia. The margrave of Ansbach concluded his treaty with England on Feb. 1, 1777, about half a year after the first publication of the play.

Figure 8. Hessian Prisoners of War, December 26, 1776. "The Hessians, surprised by General Washington on December 25, 1776, at Trenton, are brought to Philadelphia as prisoners of war." (Chodowiecki, for Sprengel, *Allgemeines historisches Taschenbuch.*)

against mutiny and desertion that "a certain number of volunteers from Waldeck" would be necessary.[208]

Fundamentally similar practices were used in all other states with contractual agreements to furnish troops. In nearly all cases their territories were too small to raise contingents of the size pledged by their sovereigns. Erhard Städtler calculated that of the 420,000 inhabitants of Ansbach-Bayreuth, no more than 22,673 were to be called to the colors in 1792, and that of these men, only 1,872 were fit for service. After subtracting those exempt from military service, there remained only 1,228.[209] Assuming that figures were similar at the time of the American war, one gets an idea of how difficult it must have been, even with recruiting abroad, to raise two regiments totaling 2,500 men.

Legally or illegally, the recruiting was bound to spread to neighboring states. The records show that recruiting took place in almost all of the larger territories between the Rhine and Elbe rivers, often by the use of questionable methods, and that attempts at recruiting were made even in territories where permission had been refused.[210] Secret recruiting went on in Württemberg, Upper Swabia, and Switzerland.[211] The rosters of soldiers contain the names of men from Hesse and Ansbach as well as from Hamburg, Prussia, Austria, Bavaria, Tyrol, Switzerland, and the Rhineland.[212] All were put into military units, equipped by the contracting states, and handed over to English commanders, mostly at the Hanoverian ports on the North Sea.

With that, the respective German governments had fulfilled their treaty obligations. They were not the least interested in exceeding them by preparing and instructing the troops bound for America. Often they had recruited the men under false pretenses.[213] The troops generally had no idea about the

---

208. "um in fremden Ländern mit schwerem Geld Rekruten zu machen . . . daß man Ausländer genug zusammenbringen werde . . . eine gewisse Anzahl freiwilliger Waldecker": Frensdorff to Johann Hagenbusch, government official at Korbach, Mar. 9, 1776; cf. Frensdorff's letter of Apr. 14, 1776 (StadtA, Korbach).

209. Städtler, "Ansbach-Bayreuther Truppen," 27.

210. Voluminous files, so far only partially investigated, are scattered in many archives. For the recruiting of troops see the respective files in: the Staatsarchive, Coburg, Hamburg, Marburg, Wolfenbüttel, and Würzburg; the Hauptstaatsarchive, Hanover and Wiesbaden; the Stadtarchive, Ansbach and Korbach; the Geheimes Staatsarchiv, Munich; and the Kriegsarchiv, Vienna.

211. Cf. Generalrescripte (HptStA, Stuttgart); Acta den Revolutions-Handel zu Stein am Rhein betr. 1781–1784 (ZB, Zurich); Englische Werbungen (StA, Bern).

212. Cf. Georg Janssen-Sillenstede, "Eine Verlustliste verkaufter deutscher Soldaten während des nordamerikanischen Freiheitskrieges (1778–1783)," *Oldenburger Jahrbuch*, XLIV/XLV (1940–1941), 102–114.

213. Max Döllner, *Erlebnisse der ansbach-bayreuthischen Hilfstruppen im Kriege Großbritanniens gegen die Vereinigten Staaten von Nordamerika (1777–1783)* (Neustadt an der Aisch, 1933), 4. Cf. Kipping, *Truppen von Hessen-Kassel*, 43; Seume, "Mein Leben," in

aims and purposes of their expedition or about the country of their destination, except that it was called America. At best, the troops were told of the illegal actions of the rebellious colonists in terms smacking of the arguments of America's most determined adversaries.[214] England, on the other hand, was lauded to the skies, especially in states with leanings toward Prussia. The island kingdom was raised to the lofty status of a savior in the hour of need, one that had unselfishly come to the rescue of Germany, that is, Prussia and its allies, in an emergency, namely, the Seven Years' War. Now Germans had to seize the welcome opportunity to show their gratitude by unselfishly coming to the assistance of harassed Great Britain.[215]

Ansbach-Bayreuth furnishes a telling example of the massive effort to influence the judgment of soldiers and of the civilian population. Its treaty with England was not concluded until the beginning of 1777, when sympathy with the Americans was much more widespread than in the previous year. In order to stem this rising tide of enthusiasm for America, numerous publications, as well as sermons and prayers for various occasions, defended the policy of the local ruling family.[216]

---

his *Werke*, I, 59–62; Johann Carl Büttner, *Büttner, der Amerikaner: Selbstbiographie*, 2d ed. (Camenz, 1828), 40–41; Johann Ludwig Graf von Sayn und Wittgenstein to Franklin, Jan. 25, 1780 (Franklin Papers, XVII, 50, APSL, Philadelphia). See also Bertolt Brecht's socio-critical adaption of George Farquhar's *The Recruiting Officer, Pauken und Trompeten* (1954) in Brecht, *Gesammelte Werke in acht Bänden*, ed. Suhrkamp Verlag (Frankfurt, 1967), III, 2617–2710.

214. Barthold Koch, "Kurze Kriegsgeschichte," 39 (privately owned by Fritz Koch, Kassel); Heusser, "Journal," 1 (StA, Marburg); "Die Hessen nach Amerika, 1777," in Marion Dexter Learned, "Gesang nach Amerika Anno 1777," *AG*, I (1897), 86; *Sr. Excellenz dem Herrn Geheimen Rath von Keller . . . von der glorreichen Eroberung des Forts Klinton* (Heiligenstadt, 1778), 3; Johann August Weppen, *Gedichte* (Karlsruhe, 1783), 352–353.

215. Cf., e.g., *Gesang bey dem Abmarsch der hochfürstlich Brandenburg-Anspach-Baireuthischen Auxiliar-Truppen nach Amerika* (Ansbach, 1777). Slightly different is the manuscript in the Historischer Verein für Mittelfranken, Ansbach, and the text published by Learned, *Americana Germanica*, I (1897), 87–88. See also Krauseneck, "Abschied eines Teutschen von seiner Geliebten, beym Feldzug nach Amerika" (1777), in his *Gedichte*, II, 101.

216. Cf. *Vier neue Arien* (n.p., 1777), 1; Johann Ernst Heim, *Schreiben eines Geistlichen, an seinen gewesenes Beicht-Kind, einen in das Feld gehenden Soldaten* (n.p., 1777), 2; Johann Georg Maison, *Das den 24 Junii 1777 von neuem feyerlich zu begehende höchst erwünschte Geburts-Fest der Durchlauchtigsten Fürstin und Frauen Frauen* [sic] *Friderica Carolina Marggräfin zu Brandenb . . .* (Kulmbach, 1777), 4–5, 10; *Gebet für die in Königl. Groß-Britannische Kriegs-Dienste überlassene Hochfürstl. Brandenburgische Kriegs-Völcker . . .* (n.p., 1777), 2–3; [Johann Christoph Krauseneck], *Feldgesang eines teutschen Grenadiers in Nordamerika* (Bayreuth, 1778), 9, 11; Johann Philipp Erb, *Antrittspredigt . . . bey Windmill Hill auf Rhod-Island vor beyden Hochfürstlich Anspachischen Regimentern* (Bayreuth, 1779); *Gebetsformel um die glückliche Rückreise der nach erfolgten Frieden aus America zurückgehenden Hochfürstlich Brandenburgischen Truppen . . .* (n.p., 1783); *Dankgebet nach der im Monat November 1783 erfolgten Zurückkunft der ansbachischen Truppen* (Bayreuth, 1783); Friedrich Wilhelm Philipp Ernst Freiherr von Reitzenstein, *An die aus*

Given the composition of the troops, it is understandable that most of the soldiers were not eager to sail off to America. Too many had been pressed into service.[217] Discontent and resistance were widespread, depressing the mood of the soldiers even more, especially on the day of departure.[218] Their march through Germany to the ports of embarkation was by no means a happy event, since all along the way they were guarded to prevent desertion. In a letter to Johann Kaspar Hirzel, the Zurich canton medical officer, Johann Heinrich Merk described the scene from Göttingen: "The auxiliary troops from Hesse passed through here yesterday and the day before on their way to America to serve England. Poor devils! Most of them were very gloomy about it, others showed forced mirth. I think only a few of them will ever come home again."[219] The morale of these troops naturally was low. Small wonder: they of all people were to stick out their necks to keep the British empire from falling apart.[220]

General ill-humor could easily combine with discontent to produce violence. On March 10, 1777, open mutiny broke out among the Ansbach troops destined for America. The troops had marched to Ochsenfurt on the Main River the day before. They were to be transported from there in an insufficient number of river boats and under unbearable circumstances. After spending one night on board, they refused to stay aboard any longer and to follow their officers' commands. When the resistance grew more serious, and several shots had been fired and some soldiers had already deserted, news was sent to the margrave, who immediately hurried to Ochsenfurt. By the time he arrived

---

America zurückgekommenen Bayreuthischen Krieger (Kulmbach, 1783), 3–4; Georg Müller, *Der Englische Friedensplan wurde bey der höchsterfreulichen Zurückkunft der Hochfürstl. Brandenb. Onolz-Culmbachischen Kriegstruppen aus Amerika . . .* (Bayreuth, 1784).

217. Cf. Seume, *Werke*, I, 57; Johann Friedrich Normann to Johann Wilhelm Ludwig Gleim, Oct. 17, 1786 (MSS collection, XCII, 6, no. 1, GH, Halberstadt); Johann Heinrich Scherber, *Gemeinnütziges Lesebuch für die Bayreuthische Vaterlandsgeschichte*, 2 vols. (Hof, 1796–1797), II, 290–291.

218. Cf. *Lied eines deutschen Kriegers in Amerika* (Bayreuth, 1778), 2; "Auszüge aus dem Tagebuche eines vormaligen kurhessischen Offiziers über den Nordamerikanischen Freiheitskrieg 1776 und 1777. Mitgetheilt durch den Lieut. von Heister," *Zeitschrift für Kunst, Wissenschaft und Geschichte des Krieges*, XII, no. 3 (1828), 223–224; Wasmus, "Aufzeichnungen," I, 64 (StA, Wolfenbüttel); Valentin Asteroth, "Erinnerungen aus dem nordamerikanischen Krieg 1776–1784," 3 (MB, Kassel); Koch, "Kurze Kriegsgeschichte," 39 (privately owned by Fritz Koch, Kassel).

219. "Gestern und vorgestern sind hier die hessischen Hülfstruppen durchpassiert, die nach Amerika in englischen Diensten gehen. Die armen Teufel! Die meisten waren gar nicht wohl zumute dabei, andere zwangen sich, lustig zu sein. Es werden recht wenige davon wieder nach Hause kommen": Merk to Hirzel, Mar. 2, 1776 (Nachlaß Hirzel, CCCX, ZB, Zurich).

220. Cf. *Vier neue Arien*, 2–3; *Gesang bey dem Abmarsch*, 2; Johann August Weppen, "Klage einer Hessin bei dem Abschied ihres Geliebten," in his *Gedichte*, 352–353 (the poem was first published in Voss's *Musenalmanach* in 1778); Städtler, "Ansbach-Bayreuther Trup-

there on the following morning, the mutiny had already been crushed at the cost of several dead and wounded.[221] Döhla described the ensuing scene: "Our two regiments were marched up at once, and the margave went to each man and asked him what his complaint was, promising mercy and his lordship's favors to all those willing to go along to America in the service of England; those, however, who did not want to go were to step forward, but they would lose all they owned, their fatherland, and his favors."[222] Döhla does not mention the result of this questioning, but Friedrich von Schiller, in his play *Kabale und Liebe*, gave a brief version of the Ochsenfurt mutiny and the way it might have ended: "Our most merciful sovereign ordered all regiments to stand in line on the parade ground and the braggarts to be shot. We heard the cracks of their rifles and saw their brains spatter on the pavement, and the whole army cried, 'Hooray, to America!' "[223]

Discontent among the soldiers did not abate in America. Often there were disputes with British soldiers that sometimes turned into wild brawls.[224]

---

pen," 53. See, however, the uncritical defense by Joseph G. Rosengarten, "A Defense of the Hessians," *PMHB*, XXIII (1899), 161.

221. Cf. the diaries in the Historischer Verein für Mittelfranken, Ansbach; "Popp's Journal, 1777–1783," *PMHB*, XXVI (1902), 27; also the file "Betr. den Marsch der Ansbachischen Truppen nach Amerika 1777–1782" (StA, Würzburg; copy in LC, Washington, D.C.); Oskar Bezzel, "Ansbach-Bayreuther Miettruppen im Nordamerikanischen Freiheitskrieg, 1777–1783," *Zeitschrift für bayerische Landesgeschichte*, VIII (1935), 196–197. See also the novel by Johannes Berbig, *Revolte in Ochsenfurt. Deutsches Blut für englische Pfunde* (Leipzig, 1944), though it is of little literary value and heavily stamped by the opinions of its time.

222. "Unsere 2 Regimenter wurden sogleich aufgestellt und der Markgraf ging Mann für Mann durch und fragte einen jeden, was seine Einwendungen wären und versprach dabei alle Gnade und Fürstengunst allen denen, die mit nach Amerika in engl. Solde gehen würden; die aber so nicht wollten, sollten heraustreten und dagegen aber ihres Vermögens samt ihren Vaterlande und aller fürstl. Gnade verlustig sein": Döhla, "Tagebuch," AGAO, XXV, no. 1 (1912), p. 90. See also the narratives of the mutiny, based on Döhla, by Max von Eelking, *Die deutschen Hülfstruppen im nordamerikanischen Befreiungskriege, 1776 bis 1783*, I (Hanover, 1863), 173–175, and Kapp, *Soldatenhandel deutscher Fürsten*, 126–129.

223. "Aber unser gnädigster Landesherr ließ alle Regimenter auf dem Paradeplatz aufmarschieren und die Maulaffen niederschießen. Wir hörten die Büchsen knallen, sahen ihr Gehirn auf das Pflaster sprützen, und die ganze Armee schrie: 'Juchhe, nach Amerika!' ": Schiller, *Werke*, National ed., V, 28–29. Scholars so far have failed to recognize the probability that Schiller's play *Kabale und Liebe* alludes to Ansbach-Bayreuth. Not only the obvious parallels in this singular event, but also the persona of Lady Milford (actually Lady Craven) as the English mistress of the margrave of Ansbach strongly suggest that Schiller was thinking of this margravate while he wrote the play. Instead, scholars have looked almost exclusively at Württemberg when explaining the background of Schiller's early plays. E.g., Buchwald, *Schiller*, I, 401, writes of this very episode: "If any scene in *Kabale und Liebe* is situated in Württemberg, it is this one." Benno von Wiese gives a similar opinion in his standard biography, *Friedrich Schiller*, 3d ed. (Stuttgart, 1963), esp. 192, 202.

224. Cf. the entry for June 10, 1777, in Friedrich Julius von Papet, "Journal," I, 103–104 (StadtA, Brunswick); also Kipping, *Truppen von Hessen-Kassel*, 22–23.

Never really convinced of the sense of the entire venture while still in Germany, many of the soldiers found it even more difficult to understand once they reached America. Many members of the auxiliary forces suffered from being separated from their families and wanted nothing more than to go home as soon as possible. Desertion, a common occurrence at the time, could easily reach a new height under these circumstances,[225] all the more since it was consciously—and in part successfully—encouraged by the Americans.[226] The rich, fertile, and wonderful country, with its freedom and its economic possibilities, furnished additional incentives for desertion. Thousands seized the opportunity to start a new and better life, free of the fetters imposed on them in Europe. Although exact data are lacking, it can safely be said that hardly more than half of the approximately thirty thousand German soldiers returned home from America, while no more than a third of the remaining twelve to fourteen thousand had fallen victim to the war.[227]

If the treaties had produced discontent among those recruited for service, they also brought acute suffering for relatives at home, who lost the working power and income of husbands, fathers, and sons without equivalent replacement.[228] In Hesse-Kassel, which had only three hundred thousand inhabitants yet furnished more than half of the auxiliary troops, destitution was beyond conception. Large areas suffered so unmercifully that even the government could not help but notice. In a declaration addressed to the landgrave, a local official from Schweinsberg, near Marburg, described the alarming consequences of the treaties so impressively that he will be quoted here in full:

225. Information on desertion is in most of the war diaries. See also Mr. S. to Haenichen, Jan. 29, 1776 (1 Alt 22, no. 1505, StA, Wolfenbüttel); Gottfried C. Querner, "Aufsätze" (c. 1840), 62 (StA, Wolfenbüttel); Eelking, *Leben und Wirken Riedesels*, II, 343, III, 226; Bezzel, "Ansbach-Bayreuther Miettruppen," *Zeitshcrift für bayerische Landesgeschichte*, VIII (1935), 413. Losch, *Soldatenhandel*, 35–36, however, denies extensive Hessian desertions; cf. Simon Louis du Ry to Erasmus Ritter, Nov. 4, 1783 (Nachlaßpapiere E. Ritter, Burgerbibliothek, Bern), which is certainly more accurate.

226. Cf. Philip Davidson, *Propaganda and the American Revolution, 1763–1783* (Chapel Hill, N.C., 1941), 410; Lyman H. Butterfield, "Psychological Warfare in 1776: The Jefferson-Franklin Plan to Cause Hessian Desertion," *APSP*, XCIV (1950), 233–241; see also the booklet *Wahrheit und Guter Rath, an die Einwohner Deutschlands, besonders in Hessen* (Philadelphia, 1783).

227. Marcus Lee Hansen, *The Atlantic Migration 1607–1860: A History of the Continuing Settlement of the United States*, ed. Arthur M. Schlesinger (Cambridge, Mass., 1940), 54, believes that 12,500 soldiers did not return to Germany.

228. Cf., e.g., the file "Acta die verschiedene Gnaden Ertheilungen . . . betr. 1779–1784" (HVMF, Ansbach), and the printed edict of Feb. 20, 1783 (AM 997, StadtA, Ansbach); also the so-called Erlaß-Verordnung of Hesse-Hanau, Sept. 23, 1776 (copies in StA, Marburg, Boston Atheneum, and LC, Washington, D.C.; printed in Kapp, *Soldatenhandel deutscher Fürsten*, 80–81).

The departure of the troops has thrown some families into such depths of destitution that they can be rescued only by Your Serene Highness's mercy. Thus, in Niederwald, Fronhausen, Niederwalgern, Lohr, Langenstein, and in several other villages soldiers' wives have been left behind, some of whom, to be sure, own land and houses, but also the debts with which they are encumbered. Besides, they have many children, which they bring to me, the oldest being no more than eight or nine years, the youngest only a few months old. Some are so frail that they cannot do without the care and attention of their mothers, several of whom are pregnant. Your Serene Highness will surely be able to judge from this how little these poor women can afford to pay for their daily bread and the schooling of their children, the unbelievably many seignorial duties and services, their tributes, and all the other levies without the slightest assistance from relatives who could help them. And although your Grace decreed that these men could not be exempted because some of them do not own enough land to engage in farming, it is nevertheless certain that, as long as they were in the country and were on leave, they could pay for the family's food, take care of most of the daily chores, and tend their few plots of land. Now all this is gone; need and want are very great among these people, and the great shortage of money, resulting in reduced consumption, prevents even those who, according to the size of their estates, could be called well-to-do from helping the poor, especially since each father gave every bit of money he could get hold of to his departing son, thus sending thousands of thalers out of the country.[229]

229. "Durch den Abmarsch derer Truppen sind einige Familien in die allergrößte Bedürftigkeit versetzt worden, die nicht anders als durch Euer Hochfürstl. Durchl. Huld und Gnade gerettet werden können: So sind zum Exempel in Niederwald, in Fronhausen, in Niederwalgern, in Lohr, in Langenstein und mehreren Ortschaften von marschierten Soldaten Weiber zurückgeblieben, welche zum Teil zwar eigene Güter und Häuser, jedoch mit darauf haftenden Schulden, allein auch zugleich viele Kinder haben, die sie mir zutragen, von denen die ältesten nicht über 8 bis 9 Jahre, die jüngsten nur wenige Monate alt und einige auch so gebrechlich sind, daß sie nicht einen Augenblick des Beistandes und der Pflege ihrer teils schwangeren Mütter entbehren können. Wie wenig nun solche ohne alle Beihülfe von Anverwandten, und zwar von Anverwandten, die ihnen assistieren könnten, zurückgeliebene arme Frauens sich das Brot zum Lebensunterhalt verschaffen, vor ihre heranwachsende Kinder das Schulgeld bezahlen, dabei die unglaublich häufige Dienste leisten, die Kontribution und übrige fast nicht alle zu benennende Abgaben entrichten können, das wird gar leichtlich von Euer Hochfürstl. Durch. höchst und huldreichst ermessen werden. Und wie auf die Erlassung solcher Soldaten nach gnädigst ergangener Verordnung nicht angetragen werden können, da sie zum Teil keine anlängliche Länderei zu Betreibung des Ackerbaues besitzen, so bleibt es doch gewiß, daß, solange der Mann im Land war und Urlaub erhiele, durch seine Profession und durch seinen Verdienst Rat und notdürftiges Brot verschaffen, vor die Dienstleistung sorgen und zur Ausstellung der wenigen Äcker Anstalt machen konnte. Jetzt fällt alles dieses weg; die Not ist bei dieser Klasse von Menschen auf das höchste gestiegen und der große Geldmangel, der durch die verringerte Konsumtion sich noch mehr äußert, und da ein jeder Hausvater alles, was er noch zusammenbringen können, seinem marschierten Sohn mitgegeben hat, mithin auf eine solche Art viele Tausend Taler außer Land gebracht worden sind, verhindert auch sogar diejenige, welche nach der Größe ihre Güter unter die Wohlhabende zu rechnen wären, denen Armen und der geringern Klasse beizustehen": Moritz Schenk von Schweinsberg to landgrave, Mar. 23, 1776; cf. his report of Apr. 5, 1776 (both 11

Those responsible found it not too difficult to overlook such conditions, for subsidy funds were coming in plentifully, as is shown in the case of Ansbach, which was paid 270,000 pounds sterling for twenty-five hundred soldiers serving in America for six years.[230] Expressed in German currency, England paid 40 million thalers to its six partners between 1775 and 1785.[231] This was not all profit, however, because it had to cover such expenditures as recruiting, equipment, soldiers' pay, and transport to the coast. The amount of actual, usable revenue is not known. Nor is it known how much private profit was brought back by the soldiers by way of booty and savings. Contemporaries have calculated that in this way alone a million thalers flowed into Hesse-Kassel.[232] But if we subtract the economic loss suffered by the country as a result of the eight years' absence of the soldiers, the net sum is decidedly smaller. For the sovereigns, in any case, the treaties were a profitable business, and the advantages arising from them were mostly theirs. Given these circumstances, which of the sovereigns concerned would have been ready to balance the poorer classes' loss against his own gain?

Despite their disastrous effects, subsidiary treaties of this kind had been part of the imperial tradition in Germany for more than a hundred years, a fact often referred to by their apologists.[233] Nevertheless, these treaties were

---

F 1 d, StA, Marburg). See also [Friedrich Justinian Freiherr von Günderode], *Briefe eine Reisenden über den gegenwärtigen Zustand von Cassel mit aller Freiheit geschildert* (Frankfurt and Leipzig, 1781), 172–173; Bopp, "1. Fehler, 2. Mißbräuche, und 3. Verbesserungen in Heßen!" (c. 1778), 87 (classified as misuse) (MB, Kassel); Kipping, *Truppen von Hessen-Kassel*, 40.

230. J. A. Brand, "Geld-Empfang von England. In der Subsidien Zeit, vom Jahr 1777. biß Ende Des Jahrs 1783" (Hessian MSS, no. 47, Anspach Papers, vol. IV, pt. 2, NYPL, New York; cf. the letter of vindication of the former president of the Justiz-Collegium, June 29, 1790 (Rep. 314, no. 29, StA, Nuremberg). See also the differing statements of Eelking, *Deutschen Hülfstruppen*, I, 15, and by Kapp, *Soldatenhandel deutscher Fürsten*, 212.

231. Eelking, *Deutschen Hülfstruppen*, I, 15; Kapp, *Soldatenhandel deutscher Fürsten*, 212.

232. Simon Louis du Ry to Erasmus Ritter, Nov. 4, 1783 (Nachlaßpapiere E. Ritter, Burgerbibliothek, Bern).

233. One-sided praise of the treaties for their financial benefits is found especially in [Martin Ernst von Schlieffen], *Des Hessois en Amérique* (n.p., 1782); "Auszüge aus dem Tagebuche des Lieut. von Heister," *Zeitschrift für Kunst, Wissenschaft und Geschichte des Krieges*, XII, no. 3 (1828), 224; Wekhrlin, ed., *Chronologen*, XII (1781), 50. For further, mostly controversial, opinions see Paul Zimmermann, "Beiträge zum Verständnis des zwischen Braunschweig und England am 9. Januar 1776 geschlossenen Subsidienvertrages," *Jahrbuch des Geschichtsvereins für das Herzogtum Braunschweig*, XIII (1914), 160–176; Selma Stern, *Karl Wilhelm Ferdinand* (Hildesheim and Leipzig, 1921), 72–79; Kurt von Düring, "Der angebliche Verkauf von Landeskindern durch Reichsfürsten im 17. und 18. Jahrhundert," *Hanauisches Magazin*, XII (1933), 87–93; Losch, *Soldatenhandel*, 7–14, 24–25, 30; Ernst Singer, "Der Soldatenhandel deutscher Fürsten im 18. Jahrhundert in der schönen Literatur" (unpubl. Ph.D. diss., University of Vienna, 1935), 32 (Singer relies heavily on Kapp, *Soldatenhandel deutscher Fürsten*; his knowledge of contemporary literature is, however,

widely condemned; Mirabeau's appeal is the best-known example.[234] But only in later years, and rarely even then, were they condemned on principle, with arguments that threatened the very essence of hierarchy and government in these times of princely absolutism. In 1793–1794 the famous Swiss pedagogue Johann Heinrich Pestalozzi wrote: "Friends of mankind will condone a sovereign's selling his subjects piecemeal to let them get shot somewhere if he can make money that supports courtesans and idlers; but they will not condone a single murder committed by the people in search of liberty."[235] Opposition on military, political, and economic grounds was also rare, one of the few exceptions being the Saxon diplomat in the Netherlands, Johann Peter Isaak Dubois, who stated that the subsidiary treaties should be looked upon "as a new emigration favoring the colonies, since one can take it for granted that all the troops will be lost."[236]

It is characteristic of the mental state and the political self-understanding of the German bourgeoisie that in condemning the treaties they hardly ever used arguments like the above. They usually spoke in general terms and on less clearly defined grounds, basing their objections to the treaties on their conviction that the Americans were fighting for liberty. They approved of the American cause, just as they disapproved of everything opposed to it. To suppress by brutal force a struggle for liberty seemed to the contemporaries of the late Enlightenment an extremely contemptible thing on moral grounds.

---

much too limited); H. D. Schmidt, "The Hessian Mercenaries: The Career of a Political Cliché," *History*, LVIII (1958), 209–210.

234. [Honoré Gabriel Riquetti, comte de Mirabeau], *Avis aux Hessois et autres peuples de l'Allemagne Vendus par leurs Princes à l'Angleterre* (Cleves, 1777), and its German translation, *Nachrichten und Erinnerungen an verschiedene teutsche Völker, die von ihren Fürsten nach America geschickt worden sind* (n.p., 1778). See also [Charles John Ann Hereford], *Frankreichs Geschichte von der ersten Gründung der Monarchie, bis zu der gegenwärtigen Umänderung*, trans. from the English, 3 vols. (Frankfurt and Leipzig, 1792), III, 120; Kapp, *Soldatenhandel deutscher Fürsten*, 189.

235. "Daß ein Fürst Tausende seiner Untertanen stückweise verhandle, um sie irgendwo totschießen zu lassen, wenn damit Geld zu verdienen ist, wovon nachmahl Buhlerinnen und Müßiggänger unterhalten werden, das erlauben ihm die Menschenfreunde, aber dem Freiheit suchenden Pöbel verzeihen diese Menschenfreunde keinen Mord": Pestalozzi, note on Adolf Freiherr von Knigge's *Joseph von Wurmbrand* in Pestalozzi's *Sämtliche Werke*, ed. Arthur Buchenau *et al.* (Berlin, 1927–), X, 235. See also [August Wilhelm Leopold von Rahmel], *Ueber den Dienst, von einem, ehemals unter der preußischen Armee gestandenen . . .* (Boston [i.e., Breslau], 1783), 14–15, and [Andreas Georg Friedrich von Rebmann], *Der politische Thierkreis, oder die Zeichen unserer Zeit*, 2d ed., 2 vols. (Strasbourg, 1800), I, 176.

236. "comme une nouvelle émigration en faveur des colonies, puis que l'on peut compter d'avance toutes ces troupes pour perdues": to Sacken, Jan. 26, 1776 (Locat 2862, vol. XXXIII, StA, Dresden). See also Frederick II, "Histoire de mon temps," in Johann David Erdmann Preuß, ed., *Oeuvres de Frédéric le Grand*, 30 vols. (Berlin, 1846–1856), VI, 117–118, and [Friedrich Karl Freiherr von Moser], *Ueber Regenten, Regierung und Ministers* (Frankfurt, 1784), 365–366.

The best-known castigation of the treaties was that of Johann Gottfried Seume, himself one of their victims.[237] Johann Christoph Krauseneck used it as material for a comedy (not without critical undertones) that quickly became very popular.[238] In later days, those taking a stand against the treaties were preeminently poets and writers. August Hermann Niemeyer wrote in his ode "To Germany, March 1778":

> And is, then, Albion still not yet replete
> With blood of Germans brave and bold
> Who fought in others' fights for freedom doomed to meet
> Their deaths, paid for by gold?[239]

Leopold Friedrich Günter von Goeckingk, Gottlieb Konrad Pfeffel, Friedrich Leopold Graf zu Stolberg, and numerous others expressed similar sentiments in those years.[240] Only a few were as direct as Christoph Friedrich Bretzner: "By rights no honest man should raise his hand against a people fighting for the rights of mankind, for liberty, and for their country."[241]

Most Germans, even those who apparently disapproved of the treaties, confined themselves to essentially noncommital remarks; yet it would seem that there were numerous reasons to speak out against the treaties in no uncertain terms. Some authors no doubt intended to express criticism by using such terms as *sale* to describe the hiring of soldiers, but the objectionable nature of the practice surely merited a sharper attack. It is also remarkable that condemnation came mostly from one group, namely poets and writers. Of course, other members of the bourgeoisie, in particular those with pro-American sentiments, could not deny the connection between one's attitude

237. Seume, *Werke*, I, 59, 97.
238. Krauseneck, *Werbung für England*.
239. "Hat Albion nicht satt das Schwert geschwungen,/Genug der Edlen hingewürgt,/ Eur deutsches Blut, zu fremder Freiheitsschlacht gedungen,/Mit Golde sich verbürgt?": Niemeyer, *Gedichte* (Leipzig, 1778), 236.
240. Goeckingk, *Gedichte*, 3 vols. (Leipzig, 1780–1782), III, 75–80; Pfeffel, *Poetische Versuche*, 4th ed., 10 vols. (Tübingen, 1802–1820), II, 70–72; Friedrich Leopold zu Stolberg, "Die Zukunft," ed. Otto Hartwig, *Archiv für Literaturgeschichte* (hereafter cited as *ALG*), XIII (1885), 269; Goethe, "Das Neueste aus Plundersweilen," in his *Werke*, Weimar ed., 1/XVI, 45 (on this see Richard Friedenthal, *Goethe. Sein Leben und seine Zeit* [Munich, 1963], 365–366); Weppen, *Gedichte*, 353; [Johann Pezzl], *Faustin, oder das philosophische Jahrhundert*, 3d ed. ([Zurich], 1785), 222–223; Thomas Paine, *Untersuchungen über wahre und fabelhafte Theologie*, trans. from the English, 2 vols. ([Lübeck], 1794–1797), I, 8–9, 12 (preface of the German translator). See also W. A. Fritsch, "Stimmen deutscher Zeitgenossen über den Soldatenhandel deutscher Fürsten nach Amerika," *Deutsch-Amerikanisches Magazin*, I (1887), 589–593.
241. "Wider eine Nation, die für die Rechte der Menschheit, für ihre Freiheit, für ihr Vaterland ficht, sollte von Rechts wegen kein rechtschaffener Mann den Arm aufheben": Bretzner, *Das Räuschgen* (Leipzig, 1786), 150.

toward the subsidiary treaties and toward the American Revolution. But during the war, public statements from them were few; they were more inclined simply to accept the situation.[242] Their attitude was also proof that they hardly knew how to express themselves politically.[243]

242. Cf. Kapp, *Soldatenhandel deutscher Fürsten*, 206; Heinrich Schneider, "Lessing und Amerika," *Monatshefte für Deutschen Unterricht*, XXX (1938), 424, 430–432. See also the more general comments of Rudolf Vierhaus, "Deutschland vor der Französischen Revolution" (unpubl. Habilitationsschrift, University of Münster, 1961), 253–254.

243. Cf. Valjavec, *Politische Strömungen*, 108–109, who has a more positive opinion of these critical comments.

5. *The Principles of the American Revolution*

The American Revolution as an Outstanding Event

Interest in what was happening in faraway America increased only slowly among the German bourgeoisie during the first half of the 1770s. Such bits of information as were carried in the newspapers remained mostly unheeded. The same people who in later years evinced profuse interest in America were not occupied with the colonies in the early days of the Revolution, or even aware of the importance of events there. Around 1770 Swiss poet Johann Jakob Bodmer showed little interest in the American colonies, but in 1778 he claimed that his recent political plays were "so very American and wholly in line with Samuel Adams's thought."[1]

Not until the middle of the decade did attitudes begin to change. As events became more spectacular and were more widely reported in the press, the German contemporaries became convinced that they were witnessing historic developments. In the late 1760s large sections of the American population had thought of the crisis as a family quarrel with Great Britain, to be settled within the framework of the British constitution.[2] Around 1775, many people in Germany adopted this view and looked upon the conflict between Britain and its colonies mostly from the standpoint of commercial or foreign politics. They were interested to see what repercussions the conflict would have on the island kingdom, the Bourbon courts, the overall European constellation of powers, and world trade.[3] These were crucial topics, and

1. "so amerikanisch, so ganz in der Denkart Samuel Adams' sind": Bodmer to Johann Heinrich Meister, July 15, 1778 (MS Bodmer XIX, 338, ZB, Zurich). For Bodmer's earlier attitude see his incidental remark on America in his letter to Johann Heinrich Schinz, Mar. 22, 1772 (*ibid.*, XIV, 215).

2. Cf. James Otis to the earl of Buchan, July 18, 1768: "The cause of America is, in my humble opinion, the cause of the whole British Empire" (James Otis Papers, Massachusetts Historical Society [hereafter cited as MHi], Boston).

3. See, generally, the diplomatic correspondence during these years. Also, Korn, *Geschichte der Kriege*, I, [3–4]; *Chronologen*, IV (1779), 308; Remer, *Geschichte des Krieges*,

they remained dominant during the entire war, especially in government circles.

But another aspect of the struggle far transcended the borders of America and became of epoch-making importance for the majority of the bourgeoisie. Early in 1777 Helferich Peter Sturz had reduced the dispute about the American Revolution to the following polarity: "What is at stake in America? Eternal or temporal happiness, life, and honor? Or is it a dispute merely over the question of whether the colonies should supply, without their consent, part of their income for the needs of the state?"[4] Sturz, whom Stolberg thought to be "basically . . . a good man, but misled by wrong ideas,"[5] emphatically denied the presence of any higher principles. This was the way English opponents of the war usually dealt with questions of higher principle. "Some howl about rebellion and robbery and get terribly excited about the godlessness of the Americans who do not dread to revolt against their rightful government. Others howl just as loud about tyranny and violence and lament the injustice of a court that wants to enslave free people."[6] But in the second half of the 1770s and in the 1780s only a few Germans belonged to Sturz's faction. The majority believed that the Americans were fighting for principles and ideals. "Their motto is death or slavery."[7] Thus, in the eyes of an increasing number of Germans the conflict had gained so much in significance that it concerned much more than the British empire; the developments "ranked with the most memorable events . . . of the eighteenth century."[8]

3–4; more limited, *Frankfurter gelehrte Anzeigen*, 1776, 698; Christian Wilhelm von Dohm in *Teutscher Merkur*, Jan. 1777, 77–78; Russell, *Geschichte von Amerika*, I, ix–x.

4. "Ist in Amerika ewiges, ist auch nur zeitliches Glück, ist Leben und Ehre auf dem Spiel? Oder dreht sich nicht der Streit einzig um die Frage, ob Kolonien einen Teil ihrer Einkünfte zur Notdurft des Staats ungefragt liefern sollen?": article first appearing anonymously in the *Deutsches Museum*, Feb. 1777, 188. It was anonymously reprinted in the Schaffhausen, Switzerland, *Hurtersche Zeitung*, Mar. 26, 1777, and again in Sturz's *Schriften*, II, 355, which was edited by the editor of the *Deutsches Museum*, Heinrich Christian Boie.

5. "im Grunde . . . ein guter Mann, aber falsche Ideen haben ihn mißleitet": Stolberg to Luise von Gramm, Oct. 22, 1776, in Stolberg, *Briefe*, ed. Behrens, 86. On Sturz see also J.F.L. Theodor Merzdorf, "Helferich Peter Sturz," *Archiv für Litteraturgeschichte*, VII (1878), 33–92, and Adalbert Schmidt, *Helferich Peter Sturz. Ein Kapitel aus der Schrifttumsgeschichte zwischen Aufklärung und Sturm und Drang* (Reichenberg, 1939), esp. 41–42.

6. "Der eine schreit über Rebellion und Räubereien und ereifert sich entsetzlich über die Gottlosigkeit der Amerikaner, die sich nicht scheuen, sich gegen ihre rechtmäßige Obrigkeit zu empören. Der andre schreit ebenso sehr über Tyrannei und Gewalttätigkeit und ärgert sich über die Ungerechtigkeit des Hofes, welcher freie Leute zu Sklaven machen will": Loewe, *Beschreibung der zwölf Vereinigten Kolonien*, 133–134.

7. "Sterben oder Sklaverei ist ihr Motto": *Freytags-Zeitung*, Jan. 12, 1776.

8. "au rang des événements les plus mémorables . . . du XVIIIeme siècle": "Discours sur la grandeur et importance de la dernière révolution de l'Amérique septentrionale" (Milan, 1783), fol. 29v (Codex 12613, NB, Vienna).

Figure 9. Surrender at Saratoga, October 17, 1777. "The Americans take the corps of General Bourgoyne prisoners, at Saratoga, October 16, 1777." (Chodowiecki, for Sprengel, *Allgemeines historisches Taschenbuch.*)

Courtesy John Carter Brown Library, Brown University, Providence, R.I.

How did it happen that Germans thought the developments in faraway America deserving of such a conspicuous place in the annals of mankind? After all, the century had already witnessed many memorable events: the struggle over the Spanish monarchy's continued existence; the contest between Sweden and Russia and its consequences; the British-French dispute and its European and global significance; the struggle between Prussia and Habsburg, which developed into a life-and-death struggle for the state of Frederick II; and the Corsicans' fight for freedom. Yet an ever-increasing number of people came to believe that, however momentus these events may have been, the American conflict was not a conventional war but an event of much greater significance, namely, a revolution that concerned all mankind.[9]

The term *revolution* still bore the stamp of the Glorious Revolution of 1688, a total turnover of the political scene, combined with ideas of liberation and freedom.[10] In the German-language area the term was at this time in common use in the political as well as in the nonpolitical domain.[11] But a change was taking place under the influence of the American Revolution. Up to then the word *revolution* had meant an impersonal event in the past, when certain happenings had made or caused a great political change, and men had to tolerate it.[12] Revolutionaries were as yet unknown—and so they had to be, in view of traditional attitudes.[13] Inevitably, however, the immediacy of the events in America had some effect on the meaning of the word *revolution*.

As early as the mid-1770s the intellectual leaders of the American Revolution had started to interpret the developments in the colonies as a revolution.[14] This became possible because the term *revolution* developed together

9. E.g., *Frankfurter gelehrte Anzeigen*, 1776, 698; *Teutscher Merkur*, Jan. 1777, 77–78; Russell, *Geschichte von Amerika*, I, ix–x; Soulès, *Revolution in Nord-Amerika*, I, iii–iv (preface by Hammerdörfer); Thomas Paine [pseud.], *Kurze Darstellung der Begebenheiten aller bisherigen Staaten in der Welt* (Leipzig, 1797), II, 479.

10. Rosenstock, "Revolution als politischer Begriff," in *Festgabe für Paul Heilborn*, 97–98; Hannah Arendt, *On Revolution* (New York, 1963), 36. See also Richard Watson, *Les Principes de la Révolution* (London, 1777), bearing on the Glorious Revolution of 1688. For greater detail with regard to the Revolutionary period see Dippel, "Concept of 'Revolution,'" in Angermann *et al.*, eds., *New Wine in Old Skins*, 115–134.

11. E.g., Isaak Iselin, *Geschichte der Menschheit*, 3d ed., 2 vols. (Zurich, 1770), II, 366; dispatch by Freiherr von Thun, Oct. 12, 1772 (A 74, Bü. 126, HptStA, Stuttgart); Seinsheim to Haslang, Feb. 27, 1777 (Bayer. Gesandtschaft, London, no. 255, GStA, Munich); Dominik Graf von Kaunitz to Prince Wenzel Anton von Kaunitz, June 28, 1779 (Staatskanzlei, Staatenabteilung: Spanien, K. 139, fol. 93, HHStA, Vienna); *Historisches Portefeuille*, 1782, I, 2.

12. On the traditional use of the term *revolution* see Karl Griewank, *Der neuzeitliche Revolutionsbegriff, Entstehung und Entwicklung*, ed. Ingeborg Horn (Weimar, 1955), 5–6, 181, 216.

13. Rosenstock, "Revolution als politischer Begriff," in *Festgabe für Paul Heilborn*, 98.

14. E.g., Richard Henry Lee to Francis L. Lee, May 21, to Gouverneur Morris, May 28, 1775, in Ballagh, ed., *Letters of Richard Henry Lee*, I, 137, 140; also the remarks by John

with the events; a revolution had ceased to be something suffered in the past. In 1779 Richard Henry Lee, in the midst of military activities, could speak of "the progress of our glorious revolution," and in 1780 Benjamin Rush referred to "the present stage of the American Revolution."[15] It is clear that revolution had ceased to be a merely historical reference and had become a living experience, just as it had ceased to be a cause of merely passive human suffering and had become an instrument of initiative and activity, although the term *revolutionary* had not yet come into use. In view of the traditional interpretation of the events of 1688 the idea of revolution as a process with social and intellectual dimensions was altogether new. In America the term had grown beyond its traditional connotations of singularity and suddenness and away from the exclusive notion of a dramatic change in government.

Because of the interest aroused by American developments, this change of terminology easily spread beyond America. James Adair had already warned London against taking the dispute too lightly, since the Americans were "full of principles of Revolution."[16] In Germany the word *revolution* was used in connection with the events in the New World for the first time in 1775. Three days after the first shots were fired at Lexington—though of course still ignorant of this fact—the *Wienerische Diarium* reported: "The outbreak of a revolution in the American colonies was probably never nearer than it is now."[17] However, the importance of these early and somewhat vague statements must not be overrated.

The incidence of the term *revolution* increased during the years immediately following 1775, although its definition by means of historical examples remained unsatisfactory. It was often used to describe the colonists' fight against suppression and tyranny.[18] Later, Pierre Ulric Du Buisson's *Abrégé*

Adams during July 1776 in Lyman H. Butterfield *et al.*, eds., *Adams Family Correspondence* (Cambridge, Mass., 1963–), II, 28, 34, 43, 289.

15. R. H. Lee to Jefferson, May 3, 1779, in Boyd *et al.*, eds., *Jefferson Papers*, II, 262. Rush to William Shippen, Nov. 18, 1780, in Lyman H. Butterfield, ed., *Letters of Benjamin Rush*, 2 vols. (Princeton, N.J., 1951), I, 260.

16. "voller Revolutionsgrundsätze": Adair, *Amerikanische Indianer*, trans. Schatz, 418. The original English text appeared in 1775.

17. "Es dürfte wohl nie in den amerikanischen Kolonien eine Revolution ihrem Ausbruche näher gewesen sein als dermal": *Wienerisches Diarium*, Apr. 22, 1775. See also Hans Moritz Graf von Brühl to Sacken, Aug. 18, 1775 (Locat 2685, conv. XI, fol. 329v, StA, Dresden); Raynal, *Europäer in beiden Indien*, II (1775), 26–27 (note by Mauvillon).

18. E.g., *Gedanken über den Aufstand der englischen Colonien*, 5–6; Johannes von Müller, *Sämtliche Werke*, ed. Johann Georg Müller, 40 vols. (Stuttgart and Tübingen, 1831–1835), XXXVII, 102–106; Lidner, *De Iure revolutionis Americanorum*, 7, 13, 15; Buchenröder, *Nord-Amerika*, II, 130–131; Korn, *Geschichte der Kriege*, III, 39, IX, 70; Edmund Burke, *Jahrbücher der neuern Geschichte der Englischen Pflanzungen in Nord-Amerika seit dem Jahr 1755. bis auf itzige Zeiten*, trans. from the English by Samuel Wilhelm Turner, 4 vols. (Danzig, 1777–1781), II, pt. 2, 85.

de la révolution de l'Amérique Angloise influenced the development of the term *revolution* by using it, probably for the first time in Europe, as the title of a book dealing with occurrences in the Western Hemisphere.[19] He spoke of a "révolution actuelle,"[20] referring to present happenings and leaving the future open, thus underlining its "process" character, just as Lee and Rush had. He also mentioned the revolutionaries, whom he called "coopérateurs."[21] Du Buisson's translator—probably a Swiss—did not know what to do with a term never before used in this context, and so he depersonalized it to "collateral causes."[22] In Germany, too, the new conception that revolutions are the manifestation of political actions took root, and even before the end of the war one could read of "the great revolution undertaken by his [Washington's] countrymen in such bold spirit and to the amazement of all Europe."[23] The phrases "present revolution in America"[24] or "révolution américaine"[25] were ever more widely used during the fifteen years before 1789, though they expressed as yet no more than a rudimentary idea that was continuously gaining wider acceptance.[26] Thus, events in America, rather than, as is often assumed, the subsequent upheaval in France, initially gave rise to the more modern connotations of the term *revolution*.[27]

That contemporaries considered the developments in America to be a "great revolution,"[28] and even "the greatest and most honorable revolution

19. (Paris, 1778).

20. "révolution actuelle": Du Buisson, *Abrégé*, 3; cf. 4, 430.

21. "coopérateurs": *ibid.*, 1.

22. "mitwirkenden Ursachen": Du Buisson, *Historischer Abriß* (1779), iii. A second edition of this work appeared under the title *Vorstellung der Staatsveränderung in Nordamerika* (Bern, 1784), iii.

23. "großen Revolution, die seine Landsleute zur Verwunderung von ganz Europa mit so kühnem Geiste unternommen haben": Heinrich Georg Hoff, *Kurze Biographien oder Lebensabriße merkwürdiger und berühmter Personen neuerer Zeiten*, 4 vols. (Brünn, 1782), III, 5.

24. "gegenwärtiger Revolution in Amerika": Zinner, *Merkwürdige Briefe und Schriften*, 66.

25. "révolution américaine": Zinzendorf, Tagebuch, XXV, fol. 43, entry of Mar. 9, 1780 (HHStA, Vienna).

26. E.g., Sprengel, *Geschichte der Europäer*, [12], 113; *Deutsche Encyclopädie*, VI (1782), 75a; Abbé Robin, *Neue Reise durch Nordamerika in dem Jahr 1781, nebst dem Feldzuge der Armee des Herrn Grafen von Rochambeau*, trans. from the French (Nuremberg, 1783), 24, 144, 160, 162, 164; Schoepf, *Reise*, I, 512; Dietrich Johann Heinrich Stöver, *Historisch-statistische Beyträge zur nähern Kenntniß der Staaten und der neuern Weltbegebenheiten* (Hamburg, 1789), 248; Ebeling, *Erdbeschreibung*, II, 457, V, 763–764.

27. That it was the French Revolution that brought about this change is maintained by Rosenstock, "Revolution als politischer Begriff," in *Festgabe für Paul Heilborn*, 107, Griewank, *Neuzeitliche Revolutionsbegriff*, 230, 233, 235, 240, and Arendt, *On Revolution*, 40–41.

28. "große Revolution": Robin, *Neue Reise durch Nordamerika*, I (preface by the translator). See also Johann Jakob Moser, *Nord-America nach den Friedensschlüssen*, I, 793;

that has ever amazed the world,"[29] does not make clear why they called these occurrences a revolution. Our modern idea of revolution has been influenced mostly by events after 1789 and does not correspond to the meaning current around 1780. When we describe a modern revolution as bourgeois or socialist, the criteria are, if not ideologically preconditioned, determined by the extent to which the revolution implements liberty and equality as well as a new political order for human coexistence.[30] But whether bourgeois or socialist, both kinds of revolutions lay claim to ideals that are generally applicable and binding for all mankind, first and foremost the ideas of liberty and equality. These ideas are the connecting link between the concept of revolution, the developments in America, and the understanding of the German contemporaries. At an early stage the patriot leaders placed the idea of liberty in the foreground of their disputes with Great Britain in order to create a more general and more binding framework for their efforts, for they thought it necessary "to convince the world that we are as firm and unanimous in the cause of Liberty as so noble and exalted a principle demands."[31] The same intention is expressed by the reference in the Declaration of Independence to "decent respect to the opinions of mankind," and in Washington's surprisingly simple formula: "Our cause is noble, it is the cause of Mankind."[32] Moreover, the idea of a new political beginning, a break with the past, a *novus ordo saeculorum*, had been expressed in many ways,[33] although for a variety of reasons this was not done as radically in America as it was done later in the French Revolution.

Michel René Hilliard d'Auberteuil to Jefferson, Feb. 17, 1786, in Boyd *et al.*, eds., *Jefferson Papers*, IX, 289; Guillaume-Thomas-François Raynal, *Geschichte der Revolution von Nord-America . . .*, trans. from the French [by F. H. Wernitz] (Berlin, 1786), iii–iv (preface by Wernitz), vii (remark by Christian Wilhelm von Dohm).

29. "die größte und ehrenvollste Revolution, welche jemals die Welt in Erstaunen gesetzt hat": Paine, *Sammlung verschiedener Schriften*, 141 (the passage is from *American Crisis*, no. XIII). See also Johann Georg Meusel in his *Neueste Litteratur der Geschichtkunde*, I, no. 2 (1779), 91–92, and Robin, *Neue Reise durch Nordamerika*, 57.

30. See Griewank, *Neuzeitliche Revolutionsbegriff*, 5–6; Bloch, *Naturrecht und menschliche Würde*, 188–190, 192–200; Arendt, *On Revolution*, 2–110.

31. R. H. Lee to Landon Carter, June 22, 1765, in Ballagh, ed., *Letters of Richard Henry Lee*, I, 8. See also Lee to Carter, Feb. 2, 1766, and to Gouverneur Morris, May 28, 1775, *ibid.*, 12–13, 140–141; also Rush to Thomas Ruston, Oct. 29, 1775, in Butterfield, ed., *Letters of Benjamin Rush*, I, 92.

32. To James Warren, Mar. 31, 1779, in John C. Fitzpatrick, ed., *The Writings of George Washington from the Original Manuscript Sources, 1745–1799*, 39 vols. (Washington, D.C., 1931–1944), XIV, 313.

33. Cf. Robert E. Brown, *Middle-Class Democracy and the Revolution in Massachusetts, 1691–1780* (Ithaca, N.Y., 1955), 266–267; William H. Nelson, "The Revolutionary Character of the American Revolution," *AHR*, LXX (1964–1965), 1013; Bailyn, *Ideological Origins*, 18–19.

Thus we see why contemporaries at the end of the eighteenth century could talk about an American "revolution." But at the same time, the question arises: When did they start fully to appreciate the revolutionary nature of events in America? Since the beginning of the war the conviction had been spreading that people in America were fighting for liberty and against oppression, and that the importance of this struggle was not limited to the New World. This gave the German contemporaries a standard for consent or rejection, a standard that Friedrich Gottlieb Klopstock expressed in 1781 in his ode, "The Contemporary War":

> Humanity ingenious and lofty
> Inspires you!
> You are the rosy morning
> Of greater days to come![34]

This was the "grand and superb spectacle" for the enjoyment of which the Europeans should, according to some Americans at least, have paid a little more by way of financial support.[35]

Statements made by Germans during the war years were usually not precise enough to throw much light on the question of what they thought was the specific factor that distinguished the American Revolution in the course of human events. They got some early, detailed information along these lines from Guillaume-Thomas-François Raynal's *Révolution de l'Amérique* and its several German editions. Raynal thought the dispute had developed into a war for reasons that were very different from the usual, namely, reasons of principle.[36] He was convinced that this was a great revolution for the political liberty of a nation.[37] Matthias Christian Sprengel seized on this idea and developed it further. From his point of view the war was the struggle of a peaceful, scattered, agrarian population of some three million souls who, without the least preparation, "suddenly leave their ploughs and start to fight for reasons more noble than those of princes; not for thirst of glory or

34. "Ein hoher Genius der Menschlichkeit / Begeistert dich! / Du bist die Morgenröte / Eines nahenden großen Tags!": Klopstock, *Sämmtliche Werke*, 12 vols. (Karlsruhe, 1818–1822), VI, 33.

35. "grand et superbe spectacle": Friedrich Melchior Grimm, *Correspondance littéraire, philosophique et critique par Grimm, Diderot, Raynal, Meister, etc.*, ed. Maurice Tourneux, 16 vols. (Paris, 1877–1882), XII, 133.

36. Raynal, *Staatsveränderung von Amerika*, 76.

37. Guillaume-Thomas-François Raynal, *Révolution de l'Amérique* (London and The Hague, 1781), 163; see also *Beschreibung der dreizehn unabhängigen Nordamerikanischen Staaten*, 6–7; [Alexander Cluny], *Reisen durch Amerika . . . Nebst einem Abriß von Nord-Amerika . . . [von Joseph Mandrillon]*, trans. from the English and the French (Leipzig, 1783), 168.

Figure 10. Benjamin Franklin, Silas Deane, and Arthur Lee Officially Received by Louis XVI, March 20, 1778. "Dr. Franklin, as ambassador of the American republic, gets his first audience in France, at Versailles, March 20, 1778." (Chodowiecki, for Sprengel, *Allgemeines historisches Taschenbuch.*)

Courtesy John Carter Brown Library, Brown University, Providence, R.I.

conquest, but for the most sacred rights of mankind: for liberty and the protection of property." He believed that a similar revolution in Europe would be impossible because of the greater military power available there. And he chided those not interested in the American Revolution "never to boast of having an open mind for great things but to keep on vegetating."[38]

Sprengel articulated with absolute certainty in 1783 why the developments in the West were so important to his contemporaries. In America there was no petty, egotistical conflict of interest at stake: there was a dispute of revolutionary significance over principles and ideals regarded as valid in bourgeois circles east and west of the Atlantic, and which now, for the first time, were transformed into political reality. Sprengel interpreted those events so convincingly that his ideas quickly gained ground with the German bourgeoisie.[39] Because the American ideals were part of the common thought processes of the time, it was easy to regard the American Revolution as "perhaps the only one that is approved of by philosophy."[40]

The conception that valid revolutionary principles were at work in America stood up even under the pressure of events during the French Revolution. As late as the end of the century, Friedrich von Gentz expressed the same view, though with different undertones, when he wrote: "Rarely did a violent undertaking such as this one have such strong motives and such convincing excuses to offer. Never before had a rebellion been initiated and carried out in such an orderly, regular, and methodical fashion as this one; never before had the leaders of a revolution taken refuge in such general

38. "plötzlich seine Pflugscharen verläßt, und für etwas edleres, als warum die Fürsten einander bekriegen, aus Ruhmsucht nicht, nicht aus Eroberungsgeist, sondern für die heiligsten Rechte der Menschheit, für Freiheit und Sicherheit des Eigentums zu fechten beginnt . . . rühme sich nie, für irgend etwas Grosses Sinn zu haben, sondern vegetiere fort": Sprengel, *Allgemeines historisches Taschenbuch*, 28.

39. See in addition to the already quoted sources: "Discours," fols. 6v–8, 43v (NB, Vienna); Chevalier [Pierre Delauney?] Deslandes, *Discours sur la grandeur et l'importance de la révolution qui vient de s'operer dans l'Amérique Septentrionale* (Frankfurt and Paris, 1785), 70, 74–75, 83; Richard Price, "Bemerkungen über die Wichtigkeit der americanischen Revolution," in Mirabeau, *Sammlung einiger Schriften*, 153–154; Karl Hammerdörfer, *Allgemeine Weltgeschichte*, 4 vols. (Halle, 1789–1791), IV, 741. These citations may be sufficient to refute the opinion of Rosenstock, "Revolution als politischer Begriff," in *Festgabe für Paul Heilborn*, that the term *American Revolution* only appeared after 1789 and could not have come into use before that date.

40. "die einzige, welche die Philosophie vielleicht gebilligt hat": Mirabeau, *Sammlung einiger Schriften*, 1. Cf. Eugen Rosenstock-Huessy, *Die europäischen Revolutionen und der Charakter der Nationen*, 2d ed. (Stuttgart and Cologne, 1951), 325, who misunderstood the importance of the American Revolution: "The first and only philosophical and idealistic world revolution, however, is the revolution of 1789."

maxims, such abstract, all-embracing, and therefore such very tempting principles."[41]

The Idea of Liberty

The idea of liberty, though certainly not the only ideal of the American Revolution, towered above all others from the point of view of German contemporaries. "During the American War, when the inhabitants of that land rose against England, the only talk in Europe was about liberty."[42] In order to grasp better the German bourgeoisie's confrontation with this principle, it is necessary first to discuss the meaning of liberty in the colonies as it is understood by scholars today.

Compared with continental European conditions, the English colonies in North America had always presented a picture of a liberal social order. Religious tolerance, especially in Pennsylvania and Rhode Island, and a relative equality of economic opportunities were merely its best-known features. Immigrants, especially from the British Isles and Germany, were attracted to the colonies all through the eighteenth century. This liberal tradition, as described by Louis Hartz,[43] can be traced back to far earlier times than 1776.[44]

The structure of American society and its dominant element, the middle classes, who understood liberty to be the exercise of their natural rights

41. "Selten hatte ein gewaltsames Unternehmen wie dieses so starke Motive und so eindringende Entschuldigungsgründe für sich gehabt. Noch nie war eine Rebellion mit solcher Ordnung, mit solcher Regelmäßigkeit, mit solcher Methode eingeleitet und ausgeführt worden: noch nie hatten die Häupter einer Revolution zu so allgemeinen Maximen, zu so abstrakten, so viel umfassenden und eben deshalb so verführerischen Grundsätzen ihre Zuflucht genommen": Gentz, "Ueber den Gang der öffentlichen Meinung in Europa in Rücksicht auf die französische Revolution," *Historisches Journal*, I, no. 1 (1799), 286. See also *Lebensgeschichte Ludwig XVI.* (Vienna, 1793), 28–29; Christoph Girtanner, *Schilderung des häuslichen Lebens, des Karakters und der Regierung Ludwigs des Sechzehnten* (Frankfurt and Leipzig, 1793), 124; *Reise von Hamburg nach Philadelphia*, 101.

42. "Im amerikanischen Kriege, da die Inwohner dieses Landes sich wider England aufgelehnt hatten, hörte man nichts in Europa als das Wort Freiheit": Moritz Flavius Trenck von Tonder in *Politische Gespräche der Toten*, II (1787), 433, reprinted in J. Hansen, ed., *Quellen zur Geschichte des Rheinlandes*, I, 201.

43. Louis Hartz, *The Liberal Tradition in America: An Interpretation of American Political Thought since the Revolution* (New York, 1955).

44. See, e.g., John C. Miller, *Triumph of Freedom 1775–1783* (Boston, 1948), 341; Max Savelle, *Seeds of Liberty: The Genesis of the American Mind* (New York, 1948), 351–354, 584–587; Hartz, *Liberal Tradition*, 35–86; Bailyn, *Ideological Origins*, 66.

within the limits set by existing laws,[45] became in the 1760s and 1770s the decisive factors in the outbreak, direction, and course of the Revolution. In the beginning the struggle was merely in defense of some rights threatened by the English government. But in the course of several years, political argumentation progressed toward a general defense of freedom itself (being the sum total of all civil and political liberties) against despotism and tyranny allegedly threatening from the government in London. Many Americans thought of their country as increasingly animated by a "spirit of liberty" that was being suppressed by England through arbitrary and unlawful actions. When the war against the mother country broke out, one of the patriots' principal aims was the preservation of their liberal social order.[46] Even England's most passionate adversaries did not dream of anarchistic, unlimited freedom. They sought constitutional liberty as the fundamental principle of a future political order.[47]

The idea of liberty was not limited to America. In Germany, too, at the beginning of the war, it was backed by an intellectual tradition and energetically sponsored by the Enlightenment. For enlightenment without liberty was unthinkable. Only he who freely used his intelligence could ever raise himself out of man's "self-imposed nonage" to gain true dignity.[48] Like Immanuel Kant, many widely known French writers of the Enlightenment, such as Voltaire, Montesquieu, and also Rousseau, had put fresh life into the idea of liberty. In Germany, Klopstock, Stolberg, Voss, and others sang of liberty in their poems before its idea was revived by events in America.[49] Traces of past

45. Bailyn, *Ideological Origins*, 79.

46. E.g., Henry Marchant to Robert Treat Paine, Dec. 24, 1765 (Robert Treat Paine Papers, MHi, Boston); Benjamin Rush to Ebenezer Hazard, Nov. 8, 1765, probably to J. Rush, Jan. 19, 1769, to Charles Lee, July 23, 1776, all in Butterfield, ed., *Letters of Benjamin Rush*, I, 18, 72, 103; John Dickinson to Otis, Dec. 5, 1767, in *The Warren-Adams Letters* (Boston, 1917–1925), I, 4; Dickinson to Arthur Lee, Nov. 25, 1769 (Arthur Lee Papers, I, 58, Harvard College Library, Cambridge, Mass.); R. H. Lee to Samuel Adams, June 23, 1774, in Ballagh, ed., *Letters of Richard Henry Lee*, I, 111–113; "Diary of James Allen," *PMHB*, IX (1885), 185 (July 26, 1775); *Erklärung der Repräsentanten der vereinigten Colonien*, 17–18.

47. See Richard Hofstadter, *The American Political Tradition and the Men Who Made It* (New York, 1948), 10; Miller, *Triumph of Freedom*, 687; Rossiter, *Seedtime of the Republic*, *passim*; Edmund S. Morgan, "The American Revolution: Revisions in Need of Revising," *WMQ*, 3d Ser., XIV (1957), 11–12; Gilman Ostrander, *The Rights of Man in America 1606–1861* (Columbia, Mo., 1961), 71–91; Dan Lacy, *The Meaning of the American Revolution* (New York, 1966), 216–236; Bailyn, *Ideological Origins*, 94–95; R. B. Morris, *American Revolution Reconsidered*, 3.

48. Kant, "Beantwortung der Frage: Was ist Aufklärung?" in his *Werke*, ed. Wilhelm Weischedel, 6 vols. (Wiesbaden and Darmstadt, 1960–1964), VI, 55–61.

49. E.g., Klopstock, "Feldgesang vor einer Freyheitsschlacht," in *Musenalmanach für das Jahr 1775* (Göttingen, 1774), 52–59; Stolberg, "Die Freyheit," *ibid.*, 221; Voss, "Trinklied für Freye," in Voss, ed., *Musenalmanach für 1776* (Lauenburg, 1775), 108.

liberty in the free imperial cities, in southwest Germany, and in Switzerland received new attention. The legend of William Tell experienced a renaissance and veiled Switzerland in the aura of a land of liberty.[50] But in cultivated circles of the bourgeoisie, especially those influenced by Voltaire and Montesquieu, England was the undisputed land of liberty up to the middle of the 1770s.[51] It often served as a model for the liberty enthusiasts in Germany.[52]

Although the word *liberty*, which had meanwhile become fashionable,[53] evoked much enthusiasm among the German bourgeoisie in the 1770s and 1780s, the term itself remained ambiguous.[54] Most conceptions still held something of the old idea that liberty was a kind of order based on granted privileges. Thus, liberty itself was nothing but a privilege.[55] These ideas arose out of the conception of estates and corresponded to the German experience before the French Revolution. After all, it was precisely the realm of estates that was revived in those years.[56] Civil liberty as an inviolable sphere of free-

50. Eduard Ziehen, *Die deutsche Schweizerbegeisterung, 1750–1815* (Frankfurt, 1922), 33–106; Erwin Hölzle, "Bruch und Kontinuität im Werden der deutschen modernen Freiheit," in Theodor Mayer, ed., *Das Problem der Freiheit in der deutschen und schweizerischen Geschichte (Vorträge und Forschungen, II)* (Lindau, 1955), 171. See also Hölzle's "Justus Möser über Staat und Freiheit," in *Aus Politik und Geschichte. Gedächtnisschrift für Georg von Below* (Berlin, 1928), 167–181.

51. E.g., Schubart, ed., *Deutsche Chronik*, May 2, 1774, 73; also Alexander James Carlyle, *Political Liberty: A History of the Conception in the Middle Ages and Modern Times* (1941; repr. London, 1963), 150–157.

52. On the German idea of liberty, in general see Leonard Krieger, *The German Idea of Freedom: History of a Political Tradition* (Boston, 1957); Jürgen Schlumbohm, *Freiheit. Die Anfänge der bürgerlichen Emanzipationsbewegung in Deutschland im Spiegel ihres Leitwortes, ca. 1760–ca. 1800* (Düsseldorf, 1975); Schlumbohm, *Freiheitsbegriff und Emanzipationsbewegung* (Göttingen, 1973); rather poor, Carlo Antoni, *Der Kampf wider die Vernunft. Zur Entstehungsgeschichte des deutschen Freiheitsgedankens*, trans. from the Italian by Walter Goetz (Stuttgart, 1951); also Kurt von Raumer, "Deutschland um 1800," in Leo Just, ed., *Handbuch der Deutschen Geschichte* (Constance, 1960–), III, pt. 1, 16; Hertz, *German Public Mind*, II, 354.

53. Cf. Wolfgang Stammler, "Politische Schlagworte in der Zeit der Aufklärung," in *Lebenskräfte der abendländischen Geistesgeschichte. Dank- und Erinnerungsgabe an Walter Goetz zum 80. Geburtstag* (Marburg, 1948), 202–216; Kyösti Julku, *Die revolutionäre Bewegung im Rheinland am Ende des achtzehnten Jahrhunderts*, I (Helsinki, 1965), 136; not quite correct, John L. Snell, "The World of German Democracy, 1789–1914," *Historian*, XXXI (1968–1969), 524.

54. See Gaetano Salvemini, "The Concepts of Democracy and Liberty in the Eighteenth Century," in Conyers Read, ed., *The Constitution Reconsidered*, rev. Richard B. Morris (New York, 1968), 111–116.

55. Cf. Buchenröder, *Nord-Amerika*, I, xxviii–xxix, 89, and his *Grundriß von Nordamerika*, xxiv–xxv. Also Otto Brunner, "Die Freiheitsrechte in der altständischen Gesellschaft," in his *Neue Wege der Verfassungs- und Sozialgeschichte*, 2d ed. (Göttingen, 1968), 193, 197.

56. Karl Otmar Freiherr von Aretin, *Heiliges Römisches Reich 1776–1806. Reichsverfassung und Staatssouveränität*, 2 vols. (Wiesbaden, 1967), I, 32, 34.

dom and a fundamental right of each citizen, individually guaranteed and based on general legal principles, was less congenial to the German bourgeoisie.[57] Before 1789, German views moved along the paths of tradition. The conventional idea of liberty was not yet questioned by the great masses of people. If there was any thought about it at all, it was usually a mere repetition of Montesquieu's phrase that liberty is "ce que l'on doit vouloir."[58]

In view of these facts it is easy to explain why the bourgeoisie did not have a clear understanding of the meaning of the idea of political liberty as an aspect of modern constitutionalism, such as was exported from America. Even those statements that directly associated the idea of liberty with what was happening in the Western Hemisphere are hardly exceptions. There was a general lack of in-depth analyses of the essence of liberty and the structure of human society. Only America's adversaries made some beginning at dealing with the idea of political liberty, not, however, in order to subject it to a detailed analysis, but to use it in their condemnation of the insurgents. "The mob in North America scream for nothing but liberty. The European mob rejoice in the echo. What is liberty? Something that never existed in this world and never will exist, a phantom."[59] Martin Ernst von Schlieffen, a Hessian minister of state, dismissed the idea of political liberty in a similar manner a little later.[60] But these few negative comments do not disprove that the vast majority of the German bourgeoisie found it difficult to grasp the meaning of political liberty as it developed during the war years. The effects of the American Revolution on the idea of political liberty in Germany brought only late fruits. Debates on political liberty that led to new avenues

57. For a similar opinion see Kurt von Raumer, "Absoluter Staat, korporative Libertät, persönliche Freiheit," *HZ*, CLXXXIII (1957), 58, 70, 92. The article is reprinted in *Beiträge zur europäischen Geschichte*, I (Munich, 1958), 55–96. See also Hölzle, "Bruch und Kontinuität," in Mayer, ed., *Problem der Freiheit*, 167–169.

58. Charles de Secondat, baron de La Brède et de Montesquieu, "De l'esprit des lois," bk. XI, chap. 3, in his *Oeuvres complètes*, ed. Roger Caillois, 2 vols. (Paris, 1949–1951), II, 395, cf. 395–407. Also, Martin Ehlers, *Discours sur la liberté*, trans. from the German (Dessau and Leipzig, 1783), 86–87; August Hennings, *Philosophische und Statistische Geschichte des Ursprungs und des Fortgangs der Freyheit in Engeland* (Copenhagen, 1783), 368; *Deutsche Encyclopädie*, X (1785), 509a; L. Brackebusch, "Unvorgreifliche Gedanken über Freiheit und Gleichheit," *Schleswigsches ehemals Braunschweigisches Journal*, III (Sept. 1792), 68; *Entwurf der neuesten Culturgeschichte*, 19.

59. "Der Pöbel in Nordamerika schreiet nichts als Freiheit. Der Pöbel in Europa ist vom Widerhall entzückt. Was ist Freiheit? Ein Ding, das niemals in der Welt war, das niemals in der Welt sein kann, ein Phantom": Wekhrlin, ed., *Chronologen*, I (1779), 166.

60. [Martin Ernst von Schlieffen], *Von den Hessen in Amerika, Ihrem Fürsten und den Schreyern*, trans. from the French ([Dessau], 1782), 19–21. See also Wekhrlin, ed., *Das graue Ungeheuer*, III (1784), 186. For related ideas of Friedrich Karl von Moser see Notker Hammerstein, "Das politische Denken Friedrich Carl von Mosers," *HZ*, CCXII (1971), 329–335, and Johann Heinrich Jung-Stilling, *Über den Revolutions-Geist unserer Zeit zur Belehrung der bürgerlichen Stände* (Marburg, 1793), 31, 36.

of discussion did not rise until the years of the French Revolution. All that the American Revolution did in the 1770s and 1780s was to further popularize the term *liberty*.

Yet the American patriots could hardly have wished for a more favorable mood in Europe for the reception of their slogans of liberty. After the outbreak of open conflict it quickly became fashionable to talk about liberty in connection with happenings in America.[61] In the years of the French Revolution, Christoph Girtanner, a physician and political historian from Göttingen, wrote with somewhat faulty chronology: "After the end of the American war, ideas of liberty and independence spread increasingly."[62] However, the views expressed were, as a rule, lacking in clarity. It took a long time before it became clear that the Americans had not revolted to defend political liberties and privileges guaranteed in their "liberty letters," as the colonial charters were mostly called.[63] For there was a vast difference, as Jefferson had clearly stated in the Declaration of Independence, between a people's uniting to defend some constitutional guarantees, and uniting to defend their liberty in general against despotism and slavery. To be sure, despotism was hardly the intention of the English government, as some German commentators did not fail to observe.[64] But after the first war years, American arguments became not only more generally known but also more and more accepted by the German bourgeoisie.[65]

Today we are perhaps even more inclined than were people in the eighteenth century to see the idea of liberty in the frame of reference of internal politics. But we must not forget that it is also a question of external politics. It was this dual aspect that created some confusion at the time of the American Revolution, especially because of the colonial status of the country. The

61. *Hamburgischer Correspondent*, Feb. 23, 1773; *Freytags-Zeitung*, Feb. 18, 1774, Apr. 28, 1775, May 3, 1776; Schubart, ed., *Deutsche Chronik*, Sept. 12, 1774, 377–378, Jan. 11, 1776, 31; Iselin to Jean Rodolphe Frey, Apr. 19, 1775, and Iselin, Tagebuch, Jan. 27, 1776 (Nachlaß Iselin, LV, no pagination, XV, 23–24, StA, Basel); Jacobi, ed., *Iris*, June 1775, 161, Sept. 1775, 180–181; *Leipziger Zeitung*, May 1, 1776; Buchenröder, *Gesammlete Nachrichten*, xxxiv–xxxv; *Briefe über die jetzige Uneinigkeit*, 89–91.

62. "Nach dem geendigten amerikanischen Kriege wurden die Ideen von Freiheit und von Unabhängigkeit immer allgemeiner und ausgebreiteter": Girtanner, *Ludwig der Sechzehnte*, 124.

63. E.g., Achenwall, *Anmerkungen über Nordamerika* (1769), 87, 2d ed. (Helmstedt, 1777), 50–51; *Freytags-Zeitung*, Aug. 10, 1770; Buchenröder, *Nord-Amerika*, I, xxviii–xxix; Sprengel, *Briefe*, 29, 33, 84–85.

64. An example is Meister's letter to Bodmer, June 12, 1778 (MS. Bodmer X, 355, ZB, Zurich).

65. See such works from the end of the century as: *La Fayette als Staatsmann*, [11] (preface by Johann Reinhold Forster); Milbiller, *Allgemeine Geschichte: Engelland*, III, 358–359; Seidel, *Neueste Geschichte von Europa*, II, 126, 227; Johann Isaak von Gerning, *Das achtzehnte Jahrhundert. Saecularischer Gesang* (Gotha, 1802), 11–12.

Americans' desire for liberty was sometimes, especially in the 1770s, represented as a matter of external politics, namely, a wish for freedom from Great Britain. Since the Declaration of Independence dealt with domestic as well as foreign politics, and since only a few phrases of its contents were known widely in Germany, the Declaration probably contributed toward making the boundaries between the two conceptions less well defined and toward equating liberty with independence.[66]

More important, however, were the voices of those who dealt with the internal context of liberty. Whether or not the insurgents were fighting for the ideal of liberty became the determining criterion for bourgeois attitudes toward America. This is shown most clearly by the comparatively small group of America's adversaries. They knew that the leaders of the Revolution claimed to be fighting for their liberty. Since this claim found wide acceptance, it was impossible to drown it in silence. Instead, the anti-Americans took up the American argument but distorted its aims. For Christoph Heinrich Korn, a military officer turned scholar, it was a case clear as daylight: "These people want no more, for various reasons, than to be free, which to them means to live their own lives, each according to his liking, without any superior authority to prescribe laws. Some want to live a licentious life without fear of punishment, others fear renewed suppression. They lack nothing but a leader."[67] Instead of fighting for a high ideal, the Americans were animated by an "exaggerated spirit of freedom,"[68] a lust for "unbridled liberty."[69] Korn's observations flatly dismissed the idea of political liberty without ever discussing it in detail.[70]

The Revolution's adversaries usually went one step further. They not only repudiated the idea of political liberty, they disputed its very existence. "In no civilized nation and perhaps nowhere in this world are there men living in complete freedom."[71] If, according to this point of view, there could

---

66. See, e.g., Gottlieb Heinrich von Treuer to margrave, July 19, 1776 (Abt. 48, no. 2187, GLA, Karlsruhe); Hennings, *Geschichte der Freyheit in Engeland*, 379–380.

67. "Alle diese Leute wünschen, obwohl aus verschiedenen Ursachen, frei, das ist nach ihrer Meinung ohne alle Herrschaft, welche ihnen Gesetze vorschreiben kann, jeder nach seinem Gutdünken zu leben. Jene, ein zügelloses Leben ungestraft führen zu können; diese, aus Furcht vor einer nochmaligen Unterdrückung. Nichts fehlte solchen Leuten als ein Anführer": Korn, *Geschichte der Kriege*, II, 64.

68. "Geist der Freiheit, der bis ins Übertriebene": Schirach, *Notiz der Großbrittannischen Colonien*, 96-page ed., 64.

69. "zügellosen Freiheit": Korn, *Geschichte der Kriege*, II, 68, VII, 26.

70. E.g., *ibid.*, II, 65; Friedrich Christian Cleve, Tagebuch, May 29, Aug. 11/13, 1778, pp. 66, 119 (StadtA, Brunswick); *Chronologen*, I (1779), 167; Schroeckh, *Allgemeine Weltgeschichte*, IV, pt. 2, 251; Peter Adolf Winkopp, ed., *Bibliothek für Denker*, I, no. 3 (1783), 267, 269; Schmettau, *Kleine Schriften*, I, 95 (written about 1783–1784).

71. "Unter keiner gesitteten Nation, vielleicht nirgend auf der Welt, leben ganz freie Menschen": Korn, *Geschichte der Kriege*, VII, 108.

not be any such thing as political liberty, the Americans' claim to be fighting for it was a mere excuse. "The mob in America are thus chasing a shadow only."[72] Their true aim was complete licentiousness, the denial of all social ties and duties, in other words, pure anarchy.

> I have seen this nation a-budding;
> I wandered through all its lands.
> I've seen the chains they have wrought
> Led astray by a foolish, false pride.
>
> Moderate from weakness and sober from want,
> They seem to pay homage to virtue;
> But the liberty for which they all strive
> Is but a refusal of duty.[73]

At the beginning of the armed conflict and in the early years of the war a sizable number of Germans stood between the protagonists and antagonists of the Revolution, undecided as to which side should have their sympathies, and therefore by no means as sure of their judgment as those who had taken a definite stand. This in-between position was a transient stage for those of America's antagonists who had grown unsure of their original condemnation of the Americans. Their attitude toward the question of liberty was summed up by a parson from Alstetten, near Zurich, Hans Heinrich Schinz, who had moved away from his original anti-American attitude only under active pressure from Johann Jakob Bodmer: "If the Americans win, they will be hailed as fighters for liberty; if they lose, they will be condemned as rebels."[74]

However, judging from the majority of pertinent statements, it seems that by far the larger portion of the German bourgeoisie had adopted and broadly construed the Americans' argument that they were defending liberty. Very early, that is, toward the end of 1774, Schubart directly contradicted his

72. "Der Pöbel in Amerika haschet also einem Schatten nach": *Chronologen*, I (1779), 167. On Wekhrlin's rejection of the idea of political liberty and of the right of resistance see Vierhaus, "Deutschland vor der Französischen Revolution," 412–413.

73. "Ich habe sie gesehen, diese keimende Nation. / Ihre Gefilde habe ich all' durchwandert. / Ich habe gesehen, wie sie sich / Durch Stolz und Einbildung törichte Fesseln schmiedet. / Mäßig aus Schwachheit, nüchtern aus Mangel, / Scheint sie der Tugend zu huldigen; / Aber die Freiheit, nach der sie atmet, / Ist nichts als Abscheu an Pflichten": "Ueber die Insurgenten, Eine Handvoll Stanzen," *Chronologen*, VIII (1780), 27. Adversaries of the French Revolution condemned it as a "freedom fraud" (*Freiheitsschwindel*); cf. Leopold II to Johann Georg Zimmermann, Feb. 13, 1792 (Nachlaß Zimmermann, A I, no. 3, LB, Hanover); *Lebensgeschichte Ludwig XVI.*, 28–29.

74. "Würden die Amerikaner siegen, so würden sie Verfechter der Freiheit heißen, unterliegen sie, so wird man sie Rebellen nennen": Schinz to Bodmer, Feb. 4, 1777 (MS. Bodmer VIII, 433, ZB, Zurich).

later adversaries and their assertions by saying about the English possessions in North America: "The spirit of liberty is constantly gaining in vitality in those regions, but it is not the impetuous spirit that degenerates into licentiousness, but a spirit controlled by wisdom, moderation, and steadfastness."[75] There is no reason to assume that Schubart changed his opinion in later years. His conviction that the colonists' open resistance against the policies of the English government was justified in principle was shared by many of his fellow citizens, for, "if the law has to be violated, let it be violated for liberty's sake."[76] But, as we have noted, basic inquiries into the meaning of political freedom were to be found even more rarely among the supporters than among the antagonists of the American Revolution.

Ordinarily, there prevailed a careless enthusiasm for liberty, an enthusiasm that had found expression in the philosophy of the Age of Enlightenment and was now revived by the developments in the West. The fight for liberty against threatening despotism was honorable and fashionable enough to guide the sympathies of an enlightened age to any country that seemed to exemplify the ideal.[77] Goethe, on the other hand, criticized this shallow and uncritical attitude when he wrote:

> Yes, yes, I heard a lot of boasting over wine
> That all would give an arm for those provincials mine.
> They toasted liberty, speaking brave and bold;
> But none turned out when the roll was called.[78]

Johann Heinrich Pestalozzi condemned empty goodwill even more incisively, especially that of the nobility, who displayed enthusiasm for the oppressed American people fighting for their freedom, while toward their

75. "Der Geist der Freiheit wird in diesen Gegenden immer lebendiger, aber nicht der ungestüme Geist, der in Zügellosigkeit ausartet, sondern ein Geist, der von Weisheit, Mäßigung und Standhaftigkeit gelenkt wird": Schubart, ed., Deutsche Chronik, Oct. 20, 1774, 465.

76. "Si fas violandum est, libertatis gratia violandum est": Iselin to Peter Ochs, June 17, 1777, in Ochs, Korrespondenz des Peter Ochs (1752–1821), ed. Gustav Steiner, 3 vols. (Basel, 1927–1937), I, 104.

77. E.g., Paine, Gesunder Menschenverstand, 81; Deutsche Chronik, Jan. 11, 1776, 31; Briefe über die jetzige Uneinigkeit, 90; Bericht eines Englischen Amerikaners, 44; Neueste Mannigfaltigkeiten (1778), I, 347–348; [Jacob Duché], Briefe des Herrn T. Caspipina, trans. from the English (Leipzig, 1778), 19; Johann Reinhold Forster to Franklin, Apr. 27, 1782 (Franklin Papers, XXV, 47, APSL, Philadelphia); Schmohl, Über Nordamerika und Demokratie, 36–37, 73–74; presidential address of Johann Heinrich Füssli, in Verhandlungen der Helvetischen Gesellschaft (n.p., 1782), 35. See also Bodmer, Die Cherusken, 14.

78. "Ja, ja, bei'm Glase Wein hört' ich wohl manchen prahlen, / Er ließe Haut und Haar für meine Provinzialen! / Da lebt' die Freiheit hoch, war jeder brav und kühn, / Und wenn der Morgen kam, ging eben keiner hin": Goethe, Die Mitschuldigen, 3d version (1780–1783), act I, scene i, in his Werke, Weimar ed., 1/IX, 44.

subjects they still behaved like petty, self-righteous despots.[79] Bengt Lidner, on the other hand, concluded his dissertation with the wish that the Americans could soon partake of the freedom he and his fellow citizens already rejoiced in.[80] With a great deal of complacency, many Europeans believed that it was their very own enlightened ideals that were triumphant on America's battlefields.

America and *liberty* more and more became interchangeable terms. If England had become tyrannical, and if Americans were forced to take arms against this former shelter of liberty in order to defend liberty, then "the American cause, or in other words, the cause of liberty itself,"[81] was one and the same thing. This kind of infatuation with the idea of liberty was easily conveyed and grew into exuberant sympathy for the American patriots and their fight against Great Britain. Consequently, America's victory was a victory for liberty, and eventually a victory for the German bourgeoisie, whose ideals had seemingly been realized in at least one part of the world. The poem "America's Liberty," which appeared in 1783 in the *Berlinische Monatsschrift*, the leading voice of the Berlin Enlightenment, reflects this conviction:

> Free thou art! (resound in victory,
> Elated song!) Free now, free America!
> Exhausted, bent, and full of shame
> Thy foe departs, and thou triumphest.
>
> The noble fight for liberty and for country
> Was fought in glory. Take thou now
> The wreath that ends it all. And Europe's joy
> To the holiest of victories![82]

These words reveal the reasons for the enthusiastic support that the large majority of the German bourgeoisie gave to the Americans' defense of

79. Pestalozzi, *Ein Schweizer-Blatt*, Jan. 24, 1782, reprinted in his *Sämtliche Werke*, ed. Buchenau *et al.*, VIII, 23–30.

80. Lidner, *De Iure revolutionis Americanorum*, 18. See also the nonpolitical work by J. C. Ildebald, *Reise nach dem Lande der Freiheit in den Jahren 1780 bis 1790* (Berlin, 1793). Rudolf Stadelmann, "Deutschland und die westeuropäischen Revolutionen," in his *Deutschland und Westeuropa* (Laupheim, 1948), 21–22, regards German enthusiasm for America's liberty only as an expression of proud self-complacency.

81. "die Sache Amerikas oder, mit andern Worten, der Freiheit": Posselt, ed., *Europäische Annalen*, May 1795, 102. Cf. Schubart, ed., *Chronik*, Sept. 3, 1790, 603; Carlyle, *Political Liberty*, 161.

82. "Frei bist du! (sag's im höheren Siegeston, / Entzücktes Lied!) frei, frei nun, Amerika! / Erschöpft, gebeugt, bedeckt mit Schande, / Weichet dein Feind, und du triumphierest. / Der edle Kampf für Freiheit und Vaterland, / Er ist gekämpfet, rühmlich gekämpfet. Nimm' / Den Kranz am Ziel! Europens Jubel / Feire den heiligsten aller Siege": *Berlinische Monatsschrift*, Apr. 1783, 386.

Figure 11. French Army at Newport, July 11, 1780. "Landing of a French auxiliary army in America, at Rhode Island, July 11, 1780." (Chodowiecki, for Sprengel, *Allgemeines historisches Taschenbuch*.)

Courtesy John Carter Brown Library, Brown University, Providence, R.I.

liberty. But they are by no means a demand for political liberty in the context of modern constitutionalism. Rather, they express a partly self-righteous, partly romantic inclination, though this too had its political consequences in later years. As early as 1776 Schubart had shown the way for all freedom enthusiasts when he sang in his "Colonist's Song of Freedom":

> Swim over! For liberty lives that way!
> Here flames its altar![83]

After eight years of fighting "over liberty and submission" and risking "all for the cause of liberty,"[84] victory seemed to guarantee that "the spirit of liberty" now would "spread its protecting wings over America."[85] The new republic in the West had become a shining example to a faraway bourgeoisie, who in their blind enthusiasm for the idea of liberty were prepared to think of America as a dream turned into reality and, with Paine, as an asylum for all mankind.[86] What England had been for the enlightened, educated bourgeoisie up to the mid-1770s, America became by 1783 at the latest: the land of liberty, though very far away.[87] This caused the break with the Voltaire-Montesquieu tradition that was sealed in the Treaty of Versailles.[88]

Although the political consciousness of the German bourgeoisie underwent decisive changes under the influence of the French Revolution, large sections of the population retained the opinion that the United States, and not Britain or France, was "the mother country of liberty."[89] Even leading German Jacobins like Georg Forster believed as late as 1793 that it was not the French but the North American republic that had "the most liberal"

83. "Schwimm her! hier wohnt die Freiheit, hier! / Hier flammt ihr Altar!": reprinted in Schubart, *Schriften*, IV, 287. Cf. his *Deutsche Chronik*, Sept. 12, 1774, 377–378. See also *Freytags-Zeitung*, Apr. 28, 1775, May 3, 1776; *Leipziger Zeitung*, May 1, 1776.

84. "über Freiheit und Unterwürfigkeit . . . alles für die Sache der Freiheit": Sprengel, *Allgemeines historisches Taschenbuch*, 144–145.

85. "Geist der Freiheit . . . mit weitumschattendem Flügel über Amerika wehen": Stolberg, "Die Zukunft," ed. Hartwig, *ALG*, XIII (1885), 270.

86. Paine, *Gesunder Menschenverstand*, 81. See also Karl Ritter von Qureille to Franklin, July 30, 1783, and Johann Valentin Embser to Franklin, Feb. 28, 1783 (Franklin Papers, LIX, 8, XXVII, 150, APSL, Philadelphia); *Beschreibung der dreizehn unabhängigen Nordamerikanischen Staaten*, 5, 32–33, 58; Mazzei, *Geschichte und Staatsverfassung*, II, 6.

87. As a further example see Brissot de Warville, *Neue Reise*, Bayreuth ed., I, 66, 80.

88. François Marie Arouet de Voltaire, "Lettres philosophiques," no. 9 (1734), in his *Oeuvres complètes*, 46 vols. (Paris, 1875–1891), XXIII, 66–67. See Montesquieu, "Notes sur l'Angleterre" (1729–1732): "L'Angleterre est à présent le plus libre pays qui soit au monde." See also his "De l'esprit des lois" (1748), bk. XI, chap. 6, both in his *Oeuvres complètes*, I, 884, II, 396–407.

89. Christoph Daniel Ebeling to Mathew Carey, Sept. 25, 1792 (Lea and Febiger Coll., PHi, Philadelphia). See also Ebeling's letter to George Washington, Oct. 10, 1793 (Miscellaneous Letters Received by the Department of State, Record Group 59, NA, Washington, D. C.).

constitution "known to us in a large state."[90] When Britain's esteem rose again among the German liberals of the *Vormärz* and St. Paul's Church era of early 1848, there resulted a dualism that found its constitutional and political models in Great Britain as well as in America.[91]

The Idea of Equality

Owing to the lack of estates and privileged groups, Americans had enjoyed some measure of equality even in colonial times. To be sure, theirs was not an egalitarian society as we understand it today, yet it was clearly in advance of the *ancien régime* and enlightened despotism. One of the characteristics of America that constantly attracted new settlers was the relative equality of economic opportunity.[92] Yet at the time of the American Revolution there was much to criticize with regard to political equality, particularly in such areas as the electoral franchise, parliamentary representation of newly settled regions of states, and differences in political power among the individual states, not to mention the condition of Negro slaves, who were politically powerless.

Whether and how far the Revolution can be linked with progress toward equality is still a central topic of investigation for historians. The question

90. "die freieste . . . die wir in einem großen Staate kennen": Georg to Therese Forster, Aug. 21, 1793, in Georg Forster, *Johann Georg Forster's Briefwechsel. Nebst einigen Nachrichten von seinem Leben*, ed. Theresa Heyne Huber, 2 vols. (Leipzig, 1829), II, 551. See also Meister, *Historische Unterhaltungen*, 216; *Historisch-geographische Unterhaltungen oder Reisen des Herrn * * * durch alle vier Welttheile. Ein unterrichtendes Lesebuch für die Jugend. Mit Landcharten*, trans. from the French, 2 vols. (Brunswick, 1790), II, 144; Brissot de Warville, *Neue Reise*, Bayreuth ed., I, 35; Ebeling, *Erdbeschreibung*, I, iii; Seidel, "Staatsverfassung," in Ramsay, *Amerikanische Revolution*, IV, 15, 58; [Andreas Georg Friedrich von Rebmann], *Hans Kiekindiewelts Reisen in alle vier Welttheile und den Mond* (Leipzig and Gera, 1794), 437–445; *Genius der Zeit*, Oct. 1795, 180; Milbiller, *Allgemeine Geschichte: Engelland*, III, 348–349, 358, *Die vereinigten nordamerikanischen Provinzen*, II, 488.

91. Cf. Eckhart G. Franz, *Das Amerikabild der deutschen Revolution von 1848/49. Zum Problem der Übertragung gewachsener Verfassungsformen* (Heidelberg, 1958), 3–14, 30–38; Snell, "German Democracy," *Historian*, XXXI (1968–1969), 524; Erich Angermann, "Der Frühkonstitutionalismus und das amerikanische Vorbild," *HZ*, CCXIX (1974), 1–32. Friedrich Christoph Dahlmann, *Geschichte der englischen Revolution*, 2d ed. (Leipzig, 1844), esp. 392–393, discusses an essential part of the political program of German liberalism during the *Vormärz*.

92. Russel B. Nye, *This Almost Chosen People: Essays in the History of American Ideas* (East Lansing, Mich., 1967), 312.

according to Carl Becker, was one "of who should rule at home."[93] Four important and inspiring essays written by J. Franklin Jameson, entitled *The American Revolution Considered as a Social Movement*,[94] emphasize the same point. Elisha P. Douglass is a more recent exponent of the idea that developments during the Revolutionary decades clearly resulted in a democratization of state and society.[95]

This interpretation could not go for long without a rebuttal, which gained emphasis during the 1950s and 1960s. The opposing historians maintain that the American Revolution did not possess any component aimed at social improvement or democratization, that it did not change either the social or the basic political structure of government as it existed in the colonial period, and that it left the degree of equality (or inequality) more or less unchanged, a rather controversial position associated particularly with Robert E. Brown.[96] It has been shown that egalitarian traits were more prominent in New England than in the southern states.[97]

Although both sides have furnished some convincing and ingenious arguments on specific points, it seems to me that the middle path between the two extremes—decisive changes toward democratization versus no changes at all—is the most productive. Moreover, local studies available today seem to indicate that the effects and results of the Revolution differed widely in individual towns, cities, and areas.[98] One should probably not overrate the

93. Becker, *The History of Political Parties in the Province of New York, 1760–1776* (1909; repr. Madison, Wis., 1960), esp. 22.

94. (Princeton, N.J., 1926).

95. Douglass, *Rebels and Democrats: The Struggle for Equal Political Rights and Majority Rule During the American Revolution* (Chapel Hill, N.C., 1955). See also Friedenwald, *Declaration of Independence*, 201–202; Thomas V. Smith, *The American Philosophy of Equality* (Chicago, 1927), 19; Aptheker, *American Revolution*, II, 50, 229–257. Also, the not entirely convincing articles by Richard Buel, Jr., "Democracy and the American Revolution: A Frame of Reference," *WMQ*, 3d Ser., XXI (1964), 165–190, and Jackson Turner Main, "Government by the People: The American Revolution and the Democratization of the Legislatures," *ibid.*, XXIII (1966), 391–407.

96. Brown, *Middle-Class Democracy*; Robert E. and B. Katherine Brown, *Virginia 1705–1786: Democracy or Aristocracy?* (East Lansing, Mich., 1964), 284–302.

97. E.g., Ephraim D. Adams, *The Power of Ideals in American History* (New Haven, Conn., 1926), 129–130; Charles S. Sydnor, *Gentlemen Freeholders: Political Practices in Washington's Virginia* (Chapel Hill, N.C., 1952), esp. 120; David Hawke, *A Transaction of Free Men: The Birth and Course of the Declaration of Independence* (New York, 1964), 169–170, 187; Harry V. Jaffa, *Equality and Liberty: Theory and Practice in American Politics* (New York, 1965), 13–18.

98. Of the enormous number of relevant studies, special attention may be called to three articles that provide some beginning answers to these questions. All three deal with older settled areas and towns. Contrary to Bruce G. Merritt's "Loyalism and Social Conflict in Revolutionary Deerfield, Massachusetts," *Journal of American History*, LVII (1970–1971), 277–289, the developments at Deerfield seem to suggest a political rather than a social conflict, as

importance of the social component in American developments, since the ideological, as well as the practical, prerequisites were lacking. The national leaders of the Revolution in general had no intention of implementing political equality in the states, with all of its social and other consequences,[99] though, of course, individual opinions varied widely on just how far to go. There were the differences between Jefferson's democratic notions of property and his successful effort to abolish primogeniture and entail in Virginia on the one hand, and the aristocratic sentiments of a man like Gouverneur Morris on the other. Social barriers in the American colonies before 1776 were undoubtedly lower than those in France before 1789 or in Russia before 1917. Nevertheless, the American Revolution, and the events preceding it as a consequence of the Seven Years' War, released specific forces in favor of social change. Sometimes there were violent efforts, as the Regulator movement of the Carolinas or the march of the Paxton Boys in Pennsylvania.[100] All in all, in spite of the definitely moderate, middle-class tone of the American Revolution, one can surely say that it fostered some tendencies toward a greater degree of social and political equality.[101]

---

some wealthy families made use of the situation to gain more political influence at the expense of those who had earlier held political power. With rich statistical material, Allan Kulikoff, "The Progress of Inequality in Revolutionary Boston," *WMQ*, 3d Ser., XXVIII (1971), 375–412, proves that "inequality rapidly advanced in Boston during the Revolutionary period. Wealth was less evenly distributed than before the war, and the proportion of wealth held by the poor and middling classes declined" (p. 409). In Chester Co., Pa., a similar development took place through the entire 18th century, accelerated by the Revolution; cf. James T. Lemon and Gary B. Nash, "The Distribution of Wealth in Eighteenth-Century America: A Century of Change in Chester County, Pennsylvania, 1693–1802," *Journal of Social History*, II (1968–1969), esp. 10–14, 24.

99. See Nye, *This Almost Chosen People*, 315. For an example of the different views on political equality compare the letters of John Adams to Francis Adrian Van der Kemp, Jan. 8, 1806, Sept. 1, 1812 (Letters to Van der Kemp, 45, 65, PHi, Philadelphia), and Benjamin Rush to [Jacob Rush], Jan. 19, 1769, in Butterfield, ed., *Letters of Benjamin Rush*, I, 72.

100. Brooke Hindle, "The March of the Paxton Boys," *WMQ*, 3d Ser., III (1946), 461–486. See also, more recently, James H. Hutson, "An Investigation of the Inarticulate: Philadelphia's White Oaks," *ibid.*, XXVIII (1971), 14–17, and Hutson, *Pennsylvania Politics, 1746–1770: The Movement for Royal Government and its Consequences* (Princeton, N.J., 1972), 84–121.

101. See among others: three works by Merrill Jensen, *The Articles of Confederation: An Interpretation of the Social-Constitutional History of the American Revolution, 1774–1781* (Madison, Wis., 1940), 6–7, *The Founding of a Nation: A History of the American Revolution, 1763–1776* (New York, 1968), 662, and "The American People and the American Revolution," *Journal of American History*, LVII (1970–1971), 3–35; three by Richard B. Morris, *The American Revolution: A Short History* (New York, 1955), 83–86, "Class Struggle and the American Revolution," *WMQ*, 3d Ser., XIX (1962), 3–29, and *American Revolution Reconsidered*, 68; Edmund S. Morgan, *The Birth of the Republic, 1763–89* (Chicago, 1956), 99–100; Frederick B. Tolles, "The American Revolution Considered as a Social Movement: A Re-evaluation," *AHR*, LX (1954–1955), 1–12; Chilton Williamson, *American Suffrage:*

At this time the black population constituted nearly one-fifth of the inhabitants of the thirteen colonies and consisted almost exclusively of slaves. Their economic, social, and political status remained essentially untouched by events, showing that the ideology propounded by the American patriots was conservative as compared with the French Revolution, which abolished slavery, and that the American Revolution was not supported by the lofty ideal of creating a society of political equals. Even Thomas Jefferson, a leading theoretician and staunch follower of the Enlightenment, was convinced of the inferiority of his black countrymen.[102] In spite of his wordy pleas for humanity and human dignity, he personally was unable to act accordingly to free his own slaves.[103] In view of this contradiction in the thought and behavior of one of the leading representatives of the Enlightenment in the New World, it is perhaps understandable that the German bourgeoisie, influenced by the Enlightenment, paid little attention to the slavery problem in America and did not view emancipation as a contemporary political goal.[104]

Yet the notion of equality was widespread in Germany in the 1770s. Although it was not as popular a conception as liberty, the idea of equality was closely linked with the philosophy of the Enlightenment. In those decades lively discussions on the question of equality were especially numerous

From Property to Democracy, 1760–1869 (Princeton, N.J., 1960), 96, 115–116; David Hawke, *In the Midst of a Revolution* (Philadelphia, 1961), *passim*; E. Wright, *Fabric of Freedom*, 140–146, 152–153; Ostrander, *Rights of Man in America*, 95–118; three works by Jackson Turner Main, *The Social Structure of Revolutionary America* (Princeton, N.J., 1965), *passim*, *The Upper House in Revolutionary America 1763–1788* (Madison, Wis., 1967), esp. 188, and "The Results of the American Revolution Reconsidered," *Historian*, XXXI (1968–1969), 542–543; Lacy, *Meaning of the American Revolution*, 216–236, 282–283; Dumbauld, *Declaration of Independence*, 56–58; Jesse Lemisch, "The American Revolution Seen from the Bottom Up," in Barton J. Bernstein, ed., *Towards a New Past* (New York, 1968), 3–45; John R. Alden, *A History of the American Revolution* (New York, 1969), 348–369.

102. Winthrop D. Jordan, *White over Black: American Attitudes Toward the Negro, 1550–1812* (Chapel Hill, N.C., 1968), 435–440; William Cohen, "Thomas Jefferson and the Problem of Slavery," *Journal of American History*, LVI (1969–1970), 503–526; and, more generally, Benjamin Quarles, *The Negro in the American Revolution* (Chapel Hill, N.C., 1961), 182–200.

103. For similar reasoning see Bloch, *Naturrecht und menschliche Würde*, 189–190.

104. Among the relatively small number of related books are Sprengel, *Ursprung des Negerhandels*; Johann Gottlieb Franz Friedrich Koch, *Versuch eines Kriegs-Rechts der Negern in Afrika und Indianer in Amerika* . . . (Tübingen, 1781); [Johann Ernst Kolb], *Erzählungen von den Sitten und Schiksalen der Negersklaven* . . . (Bern, 1789); Alexander Falconbridge and Thomas Clarkson, *Bemerkungen über die gegenwärtige Beschaffenheit des Sclavenhandels und dessen politische Nachtheile für England*, trans. from the English by Matthias Christian Sprengel (Leipzig, 1790); Johann Jakob Sell, *Versuch einer Geschichte des Negersclavenhandels* (Halle, 1791). The tendency of these books is generally historical or moralistic.

in France.[105] The Dijon Academy prize question of 1753 comes to mind, and Rousseau's famous answer, the *Discours sur l'origine et les fondements de l'inégalité parmi les hommes*, which was widely read in Germany. His *Contrat social* also often dealt with this problem.[106] As in France, though not to the same extent, *equality* had become a fashionable word in Germany in the 1760s and 1770s.[107]

The idea of equality became associated with the American Revolution somewhat later than the idea of liberty. It was not used in that context until the end of the 1770s, and then mostly by antagonists of the Revolution, who publicly voiced the view that in America one could see developing "the fanciful principles of absolute equality."[108] In Germany, as in France, the association of America with the idea of equality spread so rapidly during the following years that there was no longer a need to adduce reasons for this conviction. Mirabeau for one merely stated: "Natural equality, political equality, civil equality: These are the tenets of the American legislators."[109] Surely, this interpretation was of signal importance when *égalité* was chosen to be one of the slogans of the French Revolution. And, as we have noted, an increasing number of Germans believed that the idea of equality was connected with the American Revolution.[110] Thus, Filippo Mazzei, originally from Florence and an American by choice, quickly found adherents to his idea that the United States was a country "where freedom and equality are

105. See among others Jacob L. Talmon, *The Origins of Totalitarian Democracy* (London, 1952); Echeverria, *Mirage in the West*, 35; Bernhard Weissel, *Von wem die Gewalt in den Staaten herrührt. Beiträge zu den Auswirkungen der Staats- und Gesellschaftsauffassungen Rousseaus auf Deutschland im letzten Viertel des 18. Jahrhunderts* (Berlin, 1963), 67–68, 70–72; Sanford A. Lakoff, *Equality in Political Philosophy* (Cambridge, Mass., 1964), 89–125; Artur Greive, "Die Entstehung der französischen Revolutionsparole 'Liberté, Egalité, Fraternité,'" *Deutsche Vierteljahrsschrift für Literaturwissenschaft und Geistesgeschichte*, XLIII (1969), 735–741.

106. Jean Jacques Rousseau, "Discours" (1755), "Contrat social" (1762), bk. I, chap. 9, bk. II, chaps. 4, 11, bk. III, chaps. 1, 4, and *passim*, in Rousseau, *Oeuvres complètes*, ed. Bernard Gagnebin and Marcel Raymond, III (Paris, 1964), 111–237, 367, 373, 391–392, 397, 405. Regarding the "Discours," see also Lessing's review in the *Berlinische Privilegierte Zeitung*, July 10, 1755, reprinted in Lessing, *Werke*, ed. Göpfert, III, 251–252.

107. Stammler, "Politische Schlagworte," 232–239.

108. "die schwärmerischen Grundsätze einer völligen Gleichheit": Geschichte der en-gländischen Colonien und des Krieges Englands mit denselben," *Militärischer Almanach auf das Jahr 1780* (Leipzig, n.d.), 243.

109. "Natürliche Gleichheit, politische Gleichheit, bürgerliche Gleichheit: Das ist die Lehre der amerikanischen Gesetzgeber": Mirabeau, *Sammlung einiger Schriften*, 28.

110. See among others *Anmerkungen aus der neuen und alten Welt bey Gelegenheit der Beschreibung des Siebenjährigen Seekrieges zwischen England und den amerikanischen Staaten . . .* (Berlin, 1786), 2d ed. (Berlin, 1788), both p. 36; also Christoph Daniel Ebeling's comment on the National Bank of America, in Johann Georg Büsch and Ebeling, eds., *Handlungsbibliothek*, 3 vols. (Hamburg, 1785–1797), II (1789), 159–160.

the cornerstones of the Constitution."[111] In the early 1790s Georg Forster held quite similar views.[112] But we will have to go a step further to learn why so many Europeans thought that the principle of equality had materialized in the United States.

As the European *ancien régime* saw it, the lack of any kind of legal aristocracy constituted incontrovertible proof that "sweet equality dwelt" in the new republic.[113] "The states want to smother patricians and nobles at birth and will not put up with them."[114] Among the bourgeoisie, of course, there was little resistance to this kind of equality.[115] An enlightened age, that stressed reason and everything reasonable approved highly of this lack of social privileges and estates, although their existence was the rule in Germany as well as in France. This "equality of estates,"[116] which knew no privileges contrary to reason, seemed almost an earthly paradise to many members of the bourgeoisie. "The American state, where there is a general equality of estates, where birth is nothing and merit is everything, will be mankind's happiest land, a country where happiness and joy smile on the citizens of this world who are so often driven away from home by prejudices of birth and rank."[117] In America each individual appeared to be his own master, and

111. "wo Freiheit und Gleichheit die Grundpfeiler der Verfassung sind": Mazzei, *Geschichte und Staatsverfassung*, II, 100; cf. 227. See also Delacroix, *Verfassung*, II, 271; *Entwurf der neuesten Culturgeschichte*, 13.

112. Georg Forster, *Kleine Schriften*, III, 155–156; see also *Berlinische Monatsschrift*, Nov. 1796, 464.

113. "süße Gleichheit wohnet": "Die Freiheit Amerika's," *Berlinische Monatsschrift*, Apr. 1783, 390.

114. "Die Staaten wollen Patrizier und Adel in der Geburt ersticken und durchaus nicht leiden": *Historisches Portefeuille*, July 1784, 119; cf. Zinzendorf, Tagebuch, Dec. 29, 1783 (XXVIII, fols. 195v–196, HHStA, Vienna).

115. Cf. Justus Möser, *Sämtliche Werke*, ed. B. R. Abeken, 10 vols. (Berlin, 1842–1843), I, 425; Möser, *Werke*, ed. Akademie der Wissenschaften zu Göttingen (Oldenburg, 1944–), V, 214–217, VII, 30–31, 222–223, IX, 377. Möser postulated a pyramidal structure of the state and was therefore opposed to the absence of a nobility as well as to the equality of all citizens. See also Georg Kass, "Möser und Goethe" (publ. Ph.D. diss., University of Göttingen, 1909), 116–122; Franz Blanckmeister, "Justus Möser, der deutsche Patriot, als Apologet des Christentums," in *Sammlung von Vorträgen für das deutsche Volk*, ed. Wilhelm Fromm and Friedrich Pfaff, XIV, no. 10 (Heidelberg, 1885), 395–436. For another opposing voice see Schlözer to Woldemar Friedrich Graf von Schmettau, July 19, 1790, in C. von Schlözer, *August Ludwig von Schlözer*, II, 169.

116. "Gleichheit der Stände": Johann David Schoepf, *Von der Wirkung des Mohnsafts in der Lustseuche*, ed. Heinrich Friedrich von Delius (Erlangen, 1781), 35. See also Ingenhousz, "Remarques," 13 (HHStA, Vienna); *Entwurf der neuesten Culturgeschichte*, 21.

117. "Der amerikanische Staat, wo eine allgemeine Gleichheit der Stände herrscht, wo Geburt nichts und Verdienst alles entscheidet, wird der glücklichste Aufenthalt des Menschengeschlechts und der Ort werden, wo Glück und Freude auf allen Fluren den Weltbürgern entgegenlächelt, die so oft durch die Vorurteile der Geburt und des Ranges verscheucht werden": Julius Friedrich Knüppeln, *Die Rechte der Natur und Menschheit, ent-*

eventually a trustee of American liberty,[118] since there were no limits to personal development and everybody enjoyed the same rights.[119] Apart from the blacks, these aspects of civil and legal equality were indeed to be found throughout the America of those years. But they had existed even before 1776. They were not, as was often wrongly assumed,[120] a result of the American Revolution.

America's antagonists frequently referred to another aspect of New World society in order to justify their argument that the insurgents were striving for complete equality contrary to nature. At a time when even one of the most enlightened German sovereigns did not permit anyone of less than noble birth to become a high-ranking officer in his army,[121] most of the American generals, as judged by their professional and social status, came from the lower strata of society.[122] "A farmer, now an officer"[123] was an idea that to them seemed militarily and socially grotesque and nonsensical. The best example of this situation was General Benedict Arnold, who was said to have been a horse trader in civilian life.[124] To the opponents of the American Revolution, these conditions were an expression of complete equality, if not anarchy, and ran completely contrary to all their principles of an orderly state.

A third aspect of American society, the idea of political equality, was of a

---

weiht durch Menschen. Szenen aus der heutigen Welt, für den Menschen, Bürger und Richter (Berlin, 1784), 147.

118. Seidel, "Staatsverfassung," in Ramsay, Amerikanische Revolution, IV, 15; Entwurf der neuesten Culturgeschichte, 19.

119. Michel Guillaume Hector St. John de Crèvecoeur, Sittliche Schilderung von Amerika, in Briefen eines Amerikanischen Guthsbesitzers, trans. from the English by Karl Gottfried Schreiter (Liegnitz and Leipzig, 1784), 102–103. Cf. the other edition of this work, Briefe eines Amerikanischen Landmanns, III, 502; Berichte über den Genesee-Distrikt, 21.

120. See among others Friedrich Gentz, "Über die Moralität in den Staatsrevolutionen," in his Betrachtungen über die französische Revolution. Nach dem Englischen des Herrn Burke (Berlin, 1793), II, 165–166.

121. Frederick II to his minister in Russia, Viktor Friedrich Graf Solms zu Sonnenwalde, July 26, 1774, in Volz, ed., Politische Correspondenz Friedrichs des Grossen, XXXV, 453. See also Vierhaus, "Deutschland vor der Französischen Revolution," 197.

122. Cf. the list of American generals, including their civil occupations, as it appeared in Schlözer, ed., Briefwechsel meist historischen und politischen Inhalts, VIII, no. 43 (1781), 3–5. Schlözer received his information from Sweden; cf. Harald Elovson, Amerika i svensk litteratur 1750–1820. En Studie i komparativ litteraturhistoria (Lund, 1930), 99. Duke Ludwig Ernst of Brunswick found this list so interesting that he had a copy made of it (1 Alt 22, no. 854, StA, Wolfenbüttel).

123. "Der Bauer, jetzo Offizier": Bartholomäi, Eroberung von Charlestown, 61.

124. See among others "Journal vom 15ten Mertz 1776 an," entry of June 2, 1776 (MS no. 1640, p. 57, Geschichtsverein, Hanau; copy in LC, Washington, D.C.); Haller to Gemmingen, Nov. 5, 1777, in Haller, Briefwechsel mit Gemmingen, 138; also J. G. Zimmermann to Jean André de Luc, Nov. 7, 1777 (StA, Aarau).

Figure 12. Capture of Major John André at Tarrytown, September 23, 1780. "Major André, captured by three Americans at Tarrytown, September 23, 1780." (Chodowiecki, for Sprengel, *Allgemeines historisches Taschenbuch*.)

Courtesy John Carter Brown Library, Brown University, Providence, R.I.

different nature altogether. It was the most difficult of all to relate to the Europe of the time, and it seems to have inspired little discussion in German-speaking countries. Hardly anyone took a firm stand on the principles involved, and those who did rejected them.[125] Only a few contemporaries drew conclusions from the apparent political equality in America or attempted to explain it; Adam Smith was among the foreigners who commented on it and whose works were also read in Germany.[126] An officer from Ansbach gave his view of the consequences of the Revolution: "Congress consists mostly of people who before this war either were nobody or had nothing."[127] An assertion like this was surely justified in individual cases, but generalized as it is here, it is hardly a true interpretation. Nevertheless, it is remarkable that some contemporaries realized that the Revolution brought about some social changes that moved the United States somewhat closer to the establishment of full political equality.

There is one opinion among all these that deserves special mention. Matthias Christian Sprengel, who had so clearly affirmed the existence of ideals in the American Revolution beyond simply political interests, did not merely believe that the Americans had expanded the measure of their liberty and abolished social classes and hereditary privileges; he was convinced that one result of the Revolution meant complete political equality. "Any citizen with understanding, knowledge, and the capacity for action can claim a post as a member of government, or a deputy in Congress, or its president."[128] This assumption hinted at a development altogether unthinkable under European conditions. It was so far beyond the range of experience and imagination of the average member of the German bourgeoisie that it found hardly any response. Only at the time of the French Revolution, with the resulting political

125. E.g., Johannes von Müller, "Politisch-philosophische Betrachtungen, 1774–1776," 100 (Msc. Mü. 22, StadtB, Schaffhausen); Johann Caspar Ruef, "Freyheit des Glaubens in Amerika" (UB, Freiburg, Germany); Oskar Vogt, *Der goldene Spiegel" und Wielands politische Ansichten* (Berlin, 1904), 67–69, 76. On Wieland's *Goldener Spiegel* see among others Vierhaus, "Deutschland vor der Französischen Revolution," 184–185.

126. [Adam Smith], *Abhandlungen über die Colonien überhaupt und die Amerikanischen besonders* (Bern, 1779), 120.

127. "Erstlich bestehet der Kongreß aus Leuten, die vor diesem Kriege entweder nichts waren oder nichts hatten": "Zustand des Amerikanischen Krieges in der ersten Hälfte des Jahrs 1781, von einem ansbachischen Offizier," in Johann Georg Meusel, ed., *Historische Litteratur*, Dec. 1781, 558. See also François Jean, marquis de Chastellux, *Reisebeobachtungen über Amerika*, trans. from the French (Hamburg, 1785), 171. Only a few hints are in Schoepf, *Reise*, I, 513, 566.

128. "Jeder Einwohner von Einsicht, Kenntnissen und Tätigkeit kann auf die Stelle eines Gliedes der Regierung, eines Deputierten im Kongreß oder dessen Präsidenten Anspruch machen": Sprengel, *Allgemeines historisches Taschenbuch*, 147.

and intellectual changes, did this somewhat too idealistic judgment of Sprengel's meet with increased interest and occasional counterstatement.[129]

Before Sprengel, only Schmohl wrote in a similar vein in Germany, but his position was more consequential than Sprengel's. Schmohl started from the idea of democracy, which to him was synonymous with complete equality. He believed, however, that neither could exist in its absolute form. Reduced to what was practical in reality, democracy was to him the best political order, since it held the smallest measure of inequality.[130] "No government as yet has . . . approached the ideal of pure democracy closer than the thirteen United States of North America, where every citizen is a warrior with a vote in the legislative body . . . where every head of family, with ability and merit, can rise to the very loftiest position, to president of the federal Congress."[131] Whereas Sprengel had treated this form of equality simply as an interesting phenomenon that did not deserve much attention and was not as important to him as the idea of liberty,[132] it was for Schmohl the overall central theme: a democratic state of citizens legally, politically, and socially equal.

Schmohl, and after him, Sprengel, were not the only ones who detected democratic structures in the United States.[133] But most other contemporary statements were more like hints, comparable to Sprengel's reference to the democratic constitutions of Rhode Island and Connecticut rather than to Schmohl's thorough understanding of political categories. Before 1789 the German bourgeoisie in general did not recognize the explosive potential of

129. Cf. Schlözer, ed., *Stats-Anzeigen*, IV, no. 13 (1783), 143; Georg to Therese Forster, Aug. 21, 1793, in G. Forster, *Briefwechsel*, ed. Huber, II, 551; Luigi, conte Castiglioni, *Reise durch die vereinigten Staaten von Nord-Amerika, in den Jahren 1785, 1786 und 1787*, trans. from the Italian by Magnus Petersen (Memmingen, 1793), I, 222–223; Seidel, "Staatsverfassung," in Ramsay, *Amerikanische Revolution*, IV, 11–14; E.A.W. Zimmermann, *Frankreich und die Freistaaten*, I, 2; Milbiller, *Allgemeine Geschichte: Vereinigten nordamerikanischen Provinzen*, II, 483–484; Remer, *Handbuch der neuern Geschichte*, 567; Remer, *Handbuch der Geschichte unserer Zeiten*, 39.
130. Schmohl, *Über Nordamerika und Demokratie*, 78–79, 126–127.
131. "Noch keine Regierung ist . . . dem Ideal der reinen Demokratie näher gewesen als die dreizehn Vereinigten Staaten in Nordamerika, wo jeder Bürger Kriegsmann ist und seine Stimme bei der gesetzgebenden Gewalt hat . . .; wo jedes Familienhaupt, hat es Kräfte und Verdienste darzu, noch zum Ersten, zum Präsidenten des Generalkongresses hinaufsteigen kann": *ibid.*, 188.
132. Sprengel, "Neuester Zustand von Connecticut," in J. R. Forster and Sprengel, eds., *Beiträge zur Völker und Länderkunde*, II (1782), 186; Sprengel, *Allgemeines historisches Taschenbuch*, 28, 45–46.
133. See among others Burke, *Europäischen Kolonien in Amerika*, II, 296–297; *Kurze Geographie von Asia, Afrika, Amerika und den Südländern* (Nuremberg, 1790), 400–401; Friedrich Osterwald, *Historische Erdbeschreibung . . .*, 5th ed. (Strasbourg, 1791), II, 114; Ebeling, *Erdbeschreibung*, I, 141–142.

such ideas. Thus, there was not much discussion about them in the 1770s and 1780s, and only a few voices were raised against democratic forms of government.[134]

Germans believed that the events in America were largely of a socio-revolutionary nature, without usually being clear in their own minds about the implications necessarily arising from such events. The average commentator was content to make noncommittal statements, and perceptive interpretations were rare. They either pointed to developments dating far back in colonial times or they overrated recent events. But the principal reason why the discussion of the problem of equality in the American Revolution fell short of its goal was the vagueness of the term *equality*. Most of the few definitions that were available did not go beyond Montesquieu, who already had stressed the close connection between democracy and equality and had defined the latter as equality before the law.[135] Since the term *political equality* meant next to nothing to the vast majority of the German bourgeoisie in the 1770s and 1780s, it was not discussed in any detail.[136] Most of the deliberations stopped at the idea of civil equality, in the sense of legal equality, and the abolition of privileges—and even these were never fully explored.

The analysis of equality as an essential principle of the American Revolution took a peculiar turn in German-speaking areas. Equality of economic opportunity, equality before the law, and the absence of a traditional class structure and of hereditary privileges had all existed before the Revolution more or less in their later form. The Revolution had merely made these ideas more intelligible to contemporaries. But the German bourgeoisie seized especially upon these ideas because they, more than anything else, conformed with their own ideals and fancies. In their eyes the American Revolution was directly associated with the implementation of civil or legal equality, and they greeted the Revolution with enthusiasm because it was said to serve this aim as well as that of liberty. True innovations in America in the field of political equality, such as the lowering of property qualifications for the suffrage, usually went almost completely unnoticed. Seen from the American point of view, the discussion in Germany on equality as a goal of the American Revolution left the decisive questions unasked and unanswered; but for

134. Cf. *Chronologen* (1781), XI, 81.

135. Montesquieu, "De l'esprit des lois," bk. V, chaps. 3–5, bk. VIII, chaps. 2–3, in his *Oeuvres complètes*, ed. Callois, II, 274–279, 349–352. See also *Deutsche Encyclopädie*, X (1785), 509a; *Schleswigsches ehemals Braunschweigisches Journal*, Sept. 1792, 67–68; *Entwurf der neuesten Culturgeschichte*, 16. On another aspect of civil equality in America—as equal chance in education—compare *Genius der Zeit*, Oct. 1795, 180.

136. E.g., [Johann Jakob Bodmer], *Haß der Tyranney und nicht der Person, Oder: Sarne durch List eingenommen* (n.p., 1775), 4; *Das graue Ungeheuer* (1784), III, 186.

an understanding of the German bourgeoisie, the discussion is of intrinsic importance.

Rights of Man

A proclamation of the rights of man is an essential characteristic of any modern constitutional state.[137] The American Revolution deserves credit for having propagated this idea with determination. Of course, concern for human rights was not exactly new in 1776; British legal thought had incorporated such concerns for a long time.[138] Also, in America, with certain limitations, they had been part of political practice before the Revolution, and they were understood to be part of the privileges of European settlers. Even so, what is meaningful about the Virginia Bill of Rights of June 12, 1776, and succeeding similar declarations is that their reasoning was no longer based on British legal thought but on natural law.[139] What was new was not the proclamation of certain liberties; these had been discussed in Europe as well, in connection with natural law theory. Even the changeover to arguing on the basis of the principles of natural law did not constitute a complete break with the past. The decisive difference from preceding discussions and uses was that these declarations made clear for the first time that

137. Carl Joachim Friedrich, *Der Verfassungsstaat der Neuzeit* (Berlin, 1953), 177–181; see also Bloch, *Naturrecht und menschliche Würde*, 79–81, 199–200.

138. Josef Bohatec, *England und die Geschichte der Menschen- und Bürgerrechte. Drei nachgelassene Aufsätze*, ed. Otto Weber (Graz and Cologne, 1956). See also, with illuminating sidelights on Switzerland, Fritz Ernst, *Die Sendung des Kleinstaats. Ansprachen und Aussprachen* (Zurich, 1940), 35–57.

139. See Benjamin F. Wright, Jr., *American Interpretations of Natural Law: A Study in the History of Political Thought* (Cambridge, Mass., 1931), 91–92, 98–99; Robert A. Rutland, *The Birth of the Bill of Rights 1776–1791* (Chapel Hill, N.C., 1955), 77; Gordon S. Wood, *The Creation of the American Republic, 1776–1787* (Chapel Hill, N.C., 1969), 271–273; Georg Jellinek, *Die Erklärung der Menschen- und Bürgerrechte*, 4th ed. (Munich, 1927), 2. Controversial opinions on the origins of the American Bills of Rights can be found in McIlwain, *American Revolution, passim*; Justus Hashagen, "Zur Entstehungsgeschichte der nordamerikanischen Erklärungen der Menschenrechte," *Zeitschrift für die gesamte Staatswissenschaft*, LXXVIII (1924), 461–495; Gustav Adolf Salander, *Vom Werden der Menschenrechte* (Leipzig, 1926); Otto Vossler, "Studien zur Erklärung der Menschenrechte," *HZ*, CXLII (1930), 516–545; Gerhard Ritter, "Ursprung und Wesen der Menschenrechte," *ibid.*, CLXIX (1949), 243–244; Gerhard Oestreich, *Die Idee der Menschenrechte in ihrer geschichtlichen Entwicklung* (Hanover, 1961); Oestreich, *Geschichte der Menschenrechte und Grundfreiheiten im Umriß* (Berlin, 1968), 57–63; also Sigmar-Jürgen Samwer, *Die französische Erklärung der Menschen- und Bürgerrechte von 1789/91* (Hamburg, 1970), 330–375.

these rights were to be considered binding. They were no longer understood to be privileges handed out most graciously by a ruling prince; rather, they were generally applicable, positive, legal rights that could be codified. As Georg Jellinek has shown, demands of that nature were unknown in Europe before 1776.[140]

Human rights became more and more important in the political thinking of the leading American patriots in the 1770s, although it is true that what was to become an essential part of constitutionalism under the slogan "rights of man," or "droits de l'homme et du citoyen," had not yet been defined in America in the mid-1770s. There was talk variously of "the rights of humanity,"[141] "the rights of human nature,"[142] and "the rights of mankind."[143] But the lack of a term generally accepted and used does not mean that the ideas connected with it did not constitute a concrete and articulate political program. It encompassed those "certain inalienable rights" that were mentioned in the Declaration of Independence and codified in the constitutions adopted by most of the individual states during the time of the Revolution, as well as in the supplementary articles of the federal Constitution of 1787. Thus, the absence of the term "rights of man" around the mid-1770s is only etymologically relevant at best.

Although ideas on natural rights had penetrated into Germany by 1776, they had failed to call forth a widespread response among the bourgeoisie. The way in which the bourgeoisie dealt with the declaration of human rights in the American Revolution is another example of their incapacity to grasp this problem.

Isaak Iselin, like several others at that time, had briefly mentioned the rights of man in his *Geschichte der Menschheit* as early as the first half of the 1760s.[144] In 1776, however, the American Revolution did not significantly stimulate interest in this idea in Germany. Only in 1782 did Johann Valentin

---

140. Jellinek, *Erklärung der Menschen- und Bürgerrechte*, 15. See also Jürgen Habermas, *Theorie und Praxis. Sozialphilosophische Studien*, 2d ed. (Neuwied, 1967), 52–61.

141. Patrick Henry to [?], Jan. 18, 1773, in Henry, *Patrick Henry: Life, Correspondence, and Speeches*, ed. William Wirt Henry, 3 vols. (New York, 1891), I, 152; John Adams to James Warren, Oct. 13, 1775, in *Warren-Adams Letters*, I, 137; R. H. Lee to Washington, Nov. 26, 1775, in Ballagh, ed., *Letters of Richard Henry Lee*, I, 159; A. Lee to the earl of Shelburne, Dec. 10, 1777 (Miscellaneous Papers of the Continental Congress, 1774–1789, M 332, Roll 3, NA, Washington, D.C.).

142. Boyd *et al.*, eds., *Jefferson Papers*, I, 134.

143. Samuel Adams to Warren, Apr. 17, 1777, in *Warren-Adams Letters*, I, 314; resolution of the New York convention, Aug. 2, 1776, in Force, ed., *American Archives*, 5th ser., I, 1470.

144. [Isaak Iselin], *Über die Geschichte der Menschheit*, 2 vols. (Frankfurt and Leipzig, 1764), II, 219 (the same phrase through all following editions). See also Oestreich, *Geschichte der Menschenrechte*, 55, 64–67.

Embser of Zweibrücken speak of "les droits sacrés de l'humanité" while referring to events in America.[145] Thereafter, up to the outbreak of the French Revolution, Germans more often connected the recent events in the Western Hemisphere with the assertion of human rights.[146] Though small, the increase was nonetheless noteworthy; it gave the impression that there had been "a great deal of discussion in our times" on the question. Moreover, the phrase was transferred to other situations, such as calling the defenders of serfdom in Mecklenburg "tyrants . . . who rebel against the rights of man."[147]

Yet the idea of human rights was not nearly as popular as the ideas of liberty and equality. Wolfgang Stammler probably goes too far when he calls the rights of man a "political slogan" or even a fashionable phrase in Germany before 1789.[148] On the whole, the discussion of human rights remained sporadic and limited to a few observers. In fact, the term itself, *human rights* or the *rights of man*, is encountered only rarely before the French Revolution. Discussion centered occasionally on "the rights of mankind," which in some instances was equated with international law.[149] In contrast to America, the uncertainty of the term in Europe was a consequence of the obvious obscurity of its definite meaning and confusion about the importance human rights might have in a political order. The rights of man were hardly understood to be a concrete political requisite of modern constitutionalism. The pertinent ideas lay dormant in "the writings of philosophers and economists,"[150] or

145. Embser to Franklin, Jan. 6, 1782 (Franklin Papers, XXIV, 10, APSL, Philadelphia).

146. E.g., Friedrich Aloys Graf von Brühl to Washington, Sept, 4, 1783 (Washington Papers, Reel 93, LC, Washington, D.C.); Martin Ernst von Schlieffen to Johannes von Müller, Dec. 3, 1783 (Msc. Mü. C/2a, 22, StadtB, Schaffhausen); Knüppeln, *Rechte der Natur und Menschheit*, 13–14; *Merkwürdige Schriften zum Andenken des philosophischen Jahrhunderts* (Nuremberg, 1785), 113; Bretzner, *Das Räuschgen*, 150–151; Price, "Americanische Revolution," in Mirabeau, *Sammlung einiger Schriften*, 157; [François Jean, marquis de Chastellux], *Abhandlung über die Vortheile und Nachtheile die für Europa aus der Entdekkung von Amerika entstehen*, trans. from the French by Johann August Eberhard (Halle, 1788), 80–81. See also Gottfried Heinrich Mauchart, *Uber die Rechte des Menschen vor seiner Geburt* (Frankfurt and Leipzig, 1782), a book written strictly in terms of law, with no mention of the political implications and the natural law aspects of the rights of man idea.

147. "in unsern Zeiten ziemlich auseinandergesetzt. . . . Tyrannen . . . sich gegen die Menschenrechte empören": *Bibliothek für Denker* (1785), III, no. 2, 175.

148. Stammler, "Politische Schlagworte," in *Lebenskräfte der abendländischen Geistesgeschichte*, 247–252. Ernst Cassirer, *Die Philosophie der Aufklärung*, 2d ed. (Tübingen, 1932), 332–339, gives only French examples to prove the acceptance of the idea of the rights of man by the Enlightenment.

149. Cf. August Hennings, *Sammlung von Staatsschriften, die, während des Seekrieges von 1776 bis 1783 . . . öffentlich bekannt gemacht worden sind . . .*, 2 vols.(Altona, 1784–1785), I/1, 5: "Die Rechte der Völker oder, welches einerlei ist, die Rechte der Menschheit. . . ."

150. "in den Schriften der Philosophen und Ökonomen": *Europäische Annalen*, May 1795, 102.

else contemporaries thought these rights to be "not a historical fact but an ethical imperative," as Ernst Cassirer has put it.[151]

This situation did not change until the outbreak of the French Revolution and its "Déclaration des droits de l'homme et du citoyen." It was only then, and not ten years earlier, as Ernst Ludwig Posselt believed in retrospect, that the rights of man became "a topic of daily conversation."[152] When the *Berlinische Monatsschrift*, a leading voice of the Enlightenment, offered a platform for the discussion of the problems confronting the public, there appeared, in June 1790, Justus Möser's essay "On the Right of Humanity as the Basis of the New French Constitution."[153] Yet Möser, who was not uninformed about the American Revolution, knew nothing about the idea of the rights of man in the United States. He saw them only in France. A reply to Möser's article did not contain a single word about America, even though the author tried to dispute the uniqueness of the French declaration of human rights by adducing examples from history.[154] Eventually, the editor, Johann Erich Biester, entered the fray, declaring formally that the entire discussion belonged in the field of pure theory and not in that of practical politics: "As everybody knows, philosophers dispute whether there is such a right or not; and this dispute can only concern philosophers, since we have had no experience with such a pure state of mankind and nature, it being mere metaphysical speculation."[155]

This noticeable misinterpretation of the political reality in America and France makes clear how ineffective the American Revolution was in this respect. The belief that human rights were discussed in the United States only after the French Revolution was held even by a man like Dietrich Heinrich Freiherr von Bülow, who, having spent some very busy years in America at the end of the century, was much preoccupied with the young republic.[156] It may well be true that the term *rights of man* did not appear in America until after the French Revolution, but that is hardly relevant since the idea was

151. Ernst Cassirer, *Die Idee der republikanischen Verfassung. Rede zur Verfassungsfeier am 11. August 1928* (Hamburg, 1929), 24.
152. "der Stoff aller Tagesgespräche": *Europäische Annalen*, May 1795, 102.
153. *Berlinische Monatsschrift*, June 1790, 499–506. Möser's article appeared first in the *Westfälische Beiträge*, Apr. 17, 1790, cols. 121–128. It is reprinted in his *Werke*, ed. Akademie der Wissenschaften, IX, esp. 140.
154. Cf. the article by Eduard von Clauer in *Berlinische Monatsschrift*, Sept. 1790, 197–209.
155. "Bekanntlich streiten die Philosophen, ob es ein solches Recht gibt; und dieser Streit kann auch bloß für die Philosophen gehören, da die Erfahrung uns nirgend einen so reinen Stand der Menschheit und Natur gezeigt hat, sondern derselbe bloß eine metaphysische Spekulation ist": Biester, *ibid.*, 210.
156. Bülow, *Freistaat von Nordamerika*, II, 232.

pervasive.[157] In the 1790s, as compared with the 1780s, we find even fewer German commentators who saw any connection between the idea of human rights, the events of the previous two decades, and the new American constitutions.[158] Thus, the German bourgeoisie accorded much less importance to the idea of the rights of man in the American Revolution than had the Americans themselves.

Republicanism

Comparable to later developments in France, but in contrast to the early concern with liberty, republicanism was not one of the American patriots' original demands. However, with the striving for independence and the concomitant question of a new national order, republicanism began to be discussed as a revolutionary goal. "The first question that offers itself is, whether the general form and aspect of government be strictly republican? It is evident that no other form would be reconcilable with the genius of the people of America; with the fundamental principles of the revolution."[159] According to these words of Madison's in Federalist No. 39, there was practically no other choice once the principles of the English constitution had been abandoned. In view of the complexity of the idea as it was understood in America, this program meant much more than the mere renunciation of a monarch. The novel element in this political aim was, first of all, that a republican system was interpreted as vesting the people with the power of government as an institutional safeguard against any form of arbitrary power. Second, republicanism implied the general and equal rule of law. Thus, the demand for a republic cannot really pass for an additional revolutionary ideal; rather, it was a consequence of the other principles and was closely connected with them.[160]

157. Perhaps the term *rights of man* made its appearance in America only as a translation of the French *les droits de l'homme*. Jefferson at least seems to have grown confident with the term only during his very last years in France; cf. Jefferson to the citizens of Albemarle Co., Va., Feb. 12, 1790, in Boyd *et al.*, eds., *Jefferson Papers*, XVI, 179.

158. E.g., Delacroix, *Verfassung*, II, 287; "Nachricht von der Stadt Washington in dem Gebiet Columbia," in Sprengel, ed., *Auswahl der besten ausländischen geographischen und statistischen Nachrichten*, V (1796), 231–232; *Entwurf der neuesten Culturgeschichte*, 6–7.

159. James Madison, Federalist No. 39, in *The Federalist*, ed. Cooke, 250.

160. On republicanism and its importance in the American Revolution see among others Jefferson to Franklin, Aug. 13, 1777, in Boyd *et al.*, eds., *Jefferson Papers*, II, 27; Rush to Horatio Gates, Sept. 5, 1781, in Butterfield, ed., *Letters of Benjamin Rush*, I, 265. Also

Neither in theory nor in practice was the idea of a republican state unknown in Europe. The free imperial cities of Germany, the members of the Swiss confederation, Geneva, the Italian city-states, the Republic of the United Netherlands, and even Poland, are examples. There was also the England of the Puritan revolution and, finally, going further back in history, Rome's republican era and the Greek city-states of classical antiquity. Republicanism was also discussed in theory (though not as much as liberty and equality), especially in Switzerland and France.[161] But with the exception of the few republican structures within the German-language area, republicanism seems to have been regarded in Germany in the 1770s only incidentally as a question of imminent practical politics. More often, republicanism was treated as a moral and intellectual problem, as had also been done in the 1760s.

When practical politics were involved, the word changed color frequently. Sometimes, as was the case when Poland was called a republic, it merely meant a form of government in contrast to the reign of an individual. Others interpreted it as a particularly desirable structure of government, as the Americans did and as Rousseau had done before them, bringing together the term *republic* with *liberty* and *justice*.[162] Despite all of this, most Euro-

---

George M. Dutcher, "The Rise of Republican Government in the United States," *Political Science Quarterly*, LV (1940), 214; Cecelia M. Kenyon, "Republicanism and Radicalism in the American Revolution: An Old-Fashioned Interpretation," *WMQ*, 3d Ser., XIX (1962), 165, 167–169; Wood, *Creation of the American Republic*, 46–90; Willi Paul Adams, "Republicanism in Political Rhetoric Before 1776," *Political Science Quarterly*, LXXXV (1970), 406–421; Adams, *Republikanische Verfassung und bürgerliche Freiheit. Die Verfassungen und politischen Ideen der amerikanischen Revolution* (Darmstadt and Neuwied, 1973; forthcoming English ed.); Stourzh, *Hamilton and Republican Government*, 40–70; Robert E. Shalhope, "Toward a Republican Synthesis: The Emergence of an Understanding of Republicanism in American Historiography," *WMQ*, 3d Ser., XXIX (1972), 49–80; Pauline Maier, "The Beginnings of American Republicanism 1765–1776," in *The Development of a Revolutionary Mentality*, Library of Congress Symposia on the American Revolution (Washington, D.C., 1972), 99–117; Jack P. Greene, "The Preconditions for American Republicanism: A Comment," *ibid.*, 119–124.

161. See among others Montesquieu, "De l'esprit des lois," bk. VIII, chap. 16, in his *Oeuvres complètes*, ed. Caillois, II, 362, and Rousseau, "Contrat social," bk. II, chap. 6, in his *Oeuvres complètes*, ed. Gagnebin and Raymond, III, 380. The first version of the "Contrat social" appeared with the subtitle, "ou Essai de la forme de la république." See also Rousseau's "Considérations sur le gouvernement de Pologne," in *ibid.*, 966, and Jacques Godechot, *La Contre-Révolution. Doctrine et action 1789–1804* (Paris, 1961), 13, 41–42. Julku, *Revolutionäre Bewegung im Rheinland*, I, 136, is of opinion that republican ideas were widespread in the Rhineland during the 1770s and 1780s.

162. Rousseau, "Considération sur le gouvernement de Pologne" (1771/1782), in his *Oeuvres complètes*, ed. Gagnebin and Raymond, III, 966; cf. his "Contrat social," bk. II, chap. 6, *ibid.*, 380. Similarly, a little later, Kant, "Zum ewigen Frieden" (1795), in his *Werke*, ed. Weischedel, VI, 204–208, and Friedrich Schlegel, "Versuch über den Begriff des Republikanismus" (1796), in his *Kritische Ausgabe*, ed. Ernst Behler (Munich, 1958–), I/VII, 11–25.

Figure 13. Surrender at Yorktown, October 19, 1781. "The Americans take Lord Cornwallis and his army prisoners, at Yorktown, October 19, 1781." (Chodowiecki, for Sprengel, *Allgemeines historisches Taschenbuch*.)

Courtesy John Carter Brown Library, Brown University, Providence, R.I.

peans shared Montesquieu's authoritative and apodictic conviction that "it is the nature of a republic to comprise only a small territory."[163] If we further take into account the general ill repute in which republics were held—as unstable states exposed to collapse—the establishment of a republic in North America was in every way an epoch-making event.

At first, the reaction of the German bourgeoisie to this event seems in no way appropriate to its outstanding and fundamental importance. To be sure, in Switzerland and in the other German-speaking territories there were several prominent personalities in the 1770s and 1780s who were excited about questions of governmental structure, figures such as Justus Möser, Ewald Friedrich Graf von Hertzberg, Friedrich Karl Freiherr von Moser, and August Ludwig von Schlözer.[164] Their deliberations were doubtlessly inspired by events in America. Yet in large sections of the bourgeoisie there was no serious public discussion of these matters. In direct reference to the problems raised by America, there were at first only a number of skeptical statements either doubting the durability of the experiment,[165] or disputing outright all possible advantages of a republic.[166] It is not surprising that there was widespread condemnation of the republican idea among the nobility and among the upper layers of the bourgeoisie. In their argumentation they could easily refer to examples in history and to Montesquieu. As Schubart pointed out, similar arguments were being used up to the mid-1770s by the advocates of Britain and its "mixed constitution," which included a monarch.[167]

Eventually, however, the American Revolution produced a decisive change, for the enthusiasm of the bourgeoisie did not stop with the peace of 1783 but carried over without break to the new state that was the product of this revolution. Whether this state was called "republican"[168] or a "demo-

---

163. Montesquieu, "De l'esprit des lois," bk. VIII, chap. 16, in his *Oeuvres complètes*, ed. Caillois, II, 362.

164. Möser, "Patriotische Phantasien und verwandte Handschriften," in his *Werke*, ed. Akademie der Wissenschaften, V, 214–217, VII, 222–223, IX, 377; Schmohl, *Über Nordamerika und Demokratie*, 62; Hertzberg, "Sur la forme des Gouvernemens, et quelle est la meilleure?" (1784), in his *Huits Dissertations* . . . (Berlin, 1787), esp. 147; Moser, *Regenten, Regierung und Ministers, passim*; *Merkwürdige Schriften*, 170; Schlözer, "Regierungsformen," and "Politik" (both in KB, Aarau).

165. E.g., Schubart, ed., *Deutsche Chronik*, Oct. 10, 1774, 441–442; Erich Franzen, "Europa blickt auf Amerika," *Der Monat*, V (1952), 132; Hertzberg, *Huits Dissertations*, 147. See also J. Q. Adams on his conversation with Prince Heinrich of Prussia, Dec. 8, 1797, in Charles Francis Adams, ed., *Memoirs of John Quincy Adams, Comprising Portions of his Diary from 1795–1848*, 12 vols. (Philadelphia, 1874–1877), I, 210.

166. E.g., Schlieffen, *Von den Hessen in Amerika*, 19–21.

167. Cf. W. P. Adams, "Republicanism in Political Rhetoric," *Political Science Quarterly*, LXXXV (1970), 398–399.

168. "republikanisch": *Beschreibung der dreizehn unabhängigen Nordamerikanischen Staaten*, 58.

cratic free state,"[169] it had the same measure of sympathy from its enlightened contemporaries as the Revolution had had before. Schubart, as well as other protagonists of the American Revolution, thought it no longer necessary to be skeptical and saw no reason for doubts about the future of the new republic.

For large circles in Germany after 1783 the idea of a republic had generally lost its negative and derogatory flavor, not because the idea of republicanism had been adequately expounded in the meantime, but because in America there had been born a new state based on liberty. Since many thought of themselves as adherents of the ideal of liberty, which had been realized in America, they could no longer reject republicanism, the result of this realization. This change in attitude toward a republican structure of government can doubtlessly be ascribed to the American Revolution, but it differs markedly from the changes in German thinking we have already noted. Although the announced principles of the Revolution clearly encouraged the ideals of liberty and equality in Germany (without having much influence on the doctrine of the rights of man), it was the practical embodiment of revolutionary ideas and actions that evoked a change of attitude toward republicanism. Before 1776, republicanism was not even a subject of controversy in Germany; the sudden shift in thinking could hardly have been brought about by purely theoretical dispute.

Popular Sovereignty and Other Principles

One of the most significant permanent political achievements of the American Revolution was the elevation of the idea of popular sovereignty to the status of a concrete constitutional principle. This idea had emerged in the colonies during the early years of the dispute with England and had spread as the years went by. The new constitutions of the individual states, formulated "under the authority of the people," and the Declaration of Independence and the federal Constitution of 1787 all illustrate the use of the principle.[170]

169. "demokratischer Freistaat": *Kurze Geographie*, 400.
170. J. Adams to Isaac Smith, Sr., June 1, 1776, in Butterfield *et al.*, eds., *Adams Family Correspondence*, II, 1. See also Miller, *Triumph of Freedom*, 687; Merrill Jensen's commentary in Randolph Greenfield Adams, *Political Ideas of the American Revolution: Britannic-American Contributions to the Problem of Imperial Organization 1765 to 1775*, 3d ed. (New York, 1958), 30–31; Bailyn, *Ideological Origins*, 228; W. P. Adams, *Republikanische Verfassung*, 121–140; Wood, *Creation of the American Republic*, 344–389; Stourzh, *Hamilton and*

It was the proclamation of this principle as the basis of all governmental power that, according to Jefferson, constituted the fundamental difference between the American theory of the state and that of European absolutism. Jefferson believed that the liberty of a nation can be permanently safe from outbreaks of despotism only if the people can effectively control the government. If there is no control, he warned, an unbridgeable rift between the ruling and the ruled is bound to occur, which would be equally detrimental to the welfare of the state and to the liberty of the citizens.[171] But if the idea of popular sovereignty constitutes "the culminating point of the revolutionary principle in America,"[172] it also presents us with the central theme for answering the question of the German bourgeoisie's understanding of the American Revolution.

The idea of popular sovereignty was doubtlessly not American in origin. In the discussion about state law and natural law it had turned up again and again in recent times, from the monarchomachists to Rousseau.[173] Yet at the time of the American Revolution the diffusion of the idea among the German bourgeoisie was limited and in no way comparable to that of the idea of liberty. If popular sovereignty was discussed at all, it was, like the idea of liberty, dealt with in the context of a political system of estates, for example, the sovereignty of "the burgers organized in a guild."[174]

It seems that the American Revolution did not do much in Germany to popularize the idea of the sovereignty of the people. The first to take up the notion were apparently the opponents of America, who could use it as another reason for condemning the Revolution, because—so they believed—a state "cannot flourish . . . where all authorities and persons in public office depend wholly on the people."[175] Of all the German protagonists of the

Republican Government, 48–56; and, with different emphasis, Buel, "Democracy and the American Revolution," WMQ, 3d Ser., XXI (1964), 179–180.

171. Jefferson to Edward Carrington, Jan. 16, 1787, in Boyd et al., eds., Jefferson Papers, XI, 48–49.

172. Elisabeth Charlotte Engel, "Über das Wesen der amerikanischen 'Revolution'," in Historische Forschungen und Probleme. Festschrift Peter Rassow (Wiesbaden, 1961), 211; cf. Wood, Creation of the American Republic, 354.

173. Cf. Wolzendorff, Staatsrecht und Naturrecht, 131–132, 351–359; Gierke, Althusius, 157–162; Wolf, Rechtsdenker, 189–192, 202; Robert Redslob, Die Staatstheorien der französischen Nationalversammlung von 1789 (Leipzig, 1912), 46–74; also Friedrich Hermann Schubert, "Volkssouveränität und Heiliges Römisches Reich," HZ, CCXIII (1971), 91–122.

174. "der zünftigen Bürgerschaft": Franz Dautzenberg, Oct. 1788, quoted in Hansen, ed., Quellen zur Geschichte des Rheinlandes, I, 319. See also Wolzendorff, Staatsrecht und Naturrecht, 132–134, and Schubert, "Volkssouveränität," HZ, CCXIII (1971), 95.

175. "nicht gedeihen kann . . . wo alle Obrigkeiten und Personen, die in Ämtern stehen, gänzlich vom Volke abhängen": Baumann, Staatsverfassung der vornehmsten Länder in Amerika, 700.

American Revolution, it was probably Schmohl who first emphatically mentioned the principle of popular sovereignty in America. True to his predecessors among the modern theoreticians of natural law, he was convinced "that originally (and historically!) the authorities of all peoples were elected by the members of the society itself as freely as is humanly possible."[176] In his eyes, the exemplary character of the American Revolution lay in its revival of this original right of all men and its use of "popular sovereignty" as a counterbalance to tyrannical usurpation of power.[177] With this interpretation, Schmohl came close to Jefferson's ideas.

But even Schmohl could not popularize in Germany the concept of the sovereignty of the people. It was not until the 1790s, under the impact of the French Revolution, that the idea became widespread. Even at this time, however, we find no explanation of the term with respect to its concrete political and constitutional significance.[178] The only effort at a meaningful explanation in the mid-1790s was probably made by Günther Karl Friedrich Seidel, who took up the original reproach cast by the antagonists of the American Revolution and divested it of all derogatory connotations. "It is a fundamental principle of the American Constitution that all power originally rests with the people and is delegated only by them; and that the various government officials holding legislative, executive, or judicative power are only the people's representatives and perpetually responsible to them."[179] Seidel's remark is reminiscent of a clause in the Virginia Bill of Rights of 1776: "That all power is vested in, and consequently derived from, the people; that magistrates are their trustees and servants, and at all times amenable to them."[180]

In general, then, the idea of popular sovereignty hardly penetrated the German bourgeoisie, at least not before 1789, although the Americans had emphatically propagated it and incorporated it into their new constitutions. However, it was not only the principle of popular sovereignty that was rela-

176. "daß die Obrigkeiten bei allen Völkern ursprünglich (und historisch!) mit aller unter Menschen möglichen Freiheit von den Gliedern der Gesellschaft selbst gewählt worden sind": Schmohl, *Über Nordamerika und Demokratie*, 7.

177. "Volkssouveränität": *ibid.*, 75; cf. p. 62 and *passim*.

178. *Europäische Annalen*, May 1795, 102; *Examen impartial*, 78; Milbiller, *Allgemeine Geschichte: Die vereinigten nordamerikanischen Provinzen*, II, 483. See also the short, paraphrasing remarks by Crèvecoeur, *Sittliche Schilderung von Amerika*, 102–103, and in his *Briefe eines Amerikanischen Landmanns*, III, 502; *Berichte über den Genesee-Distrikt*, 21.

179. "Es ist ein Fundamentalgrundsatz der amerikanischen Staatsverfassung, daß alle Gewalt ursprünglich in dem Volke ruht, und nur von ihm abgeleitet ist; und daß die verschiedenen Beamten der Regierung, welche die gesetzgebende, ausübende und richterliche Gewalt besitzen, nur die Stellvertreter des Volkes und demselben jedesmal verantwortlich sind": Seidel, "Staatsverfassung," in Ramsay, *Amerikanische Revolution*, IV, 27.

180. Virginia Bill of Rights, Sec. 2, in Thorpe, ed., *Federal and State Constitutions*, VII, 3813.

tively little discussed in Germany in those years. Federalism, too, was an idea known in Europe before the Articles of Confederation and the federal Constitution. It was mostly understood to be a synthesis of inner freedom with external power and security, arrived at by numerous small, free republics merging into a sufficiently large and powerful union.[181] Protagonists of this political structure had existed before 1776, not only in Switzerland and the Netherlands, but also in the American colonies.[182]

The majority of the German bourgeoisie could not see federalism as a matter of concern to them, although the Swiss viewed things somewhat differently. But the observers in both countries failed to develop an understanding of the tangible aspects of American federalism or the legal structure of the Union's constitution. The mere indication that the organization of the American republic "was very similar to the Swiss and former Batavian" organization was deemed sufficient.[183] The prevalent political understanding of the time was oriented toward the conception of "centralism" and its nominal opposite, "federalism." There was no such thing as our modern differentiation between a confederation and a federation of states, although the distinction could have been found in *The Federalist* if that publication had been known in Germany.[184]

Only a few German contemporaries ever arrived at a deeper understanding of the federalism established in the federal Constitution of 1787. Seidel, for example, declared: "Thus each individual state is a part dependent on the whole united body of states and is endowed with its own legislative, executive, and judicial power; but each state has only sufficient power to govern itself and promote the happiness of its people according to its local and special needs, without infringing on the rights of the entire federation. . . . The total power of all states is concentrated in the unified government of the

181. Montesquieu, "De l'esprit des lois," bk. IX, chaps. 1–3, in his *Oeuvres complètes*, ed. Caillois, II, 369–372; Rousseau, "Considérations sur le gouvernement de Pologne," in his *Oeuvres complètes*, ed. Gagnebin and Raymond, III, 1010. See also Maurice Möckli-Cellier, *La Révolution française et les écrivains suisses-romands (1789–1815) (groupe genevois)* (Paris, 1931), 18. This opinion is fully in line with the interpretation of the United States by Walther, *Neueste Erdkunde*, 251.

182. Stourzh, *Hamilton and Republican Government*, 153–161.

183. "große Ähnlichkeit mit der des Helvetischen und weiland Batavischen": [Raphael Kleinsorg], *Abriß der Geographie*, 3d ed., 2 vols. (Salzburg, 1797), II, 763. It may be noted that this or a similar wording is not found in a previous edition. For like opinions see Meister, *Historische Unterhaltungen*, 228–229; Friedrich Christian Franz, *Lehrbuch der Länder- und Völkerkunde in zween Theilen* (Stuttgart, 1788–1790), II, 216–217; *Beschreibung aller Länder und Völker der Erde zur Belehrung und Unterhaltung* (Halle, [1796]), 449.

184. On the scant influence of the American idea of federalism in Germany at the end of the 18th century see Rudolf Ullner, *Die Idee des Föderalismus im Jahrzehnt der deutschen Einigungskriege* (Lübeck and Hamburg, 1965), 10–13.

United States."[185] Johann Georg Büsch, co-director of the Hamburg Handlungsakademie, was aware of the political difficulties that had to be overcome in drafting this constitution. It was a question, he observed, of uniting the very "different interests of the states and giving sufficient power to the federal government, while not infringing too much on the individual states' sovereignty."[186] Though such explanations lacked concrete constitutional examples to back up their abstract formulation, they nevertheless came very close to the basic principle of the American state structure.

To the civilian leaders of the American Revolution the security of property was of decisive importance; in general, it was not to be violated but to be safeguarded, and especially against alleged British outrages.[187] The French *philosophes* had for some time been discussing the idea and the role of property. But even the French Revolution—with the exception of the unsuccessful faction represented by Babeuf and several others on the left—did not deny the right of private property, and expressly protected it in the convention's constitution of 1793.[188] Property was just as sacrosanct to the German bourgeoisie of the 1770s and 1780s, and they rightly did not believe that the unrestricted right to private property was jeopardized by the American Revolution, especially since protection of property had been one reason for resistance against British policy. That the loyalist question commanded no attention whatever in Germany may also have influenced their thinking.

185. "Ein jeder einzelner Staat ist also ein abhängiger Teil des ganzen vereinigten Staatenkörpers, der aber eine eigene gesetzgebende, ausübende und richterliche Gewalt besitzt, die zusammen nur so viel Macht in sich vereinen, daß sie ihn nach seinen örtlichen und besondern Bedürfnissen, ihrem eigenen Gutbefinden zufolge, im Innern regieren und seine innere Glückseligkeit, ohne die Rechte des ganzen Bundes zu schmälern, befördern können.... Die ganze Kraft aller einzelnen Staaten konzentriert sich aber in der Unionsregierung der Vereinigten Staaten": Seidel, "Staatsverfassung," in Ramsay, *Amerikanische Revolution*, IV, 6, cf. 7, 32, 48. See also Paine [pseud.], *Begebenheiten aller bisherigen Staaten*, II, 485.

186. "das so verschiedene Interesse der Staaten zu vereinigen, keinem seine Souveränität zu sehr zu schmälern und doch dem Bundesregiment Kraft zu geben": Büsch, *Grundriß einer Geschichte der merkwürdigsten Welthändel neuerer Zeit*, 3d ed. (Hamburg, 1796), 488, cf. 489, 492. Also Remer, *Lehrbuch der algemeinen Geschichte*, 629–630.

187. E.g., the New York petition to the House of Commons, Oct. 18, 1764, in Edmund S. Morgan, ed., *Prologue to Revolution: Sources and Documents on the Stamp Act Crisis, 1764–1766* (Chapel Hill, N.C., 1959), 9–10; *Bericht eines Englischen Amerikaners*, 5–6; Ramsay, *Amerikanische Revolution*, I, 246–247; Arthur M. Schlesinger, *Nothing Stands Still*, ed. Arthur M. Schlesinger, Jr. (Cambridge, Mass., 1969), 91; and the illuminating study by Hans-Christoph Schröder, "Das Eigentumsproblem in den Auseinandersetzungen um die Verfassung von Massachusetts, 1775–1787," in Rudolf Vierhaus, ed., *Eigentum und Verfassung. Zur Eigentumsdiskussion im ausgehenden 18. Jahrhundert* (Göttingen, 1972), 11–67.

188. Félicien Challaye, *Histoire de la propriété*, 4th ed. (Paris, 1948), 68–84; Richard Schlatter, *Private Property: The History of an Idea* (London, 1951), 218–231; Paschal Larkin, *Property in the Eighteenth Century with Special Reference to England and Locke*, 2d ed. (New York, 1969), 212–228.

When the question of property came under discussion, occasionally in Germany, or more often in France during its revolution, no one had the least doubt that events in America had come about to "secure property."[189]

A Novus Ordo Saeculorum

In *On Revolution* Hannah Arendt arrived at the conclusion that "only where this pathos of novelty is present and where novelty is connected with the idea of freedom are we entitled to speak of revolution."[190] Both factors are present in the American Revolution, even though its leaders carried over into the post-Revolutionary period many elements of the English constitution, as well as other traditional forms. For the first time, a large state was organized as a republic and built on a foundation of liberty, popular sovereignty, separation of powers, and rejection of privileges. A state structure unknown at the time became a reality in the federalism of the federal Constitution of 1787.

All of these developments were not the product of pure chance; they were zealously striven for by the leaders of the American Revolution.[191] William Shippen remarked on this deliberate process: "I mean an opportunity of forming a plan of Government upon the most just rational and equal principles; not exposed as others have heretofore been to caprice and accident or the influence of some mad conqueror, or prevailing parties or factions of men—but full power to settle our government from the very

189. "Sicherheit des Eigentums": Sprengel, *Allgemeines historisches Taschenbuch*, 28. See also Jacobi, ed., *Iris*, Mar. 1775, 155; Schmohl, *Über Nordamerika und Demokratie*, 13, 47. E.A.W. Zimmermann, *Frankreich und die Freistaaten*, esp. II, 593–594, regarded the respective handling of the property question as the essential criterion in judging the American and the French revolutions.

190. Arendt, *On Revolution*, 27.

191. E.g., J. Adams to I. Smith, Sr., in Butterfield *et al.*, eds., *Adams Family Correspondence*, II, 1; Jefferson to Franklin, Aug. 13, 1777, to Carrington, Jan. 16, 1787, in Boyd *et al.*, eds., *Jefferson Papers*, II, 27, XI, 48–49; Rush to Gates, Sept. 5, 1781, to John King, Apr. 2, 1783, in Butterfield, ed., *Letters of Benjamin Rush*, I, 265, 298; Dagobert D. Runes, ed., *The Selected Writings of Benjamin Rush* (New York, 1947), 26. Also Boyd, *Declaration of Independence*, 3; Bernard Bailyn, "Political Experience and Enlightenment: Ideas in Eighteenth-Century America," *AHR*, LXVII (1961–1962), 344, 351; Bailyn, *Ideological Origins*, 198, 299–301; Clinton Rossiter, "The Political Theory of Benjamin Franklin," *PMHB*, LXXVI (1952), 291; David S. Lovejoy, *Rhode Island Politics and the American Revolution 1760–1776* (Providence, R.I., 1958), 193–194.

foundation *de novo*."[192] The results of these efforts set post-Revolutionary America sharply and definitely apart from the political and social realities of Europe before 1789. In this respect the United States was indeed "the first new nation,"[193] in fact, the first modern state consciously opposed to all European *ancien régime* states, as many Americans knew only too well.[194] In American eyes a *novus ordo saeculorum* had truly begun; America was inhabited by a new species of man, who, thanks to different social and national conditions, enjoyed opportunities seemingly unlimited when compared with European conditions.[195]

Even if one admits that the Americans had good reasons to call their deeds a revolution, we must nevertheless ask what aspects of the events in America were really revolutionary and novel in the eyes of European contemporaries, and especially the German bourgeoisie. Time and again in the last quarter of the century Germans referred to these events as a revolution. But considering their view of what took place, did they have a right to do so, or were they simply transferring certain notions of their own to a spectacular occurrence that could more appropriately have been called a fight for liberty? Or, vice versa, did they talk of revolution because they saw in the dispute something that was really novel? It is very difficult to find clear answers to these questions. Obviously, the events were so impressive, and there was so much agreement among the bourgeoisie, that no one thought it necessary to give the full particulars of his conviction. Observers merely mentioned in a vague and general way the "character of greatness and of novelty" that they thought to be the most obvious aspect of the events in the New World.[196]

One point of view that, because of our experiences of the most recent past we are inclined to anticipate in any discussion of revolution, should be mentioned here is the idea of colonial liberation. There is a tendency in the United States today to recommend its own past as a model for other nations striving for political independence.[197] Even though I very much doubt that large sections of the Third World's population have such interests, it is true that the United States was "the first country in a foreign part of the world

192. To Edward Shippen, July 27, 1776 (Shippen Papers, XII, 41, PHi, Philadelphia).

193. Seymour Martin Lipset, *The First New Nation* (London, 1964), esp. 15; Lipset, "The *Newness* of the New Nation," in Woodward, ed., *Comparative Approach to American History*, 62–74; Louis Hartz, *The Founding of New Societies: Studies in the History of the United States, Latin America, South Africa, Canada, and Australia* (New York, 1964), 69–82.

194. See Jefferson to Carrington, Jan. 16, 1787, in Boyd *et al.*, eds., *Jefferson Papers*, XI, 48–49; also Palmer, *Age of the Democratic Revolution*, I, 3–4.

195. E. Wright, *Fabric of Freedom*, 237–254.

196. "caractère de grandeur et de nouveauté": "Discours," fol. 17 (NB, Vienna).

197. Cf. Richard B. Morris, *The Emerging Nations and the American Revolution* (New York, 1970), ix, 1–35, 178–223.

Figure 14. British Evacuation of New York. "End of the hostilities. The English give up New York to the Americans, 1783." The official date of the evacuation, November 25, 1783, was hardly known in Germany before the very end of the year, that is, after Sprengel's book was published. (Chodowiecki, for Sprengel, *Allgemeines historisches Taschenbuch*.)

Courtesy John Carter Brown Library, Brown University, Providence, R.I.

that was liberated by Europeans from the rule of [other] Europeans."[198] Nevertheless, only a few contemporaries stressed the achievement of national independence as the really novel element in the American Revolution, and those who did were latecomers. Before 1789 the majority of the bourgeoisie probably looked for novelty on an altogether different plane, even if they appreciated independence as an important achievement.

The idea of colonial liberation was not mentioned so often as the constitutional achievements of the American Revolution. As Paine made quite clear, American constitutional ideas combined English legal traditions with notions originating in America to form something novel indeed.[199] In the federal Constitution of 1787 Schubart, too, detected elements of novelty, without, however, accurately summarizing the months of debate in the Constitutional Convention. "This constitution is not a copy, . . . instead, it was abstracted by a philosophic mind from the people's character and situation."[200] There are other statements of a similar nature, though they are not numerous. Most date from the period of the French Revolution and invoke principles such as popular sovereignty to document the novelty of the American Revolution.[201]

It is very difficult to find contemporary statements that give tangible expression to a point that was already evident to the majority of the bourgeoisie. In 1775 the Palatinate minister Heinrich Anton Freiherr von Beckers von Wetterstetten spoke prophetically about events in America: "Whatever the outcome of this affair, it seems to me that it will be wished the question had never arisen."[202] Two months later his colleague in Munich, Joseph Franz Maria Ignaz Graf von Seinsheim, voiced a similar concern.[203] Although the reasons behind these warnings are uncertain to us, there is no

---

198. "das erste Land in einem fremden Weltteile, das durch Europäer von der Herrschaft der Europäer frei gemacht worden": Dietrich Johann Heinrich Stöver, *Unser Jahrhundert . . .*, 8 vols. (Altona, 1791–1800), I (2d ed., 1795), 42. Samuel Baur used the very same wording, but without acknowledging his indebtedness to Stöver, in Baur, *Geschichtserzählungen großer und seltener Menschen unsers Zeitalters*, 2 vols. (Leipzig, 1798), I, x.

199. Paine [pseud.], *Begebenheiten aller bisherigen Staaten*, II, 484–485.

200. "Diese Konstitution ist nicht kopiert . . ., sie ist vielmehr von einem philosophischen Kopfe vom Charakter des Volks und ihrer Lage abgezogen worden": Schubart, ed., *Vaterländische Chronik*, Nov. 1787, 328.

201. E.g., Schmohl, *Über Nordamerika und Demokratie*, 75–76; Seidel, "Staatsverfassung," in Ramsay, *Amerikanische Revolution*, IV, 27–28; *Examen impartial*, 78.

202. "Quelque issue que cette affaire puisse avoir, il me paraît qu'il serait à souhaiter qu'il n'en eut jamais été question": Beckers von Wetterstetten to Josef Franz Xaver Freiherr von Haslang, Feb. 4, 1775 (Bayer. Gesandtschaft: London, no. 253, GStA, Munich).

203. Seinsheim to Haslang, Apr. 23, 1775 (*ibid.*).

doubt that the two ministers recognized something novel in American events and had a premonition of a political challenge likely to affect Europe.[204]

As the majority of the German bourgeoisie understood events in the New World, the novel and revolutionary element could only be that the Americans were fighting for something different from what Europeans were used to fighting for, namely, universally valid ideals—above all, liberty and political equality. Now, for the first time, these ideals existed in practice, although far away. The fact alone seemed to the bourgeoisie incomparably more important than the distance. "A mere look at this land of freedom" was joyful and comforting, for it harbored "no compulsory service, no gabelles, no clerical tithes, no hereditary benefices, no monopolies, no preference by birth, no waste of the people's industry by lazy courtiers or fat priests; the industrious, righteous, and clever man rises here from poverty to wealth, from a plough to the helm of state; here reason and human values rule."[205] The German bourgeoisie saw the novel and the revolutionary aspects of American events in the renunciation of the characteristics of absolutist states and in the declaration of universal and rational principles as the foundation of state and society, principles that in their eyes embodied much more than a fight for freedom or independence.

204. The first volume of Palmer's *Age of the Democratic Revolution* has as its subtitle *The Challenge*.

205. "Das bloße Hinsehen auf dies Land der Freiheit. . . . keine Frondienste, keine Gabellen, keine kirchliche Zehnten, keine erbliche Pfründen, keine Monopolien, kein Geburtsvorzug, kein Verschwenden des Volksfleißes durch faule Höflinge oder sich mästende Priester; der tätige, rechtschaffene, gescheite Mann steigt hier von der Dürftigkeit zum Wohlstande, von dem Pfluge zum Staatsruder; hier herrscht Vernunft und Menschenwert": E.A.W. Zimmermann, *Frankreich und die Freistaaten*, I, 2.

6. Historical Parallels to the American Revolution

The Question of Comparability

As our treatment of the ideals of the American Revolution has shown, the German bourgeoisie were hardly able to comprehend their own "present as a historical problem" measured against the important developments in America.[1] To make these developments more intelligible, contemporaries made great efforts to compare events in the West with ostensibly related developments in other periods of history. Such historical comparisons are always subject to question, for each event or historical process at every stage is marked by its own peculiar characteristics. Yet the effort to draw such comparisons is not improper, and if carefully done, may be useful to the scholar today, just as men in the eighteenth century found it so.[2] For our purposes an analysis of the parallels drawn by contemporaries offers not only an insight into their historical interpretations but also additional information—revealed by the selection and orientation of the parallels—on their evaluation of the American Revolution.

Retrospective glances into history, when a fitting occasion presented itself, had been common long before the American Revolution. But we shall be able to understand the special characteristics of these parallels to the American Revolution only if we are aware of how the times conditioned the reception of the Revolution in Germany and determined the aspects of it that were stressed.

1. Georg Lukács, *Geschichte und Klassenbewußtsein* (Berlin, 1923), 173.
2. Johann Gustav Droysen, *Historik. Vorlesungen über Enzyklopädie und Methodologie der Geschichte*, ed. Rudolf Hübner, 4th ed. (Darmstadt, 1960), 156–163; Ernst Bernheim, *Lehrbuch der historischen Methode und der Geschichtsphilosophie. Mit Nachweis der wichstigsten Quellen und Hilfsmittel zum Studium der Geschichte*, 5th/6th eds., 2 vols. (Leipzig, 1908), II, 606–613; Marc Bloch, "Pour une histoire comparée des sociétés européennes," *Revue de synthèse historique*, XLVI (1928), 15–50; Erich Rothacker, "Die vergleichende Methode in den Geisteswissenschaften," in Robert H. Schmidt, ed., *Methoden der Politologie. Wege der Forschung*, LXXXVI (Darmstadt, 1967), 265–286; Theodor Schieder, "Möglichkeiten und Grenzen vergleichender Methoden in der Geschichtswissenschaft," in his *Geschichte als Wissenschaft* (Munich, 1965), 187–211.

The Example of Antiquity

The years with which we are dealing span the period that historians of German literature call Das Zeitalter der Klassik. The name denotes an approach toward antiquity that was significant for the whole Western world in the eighteenth century. Enthusiasm for this time of past greatness had been constantly growing, as was the number of contemporaries inspired by it. Dryden's edition of Virgil, Montesquieu's *Considérations sur les causes de la grandeur et de la décadence des Romains* (1734), and Gibbon's great opus on the *Decline and Fall of the Roman Empire* (the first volume of which appeared in 1776), are only some of the better-known instances of the great adulation of antiquity.

The use of examples from antiquity as arguments in colonial political disputes became common practice in Great Britain and in North America beginning in the 1760s, and later appeared in revolutionary France as well.[3] There were two basic reasons for this. First, Greek, Carthaginian, and Roman history included numerous instances of problems between colonies and mother countries.[4] Second, the great political personalities and defenders of the Roman Republic were referred to by the leaders of the American Revolution and their followers to justify their deeds, just as the French revolutionists did after 1789.[5]

As is well known, German thought in the last third of the eighteenth century followed a different path, one charted by Johann Joachim Winckelmann. Led by his inspiring influence, which dominated German thought well beyond his death in 1768, the educated German bourgeoisie concentrated their enthusiasm not on ancient Rome but on classical Greece, its art, poetry, and mythology. Rather than emphasizing political or social points of view, their enthusiasm was oriented toward the esthetic perfection of classical Hellas, which made the Romans seem mere undistinguished imitators. Gotthold Ephraim Lessing, Johann Gottfried Herder, Johann Heinrich Voss, and

3. See among others Richard M. Gummere, *The American Colonial Mind and the Classical Tradition: Essays in Comparative Culture* (Cambridge, Mass., 1963), 120–197; Howard Mumford Jones, *O Strange New World: American Culture; The Formative Years* (New York, 1964), 227–272; Bailyn, *Ideological Origins*, 23–26.

4. E.g., Stephen Hopkins, *The Rights of Colonies Examined* (Providence, R.I., 1765), reprinted in Bernard Bailyn, ed., *Pamphlets of the American Revolution* (Cambridge, Mass., 1965–), I, 507–522. In general see Michael Kammen, "The Meaning of Colonization in American Revolutionary Thought," *Journal of the History of Ideas*, XXXI (1970), 342, 345–350, 351–354; also Barron, *Geschichte der Kolonisirung der freien Staaten*.

5. Harold T. Parker, *The Cult of Antiquity and the French Revolutionaries* (1937; repr. New York, 1965), 17–20, 35, 70.

Friedrich Hölderlin were influenced by this notion of antiquity; Goethe and Schiller paid their tributes in *Prometheus, Iphigenie*, and *Die Götter Griechenlands*.[6] Switzerland, however, did not entirely share the separate position that Germany occupied with respect to the other West European countries and North America. Because the country was a republic and culturally influenced by France, enthusiasm for classical Greece could not suppress the regard for ancient Rome among the Swiss bourgeoisie to the same extent as among the comparable German classes.[7]

Contrary to the intentions of the American pamphleteers, their examples from antiquity, as viewed in Germany, did not serve as political justifications but rather as embellishments or ornaments, and often as additional aureola. Direct points of contact with Anglo-American arguments were rarely in evidence. The problem of the colonies' relationship to the mother country was seldom discussed in classical terms.[8] On the other hand, the armed conflict in the New World could be linked to past wars, the Roman Marsic or Social War (91 to 89 B.C.), for example, as was done by Christian Gottlob Heyne in his address at the forty-sixth anniversary of the University of Göttingen.[9] Others were more inclined to rank the triumphs of the Americans with venerable victories in the ancient Greek struggle for freedom, such as those at Marathon, Salamis, or Plataeae.[10]

Parallels to the heroes of republican Rome, common in the West, were drawn relatively late in the German-speaking countries apart from Switzerland. Even occasional mention of names like Cato, Cicero, or Regulus, to cite only a few,[11] cannot erase the impression that such parallels were not very

6. Wolfgang Schadewaldt, *Goethe und das Erlebnis des antiken Geistes* (Freiburg, Germany, 1932); Schadewaldt, *Goethestudien* (Zurich, 1963), 9–126; E. M. Butler, *Deutsche im Banne Griechenlands*, trans. from the English by Erich Rätsch (Berlin, 1948), 95–237; Walter Rehm, *Griechentum und Goethezeit*, 3d ed. (Munich, 1952), 11; Rehm, *Europäische Romdichtung*, 2d ed. (Munich, 1960), 167–192; Fritz Wagner, "Herders Homerbild, seine Wurzeln und Wirkungen" (publ. Ph.D. diss., University of Cologne, 1960); Elizabeth Rawson, *The Spartan Tradition in European Thought* (Oxford, 1969), 308–309.

7. Paul Wernle, *Der schweizerische Protestantismus im XVIII. Jahrhundert* (Tübingen, 1923–1925), II, 15–23; also Ludwig Meyer von Knonau, *Lebenserinnerungen*, ed. Gerold Meyer von Knonau (Frauenfeld, 1883), 29–30.

8. For exceptions see Achenwall, *Anmerkungen über Nord-Amerika* (2d ed., 1777), 4, and *Chronologen* (1779), I, 164.

9. [Christian Gottlob Heyne], *De Belli Romanorum Socialis Caussis et Eventu, respectu ad bellum cum Coloniis Americanis gestum habito* (Göttingen, [1783]), reprinted in his *Opuscula academica collecta et animadversionibus locupletata*, 6 vols. (Göttingen, 1785–1812), III (1788), 144–161.

10. August Christian Borheck, *Versuch eines tabellarischen Grundrisses der Weltgeschichte...*, 2 vols. (Halle, 1783–1784), II, 240; see also "Discours," fol. 16v (NB, Vienna).

11. *Teutscher Merkur*, Oct. 1775, 88–89; *Deutsche Chronik*, Jan. 1, 1776, 5; Ramsay, *Amerikanische Revolution*, I, vi (preface by Seidel); *Europäische Annalen*, Nov. 1796, 161.

popular east of the Rhine. More impressive and more common in Germany, as elsewhere, were the popular comparisons of Washington to Quintus Fabius Maximus, called Cunctator—both were equally respected for their wise avoidance of too-risky open battle—and to Lucius Quinctius Cincinnatus, a plain and unpretentious country squire who saved his country when it called upon him and then returned to his plow.[12]

Another tone emerged in the discussion in the late 1780s and the 1790s, when the idea of republicanism was inspired by the American example. Obvious parallels now seemed to connect republican America with the pattern of antiquity.

Republican Rome and young America were each considered countries of unspoiled virtue. Both states stood out among all others in their time and were equated as republics no less liberty-loving than they were virtuous.[13] The effect of the French Revolution was to strengthen the identity of the United States as the true New Rome, for it was only in America that the perfect combination of republicanism and virtue was to be found. Ancient Rome had ceased to exist, living only in memory as a symbol of august grandeur. But now a new and magnificent empire had been born "in the true republican spirit," applauded by Europe and glorified from afar. Like ancient Rome, the liberty-loving American republic had achieved this goal through a heroic and astounding struggle against the world's strongest power. In this its glory exceeded all past glories. "Thus, *Roma æterna*, reborn more beautifully, lives on in the New World."[14]

See also the London news in *Hamburgischer Correspondent*, Jan. 13, 1775, and in *Wienerisches Diarium*, Jan. 25, 1775.

12. E.g., Lambert to Franklin, Basel, Dec. 26, 1777 (Franklin Papers, LXII, 62, APSL, Philadelphia); Cluny, *Reisen durch Amerika*, 179; Johann Wilhelm von Archenholtz, "General Washington auf einer Reise," in Archenholtz, ed., *Litteratur und Völkerkunde*, Feb. 1785, 176; Delacroix, *Verfassung*, II, 311.

13. For more modern appreciations of the Roman Republic see Ulrich von Lübtow, *Blüte und Verfall der römischen Freiheit* (Berlin, 1953), 38, 44; Joseph Vogt, *Römische Republik* (Freiburg, Germany, 1962), I, 86–93; more critical, Franz Hampl, "Römische Politik in republikanischer Zeit und das Problem des 'Sittenverfalls,'" *HZ*, CLXXXVIII (1959), 497–525.

14. "im wahren republikanischen Geist. . . . So wirkt die Roma aeterna nach einer schönern Wiedergeburt in der Neuen Welt fort": Carl August Böttiger, "Washington, Neu-Rom in Amerika," *Neuer Teutscher Merkur*, Nov. 1793, 221, 231.

Parallels to Switzerland and the Netherlands

In justifying their actions, the leaders of the American Revolution and their followers in Europe cited any and all historical parallels, however remote, that showed real or imagined similarity of action. The origin of the Swiss confederacy and of the Netherlands seemed obvious incidents for comparison, for in both cases a people had attained its liberty in a heroic struggle against a faraway, superior power.[15] The general popularity in Europe, and especially among the German bourgeoisie, of American ideas of liberty worked its magic on the interpretation of history and easily combined with the distinctly sympathetic feeling toward the past struggles for liberty of the Swiss and the Dutch. Enthusiasm for the origins of both of these countries was more often than not expressed in literature, as Goethe's *Egmont*, Schiller's *Abfall der Niederlande*, and Bodmer's and Schiller's dramatizations of the William Tell material easily document.[16] Sympathy was especially noticeable, of course, among the Swiss bourgeoisie.

Because of the existing cultural sympathy for Switzerland and the Netherlands, comparisons of those nations to America became much more popular in Germany than comparisons to antiquity. Moreover, the two kinds of comparisons were used for somewhat different purposes. When Americans or their German supporters drew analogies to republican Rome, their purpose was mainly to legitimize their patriotic arguments, or, in some cases, to embellish their rhetoric. The purpose of adducing the Swiss and Dutch examples was to persuade Germans and other eighteenth-century Europeans that the American Revolution was as justifiable as the long-past struggles for liberty in two of Germany's neighboring countries.

The idea that the Swiss confederacy had arisen from a struggle between liberty and oppression, that free peasants had defended themselves against a feudal nobility in the process of expanding its power and were finally victori-

15. E.g., [John Joachim Zubly], *Eine kurzgefaßte Historische Nachricht von den Kämpfen der Schweitzer*, trans. from the English (Philadelphia, 1775). Zubly (1724–1781), born at St. Gall, Switzerland, emigrated to America in his twenties; John to John Quincy Adams, July 27, 1777, in Butterfield *et al.*, eds., *Adams Family Correspondence*, II, 290. Also, though not convincing, Leo Schelbert, "Der Wilhelm-Tell-Mythos in der Tradition der Vereinigten Staaten von Nordamerika," in Lilly Stunzi, ed., *Tell: Werden und Wandern eines Mythos* (Bern, 1973), 76, 314–316. Concerning the Netherlands see *Entretiens . . . sur la Révolution ancienne des Pays-Bas et les Affaires actuelles d'Amérique* (London and Paris, 1776).

16. See Ricco Labhardt, "Wilhelm Tell als Patriot und Revolutionär 1700–1800" (publ. Ph.D. diss., University of Basel, 1947), 147; Franz Heinemann, *Tell-Iconographie. Wilhelm Tell und sein Apfelschuss im Lichte der bildenden Kunst eines halben Jahrtausends (15.–20. Jahrhundert). . .* (Lucerne and Leipzig, 1902), 32–41.

ous, has a long tradition. According to the view of the eighteenth century, this was the proper way to interpret the three-canton league of 1291 and the Battle at the Morgarten in 1315. It harmoniously incorporated the legend of the oath on the Rütli and that of William Tell. How the American Revolution was related to legendary events in Switzerland is shown in a statement by Andreas Friedrich Loewe: "If the Americans succeed in maintaining their liberty, posterity will some day talk about Hancock, Adams, Franklin, Washington, and others just as sympathetically as they are now . . . talking . . . about Stauffacher, Melchthal, and Fürst,"[17] the three initiators of the oath on the Rütli (1291). William Tell was ranked with Washington, and the two were revered as "heroes of the old liberty."[18]

From the point of view of scientific history, all of these ostensible analogies are seriously open to question. First of all, they relate only to the supposed struggle for liberty, omitting all other phases and principles of the American Revolution. Second, the presentation of the origin of Switzerland is hopelessly cliché-ridden. It is not even necessary to mention the most recent research, which shows that these medieval events were not so much the result of superior general principles but rather of local and quite concrete economic and political conflicts and disputes with the House of Habsburg.[19] But if a few commentators in the eighteenth century had doubts as to the suitability of the comparison, it was not for these or even similar reasons. They considered the analogy faulty because the Swiss, as well as the Dutch later, had no alternative but to fight openly for liberty and separation from the Habsburgs. The Americans, however, could claim no such excuse, for according to this interpretation, if the Americans had been more moderate, they could have come to a cordial agreement with England.[20]

17. "Wenn es den Amerikanern gelingt, ihre Freiheit zu behaupten, so wird die Nachwelt dereinst von einem Hankok [*sic*], Adams, Franklin, Washington und andern ebenso vorteilhaft sprechen, als es jetzt . . . von einem Stuffacher [*sic*], Melchtal und Fürst . . . geschiehet": Loewe, *Beschreibung der zwölf Vereinigten Kolonien*, 137.

18. See also the contemporary anonymous copper of Tell and Washington. Contrary to the opinion in Stunzi, ed., *Tell*, 109, 114, I presume that the copper was engraved in the late 1770s and not sometime around 1793. The first date would be closer to the evidence of contemporary opinions; moreover, the portrait of Tell is more detailed than the copy on a copper of the early 1790s. See also Lambert to Franklin, Dec. 26, 1777 (Franklin Papers, LXII, 62, APSL, Philadelphia); furthermore, *Fliegende Blätter*, Feb. 1794, 98–99, Aug.-Sept. 1794, 792.

19. See the illuminating study by Andreas Riggenbach, "Der Marchenstreit zwischen Schwyz und Einsiedeln und die Entstehung der Eidgenossenschaft" (publ. Ph.D. diss., University of Zurich, 1965), *passim*. For a more traditional view see Wolfgang von Wartburg, *Geschichte der Schweiz* (Munich, 1951), 29–42.

20. E.g., Johann Heinrich Meister to Johann Jakob Bodmer, Apr. 25, 1777, June 5, 1778 (MS Bodmer, X, 333, 354, ZB, Zurich); Struensee, *Beschreibung der Handlung*, I, 173–174.

Figure 15. Washington and Tell: The Heroes of the Old Liberty (n.p., [1777–1779]). This anonymous engraving has also been dated c. 1793, the date of publication of an identical, anonymous French engraving called "Les Vertues Républicains" (Lilly Stunzi, ed., *Tell: Werden und Wandern eines Mythos* [Bern, 1973], 109, 114). However, the French version is less detailed and less accurate, which suggests that it was actually the later one. Also, the intellectual climate in Germany during the second half of the 1770s would have been favorable for the publication of the German portrait during those years.

Courtesy Universitätsbibliothek, Karl Marx University, Leipzig

It is notable that even in the denials of a possible parallel between the origin of the Swiss confederacy and that of the United States the arguments revolved around the struggle for liberty. This emphasis was characteristic of the second half of the 1770s. In the 1780s, when the American Revolution had become more meaningful to the German bourgeoisie and was linked increasingly with the idea of civil and legal equality and less exclusively with the idea of liberty, the parallels with the origin of Switzerland lost their meaning. The novelty of events in the Western Hemisphere seemed less comparable to an alleged medievel struggle for liberty.

References to the Dutch revolt against Spanish rule met with a similar fate. Most such references also originated between 1777 and 1779. In western and northern Germany they seem to have been more popular than the comparisons with Switzerland. Here again the fight for liberty was the central point of comparison,[21] while events were portrayed in clichés. Although there may be parallels in the political situations of the Dutch provinces and the American colonies at the beginning of their respective conflicts, the comparison ends with the early merger of the Dutch uprising into a conflict between Calvinists and Catholics. Moreover, the English colonies knew no formal social classes, whereas the Dutch uprising clearly bears the mark of premodern society—with the fronde of the seigneurs at the top, followed by the lower nobility and the upper middle classes—a situation that gave it a social basis completely different from that of the American Revolution.[22]

It was on this last point that isolated criticism of the comparison, so popular with the bourgeoisie, fastened. "The Dutch had a prince for a leader. . . . What are Hancock and Adams? Creatures of democracy, which first worships its idols and then annihilates them one by one."[23] Helferich Peter Sturz believed that for this reason the parallel with Holland was just as devious and misleading as the idea that the Americans were fighting for lofty

21. E.g., Schlözer, ed., *Briefwechsel* (1777), I/1, 40–41; Meister to Bodmer, Apr. 25, 1777 (MS Bodmer, X, 333, ZB, Zurich); Frederick II to Prince Heinrich, July 25, 1777, in Volz, ed., *Politische Correspondenz Friedrichs des Grossen*, XXXIX, 271; Loewe, *Beschreibung der zwölf Vereinigten Kolonien*, 137; Büsching, ed., *Wöchentliche Nachrichten*, Apr.–May 1778, 113–116, 145–147; Struensee, *Beschreibung der Handlung*, I, 173–174; L. F., Baron van Wynbergen, from Wesel, to Franklin, May 21, 1779 (Franklin Papers, XIV, 128, APSL, Philadelphia); *Fliegende Blätter*, Feb. 1794, 98–99, Aug.–Sept. 1794, 792.

22. See J. W. Smit, "The Netherlands Revolution," in Robert Forster and Jack P. Greene, eds., *Preconditions of Revolution in Early Modern Europe* (Baltimore, 1972), 19–54; and most recently, Heinz Schilling, "Der Aufstand der Niederlande: Bürgerliche Revolution oder Elitenkonflikt?" *200 Jahre amerikanische Revolution und moderne Revolutionsforschung. Geschichte und Gesellschaft, Sonderheft*, II (1976), 177–231.

23. "Die Niederländer hatten einen Fürsten zum Anführer. . . . Was sind Hancock und Adams? Geschöpfe der Demokratie, die ihre Götzen eins ums andere anbetet und vernichtet": Sturz, *Schriften*, II (1782), 357–358, cf. 355–356. See also *Chronologen* (1779), I, 164.

human ideals and not merely against taxation. But convinced antagonists of the American Revolution like Sturz were not the only ones who rejected these analogies, often without sufficient knowledge of either event. Even among the protagonists of America's cause there were those who, like Jakob Mauvillon, questioned the necessity of the Declaration of Independence, thus denying the right of self-defense to the Americans while granting it to the Dutch. Such men believed that the Americans could have achieved their goals without breaking with the mother country.[24]

During the 1780s, comparisons of the American Revolution with the origins of Switzerland and the Dutch uprising continued, but few centered specifically on the idea of a fight for liberty. After 1783 a different kind of comparison of America and the two European republics became popular: the analogy of the fight for liberty was supplanted by analogies drawn to the structure of the state. As we have already seen, the popularity of this new analogy did not result in the idea of American federalism becoming a serious topic of discussion. People were content both in and outside of Germany[25] simply to make the general observation that the state structure was "similar to that of the united Netherlands" or to that of Switzerland.[26]

Written at the time of the Articles of Confederation, these remarks seem to us a gross simplification, but they were not completely unjustified. These superficialities were more serious, however, when they were repeated as late as the 1790s.[27] Fortunately, more informed contemporaries understood that parallels appropriate at the time of the Articles of Confederation were no longer applicable after the decisive changes brought about by the new federal Constitution of 1787. For "by virtue of the Constitution of 1787 the individual states did not merely renounce their sovereignty in all cases relating to their foreign affairs but also in some of the most important affairs of internal politics, delegating them undivided to a federal government."[28] In view of

24. Mauvillon, *Sammlung von Aufsätzen*, II, 8–9; see also his note to his translation of Raynal, *Europäer in beiden Indien*, VI (1777), 545–547.

25. E.g., Charles Joseph Mayer, *Les Ligues achéenne, suisse et hollandoise; et révolution des Etats Unis de l'Amérique*, 2 vols. (Geneva and Paris, 1787).

26. "nach Art der vereinigten Niederlande": [Gotthilf Christian Reccard], *Lehr-Buch*, 6th ed., ed. Peter Johann Hecker (Berlin, 1782–1783), II, 533. See also [Jakob Kloppenburg], *Geographie für Jedermann*, 2 vols. (Schleswig, 1785–1786), II, 251; [Georg Lorenz Bauer], *Neuestes Lehrbuch der Erdbeschreibung* (Nuremberg, 1787), 686; also the letters by Jean Rodolphe Vautravers to Franklin (Franklin Papers, APSL, Philadelphia).

27. E.g., Meister, *Historische Unterhaltungen*, 228–229; *Beschreibung aller Länder und Völker*, 449; Kleinsorg, *Abriß der Geographie*, 3d ed. (1797), II, 763.

28. "Durch die Konstitution von 1787 entsagten die einzelnen Staaten ihrer Souveränität nicht nur in allen Fällen, welche ihre äußere Verhältnisse betreffen, sondern auch in einigen der wichtigsten Angelegenheiten der innern Regierung, und übertrugen sie ungeteilt einer Unionsregierung": Seidel, "Staatsverfassung," in Ramsay, *Amerikanische Revolution*, IV, 4. See also Franz, *Lehrbuch der Länder- und Völkerkunde*, II, 216–217.

these new facts, Johann Georg Büsch rejected every comparison when he remarked: "Moreover, this constitution differs very much from those of the two federal republics which have sprung up in Europe in modern times, Switzerland and the United Netherlands. Their constitutions, very much the products of accident and necessity, were left incomplete, and even under changed circumstances, nothing was done to improve them and to tighten the bond that had been too slack from the beginning."[29]

The discussion of possible parallels between the state structures of the United States, Switzerland, and the Netherlands did not live to see the end of the century. The coup de grâce was delivered by the French Revolution at the time when the two old confederations broke down under the impact of French revolutionary armies and when the multitude of small confederated states was replaced by one centralized republic. The idea of comparing the three states, which had intrigued bourgeois circles in Germany for twenty years, was dead. The fight for liberty was no longer so important because the American Revolution, as they saw it, had grown beyond this notion; and the comparison with the federal state structure no longer applied because it had changed in all three countries.

Other Comparisons

The comparison of the Revolution with the Reformation, if it was not meant to be derogatory from the very start, was necessarily limited to the Protestant part of the German population. But here, too, it remained a marginal phenomenon, worthy of notice not because of its popularity (limited in any case) but because of the nature of the comparison.

As early as 1777 Jakob Mauvillon had called the American Revolution "the most memorable spectacle . . . enacted on our planet since the discovery of America and the Reformation."[30] By the beginning of the 1790s we find a

29. "Auch unterscheidet sich diese Konstitution gar sehr von denen der beiden föderierten Republiken, welche Europa in neuern Zeiten bekommen hat, der Schweizer und der V. Niederländer, in welche so viel Zufälliges und Umstände einer dringenden Notwendigkeit einwirkten, die man aber in ihrer Unvollkommenheit gelassen hat, ohne in geänderten Umständen etwas daran zu bessern und das von Anfang an zu schlaffe Band fester zu knüpfen": Büsch, *Geschichte der merkwürdigsten Welthändel*, 3d ed. (1796), 492.

30. "das denkwürdigste Schauspiel . . . das sich seit der Entdeckung von Amerika und seit der Reformation auf unsrer Erdkugel gezeigt habe": note by Mauvillon in his translation of Raynal, *Europäer in beiden Indien*, VI, [7].

detailed comparison that already included the French Revolution. Its basic idea was that "in the history of Europe there are two outstanding moments in time which are remarkable and fruitful because, by virtue of surprisingly similar facts, they exerted a great influence on the complete transformation of contemporary thought and attitudes, and the evolution of mankind toward the loftier purposes of existence. These two moments fall into the sixteenth and eighteenth centuries. The first resulted in the Reformation, the second in the American and French revolutions; the first in the overthrow of hierarchy, and the second in the overthrow of despotism; the first in clerical freedom, the second in civil liberty."[31] The central idea of this comparison was again liberty, which furnishes another reason why parallels like these were not very popular: the majority of the German bourgeoisie had long ceased to regard the American Revolution exclusively as a fight for liberty.

The emphasis on liberty entered also into other cursory analogies, namely, those referring to the Corsican fight for liberty and to its hero, Pasquale Paoli. Especially in the 1760s, Paoli's fame was spreading beyond Europe to North America.[32] Since here again the idea of liberty was the only analogy, this parallel was likewise doomed to failure, especially since Paoli's fight had foundered in 1769. The Corsican analogy fell victim to the German bourgeoisie's developing views on the American Revolution.[33]

Finally, it is impossible to pass over the inescapable parallels between events in America and those in England in the seventeenth century, especially

31. "In der Geschichte von Europa zeichnen sich zwei Zeitpunkte aus, die durch überraschende, einander äußerst ähnliche Begebenheiten durch einen gleich großen Einfluß auf die gänzliche Umformung der Denkungsart und der Gesinnungen der Zeitgenossen und auf die Ausbildung der Menschheit zu den höhern Zwecken ihres Daseins äußerst merkwürdig und fruchtbar sind. Diese zwei Zeitpunkte fallen in das 16. und in das 18. Jahrhundert, wovon das erste die Reformation, das zweite die amerikanische und Französische Revolution—das erste den Umsturz der Hierarchie, das zweite den Umsturz des Despotismus—das erste die kirchliche, das zweite die bürgerliche Freiheit hervorbrachte": "Einige Aehnlichkeit der Reformation und der Revolution," *Schleswigsches ehemals Braunschweigisches Journal*, June 1792, 173; cf. pp. 181–182, 191–192, 197.

32. See among others Rousseau, "Contrat social," bk. II, chap. 10, in his *Oeuvres complètes*, ed. Gagnebin and Raymond, III, 391; Peter Adam Thrasher, *Pasquale Paoli: An Enlightened Hero, 1725–1807* (London, 1970), 133, 157–158, and *passim*; Franco Venturi, *Italy and the Enlightenment: Studies in a Cosmopolitan Century*, trans. from the Italian by Susan Corsi, ed. Stuart Woolf (London, 1972), 143–146. See also Goethe's remarks on Paoli's esteem throughout Europe and on his stay at Frankfurt, in Goethe, "Dichtung und Wahrheit," bk. XVII, in his *Werke*, Weimar ed., 1/XXIX, 68. Also, Michael Kraus, "America and the Utopian Ideal in the Eighteenth Century," *Mississippi Valley Historical Review*, XXII (1935–1936), 493: "He was an inspiration to the colonial Sons of Liberty."

33. It may be noted as an interesting point in the history of ideas that Goethe substituted for his remarks on Paoli in the first and second versions of the "Mitschuldigen" of 1769, an allusion to the events in America in his third version (1780–1783); cf. his *Werke*, Weimar ed., 1/IX, 44, 89, 465, 487.

the Puritan Revolution and the Glorious Revolution. From the standpoint of the present, we are almost inclined to consider such parallels obvious. Were there not many features of the American developments that recalled the reign of Charles I and the ensuing years of war and revolution? The Commons in the 1620s and 1630s, like the eighteenth-century Americans, regarded themselves as the defenders of good old English law, and, like the Americans, they turned against seemingly unjust and unlawful taxation, resisted the billeting of troops in peacetime, and protested religious and economic oppression. Both fought for citizens' liberty and against unlawful usurpation of power; questions of objective and subjective rights were central concerns in both cases.[34] Similarly, the English revolution of 1688–1689 resembled events in America in numerous ways, especially in the intrinsic characteristics of its results as compared with the prerevolutionary situation. As we understand these developments now, it is possible to attribute to the American Revolution virtually the same liberal-conservative characteristics that George M. Trevelyan ascribed to the results of the 1688–1689 revolution.[35]

If it was considered necessary to compare the events in America to anything at all, parallels to England would have been much more obvious than all others. The Americans were well aware of the English parallels, and it was not by accident that in their arguments they often cited the ideas of such pamphleteers and theoreticians of the seventeenth century as John Milton, James Harrington, Marchamont Nedham, Henry Neville, Algernon Sidney, and John Locke, or Sir Edward Coke among the jurists.[36] But in German-speaking areas, including Hanover, this epoch of British history was seldom mentioned in this context. Memories of the Glorious Revolution had not really remained alive in Germany, and even the centennial celebration in 1788 did little to change this.

Although the German bourgeoisie paid little attention to possible analogies between the Puritan and the American revolutions, some scattered allu-

34. The most recent work on these questions is Hans-Christoph Schröder, "Die amerikanische und die englische Revolution in vergleichender Perspektive," *200 Jahre amerikanische Revolution und moderne Revolutionsforschung. Geschichte und Gesellschaft, Sonderheft,* II (1976), 9–37.

35. George Macaulay Trevelyan, *The English Revolution 1688–1689* (1938; repr. London, 1963), 134. See also David Ogg, *England in the Reigns of James II and William III* (Oxford, 1963), 223; Maurice Ashley, *The Glorious Revolution of 1688* (London, 1966), 197–198. Cf. Peter Marshall, "Radicals, Conservatives and the American Revolution," *Past and Present*, XXIII (1962), esp. 50.

36. See Angermann, "Ständische Rechtstraditionen," *HZ*, CC (1965), 84–86.

37. As Sigismund Graf von Haslang wrote shortly afterward to Matthäus Graf von Vieregg, Nov. 7, 1788: "Le 4 de ce mois, le parti des Whigs, c'est-à-dire, Anti-Royalistes, ayant célébré le centenaire de la révolution arrivée en l'année 1688" (Kasten schwarz 15389, GStA, Munich).

sions to the former did turn up in 1776–1777. They came almost exclusively from America's antagonists, however, and, in keeping with the personality-oriented view of history generally held at the time, they dwelt on the figure of Oliver Cromwell. He was depicted as a cruel regicide and a fanatically obsessed, dogmatic, hypocritical Puritan, unsoftened by humaneness and tolerance.[38] To many contemporaries in the eighteenth century, Cromwell appeared as a horror to be related to America only as a way of summarily condemning what was going on there. "The light in which the colonists present their uprising is seductive to the uninformed; but it cannot shield the passion for anarchy that starts the revolt; and anarchy leads to despotism: Cromwell's ghost slinks about in America."[39]

Such allusions to the Lord Protector soon subsided. In the 1780s it was even occasionally possible to mention Cromwell in connection with the United States without derogatory connotations,[40] as the American patriots themselves had done during the Revolution.[41] But the casual hints of the time cannot really make up for the otherwise complete lack of analytic comparison between the American and the Puritan revolutions. These scattered comments throw more light on the image of Cromwell and on the political comprehension of the German bourgeoisie than on their appreciation of events in the New World.

38. Maurice Ashley, *The Greatness of Oliver Cromwell* (1957; repr. New York, 1962), 14–20; Christopher Hill, *God's Englishman: Oliver Cromwell and the English Revolution* (London, 1970), 266–267.

39. "Der Anstrich, den die Kolonisten ihrem Aufstande geben, ist für Ununterrichtete verführerisch; aber er kann die Sucht nach Anarchie nicht verbergen, die den Aufstand erregt hat; und Anarchie führt zum Despotismus: Cromwells Geist schleicht in Amerika": *Über den Aufstand der englischen Colonien*, 18, reprinted in Korn, *Geschichte der Kriege*, II, 75. See also Schirach, *Notiz der Großbrittannischen Colonien in America*, 96-page ed., 83; Seinsheim to J.F.X. von Haslang, Apr. 6, 1777 (Bayer. Gesandtschaft: London, no. 255, GStA, Munich).

40. Cf. *Anmerkungen aus der neuen und alten Welt* (1786), 166; the same in the 1788 edition.

41. Hill, *God's Englishman*, 272–273.

7. Expected Consequences of the American Revolution

General Expectations

In view of the great importance assigned to the American Revolution by German contemporaries, it was only logical for them to expect manifold and far-reaching results. At the beginning of the war it was difficult to predict anything with certainty, but Christoph Heinrich Korn asked as early as 1776: "Are we at the beginning of an epoch in history that will forever remain remarkable to posterity? Isn't the foundation stone being laid right now on the other side of the ocean for a powerful state that in the future, when American fleets will cover the seas, might terrify the European powers?"[1] To antagonists of the American Revolution this seemed a gloomy and remote possibility, but to some Germans the prospect was thoroughly enjoyable. Thus, in 1783 Georg Forster rejoiced in the obvious manifestations of enlightened European progress spreading through non-European parts of the globe. "America and Asia Minor set a-going at the same time; sciences, agriculture, arts, European luxury introduced on both sides: This is indeed a long step toward the great revolution of this planet."[2] These statements by Korn and Forster express a conviction that we may assume was shared by large sections of the German population at the time. As much as two generations later it was echoed by Alexis de Tocqueville. The American Revolution,

1. "Sollten wir wohl am Anfange einer Epoche in der Geschichte stehen, welche der Nachkommenschaft auf immer merkwürdig sein wird? Sollte wohl jetzt jenseits des Ozeans der Grund zu einem mächtigen Staate gelegt werden, der vielleicht in Zukunft die europäischen Mächte in Schrecken setzen könnte, wenn amerikanische Flotten die Meere bedecken werden?": Korn, *Geschichte der Kriege*, I, [4].
2. "Amerika und Kleinasien zu gleicher Zeit in Tätigkeit gebracht, Wissenschaften, Landbau, Künste, europäischer Luxus auf beiden Seiten eingeführt: Das ist in der Tat ein großer Schritt zu der großen Revolution des Erdballs": Georg to Johann Reinhold Forster, Feb. 13, 1783, in G. Forster, *Briefwechsel*, ed. Huber, I, 321–322. See also Isaak Iselin to Johann Georg Zimmermann, Mar. 20, 1782 (Nachlaß Zimmermann, A II, no. 47a, fol. 132, LB, Hanover).

he said, "was like the voice of John crying in the wilderness that new times are near."[3]

There were some German contemporaries, however, who toward the end of the eighteenth century tried to express their conjectures as to the effects of the American Revolution in a more concrete way than did Korn, Forster, and Tocqueville. Here, too, the point of departure was the idea of liberty. In his pamphlet *Common Sense*, Thomas Paine had exhorted the Americans to establish an asylum for freedom, which had been hunted round the globe.[4] The victorious ending of the war seemed to have implemented this plan, and Richard Price told Jefferson in 1785 that "the eyes of the friends of liberty and humanity are now fixed on that country."[5] The idea of a refuge for freedom in the new American republic was so potent with the German admirers of the Revolution that Friedrich Leopold Graf zu Stolberg was able to say in his poem, "Die Zukunft," written about 1780:

> For America will be free! And if it can, may it comfort you,
> Britons, that among the sons of liberty
> Your brothers will be the first. On wise laws
> Their empire will be based. . . .[6]

Like Stolberg, other contemporaries expressed the hope that this sanctuary for liberty might be blessed and be part of humanity "until the end of all days."[7]

These selected statements show that the comparatively reserved character of the American Revolution was in accord with the political comprehension of the German bourgeoisie. Both Americans and Germans believed that the object of the Revolution was America alone, even if a few Americans had expressed their conviction that their actions would serve as an example to mankind and especially to the oppressed parts of it.[8] But the idea of a world

3. Alexis de Tocqueville, "L'Ancien Régime et la Révolution," in his *Oeuvres complètes*, ed. J.-P. Mayer (Paris, 1951–), II/2, 45.

4. Paine, *Gesunder Menschenverstand*, 81.

5. Mar. 21, 1785, in Boyd *et al.*, eds., *Jefferson Papers*, VIII, 53.

6. "Denn frei wird Amerika sein! Und kann es Euch Trost sein, / Briten, so sei es Euch Trost, daß unter den Söhnen der Freiheit / Eure Brüder die Erstlinge sind. Auf weise Gesetze / Werden sie gründen ihr Reich": Stolberg, "Die Zukunft," ed. Hartwig, *ALG*, XIII (1885), 269.

7. "bis ans Ende der Welt erhalten": Karl Ritter von Qureille to Franklin, July 30, 1783 (Franklin Papers, LIX, 8, APSL, Philadelphia). See also Isidor Bianchi, in Gian Rinaldo Carli, *Briefe über Amerika*, trans. from the Italian by Christian Gottfried Hennig, 3 vols. (Gera, 1785), I, vii; *Paul-Jones, ou prophéties sur l'Amérique* (Basel, 1781), 15, 20.

8. E.g., Philipp Waldeck, *Diary of the American Revolution*, ed. Marion Dexter Learned (Philadelphia, 1907), 75 (entry of July 15, 1778); Rush to the ministers of the gospel, June 21,

revolution based on a worldwide overthrow of established power structures was as alien to German contemporaries before 1789 as it was in France during the early phase of the French Revolution.

Yet a few antagonists doubtlessly sensed something of the challenge to the traditional European systems of government presented by the American Revolution. They did not assume, however, that it would have any concrete sequels in France, despite that country's support of the Americans. Only in the 1790s was it suggested that the French had imported their revolution by giving aid to the Americans a decade earlier. The author of one of the very first anti-American pamphlets published in Germany wrote: "Since the interest of every sovereign is to suppress rather than to support a rebellion, the Americans cannot hope for foreign aid."[9] Seinsheim, the Bavarian minister who had for some time been worried about England and the outcome of the American conflict, had gloomy forebodings: "May God grant that they have good fortune and that this intestine war will end satisfactorily in every respect for His Britannic Majesty! What misfortune and what consequences if the insurgents should come out on top!"[10] Korn warned a little later: "God help all monarchs if their subjects should agree with the Americans' principles, which arise from a perverted and fanatical interpretation of liberty."[11] Similar warning voices were heard again during the French Revolution. But time showed that events in America did not directly endanger the German system of government, so that such forebodings virtually ceased in the following years.

The few predictions of a wider influence for the American Revolution usually crossed the Rhine from France. They could not engender feelings of serious danger, but they are still worthy of notice. Peter Ochs, the future revolutionary from Basel, thought that the Americans' success was "a new

---

1788, in Butterfield, ed., *Letters of Benjamin Rush*, I, 466; John Quincy Adams, *Beantwortung der Paineschen Schrift von den Rechten des Menschen*, trans. from the English by W.H.F. Abrahamson (Copenhagen, 1793), 15.

9. "Fremde Hülfe dürfen die Amerikaner umso weniger hoffen, da es das Interesse eines jeden Souverän erfordert, eine Rebellion eher unterdrücken als befördern zu helfen": *Gedanken über den Aufstand der englischen Colonien*, 39.

10. "Dieu fasse, qu'elles soient heureuses et que cette guerre intestine finisse à tous égards à la satisfaction de Sa Mté. Britannique! Quel malheur et quelles suites, si les insurgents prenaient le dessus": Joseph Franz Maria Ignaz Graf von Seinsheim to Joseph Franz Xaver Freiherr von Haslang, Apr. 28, 1776 (Bayer. Gesandtschaft: London, no. 254, GStA, Munich). Cf. Heinrich Anton Freiherr von Beckers von Wetterstetten to Haslang, Feb. 19, Nov. 12, 1774, and Seinsheim to Haslang, Jan. 22, Feb. 19, Dec. 24, 1775 (*ibid.*, nos. 252, 253, 254).

11. "Wehe allen Monarchen, wenn die ihnen unterwürfigen Völker diesen Grundsätzen der Amerikaner beipflichten sollten, die aus einem verkehrten und fanatischen Begriffe von der Freiheit entstehen": Korn, *Geschichte der Kriege*, VII, 25. See also Charles Bonnet to Albrecht von Haller, Oct. 17, 1777 (Korrespondenz Albrecht von Hallers, Burgerbibliothek, Bern).

lesson to despots."[12] Others, too, believed that the American Revolution had had an enlightening effect on ideas about the nature of government.[13] In their enthusiasm for its ideals, some even went so far as to claim that it was "a lesson to princes who cannot believe that the spirit of freedom might ever rouse their subjects and fire them to resist their usurpation; a lesson to statesmen who are under the delusion that a people is an animal to be saddled and bridled at will and to be subjected to the whims and wants of its masters by standing armies."[14] But these few statements from self-conscious sections of the bourgeoisie cannot erase the fact that most members of the German middle-class still did not think of themselves as political activists and did not take up the challenge emanating from America.

Effects on the Domestic Development of the United States

The future prospects of the young state in the New World seemed to German contemporaries to be much more inspiring and interesting than the effects in Europe of the American Revolution. The idea of America's future greatness was altogether intoxicating during the mostly optimistic years before the French Revolution. As early as the mid-1760s Christoph Daniel Ebeling had prophetically surmised that the Western Hemisphere might one day exceed even Europe in the economic, political, and cultural fields.[15] The title of his article made it clear, however, that he thought that this development would take centuries. But after 1776 the American Revolution made

12. "une nouvelle leçon aux despotes": to Iselin, May 2, 1777, in Steiner, ed., *Korrespondenz des Peter Ochs*, I, 102. See also Raynal, *Staatsveränderung von Amerika*, 102.

13. E.g., "Discours," fols. 65, 69v (NB, Vienna).

14. "belehrend für die Fürsten, welche nicht glauben, daß jemals Freiheitsgeist ihre Untertanen beleben und zu Widersetzlichkeit gegen ihre Usurpation entflammen könne; für Staatsmänner, welche in dem Wahne stehen, daß das Volk ein Tier sei, das sich sattein und zäumen lasse nach Belieben und durch stehende Armeen zu allem genötigt werden könne, wozu Laune und Bedürfnis seiner Gebieter es nötigen will": Soulès, *Revolution in Nord-Amerika*, I, v (preface by Hammerdörfer). For a similar statement see [Christian Gottlob Hempel], *Kurzer Abriß der neuesten europäischen Denkwürdigkeiten*, 2 vols. (Berlin, 1788–1789), I, 43; see also Brissot de Warville, *Neue Reise*, Bayreuth ed., III, 19.

15. Ebeling, "Fragen, welche erst nach einigen Jahrhunderten können aufgelöst werden," *Hannoverisches Magazin*, Nov. 15, 1765, cols. 1447–1448.

16. E.g., Elbridge Gerry to James Warren, Nov. 8, 1778, in *Warren-Adams Letters*, II, 65.

17. Cf. among others the scientific and medical tracts by Johann Philipp Du Roi, Friedrich Kasimir Medicus, Heinrich Christoph Moser, Georg Wolfgang Franz Panzer, Johann David Schoepf, Friedrich Adam Julius von Wangenheim, and Joseph von Weber.

the wheels of history seem suddenly to turn much faster, so that even some Americans predicted that the former colonies would develop into a state surpassing in power and wealth every other empire past or present.[16]

This view spread to Germany very rapidly. America's increasing importance for European science[17]—the Revolution had given strong impetus to the development of science in the former colonies[18]—caused the German bourgeoisie of the mid-1770s to believe that the young republic would rise to be a center of science and culture.[19]

As early as 1776 the southern German periodical *Neueste Geschichte der Welt* thought that America's future greatness would be even more imposing: "The Americans will rise to independence, power, and all the grandeur of the most famous nations because they are building their state on the firm ground of public liberty."[20] In October of the same year, Isaak Iselin summed up clearly why large sections of the bourgeoisie believed that the state in the New World would be exemplary in every respect, provided that Americans remained true to the principles that guided them initially: "They will become a truly flourishing nation, and they will show the world to what levels the prosperity of a society can be raised through true and genuine liberty."[21] In these statements, to which many similar ones could be added,[22] we encounter again the bourgeois ideal of liberty.

But there is another basis for such far-reaching prognoses, as had already been suggested by Iselin, namely, economics. The notion that the Americans were prosperous was widespread in Germany in 1776.[23] However, some observers, especially antagonists of the Revolution, thought that the great debts incurred from the war, and the oppressive taxation that would necessarily follow, would ultimately destroy the citizens' economic

18. Evarts B. Greene, "Some Educational Values of the American Revolution," *APSP*, LXVIII (1929), 185–194; Brooke Hindle, *The Pursuit of Science in Revolutionary America, 1735–1789* (Chapel Hill, N.C., 1956), 382–385.

19. E.g., Schubart, ed., *Deutsche Chronik*, May 5, 1774, 81–84; Loewe, *Beschreibung der zwölf Vereinigten Kolonien*, 80–81; more skeptical, Crome, *Nordamerikanischer Freystaat*, 61.

20. "Die Amerikaner werden zur Unabhängigkeit, Macht und jeder Größe der berühmtesten Staaten emporsteigen, weil sie auf den festen Grund der öffentlichen Freiheit bauen": *Neueste Geschichte der Welt* (1776), II, 87.

21. "Alsdenn auch werden sie ein wahrhaft blühendes Volk werden und der Welt ein Beispiel geben, wie hoch der Wohlstand einer Gesellschaft durch wahre und echte Freiheit gebracht werden kann": *Ephemeriden der Menschheit*, Oct. 1776, 107.

22. E.g., *Briefe über den gegenwärtigen Zustand von England*, I, 69–70; Sprengel, *Über den jetzigen Nordamericanischen Krieg*, 3; Robin, *Neue Reise durch Nordamerika*, 142.

23. E.g., *Über den Aufstand der englischen Colonien*, 7–8; Korn, *Geschichte der Kriege*, II, 70–71.

well-being.[24] Others believed that "the moral and political character of the inhabitants," rebellious and fanatical as they were, would not fail to have long-term negative results for the well-being of the people.[25]

Of course, German protagonists of the Revolution did not share this pessimism, and their views often showed what they predicted for the new state. August Wilhelm Friedrich Crome believed that "geography, climate, and fertility are generally such as to reward the farmer's labors as well as do Europe's best countries. . . . Everything depends on there being a sufficient number of inhabitants, and America will have them if it gladly admits every stranger and grants as much latitude to trade and commerce as to the various religions."[26] Karl Philipp Michael Snell had as much confidence in these developments as Crome did, for America has "been amply provided by nature with the most glorious products of all kinds," and it has raised itself "out of nothingness" to "freedom and power so radiant and advantageous as to be unrivaled by any state. It is easy to predict the quick growth of this happy state, and it will take no more than one generation to see it in its admirable grandeur."[27] Matthias Christian Sprengel presented his views on the economic prospects and the inexorable rise of America with the same firm conviction and without the slightest doubt of the republic's future greatness.[28] Economic independence from England, even in manufactures, would follow speedily, it was believed, thus constituting, in conjunction with liberty, a secure foundation for the happiness and well-being of the new republic.[29]

24. See Peter Hasenclever to Gottlob Benedikt von Schirach, Nov. 13, 1781, in A. Hasenclever, ed., *Peter Hasenclever*, 149.

25. "der moralische und politische Charakter seiner Bewohner": [Franz Dominicus?] Häberlin, "Über den Einfluß der Unabhängigkeit der vereinigten Staaten von Nord-America, auf den politischen Zustand Europas," *Göttingisches Magazin der Wissenschaften und Litteratur*, III/5 (1783), 695.

26. "Lage, Klima und Fruchtbarkeit sind durchgängig von der Art, daß sie bei gehöriger Benutzung den Fleiß des Landmanns ebenso sehr belohnen als die besten Länder Europens. . . . Nur auf die hinlängliche Anzahl von Bewohnern kommt alles an; und diese wird Amerika erhalten, wenn es einen jeden Fremdling gern aufnimmt und Handel und Wandel ebenso gern freien Lauf läßt als den verschiedenen Religionsübungen": Crome, *Nordamerikanischer Freystaat*, 60.

27. "von der Natur mit den herrlichsten Produkten aller Art reichlich versehen . . . aus seinem Nichts . . . Besitz einer Freiheit und Macht, so glänzend und vorteilhaft, als sie je ein Staat gehabt hat. Man kann den bevorstehenden schnellen Wachstum dieses glücklichen Staates leicht voraussehen, und es wird nicht mehr als ein Menschenalter dazu erfordert werden, um denselben in einer bewundernswürdigen Größe zu erblicken": Snell, *Von den Handlungsvortheilen, welche aus der Unabhängigkeit der vereinigten Staaten von Nord-Amerika für das russische Reich entspringen* (Riga, 1783), 5–6.

28. Sprengel, *Allgemeines historisches Taschenbuch*, 146–147.

29. E.g., Schmohl, *Über Nordamerika und Demokratie*, 77–78; *Historisches Portefeuille*, June 1784, 789–790; Wendeborn, *Grosbritannien*, I, 287–288.

The American Revolution, the victory over England, the state built "as by a miracle"[30]—all had opened prospects of a happy and great future. People were only too inclined to believe that this republic would be "some day among the first states of the world," spreading its power and its wealth by free trade to all the countries of the world, and, of course, to all Europe.[31]

There were some contemporaries, however, who had a more skeptical attitude toward the economic and commercial consequences of American independence. They believed that general European trade would not benefit from the Revolution, since the Americans would continue to be economically dependent upon Great Britain for years to come.[32] This view contradicted indirectly the opinion expressed in private in 1778 by Rochus Friedrich Graf von Lynar of Saxony, who condemned France's support of the Americans as shortsighted, since it would lead to "the inhabitants of the New World becoming masters of the Old World's trade."[33]

Lynar's assertion touched on a point that constituted the true import of the American Revolution for those parts of the European bourgeoisie who were interested in overseas trade, especially in France. Many contemporaries disagreed with Lynar: "Europe should look with satisfaction upon a revolution that assures freedom of the seas and the universality of commerce."[34] The sacrifice made by France in participating in the war had, in their opinion, been more than balanced by achieving freedom of trade and of the seas.[35] They felt sure that the young republic would have an important place in world trade by virtue of its wealth alone.[36]

It may surprise us today to note the optimistic outlook of many contemporaries about the immediate economic future of the new United States.

---

30. "wie durch ein Wunder": Schubart, ed., *Vaterlandschronik*, Jan. 8, 1788, 21.

31. "dereinst einer der ersten Staaten in der Welt": Karl Ehregott Mangelsdorf, *Allgemeine Geschichte der europäischen Staaten* (Halle, 1784–1794), V (1787), 248.

32. See [August von Hennings], "Welchen Einfluß wird die Unabhängigkeit von America auf den Handel, und überhaupt auf den politischen Zustand von Europa haben?" *Politisches Journal* (1782), II, 403–406. The article was published anonymously; I happened to find a manuscript draft in Hennings's hand in the Nachlaß Hennings, XXVII, fols. 34–74v, SuUB, Hamburg. See also Häberlin, "Über den Einfluß der Unabhängigkeit der vereinigten Staaten," *Göttingisches Magazin*, III/5 (1783), 685–734.

33. "die Bewohner der Neuen Welt Meister vom Handel der Alten werden": Lynar to Zacharießen, Sept. 1, 1778 (Nachlaß Lynar, XXVII, 587, StA, Oldenburg). See also Lynar to Zacharießen, June 9, 1778 (*ibid.*, XXVI/XXVII, 574–575).

34. "L'Europe doit voir avec satisfaction une révolution qui assure la liberté de la mer et la généralité du commerce": Accarias de Sérionne, *Situation politique*, 129.

35. Cf. Raynal, *Considérations sur la paix*, 3, 24; *Beschreibung der dreizehn unabhängigen Nordamerikanischen Staaten*, 55–56.

36. E.g., Wendeborn, *Grosbritannien*, I, 290; Hammerdörfer and Kosche, *Amerika*, I, 359–360; "Bericht über die politischen und wirtschaftlichen Verhältnisse in Nordamerika" (1790) (HptStA, Hanover).

After all, the American economy had been severely strained at the time, and the consequences of the war had by no means been overcome as late as the mid-1780s.[37] Great Britain's headstart in industrial production, as well as in overseas trade, was greatly underrated in the pro-American statements, as subsequent developments proved.

Other elements of American internal life and its future development received scant treatment. To be sure, Doctor Johann David Schoepf noted some of the social contradictions between the North and the South during his travels through several states immediately after the war. He prophesied that the slave question in the South would develop into one of America's great problems, and that only after its solution would there be a happy and great future.[38] But Schoepf's views were those of only one perceptive individual. The large majority of the bourgeoisie paid little attention to the problem and consequently had no idea of the extent, the causes, and the future of slavery in the United States. Thus, Johann Jakob Sell, as overly optimistic as many Americans at that time,[39] believed that the Revolution had seriously weakened the institution of slavery and that it would soon die out.[40] But the prevailing indifference was such that this view seems to have commanded just as little attention as Schoepf's.

Effects on the Western Hemisphere

For many German contemporaries the possible effects of the Revolution on colonialism, and especially on the future of the European domains in Latin America, were more interesting than the opaque problems of black slavery.

It is mainly among the physiocrats that we find some opposition to colonialism in the 1770s and 1780s. One of their most important representa-

37. Merrill Jensen, *The New Nation: A History of the United States During the Confederation 1781–1789* (New York, 1950), 179–233, sees economic development after 1783 positively; more critical is Curtis P. Nettels, *The Emergence of a National Economy, 1775–1815* (New York, 1962), esp. 45–64. Douglass C. North, *The Economic Growth of the United States, 1790–1860* (Englewood Cliffs, N.J., 1961), esp. 17–23, holds a convincing middle line; see also North's *Growth and Welfare in the American Past* (Englewood Cliffs, N.J., 1966), 50–63.
38. Schoepf to Johann Kaspar Hirzel, Apr. 1, 1783 (Familienarchiv Hirzel, CCCXV, ZB, Zurich). Cf. Staughton Lynd, *Class Conflict, Slavery, and the United States Constitution* (Indianapolis, Ind., 1967), esp. 185–213.
39. Cf. E. Wright, *Fabric of Freedom,* 149.
40. Sell, *Geschichte des Negersclavenhandels,* 200–201.

tives in the German-language area at the time was Iselin, who considered any form of colonial oppression to be an "injustice,"[41] and who hoped that Britain's "mercantile tyranny" would be brought to an end by the disputes in America.[42] Very early he espoused the view that "the dispute between the colonies and their metropolis is probably not as important politically as it is economically. As a struggle between freedom and tyranny and between liberty and righteous power, it is a grand and interesting spectacle, promising considerable results to the world. But as a struggle of oppressed diligence against oppressive greed, though it is not as spectacular, it is basically of much greater importance to the contesting parties and to all mankind."[43]

Iselin was not the only one in the German-language area who welcomed the American Revolution because of its probable consequences for colonialism and unhindered commercial enterprise. Karl Graf von Zinzendorf, to name just one more example, also believed in the necessity of the "independence of each state."[44] Even Heinrich Christian Boie, though certainly not a defender of the American Revolution, welcomed independence in the belief that "thus all European colonies in other parts of the world will one day be independent states. It is unjust and unfair for merchants to rule and suppress where they should merely trade."[45]

This antimercantilist and anticolonialist thinking often ended in the expectation that the American Revolution would have direct colonial consequences, above all for the Spanish dominions in Latin America. In German governmental circles anxious suspicions emerged very soon that the Spanish colonies in the Western Hemisphere might follow the example of the British

---

41. "Ungerechtigkeit": Iselin, Tagebuch, Jan. 11, 1774 (Nachlaß Iselin, XIV, 168–169, StA, Basel).

42. "merkantilistischen Tyranneien": to Salomon Hirzel, Nov. 27, 1774; cf. his letters to Jean Rodolphe Frey, Apr. 18, 1779, Dec. 10, 1780, Feb. 11, 1781 (*ibid.*, LXII, 39, LVI, 216–217, 276, 281).

43. "Die Streitigkeiten der englischen Kolonien mit ihrer Metropole ist dem politischen Gesichtspunkt wohl nicht so wichtig als in dem wirtschaftlichen. Als ein Kampf zwischen der Freiheit und der Tyrannei oder zwischen der Ungebundenheit und der gerechten Gewalt ist sie freilich ein großes, ein interessantes Schauspiel und verspricht sie der Welt schon sehr beträchtliche Folgen. Aber als der Kampf der unterdrückten Emsigkeit wider die unterdrückende Habsucht hat sie zwar kein so glänzendes Ansehen, sie ist aber im Grunde für die entzweiten Parteien und für die ganze Menschheit von einem weit größern Belange": *Ephemeriden der Menschheit*, Jan. 1776, 116–117. Cf. Im Hof, *Iselin und die Spätaufklärung*, 143.

44. "indépendance de chaque Etat": Zinzendorf, Tagebuch, Dec. 29, 1779 (XXIV, fol. 273v, HHStA, Vienna).

45. "So werden einst alle europäische Kolonien in fremden Weltteilen für sich bestehende Staaten werden. Es ist unrecht und unbillig, daß Kaufleute dort herrschen und unterdrücken, wo sie bloß handeln sollten": to Louise Mejer, Jan. 20, 1782 (SuUB, Göttingen). Cf. the printed version in Boie, *Ich war wohl klug*, 128; see also Girod-Chantrans, *Reisen eines Schweizers*, 293, 295.

colonies. Eberhard Friedrich von Gemmingen, a high-ranking Württemberg official, ruminated: "I am almost led to believe that it is impossible everywhere to keep colonies like those in North America dependent on the mother country for any length of time."[46] A little later the Hesse-Kassel emissary, Christian Moritz Freiherr von Kutzleben, saw an even more concrete danger: "Spain fears that its colonies in South America will follow the example of the English colonies."[47] In German bourgeois circles this prospect, which was discussed in the 1780s, generally had no negative implications, as Iselin's and Boie's statements document. The idea that the Latin American colonies might in a relatively short time follow the example of the United States seemed to them to be as much to be hoped for as it was necessary.[48]

Historical developments have proven that these views were by no means unjustified. Within the next two generations nearly all Latin American dominions freed themselves from colonial bondage and became independent states. But although the American Revolution and the federal Constitution of 1787 did have some influence on the Latin American revolutions at the beginning of the nineteenth century, these revolutions cannot be interpreted without taking into consideration the French Revolution and the Napoleonic wars and their impact on the Iberian peninsula.[49]

46. "Beinahe komme ich auf den Gedanken, daß es überall unmöglich sei, Kolonien von der Art der nordamerikanischen in die Länge von dem mütterlichen Lande abhängig zu erhalten": to Albrecht von Haller, Aug. 7, 1777, in Haller, *Briefwechsel zwischen Haller und Gemmingen*, ed. Fischer, 129. Cf. Haller to Gemmingen, Mar. 29, 1776, *ibid.*, 91; Seinsheim to Haslang, Apr. 23, 1775 (Bayer. Gesandtschaft: London, no. 253, GStA, Munich); Hans Moritz Graf von Brühl zu Martinskirch to Graf von Sacken, Aug. 18, 1775 (Locat 2685, conv. XI, fol. 330, StA, Dresden); Lynar to Zacharießen, June 9, 1778 (Nachlaß Lynar, XXVI/XXVII, 574–575, StA, Oldenburg).

47. "L'Espagne craint que ses colonies dans l'Amérique méridionale suivraient l'example des colonies anglaises": Kutzleben to the landgrave of Hesse-Kassel, Oct. 17, 1780 (300 Philippsruhe E 11/6, V, fol. 159, StA, Marburg).

48. E.g., Stolberg, "Die Zukunft," ed. Hartwig, *AGL*, XIII (1885), 272; Johann August Weppen, "Eine Parabel am 20sten Januar 1783. als am Tage des Friedensschlusses zu Versailles," *Musenalmanach für das Jahr 1784* (Göttingen, 1783), 187–188; Friedrich von Matthisson to [?], Dec. 21, 1791, in his *Briefe*, 2d ed. (Zurich, 1802), 125.

49. See Arthur P. Whitaker, *The United States and the Independence of Latin America, 1800–1830* (1941; repr. New York, 1964), 61–99; Salvador de Madariaga, *The Fall of the Spanish American Empire* (New York, 1948), 302–305; Boleslao Lewin, *Los movimientos de emancipación en Hispanoamérica y la independencia de Estados Unidos* (Buenos Aires, 1952), 7–56, 186; Ricardo Levene, *El mundo de las ideas y la revolución hispanoamericana de 1810* (Santiago de Chile, 1956), 157–178; Charles C. Griffin, *The National Period in the History of the New World: An Outline and Commentary* (Mexico City, 1961), 10–19; Pierre Chaunu, *L'Amérique et les Amériques* (Paris, 1964), 189–206; Robert A. Humphreys and John Lynch, eds., *The Origins of the Latin American Revolution 1808–1826* (New York, 1965), 75–110; Carlos Restrepo Canal, "Causas de la independencia de los países hispanoamericanos e ideas de sus libertadores," *Revista de Indias*, XXVIII, nos. 111/112 (1968), 143–167.

A noteworthy number of contemporaries went further than these prognoses; they speculated about the future role of the United States in the New World and its relationships with other areas of the hemisphere. The questions arising from such considerations, which included both domestic and foreign politics, were summed up by August von Hennings: "Will America become a warlike state? Will it conquer Mexico and Canada, occupy the West Indies, and monopolize the fishing grounds off Newfoundland? Or will America become a mercantile state?"[50] Before the war was over, there were some, at first even among the protagonists of the Revolution, who voiced the conviction that the United States would soon conquer all neighboring colonies and expand its political and military hegemony over the entire continents of North and South America.[51] "The United States will be masters of both Americas before another century has passed," one author concluded.[52]

These visions of the future reveal the impact of the American Revolution on the imaginations of large parts of the German bourgeoisie. For these expectations were hardly realistic if compared with the actual instruments of political and military power in America in those years. Toward the end of the eighteenth century the United States could certainly not be called militaristic and imperialistic in a nineteenth-century European sense, however vaulting its ambitions.[53] After the Treaty of Paris this realization quickly spread in Germany, and the number of such grand conjectures decreased sharply. Later, in the 1790s, Dietrich Heinrich Freiherr von Bülow held the view that the United States would expand toward the West but would be prevented by Mexico from reaching the Pacific.[54]

50. "Wird Amerika ein kriegerischer Staat werden, Mexiko und Kanada erobern oder die westindischen Inseln in Besitz nehmen und die Fischerei in Terreneuve an sich zu bringen suchen, oder wird Amerika ein handelnder Staat werden": Hennings, "Einfluß der Unabhängigkeit von America?" *Politisches Journal* (1782), II, 403.

51. E.g., Jan Ingenhousz to Franklin, Dec. 14, 1777 (Franklin Papers, I, 41, University of Pennsylvania Library, Philadelphia); Lynar to Zacharießen, June 9, 1778 (Nachlaß Lynar, XXVI/XXVII, 575, StA, Oldenburg); Georg Christoph Lichtenberg to Johann Andreas Schernhagen, Dec. 23, 1782, in Albert Leitzmann, ed., "Neues von Lichtenberg," *Zeitschrift für Bücherfreunde*, N.S., IV, no. 1 (1912), 125.

52. "und daß, ehe ein Jahrhundert vergeht, die Vereinigten Staaten Herren von beiden Amerikas sein werden": Köster, ed., *Neueste Staatsbegebenheiten*, Feb. 1782, 160.

53. See Marcus Cunliffe, *Soldiers & Civilians: The Martial Spirit in America 1775–1865* (Boston and Toronto, 1968), esp. 65–98; Hans-Ulrich Wehler, "1889: Wendepunkt der amerikanischen Außenpolitik," *HZ*, CCI (1965), 57–60; Robin W. Winks, "Imperialism," in C. Vann Woodward, ed., *Comparative Approach to American History* (New York, 1968), 253–270; Richard H. Miller, ed., *American Imperialism in 1898: The Quest for National Fulfillment* (New York, 1970), 1–15, 21–32, 179–190.

54. Bülow, *Freistaat von Nordamerika*, II, 200.

Given the date when von Bülow made this prediction, wrong as it was in the end, he could surely claim a greater measure of realism than could the prophets of about 1780. Their visions may have sounded incredible near the end of the eighteenth century, but they were not completely irrational, as is proven by American history during the nineteenth and twentieth centuries, in particular the War of 1812, the Mexican War, the Spanish War of 1898, and America's policy toward Latin America to the present.

During the war years and the period immediately thereafter, there were hardly any prophecies of similar reach and scope pertaining to American political relations with Europe. Comparable speculations concerning the United States and Europe were essentially an outgrowth of the French Revolution and will be discussed later.

8. Criteria of Judgment
on the American Revolution

The Englandbild

So far we have inquired into the various kinds of views on the American Revolution that were held in the 1770s and 1780s by German contemporaries, especially the bourgeoisie. I have tried to show that the actions of the American patriots evoked a wave of sympathy in Germany, as Edmund Burke more generally remarked when he wrote that in all European countries where public affairs could be discussed, opinion was generally in favor of the Americans. Burke did not consider this a pleasant thought, but he knew it was one of some significance.[1] The British government, however, was not entirely without friends in Germany, even though they were far fewer in number than their opponents.

But no matter where one stood, there was remarkable agreement that the Revolution was a divisive event, one that compelled men to form opinions and take sides. The *Leipziger Zeitung*, for example, could state unequivocally as early as 1776 that "England's dispute with its colonies is at present undoubtedly the most important public topic. Everyone participates in it, and everyone judges it as he sees fit."[2] This was a report not from London but from Leipzig, and it agrees with what was said elsewhere a little later: "Everyone participates in it, everyone draws his own conclusions."[3] In September 1777 a commentator said the same in the *Frankfurter Gelehrten Anzeigen*: "Everybody now wants to pass judgment on the American war."[4] Even sev-

---

1. "Es ist kein angenehmer, vielleicht aber kein ganz unbedeutender Umstand, daß in allen Ländern Europens, wo man von öffentlichen Angelegenheiten reden und schreiben darf, die allgemeine Stimme für die Amerikaner gewesen ist": Burke, *Geschichte der Englischen Pflanzungen*, IV, 136. Cf., however, the contradictory remark of the translator.
2. "Der Zwist Engellands mit seinen Kolonien ist gegenwärtig unstreitig die wichtigste unter den öffentlichen Angelegenheiten. Jedermann nimmt daran Anteil, und jedermann urteilt darüber, so wie es ihn gut dünkt": *Leipziger Zeitung*, Feb. 6, 1776. For a similar statement in a report from London see *ibid.*, May 14, 1770.
3. "Jeder nimmt teil daran, jeder urteilet darüber": *Geographische Belustigungen*, I, [4].
4. "Jedermann will jetzt über den amerikanischen Krieg urteilen": p. 565.

eral years later interest was still lively, for "everybody takes sides in this matter, while very few are knowledgeable enough to judge the dispute truly and properly."[5]

As for the image of England, the question arises: In what way did it influence German views on the American Revolution at the time, and was there a significant influence? To inquire into this we will have to sketch briefly the German bourgeoisie's *Englandbild* at the beginning of the American war.

Especially since the days of Montesquieu and Voltaire, England was believed to be Europe's freest country, enjoying the world's best constitution. But after the Seven Years' War, despite the influence of works by anglophiles, there gradually spread a feeling increasingly ill-disposed toward an all-too-powerful, proud, and boastful Albion.[6] On the one hand, England thrived under a relatively free political order; on the other, it displayed an arrogant boastfulness based on a dominant political and economic position. This combination produced an inner rift in the German bourgeoisie, who admired England's constitution while they abhorred its "mercantile tyrannies."[7] Like no other event, the American Revolution was able to clarify this somewhat ambiguous picture, offering, as it did, equally clear starting points to both protagonists and antagonists of the patriots.

While the German governments' relations with Great Britain were determined fundamentally by political and economic considerations, the bourgeoisie's attitude toward England was focused on the idea of liberty, which was associated with both England and the American Revolution. If the American patriots were really fighting for liberty, then Britain could not be its homeland. But if the Americans' arguments were unjustified, there was no contradiction in being both an enthusiast for liberty and an anglophile. And if the Americans were insurgents and rebels who, out of base motives, aimed to destroy the established order, then England could claim to be a trustee of the status quo without impairment of its reputation for having an exemplary political order. These three opinions represent the basic attitudes concerning England and America that we find among the German bourgeoisie of the 1770s and 1780s.

5. "da jedermann in dieser Sache Partei nimmt und doch so wenige diejenige Kenntnis besitzen, welche zu einem wahren und richtigen Urteile in diesem Streite erfordert wird": German editor's preface to Russell, *Geschichte von Amerika*, I, iii.

6. Palmer, *Age of the Democratic Revolution*, I, 248; see also *Beschreibung der dreizehn unabhängigen Nordamerikanischen Staaten*, 43. Frederick II's antipathy toward England following the Seven Years' War is another, well-known example of these resentments.

7. "merkantilischen Tyranneien": Isaak Iselin to Salomon Hirzel, Nov. 27, 1774 (Nachlaß Iselin, LXII, 39, StA, Basel). Further proof of Iselin's ambiguous attitude toward England is in his *Geschichte der Menschheit*, 3d ed. (1700), II, 338; also in the fourth edition (Basel, 1779), II, 367. See also Im Hof, *Iselin und die Spätaufklärung*, 128–129, 143–146.

Up to the mid-1770s nearly all those members of the bourgeoisie who later acclaimed America's liberty still hailed England, "which by virtue of its government and liberty, is the world's first nation."[8] Jakob Mauvillon, Isaak Iselin, Jan Ingenhousz, and nearly all others were enthusiastic about English liberty in those years. But after 1775 their enthusiasm, together with Christoph Daniel Ebeling's and Matthias Christian Sprengel's, turned from the island kingdom and moved to America, with the ideal of liberty as its vehicle. How much England's image was tarnished in the transitional phase around the middle of the decade is illustrated by the case of Friedrich Wilhelm Taube. He was born in England, and though he spent many years in the service of Austria, his ideal was "English liberty."[9] But in spite of his love for the country of his birth, he could not bring himself to condemn the Americans in their war, which was becoming more destructive all the time. His attitude toward both sides became increasingly neutral,[10] but his early death prevents us from learning what his final decision on the conflict would have been.

Christian Friedrich Daniel Schubart's attitude, however, is unequivocal and easily understood. As late as 1774–1775, he divided his love of liberty— originally reserved for England alone—between the mother country and its colonies. But by 1776 he had decided clearly for America, praising it as the only country of liberty.[11] This attitude is representative of many other liberty enthusiasts, who, the more they believed that the American patriots were defending liberty, the more they thought that Britain was tyrannical. The Rockingham Whigs, who took over the leadership of the British government in the spring of 1782 after long years of opposition to Lord North's American policy, were the only group that did have a few followers among the German champions of liberty.[12] But by 1783 the German devotées of liberty, notwithstanding occasional breakaways, were less inclined toward the En-

8. "die durch ihre Regierungsform und ihre Freiheit die erste Nation des Erdbodens ist": note by Jakob Mauvillon to his translation of Raynal, *Philosophische und politische Geschichte*, III, (1775), [5]. See also Mauvillon, *Sammlung von Aufsätzen*, I, 99, 128–129.

9. "engländische Freiheit": Friedrich Wilhelm Taube, *Historische und politische Abschilderung der Engländischen Manufacturen* (Vienna, 1774), 178; the same in his *Abschilderung der Engländischen Manufacturen*, 2d ed. (Vienna, 1777–1778), II, 270.

10. Cf. all three editions of Taube's *Abschilderung*, 1774, 1776, and 1777–1778.

11. Cf. Schubart's *Chronik*; also Schubart to Balthasar Haug, May 10, 1776, in Schubart, *Leben in seinen Briefen*, ed. David Friedrich Strauss (Berlin, 1849), I, 333. See also, though not always correct: Gustav Hauff, *Christian Friedrich Daniel Schubart in seinem Leben und seinen Werken* (Stuttgart, 1885), 345; Gallinger, "Haltung der deutschen Publizistik," 12; J. A. Walz, "Three Swabian Journalists," *GAA*, I (1903), 209–212; Ford, "Two German Publicists," *JEGP*, VIII (1909), 168; Schairer, "Schubart als politischer Journalist," 24, 155; King, "Echoes of the American Revolution," *PMP*, XIV (1930), 177.

12. Cf. the following issues of the *Historisches Portefeuille* of 1782: Jan., 92; Apr., 404–405; May, 626; June, 715–745.

glish constitution, acclaiming instead, and almost exclusively, the new republic in the New World as their ideal state.

Among these bourgeois champions of liberty we must distinguish certain factions, especially in Hanover. To be sure, the Hanoverians followed general opinion, but at the same time they retained a more lasting predilection for Great Britain. England, tied to Hanover as it was by dynastic relations, continued to be their intellectual haven and political homeland. Whether August Ludwig Schlözer was really a member of one of these factions is debatable. But Georg Christoph Lichtenberg, the physicist and satirist from Göttingen, surely was. His personal friends and acquaintances in England influenced his views on America and the American Revolution, which were never very favorable; he always condemned the revolt. But like Schlözer, Lichtenberg shared the German bourgeoisie's enthusiasm for the French Revolution during its first years. This fact at least illustrates that Lichtenberg was not opposed to the bourgeois ideal of liberty. His siding with Great Britain during the American Revolution can presumably only be explained by his lasting attachment to England.[13]

The enthusiasm of these factions for Britain, which in Lichtenberg's case lasted until after 1783, clearly sets them apart from those contemporaries who, like Sprengel or Ebeling,[14] very much favored England at the outset of the war but later became convinced that their longing for liberty was best satisfied by the American example. In Ebeling's case the brusque opposition that replaced his affection for Britain preserved its intensity unchanged during the French Revolution.[15] But most of the anglophile liberty enthusiasts in Hanover remained unperturbed in their conviction that the English constitution was exemplary.

Another group of British protagonists that should be set apart was made up of those who opposed American revolutionary ideals on principle. A group heterogeneous in composition, its position toward England was not necessarily an expression of deep sympathy, but rather a declaration of

13. Cf. Lichtenberg's letters to Johann Andreas Schernhagen, most of which have been published; also, the diary of his journey to England in 1774–1775, and a resolution of the Rockingham Whigs brought home and kept by Lichtenberg (all in Nachlaß Lichtenberg, SuUB, Göttingen). Wolfgang Rödel, *Forster und Lichtenberg. Ein Beitrag zum Problem deutsche Intelligenz und Französische Revolution* (Berlin, 1960), ignores these matters since he pays no attention to Lichtenberg's attitude toward the American Revolution.

14. For information on Lichtenberg's relations with Sprengel, who at this time still lived in Göttingen, and on the attitudes of both toward England, see Lichtenberg to Schernhagen, Feb. 8, 1778 (Nachlaß Lichtenberg, SuUB, Göttingen). On Ebeling's attitudes see his *Erdbeschreibung*, I, ii.

15. Cf. Ebeling to Mathew Carey, Mar. 12, 1794 (Lea and Febiger Coll., PHi, Philadelphia), to Ezra Stiles, June 26, 1794, in Massachusetts Historical Society, *Collections*, 2d Ser., VIII (1826), 273, and to Joel Barlow, Mar. 16, 1796, in Lane, ed., *Letters of Ebeling*, 18.

loyalty to a country that in the present conflict was acting as a trustee of the existing order.[16] Of course, there could also be traces of anglophilia in this point of view. Albrecht von Haller probably best exemplifies this attitude. He championed Britain not because of its liberal constitution but because of his devotion to the constitutional orders of aristocracy and monarchy. He hated the Wilkesites, as well as all efforts tending toward a democracy.[17] It was therefore only natural that he closely followed the war in the colonies, which broke out shortly before his death, while at the same time he condemned the aims of the American patriots.[18]

There were numerous others who shared this predilection for England's aristocratic features and rejected the bourgeois idea of liberty. Johannes von Müller, who was at least skeptical about the American Revolution, seems to have had similar ideas when he called England "the country of true liberty."[19] The same may be said of Adam Friedrich Geisler, a writer from Leipzig; Johann Georg Zimmermann, the doctor from Hanover; Georg Friedrich Brandes, a civil servant; and Christoph Gottlob Heyne—to mention only a few.[20] When the French Revolution began, this faction set itself apart from both the bourgeois liberty enthusiasts and men like Georg Christoph Lichtenberg by uniting in condemnation of the events in France, just as they had done earlier in response to the happenings in the New World. They believed that an aristocratic England was the only guarantor of a threatened political order.

The true depth of the impression made by the American Revolution on the German bourgeoisie may be measured by recognizing that their attitude toward it was not a result of any preceding image of England. On the contrary, it was the events in the Western Hemisphere that changed the image of Britain in the minds of large sectors of the German public. In an era that

16. E.g., Korn, *Geschichte der Kriege*, II, 81, III, 59; A. J. Pföter, *Betrachtungen über die Quellen und Folgen der merkwürdigsten Revolutionen unseres Jahrhunderts* (Vienna, 1794), 284.

17. See among others his reviews in the *Göttingische Anzeigen von gelehrten Sachen*, Mar. 12, 1770, Mar. 21, 1772; also his letters to Friedrich von Gemmingen, Apr. 30, 1772, Jan. 23, 1774, in Haller, *Briefwechsel zwischen Haller und Gemmingen*, ed. Fischer, 23, 65. In addition, Max Widmann, *Albrecht von Hallers Staatsromane* (Biel, 1894), 193, and Anneliese Frey, "Albrecht von Hallers Staatsromane" (publ. Ph.D. diss., University of Freiburg, Germany, 1928), 23–26, 29–32, 64–65.

18. See his letters to Gemmingen during 1777, in his *Briefwechsel zwischen Haller und Gemmingen*, ed. Fischer, 101, 118–119, and *passim*.

19. "le pays de la vraie liberté": to Georg Forster, Mar. 18, 1790, in Forster, *Briefwechsel*, ed. Huber, I, 866.

20. Geisler, *Königlich Grosbritannischen Kriegsmacht*, 354, 356–357, 365–366, 369–370, 373, 399. On Johann Georg Zimmermann see especially his letters to Jean André de Luc during the years 1777–1795 (StA, Aarau). On Brandes and Heyne see the letters by Brandes in

acclaimed Frederick II of Prussia, Britain's official foreign policy did not have many champions in Germany anyway. This dislike, however, was not the deciding factor. Opinion was determined primarily by whether one preferred a government based on civil liberty, or a government predominantly monarchical and aristocratic. Up to the mid-1770s adherents of both sides used Britain as a basis for their argumentation. The American Revolution changed that: after 1783 at the latest, but mostly since the end of the 1770s, the majority of the educated bourgeoisie shared the American patriots' conviction that Britain was no longer a haven of liberty and an exemplary state. German bourgeois sympathies generally were transferred, without restriction, to the United States as the embodiment of their ideals.[21] It was only during that brief transitional phase—from being an advocate of liberal Britain to becoming an advocate of the American Revolution—that the prevailing *Englandbild* influenced large groups in their judgment of the American Revolution. In the long run, only the Hanoverian liberty enthusiasts remained completely under the spell of their earlier sympathies for Britain. Although they were emphatically in favor of the bourgeois ideal of liberty, it was their *Englandbild* that kept them for years from accepting the American Revolution.

Regional Aspects

If the strength of the German image of England was conditioned in part by regional factors, we might ask further, how important in general were territorial connections in influencing German appraisal of the events in the Western Hemisphere? Many investigators have stated that regional characteristics within Germany were of decisive importance in the formation of responses to the American Revolution, and that there was real interest in the Revolution only along an imaginary axis from Bern to Berlin. They also have insisted that, because Hanover belonged to the English crown, judgments on the American Revolution by Hanoverians were different from those made by all other Germans who had any interest at all in what was happening on the other side of the Atlantic. The extent of interest, they believe, varied with the territory, the

---

the Nachlaß Heyne (SuUB, Göttingen). See also Johann Conrad Ruff, "Tagebuch von Braunschweig nach America," Mar. 19, 1778 (StadtA, Brunswick).

21. Cf. King, "Echoes of the American Revolution," *PMP*, XIV (1930), 186.

centers having been in central and northern Germany, in fact, in Göttingen and Kassel.[22]

These views need correction. That regional connections really constituted a decisive criterion still needs to be proven; at the same time, there is no question that interest in American events was much greater everywhere in Germany than has been assumed until now. This may be shown by an analysis of numerous contemporary statements, both public and private, a survey of the published literature, including consideration of what it reveals about the authors, and by an account of the opinions of personalities with known views.

Let us return once more to German book production in general, and to the publication of Americana Germanica in particular. Johann Goldfriedrich has ranked German places of publication according to the quantity of books published at each in the last decades of the eighteenth century.[23] If we compare this ranking with that for publishing locations for literature on America, Vienna and Hamburg change places, but the rest of the eight most important cities hold to almost the same order. Shifts in the sequence that are worth mentioning occur only farther down, with Dresden, Jena, Prague, and Zurich losing in favor of Bern and Barby.[24]

But if our standard is the one-quarter of the Americana Germanica that is concerned exclusively with America, a comparison of their places of publication with Goldfriedrich's general ranking sets Hamburg apart even more clearly as one of the late eighteenth-century centers for studies on America. The city of Halle loses ground appreciably, while Bern is still distinctly above Goldfriedrich's ranking.[25] If we group the publishing locations under terri-

22. See Gallinger, "Haltung der deutschen Publizistik," 33, 56; Weber, *America in Imaginative German Literature*, 10; Desczyk, "Amerika in der Phantasie deutscher Dichter," *Deutsch-Amerikanische Geschichtsblätter*, XXIV–XXV (1925), 32; Palmer, *Age of the Democratic Revolution*, I, 248. For a similar statement concerning the German response to the French Revolution see Jacques Droz, *L'Allemagne et la Révolution française* (Paris, 1949), 18.

23. According to Goldfriedrich, *Geschichte des deutschen Buchhandels*, III, 471–472, the top 20 publishing places ranked as follows: Leipzig, Berlin, Vienna, Halle, Frankfurt, Nuremberg, Hamburg, Göttingen, Breslau, Augsburg, Dresden, Jena, Prague, Brunswick, Erlangen, Hanover, Strasbourg, Zurich, Tübingen, and Basel.

24. The most important publishing centers for literature on America, with the number of books published from 1770 to 1800, were: Leipzig (119); Berlin (90); Hamburg (51); Frankfurt (35); Halle (33); Nuremberg (26); Vienna (25); Göttingen (23); Brunswick (14); Bern (13); Augsburg (12); Breslau (12); and Barby (11). Bern ranked 38th in Goldfriedrich; here it is 10th. Barby, ranked 13th here, is not even in Goldfriedrich's list of more than 90 places. When more than one publication place was given on a title page, I generally considered only the first one.

25. More than five works of Americana Germanica were published, 1770–1800, at Leipzig (32), Berlin (29), Hamburg (28), Frankfurt (16), Göttingen (9), and Vienna (6). Four were

torial and denominational categories, we are struck by the clearly dominant position of the free imperial cities as well as the position of the duchy of Brunswick-Wolfenbüttel, while the Catholic territories, and especially the Habsburg possessions, clearly fall off.[26]

The publishing centers for Americana Germanica vary markedly from those for overall German book production. Censorship legislation, which was often arbitrary and administered irrationally,[27] may have had some influence here, in spite of the possibility of circumventing it by publishing anonymously or choosing a more favorable publishing center. It is undisputed that strict censorship had a crippling effect on cultural life and public political discussion.[28] But even with these limitations, publishing centers were scattered from the Alps to the Baltic and from the Rhine to Breslau and Königsberg.

One additional source gives us valuable hints: between 1777 and 1785, especially before the conclusion of the peace negotiations, nearly two hundred Germans from practically all social classes of the German-language area wrote letters to Benjamin Franklin. Generally, these letters have a friendly tenor toward Franklin and America, though it is true that some were intended merely to curry Franklin's favors and help. But writing to representatives of foreign countries living abroad was not a common practice for private persons in the eighteenth century, which makes this collection of documents an

---

published at Bern and three at Halle. If we take the turn of the year 1783–1784 to be a caesura, in the period 1770–1783 the leading centers of this kind of publishing were Frankfurt (14), Leipzig (13), Hamburg (10), and Göttingen (9). For the years 1784–1800, Berlin (25), Leipzig (19), and Hamburg (18) ranked highest.

26. Free imperial cities (55), Prussia (42), electorate of Saxony (35), electorate of Hanover (11), duchy of Brunswick-Wolfenbüttel (8), Switzerland (6), and Habsburg territories (6). In Bavaria and in the ecclesiastical territories, save the electorate of Salzburg, no work of Americana Germanica, in its narrower sense, was published. Salzburg ranked 33d in general publishing and therefore was far more important in this regard than any other city belonging to an ecclesiastical territory; cf. Goldfriedrich, *Geschichte des deutschen Buchhandels*, III, 343–434, 472, and Robert Haass, *Die geistige Haltung der katholischen Universitäten Deutschlands im 18. Jahrhundert. Ein Beitrag zur Geschichte der Aufklärung* (Freiburg, Germany, 1952), esp. 160–165.

27. For a survey of censorship in the most important German territories during this time see Goldfriedrich, *Geschichte des deutschen Buchhandels*, III, 343–434. A singular, but nonetheless illuminating, event in practical censorship is told by Isabel Heitjan, "Zur stadtkölnischen Bücherzensur am Ende des 18. Jahrhunderts," *Gutenberg-Jahrbuch*, XLII (1967), 204–207; see also King, "Echoes of the American Revolution," *PMP*, XIV (1930), 26–27.

28. Cf. Stadelmann, *Deutschland und Westeuropa*, 21; Otto Borst, "Die Kulturbedeutung der oberdeutschen Reichsstadt am Ende des alten Reiches," *Blätter für deutsche Landesgeschichte*, C (1964), 159–246.

extremely valuable supplement to any inquiry into the regional influences upon German appraisals of the American Revolution.[29]

If we disregard combatants in the auxiliary forces, Franklin's correspondents, and diplomats (because of their special position), and consider only authors and other personalities whose views on the American Revolution we know from before 1789, we come up with some ninety persons from the entire German-language area. Even though this group is in no way representative, it shows a high percentage of writers from northern Germany, Prussia, and Switzerland, whereas there are nearly none from the ecclesiastical territories and the electorate of Bavaria. This distribution merely reaffirms the well-known fact that political awareness was not a conspicuous feature of these latter areas.

We get similar results when we classify Franklin's German correspondents according to geographical origin. Again, the writers come from the entire German-language area. If we try to cut this area approximately in half and assume the dividing line to be the Main River and the northern boundaries of the Habsburg possessions, then the number of letter writers from the north is only slightly higher than that from the south. If we assume a north-south dividing line nearly identical with West Germany's eastern border today, two-thirds of the letters originated in the western areas, including German-speaking Switzerland. If we consider only the strip of territory lying between Bern, Frankfurt, and Hamburg to the west, and Zurich, Nuremberg, Leipzig, and Berlin to the east—an area generally thought of as the cultural center of Germany, with three-quarters of Goldfriedrich's twenty most important publishing locations—only an insignificantly larger number of letters were written to Franklin from this part of Germany as compared with the rest of the German-language area.

As a result of this first inquiry, we can say that confrontation with the American Revolution by the bourgeoisie was not limited to certain regions within the German-language area but occurred everywhere, although there are some parallels to the usual centers of literary life. Now the question remains: Do the regional affiliations of German contemporaries suffice to explain the differences in their appraisal of events in the New World, or was this influence generally of only secondary importance, as we found was the case with preconceptions of England?

Starting our survey of German-speaking countries with the area north of the Elbe River, we meet with at least two statements dating from the 1780s

---

29. By far, the largest collection of these letters is presently in the American Philosophical Society Library, Philadelphia. Franklin received many more letters of this sort from France than from Germany, but the significance of the German material is unquestionable.

that refer to the prevalence of pro-English feelings. Emanuel Mathias, the British envoy to Hamburg, reported to London that it seemed to him that the major part of the city and of all Germany had clearly sided with England.[30] Near the end of the decade Johann Hermann Stöver recollected that America's cause had been espoused in northern Germany only by the Hamburg journalist and lawyer Albrecht Wittenberg, much to his own detriment.[31] And after 1781 Gottlob Benedikt von Schirach's anti-American periodical, the *Politisches Journal*, was published in this city.

In view of the many personal sentiments and business ties linking this area with Great Britain, statements like the above seem at first wholly credible. Ebeling himself said later that he had been anti-American during his first years in Hamburg.[32] Judging from his publications, Ebeling's friend Johann Georg Büsch, who was closely linked to Hamburg's commercial and economic circles, appears to have sided with England at least to the end of the war.[33] But Ebeling also emphasized that it was mostly the influence of his pro-American friends in Hamburg that made him change his opinion. And we must not forget Friedrich Gottlieb Klopstock, who threw the entire weight of his reputation on the American side, just as did Friedrich Leopold Graf zu Stolberg. It is also notable that in the very first years of the war Johann Nikolaus Karl Buchenröder published pro-American works in Hamburg and Schwerin with remarkable success, the former being the publication place of much Americana Germanica toward the end of the eighteenth century. Johann Georg Möller, a historian from Greifswald, was certainly anti-American, but Peter Ahlwardt, the professor of philosophy under whom Bengt Lidner wrote his dissertation, definitely was not. The north German bourgeoisie obviously were not as unanimously pro-British as Stöver and as Mathias would have us believe; on the contrary, within our limited sample this area produced more pro-American statements than pro-English ones. But, generally speaking, Britain seems to have had a sizable number of supporters in northern Germany.

Comments from farther east, from Prussia's eastern provinces, including Danzig, are relatively few in number, but those that have come to our attention are almost exclusively pro-American. The Pomeranian mathematician in Stettin, Johann Jakob Meyen, lauded Franklin to the skies, and Burke's

---

30. Emanuel Mathias to David Murray, Viscount Stormont, July 14, 1780 (S.P. 82/98, PRO, London).

31. [Stöver], *Niedersachsen*, 3 vols. (Rome [i.e., Berlin], 1789), I, 215–216.

32. Ebeling, *Erdbeschreibung*, I, ii.

33. Cf. the first and second editions of his *Grundriß einer Geschichte der merkwürdigsten Welthändel* of 1781 and 1783. Only the third edition of 1796 is distinctly friendly toward America.

Jahrbücher, in which the policies of the English government were widely criticized, were published in Danzig. A Königsberg publishing house, Wagner, brought out Johann Christian Schmohl's great defense of the American Revolution, though anonymously. Johann Brahl, the publisher of a German edition of Mirabeau's pro-American writings, came from the same city. As for the province of Silesia, the *Bunzlauische Monatsschrift* comes to mind, as well as Andreas Friedrich Loewe of Bunzlau, the patriots' defender. And the first German edition of Crèvecoeur was published in Liegnitz.[34]

Doubtlessly, literary life was more lively in Prussia's central provinces because of the intellectual centers of Berlin and Halle. Herbert P. Gallinger was of the opinion that there was a sizable pro-British group in Berlin, whereas P. C. Weber thought that Prussia was pro-American almost throughout.[35] However, we know, for example, that Johann Georg Sulzer, a Swiss who resided in Berlin for decades, and Ludwig Adolf Baumann, a deputy headmaster from Brandenburg, were anti-American.[36] On the other hand we know of more pro-Americans: the Berlin Councillor for War, Johann Friedrich Borchmann; young Ludwig Gedike, who was to become a noted pedagogue;[37] the poet Leopold Goeckingk; and the Berlin lawyer Friedrich Julius Knüppeln, to name only a few. *Mannigfaltigkeiten*, a Berlin weekly, and the *Berlinische Monatsschrift*, which was published by Ludwig Gedike's brother Friedrich and by Johann Erich Biester, lent weighty support to the Americans. Numerous publications on America, mostly by Prussian citizens, appeared in Berlin, and hardly one of them condemned the patriots' actions. Matthias Christian Sprengel's *Geschichte der Revolution von Nord-Amerika* was one of the major local publications. The historian from Halle, together with his father-in-law, Johann Reinhold Forster, and Johann August Eberhard, was one of America's most reputable protagonists at Prussia's great university.[38]

Not far from Halle there was not only the principality of Anhalt-Zerbst, one of the states that sent auxiliary troops, but also the principality of Anhalt-Dessau, whose capital, in contrast to Zerbst, developed a vigorous cultural life, Johann Bernhard Basedow's Philanthropinum being one of the centers. Of the educators active during those years, we know that at least one, August Friedrich Wilhelm Crome, was pro-American. *Litteratur und Völkerkunde*, a periodical published by Johann Wilhelm von Archenholtz in Dessau, was

---

34. Its translator was 28-year-old Karl Gottfried Schreiter.

35. Gallinger, "Haltung der Deutschen Publizistik," 69. Weber, *America in Imaginative German Literature*, 10.

36. For Sulzer see his letter to Johann Georg Zimmermann, Jan. 19, 1777, in Zimmermann, *Leben und Briefe*, ed. Bodemann, 261.

37. See his letter to Franklin, June 11, 1779 (Franklin Papers, LIX, 61, APSL, Philadelphia).

38. Eberhard was the translator of Chastellux's *Vortheile und Nachtheile*.

part of the same trend. While the prestigious Buchhandlung der Gelehrten issued Martin Ernst von Schlieffen's anti-American booklet in 1782,[39] it also published a few years later an edition of Franklin's collection of American constitutions and documents.

There is astonishingly little material from Saxony and Thuringia for the 1770s and 1780s. Yet the American Revolution aroused interest in these areas as well. After all, the *Leipziger Zeitung* had reported that everybody in Leipzig was discussing the developments. We have already mentioned the interest of the Saxon government and the eminent collection of contemporary literature on America in the Dresden library. And in Leipzig more books on America were published than in any other German city, although this is not extraordinary in view of the leading position held by this city in the field of publishing in general. Nevertheless, concrete statements on the Revolution from these areas did not begin to appear in appreciable numbers until the 1790s. From earlier years we have Graf Rochus Friedrich von Lynar's private comments on his opposition to the American Revolution.[40] His views were shared by Johann Matthias Schroeckh, professor of history in Wittenberg and an eminent authority on church history, as well as by the Leipzig writer, Adam Friedrich Geisler. On the other hand, we know that Christoph Friedrich Bretzner, a popular writer of plays and novels who hailed from Leipzig, was an admirer of the Americans. *Nichts Neues, aber doch manches Brauchbare*, a Dresden weekly, also emphatically sided with the patriots, and Wieland's *Teutscher Merkur* was not unfriendly toward them either. Thus, the pro-American camp seems to have had more publicity than the pro-British side, and the assumption that, other than in the areas previously discussed, America's antagonists were in the majority among the bourgeoisie is unwarranted. Moreover, the number of Franklin's correspondents and their statements do not permit such a conclusion.[41]

The picture changes somewhat in northwestern Germany, especially in Hanover, Oldenburg, and Brunswick. These territories had close connections with Great Britain, only one of which was the dynastic tie between

39. This information is drawn from the catalog of the Leipzig book fair, fall 1782, p. 426, and refers to the German translation of Schlieffen's booklet.

40. See his letters to Zacharießen, the Oldenburg chancellery councillor, during the war years (StA, Oldenburg).

41. See the letters by Christian Emanuel Froelich, from Görlitz, Apr. 7, 1781; Sebastian Hartwig, Gotha, Apr. 28, 1778, May 9, 1783; von Leidenfal, Gotha, Nov. 10, 1783; Reyhermann, Wersdorf, near Apolda, Apr. 7, 1780; Johann Wilhelm and Johann Gottfried Spangenberg, Ruhla, Saxony, Mar. 14, 1783; Karl Heinrich Titius, Dresden, July 2, 3, 1783; and Johann Kaspar Weinlandt, Römhild, near Coburg, Feb. 23, 1784 (Franklin Papers, XXI, 135, LIX, 80, 68, XXX, 83, LIX, 21, XXVII, 193, LIX, 48, XXIX, 7, 9, LIX, 28, APSL, Philadelphia).

Great Britain and Hanover.[42] Therefore, we may expect them to have been somewhat more London-oriented than were Prussia or Saxony. Among the antagonists of the American Revolution, there were some influential state officials, such as Helferich Peter Sturz, Georg Friedrich Brandes,[43] and Johann Andreas Schernhagen.[44] Pro-Britishers from other sections of the population were: Johann Georg Zimmermann, the physician from Brugg (Switzerland) and a resident of Hanover from 1768 to his death in 1795;[45] professors at the universities of Göttingen and Helmstedt like Heyne, Lichtenberg, Schirach; and Abraham Gotthelf Kästner, a mathematician and poet from Göttingen.[46] Christian Leiste, a teacher in Wolfenbüttel, and Albrecht Anton Watermeyer, a preacher from Stade, also deserve mention among the antagonists of the American Revolution.

Even though more of the American patriots' adversaries came from these areas than from the other German-speaking regions, it would be a mistake to assume that in the 1770s and 1780s the bourgeoisie here were generally anti-American. Letters to Franklin were sent from this area, too, and by no means just a few of them.[47] We must not forget Julius August Remer's work in Brunswick and later in Helmstedt, and among the professors in Göttingen, Schlözer presumably was not a convinced adversary of the Americans. Others had come to know and respect Franklin during his stay in Göttingen, including the historian and jurist Gottfried Achenwall, the orientalist Johann David Michaelis, and Johann Stephan Pütter, a professor of international law.[48] Moreover, we must not forget that it was a Hanover

42. The House of Brunswick-Wolfenbüttel is a collateral line of the House of Brunswick-Lüneburg (Hanover). On Oldenburg see the correspondence of Prince Peter Friedrich Ludwig with Duke Friedrich August, following the year 1775 (StA, Oldenburg).

43. See Brandes's letters to Christian Gottlob Heyne, especially during the years 1776–1783 (Cod. MS Heyne, CXXVI–CXXIX, SuUB, Göttingen), as well as the genealogically interesting article on the relationship between Brandes and Heyne by Carl Haase, "Göttingen und Hannover. Geistige und genealogische Beziehungen im ausgehenden 18. Jahrhundert," *Göttinger Jahrbuch* (1967), 95–124.

44. See Georg Christoph Lichtenberg's letters to Schernhagen in Lichtenberg's *Briefe*, ed. Leitzmann and Schüddekopf; some additional manuscript letters are in the Nachlaß Lichtenberg (SuUB, Göttingen).

45. See his correspondence with Jean André de Luc (StA, Aarau, LB, Hanover, and HptStA, Hanover).

46. See Kästner to Heyne, Dec. 1790 (Chron. XXIII, 49, AAW, Göttingen).

47. E.g., the letters of Johann Wilhelm Backhaus, from Hanover, Jan. 20, Feb. 7, 1783; Johann Christoph Bauer, Göttingen, Sept. 8, 1783; Friedrich Wilhelm, freiherr von Bessel, Hanover, July 6, 1779; Karl Grosett, Brunswick, Jan. 17, 1784; Johann Schmoldt, electorate of Hanover, c. 1783, July 16, 1784; and A. C. Schüler, Brunswick, Oct. 8, 1779, Mar. 7, 1780 (Franklin Papers, XXVII, 35, 90, LIX, 25, XV, 22, XVI, 10, XXXI, 30, LVII, 49, LIX, 70, XVII, 114, APSL, Philadelphia).

48. Cf. Achenwall, *Anmerkungen über Nord-Amerika* (1769), 2d ed. (1777), first pub-

publishing house that issued one of the first emphatic justifications of the American patriots' actions.[49] Periodicals like the *Göttingische Gelehrte Anzeigen* or the *Hannoverisches Magazin* were not strictly anti-American but were cautious of what they said during the war years. We may then assume that the Americans did have followers in those areas, notwithstanding that the prevailing image of England probably played a greater role here than elsewhere and that observers respected the special interests of their governments, in spite of the considerable measure of academic freedom in Göttingen.[50]

The intellectual situation in Brunswick-Wolfenbüttel differed from the majority of the other subsidiary states. In Kassel in 1776–1777, for instance, Jakob Mauvillon was allowed to espouse the American cause publicly and vehemently. One of his colleagues at the Collegium Carolinum, Christian Wilhelm Dohm, who later became a noted Prussian diplomat, published the first German translation of Paine's *Common Sense* in 1777. True, the other camp was also represented, by the Hesse-Kassel minister of state, Schlieffen, and by numerous scribblers in Ansbach-Bayreuth, but all in all they seem merely to have expressed a certain reflex reaction to the strong pro-American sentiment in this territory. Indeed, a sizable number of Franklin's correspondents lived in Ansbach-Bayreuth.[51] While Johann Georg Meusel, a history professor at Erlangen, wrote his *Historische Litteratur* in the 1780s in a very neutral style, Friedrich Ludwig Walther, who was born in Ansbach and later became a noted cameralist and botanist, openly sided with the Americans in 1785. We cannot speak of a general ideological consensus in these states about English policy; but it seems they were strongly pro-American.

There is nothing to show that there was less interest in the American Revolution in western and southwestern Germany. The Rhine countries and the bordering areas of Westphalia, Hesse, and the Palatinate have a noticeable number of Franklin correspondents.[52] As early as the spring of 1775,

---

lished as an article in the *Hannoverisches Magazin* in 1767; Michaelis, *Lebensbeschreibung*, 110–111; Pütter, *Selbstbiographie*, II, 490–491.

49. *Briefe über die jetzige Uneinigkeit.*

50. Sigmund Skard, *American Studies in Europe: Their History and Present Organization*, I (Philadelphia, 1958), 218.

51. E.g., the letters by Friedrich Wilhelm Ferdinand von Brandenstein, from near Bayreuth, c. 1783; Capt. von Doppelmair, Ansbach, Jan. 8, 1780; von Flachenfeld, Erlangen, Sept. 25, 1779; Gottlieb Christian von Weckherlein, Ansbach, Jan. 8, 1780 (Franklin Papers, XLIV, 28, LIX, 20, XV, 218, LIX, 19, APSL, Philadelphia).

52. E.g., the letters by Georg Arnold, Mainz, Dec. 27, 1777, May 13, 1778; Johann Adolf Behrends, Frankfurt, Oct. 28, 1778; J. C. Freiherr von Berger, Münster, Aug. 10, Nov. 2, 1779; Franz von Brahm, Koblenz, Apr. 20, 1777, Apr. 27, 1783; Alexander Gillon, Frankfurt,

Johann Georg Jacobi of Düsseldorf, brother to the more famous Friedrich Heinrich Jacobi, used powerful words in defense of the American patriots in his periodical, *Iris*. One of the most unconditional justifications of the Revolution ever published appeared in the city of Cologne.[53] We also know that August Christian Borheck, headmaster in Bielefeld, was pro-American in the 1780s. Heinrich Martin Gottfried Köster, who was born in the middle Rhine region and became professor of history at Giessen in 1773, spoke out against the Americans in his periodical, the *Neueste Staatsbegebenheiten*, but his attitude does not seem to have had any noteworthy influence in this area. Jakob Rieger, an officer in the American service, reported to Franklin that everyone in the Palatinate, which he had visited, was very sympathetic toward the Americans' struggle for liberty.[54] A few years later, publishing houses in Frankenthal and Speyer, places otherwise relatively unimportant for our purpose, produced reprints of Matthias Christian Sprengel's *Geschichte der Revolution*. And in 1792 one of the first German editions of Brissot de Warville's *Nouveau Voyage* appeared in Bad Dürkheim. It was edited by a citizen of Strasbourg, Theophil Friedrich Ehrmann. We also know that Zweibrücken professor Johann Valentin Embser was pro-American,[55] as was the court in this duchy[56] and the court of Baden, in Karlsruhe.[57]

Looking at Württemberg and Swabia, we find that investigators are remarkably unanimous in their opinion that enthusiasm for the Americans was general in these areas.[58] This is astonishing insofar as statements from this region made in the 1770s and 1780s are by no means numerous. In defense of their argument, researchers have usually referred to the eminent personality of Schubart and his outstanding *Chronik*. But there were views to the

---

Dec. 1, 1779; Edmund von Harold, Düsseldorf, Oct. 28, Dec. 3, 1777; Jakob Hemmer, Mannheim, Oct. 8, 1778, Aug. 8, 1780; H. Adolf Hoffmeister, Heidelberg, Dec. 29, 1781, Mar. 31, 1783; Johann Wilhelm Karl Adolf Freiherr von Hüpsch von Lontzen, Cologne, June 7, 1778; Johann Wilhelm Jaeger, Frankfurt, Dec. 20, 1777; Philipp Konrad Katz, Bündingen, Aug. 9, 1778; etc. (*ibid.*, LIX, 12, IX, 158, XII, 92, XV, 115, XVI, 90, V, 159, XXVIII, 66, XVI, 137, VII, 87, 128, XII, 28, LXX, 114, XXIII, 149, XXVII, 235, X, 22, VII, 165, LIX, 85).

53. *Beschreibung der dreizehn unabhängigen Nordamerikanischen Staaten.*

54. Rieger to Franklin, Oct. 10, 1778 (Franklin Papers, XII, 40, APSL, Philadelphia).

55. See his letters to Franklin, Jan. 6, May 9, 1782, Feb. 28, 1783 (*ibid.*, XXIV, 10, XXV, 63, XXVII, 150).

56. See the letters of Gräfin von Forbach to Franklin, Aug. 18, Sept. 1, 1778, Feb. 14, 1779, c. Mar. 20, Apr. 13, 21, 1783, and those of the Chevalier de Keralio, Oct. 17, 1779, Feb. 27, 1781, Jan. 27, 1783 (*ibid.*, XI, 57, LXX, 95, XIII, 104, XLIV, 251, XLI, 52, 43, XVI, 47, XXI, 83, XXVII, 52).

57. See especially the letters by P. P. Burdett to Franklin, Apr. 5, June 1, 1777, Jan. 17, 1786, Aug. 19, 1787 (*ibid.*, V, 138, VI, 41, XXXIV, 11, XXXV, 108).

58. Cf. Gallinger, "Haltung der deutschen Publizistik," 15; J. A. Walz, "Three Swabian Journalists," *AG*, IV (1902), 97–98; Weber, *America in Imaginative German Literature*, 10.

contrary, as expressed by Wilhelm Ludwig Wekhrlin in his periodicals or by Christoph Heinrich Korn, a private scholar from Stuttgart who, after all, had been editor of the periodical *Neueste Geschichte der Welt* before Schubart became editor in 1776.[59] Yet it is true that Schubart was the most powerful and influential publicist in this area. Also, numerous letters to Franklin indicate widespread sympathies for the Americans throughout the region.[60] But it would be a mistake to overlook representatives of the opposition as well, especially since Württemberg and Swabia, as Schubart himself showed, had strong intellectual ties to England. Contemporaries were fond of comparing Württemberg's constitution with England's, for example.

In German-speaking Switzerland there surely was no less interest in the American Revolution than in the more northerly states, although the reports that we have are by no means unanimous. In 1777 Lambert told Franklin from Basel that Switzerland was pro-American throughout.[61] But a few years later, Louis Braun, secretary to the British embassy in Bern and son-in-law of the late Albrecht von Haller, reported repeatedly to London that all the influential citizens of Bern, and even the general public, were in favor of a British victory.[62]

When evaluating these two reports, it seems appropriate to keep in mind who wrote them and to whom they were written. The group that had formed in Bern around Albrecht von Haller, one of the greatest universal scholars of the Swiss Enlightenment, probably had scant sympathy for the Americans. Johannes von Müller, an eminent Swiss historian, seems to have been another influential personality more inclined to favor Britain than America.[63] But we know of a much larger number of supporters of the American Revolution,

59. On the question of editorship see Kirchner, *Grundlagen des deutschen Zeitschriftenwesens*, II, 148.

60. E.g., the letters by Johann Baptist Kaspar Anton [?] Auer, from Ebingen (Württemberg), Aug. 4, Sept, 7, 1779, June 20, 1780, Sept. 1, 1781, Oct. 21, 1782; J. Thaddeus Ehet, Augsburg, Dec. 4, 1780, Nov. 16, 1782 (2); Joseph Mayer, Constance, July 16, 1781; Mehl, Schorndorf (Württemberg), July 1, 1777; Jakob Lambert Ransier, Augsburg, July 7, Fürth, Aug. 12, 1783; Ferdinand von Rembau und Dupont, Donaueschingen, Apr. 5, 1782; Gottlob Friedrich Ruthardt, Ludwigsburg, Oct. 31 (two letters), Dec. 9, 1780; comte de Tende, Stuttgart, Nov. 20, 1780; Maj. von Wolff, Stuttgart, Mar. 4, 1784; Heinrich Hartmann Zeller, Nußbaum (Württemberg), Dec. 4, 1782 (Franklin Papers, LIX, 35, 37, 82, XXII, 130, XXVI, 23, LIX, 75, 51, XXVI, 65, LIX, 5, 38, XXIX, 16, 79, XXV, 7, XLIV, 259, LIX, 74, 72, XX, 79, XXXI, 103, LIX, 52, APSL, Philadelphia).

61. Lambert to Franklin, Dec. 26, 1777 (*ibid.*, LXII, 62).

62. Louis Braun to Wills Hill, 2d Viscount Hillsborough, July 1, 22, 1780 (S.P. 96/48, PRO, London).

63. See among the papers in the Nachlaß Müller (StadtB, Schaffhausen) his essay "De l'Empire Britannique," written about 1780 (Msc.Mü. LI, 6). Müller was befriended by the American loyalist Francis Kinloch, a Southerner who returned after the war to Albemarle Co., Va. (cf. Msc.Mü. LXXXV).

including citizens no less influential and respectable than Haller and Müller: Isaak Iselin and his *Ephemeriden der Menschheit*; Peter Ochs; and Emanuel Wolleb, a jurist and member of the Grand Council in Basel.[64] In Zurich there was Johann Jakob Bodmer, Johann Heinrich Pestalozzi, and Johann Georg Schulthess,[65] while Johann Georg Heinzmann of Bern and Jean Rodolphe Vautravers of Biel should also be mentioned.[66] We have already referred to Bern as a noteworthy publication center of Americana Germanica; two German editions of Pierre Ulric Du Buisson's *Révolution en Amérique* were among the works published there. If we again bring in Franklin's correspondents, we can surely speak of a broad wave of assent to the American Revolution, even in influential Bern families, in spite of the obvious existence of antagonists to the patriots.[67]

We know of far fewer statements from Bavaria. As opposed to the literary centers on the other side of the border, such as Augsburg, Nuremberg, or Salzburg, no specialized books on America were published here. But books published in those cities probably became known in Bavaria, just as Schubart's and Wekhrlin's periodicals influenced at least the western part of Bavaria to no small degree. The small amount of literary production does not necessarily indicate a general lack of interest. That the number of Franklin's correspondents from this area, and especially from Munich, was not below the general average is further proof of interest in North America.[68] By the 1790s a number of personalities in Bavaria did become engaged in literary work on America: Albrecht Christoph Kayser, librarian to the court of Thurn and Taxis and translator of the only complete German edition of Brissot de

64. Cf. Wolleb's letter to Franklin, Jan. 3, 1778 (Franklin Papers, VIII, 9, APSL, Philadelphia).

65. On Schulthess see his correspondence with Bodmer, especially his letter of Aug. 13, 1778 (MS Bodmer 4c. XIX, 46, ZB, Zurich).

66. See Vautravers's numerous letters to Franklin, Washington, and others (Franklin Papers, APSL, Philadelphia; Washington Papers, LC, Washington, D.C.). Vautravers's desire to show off was close to pathological; cf. Hans Utz, "Rousseaus Schatten über Biel," *Neues Bieler Jahrbuch* (1962), 51.

67. E.g., the letters by Abraham von Erlach Freiherr zu Riggisberg, Dec. 22, 1778; Iselin, from Basel, July 28, 1778; Samuel Marcel, Bern, Mar. 20, 1779; Stokar zur Sonnenburg, Schaffhausen, Dec. 6, 1781, Aug. 3, 1782, Apr. 14, July 3, 1783; Johann Rudolf Tschiffeli, Bern, Aug. 1, 1778; David Salomon von Wattenwil (von Belp), Bern, Aug. 25, 1776; Franz Rudolf Weiss (von Daillens), Bern, Dec. 2, 1778 (Franklin Papers, XII, 211, X, 154, XIII, 207, XXIII, 100, XXV, 149, XXVIII, 38, XXIX, 8, XI, 9, IV, 108, XII, 170, APSL, Philadelphia). See also the letters by Lambert, Vautravers, and Wolleb already cited.

68. E.g., the letters by Ritter von Forstner, from Munich, Mar. 28, 1779; Johann Georg von Grünberger, Munich, May 4, 1778; von Kemtenstrauss, Munich, Nov. 5, 1780; Ignatius Salern, Munich, May 4, 1778; Freifrau von Seckendorff, née Gräfin von Gronsfeld, Oberzenn, Dec. 18, 1781; Josef von Utzschneider, Munich, Apr. 10, 1783 (*ibid.*, XIII, 227, LX, 105, XX, 63, LX, 105, XXIII, 126, XXVIII, 22).

Warville's *Nouveau Voyage*, as well as the writers Joseph Milbiller and Josef von Sartori, who were then living in Vienna.

Finally, in the Habsburg crown dependencies in the southeast of the German-speaking area we find a substantially higher number of statements than have survived from Bavaria. In the 1770s and 1780s several influential advocates of America's cause lived in Vienna, among them Jacques Accarias de Sérionne, Jan Ingenhousz, Friedrich Wilhelm Taube, and Karl Graf von Zinzendorf. None of them was Austrian-born, but all had been residents of the capital since the 1760s. Their inclinations were obviously shared by numerous Austrians, including Johann Zinner and Heinrich Georg Hoff, who published their views. At the end of the eighteenth century Vienna itself produced somewhat fewer books on America than would have been in keeping with the city's rank among German publishing centers, although a few informative works on America did originate there. But the number of known Franklin correspondents from that area is amazing.[69] They confirm the impression that pro-American sympathies were widespread in this area, which was relatively little affected by England.

Summing up the results of this short survey, we find that the level of interest in the American Revolution, notwithstanding certain fluctuations, was roughly the same throughout. There seems to have been a relatively high percentage of pro-English sentiment in northern Germany, especially in Hanover, because of political and economic ties and because of England's positive image there. Nevertheless, this analysis shows that regional differences seem to have had an almost negligible effect on German responses to the Revolution. In individual cases regional interests played a certain role, but assent to the American Revolution was general among German contemporaries, even if it differed in intensity. A conclusion that territorial questions were decisive factors in the formation of opinion appears to be untenable.

Social Factors

If regional factors do not seem to have significantly conditioned German opinion about the American Revolution, there remains the question of whether social position was any more important as an influence upon indi-

---

69. E.g., the letters by Bek, from Vienna, June 10, 1779; Ignaz Ritter von Born, Vienna, Nov. 21, 1783; Joseph Cauffmann, Vienna, Apr. 23, 1777; Karl Freiherr von Emerich, Brandeis, Bohemia, Dec. 4, 1777; Graf von Grävenitz-Walheim, Vienna, June 26, 1783; J. Nekrep,

vidual responses to American events. In order to answer this question, I have resorted again to authors and their works, to evidence from Franklin's correspondence, and to statements of known personalities.

We have already seen that the sovereigns and their ministers hardly thought of America as a challenge to the European system of government. Consequently, they did not unequivocally condemn America's revolutionary principles, but at the same time they were not highly enthusiastic about them either. Their position was motivated mainly by external factors, especially policy toward England. Thus, late in 1777 Vautravers was not just using pleasing words when he wrote to Franklin from Mannheim: "No court of any weight in Europe sides with the cause of G. Britain, but rather rejoices at its humiliation."[70] The general attitude was neutral, if not uninterested. The political orientation of the Catholic and south German governments especially was more closely linked with France's policy than with Britain's, and the British emissary to the three Catholic electors on the Rhine considered only the prince-bishop of Würzburg among all the Catholic German rulers to be Britain's friend.[71] The subsidiary treaties concluded with London by six of the Protestant sovereigns were made not primarily because of ideological agreement with England's American policy but mainly for economic or financial reasons. So the Prussian viewpoint communicated by Frederick II to his emissary in London late in 1775 has a ring of truth in it: "What is very certain is that almost all Europe takes sides with the colonies and defends their cause and that the court has neither supporters nor promoters."[72] The Prussian king was surely not thinking of an ideological consensus; there is no indication of any such idea in his other statements concerning events in the Western Hemisphere. It seems rather that the point of view of power-politics was uppermost in his thoughts.

Ideology commanded more attention on the level of ministers and high civil servants. It is here and among the nobility that we find relatively wide-

---

Vienna, June 12, 1784; Jakob Oberleithner, Vienna, Jan. 9, 1778; Josef Pellegrini, Vienna, July 19, 1779; Johann Christian Schuster, Vienna, Feb. 8, 1783; Capt. Siegmüller, Linz-on-the-Danube, Feb. 13, 1783; Josef von Weinbrenner, Vienna, Feb. 19, 1783; Johann Karl von Zinner, Buda, Oct. 26, 1778 (ibid., XIV, 169, XXX, 99, V, 163, LIX, 83, 50, XL, 128, VIII, 24, XV, 52, XXVII, 92½, XXVII, 107, 132, XII, 84).

70. Dec. 4, 1777 (ibid., VII, 130).

71. George Cressener to Thomas Howard, earl of Suffolk, Apr. 14, 1777 (S.P. 81/155, PRO, London).

72. "Ce qu'il y a de très certain, c'est que toute l'Europe presque prend le parti des colonies et défend leur cause, et que celle de la cour ne trouve ni fauteurs ni promoteurs": Frederick II to Joachim Karl Graf von Maltzahn, Dec. 18, 1775, in Volz, ed., Politische Correspondenz Friedrichs des Grossen, XXXVII, 336–337. See also the remarks on Prussian political sympathies by Graf Lynar in his letter to Zacharießen, Jan. 17, 1778 (Nachlaß Lynar, XXXIV, 751–753, StA, Oldenburg).

spread condemnation of bourgeois revolutionary ideals. These circles were convinced that liberty was a "phantom . . . slavery in disguise, a chimerical goddess prayed to by ambitious enthusiasts and adored by the simple-minded." It was better to obey a king "whose power is limited by law and even preferably by sentiment than to be ruined by some fellow citizens whom money or cabal have made magistrates."[73] The idea that aristocratic-monarchical government was preferable so far as their own interests were concerned was shared by men like the Palatinate minister Beckers von Wetterstetten; his colleagues from Munich and Kassel, Seinsheim and Schlieffen; Georg Friedrich Brandes; Eberhard Friedrich von Gemmingen, a high-ranking official of Württemberg; Graf Lynar of Saxony, who had been in Danish services for decades; Justus Möser; Friedrich Freiherr von Reitzenstein, from Bayreuth; Schernhagen from Hanover; Woldemar Friedrich Graf von Schmettau; and Helferich Peter Sturz.[74] It is perhaps not surprising that numerous proponents of this view, whose pro-monarchic and pro-aristocratic leanings were just as manifest as their rejection of the American Revolution, had themselves been elevated into the nobility at some time in their lives, as were Albrecht von Haller, Johannes von Müller, Gottlob Benedikt von Schirach, and Johann Georg Zimmermann.[75]

Unquestionably, some who sympathized with events in the New World were also ennobled, but this seems to have happened, if not more rarely, then at least not to any staunch supporters of the patriots while the war was in progress.[76] In the highest government ranks, apart from the Viennese count Karl von Zinzendorf, there are almost no known advocates of the American Revolution. Among the nobility, however, we do find a respectable number

73. "phantome . . . un esclavage masqué, une divinité chimérique, que l'ambitieux enthousiasme prêche et que la simplicité trompée adore . . . dont la loi, et ce qui vaut encore mieux, le sentiment limite le pouvoir, que d'être tira nuisé par quelques concitoyens, que l'argent ou la cabale ont élevés à la magistrature": Lynar to Zacharießen, Nov. 11, 1780 (Nachlaß Lynar, XXIX, 630, StA, Oldenburg).

74. In general see the correspondence of: Beckers von Wetterstetten and Seinsheim with Haslang (Bayer. Gesandtschaft: London, GStA, Munich); Brandes to Heyne (Nachlaß Heyne, SuUB, Göttingen); Gemmingen and Haller, in Haller, *Briefwechsel zwischen Haller und Gemmingen*, ed. Fischer; Lynar to Zacharießen (Nachlaß Lynar, StA, Oldenburg); and Lichtenberg to Schernhagen, in Lichtenberg, *Briefe*, ed. Leitzmann and Schüddekopf.

75. Haller became a member of the *Reichsadel* in 1749. Müller was elevated by the emperor to the *Reichsritterstand* in 1791; cf. Karl Schib, *Johannes von Müller 1752–1809* (Thayngen and Schaffhausen, 1967), 166. Schirach was ennobled by Empress Maria Theresa in 1776. And Zimmermann was created Knight of the Vladimir Order by Empress Catherine II in 1786; cf. J. G. Zimmermann, *Leben und Briefe*, ed. Bodemann, 122. When no other reference is given, the information is drawn from the *Neue* or the *Allgemeine Deutsche Biographie*.

76. Taube, for example, was created knight in 1777, whereas Dohm and Goeckingk were ennobled by the Prussian king in 1786 and 1789, respectively.

of protagonists of the Revolution, just as later the French Revolution in its early phases attracted some aristocratic support. Numerous counts and barons corresponded with Franklin.[77] Other admirers of America, like Johann Wilhelm von Archenholtz and August Wilhelm Leopold von Rahmel were of the lesser nobility.[78] But these examples cannot conceal the general condemnation of the American Revolution that was widespread among the highest social classes. The extent of interest in the controversy is expressed in a letter written at the end of the war by Louise Mejer to the man she later married, poet Heinrich Christian Boie, an antagonist of the Revolution: "Pestel and I are English, Luise sides with the Americans."[79]

Interest in the events in the Western Hemisphere was not confined to the nobility, as we know. "For years the disputes between the British and their North American brothers have kept busy the brains of all true and would-be politicians, being the major topic of discussion where champagne is drunk from etched glasses as well as where beer is drunk from mugs and pewter cans."[80] How the judgment of the various social classes might differ was expressed in a letter by young Friedrich Otto Wilhelm Gärtner of Brunswick, written to Adam Friedrich Oeser's daughters in Leipzig: "Brunswick is divided into two camps almost like England. All those attached to the court side with the English, but all others are for the Americans."[81] All others, to

77. E.g., the letters by Friedrich Wilhelm Freiherr von Bessel, July 6, 1779; Ignaz Ritter von Born, Nov. 21, 1783; Karl Freiherr von Emerich, Dec. 4, 1777; August Freiherr von Haxthausen, Feb. 26, 1783; Johann Wilhelm Franz Freiherr von Krohne, June 23, 1777; Freiherr von der Marck und Stein, Mar. 23, 1783; Karl Ritter von Qureille, July 30, 1783; Johann Ludwig Graf von Sayn and Wittgenstein, Jan. 25, 1780; Franz Anton Freiherr von Seyffertitz, Sept. 13, 1778; Graf von Wied-Runkel, Mar. 19, 1783; L. F., baron van Wynbergen, May 21, 1779 (Franklin Papers, XV, 22, XXX, 99, LIX, 83, XXVII, 147, VI, 76, XXVII, 214, LIX, 8, XVII, 50, XI, 135, LIX, 69, XIV, 128, APSL, Philadelphia).

78. See the letters from the ranks of the lower nobility, e.g., Karl von Dyke, July 13, 1780; Christian von Francken, Apr. 30, 1779; von Leidenfal, Nov. 10, 1783; Capt. de Lenoble, Feb. 4, 1783; August Friedemann Rühle von Lilienstern, Mar. 14, Apr. 3, 1783; Gottlieb Christian von Weckherlein, Jan. 8, 1780; Josef von Weinbrenner, Feb. 19, 1783; Lt. von Woedtcke, Mar. 10, 1781; von Wolff, Mar. 4, 1784 (ibid., XIX, 6, LIX, 39, XXX, 83, XXVII, 81, LIX, 69, 9, 19, XXVII, 132, XXI, 99, XXXI, 103).

79. "Pestel und ich sind englisch und Luise auf der Amerikaner Seite": Jan. 13, 1782, in Boie, Ich war wohl klug, 126, which refers to Friedrich Justus von Pestel, councillor at the Superior Court of Appeals at Celle, and his wife Luise, née von Grävemeyer.

80. "Die Streitigkeiten zwischen den Engländern und ihren Brüdern in Nordamerika beschäftigen seit einigen Jahren das Gehirn aller wahren und Afterpolitiker und sind in allen Gesellschaften, wo Champagner aus geschliffenen Gläsern oder Stadtbier aus Krügen und Schleifkannen getrunken wird, ein Hauptgegenstand der Untersuchung": Nichts Neues, aber doch manches Brauchbare, May 22, 1778, 25.

81. "Übrigens ist Braunschweig fast wie England in zwei Parteien geteilt. Alles, was dem Hofe angehört, ist auf der Engländer Seite. Aber alle andre sind für die Amerikaner": Apr. 7, 1777, quoted in P. Zimmermann, "Braunschweigs und Englands Subsidienverträge," Jahrbuch des Geschichtsvereins für das Herzogtum Braunschweig, XIII (1914), 173.

Gärtner, probably meant first of all himself and his own social class, the bourgeoisie, which at the end of the eighteenth century consisted mostly of businessmen and professionals, united by the bond of education. They understood *bourgeoisie* or *Bürgertum* to mean the educated middle class, thus separating themselves from the uneducated, mostly manually occupied, people, such as employed artisans, low civil servants and clerks, servants, workers of all kinds, peasants, teachers at village schools who depended for their living on supplementary farming, and so on.[82]

As we have noted several times before, even the bourgeoisie did not always side with the Americans. Leopold Friedrich Günther von Goeckingk exemplifies this in a description of his daily activities sent to the poet Gottfried August Bürger: "Now I write a preface to the *Musenalmanach*, then I draft an official lease deed, or do some copying of the *Adlerkant*, or debate the American war with the syndic of Nordhausen."[83] Hans Heinz Schinz, the parson from Alstetten, was disposed to imagine that Johann Georg Sulzer was right in "thinking against the Americans."[84] Differences of opinion may have existed on other than individual grounds. In the mid-1770s, for example, Johann Georg Jacobi was convinced that sympathy with the patriots was especially widespread among bourgeois women.[85] But on the whole, the bourgeoisie seem to have been overwhelmingly enthusiastic about the American Revolution and its ideals.[86]

This general impression is confirmed when we classify socially those per-

82. For a very searching socioeconomic definition of the bourgeoisie see Robin, "Idéologies et bourgeoisie," *La nouvelle critique*, N.S., XXXII (Mar. 1970), 42–45, 48. For partly analogous definitions by contemporaries and modern scholars compare among others *Schleswigsches Journal*, July 1793, 284; Elinor G. Barber, *The Bourgeoisie in 18th Century France* (Princeton, N.J., 1955), 14–33; Habermas, *Strukturwandel der Öffentlichkeit*, 83–84. Riedel, "Bürger, Staatsbürger, Bürgertum," in Brunner *et al.*, eds., *Geschichtliche Grundbegriffe*, I, 683–698, demonstrates that in Germany during the second half of the 18th century the bourgeoisie increasingly became antagonistic to the nobility and to what came to be called the Fourth Estate, or the lower strata of the population, especially in the cities (workers, day laborers, etc.). For a further characterization of the differences within the bourgeoisie between the grande and the petite bourgeoisie see the remarks on the latter in Möller, *Kleinbürgerliche Familie*, 2–8.

83. "Da hab ich bald eine Vorrede zu dem Musenalmanach geschrieben, bald einen Amtspachtkontrakt gemacht, bald am Adlerkant kopiert, bald den Krieg in Amerika mit dem Nordhausischen Syndikus entschieden": Sept. 8, 1777, in Bürger, *Briefe*, ed. Strodtmann, II, 124.

84. "wider die Amerikaner denke": to Bodmer, July 15, 1776 (MS Bodmer, VIII, 396, ZB, Zurich).

85. *Iris*, Sept. 1775, 180–181.

86. Cf. Paul B. Baginsky, *German Works Relating to America 1493–1800* (New York, 1942), ix; Gallinger, "Haltung der deutschen Publizistik," 74; J. A. Walz, "American Revolution and German Literature," *MLN*, XVI (1901), 411–412, which stands in need of correction; and Skard, *American Studies in Europe*, I, 210.

sons whose attitudes we know with regard to events in the West. The great majority of the total of authors, correspondents of Franklin, and others belonged to the bourgeoisie. If we look at the group of ninety persons whose leanings we know, we find that 90 percent of the protagonists of the American Revolution were of bourgeois descent. Of the much smaller number of antagonists, only half were from the bourgeoisie, constituting a mere 20 percent of the total ninety. (I include government officials, such as Justus Möser and Georg Friedrich Brandes, with the nobility, which was really the class nearest to them.) Confrontation with the American Revolution was therefore not primarily a bourgeois affair, but as Mauvillon correctly put it: "The major part of enlightened Germany disapproved of Britain's actions against its colonies."[87]

We know little about the lower social classes, such as craftsmen, laborers, servants, and peasants. Antagonists of the Revolution believed that enthusiasm for the Americans was general among the uneducated.[88] Jakob Rieger confirms this for the Palatinate, where he met with general sympathy "from the lord to the peasant."[89] In Swabia, Schubart had some influence on these circles. We may safely assume that several of Franklin's correspondents came from these classes, although biographical data about them are difficult to come by.[90] Scanty as our information is from direct statements—the emigration movement will be dealt with later—nothing seems to indicate that they were reluctant to show sympathy for the American Revolution.

The influence of social factors on German appraisal of events in the New World becomes clearer when we analyze specific professional groups and the educational levels of the appraisers. We have already mentioned that a noteworthy number of antagonists to the Revolution can be found among the highest government officials. But the picture changes noticeably when we descend one step, to the level of middle and higher state and administration officials. Although we know that some antagonists of the Revolution, like Heinrich Christian Boie, were among this group, the protagonists are much more numerous, for instance, Johann Friedrich Borchmann, Johann Brahl, Goeckingk, Hennings, Karl Gotthelf Lessing, Rahmel, and Friedrich Leopold Graf zu Stolberg. It seems that support for the Americans was more widespread among the subordinates than at the top, increasing in intensity in reverse ratio to position in the hierarchy of government and administration.

87. "der größte Teil des erleuchteten Deutschlands das Verfahren Englands gegen die Kolonien mißbilligte": Mauvillon, *Sammlung von Aufsätzen*, I, 141–142.
88. Cf. *Über den Aufstand der englischen Colonien*, 6.
89. Rieger to Franklin, Oct. 10, 1778 (Franklin Papers, XII, 40, APSL, Philadelphia).
90. E.g., the letters of Auer to Franklin, Aug. 4, Sept. 7, 1779, June 20, 1780, Sept. 1, 1781, Oct. 21, 1782 (*ibid.*, LIX, 35, 37, 82, XXII, 130, XXVI, 23).

When we compare university professors with teachers in high schools and secondary schools, we get a similar impression of social layers. Dealing first with the universities, it seems that the Revolution was not as broadly rejected as among the highest government officials, but it was not only in Göttingen that a sizable number of antagonists to the patriots' aims could be found. There was Köster in Giessen, Möller in Greifswald, Johannes von Müller in Kassel, Schirach in Helmstedt, and Johann Matthias Schroeckh in Wittenberg. Of course, there were supporters of the Revolution among the professors as well. Controversies often cut right across the universities. During the war years this happened in the cases of Peter Ahlwardt and Möller in Greifswald, Julius August Remer and Schirach in Helmstedt, and Mauvillon and Christian Wilhelm Dohm on one side and Müller on the other at Kassel. In Göttingen, Christoph Gottlob Heyne, Abraham Gotthelf Kästner, and Georg Christoph Lichtenberg stood as convinced antagonists of the patriots, but at the end of the 1770s, Johann August Eberhard, Johann Reinhold Forster, and Sprengel led groups of sympathizers at the University of Halle. It is debatable whether among the professors the number of antagonists of the Revolution was higher than the number of supporters,[91] but opposition to the patriots was relatively widespread in their circles.

This antagonism toward the Americans was much less prevalent among high school and secondary school teachers. We do know that Ludwig Adolf Baumann of Brandenburg, Christian Leiste of Wolfenbüttel, and Johann Georg Maison of Kulmbach, all of whom were deputy headmasters, were anti-American. But they are more than matched by the number of pro-Americans, including August Christian Borheck, headmaster in Bielefeld; August Friedrich Wilhelm Crome of Dessau; Johann Valentin Embser of Zweibrücken; Friedrich and Ludwig Gedicke and Johann Jakob Meyen of Stettin; and Karl Philipp Michael Snell, Hesse-born and teacher for some time at the Domschule in Riga.

Much sympathy for the Americans is also to be found among other bourgeois professions. Physician Johann Georg Zimmermann was anti-American, but Johann Adolf Behrends of Frankfurt and Jakob Oberleithner, Josef Pellegrini, and Ingenhousz, all of Vienna, were ardent pro-Americans.[92] To give another example, among the lawyers we know Dr. Hennesienne of Vienna, Friedrich Julius Knüppeln of Berlin, August Friedmann Rühle von

91. See also Doll, "American History," *APST*, N.S., XXXVIII (1948), 454; Sigmund Skard, *The American Myth and the European Mind: American Studies in Europe, 1776–1960* (Philadelphia, 1961), 21.

92. See the respective letters of Behrends, Oberleithner, and Pellegrini to Franklin, Oct. 28, Jan. 9, 1778, July 19, 1779 (Franklin Papers, XII, 92, VIII, 24, XV, 52, APSL, Philadelphia).

Lilienstern of Dillenburg, Josef von Utzschneider of Anger, Albrecht Witten-berg of Hamburg, and Emanuel Wolleb of Basel, to have had pro-American sentiments.[93] The clergy, at least the Protestants, seem to have formed their opinions in a similar way. To be sure, Albrecht Anton Watermeyer of Stade, was against the Revolution, but among the advocates were Johann August Ephraim Goeze, Johann Leonhard Neusinger, Johann Georg Schulthess, and Gebhard Friedrich August Wendeborn.[94]

Historical research up to now has given preponderant attention to poets, writers, and journalists. Some authorities have believed them to be over-whelmingly pro-American;[95] others have argued that their reactions were divided and conflicting, with the exponents of "Sturm und Drang" being enthusiasts and the exponents of classicism being opponents.[96] This is proba-bly essentially correct, though the deciding factor may not have been adher-ence to some literary school so much as membership in a certain social class. The attitude of poets and writers corresponds largely to that of the general bourgeoisie. We know of exponents of Sturm und Drang, like Friedrich Maxi-milian Klinger and Jakob Michael Reinhold Lenz, who obviously had as lit-tle interest in the American Revolution as had Goethe and Schiller among the classicists, both of whom, after all, had gone through a Sturm und Drang pe-riod themselves. To be sure, there were representatives of Sturm und Drang who were enthusiastic about the patriots' ideals, foremost of all, Christian Friedrich Daniel Schubart. But convinced supporters, of the Americans, like Bodmer and Klopstock, and the poets who had close connections with the Anacreontics or the Göttingen Hainbund, like Goeckingk, Hennings, and Stolberg, cannot be related directly to the Sturm und Drang school. The same qualification probably applies to Wieland's *Teutscher Merkur*, which cer-tainly was not unfriendly toward the Americans, as well as to Christoph Friedrich Bretzner and the younger Lessing.

93. See the respective letters of Hennesienne, Rühle von Lilienstern (two letters), Utzschneider, and Wolleb to Franklin, Sept. 28, 1778, Mar. 14, Apr. 3, Apr. 10, 1783, Jan. 3, 1778 (*ibid.*, XLIX, 21, LIX, 69, 9, XXVIII, 22, VIII, 9).

94. See Schulthess to Bodmer, Aug. 13, 1778 (MS Bodmer, 4c. XIX, 46, ZB, Zurich).

95. Walter Wehe, "Das Amerika-Erlebnis in der deutschen Literatur," *Geist der Zeit*, XVII (1939), 98.

96. Hildegard Meyer, *Nord-Amerika im Urteil des Deutschen Schrifttums bis zur Mitte des 19. Jahrhunderts. Eine Untersuchung über Kürnbergers "Amerika-Müden"* (Hamburg, 1929), 6–11; also Rolf Engelsing, "Deutschland und die Vereinigten Staaten im 19. Jahrhun-dert," *Welt als Geschichte*, XVIII (1958), 140–141; J. A. Walz, "American Revolution and German Literature," *MLN*, XVI (1901), 459; King, "Echoes of the American Revolution," *PMP*, XIV (1930), 174; Fraenkel, *Amerika im Spiegel des deutschen politischen Denkens*, 19–20; Jantz, "Amerika im deutschen Dichten und Denken," in Stammler, ed., *Deutsche Philologie im Aufriß*, 330–332.

Of course, some poets and writers were opposed to the American Revolution. Heinrich Christian Boie, mentioned several times before, represents many others. But the general impression is that the opinions of the poets and writers were closely related to those held by mid-rank and higher civil servants and by high school teachers, that is, essentially by the bourgeois professions. Overall, it seems, we meet with widespread pro-Revolutionary sentiments among these groups, whereas the number of antagonists is relatively small.

As far as we can tell, the same applies to commercial circles. Many observers believed that there was an identity of interest between the American revolutionaries and German merchants, since American independence would mean an end to the Navigation Acts and the opening of the American market to all Europe. Economic liberalism at home and abroad appeared to be one of the great achievements of the American Revolution in the eyes of physiocrats and economists. Considerations like these prompted many merchants and commercial houses to try to contact Franklin[97] and to welcome events in the West, in some cases very eagerly. Only rarely did dissenting voices express the fear that developments in the New World could be indifferent to their own interests, and even detrimental. Thus, Silesian linen merchants believed for some time that their own exports would be endangered by independence for the colonies, since after the abolition of all English economic restrictions the colonies would not only satisfy their own demand but would furnish goods to foreign markets at cheaper prices.[98] Reserved opinions like these were shared to a limited extent by a few others, for example, the co-director of the Hamburg Handlungsakademie, Johann Georg Büsch.

As this survey suggests, German assent to the American Revolution, though subject to individual peculiarities, resided mainly with the bourgeoisie. In view of the educational ambitions of this class, it is not surprising that most of its spokesmen were university trained. While this point deserves no special mention, the choice of universities does. Of the American oppo-

97. E.g., the letters to Franklin by Becker & Saltzmann, from Berlin, Apr. 20 (2), July 3, 23, 1779; J.A.C. Sieck, Berlin, May 15, 17, Aug. 19, 23, 1783; Arnold Delius, Bremen, Feb. 7, 1783; Hermann Heyman, Sohn, Bremen, Feb. 17, July 31, 1783, Jan. 19, 1784; Johann und Kaspar Halbach und Sohn, Remscheid, Apr. 11, 1783; Jakob Lambert Ransier, Augsburg, July 7, Fürth, Aug. 12, 1783; Konrad Walter & Co., Hildesheim, Mar. 15, 1784; also the letters by Karl Gottfried Paleske, Mar. 7, 1783; Josef von Weinbrenner, Feb. 19, 1783, and others (Franklin Papers, XIV, 49, 50, XV, 11, 59, LIX, 63, 65, 22, 24, XXVII, 91, XXVIII, 123, XXIX, 61, XXXI, 38, XXVIII, 29, XXIX, 16, 79, XXXI, 115, XXVII, 176, 132, APSL, Philadelphia).

98. See the memorial of the elders of the Breslau merchants to Silesian minister Karl Georg Heinrich Graf von Hoym, Jan. 20, 1779 (Acta vom mutuellen Commercio, I, fol. 39v, StA, Breslau; copy in LC, Washington, D.C.).

nents whose education we know something about, almost 50 percent had studied entirely or partly at Göttingen, and only a scant 15 percent at Halle, the second university in Germany that was considered "modern" at the time. American supporters, however, were scattered almost equally throughout both universities. Moreover, as contrasted with the admirers of the Revolution, the antagonists who had been educated at Göttingen became in later life, almost without exception, members of the nobility or the upper layer of the bourgeoisie. Protagonists of the Revolution, though university educated, tended to fall below the top level in society and government and thus were more often confronted with the barriers raised by a society firmly based on privilege.

Of the variety of social factors that may have conditioned German attitudes toward the American Revolution, we have not yet directly considered the influence of religion. In this regard, we have to keep in mind that interest in public affairs and intellectual awareness in general were not the same all over Germany and were noticeably low in the ecclesiastical territories.[99] It is, however, open to question whether this greater apathy applied to the middle and upper levels of the bourgeoisie, proud as they were of their education, and whether religious affiliation really can account for significant variations at all social levels. Our survey of the several territories has shown that the letters Franklin received came in virtually equal numbers from predominantly Protestant Prussia, the Catholic Habsburg holdings, and the ecclesiastical territories, including the electorate of Bavaria.[100] Therefore, a superficial separation into Protestant and Catholic population areas seems to be inappropriate and inapplicable.

But there are some other possible viewpoints. We know of the important influence exerted by the Protestant parsonage on the intellectual and literary history of the eighteenth century.[101] If we look at the group of about ninety authors, plus others in the period of the 1770s and 1780s whose attitudes we know, we find that almost 50 percent of the bourgeois antagonists, of whose parents we know something, were born into Protestant parsons' families, whereas only slightly more than a third of the protagonists seem to have been children of such families. This ratio, vague as it is, suggests that perhaps Lutheran ideas of authority were responsible for a greater detachment from Revolutionary ideology. Indeed, nearly 80 percent of the known anti-Americans

99. Cf. Stadelmann, *Deutschland und Westeuropa*, 21.

100. More than a quarter of the known German correspondence to Franklin came in almost equal parts from these three areas.

101. See Lydia Rösch, "Der Einfluß des evangelischen Pfarrhauses auf die Literatur des 18. Jahrhunderts" (publ. Ph.D. diss., University of Tübingen, 1932); Vierhaus, "Deutschland vor der Französischen Revolution," 210–213.

seem to have been Lutherans, compared to a very low percentage of Calvinists. Moreover, hardly more than half of the known pro-Americans were Lutherans, while a quarter were Calvinists. If we consider that in eighteenth-century Germany the number of Lutherans by far exceeded that of Calvinists, these figures become quite telling.

Among the protagonists of the Revolution there were a number of Catholics (including converts—some later in life—such as Stolberg, Taube, and Zinzendorf). This seems to indicate that the Catholic sector of the population was not antirevolutionary to an unusual degree, and may even have been somewhat sympathetic toward the events in America.

We can hardly say anything definite about other groups, like the Freemasons, whose opponents later linked them often with the French Revolution and with revolutionary ideas in general. We do know that Johann Wilhelm von Archenholtz was sympathetic toward the patriots, while Helferich Peter Sturz was on the other side. The best we can do here is to make a negative statement: Nothing seems to indicate that the Freemasons' response to the Revolution was completely atypical, compared with that of other religious and social groups.

Another possible influence upon German political opinion of the Revolution is the factor of urban versus rural residence. In the late eighteenth century the vast majority of Germans lived in the country.[102] Only Vienna, Berlin, and Hamburg had more than 100,000 inhabitants, and these were followed by only a few, much smaller cities. Since our analysis has shown that confrontation with the American Revolution was a concern principally of the bourgeoisie, who were urban by nature, though not restricted to cities and towns,[103] it is nearly self-evident that most of the supporters and opponents of the Revolution are to be found within the urban population. We can therefore hardly ascribe a lasting influence on an individual's judgment to his residence in the city or country.

We do have to be careful, however, not to credit only the cities and their bourgeois population with having responded to the events in the West. Jakob Rieger has left us some idea of the sympathies of the country population,[104] as Lafayette did later when he journeyed through Germany.[105] Franklin's

102. See Reinhold Aris, *History of Political Thought in Germany from 1789 to 1815* (1936; repr. London, 1965), 31.
103. See Régine Pernoud, *Les Origines de la bourgeoisie*, 4th ed. (Paris, 1969), 15–16; Robin, "Idéologies et bourgeoisie," *La nouvelle critique*, N.S., XXXII (Mar. 1970), 49; Riedel, "Bürger, Staatsbürger, Bürgertum," in Brunner *et al.*, eds., *Geschichtliche Grundbegriffe*, 672, 676–678, 681–683.
104. Rieger to Franklin, Oct. 10, 1778 (Franklin Papers, XII, 40, APSL, Philadelphia).
105. Gottschalk, *Lafayette between the Revolutions*, 181–201.

correspondents are the best proof of rural sympathies. They wrote not only from capitals, university towns, trade centers, and free imperial cities, but also from villages like Haselünne in the Emsland, Bärwalde in Pomerania, Brieg in Silesia, Römhild in Thuringia, Felsberg in Hesse, Simmern in the Hunsrück Mountains, and Schorndorf, near Stuttgart.[106]

Age is another social criterion that may be found to have had some influence upon German opinion of the American Revolution. The youngest adversary of the patriots thus far mentioned was Johann Hermann Stöver, an Altona-born writer and private secretary to Gottlob Benedikt von Schirach. Stöver was all of twelve years old in 1776, and twenty-five when his book on Lower Saxony appeared. The two oldest adversaries, Albrecht von Haller and Graf Lynar, were sixty-eight in 1776. Notwithstanding this broad spectrum, there were very few in the younger age group—those not yet thirty in 1776—who condemned the Revolution, and only a small number of derogatory statements are known to have come from persons sixty and over. But the age group from thirty to fifty-nine, virtually spanning a generation, gives us nearly 80 percent of the antagonists we know by name. Most of the signers of the Declaration of Independence came from the same age group, also about 80 percent.

The age structure of the protagonists of the American Revolution differs completely. Johann Jakob Bodmer, the oldest protagonist, was almost eighty in 1776, but 50 percent of the American patriots' admirers known to us were not older than thirty in that year. While the Americans had numerous friends in Germany among the other age groups, the number was considerably smaller among the thirty- to forty-year-olds, and constantly decreased with increasing age, probably not atypically for demographic reasons. More than 70 percent of the protagonists that we know of had not reached forty in 1776. The overwhelming majority of that age group, and particularly the age group under thirty, seems to have sided with the Americans, especially in bourgeois circles. (See Chart 2.)

The very young, it seems, were equally enthusiastic about the American Revolution. Josef von Sartori, born in 1749 in Öttingen-Wallerstein, reminisced in the 1790s: "The concern felt in Germany and in all other nations about this event and its impression on our minds was extraordinary. Boys shed tears at American losses and were nearly inconsolable."[107] But, of

106. See the letters by Alexander Niehaus, from Emsland, Oct. 10, 1778; I. M. Steuben, Bärwalde, Feb. 13, 1782; Adam Christian Kümmel, Brieg, Jan. 28, 1783; Johann Kaspar Weinlandt, Römhild, Feb. 23, 1784; Maj. Führer, Felsberg, Dec. 20, 1780; Freiherr von Strasser, Simmern, July 20, 1782; Mehl, Schorndorf, July 1, 1777 (Franklin Papers, LIX, 84, 44, XXVII, 57, LIX, 28, XX, 132, XXV, 123, LIX, 38, APSL, Philadelphia).

107. "Der Anteil, welchen Deutschland und die übrigen Nationen an dieser Begebenheit nahmen, war außerordentlich, so wie der Eindruck derselben auf alle Gemüter. Knaben ver-

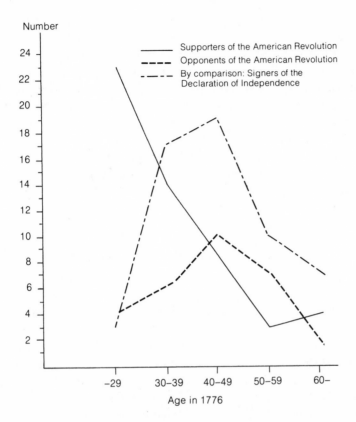

Chart 2. Age as a Factor in German Attitudes toward the American Revolution (c. 1776–1790)

course, enthusiasm for the Americans was not youth's only sentiment. We know that at the Karlsschule in Stuttgart pro-British and pro-American factions formed at once, with the young Schiller belonging to neither.[108] This formation of factions may have been owing to the pro-British sentiments peculiar to the Württemberg bourgeoisie up to the mid-1770s. Then there was Ludwig Meyer von Knonau, only seven years old in 1776, who at first was anti-American because of infantile sentiments but soon joined in youth's general enthusiasm.[109] We learn that Heinrich Büttner of Ansbach (born in

gossen Tränen, wann die Amerikaner einen Verlust erlitten, und waren beinahe untröstlich": Sartori, "Nord-Amerika" (c. 1792), fol. 68v (Cod. ser. nov. 1640, NB, Vienna).

108. Buchwald, *Schiller*, I, 256; see also Adolf Wohlwill, *Weltbürgertum und Vater-landsliebe der Schwaben* (Hamburg, 1875), 26–27.

109. Meyer von Knonau, *Lebenserinnerungen*, 10–11.

1766) and his friends sometimes turned to matters more general, "feeling deep compassion with the Americans' War of Independence and bewailing the sad fate of our fellow countrymen destined to fight against Washington and his cohorts."[110] Even Henrich Steffens, born in 1773, remembered much later the prevailing enthusiasm for the Americans, which also infected him.[111]

Summarizing the results apparent up to now, it seems that the American Revolution met with a broad wave of sympathy from the younger generation of the bourgeoisie of the German-language area. Approval does not seem to have been so one-sided among the older people. It was above all the young, aspiring members of the bourgeoisie who identified themselves with the ideals of the American patriots.

The Emigration Movement After 1783

Our investigation so far has been limited mainly to evaluating comments from the nobility and bourgeoisie. It can therefore lay no claim to reflecting "public opinion," a phenomenon that, in any case, was just starting to take shape at this time.[112] The millions of craftsmen, workers, farmers, and day laborers, who are also part of a public, have heretofore been almost non-existent in this study because, as a rule, they seldom produced any literary documents and have left only a few isolated written notes from which we can examine their opinions on the questions that concern us here. Therefore, we must try to find indirect hints of their opinions. An extraordinarily useful means for doing this is an examination of emigration from Germany to the New World.

Germans had emigrated to North America throughout the eighteenth century, but not always at the same rate. The German exodus to the Western Hemisphere reached its peak in the beginning and the middle of the century, mostly for reasons of religion or economic need. Between 1700 and 1776 some seventy thousand to eighty thousand Germans sought new homes in the British colonies on the North American continent. But apart from a brief rise

110. "innigen Teil nehmend am Freiheitskriege der Amerikaner und das traurige Los unserer Landsleute beseufzend, die gegen Washington und seine Kohorten kämpfen sollten": Büttner, "Selbstbiographie," 48 (HVMF, Ansbach).

111. Steffens, *Was ich erlebte* (Breslau, 1840–1844), I, 78, 80–81; see also Adolf Hermann Ludwig Heeren, "Schreiben an einen Freund, biographische Nachrichten enthaltend," in his *Vermischte historische Schriften*, I (Göttingen, 1821), xix.

112. Cf. Vierhaus, "Deutschland vor der Französischen Revolution," 413–419; Habermas, *Strukturwandel der Öffentlichkeit*, 102–116; Schneider, *Pressefreiheit*, 11, 81–100.

in the early 1770s, emigration figures decreased after the middle of the century. In Germany the economic situation improved, religious oppression diminished in the Age of Enlightenment, and the imperial and state governments tried valiantly to prevent emigration of their subjects. (Many more emigrants went to Eastern and Southeastern Europe than to America.) When hostilities broke out in the colonies, emigration to the West practically stopped, though a few people may have gone in the first war years.[113]

The peace of 1783 was, at least theoretically, a sign to start anew. But was there really an emigration movement to America, especially in the subsidiary states, immediately after 1783? Germany was not ravaged by war, nor was it a time of great famines or religious coercion. In many cases the fear of the unknown and of a dangerous and wearisome voyage was a decisive restraint. In addition, German emigration in the latter third of the century was generally rendered very difficult by governments that often resorted to confiscation of property to prevent their abused and economically distressed subjects from emigrating.[114]

The world of 1783 was different from that of the years prior to 1776. The American Revolution had left a deep impression on Europeans. Their own situation and, more than ever before, their knowledge of political, economic, and social conditions in the United States influenced those willing to emigrate. These considerations carried weight with the lower classes in the areas to which the auxiliary troops returned after the war. Now even the

113. See the tin bowl from Frankfurt on which the words were engraved: "Adieu Deutschland. Wir fahren nach Amerika. Vivat Frankfurt 1777." The authenticity of the bowl is open to doubt, however. A photograph of the engraving is in Waldemar Kramer, ed., *Bilder zur Frankfurter Geschichte* (Frankfurt, 1950), 98, 222, pl. 255. See also the "Munstering Book of the Brittannia of James Peters from Rotterdam to Philadelphia," July 1, 1773 (PHi, Philadelphia), and Adolf Gerber, *Die Nassau-Dillenburger Auswanderung nach Amerika im 18. Jahrhundert. Das Verhalten der Regierungen dazu und die späteren Schicksale der Auswanderer* (Flensburg, 1930), 33–45.

114. On emigration to America see the emigration files and corresponding edicts in: the Staatsarchive, Coburg, Hamburg, Koblenz, Ludwigsburg, Sigmaringen, Speyer, and Würzburg; the Stadtarchive, Frankfurt and Mainz; the Hauptstaatsarchive, Stuttgart and Wiesbaden; the Geheimes Staatsarchiv and the Staatsarchiv für Oberbayern, Munich; and the card register of emigrants in the Staatsarchiv, Darmstadt. Also, Hermann Wätjen, *Aus der Frühzeit des Nordatlantikverkehrs. Studien zur Geschichte der deutschen Schiffahrt und deutschen Auswanderung nach den Vereinigten Staaten bis zum Ende des amerikanischen Bürgerkrieges* (Leipzig, 1932); Ralph Beaver Strassburger, *Pennsylvania German Pioneers: A Publication of the Original Lists of Arrivals in the Port of Philadelphia from 1727 to 1808*, ed. William John Hinke, 3 vols. (Norristown, Pa., 1934); John D. Brite, "The Attitude of European States toward Emigration to the American Colonies and the United States, 160–1820" (unpubl. Ph.D. diss., University of Chicago, 1937), 45–62; Abbot Emerson Smith, "Some New Facts About Eighteenth-Century German Immigration," *Pennsylvania History*, X (1943), 105–117; Eva Schünzel, "Die deutsche Auswanderung nach Nordamerika im 17. und 18. Jahrhundert" (unpubl. Ph.D. diss., University of Würzburg, 1959).

poorest social strata were able to get firsthand information by listening to the recollections and impressions of the soldiers. After all, those who returned home were not exclusively antagonistic toward the Revolution but included innumerable sympathizers. Many of the latter returned to America in later years. But did their enthusiasm for the new state really leave a traceable influence on the lower classes of the former subsidiary states and the large recruiting areas, and does the emigration movement of 1783 to 1785 furnish a standard for measuring this influence?

We have no direct information on the tales told by returning soldiers, but the notes and letters written by them during the years of their stay in the New World reveal some of their most enduring impressions, which probably appeared again in later accounts. To judge the soldiers' situation properly, we have to keep in mind that many left home in the drabness of late winter and arrived in America in early summer after a wretched and risky voyage of several weeks. Almost all the soldiers from Brunswick and Hanau landed in Canada, and their first glimpse of land after a dangerous journey was the barren coasts of Labrador and Newfoundland. The majority of the Hesse-Kassel and Ansbach troops, however, landed in New York harbor and were overwhelmed by the beauty of the countryside. A "real paradise" took the place of an almost endless waste of water.[115] Dr. Johann David Schoepf impressively described this contrast to his parents, though he tried to minimize the dangers of the voyage.[116]

First impressions tended to determine future attitudes. Even after the soldiers became better acquainted with America, they thought of it as an incomparably beautiful country, abundantly rich and incredibly fertile. They marvelled at well-constructed houses, streets lit at night in the larger cities, and papered walls in even farmers' houses. A simple man enjoyed affluence seemingly unattainable by a farmer from Hesse or Ansbach.[117] Their very

115. "wahres Paradies": Johann Ernst Prechtel, Tagebuch, June 1777, 53 (KA, Munich).

116. Schoepf to his parents, Aug. 20, 1777 (Anspach Papers, II/1, no. 17, Hessian MSS No. 47, NYPL, New York).

117. See among others Waldeck, Diary of the American Revolution, ed. Learned, 16 (entry of Oct. 17, 1776); Ansbachisches Kriegstagebuch, June 3, 1777, fol. 6v (HVMF, Ansbach); Döhla, "Tagebuch," AGAO, XXV, no. 1 (1912), 102, 103 (entries of June 3, 4, 1777); Prechtel, Tagebuch, Nov. 27, 1777, Feb. 1, 1782, 115–116, 549 (KA, Munich); Capt. O'Connel to Schrader, Dec. 1, 1777 (No. 3152, Landschaftliche Bibliothek Brunswick, at StA, Wolfenbüttel); Schlözer, ed., Briefwechsel, II/8 (1777), 107, 108, III/13 (1778), 27–35; Baron von Knoblauch to Heinrich Adrian Graf von Borcke, Oct. 22, 1780 (Rep. 92 von Borcke III, no. 53, VIII, fols. 223–224, DZA, Merseburg); Acomb, "Journal of Baron Von Closen," WMQ, 3d Ser., X (1953), 66; Wilhelm Graf von Schwerin to the ruling Graf von Wied, Dec. 20, 1781 (Fürstlich Wiedisches Archiv, Neuwied; copy in LC, Washington, D.C.); Charlotte S. J. Epping, trans., Journal of Du Roi the Elder, Lieutenant and Adjutant, in the Service of the Duke of Brunswick, 1776–1778 (New York, 1911), 144, 155–160. For the opposing impres-

first experiences showed that the lower strata of the American population were far better off than they could ever hope to be at home. Officers, who viewed the war from a more professional standpoint than did the common soldier,[118] rarely contradicted this belief,[119] even though their attitudes toward the Revolution were sharply divided and generally more negative than positive.[120]

Impressions of the beauty, the riches, and the economic opportunities of the country deeply affected the common soldiers, although it was by no means confined to them. As late as the end of the century travelers thought of America as "a genuine earthly paradise."[121] The German bourgeoisie were moved by this idea of a promised land.[122] Goethe, looking back, gave a telling description of the situation when he wrote: "Then, perhaps even more than now, America was Eldorado to all who momentarily were in a distressing situation." But Goethe himself had rejected this utopian fantasy years before.[123]

Utopian ideas of America were not derived from its affluence alone. On the contrary, this view was generally associated with the principles of the American Revolution, the notions of liberty and civil equality. Not only did the country appear to offer every material prerequisite for prosperity and happiness, but state and society as well, by the abolition of special privilege, proffered a basis for free and unfettered activity. All this could not but make an impression, and it prompted thousands of soldiers to defect and start a

---

sions of the regiments that landed in Canada see Melzheimer, *Reise der Braunschweigischen Auxiliär Truppen*, 21.

118. See Hans Huth, "Letters from a Hessian Mercenary," *PMHB*, LXII (1938), 491.

119. See Marion Dexter Learned, ed., "Tagebuch des Capt. [Bernhard Wilhelm] Wiederholdt," *AG*, IV (1902), esp. 45–46.

120. For diverging attitudes see the two Hessian noblemen Karl Ludwig Freiherr von Dörnberg, *Tagebuchblätter eines hessischen Offiziers aus der Zeit des nordamerikanischen Unabhängigkeitskrieges*, ed. Gotthold Marseille, 2 vols. (Pyritz, 1899–1900), and Friedrich von der Malsburg, Tagebuch (StA, Marburg). Whereas Dörnberg opposed the Revolution, Malsburg had a more sympathetic view.

121. "ein wahres irdisches Paradies": *Reise von Hamburg nach Philadelphia*, 49.

122. E.g., Isaak Iselin to Salomon Hirzel, Sept. 18, 1771 (Nachlaß Iselin, LXI, 174, StA, Basel); Iselin to Franklin, July 28, 1778 (Franklin Papers, X, 154, APSL, Philadelphia); Krauseneck, *Werbung für England* (1776 ed.), 5–6; Ingenhousz, "Remarques," 2 (HHStA, Vienna); Friedrich Leopold to Christian Stolberg, Dec. 23, 1777, in F. L. Stolberg, *Briefe*, ed. Behrens, 99; "Schilderung des gesellschaftlichen Lebens u.s.w. in den vereinigten Staaten von Amerika" (c. 1800) (LB, Gotha). See also Kraus, "America and the Utopian Ideal," *Mississippi Valley Historical Review*, XXII (1935–1936), 487–504.

123. "Amerika war damals vielleicht noch mehr als jetzt das Eldorado derjenigen, die in ihrer augenblicklichen Lage sich bedrängt fanden": Goethe, "Dichtung und Wahrheit," bk. XIX. See also his "Wilhelm Meisters Lehrjahre," bk. VII, chap. 3, with the famous exclamation: "Hier oder nirgend ist Amerika." Both are in Goethe, *Werke*, Weimar ed., 1/XXIX, 156, 1/XXIII, 20.

new life in America. Many of the soldiers who returned home were also deeply affected and tried to communicate their feelings to friends and relatives in Germany.

What happened next did not surprise many observers. As early as 1777 Johann Nikolaus Karl Buchenröder had stated unequivocally that emigrants from Germany would flock to the New World after an American victory.[124] At the end of the war Georg Christoph Lichtenberg presumed the same: "A kind of *Völkerwanderung* will set in. Perhaps we will live to see professors from Göttingen getting a call to the Alma Philadelphica and book dealers from Philadelphia at the Leipzig fair."[125] Sprengel, too, believed that "the repute of American freedom might increase emigration from Germany and Great Britain."[126] Franklin, who had written a small guidebook for emigrants to America, diagnosed the situation similarly: "I think there will be great emigrations from England, Ireland, and Germany."[127]

The question remains, however, was there actually a sizable emigration of the lower classes to this promising land? Let us look at those regions to which a large number of veterans returned, since here is where one might expect to find evidence of the influence of their experiences and impressions of America. In 1784–1785 the developments are interesting. Although we have no statistics or official lists, it seems that emigration to America markedly increased from those areas, especially during the first two postwar years. In Brunswick the increase was so sharp that on March 29, 1784, the duke issued a decree emphatically reconfirming the old ban on emigration, because in recent times, he said, "several local subjects seem to have decided to leave this country and to go to America in spite of everything."[128] It is not likely that only a few isolated cases would have been sufficient to rouse the sovereign's discontent.

124. Buchenröder, *Nord-Amerika*, III, vii–viii.

125. "Es wird eine förmliche Völkerwanderung dorthin geschehen. Vielleicht erleben wir noch Vokationen Göttingischer Professoren nach der Alma Philadelphica und sehen Philadelphische Buchhändler auf der Leipziger Messe": to Schernhagen, Dec. 30, 1782, in Leitzmann, ed., "Neues von Lichtenberg," *Zeitschrift für Bücherfreunde*, N.S., IV, no. 1 (1912), 126.

126. "der Ruf der amerikanischen Freiheit die Auswanderungen aus Deutschland und Großbritannien vermehren könnte": Sprengel, *Allgemeines historisches Taschenbuch*, 149. See also August Friedemann Rühle von Lilienstern to Franklin, Mar. 14, 1783, and Karl Gottfried Paleske to Franklin, May 27, 1783 (Franklin Papers, LIX, 69, XXVIII, 120, APSL, Philadelphia).

127. To Robert R. Livingston, Apr. 15, 1783, in Smyth, ed., *Writings of Franklin*, IX, 34; cf. Franklin to Livingston, July 22, 1783, *ibid.*, 71.

128. "dennoch verschiedene hiesige Untertanen den Entschluß gefaßt haben sollen, sich von hier weg und nach Amerika zu begeben": "Serenissimi Edict, gegen das Auswandern der Unterthanen in fremde Lande, und insonderheit nach Amerika. d.d. Braunschweig, den 29 März 1784" [printed] (StA, Wolfenbüttel).

Early in 1785 the Fulda government also thought it necessary to refer again to the existing emigration regulations, after a certain Karl Rooss from America "talked several of his friends in Hettenhausen and Gersfeld into going to America with him." The word "depopulation" was even used in this context.[129] And in 1784–1785 numerous citizens emigrated "even to America" from the Hanau territory, most of them without the sovereign's permission and often in desperate economic straits.[130] Also, in May 1785, the nearby principality of Isenburg announced that "several subjects . . . have emigrated as far as America."[131]

Most decrees and written announcements made no specific mention of aims or plans of emigrants. But since this was done in the cases referred to above, we may conclude that officials must have thought the phenomenon to be noteworthy. It is most improbable that the examples quoted were singular cases unconnected with the return of the auxiliary troops. Their combined incidence and the temporal connection to the soldiers' return from North America are too obvious. The assumption that the emigration was limited to Brunswick and Hanau alone and did not affect the other subsidiary states also seems baseless; it is contradicted by the simple fact that in the same years many emigration bans, even if not specifically referring to America, suddenly were proclaimed in neighboring territories, such as Nassau, the electorate of Mainz, and the entire Rhine-Main area.[132]

It was probably not an accident that in 1784–1785 emigration to America made itself felt in exactly those states whose soldiers had returned shortly before. And if those veterans' tales could really influence numerous Germans to overcome the fear of hardships and risks and to launch on a voyage almost totally unknown in order to start a new life in America, then we must assume that this new country and its Revolution enjoyed much

129. "verschiedene seiner Freunde von Hettenhausen und Gersfeld beredet, mit nach Amerika zu ziehen. . . . Entvölkerung": J. Weitar to the government at Fulda, Jan. 28, 1785 (98 d X no. 1, fols. 56r–v, StA, Marburg).

130. "sogar nach Amerika": May 6, 1785 (98 d X no. 9, StA, Marburg; also as Ugb. A 9 no. 7, StadtA, Frankfurt).

131. "verschiedene Untertanen . . . bis nach Amerika emigriert": local administrators at Meerholtz to the government at Hanau, May 18, 1785 (86 no. ∝2812, fol. 152, cf. fol. 65, StA, Marburg).

132. See among others the emigration files and respective edicts in the Staatsarchiv Koblenz, Stadtarchiv Mainz, and Hauptstaatsarchiv Wiesbaden; also Franklin, *Bericht für diejenigen, welche nach Nord-Amerika sich begeben*. The translator was Vautravers; cf. his letters to John Adams, Dec. 7, 1791, and to Washington, June 6, 1792 (Reel 101, 102, Washington Papers, LC, Washington, D.C.). See also the rather poor studies by Karl Hartnack, "Ein Beitrag zur Geschichte der waldeckischen Auswanderung nach Nordamerika," *Geschichtsblätter für Waldeck und Pyrmont*, XXIX/XXX (1931), 133–139, and Max Miller, "Ursachen und Ziele der schwäbischen Auswanderung," *Württembergische Vierteljahrshefte für Landesgeschichte*, XLII (1936), 184–218.

sympathy among the lower classes, even though they had but little factual knowledge. The postwar emigration movement permits us to assume that the German bourgeoisie's enthusiasm for America continued in modified form among the lower classes of the population.

All of this makes clear that England's image and the territorial affiliations of contemporary observers were, relatively speaking, of little importance in the majority's attitude toward the American Revolution. However, some social divisions were very pronounced in spite of all fluctuations. In Germany the American Revolution and its ideals roused the enthusiasm of the nonprivileged classes of the population, and the up-and-coming young middle class acted as spokesman in the articulation of this "contagion of liberty," to use Bernard Bailyn's phrase.[133] The privileged classes, notwithstanding some sympathetic declarations, were less favorably inclined toward the patriots. In growing numbers they recognized that the privileges that raised them above the common masses were threatened by American Revolutionary principles, which declared such privileges to be the common property of all men.

Washington

It was only natural, considering the time, that the bourgeoisie in their enthusiasm for the Revolution and its principles would quickly find a personification of their ideals. Obviously, and almost as a matter of course, no other patriots could rival George Washington and Benjamin Franklin.[134] Very early, John Adams had unhappily prophesied this mythical outcome: "The history of our revolution will be one continued lie from one end to the other. The essence of the whole will be that Dr. Franklin's electrical rod smote the earth and out sprung General Washington. That Franklin electrified him with his rod—and thence forward these two conducted all the policy, negotiations, legislatures, and war."[135]

The respect Washington enjoyed among his countrymen was based, on

133. Bailyn, *Ideological Origins*, the title of chap. 6. Cf. Palmer, "Einfluß der amerikanischen Revolution," in Mann *et al.*, eds., *Propyläen-Weltgeschichte*, 37, 40–41, and Palmer, *Age of the Democratic Revolution*, I, 259.

134. See Goethe, "Dichtung und Wahrheit," bk. XVII, in his *Werke*, Weimar ed., 1/XXIX, 68.

135. To Benjamin Rush, Apr. 4, 1790, in Butterfield, ed., *Letters of Benjamin Rush*, II, 1207.

the one hand, on his role as commander-in-chief of the American army in the War of Independence and, on the other, on his eight-year tenure of office as the first president of the United States. His wise and clever strategy had brought independence, which was made secure by no less successful political leadership in the difficult early phases of the republic. These accomplishments, together with the force of his character and his captivating manner, elevated him so much in the eyes of contemporary Americans and their descendants that he became a "living legend" and a "mythic figure" during his lifetime. "For later generations, even more than for his own, Washington has remained as much myth as man, as much monument as human."[136]

Most European contemporaries admired Washington just as uncritically. To be sure, there were some antagonists of America who included Washington in their condemnation of the Revolution, naming him in one breath with the much-hated Cromwell and imagining the general to be a dictator and a despot.[137] But ideas like these obviously were not widespread among the German bourgeoisie. Comments lauding Washington's military capabilities came even from England.[138] In Germany, Washington's fame increased steadily, and one of many to praise him was Freiherr von Knoblauch, formerly a Prussian and later an American officer, who called him "one of the greatest generals in this age."[139]

But esteem for Washington did not reach its peak in Germany until the end of the war, when it seemed obvious that his strategy had met with full success. Now it was clear "that the existence of the new republic had then depended merely on Washington's courage. . . . In this desperate situation, Washington showed his true greatness."[140] For he "defended America's lib-

---

136. James M. Smith's introduction to his *George Washington: A Profile* (New York, 1969), vii. See also Douglas Southall Freeman, *George Washington: A Biography*, 7 vols. (New York, 1948–1957), V, 480–501; Marcus Cunliffe, *George Washington: Man and Monument* (New York, 1960), 24, 109; James Thomas Flexner, *George Washington*, 4 vols. (Boston, 1965–1972), II, 531–552; also Gilbert Chinard, ed., *George Washington as the French Knew Him: A Collection of Texts* (Princeton, N.J., 1940), 20, 24, 31, 81, 94, 108.

137. E.g., Korn, *Geschichte der Kriege*, VII, 72, VIII, 18–19; *Politisches Journal*, June 1781, 613.

138. See the London news in the *Freytags-Zeitung*, Feb. 21, 1777; Johann Reinhold Forster to Johann David Michaelis, London, Aug. 17, 1779 (Nachlaß Michaelis, CCCXXII, fol. 331, SuUB, Göttingen); *Correspondance du Lord G. Germain*, xiii, xiv; *Vorläufige Nachricht und Beschreibung*, xii–xiii.

139. To Washington, Sept. 2, 1778 (Reel 51, Washington Papers, LC, Washington, D.C.).

140. "daß das Dasein der neuen Republik damals bloß von Washingtons Mut abhing. . . . Eben in dieser verzweifelten Lage zeigte Washington seine wahre Größe": Hoff, *Kurze Biographien*, III, 17, cf. 20–21. The same wording appeared in the reprint of this work, Hoff's *Kurze Biographien berühmter Staatsmänner, Helden, Künstler und Frauenzimmer* (Frankfurt and Leipzig, 1783), 17, 20–21.

erty" in this war[141] and was the "soul and pillar of one of the most sweeping state transformations."[142] He was the "Fabius of America . . . whose name will be handed down to the most distant generations."[143] The Americans had only him to thank, his courage, his farsightedness, and his patience, for being able to secure their liberty and put it on a solid foundation. His name was not connected with any great battle, but as commander-in-chief, he was far above all other American generals. Thus, Chastellux wrote for all German contemporaries to read: "North America, from Boston to Charleston, is one great book, each page of which sings his praise."[144] America's success in war was his merit alone, and his name was linked forever with the achievement of American liberty.[145]

The mythicizing that John Adams voiced fear of a few years later had already taken place as far as the German bourgeoisie were concerned. Washington was hardly looked upon any more as a military leader; he was the personification of America's fight against Great Britain. Lafayette gladly confirmed this idea when he reported to his friend Washington on his journey through Germany: "With your eulogium began every conversation of American affairs."[146] Washington's reputation in Germany became pure hero worship, and had grown to the extent that Friedrich Leopold zu Stolberg could seriously write in 1784: "I wish this great and noble man would die. His glory is as yet untarnished, but how often does it continue that way?"[147] The aged Saxon general Friedrich Ludwig Graf von Solms, asked for a portrait of the "greatest of all warriors," the receipt of which he confirmed by saying that it was given a place of honor in his private gallery, between the Prussian

141. "verteidigte die amerikanische Freiheit": Zinner, *Merkwürdige Briefe und Schriften*, 11.
142. "die Seele und Stütze einer der größten Staatsveränderungen": *Historisches Portefeuille*, Nov. 1782, 1381.
143. "Fabius von Amerika . . . dessen Name auf die entfernteste Nachwelt kommen wird": Cluny, *Reisen durch Amerika*, 179. See also Jäger, *Zeitungs-Lexicon*, II (1784), 842b–843a; Hanns Schlitter, ed., "Die Berichte des ersten Agenten Österreichs in den Vereinigten Staaten von Amerika Baron de Beelen-Bertholff an die Regierung der österreichischen Niederlande in Brüssel 1784 bis 1789," *Fontes Rerum Austriacarum* (hereafter cited as *FRA*), 2/XLV/2 (1891), 289, 294 (the notes are from Apr. 25, 1784, and from the beginning of 1784).
144. "Nordamerika, von Boston bis Charleston, ist ein großes Buch, von dem jedes Blatt sein Lob erzählt": Chastellux, *Reisebeobachtungen*, 28.
145. See Esmond Wright, *Washington and the American Revolution* (London, 1957), 129.
146. Lafayette to Washington, Feb. 6, 1786, in Gottschalk, ed., *Letters of Lafayette to Washington*, 306. Cf. Lafayette to Washington, Sept. 3, 1785, in *ibid.*, 302; also Gottschalk, *Lafayette between the Revolutions*, 200.
147. "Ich wollte, daß der große edle Mann stürbe. Noch ist sein Ruhm tadellos, und wie selten bleibt er das": Stolberg to [his sister?] Katharina, June 11, 1784, in Johann Heinrich Hennes, ed., *Friedrich Leopold Graf zu Stolberg und Herzog Peter Friedrich Ludwig von Oldenburg. Aus ihren Briefen und andern archivalischen Quellen* (Mainz, 1870), 243.

king Frederick II and Frederick's brother, Prince Heinrich. "You see that this is a very harmonious trio."[148]

This concept of the military hero receded somewhat in America during the years between Washington's resignation as commander-in-chief and his nomination for president of the federal Constitutional Convention of 1787, while he was living the life of a landed Virginia gentleman. But among his European admirers, esteem for Washington did not fade—just the opposite. "Washington, perhaps the one military leader in the last two thousand years most worthy of being compared to the great Fabius Cunctator, has now completely turned into Cincinnatus."[149] His fame was now based less on past military deeds than on his personality and his exemplary character, entirely in the sense in which Montesquieu had named virtue as the outstanding characteristic of a republic. Even today it is a commonplace of American folklore that Washington never told a lie.[150] "He has achieved the most radiant fame and the most unlimited power without exciting envy and arousing suspicion."[151] For this reason Stolberg thought of him as a "modest hero,"[152] while for Crèvecoeur this idol was "an enlightened citizen, a skilled general, and experienced statesman."[153] Chastellux saw in him the "idea of a perfect whole. . . . Courageous without recklessness, industrious without ambition, generous without wastefulness, noble without arrogance, virtuous without austerity."[154]

In the 1790s, after Washington had risen to the presidency, these characteristics seemed even more cogent to observers. The influential writer Jacques Pierre Brissot de Warville was of the opinion that "Washington can perhaps not be ranked with the most famous warriors, but he exemplified a perfect republican, with all the attributes, all the virtues characteristic of such a

148. "plus grand des guerriers. . . . Vous voyez, que c'est un trio fort harmonique": Solms to Washington, July 9, 1783, Aug. 4, 1785 (Reels 92, 95, Washington Papers, LC, Washington, D.C.).

149. "Washington, der vielleicht von allen Feldherrn seit 2,000 Jahren am würdigsten ist, mit dem großen Fabius Cunctator verglichen zu werden, ist jetzo ganz in den Charakter des Cincinnatus übergegangen": *Litteratur und Völkerkunde*, Feb. 1785, 176. Cf. Hoff, *Kurze Biographien*, III, 5.

150. See Cunliffe, *Washington*, 18.

151. "Er hat sich den glänzendsten Ruhm erworben, hat die unumschränkteste Gewalt erlangt, ohne den Neid zu reizen und ohne Verdacht zu erregen": *Historisches Portefeuille*, Nov. 1782, 1382.

152. "bescheidenen Helden": Stolberg, *Jamben* (Leipzig, 1784), 64.

153. "der aufgeklärte Bürger, der geschickte General, der erfahrne Staatsmann": Crève-coeur, *Briefe eines Amerikanischen Landmanns*, III, 344.

154. "Begriff eines vollkommenen Ganzen. . . . Tapfer ohne Verwegenheit, arbeitsam ohne Stolz, freigiebig ohne Verschwendung, edel ohne Hochmut, tugendhaft ohne Strenge": Chastellux, *Reisebeobachtungen*, 29.

personality."[155] Ewald Friedrich Graf von Hertzberg expressed similar views in a letter of recommendation he wrote to Washington on behalf of a Prussian merchant: "I have always admired your great virtues, and qualities, your disinterested patriotism, your unshaken courage, and simplicity of manners —qualifications by which you surpass men the most celebrated of antiquity." And he concluded his letter: "I wish you and your republic a constant prosperity."[156] A few years later Ernst Ludwig Posselt's *Europäische Annalen* called Washington "great and just . . . wise, great of soul and virtue" and ranked him with the Roman ideal embodiments of virtue, "Fabricius, Scipio, and Cato."[157]

The esteem Washington enjoyed in Europe made him one of the age's great idols, and to be able to boast of his personal acquaintance was regarded as a sign of great distinction.[158] Dozens of Germans wrote letters to him, mainly in the early 1790s, most of them asking for favors, just as they had written to Franklin at an earlier time.[159] The German bourgeoisie saw in the American president not only "one of the greatest men in recent history,"[160] whose greatness far outshone all European statesmen,[161] they also fancied him more and more as the "world's wise and noble benefactor . . . vindicator of human nature, and a friend to both worlds."[162]

155. "Washington darf vielleicht den berühmtesten Kriegern nicht an die Seite gestellt werden, aber er ist ein Muster eines vollkommenen Republikaners und zeigt alle Eigenschaften, alle Tugenden, die dieser Charakter erheischt": Brissot de Warville, *Neue Reise*, Bayreuth ed., II, 204. See also Delacroix, *Verfassung*, II, 311; Castiglioni, *Reise durch die Vereinigten Staaten*, 264–267.

156. Hertzberg to Washington, June 14, 1793 (official translation) (Reel 92, Washington Papers, LC, Washington, D.C.).

157. "großen und gerechten . . . Weisheit, Seelengröße und Tugend . . . Fabricius, Scipio und Cato": *Europäische Annalen*, Nov. 1796, 161. See also Remer, *Handbuch der neuern Geschichte*, 3d ed., 843.

158. E.g., *Historisches Portefeuille*, Nov. 1782, 1381–1383; also the letter of Matthias Blume, Feb. 14, 1790 (Abt. Grafschaft Hanau-Lichtenberg, StA, Speyer). Blume was born in Alsace and emigrated to Pittsburgh.

159. In addition to the letters to Washington already mentioned, see those by Karl von Leuchsenring, from Durlach, Mar. 18, 1788; David Friedrich Oehler, Crimmitschau, near Leipzig, Feb. 1, 1791; and those by Vautravers and others (Washington Papers, LC, Washington, D.C.). See also Christian von Mechel to Friedrich Dominikus Ring, Dec. 10, 1785 (Nachlaß Ring, XV, fol. 9v, UB, Freiburg, Germany).

160. "einen der größten Männer, den die neuere Geschichte kennt": Remer, *Darstellung der Gestalt der historischen Welt* (Frankfurt and Leipzig, 1794), 297.

161. See among others *Prophetische Muthmaßungen über die Französische Staatsveränderung* (Philadelphia, 1794); Georg Freiherr von Vega to [?], Apr. 8, 1795 (Vega, Korrespondenz, fol. 169, HHStA, Vienna).

162. "der edle weise Wohltäter der Welt . . . der Verteidiger der menschlichen Natur, der Freund beider Welten": Henry Wansey, *Tagebuch einer Reise durch die vereinigten Staaten von Nord-Amerika*, trans. from the English (Berlin, 1797), 138. See also Seidel, *Neueste Geschichte von Europa*, II, 191.

Thus, Washington had been completely transformed into a bourgeois ideal. Like the Franklin myth, the picture was further enhanced by the former president's death, which came to the attention of those living east of the Rhine in the early days of 1800. And as in the case of Franklin ten years previously, an abundance of memorials appeared, recounting Washington's merits and mourning one of mankind's benefactors:

> O liberty, mourn! Your soul arose
> To heaven, to its origin,
> The realm of infinite purity . . .
> Rejoice, O despots, for your judge
> Has left his bench! . . .
> O mankind, weep! Your friend now lies
> Bedraggled at your breast.[163]

Again they recalled memories of the American Revolution, lauding to the skies the legendary merits of the man. But the first shadows also began to fall on this bright picture. Washington was a Federalist, and the dispute of this party with the Republicans did not spare the former president. As yet there were only a few in Germany who openly criticized him, and their attacks on this American father image were unsuccessful.[164]

At the end of the eighteenth century Washington was, on the whole, the venerated idol of the bourgeois world. Johann Wilhelm von Archenholtz began his obituary of him by stating: "If ever the judgment of mankind of one of our contemporaries was unanimous, it was in the appreciation of Washington."[165]

---

163. "O traure, Freiheit! Deine Seele stieg / Zu ihrem Himmel wieder in den Schoß / Des reinen Daseins, der Unendlichkeit / . . . O jauchzt, Despoten! Euer Richter ist / Von seinem Stuhl gefallen! / . . . O weine, Menschheit! Dein Vertrauter sank / Verwelkt an deinen Busen . . .": Johann Gottfried Hagemeister, "Auf Washington's Tod," *Berlinisches Archiv der Zeit* (1800), II, 10. See also Karl von Zinzendorf, in Pettenegg, ed., *Ludwig und Karl von Zinzendorf*, 254; *Washingtons Ankunft in Elisium* (Lancaster, Pa., 1800). Washington, however, scarcely ever appeared in contemporary German novels and dramas; cf. John R. Frey, "George Washington in German Fiction," *American-German Review*, XII, no. 5 (1946), 25–26, 37; also Echeverria, *Mirage in the West*, 253–255.

164. Only a very few cautiously critical suggestions were made by Friedrich von Gentz in his *Historisches Journal* (1800), II/1, 311, 316. For sharp personal attacks, however, see K. A. Kierulf, "Bemerkungen über die berühmtesten Männer des Freistaates in Nordamerika," *Geschichte und Politik*, I (1800), esp. 116–123, and Weld, *Reisen durch die vereinigten Staaten* (Berlin: Öhmigke, 1800), I, 85–86. The same passage appears on page 76 of the edition published in the same year by Voss of Berlin; it is missing, however, in the translation published by Haude & Spener (Berlin, 1800).

165. "Wenn je über einen unserer Zeitgenossen das Urteil der Menschen ungeteilt gewesen ist, so war es das Urteil über Washington": *Minerva*, Mar. 1800, 540.

Franklin: An Idol of the Times

While Washington, in the eyes of the German bourgeoisie, was primarily the expression of the heroism and virtue of the American Revolution, Franklin was looked upon as the embodiment of American social and cultural ideals. In Germany, in contrast to America,[166] Franklin's fame outshone Washington's. Even before the beginning of the War of Independence, Franklin had enjoyed great respect in all of Europe. This reputation, resting on his fame as a scientist and moral philosopher,[167] was enhanced by his journey to Göttingen in 1766 and his election to membership in the Göttingen Akademie der Wissenschaften.[168]

Franklin's prestige as a scientist[169] was based in part on his identification with the American Philosophical Society, whose "president is the famous Mr. Benjamin Franklin."[170] The great esteem in which Franklin was held in Enlightenment circles during those years was expressed by an invitation to the margrave of Baden's court late in 1774: "He invites you to Germany upon that principle which seems to have actuated your whole life, I mean, the benefit of mankind in general and his subjects in particular."[171]

Franklin's image as represented here is that of a scientist and a sage only. His political activities and the role he played in the growing conflict with England were scarcely mentioned, although some details concerning his position had been published in Germany, including his interrogation in the House of Commons on the Stamp Act.[172] German contemporaries did not become aware of Franklin as a revolutionary leader until, having arrived in France at the end of 1776, he tried to recruit active support there for the Americans' fight for independence. Now, suddenly, sectors of the bourgeoisie saw the

166. Cunliffe, *Washington*, 20–23; Hartz, *Liberal Tradition*, 51.

167. E.g., Emilio Goggio, "Benjamin Franklin and Italy," *Romanic Review*, XIX (1928), 302–308; Antonio Pace, *Benjamin Franklin and Italy* (Philadelphia, 1958), 17–48, 120–143.

168. It may be noted that in 1793 some members of the Akademie objected to the expulsion of Georg Forster with the argument that the Royal Society had not excluded Benjamin Franklin during the American war (Pers. 66, nos. 1, 2, AAW, Göttingen).

169. E.g., Georg Christoph Lichtenberg, *Aphorismen*, ed. Albert Leitzmann (Berlin, 1902–1908), aphorism K. A. 16 (c. 1770).

170. "Präsident der berühmte Hr. Benjamin Franklin": Albrecht von Haller in a review of the first volume of the *Transactions of the American Philosophical Society*, in *Göttingische Anzeigen von gelehrten Sachen*, Zugabe, Jan. 29, 1774 (see Haller's ex libris copy in the Stadt- und Universitätsbibliothek, Bern). See also [Benjamin Franklin], *Merkwürdiger Americanischer Haushaltungs Calender* (Boston, i.e., Germany, 1771) (first German translation of the *Way to Wealth*).

171. P. P. Burdett to Franklin, Dec. 15, 1774 (Franklin Coll., I, 25, PHi, Philadelphia).

172. Torén, *Reise nach Surate*, 143–238.

great scientist and exponent of the Enlightenment in a political setting. Because of the increasing sympathies for the patriots, he was at once extolled as an eminent statesman and champion of the ideals of the American Revolution.

The letters written to Franklin during the time he was in Paris express clearly the character of the German enthusiasm for him. They display the mood of the age, invoking Franklin's fame in ever new terms. Writers were convinced that Franklin was "the most renowned man of these times,"[173] something like their spiritual father, "the prime source of all that is good,"[174] "the great man, the American Orpheus, the extent of whose merits astonishes Europe,"[175] and who had so decisively contributed "to break the chains of an oppressed people."[176] In these statements were merged Franklin's image as a sage and scientist—whose thoughts and ideas benefited all mankind—and his new identity as a spokesman of the American Revolution and its principles.

Admiration for Franklin and devotion to the patriots' ideals were, as a rule, closely allied in the bourgeois mind, bringing about the immense respect in which he was held all over Europe. Franklin, even more than Washington, was the best vehicle for the articulation of revolutionary enthusiasm,[177] and he came to symbolize the American Revolution and its ideals. His popularity was due not to his participation in the event, but rather to his position as the most eminent exponent of the Enlightenment in the New World who had thrown his whole moral weight on the side of the patriots. This also made Franklin a focal point for the appraisal of these events. The aura that emanated from him gave his public advocacy of the insurgents a powerful influence on the European judgment of the Revolution. In 1795 Franklin's biographer, Christian Jakob Zahn, reduced to a simple statement the probable interrelation between Franklin's image and the people's appraisal of the Revolution: "The question of the legality of the American Revolution and that of Franklin's moral righteousness in taking part in it are one and the same. If a discussion should end in a judgment against the Americans, Frank-

173. "l'homme le plus renommé de ces temps": Franz Streinsky to Franklin, Prague, Sept. 12, 1781 (Franklin Coll., II, 40, PHi, Philadelphia).

174. "la première source de tout le bien": Franz Anton Freiherr von Seyffertitz to Franklin, Sept. 13, 1778 (Franklin Papers, IX, 135, APSL, Philadelphia).

175. "der große Mann, der amerikanische Orpheus, der diesen Umfang der Verdienste hat, welcher Europa in Erstaunen setzt": Johann Jakob Meyen to Franklin, June 28, 1788 (*ibid.*, LIX, 29).

176. "à briser les chaines d'un peuple opprimé": August Friedrich Wilhelm Crome to Franklin, Mar. 4, 1783 (*ibid.*, XXVII, 164).

177. Among the numerous letters to Franklin see especially those by Nikolaus Paradis, Lt. Wommrad, Ludwig Friedrich Gottlob Ernst Gedike, Bek, Baron von Welffen, Johann Valentin Embser, and also those by Jean Rodolphe Vautravers (all *ibid.*).

lin would also be condemned, and vice versa."[178] It is evident from such interpretations and from Franklin's immense popularity in Europe that his share in the Revolution was much overemphasized by the German bourgeoisie.[179]

Franklin's concrete influence on German evaluation of the American Revolution can be verified in the case of many people whose former political prototype was liberal England. Jan Ingenhousz, the court physician in Vienna, is an excellent example, having been on close terms with Franklin ever since the latter's stay in England as the colonies' representative. Ingenhousz was probably the only person in the German-language area who could truly call himself Franklin's friend. Ingenhousz commonly called England his spiritual homeland. But affection for Great Britain and sympathy with the American patriots could exist harmoniously side by side for only so long; after the war broke out, he had to make a choice.

His correspondence with Franklin furnishes the key to an explanation of his final decision. Franklin had broadly expounded to Ingenhousz his motives, as well as all the consequences thereof, and this caused Ingenhousz to make up his mind. The American had convinced him; Ingenhousz now condemned English policy and told his friend: "I am fully persuaded that you act according to your best judgment for the good and the dignity of your country."[180] In a report Ingenhousz made to Empress Maria Theresa he put Franklin's moral authority in the foreground: "If Mr. Franklin, whose moderate and gentle temperament is beyond question among noted Americans as well as among those who, like myself, have been associated with him in sincere friendship, is so violently turned against the old government, then we are constrained to believe that the majority of his compatriots, who have always listened to him as the most clear-sighted among them, very much share his enthusiasm."[181]

Even in the 1790s, after Franklin's death, numerous Germans were of

---

178. "Die Frage also von der Rechtmäßigkeit der amerikanischen Revolution ist eine und eben dieselbe mit derjenigen von Franklins Moralität in Absicht auf seine Mitwirkung zu derselben. Fiele das Resultat der Erörterung gegen die Amerikaner aus, so wäre auch Franklin verdammt, und umgekehrt": [Zahn], *D. B. Franklins Leben* (Tübingen, 1795), 220.

179. Cf. Esmond Wright, *Benjamin Franklin and American Independence* (London, 1966), 90–161; Roger Burlingame, *Benjamin Franklin: Envoy Extraordinary* (New York, 1967), 121–122; also Michael G. Kammen, *A Rope of Sand: The Colonial Agents, British Politics, and the American Revolution* (Ithaca, N.Y., 1968), 240–252, 273–281.

180. Ingenhousz to Franklin, June 28, 1777 (Franklin Papers, VI, 83, APSL, Philadelphia).

181. "Si Mr. Franklin dont le tempérament modéré et doux est hors de question chez tous les Américains de note comme à tous ceux qui ont vécus dans une étroite amitié avec lui, comme moi, est si violemment exacerbé contre l'ancien gouvernement, il y a bien de croire, que la plupart de ses compatriotes, qui l'ont toujours écouté comme l'homme le plus clairvoyant parmis eux, participent beaucoup de son enthousiasme": May 18, 1777 (NB, Vienna).

this conviction. Johann Gottfried Herder wrote of him as one of his "favorites," whose "sense of humanity" he especially valued: "The greater part of the English nation knows well enough that he was no insurgent, that he made the most sensible proposals for peace and reconciliation." According to Herder, Franklin had not started the war with England; there was rather a "star of peace" shining in him.[182] At the end of the century Samuel Baur saw even more clearly this direct relationship between the justification of the American Revolution and Franklin's morality: "Franklin did everything possible to get the ministers' assent to changing their policy.... In vain! They did not listen to his wise council, but blindly pursued their own plans, leaving the colonists a choice only between unconditional submission and active resistance. The former was not compatible with the principles of liberty, which the colonists had been brought up to revere; thus, in the end, they were forced to have recourse to the latter."[183]

Interpretations like these were quite in keeping with the personalized idea of history popular at that time. Numerous bourgeois representatives obviously shared the view that the Revolution was even more justified because one of the best-known exponents of the Enlightenment took part in it.[184] We may assume that Franklin's visit to Göttingen similarly affected some individuals, especially in view of the friendly words used by the orientalist Johann David Michaelis and the professor of constitutional law Johann Stephan Pütter when reminiscing about this event in the 1790s.[185]

182. "Lieblinge... Sinn der Humanität.... Dem bessern Teil der englischen Nation ist es bekannt genug, daß er kein Aufrührer gewesen, daß er zum Frieden und zur Aussöhnung die einsichtvollesten Vorschläge getan habe.... Friedensstern": Herder, *Briefe zu Beförderung der Humanität*, 10 vols. (Riga, 1793–1797), I, 10–11, 37–38.

183. "Franklin ließ nichts unversucht, die Minister zu bewegen, ihre Einwilligung zu veränderten Maßregeln zu geben... Umsonst! Sie hörten nicht auf seinen weisen Rat. Blind verfolgten sie ihre eigenen Pläne und ließen den Kolonisten nur die Wahl zwischen unbedingter Unterwerfung und tätigem Widerstande. Jene vertrug sich nicht mit den Grundsätzen von Freiheit, in deren Verehrung sie erzogen waren: sie sahen sich also am Ende, wiewohl ungern, genötigt, ihre Zuflucht zu dem letztern zu nehmen": Baur, *Geschichtserzählungen*, II, 101, cf. 118–119. See also *Das graue Ungeheuer*, VII (1786), 252; Benjamin Franklin, *Kleine Schriften*, trans. from the English by Georg Schatz, 2 vols. (Weimar, 1794), I, [3–4] (foreword by Schatz).

184. E.g., Iselin to Jean Rodolphe Frey, July 28, 30, 1778 (Nachlaß Iselin, LVI, 146, 151, StA, Basel); Isidor Bianchi, in Carli, *Briefe über Amerika*, I, ix–x; Georg Friedrich Palm, *Adel der Menschheit* (Leipzig, 1798), 327–347; Karl August Schiller, *Gallerie interessanter Personen* (Berlin and Vienna, 1798), 264–269; *Der Unglickliche Walter oder Leiden und Verfolgungen eines Deutschen in Amerika* (Vienna and Prague, 1798), 142–146; also Benjamin Rush, *Untersuchungen über den Einfluß körperlicher Ursachen auf die Moralität*, trans. from the English (Offenbach, 1787), 93.

185. Michaelis, *Lebensbeschreibung*, 110–111; see also his letters to and from Jean Le Rond d'Alembert, June 17, Sept. 6, 1780 (Nachlaß Michaelis, CCCXX, fols. 21v, 22v–23, SuUB, Göttingen); Pütter, *Selbstbiographie*, II, 491.

Georg Forster is another case in point. He visited Franklin in Paris before he ever made any meaningful statement on the American Revolution. He returned from Paris at the age of twenty-three, full of idealism and deeply impressed by this illustrious person.[186] He took a benevolent stand on the American Revolution only in later years, but his admiration for Franklin never left him, and as late as 1791 he described Franklin as "the most venerable name ever pronounced by the eighteenth century."[187] Johann Reinhold Forster, who was influenced by England more than his son, made a similar remark: "It is one of the most pleasant memories of my life to have met the great Franklin in person."[188]

The above remarks did not ignore or reject Franklin the statesman; rather, they integrated this side of the man into the overall image. He appeared to be "a genius with few equals anywhere, equally great as philosopher and statesman."[189] And this was by no means the last stage the Franklin legend was to attain with an enthusiastic bourgeoisie. Even Johann Christian Schmohl, a usually clear-headed apologist of the American Revolution, contributed to the myth: "Franklin is the father of science and of all sound philosophy and politics in America."[190] Knowledgeable Germans could read the appraisal of Franklin by the popular Italian poet and liberty enthusiast, Vittorio Alfieri, in his ode "L'America libera": ". . . father, advisor, soul, mind / of nascent liberty."[191] A less eminent German colleague of Alfieri's, Johann Jakob Meyen, sang of Franklin a little later:

> My song is for the sage who brought the light of science
> To new-discovered lands across the northern ocean.
> His country he has freed of tyrants who oppressed it.
> By nature chosen, he assumed the leader's duty
> When Indian woods and huts gave way to provinces.

186. G. Forster, *Tagebücher*, ed. Zincke and Leitzmann, 25–26 (entry of Oct. 9, 1777).

187. "der ehrwürdigste Name, den das achtzehnte Jahrhundert ausgesprochen hat": G. Forster, *Ansichten vom Niederrhein* (1791), ed. Gerhard Steiner, in his *Werke*, ed. Deutsche Akademie der Wissenschaften, IX (Berlin, 1958), 194. See also his considerations on Franklin in his *Erinnerungen aus dem Jahr 1790* (Berlin, 1793), reprinted in his *Kleine Schriften*, VI (Berlin, 1797); Kahn, "George Forster and Franklin," *APSP*, CII (1958), 1–6.

188. "Es gehört zu den angenehmsten Erinnerungen meines Lebens, daß ich den großen Franklin persönlich gekannt habe": J. R. Forster in a note to his translation of Brissot de Warville, *Neue Reise*, Berlin ed., 105. Cf. Brissot de Warville's own remarks, *ibid.*, 94.

189. "ein Genie, dergleichen wenige gefunden werden, gleich groß als Philosoph und Staatsmann": Zinner, *Merkwürdige Briefe und Schriften*, 137.

190. "Franklin ist Vater der Naturkunde und aller gesunden Philosophie und Politik in Amerika": Schmohl, *Über Nordamerika und Demokratie*, 204.

191. ". . . padre, consiglio, anima, mente / Di libertà nascente": Alfieri, *L'America libera* (Kehl, 1784), 27.

Ennobling the spirit of liberty through his art and wisdom,
The essence of his gentle nation he created
And with it the foundation of his state.[192]

The obituaries at Franklin's death seemed to justify in every way John Adams's fears regarding the overemphasis of Franklin's role in the American Revolution. In a long necrology Friedrich Schlichtegroll praised the American's "cleverness and deftness in his dealings with France" and then concluded: "Adding to this his first efforts to disseminate lofty principles among his fellow countrymen, we can appreciate how rightfully Franklin deserves to be called the father of American liberty."[193]

Obviously, antagonists of the American Revolution did not agree with these eulogies. These individuals can be divided into two distinct groups. Those adherents of the Enlightenment ideal of liberty who were largely under the influence of England respected Franklin as a scientist and an exponent of Enlightenment philosophy while they condemned the rebel in him. This was the position of Georg Christoph Lichtenberg, for example. When Franklin died, Lichtenberg could not resist making the remark: "They should have put crape on the lightning rods to commemorate Franklin's death."[194] The Göttingen mathematician Abraham Gotthelf Kästner seems to have had similar views; on Franklin's death he wrote to Christoph Gottlob Heyne: "Franklin concerns us as a scientist. I do not think it proper to praise him as

192. "Den Philosophen besingt mein Lied, der dem neueren Weltteil / Jenseits des Mar del Nort' das Licht der Wissenschaft brachte, / Und sein seufzendes Vaterland von Tyrannen befreite, / Von der Natur gesandt, als Wälder und Hütten der Wilden / In Provinzen verwandelt, einers Führers bedurften, / Der den Geist der Freiheit durch Weisheit und Künste veredelt, / Den Nationalgeist bildet, und mit sich höher emporhebt / Die Grundfeste des Staats": Meyen, *Franklin der Philosoph und Staatsmann,* 5–6.

193. "die Klugheit und Geschicklichkeit, mit welcher der Philosoph sein Geschäft in Frankreich betrieb. . . . Nimmt man dies und seine ersten Bemühungen, den Samen großer Grundsätze unter seinen Landsleuten auszustreuen, zusammen, so sieht man, mit wie vielen Rechte Franklin den Namen des Vaters der amerikanischen Freiheit verdient": Friedrich Schlichtegroll, *Nekrolog auf das Jahr 1790,* I (Gotha, 1791), 295. For similar remarks see [Johann Georg Heinzmann], *Gemälde aus dem aufgeklärten Jahrhundert,* 2 vols. (Bern and Leipzig, 1786), I, 201–202; [Friedrich Samuel Mursinna], *Leben und Charaktere berühmter Männer* (Halle, 1792), 69; C. Milon, *Denkwürdigkeiten zur Geschichte Benjamin Franklins* (St. Petersburg, 1793), 31, 56–58, 110; Wansey, *Tagebuch einer Reise,* 132; Johann Gottfried Grohmann, *Neues Historisch-biographisches Handwörterbuch,* 10 vols. (Leipzig, 1796–1808), III (1797), 325–327; Karl Ludwig Woltmann, *Geschichte der Europäischen Staaten* (Berlin, 1797–1799), I, 310; see also Kenneth N. McKee, "The Popularity of the *American* on the French Stage During the Revolution," *APSP,* LXXXIII (1940), 479–491.

194. "Bei Franklins Tod hätte man sollen Flöre an die Blitzableiter hängen": Lichtenberg, *Aphorismen,* ed. Leitzmann, IV, 71 (c. 1790), cf. the aphorisms J 412 (c. 1790), J 503 (c. 1791), J 840 (c. 1792), and J 1125 (1793). See also Lichtenberg to Schernhagen, Nov. 25, 1779, and to Ernst Gottfried Baldinger, Nov. 1784, in Lichtenberg, *Briefe,* ed. Leitzmann and Schüddekopf, I, 336, III, 251.

the originator of American liberty. To me the Americans are merely rebels who were successful. But even if I thought differently, I would not voice his praise in the king's German countries."[195]

Those among the American Revolution's antagonists who rejected the Enlightenment and its civic ideals of liberty and equality saw no reason to differentiate between the natural philosopher and the rebel. They thought that Franklin's siding with the patriots branded him as an outlaw rebel against England. When Johann Georg Sulzer told the Hanoverian court physician Johann Georg Zimmermann about his anger at Franklin's taking part in the Revolution, he got the following answer: "You should never have taken old Franklin for a good man."[196] But Zimmermann, too, took a different stand later on; in 1791 he wrote to his friend Christoph Girtanner: "Mirabeau, Europe, America, and you have very nobly mourned Franklin's death. But only an idiot, a scoundrel, or a fool like Klopstock could ever wear a mourning band for Mirabeau in Germany!"[197] The bourgeoisie in Germany, devoted to the Enlightenment and to liberty, had so strikingly recorded Franklin's role in the American Revolution that even his adversaries made no attempt to change this.

One question still remains: What was the attitude of the several German governments toward Franklin? Franklin's stay in Britain had drawn government attention to him, and his departure for America in 1775 was duly recorded, but the governments had not formed any clear ideas about his political tasks and achievements. The diplomats ordinarily talked about the old man with a certain feeling of sympathy, fearing, however, that "the famous Dr. Franklin" might side with the rebels.[198]

195. "Franklin geht uns als Gelehrter an. Den Urheber der amerikanischen Freiheit würde ich nach meiner Empfindung nicht loben, weil ich die Amerikaner nur für Rebellen, denen es geglückt ist, erkenne. Indessen, wenn ich auch anders dächte, so würde ich doch dieses Lob in des Königs deutschen Landen verschweigen": Dec. 1790 (Chron. 23, no. 49, AAW, Göttingen). See also Georg Friedrich Brandes to Heyne, June 24, 1776 (Nachlaß Heyne, CXXVI, fol. 48, SuUB, Göttingen); Schlözer in his Briefwechsel, I/1 (1777), 49; Historisches Portefeuille, June 1785, 726–727, Nov. 1785, 674; Stöver, Unser Jahrhundert, I, 26, 505, 507, 533.

196. "Den alten Franklin soll man nie für einen guten Mann gehalten haben": J. G. Zimmermann to Sulzer, Feb. 23, 1777, in Zimmermann, Leben und Briefe, ed. Bodemann, 262. See also Sulzer to Zimmermann, Jan. 19, 1777, in ibid., 261. For similar opinions see J.F.C.E. Freiherr von Linsingen, "Beschreibung der Reise von Stade nach Quebeck" (1778), fol. 6 (LB, Karlsruhe), and the rather low-level polemics in the anti-Franklin satire, Franklins freier Wille, ein Wink für denkende Menschen über die Macht des Zufalls (Leipzig, 1787).

197. "Sehr edel haben . . . Mirabeau, Europa, Amerika und Sie für Franklin getrauert. Aber nur ein Idiot, ein Schurke oder ein Narr wie Klopstock konnte in Deutschland für Mirabeau die Trauer anlegen!": to Christoph Girtanner, Nov. 18, 1791 (GSA, Weimar).

198. "le célèbre Dr. Franklin": Hans Moritz Graf von Brühl zu Martinskirch to Sacken, Mar. 24, 1775; cf. Brühl's dispatch of Apr. 28, 1775 (Locat 2685, conv. XI, fols. 122r–v,

In December 1776 "the famous Franklin" suddenly turned up in France, and still the German emissaries in the western countries clearly felt benevolent toward him.[199] But at the same time, their reports expressed an astonishing misconception of the purpose of his journey, which they of course conveyed to their governments. Hans Moritz Graf von Brühl zu Martinskirch, the chief of the Saxon mission in London, no less than Thulemeyer at The Hague,[200] recognized and reported Franklin's true intentions, but the minister in Dresden disagreed with him,[201] and put into words what most of the politicians and diplomats were merely assuming at the time: Franklin is simply leaving the sinking ship and looking in France for a place of repose in his old age.[202] Prince Wenzel Anton von Kaunitz was also convinced that Franklin's motives were philosophical rather than political in nature. According to the English envoy in Vienna, "Prince Kaunitz . . . could by no means be brought to suppose that Franklin could be so foolish (as he called it) as to come to Paris with any prospect of inducing the French ministry to take a part in the American quarrel. The Prince seemed fully persuaded that Franklin sought for nothing more than a philosophical retirement in the French king's dominions."[203]

But when the diplomats, too, recognized the true intentions of Franklin and the American patriots, their praise and admiration for the venerated figure vanished. However, they did remain largely neutral and avoided open

---

167v/170, StA, Dresden). For more critical remarks see especially the Prussian minister to London, Maltzahn, in his letters and dispatches to Frederick II, Feb. 4, 1774, July 7, 1775, and to his colleague Thulemeyer, Mar. 21, 1775 (Rep. 96, 35A, vol. IX, fols. 42v–43v, 35B, vol. X, fols. 130r–v, Rep. 92 Thulemeier, no. 10, vol. V, DZA, Merseburg).

199. "le fameux Franklin": Seinsheim to Haslang, Dec. 29, 1776 (Bayer. Gesandtschaft: London, no. 255, GStA, Munich). See also Seinsheim to Maximilian Emanuel Freiherr von Eyck, Dec. 28, 1776 (Bayer. Gesandtschaft: Paris, no. 36, *ibid.*); Johann Adolph Graf von Loss to Sacken, Dec. 20, 1776 (Locat 2747, conv. XXII, fols. 6r–v, StA, Dresden); Belgiojoso to Prince Wenzel Kaunitz, Dec. 20, 1776 (Staatskanzlei, Staatenabteilung: England, K. 118, fol. 60v, HHStA, Vienna); Mr. S. to Haenichen, Dec. 15, 1776 (1 Alt 22, no. 1505, XIV, StA, Wolfenbüttel); more critical, Maltzahn to Frederick II, Dec. 17, 1776 (Rep. 96, 35C, vol. XI, fols. 312r–v, DZA, Merseburg), and Baron von Boden to the cabinet at Kassel, Dec. 28, 1776 (4 f Frankreich, no. 1716, StA, Marburg).

200. To Frederick II, Jan. 3, 1777 (Rep. 96, 41D, vol. XVI, fol. 2v, DZA, Merseburg).

201. Brühl to Sacken, Jan. 7, 1777, Sacken to Brühl, Jan. 12, Feb. 2, 1777 (Locat 2685, conv. XIII, fols. 17r–v, 11, 42r–v, StA, Dresden).

202. E.g., Bernhard Wilhelm Freiherr von der Goltz to Frederick II, Dec. 19, 1776 (Rep. 96, 28C, vol. IXᵇ, fols. 160v–161, DZA, Merseburg); Seinsheim to Haslang, Feb. 8, 1777 (Bayer. Gesandtschaft: London, no. 255, GStA, Munich); Boden to landgrave, Dec. 11, to the cabinet, Dec. 15, 1776 (4 f Frankreich, no. 1717, fol. 10, no. 1716, StA, Marburg); Mr. S. to Haenichen, Dec. 12, 1776 (1 Alt 22, no. 1505, XIV, StA, Wolfenbüttel). For an opposing, retrospective view see Christian Wilhelm von Dohm, *Denkwürdigkeiten meiner Zeit oder Beiträge zur Geschichte vom lezten Viertel des achtzehnten und vom Anfang des neunzehnten Jahrhunderts 1778 bis 1806*, 5 vols. (Lemgo and Hanover, 1814–1819), II, 102–103.

203. Robert Murray Keith to Suffolk, Dec. 30, 1776 (S.P. 80/218, PRO, London).

condemnations of Franklin, although a few critical remarks were made of his open allegiance to the insurgents' cause.[204] Nevertheless, when the war was over, Franklin became the "celebrated doctor" again, even in diplomatic circles.[205]

This attitude shows that the German diplomats, who believed themselves unable to assent more than minimally to the rebels' actions, were considerably influenced by Franklin's personality. In the 1780s Franklin's character was likely to arouse sympathies that in turn could affect individual attitudes toward the American Revolution. Franklin's image apparently influenced the German bourgeoisie's assessment of the American Revolution much more than did Washington's. When the enlightened bourgeoisie in Germany, enthusiastic about liberty and America, recorded their interpretations of the Revolution, they mythically glorified Franklin as a "kind of saint to every good man."[206]

204. E.g., Boden to landgrave, Mar. 24, 1779 (4 f Frankreich, no. 1718, fols. 82r–v, StA, Marburg); Schönfeld to Stutterheim, Aug. 4, 1780 (Locat 2748, conv. XXV, fol. 211, StA, Dresden); Mercy d'Argenteau to Kaunitz, Mar. 18, 1789 (Staatskanzlei, Staatenabteilung: Frankreich, K. 162, fol. 9v, HHStA, Vienna).

205. "célèbre Docteur": Brühl to Stutterheim, Oct. 1, 1782 (Locat 2686, conv. XVIII, fol. 296, StA, Dresden).

206. "jedem guten Menschen gewissermaßen ein Heiliger": *Genius der Zeit*, May 1794, 72. Cf. *ibid.*, Oct. 1794, 245–246. Also, *Neue Bunzlauische Monatsschrift*, July 1790, 207–211; *Deutsche Monatsschrift*, Sept. 1790, 3–9; Daniel V. Hegeman, "Franklin and Germany: Further Evidence of His Reputation in the Eighteenth Century," *German Quarterly*, XXVI (1953), 189; Gilbert Chinard, "The Apotheosis of Benjamin Franklin, Paris, 1790–1791," *APSP*, XCIX (1955), 440–473.

PART III

*The Age of
the French Revolution*

9. *Germany and America on the Eve of the French Revolution*

German Awareness of a Crisis before 1789

In the European world of the 1770s and 1780s unrest was spreading. Events in America were not the only contributing factor, although they had done much to keep many German contemporaries on edge. Germans had witnessed the coup d'état in Sweden, the Pugachev uprising in Russia, the grain riots and the *révolte nobiliaire* in France, and the Gordon riots in Britain. They had also seen uprisings and revolts as varied as those in Geneva and Fribourg, Ireland and the Netherlands. All of these events expressed a powerful trend that Robert R. Palmer summed up in the title of his two-volume work, *The Age of the Democratic Revolution*.[1] In spite of the possible objections to this characterization of the latter third of the eighteenth century, it was undeniably an era much less inclined than former times to accept uncritically the structures of government and order that it inherited; this era would have to come to terms with an aspiring and self-conscious bourgeoisie claiming an increased share of power.

Alert contemporaries had not failed to notice the signs of social and political transformation. "I see our times pregnant with great changes," Johannes von Müller wrote to August Ludwig Schlözer in August 1774, "and our century preparing the happiness and ruin of many to come."[2] In the mid-1770s, Isaak Iselin called for the emancipation of men and states, and a little later he predicted a great crisis for Europe.[3] Friedrich Leopold Graf zu Stol-

1. Palmer, *Age of the Democratic Revolution*, esp. I, 3–7; see also Vierhaus, "Deutschland vor der Französischen Revolution," 511–512; and three works by Jacques Godechot, *Contre-Révolution*, 2–4, *Les Révolutions (1770–1799)* (Paris, 1963), 94–113, and *La Prise de la Bastille (14 Juillet 1789)* (Paris, 1965), 11–51.
2. "Ich sehe unsere Zeit schwanger an großen Veränderungen, und unser Jahrhundert das Glück und Verderben vieler folgenden bereiten": Johannes von Müller, *Sämmtliche Werke*, ed. J. G. Müller, XXXVII, 197.
3. Iselin, in *Ephemeriden der Menschheit*, Mar. 1776, 117; Iselin, *Geschichte der Menschheit*, 4th ed. (1779), II, 466–467. The prediction does not occur in a previous edition of the book. See Im Hof, *Iselin und die Spätaufklärung*, 131–132.

berg held similar views.⁴ Georg Forster prophesied in the spring of 1782: "Europe seems on the brink of a terrible revolution," and a year later he happily contemplated a radically altered future.⁵ Other observers shared the opinion that Europe was in a period of "fermentation."⁶

Such statements express an awareness of a "crisis" that was rooted in the times before the American war. In 1774 Stolberg responded to Friedrich Gottlieb Klopstock's ode, "Weissagung," by saying, "Our nation is truly fermenting. A great fire glows among the ashes and those who are to fan the flames are perhaps already blessed by God."⁷ In the same vein Iselin wrote five years later, "Europe is now in a crisis far more extensive than any that has occurred since the beginning of organized government. This crisis should by no means instill in us the fear felt by timid observers, but should give us a consoling and hopeful outlook."⁸

It is clear from these statements that the awareness of a crisis in this period bore the stamp of the Enlightenment, with its belief in human progress. Observers like Iselin expressed the still unshaken belief in a happier future held by large parts of the German bourgeoisie. The term *crisis* did not yet have for them those pejorative connotations impressed upon it by the French Revolution and the nineteenth century. Awareness of a crisis and hopes for

4. Stolberg, "Die Zukunft," ed. Hartwig, *ALG*, XIII (1885), 272.

5. "Europa scheint auf dem Punkt einer schrecklichen Revolution": to Johann Reinhold Forster, Mar. 30, 1782, in G. Forster, *Sämmtliche Schriften*, ed. his daughter, 6 vols. (Leipzig, 1843), VII, 159. For Georg's later views see his letters to Friedrich Heinrich Jacobi, Feb. 11, 1783, and to J. R. Forster, Feb. 13, 1783, *ibid.*, 180, 183.

6. "Gärung": e.g., Jean Charles Poncelin de La Roche-Tilhac, *Philosophische Beschreibung des Handels, und der Besitzungen der Europäer in Asien und Afrika*, trans. from the French, 2 vols. (Strasbourg, 1783–1784), I, [4]. See also Schib, *Johannes von Müller*, 419; Benjamin Rush, *Über die Vortheile, welche das Aderlassen in vielen wichtigen Krankheiten gewährt*, trans. from the English by Christian Friedrich Michaelis (Leipzig, 1800), 84; Woldemar Wenck, *Deutschland vor hundert Jahren. Politische Meinungen und Stimmungen bei Anbruch der Revolutionszeit*, 2 vols. (Leipzig, 1887–1890), I, 194–195; Guido Gross, "Trierer Geistesleben unter dem Einfluß von Aufklärung und Romantik (1750–1850)" (publ. Ph.D. diss., University of Mainz, 1956), 21; Raumer, "Deutschland um 1800," in Just, ed., *Handbuch der Deutschen Geschichte*, III, pt. 1, 21, 30; Ehrenfried Muthesius, *Ursprünge des modernen Krisenbewußtseins* (Munich, 1963), 41 (rather disappointing for this period). For an opposing view see Egon Friedell, *Kulturgeschichte der Neuzeit. Die Krisis der europäischen Seele von der schwarzen Pest bis zum ersten Weltkrieg*, 18th–22d eds., II (Munich, 1948), 440–441, who denies a widespread consciousness of crisis.

7. "Unsre Nation ist wahrlich in Gärung. Ein großes Feuer glimmt in der Asche, und Gottes Segen weihet vielleicht schon diejenigen, welche die Flammen erregen sollen": Stolberg to Klopstock, Mar. 15, 1774, in Jürgen Behrens, ed., *Briefwechsel zwischen Klopstock und den Grafen Christian und Friedrich Leopold zu Stolberg* (Neumünster, 1964), 164.

8. "daß Europa sich nun in einer weit größeren Krisis befinde, als es jemals seit dem Anfange seiner Polizierung sich befunden hat; und weit entfernt, daß wir mit ängstlichen Beobachtern diese Krisis als gefährlich ansehen sollten, gibt sie uns eher tröstliche und hoffnungsvolle Aussichten": Iselin, *Geschichte der Menschheit*, 4th ed. (1779), II, 467.

the future were not contradictory but complementary: it was only through crisis, through "moral thunderstorms,"[9] that a better world would be created.

Many historical forces influenced these bourgeois ideas and contributed to the unburdened belief in progress. Undoubtedly, the Enlightenment itself had furnished a decisive cause by teaching the bourgeoisie that the practice of *sapere aude*, dare to know, alone could lead man out of his self-encumbered childhood toward a better future.[10] To the bourgeoisie, rational thinking meant criticizing existing conditions whenever they were contrary to reason.[11] As Reinhart Koselleck has shown, the concomitant demand for change caused an ever-increasing sensation of crisis.[12] On the other hand, it is obvious that in the 1770s and 1780s the occurrence of the American Revolution gave considerable support to the feeling that a crisis was impending, for the Revolution proved not only that fundamental change was indeed possible but also that the change could be realized in conformity with the bourgeoisie's own interests.

Adversaries of the Enlightenment, however, did not believe that these portents were favorable. Instead of hopeful bourgeois optimism, they felt a mounting fear of possibly threatening innovations. "For a decade," one writer commented, we have lived "under the deep shadow of revolution," with world politics growing increasingly turbulent.[13] Bourgeois hopes seemed indeed to be justified, and these hopes in turn kindled an awareness of a crisis among those supporters of the existing order who did not equate change with more happiness.[14] They were deeply troubled by the possibility of a transformation in the existing structure of power in accordance with frequently expressed bourgeois ideals. Sometimes they grasped something of that great synthesis Palmer has advanced to explain the common features in European and Ameri-

9. "moralische Ungewitter": *ibid.*, 466.

10. Cf. Immanuel Kant, "Beantwortung der Frage: Was ist Aufklärung," in his *Werke*, ed. Weischedel, VI, 53–61.

11. E.g., Knüppeln, *Rechte der Natur und Menschheit*, 15–16; *Bibliothek für Denker*, Feb. 1785, 179; *Briefe eines reisenden Punditen über Sclaverei, Möncherei, und Tyrannei der Europäer. An seinen Freund in U-pang* (Leipzig, 1787); [Christian Friedrich Daniel Schubart], *Das Wetterleuchten über Europa am Ende des Jahrhunderts gesehen im Jahre 1788* (Malta and Cairo [i.e., Düsseldorf], 1799), 6–7; Richard Price to Jefferson, Oct. 26, 1788, Jefferson to Thomas Lee Shippen, Mar. 11, 1789, in Boyd *et al.*, eds., *Jefferson Papers*, XIV, 38, 638.

12. Koselleck, *Kritik und Krise. Ein Beitrag zur Pathogenese der bürgerlichen Welt* (Freiburg and Munich, 1959), 105, and *passim*.

13. "seit einem Jahrzehnt . . . in großen revolutionsschwangern Tagen": *Deutscher Zuschauer*, June 1788, VII, 316. See also [Conrad Siegismund Ziehen], *Nachricht von einer bevorstehenden großen Revolution der Erde*, which was published for the first time around 1779–1780 and soon became very popular. Lichtenberg publicly refuted its prediction that a devastating earthquake would occur by Easter 1786.

14. E.g., *Teutscher Merkur*, Mar. 1788, 226; Woldemar Friedrich Graf von Schmettau to Schlözer, May 28, 1788, in C. von Schlözer, *August Ludwig von Schlözer*, II, 149.

can history. In 1787 Gottlob Benedikt von Schirach published in the *Politisches Journal* a paradigmatic paper entitled, "The Spirit of Unrest in Our Age. Discord, Uprisings, and Movements in Many Towns and Countries in Europe, Asia, Africa, and America." He was horrified to find that "since that uprising in the North American provinces, successful because of France's support and the countenance of the English Parliament, a dizziness of liberty has seized many brains who do not know what they want or what true liberty is." He eloquently described the dangers of this development, which could only serve to "take advantage of a deluded people" and to attack a benevolent prince from the rear. Resigned to conditions, he concluded his warning: "But fraud and falsehood prepare tumultuous revolutions and will not listen to the voice of reason."[15]

Doubtlessly, vague awareness of an impending crisis had existed in Germany before the American Revolution, but on the eve of the French Revolution the impression created by the events in America had far-reaching effects on both the bourgeoisie and the aristocracy, evoking great hopes in the former and deep-seated fear in the latter. In noteworthy contrast, however, to this influence of the American Revolution on German political consciousness was the limited amount of attention accorded to United States internal development at the time.

The American Confederation and Its Problems

At the end of the war the United States entered a new phase of development, one marked by a number of weighty problems. The young republic's finances were in dismal shape; it was burdened by an immense debt, and the economy, foreign trade, and trade between the states had to be reorganized and renewed to meet peacetime demands. National institutions had to be

15. "Geist der Unruhe unsers Zeitalters. Zwietracht, Empörungen, Bewegungen in vielen Örtern und Ländern in Europa, Asia, Afrika und Amerika. . . . daß seit jenem, durch Frankreichs Unterstützung, und des eignen Nationalparlaments Begünstigung, geglücktem Aufruhre der nordamerikanischen Provinzen ein Freiheitsschwindel sich vieler Köpfe bemeistert hat, die selbst nicht wissen, was sie wollen und was wahre Freiheit ist . . . das verblendete Volk mißbrauchen. . . . Aber der Schwindelgeist hört nicht die Stimme der Vernunft und bereitet tumultuarische Revolutionen": *Politisches Journal*, July 1787, 707, 713. See also the article by Moritz Flavius Trenck von Tonder, "Freiheits- und Gleichheitsbestrebungen in Europa seit dem Amerikanischen Freiheitskriege" in his *Politische Gespräche der Toten*, July 1, 1787, reprinted in J. Hansen, ed., *Quellen zur Geschichte des Rheinlandes*, I, 201–204.

rendered viable and fit to meet the changed situation; the army had to be demobilized, and the soldiers had to be paid back wages. It was imperative that interstate rivalries be minimized, that the executive power of the Congress be reinforced, and that federal authority be recognized at home and abroad. The government and organization of the western territories, that extensive area between the Alleghenies and the Mississippi awarded to the United States in the 1783 peace treaty, had to be removed from the grasp of competing individual states and transferred to the Congress.[16]

At the end of the last century John Fiske, the popular American historian, characterized this era as the "Critical Period."[17] An era confronted with the necessity of finding solutions to so many problems is indeed a critical period, but it is not necessarily one of crises. Researchers today are largely of the opinion that these were years of more accomplishment than Fiske's term implies.[18] Demobilization was carried out, although not without mishaps, and the cornerstone of economic and financial recovery was laid.[19] The greatest and most lasting success of this period in American history was the working out of a solution to the future political development of the western territories, as it was sketched in its essential points by the Northwest Ordinance of 1787. This ordinance proclaimed that new states could join the Union on equal terms with the old, thus rejecting forever the possibility of imperial rule of the continent by the eastern states.[20]

But not all questions could be answered as definitively by the federal government. From 1785 to 1787, especially, esteem for Congress was at a nadir. Quarrels arose between individual states, and tax increases aroused the wrath of large parts of the population. Disputes with the Indians cast more and more doubt on the validity of the existing Indian policy. In foreign affairs the republic was largely unsuccessful. And in 1787 the decline of governmental authority led to a local farmers' uprising in Massachusetts, Shays's Rebellion. It was put down quickly but was psychologically important in

16. See among others Jensen, *New Nation*; Allan Nevins, *The American States during and after the Revolution 1775–1789* (New York, 1924), 544–605.

17. John Fiske, *The Critical Period of American History 1783–1789*, first published in 1889, reprinted in his *Historical Writings*, XII (Boston, 1916); see also Richard B. Morris, "The Confederation Period and the American Historian," *WMQ*, 3d Ser., XIII (1956), 139–156.

18. See Jensen, *New Nation*, esp. 347–349; Frank Thistlethwaite, *The Great Experiment: An Introduction to the History of the American People* (Cambridge, 1955), 46–47; Morgan, *Birth of the Republic*, 113–128; E. Wright, *Fabric of Freedom*, 156–160.

19. See among others North, *Growth and Welfare*, 62–63.

20. See among others Ray Allen Billington, *Westward Expansion: A History of the American Frontier*, 3d ed. (New York, 1967), 199–220; E. Wright, *Fabric of Freedom*, 160–164.

that it shocked large sections of the American middle class. If the term "Critical Period" is to be used at all, it must be limited to those three years.[21]

Looking at pertinent statements by German contemporaries of that brief period, our impression is that those basic political phenomena did not command much interest. Georg Christoph Lichtenberg, who condemned American independence, was content to label the United States a "rogues' republic,"[22] and the German followers of the patriots did no more in those years than sing hymns of praise to the Revolution and to the liberty and independence it brought about.[23] The German bourgeoisie seem not to have been at all concerned about the postwar political problems in the Western Hemisphere.

Contemporaries in the mid-1780s did learn that "the individual states of the new republic are using the time of peace for improvements at home."[24] But what these improvements were was difficult for them to find out. Several months later it was said that "in this spacious and free state every citizen and inhabitant" was still busy repairing war damage.[25] No matter what the publication, in those years constitutional questions did not arouse any noteworthy interest.[26] To be sure, one might perhaps learn something about disputes with the Indians or about a developing consciousness of statehood,[27]

21. Forrest McDonald, E Pluribus Unum: The Formation of the American Republic, 1776–1790 (Boston, 1965), 133; Van Beck Hall, Politics Without Parties: Massachusetts, 1780–1791 (Pittsburgh, 1972), esp. 190–226.

22. "Spitzbubenrepublik": Lichtenberg, Aphorismen, ed. Leitzmann, III, 62 (presumably of 1777).

23. E.g., Johann Zinner to Congress, Sept. 23, 1783 (Franklin Papers, 2d Ser., fol. 2616, LC, Washington, D.C.); "Discours," fols. 24–25 (NB, Vienna); Historisch-geographische Beschreibung von Amerika für Jünglinge (Nuremberg, 1784), 126; von Wolff to Franklin, Mar. 4, 1784 (Franklin Papers, XXXI, 103, APSL, Philadelphia); Merkwürdige Schriften, 45, 110, 112, 170; Meyen, Franklin der Philosoph und Staatsmann, 35–36; Neusinger, Kurze Geschichte der Welt, IV, 227.

24. "Die verschiedenen Staaten dieser neuen Republik wenden die Zeit des Friedens zu innern Verbesserungen an": Historisches Portefeuille, Aug. 1784, 246.

25. "in diesem weitläufigen und freien Staaten noch jeder Bürger und Einwohner . . .": ibid., Dec. 1784, 771.

26. Staatsgesetze der dreyzehn vereinigten amerikanischen Staaten, trans. from the French (Dessau and Leipzig, 1785), was one of the few examples. See the scant remarks in Zinzendorf, Tagebuch, June 11, 1784 (XXIX, fols. 82v–83, HHStA, Vienna); Meyen, Franklin der Philosoph und Staatsmann, 37–38, 43; Anmerkungen aus der neuen und alten Welt, 165–166; note, presumably by the eldest son of Baron de Beelen-Bertholff, Nov. 27, 1787 [?] (Belgien DDB, 182d, fol. 256, HHStA, Vienna; not printed in Schlitter, ed., "Berichte des ersten Agenten Österreichs," FRA, 2/XLV/2 [1891]); Jefferson to Jan Ingenhousz, June 19, 1788, in Boyd et al., eds., Jefferson Papers, XIII, 262; see also the incomplete translation of Jefferson's Notes on Virginia, in J. R. Forster and Sprengel, eds., Beiträge zur Völker und Länderkunde, VIII (1788), 171–277, IX (1789), 1–130.

27. On Indian relations see Sigismund Graf von Haslang, from London to Matthäus Graf

but the bourgeoisie were obviously still so preoccupied with the Revolution and its ideals that they rarely focused attention on the existing political problems.

The followers of the American Revolution probably were under the general impression that the United States was well on the way toward inner consolidation according to its stated republican principles. "North America continues to create institutions of common weal. The respect enjoyed by the law and the courts of law increases, and everything promises a perfect civil order of a well-structured and flourishing state."[28] Friedrich Ludwig Walther probably spoke for many when he stated that "in all of North America there is no country that flourishes more."[29]

But during that critical phase of confederation between 1785 and 1787, negative judgments of America increased in Germany. Critics referred to Congress's loss of authority, unrest in the individual states, and general economic difficulties, and they pronounced the Confederation to be in a desolate and chaotic situation.[30] It was not just Shays's Rebellion that was instrumental in creating this impression, for little attention was paid to it;[31] it was rather a state of general anarchy that some believed they saw in America. Just before the federal Constitutional Convention and the new Constitution silenced such statements, von Schirach wrote: "North America gives the world anew the great example that freedom leads to confusion and anarchy if it is not curbed by firm laws and shaped into a civil order."[32]

---

von Vieregg, Nov. 4, 25, 1785 (Kasten schwarz 15386, GStA, Munich); on statehood see Walther, *Neueste Erdkunde*, 252.

28. "Nordamerika fährt fort, Einrichtungen zum allgemeinen Besten zu treffen. Gesetze und Gerichtshöfe kommen immer mehr in Ansehen, und es läßt sich alles zur vollkommenen bürgerlichen Ordnung eines wohleingerichteten und blühenden Staats an": *Historisches Portefeuille*, Jan. 1784, 141; cf. Mar. 1782, 331, Apr. 1782, 448, Dec. 1783, 777–778.

29. "In ganz Nordamerika ist kein blühenders Reich": Walther, *Neueste Erdkunde*, 251.

30. E.g., *Politisches Journal*, July 1785, 751, Aug. 1785, 796; *Politische Gespräche der Toten*, July 1, 1787, reprinted in J. Hansen, ed., *Quellen zur Geschichte des Rheinlandes*, I, 203; *Historisches Portefeuille*, Oct. 1785, 537–538, June 1786, 766–767; Haslang to Vieregg, Aug. 25, 1786 (Kasten schwarz 15387, GStA, Munich); Hammerdörfer and Kosche, *Amerika*, I, 359–360, 362–363.

31. For the few exceptions see among others Haslang to Vieregg, Apr. 13, 1787 (Kasten schwarz 15388, GStA, Munich); note of Beelen-Bertholff, May 24, 1787, in Schlitter, ed., "Berichte des ersten Agenten Österreichs," FRA, 2/XLV/2 (1891), 731, 733; Dietrich Hermann Hegewisch, "Geschichte der Unruhen und des innerlichen Krieges in Massachusetts in den Jahren 1786 und 87," in Hegewisch and Ebeling, eds., *Amerikanisches Magazin*, III (1796), 36–104.

32. "Nordamerika gibt der Welt das neue große Beispiel, daß Freiheit zur Zerrüttung und Anarchie führt, wenn sie nicht durch feste Gesetze eingeschränkt und zur bürgerlichen Ordnung gebildet ist": *Politisches Journal*, July 1787, 711, cf. June 1786, 649. Also, *Historisches*

These statements do not permit the conclusion that German contemporaries, as a rule, were critical of the new republic and skeptical of its achievements, as has been asserted.[33] The change in German attitudes toward republicanism and the conjectures on the future greatness of the United States that we have already seen sufficiently disprove this view. Negative comments in the years 1785 to 1787 were relatively few, and, significantly, they came almost exclusively from men long known to be antagonists of the American Revolution, men who did not share the bourgeois enthusiasm for liberty and now believed they had found some confirmation of their former suspicions. Thus, von Schirach and others talked of anarchy at this time because the American example seemed to offer them a welcome opportunity to articulate their own ideas, which were opposed to the liberal and enlightened ideals of the bourgeoisie.

Other questions concerning the new state were equally problematic. Contemporaries dealt only rarely with economic and financial problems of a public nature. It was probably highly unusual for any German to comment as Hessian regimental quartermaster Karl Bauer did in his diary shortly before the auxiliary troops left New York for home: "Fear of a new government has sent the richest and most respected merchants to England and other countries. These, and the many departed loyalists, took a lot of the money with them; our fleet also took a considerable sum of guineas." He further observed that the war in general had brought many more economic disadvantages than advantages to the Americans, that the persecution of loyalists had had detrimental effects and had depressed the price of real estate and agricultural products, and that the gigantic national debt could only be paid off by increasing taxes, which in turn would lower living standards.[34] Though not always accurate—as in his remark on agriculture[35]—Bauer at least touched

---

Portefeuille, Dec. 1785, 785, Jan., July 1786, 112, 108, Jan. 1787, 47; Schairer, "Schubart als politischer Journalist," 14–15.

33. Gerald John Ghelfi, "European Opinions of American Republicanism During the 'Critical Period' 1781–1789" (unpubl. Ph.D. diss., Claremont Graduate School, 1968), 8, and *passim*.

34. "Die reichsten und angesehensten Kaufleute hatten sich aus Furcht für einem neuen Gouvernement nach England und andern Ländern begeben. Mit diesen und denen vielen weggegangenen Loyalisten ging auch ein großer Teil des rollierenden Geldes weg; auch nahm unsere Flotte noch eine beträchtliche Summe Guineas mit": Bauer, "Journal vom Hochfürstlich-Hessischen Grenadier-Bataillon Platte," Nov. 8, 1783, 389, 392–395 (StA, Marburg). See also *Historisches Portefeuille*, June 1783, 852–853.

35. See Jensen, *New Nation*, 192–193; Jensen, "The American Revolution and American Agriculture," *Agricultural History*, XLIII (1969), 107–127; W. Augustus Low, "The Farmer in Post-Revolutionary Virginia, 1783–1789," *ibid.*, XXV (1951), 122–127; Marion Clawson, *The Land System of the United States: An Introduction to the History and Practice of Land Use and Land Tenure* (Lincoln, Neb., 1968), 28–29.

on some major American problems; but his views did not penetrate to the general public.

Often, and especially among the bourgeoisie, enthusiasm for the Revolution led to an unquestioning assumption that independence would be generally beneficial for America, as had been proclaimed by the physiocrats and antimercantilists without specific knowledge of the American situation.[36] In the end, however, it was the prospect of being able to participate in America's wealth from afar that pushed all awareness and consideration of the Confederation's present economic and financial problems into the background. The lure of America's supposed wealth generated a belief in easily accessible riches and profits.[37]

During the War of Independence, however, the German bourgeoisie had begun to grasp the relevance of events in the Western Hemisphere to the international economy, especially when they themselves literally paid for some of the results. At the end of the eighteenth century, for example, coffee and tobacco were widely used in Germany, but to buy these goods during the American war one had to pay steadily increasing prices. Coffee rose to more than three times its prewar value, and the continuously expanding war at sea led to higher prices for overseas products of all kinds (see chart 3). Not only commercial circles were affected. During the war years there were continuous complaints from the bourgeoisie about the exorbitant prices of imported consumer goods.[38]

In commercial circles such disadvantages were often balanced by respectable profits. As early as the mid-1770s business with the Americans in the supply of saddles and other leather goods had been good in and around the Hanover area. But the appearance of American ships on the Elbe River

36. E.g., Crome, *Nordamerikanischer Freystaat*, 12–13; Chastellux, *Vortheile und Nachteile*, 35–36, 56, 75–78, 83–84.

37. See among others August Friedrich Wilhelm Crome to Franklin, Mar. 4, 1783 (Franklin Papers, XXVII, 164, APSL, Philadelphia); Heinrich Friedrich Karl Reichsfreiherr vom und zum Stein to his mother, Mar. 18, 1783, in Stein, *Briefe und amtliche Schriften*, comp. Erich Botzenhart, newly ed. Walter Hubatsch, I (Stuttgart, 1957), 149; Franklin to Robert R. Livingston, July 22, 1783, in Smyth, ed., *Writings of Franklin*, IX, 67, 70–71; Konrad Walter & Co. to Franklin, Mar. 15, 1784 (Franklin Papers, XXXI, 115, APSL, Philadelphia). More skeptical, August von Hennings, "Annales dediés à la Posterité" (1777), 90–91 (Nachlaß Hennings, LIX, SuUB, Hamburg); *Chronologen* (1779), IV, 306; *Politisches Journal*, Jan. 1784, 10. Men like Ingenhousz (cf. his correspondence with Franklin in the 1780s) and Peter Ochs (Action d'Amérique, StA, Basel) had economic interests in the United States. See also K.P.M. Snell, *Handlungsvortheile*.

38. See "Chronik des Lorenz Friedrich Finger, 1766 bis 1782," Apr. 17, 1780 (StadtA, Frankfurt); *Teutscher Merkur*, May 1782, 107; *Historisch moralisch und politisch abgefaßte Belustigungen für alle Stände*, 2 vols. (Leipzig, 1780–1782), II, 27–28; Johann Georg Büsch, *Versuch einer Geschichte der Hamburgischen Handlung* (Hamburg, 1797), 164.

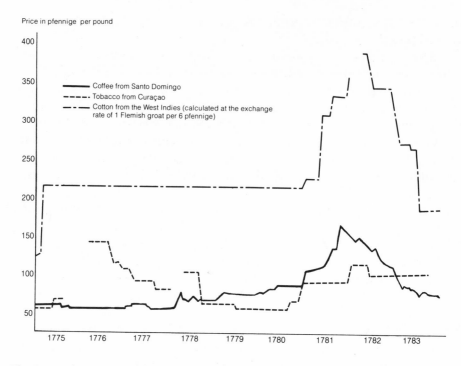

Price in pfennige per pound

— Coffee from Santo Domingo
---- Tobacco from Curaçao
—·— Cotton from the West Indies (calculated at the exchange
rate of 1 Flemish groat per 6 pfennige)

Chart 3. Changes in Prices of Selected Overseas (West Indian) Products
from January 1775 to December 1783 (according to the *Hamburgischer
Waren-Preis-Courant*)

alarmed the English government so much that extraordinary measures were
taken to prevent this trade,[39] with the crown going so far as to exert intense
pressure on Hamburg.[40]

   In other regions of Germany many merchants, especially those engaged
in the textiles and arms industries, tried to contact Franklin and other Americans with the intention of making a profit from the American war.[41] The

   39. "Betr. Bestellung von Kriegsbedürfnissen für die rebellischen Colonien in Amerika,
1775–1777"; "Aufbringung von zwei amerikanischen Rebellen-Schiffen auf der Elbe, 1776";
"Die muthmaßlich für die Americanischen Rebellen im Hannoverschen und in benachbarten
Gegenden verfertigten Kriegsbedürfnisse betr. 1775–1777"; "Acta betr. zwei zu Hamburg
arretirte Schiffe der Americanischen Rebellen, 1776" (all in HptStA, Hanover; copies of the
first two are in LC, Washington, D.C.). See also Richard Graewe, "The American Revolution
Comes to Hannover," *WMQ*, 3d Ser., XX (1963), 246–250.
   40. See "Protocollum Deputationis Commercii, 1775–1783," vol. UU, p. 272 (Feb. 20,
1775) (Kommerz-Bibliothek, Hamburg). Also the dispatches of Emanuel Mathias, the English
minister at Hamburg, for the years 1775–1776 (S.P. 82/94–95, PRO, London).
   41. E.g., Baruch Pincus von Eisenstadt to Arthur Lee, July 20, 1777 (Arthur Lee Papers,
III, 61, Harvard College Library, Cambridge, Mass.); Heinrich Walter to Franklin, Dec. 8,

Prussian economy was particularly adept at profiting from the conflict, with initiatives coming from both Prussians and Americans,[42] as is proven by Arthur Lee's stay in Berlin in 1777.[43] Early in 1778 the *Leipziger Zeitung* reported from the province of Brandenburg: "Our commerce is revived by the American trade. Sayre and Lee bought 1 ½ million's worth of our roughest textiles. . . . England is buying immense amounts of lumber. . . . Both France and England are buying much wood for shipbuilding purposes; the former is having some armed ships built in Stettin. Last summer the Dutch exported more than 3,000 hundredweight of Pomeranian and Brandenburg tobacco from Stettin, which they twist for the German troops in America."[44] A few years later Francis Dana reported similarly to the Congress from St. Petersburg: "It is to be observed that the Danzigers, the Prussians, and the Russians are improving the present opportunity which the Dutch war affords them of increasing their own navigation with the utmost industry; and the great rise of freights enables them to do it with much advantage."[45]

It is no wonder that many members of economic and trade circles had high hopes of participating in the profitable American business, in spite of their lack of information about the American situation after the war. Thus, in 1783 Josef von Utzschneider informed Franklin that a Bavarian firm was very much interested in trading with America.[46] We do not know whether he had in mind the crucible industry in Obernzell, but we do know that this firm did considerable exporting to America at the end of the eighteenth century.[47] We are also aware of some business connections with Switzerland, but the

1777 (Franklin Papers, VII, 137, APSL, Philadelphia); Johann Wilhelm and Johann Gottfried Spangenberg to Franklin, Mar. 14, 1783 (*ibid.*, LIX, 48); Justus Möser to Friedrich Nicolai, Mar. 1782, in Möser, *Briefe*, ed. Ernst Beins and Werner Pleister (Hanover, 1939), 351–352.

42. E.g., the letters of the Berlin merchants Becker & Satzmann, from 1779, and J.A.C. Sieck, from 1783 (all in Franklin Papers, APSL, Philadelphia).

43. On Prussian-American economic interests during these years see Dippel, "Prussia's English Policy," *Central European History*, IV (1971), 204–209.

44. "Unsere Handlung bekömmt durch die amerikanischen Händel einen neuen Schwung. Sayre und Lee haben für 1 ½ Millionen unserer gröbsten Tücher . . . gekauft. . . . Engelland kauft bei uns unglaublich viel Holz. . . . Frankreich sowohl als England kaufen viel Schiffbauholz, und ersteres läßt auch in Stettin armierte Schiffe bauen. Die Holländer haben in dem vorigen Sommer über 3000 Zentner pommerschen und märkischen Tobak von Stettin ausgeführt, welchen sie für die deutschen Truppen in Amerika spinnen und abführen": *Leipziger Zeitung*, Feb. 23, 1778.

45. Sept. 15, 1781, in Wharton, ed., *Revolutionary Diplomatic Correspondence*, IV, 711.

46. Josef von Utzschneider to Franklin, Apr. 10, 1783 (Franklin Papers, XXVIII, 22, APSL, Philadelphia). On Utzschneider and his activities at this time see Ilse Mackenthun, "Josef von Utzschneider, sein Leben, sein Wirken, seine Zeit (Ein Beitrag zur bayerischen Wirtschaftsgeschichte)" (publ. Ph.D. diss., University of Munich, 1958), 1–7.

47. Gerhard Slawinger, *Die Manufaktur in Kurbayern* (Stuttgart, 1966), 221–222.

Swiss seem to have been more cautious in their expectations.[48] In Thuringia, however, some people were more impatient. Friedrich Johann Justin Bertuch appointed himself advocate of their interests and included also some commercial firms in Bremen and Hamburg; but results were too meager to nourish further ambitions at that time.[49]

In the years after the Treaty of Paris private establishments and commercial firms were not alone in having their plans frustrated; the German governments interested in American affairs did not fare much better. The Saxon government, for instance, made great efforts to enter into trade with America. After its emissary in Paris had sounded out Franklin on this matter,[50] Philipp Thieriot, a Leipzig merchant, was sent to Philadelphia in 1783 to look into concrete opportunities for trade between America and Saxony. But Thieriot returned to Europe in 1785 with the most unfavorable impressions.[51]

The Austrian court and government were also interested in trade possibilities. In 1783 they too sent an agent to Philadelphia, one Baron de Beelen-Bertholff,[52] who, contrary to Joseph II's wishes, had not been accredited to Congress.[53] His primary task was to sound out the prospects of direct trade between the republic and the imperial countries and, should the opportunity arise, to take the first steps toward establishing trade relations.[54] But the

48. See Hans Conrad Peyer, "Zürich und Übersee um die Wende vom 18. zum 19. Jahrhundert," in *Beiträge zur Wirtschafts- und Stadtgeschichte. Festschrift für Hektor Ammann* (Wiesbaden, 1965), 209–212.

49. Caspar Voght to Bertuch, Oct. 22, 1785, July 9, 1791; Hagen to Bertuch, from Ilmenau, June 3, 1786; Bertuch, "Privatakte über den Kommissionshandel mit Nordamerika 1783–1786," and his "Aufzeichnungen und geschäftliche Unterlagen über die Handelsbeziehungen mit Nordamerika" (Nachlaß Bertuch, I, 3477, 1146, II, 199, 200, GSA, Weimar). Albrecht von Heinemann, *Ein Kaufmann der Goethezeit: Friedrich Johann Justin Bertuchs Leben und Werk* (Weimar, 1955), 85.

50. See Johann Hilmar Adolf von Schönfeld to Heinrich Gottlieb von Stutterheim, Sept. 19, 1782, Feb. 6, 1783 (Locat 2748, conv. XXVII, fol. 269, XXVIII, fol. 63, StA, Dresden), as well as further dispatches from 1783.

51. "Acta die Eröffnung eines unmittelbaren Handels nach Nord-Amerika und die Errichtung einer diesfalsigen Handlungs-Societät betr. 1783–1803"; also "Acta Die zu einem unmittelbaren Handel mit den Americanischen Colonien durch die Dänische Insul St. Thomas beschehenen Vorschläge betr. 1768–1770"; "Acta den Nordamerikanischen Handel betr. 1778–1801"; "Acta den Französisch-Amerikanischen Handel betr. 1779–1785" (all files in StA, Dresden). For greater detail see Dippel, "Sources in Germany for the Study of the American Revolution," *Quarterly Journal of the Library of Congress*, XXXIII (1976), 205–206.

52. Most of his dispatches have been published in Schlitter, ed., "Berichte des ersten Agenten Österreichs," *FRA*, 2/XLV/2 (1891), 225–892.

53. See Philipp Graf von Cobenzl to the Hofkammer, Nov. 12, 1792 (Abt. Kommerz, Rote no. 651, fol. 833, Hofkammerarchiv, Vienna).

54. For the years 1775–1783 see the file "Kommerz nach Ost- und Westindien 1763–1809" (*ibid.*). See also Karl Otmar Freiherr von Aretin, "Fürst Kaunitz und die österreichisch-ostindische Handelskompagnie von 1775," *Vierteljahrschrift für Sozial- und Wirtschaftsgeschichte*, XLVI (1959), 361–377; Hanns Schlitter, "Die Beziehungen Österreichs zu den

results of his efforts were so unpromising that a trade agreement between Austria and the United States was not consummated at the time. Even in the 1790s the volume of trade between the two countries was negligible, and it certainly did not warrant establishing consulates; consequently, the Austrian government regularly refused to grant requests from commercial firms intending to establish consular relations.[55]

The situation was more encouraging in the case of Prussia, even if several years had to pass before there were any tangible results. In 1785, after long negotiations, a commercial treaty with the United States was concluded, but the hopes associated with it were not fulfilled at once. Contrary to the Prussian government's wishes, there was no direct trade at first, and in 1787 Heinrich Emanuel Lutterloh's application for appointment as Prussian consul general in the United States was rejected by the king's ministry "because his subjects until now have little or no commerce with them."[56] Although the situation did not improve during the following years, the Prussian government in 1791 made merchant Karl Gottfried Paleske consul general in Philadelphia in hope of enlivening trade.[57] The same purpose was served by the appointment of John Quincy Adams as emissary in Berlin, where he stayed from 1797 to 1801, and where the Prussian-American commercial treaty of 1785 was renewed in 1799.[58] An increase in Prussian trade with America led in 1798 to the appointment of the merchant Johann Ernst Christian Schultze

---

Vereinigten Staten von Amerika" (publ. Ph.D. diss., University of Innsbruck, 1885), 51, 106; Hubert van Houtte, "Contribution à l'histoire commerciale des Etats de l'empereur Joseph II (1780–1790)," *Vierteljahrschrift für Sozial- und Wirtschaftsgeschichte*, VIII (1910), 350–393; Houtte and Edmund C. Burnett, "American Commerical Conditions, and Negotiations with Austria, 1783–1786," *AHR*, XVI (1910–1911), 567–587. See also the rather poor study by Erich Figl, "Die Wirtschafts- und Finanzpolitik Josef II." (unpubl. Ph.D. diss., University of Erlangen, 1951), 39–43; furthermore, Prince Wenzel Anton von Kaunitz to Karl Ludwig Graf von Barbiano und Belgiojoso, Mar. 11, 1780 (Staatskanzlei, Staatenabteilung: England, K. 128, fol. 7, HHStA, Vienna); Josef von Weinbrenner to Franklin, Feb. 19, 1783 (Franklin Papers, XXVII, 132, APSL, Philadelphia); Countess Dowager von Degenfeld-Schonburg to Greffier Fagel, Jan. 24, 1782 (1 Alt 22, no. 860, StA, Wolfenbüttel); Lafayette to Washington, Sept. 3, 1785, in Gottschalk, ed., *Letters of Lafayette to Washington*, 302.

55. See "Consuln in verschiedenen Ländern item in den vereinigt Nord Amerikanischen Staaten 1754–1800," fols. 806, 810, 812, 833 (Hofkammerarchiv, Vienna); also Schlitter, "Beziehungen Österreichs zu den Vereinigten Staaten," *passim*.

56. "parce que ses sujets n'y font jusqu'ici que peu ou point de commerce": May 8, 1787 (Rep. XI. 21a, conv. I, no. 7, fol. 17, DZA, Merseburg). With a patent as major from the American commissioners at Paris, Lutterloh, a former Brunswick captain, went to America in 1777, served with the army, and later became a colonel.

57. See under the dates of Aug. 9, 14, 1791: Rep. 96. 224C, Rep. XI. 21a, conv. I, no. 8, fol. 8; cf. also fols. 19–20v (*ibid.*).

58. See the files Rep. XI. 21a, conv. II, nos. 5, 7, fol. 115; the text of the treaty follows fol. 132 (*ibid.*).

as Prussian consul in Baltimore.⁵⁹ Despite these small improvements, however, a significant exchange of goods was not established during these years.

The experience of the Hanseatic cities was similar. Like Stettin and other Prussian towns, they had profited from the American War of Independence because their neutral flag was favored, and they had tried to increase this profit by additional speculation. Numerous enterprises had gambled rashly on the boom and were bound to fail when peace drastically lowered wartime demands.⁶⁰ But many entrepreneurs did not give up hope. As early as 1782 a Hamburg merchant had attempted to induce the three Hanseatic cities to undertake common trade relations with America. But Hamburg and Lübeck refused. It seemed too risky an undertaking while there was no peace. In 1783 and 1784 renewed efforts were made, this time from Bremen. Again they failed. Hamburg was not interested, and Lübeck could not see any economic profit coming from such an enterprise.⁶¹ Thus, Bremen and Hamburg went separate ways. Bremen tried as early as 1783 to get into the American trade. The beginnings, however, were troublesome and attended with disasters and failures. Altogether, the results in the 1780s remained meager. It was only after the mid-1790s—there was an American consul in Bremen by then⁶²—that a boom made Bremen one of the Americans' favorite ports in Europe.⁶³

Developments were similar in Hamburg, and that city's efforts proved

59. The installation is dated July 24, 1798 (*ibid.*, no. 6, fol. 5).
60. See Stöver, *Niedersachsen*, II, 70; Heinrich Sieveking, "Das Handlungshaus Voght und Sieveking," *Zeitschrift des Vereins für Hamburgische Geschichte*, XVII (1912), 85; Graewe, "American Revolution Comes to Hannover," *WMQ*, 3d Ser., XX (1963), 249–250.
61. "Acta und Correspondenz unter den Hansestädten den Abschluß eines Handels-Traktates mit den Nordamerikanischen Freistaaten betr. 1782–1784" (copy in Archiv der Hansestadt, Lübeck; original now at the Deutsche Zentralarchiv, Potsdam).
62. See Despatches from the United States Consuls in Bremen, 1794–1906, vol. I (NA, Washington, D.C.); Ludwig Beutin, *Bremen und Amerika. Zur Geschichte der Weltwirtschaft und den Beziehungen Deutschlands zu den Vereinigten Staaten* (Bremen, 1953), 20; see also Arnold Delius to Franklin, Feb. 7, 1783 (Franklin Papers, XXVII, 91, APSL, Philadelphia).
63. See Philipp Heineken, "Bremens Handelsbeziehungen zu den Vereinigten Staaten in ihrer 140jähr. Entwicklung," *Jahrbuch des Norddeutschen Lloyd Bremen*, 1922/1923 (Bremen, 1924), 66; Beutin, *Bremen und Amerika*, 17–18, 19; Rolf Engelsing, "England und die USA in der bremischen Sicht des 19. Jahrhunderts," *Jahrbuch der Wittheit zu Bremen*, I (1957), 46; Engelsing, "Schlesien und der bremische Leinenhandel bis zur Kontinentalsperre," *Jahrbuch der schlesischen Friedrich-Wilhelms-Universität zu Breslau*, III (1958), 155–181; Engelsing, "Geschäftsformen in den Anfängen des deutschen Nordamerikaverkehrs (1783)," in *Tradition, 5. Beiheft. Beiträge zur bremischen Firmengeschichte* (Munich, 1966), 20–32. See also the letters of Hermann Heyman Söhne, of Bremen, to Franklin between Feb. 17, 1783, and Jan. 19, 1784 (Franklin Papers, XXVIII, 123, XXIX, 61, XXXI, 38, APSL, Philadelphia); and the correspondence between John Trumbull and Friedrich Delius and Peter Godeffroy, merchants at Bremen and Hamburg, respectively, in the years 1795–1796 (John Trumbull Collection, Box 8, Yale University Library [hereafter cited as YUL], New Haven, Conn.).

even more successful in the 1790s than Bremen's. In view of its numerous commercial links with Great Britain, Hamburg at first had to proceed much more cautiously than its rival. During the war it had been forced under pressure from Britain to prevent American ships from leaving port, a policy that did not exactly recommend the city to Americans as a trading partner. In 1783 the magistrate of the city tried to make the Americans forget that episode by sending to Congress a letter of congratulations with many verbose excuses.[64] Private trading firms like that of Voght and Sieveking immediately tried their luck. Few listened to Johann Georg Büsch's earnest appeals to reason: the American market was flooded with European products, he warned, while the economy and finances of the young state still suffered from the aftereffects of war.[65] Indeed, he was only too right; it was still too early.

In Hamburg, as in Bremen, the turning point came only in the mid-1790s, although overcautious Büsch was still raising his voice in warning. In the meantime the city had also exchanged consuls with the United States,[66] and in the last years of the century a boom came to Hamburg such as it had not experienced for many years. The boom was primarily the result of that profitable trade with America that everybody had anticipated in vain for so long. The spark of new life infused into world trade in general by American independence now also came to this city, in whose port 192 ships from America docked in 1799.[67]

Thus, in the last third of the eighteenth century all German groups interested in overseas trade looked hopefully to North America. However, many had to pay dearly for their ignorance and neglect of the internal developments in America, especially in the 1780s. Profit was not as easy to come by in America as Germans had thought, and it was only after years of much disillusionment that some saw their hopes begin to be fulfilled at the end of the century.

64. Johann Ulrich Pauly to Franklin, May 20, 1782 (Franklin Papers, III, 17, PHi, Philadelphia); Rathsprotokoll-Extrakte und Aktenstücke betr. Senatus Glückwunschschreiben an den Kongreß der Nordamerik. Staaten zur erworbenen Unabhängigkeit mit Empfehlung zur Begünstigung wechselseitiger Handelsbeziehungen, 1783 (StA, Hamburg); mayor and senators of the city of Hamburg to Franklin, Apr. 1, 1783 (Franklin Papers, XXVIII, 3, APSL, Philadelphia).

65. See among others Johann Georg Büsch, "Ueber den Handel auf Nordamerika," in Büsch and Ebeling, eds., *Handlungsbibliothek*, II (1789), 9, 15, 32.

66. See Acta betr. den amerikanischen Konsul John Parish bzw. Joseph Pitcairn in Hamburg 1793–1800; Acta betr. das Hambg. GeneralConsulat zu Philadelphia, errichtet 1794 (both in StA, Hamburg). Also, Despatches from the U.S. Consuls in Hamburg, 1790–1906, vol. I (NA, Washington, D.C.).

67. See Büsch, *Hamburgische Handlung*, 165–169, 179–180, 216, 218; Ernst Baasch, *Beiträge zur Geschichte der Handelsbeziehungen zwischen Hamburg und Amerika* (Hamburg, 1892), 35–39, 66; Heinrich Sieveking, *Georg Heinrich Sieveking. Lebensbild eines*

The American Federal Constitution of 1787

While Gottlob Benedikt von Schirach in Germany was still maintaining that the United States, having sacrificed political order for liberty, was continually growing more anarchical, fifty-five delegates from twelve states—Rhode Island was the only absentee—met in Philadelphia "for the sole and express purpose of revising the Articles of Confederation."[68] But from the beginning many delegates thought of their task as that of "revising the federal system of Government."[69] After four months of intensive debate behind locked doors, the participants of the federal Constitutional Convention agreed on the draft of a new constitution for the United States on September 17, 1787.

The ideas of the signers differed in essential points from the Articles of Confederation. In place of the loose confederation of states with a weak central power, they proposed a federal state in which the government could turn directly to the citizens, bypassing the individual states, since the old way had proven to be impractical. The citizen's rights and duties were now directly bound up with the Union, as in the field of taxation. A sizable measure of sovereignty and political power was transferred from the states to the federal government. The Congress of the Confederation was to be replaced by a president, a legislature consisting of two houses, and federal courts, all organized strictly according to the principle of the separation of powers and a system of checks and balances. The constituting basis for one house of the

---

Hamburgischen Kaufmanns aus dem Zeitalter der französischen Revolution (Berlin, 1913), 343, 365–367; Percy Ernst Schramm, *Deutschland und Übersee. Der deutsche Handel mit den anderen Kontinenten* (Brunswick, 1950), 47–48; Schramm, *Neun Generationen. Dreihundert Jahre deutscher "Kulturgeschichte" im Lichte der Schicksale einer Hamburger Bürgerfamilie (1648–1948)* (Göttingen, 1963–1964), I, 261; Hermann Kellenbenz, "Der deutsche Außenhandel gegen Ausgang des 18. Jahrhunderts," in Friedrich Lütge, ed., *Die wirtschaftliche Situation in Deutschland und Österreich um die Wende vom 18. zum 19. Jahrhundert* (Stuttgart, 1964), 25.

68. Resolution of Congress, Feb. 21, 1787, in Charles C. Tansill, ed., *Documents Illustrative of the Formation of the Union of the American States* (Washington, D.C., 1927), 46.

69. See Madison's report on the debates in the Constitutional Convention, *ibid.*, 109, 113–176. On May 14, 1787, he specifically noted "revising the federal constitution" as the target of the Convention; but he afterward struck out "constitution" and substituted "system of Government" (*ibid.*, 109). Already in March and April 1787, in private letters, Madison gave it as his opinion that a completely new constitution was needed, instead of a mere revision of the Articles of Confederation; see his letters to Jefferson, Mar. 19, and to Washington, Apr. 16, 1787, in Madison, *Letters and other Writings*, 4 vols. (Philadelphia, 1865), I, 284–286, 287–292. See also Irving Brant, *James Madison*, Vol. III, *Father of the Constitution* (Indianapolis and New York, 1950), 11–16; Clinton Rossiter, *1787: The Grand Convention* (New York, 1966), 169–171; Wood, *Creation of the American Republic*, 471–475.

legislative branch, the Senate, was the equality of all states of the Union, while the other house represented the totality of all citizens. Finally, the new constitution went back to the idea of the sovereignty of the people, as expressed in 1776 in the constitutions of the individual states and in the Declaration of Independence, and it solemnly proclaimed in the preamble: "We, the People of the United States, . . . do ordain and establish this Constitution for the United States of America."[70]

After Congress had sent the new constitution to the individual states with the recommendation that it be adopted, a passionate public discussion ensued among the politically minded population, provoked by the profound changes proposed by the Convention. The discussion between protagonists and antagonists, Federalists and anti-Federalists, varied in bitterness but occurred in all the states; in Virginia and New York, two of the most important states, the controversy was most heated. The opponents of the new constitution did not reject out of hand the proposition that the Articles of Confederation needed reform; but they fought against the reduced sovereignty of the states, against the transfer of so much power to a faraway central authority, and against what they considered to be ineffective safeguards for the rights of the individual citizen.[71]

Delaware was the first state to ratify the new constitution, on December 7, 1787, and when New York, on July 26, 1788, became the eleventh state to do so, the dispute about it was practically over, for Virginia had assented one month earlier. Theoretically, nine states would have been sufficient for adoption. The new constitution became effective in 1789, even though North Carolina and Rhode Island had not yet ratified it. In lengthy but peaceful proceedings the country had given itself a new foundation and proved to the world that the republican political process in America was still working and that the alleged anarchy was far away. The proponents of the Constitution were proud of it, convinced that "the adoption of this Constitution will give us lustre and dignity throughout the world."[72]

70. See Edward Dumbauld, *The Constitution of the United States* (Norman, Okla., 1964), 59–61; Karl Carstens, *Grundgedanken der amerikanischen Verfassung und ihre Verwirklichung* (Berlin, 1954), 19–193; Wood, *Creation of the American Republic*, 471–564.

71. See Jackson Turner Main, *The Antifederalists: Critics of the Constitution 1781–1788* (Chapel Hill, N.C., 1961); Broadus and Louise P. Mitchell, *A Biography of the Constitution of the United States* (New York, 1964), 123–186; Cecelia M. Kenyon, ed., *The Antifederalists* (Indianapolis, 1966), xxi–cxvi; Robert A. Rutland, *The Ordeal of the Constitution* (Norman, Okla., 1966); William P. Murphy, *The Triumph of Nationalism* (Chicago, 1967), 267–406. See also Roger Sherman to [?], Dec. 8, 1787 (Roger Sherman Collection, YUL, New Haven, Conn.).

72. Henry Van Schaack to Theodore Sedgwick, Feb. 9, 1788 (Theodore Sedgwick Papers, A, 143, MHi, Boston). On Van Schaack see Richard E. Welch, Jr., *Theodore Sedgwick, Federalist: A Political Portrait* (Middletown, Conn., 1965), 113.

The American Federalists could well be content with their Constitution, which had no prototype anywhere in the world. But, significant as this achievement was, could it arouse appropriate interest in Europe, including Germany? Looking for pertinent statements made by German contemporaries from 1787 to 1789, we find only a few remarks of substance. A German reviewer of Mazzei's *Recherches historiques et politiques sur les États-Unis* correctly asserted that "there is much darkness lying over the constitutions of the individual states of the North American republic."[73] Yet this realization did not bring about a change in the basic level of available information. The federal Convention attracted only cursory attention. Texts of the new constitution were published in far too small a number in Germany,[74] and there was little interest in the disputes between the Federalists and anti-Federalists following the drafting of the document.[75]

Under these circumstances it is not surprising that the German bourgeoisie remained for the most part unfamiliar with the Constitution even during the years following its adoption. Many had no knowledge of it whatever, and those who did usually could describe it only in hazy and vague terms.[76] It is clear, therefore, that the outbreak of the French Revolution was not responsible for the low level of knowledge in Germany about the American Constitution of 1787; the Declaration of Independence and the Articles of Confederation had already met with a similar fate. If we look at the years from 1787 to the outbreak of the French Revolution, we find almost no evidence of cogent discussion that might have been affected by the changed circumstances following the storming of the Bastille.[77] On the contrary, the

73. "Die innere Staatsverfassung der einzelnen Staaten des nordamerikanischen Freistaats hat bisher noch manche Dunkelheit gehabt": *Göttingische Anzeigen von gelehrten Sachen*, July 14, 1788, 1125.
74. For the few exceptions see *English Lyceum*, Oct., Dec. 1787, 1–13, 299–310, Jan. 1788, 265–267 (with Franklin's speech of approval to the Convention), and *Neue Litteratur und Völkerkunde*, Jan. 1788, 3–31 (Constitution only). Both periodicals were published by Johann Wilhelm von Archenholtz. See also Mazzei, *Geschichte und Staatsverfassung*, II, 266–287; Martens, *Receuil des traités*, III, 76–95; Cooper, *Renseignemens sur l'Amérique*, appendix, 1–34.
75. Scattered remarks are to be found in Beelen-Bertholff's notes; cf. Schlitter, ed., "Berichte des ersten Agenten Österreichs," *FRA*, 2/XLV/2 (1891), 716, 727, 755, 756. See also Schubart, ed., *Vaterlandschronik*, Aug. 12, 1788, 529.
76. E.g., Hammerdörfer and Kosche, *Amerika*, I, xiii–xiv; Michael Konrad Curtius, *Grundriß der Universal Historie* (Marburg, 1790), 236; Osterwald, *Historische Erdbeschreibung*, II, 116; Johann August Philipp Hennicke, *Synchronistische Tabellen über Schröckhs Lehrbuch der allgemeinen Weltgeschichte, zum Gebrauch der niedern Classen in den Schulen* (Leipzig, 1797), last table; also Castiglioni, *Reise durch die vereinigten Staaten*, 99–100, 257–258; Franklin, *Kleine Schriften*, II, 268 (note by Schatz).
77. Fraenkel, *Amerika im Spiegel des deutschen politischen Denkens*, 23, is therefore incorrect when he suggests that there was an end to interest in America.

impression made by the French Revolution stimulated interest in fundamental questions about the formation of governments. It was this interest that in turn prompted the beginnings of a discussion of the American Constitution among the German bourgeoisie in the 1790s.

In 1795 Günther Karl Friedrich Seidel, for one, dealt with the document in detail, convinced that "the inquiry into the Constitution of the United States of North America is an essential part of the history of their Revolution, for the new Constitution is the result of these notable events; without detailed knowledge we cannot decide whether the Americans profited or lost by their independence from Great Britain."[78] He then proceeded to explain to his fellow citizens the substance of federalism, the separation of powers, the system of checks and balances, the sovereignty of the people, and other basic ideas of the American Constitution.[79] At about the same time, Dietrich Hermann Hegewisch made the same constitutional principles the center of his observations.[80] Johann Georg Büsch also showed above-average perceptiveness when he observed that "the essential difference between the Articles of Confederation of 1778 and the new Constitution is that the former concerned only the several states, while the latter concerns all individuals."[81] Julius August Remer, on the other hand, thought federalism was the most noteworthy achievement of the Constitution.[82]

These few examples indicate how far the political understanding of the German bourgeoisie had progressed over twenty years time, for the problems touched on here did not, after all, originate in the second half of the 1790s. They were much older and can be traced back in essentially the same form to at least the mid-1770s. Until after the outbreak of the French Revolution, however, the bourgeoisie had hardly considered them, other than in the

78. "Die Darstellung der Staatsverfassung der Vereinigten Staaten von Nordamerika ist ein wesentlicher Teil der Geschichte ihrer Revolution. Denn die neue Verfassung ist das Resultat dieser merkwürdigen Begebenheit; ohne eine genauere Kenntnis derselben läßt sich nicht entscheiden, ob die Amerikaner durch die Unabhängigkeit von Großbritannien gewannen oder verloren": Seidel, "Staatsverfassung," in Ramsay, *Amerikanische Revolution*, IV, iii. See also the famous remark made by Benjamin Rush in 1787, that only the first stage of the Revolution was over in Runes, ed., *Writings of Benjamin Rush*, 26; also Wood, *Creation of the American Republic*, 562–564, 606–615.

79. Seidel, "Staatsverfassung," in Ramsay, *Amerikanische Revolution*, IV, 6–7, 32, 48.

80. Hegewisch, "Historische, vergleichende Uebersicht der Konstitutionen der vereinigten amerikanischen Staaten," in Hegewisch and Ebeling, eds., *Amerikanisches Magazin*, I (1795), 1–38.

81. "Die wesentlichste Verschiedenheit der Konstitutionsartikel von 1778 und der neuen Konstitution lag darin, daß jene bloß auf die einzelnen Staaten wirkten, diese aber auf die Individuen in allen": Büsch, *Geschichte der merkwürdigsten Welthändel*, 3d ed., 488, cf. generally 488–492.

82. See three works by Remer, *Handbuch der neuern Geschichte*, 567–568, *Handbuch der Geschichte unsrer Zeiten*, 39–40, and *Lehrbuch der algemeinen Geschichte*, 629–630.

most general terms. The definite expansion of the German bourgeoisie's horizons to include more involved questions of constitutional structure does not mean that they had reached a level of political consciousness comparable to that in America, a fact that is obvious from the examples cited. But by taking up questions that were formerly devoid of interest, the bourgeoisie revealed their readiness to go beyond general comments and approach basic questions of governmental organization, particularly that of the relationship between the government and the governed. This overall change in interest and attitude was more important than any specific observation about the American Constitution, for even the most concrete statements were not always conspicuous for detailed content and analytical keenness.

10. *The American Revolution and the French Revolution*

The Outbreak and First Phase of the French Revolution

The German bourgeoisie's discussion of the American federal Constitution of 1787 bore the distinct impress of Europe's political development at the time. The relative quiet of the years after the American war came to an end with the storming of the Bastille on July 14, 1789. France and all Europe were witness to an epoch-making event. What some German contemporaries in earlier years had thought to be only a distant crisis looming on the far horizon had vehemently exploded in France, triggering events that were to leave deep traces in the history of mankind. Certainly the outbreak of the French Revolution was not a bolt out of the blue. It was a consequence of French history in the preceding months, years, decades, even centuries, as Alexis de Tocqueville showed as early as 1856.[1] But contrary to this somewhat detached perspective from later years, contemporaries were surprised and captivated by the precipitate events.

The German bourgeoisie's initial reaction to the outbreak and first phase of the French Revolution is reminiscent of its reaction to the American Revolution during the first years of the War of Independence. Friedrich Gottlieb Klopstock, who had praised events in America as a happy promise, now exclaimed:

> France has struggled free.
> The century's noblest deed arose
> To heights Olympian![2]

1. Tocqueville, "L'Ancien Régime et la Révolution," bk. III, chap. 8, in his *Oeuvres complètes*, ed. Mayer, II/1, 249–250.
2. "Frankreich schuf sich frei. Des Jahrhunderts edelste Tat hub / Da sich zu dem Olympus empor!": Klopstock, "Kennet euch selbst" (ode, 1789), in his *Sämmtliche Werke*, VI, 104, cf. 33 (1781).

Daniel Jenisch expected the French to do what had been expected of the Americans all along:

> Paris! Show your powers! Equal Sparta! Break the chain!
> And prove yourself in action! . . .
> Another Brutus and another Cato dies
> For liberty and his country
> Making Rome and Paris equal as monuments of liberty
> To heirs born free of serfdom![3]

Henrich Steffens, who as a child had experienced his family's enthusiasm for the American Revolution, remembered later that in 1789, at the age of sixteen, he had felt those first manifestations of joy as "something pure, even holy."[4] Friedrich von Gentz, disciple of Kant that he was, considered the events in France "the first practical triumph of philosophy," and in the spring of 1791 he mourned Mirabeau, "mankind's great benefactor,"[5] who himself had made similar statements about the American Revolution in the 1780s.[6] The German bourgeoisie celebrated this event as enthusiastically as they had extolled the American Revolution because the ideals involved seemed to them to be the same as their own.[7]

The similarity of reactions to the openings of the French and the American revolutions found expression not only in the celebrations of the bourgeoisie in both cases, but also in the fears of the aristocracy, which, in view of the geographical proximity of France, were even more pronounced in the later case than those voiced earlier by Joseph Franz Maria Ignaz Graf von Seinsheim, Heinrich Anton Freiherr von Beckers von Wetterstetten, and others. Thus, only a few weeks after the storming of the Bastille, the peasants' liberation, and the declaration of human rights, Herzogin Auguste von Braunschweig, the princess royal of Great Britain, wrote: "We live here in a state of

---

3. "Paris! ermanne dich! sei Sparta! brich die Kette! / und zeige Kraft und Tat . . . / Und neue Brutus werden, neue Caton's sterben / für Freiheit und für Vaterland, / und lassen Rom-Paris dem freigebornen Erben; / ein Denkmal tapfrer Hand!": *Teutscher Merkur*, Oct. 1789, 65–66.

4. "etwas Reines, ja Heiliges": Steffens, *Was ich erlebte*, I, 364. During the following years he became an outspoken critic of the French Revolution; cf. *ibid.*, IV, 53–62.

5. "der erste praktische Triumph der Philosophie. . . . Wohltäter der Menschheit": to Christian Garve, Dec. 5, 1790, Apr. 19, 1791, in Friedrich Carl Wittichen and Ernst Salzer, eds., *Briefe von und an Friedrich von Gentz*, 3 vols. (Munich, 1909–1913), I, 178, 205.

6. Mirabeau, *Sammlung einiger Schriften*, 1.

7. See among others Geiger, *Berlin*, II, 44–45; George Peabody Gooch, *Germany and the French Revolution* (London, 1920), 39; Stadelmann, *Deutschland und Westeuropa*, 22–23; Droz, *L'Allemagne et la Révolution française*, 42–43; Douglass, "German Intellectuals," *WMQ*, 3d Ser., XVII (1960), 217–218; Hertz, *German Public Mind*, II, 420–421; see also Gerhard Ritter, *Das deutsche Problem* (Munich, 1962), 42–54.

true anxiety caused by those detestable troubles which are shaking France."[8]

In view of the similar interpretations usually given to both events in their time, it is not surprising that, in spite of the dominant role of the French Revolution, the bourgeoisie very soon tried to compare it to the American. The idea of viewing the two revolutions as the single expression of a changed world, which was Thomas Paine's conception,[9] or as links in the same chain, which was the way Peter Ochs understood events,[10] has been emphasized by historians, especially since World War II. Historians have now come to believe that in the latter third of the eighteenth century certain common factors became manifest in several countries on both sides of the North Atlantic, precluding an interpretation of events only in the context of their national isolation.[11]

Shortly after July 14, 1789, the German bourgeoisie, like Paine, Ochs, and modern historical researchers, came to believe that there was a parallel between the American and the French revolutions. Their equal measure of enthusiasm for both events rested on the view that they were expressions of similar principles, principles that the vast majority of the bourgeoisie conceived to be universally applicable. The agitation over the storming of the Bastille had not yet subsided when the first, still vague comparisons to the American Revolution were made.[12] During the following months observers ever more clearly saw common elements, so that by April 1790 Johann Wilhelm Ludwig Gleim thought it advisable to warn the French against too much impetuosity with the quatrain, "The Americans to the French":

8. "Nous vivons ici dans une vraie anxiété par rapport aux troubles affreuses qui boule-versent la France": Herzogin Auguste von Braunschweig to [?], Oct. 1, 1789 (GLA, Karlsruhe).

9. Paine, *Die Rechte des Menschen. Eine Antwort auf Herrn Burke's Angriff gegen die französische Revolution*, trans. from the English [by Dorothea Margarete Liebeskind], 2d ed., 2 vols. (Copenhagen, 1793), I, 184; see also Paine, *Kurzer Abriß der Entstehung der französischen Revolution*, trans. from the French [by J. G. Dyck] (Leipzig, 1791), 11–12.

10. Ochs to Leonhard Meister, early 1792, in Steiner, ed., *Korrespondenz des Peter Ochs*, I, 325; cf. Ochs to Johannes von Müller, Dec. 28, 1789 (p. 225), and also the introduction by Steiner (pp. xxxii–xxxiv).

11. E.g., Jacques Godechot and Robert R. Palmer, "Le Problème de L'Atlantique du XVIIIème au XXème siècle," in *Relazioni del X Congresso internazionale di Scienze storiche*, V (Florence, 1955), 173–239; Palmer, *Age of the Democratic Revolution*; Godechot, *Révolutions*, 102, 259–260; Peter Amann, ed., *The Eighteenth-Century Revolution: French or Western?* (Boston, 1963); see also R. B. Morris, *American Revolution Reconsidered*, 54, 65; Sagnac, *Fin de l'Ancien Régime*, 431; Gilbert Chinard, "Notes on the American Origins of the Déclaration des Droits de l'Homme et du Citoyen," *APSP*, XCVIII (1954), 383–396; Wolzendorff, *Staatsrecht und Naturrecht*, 364–366. Strong emphasis is laid on the differences, however, by scholars such as Talmon, *Origins of Totalitarian Democracy*, 27.

12. See among others Daniel Jenisch, "Ode auf die gegenwärtigen Unruhen in Frankreich, 4. Aug. 1789," *Teutscher Merkur*, Oct. 1789, 60–66.

Don't flaunt your wisdom full of spite
Do rather all you can to remain your former self!
A kindly spirit led you to the light;
An evil one may drive you back to darkness.[13]

Others at the time, no matter whether they approved or condemned developments, expressed the conviction that both events had similar aims. Explicitly mentioned were the ideas of liberty and equality, and the antimonarchic trend,[14] which now, under the influence of the French Revolution, became more obvious to observers of the American Revolution as well.

These speculations on the ultimate aims of both movements arose out of the bourgeois notion that the American Revolution had directly affected the outbreak of the French, especially since there had been very close relations between the two countries during the preceding decade. "This contact between France and America spread the spirit of liberty even more."[15] It was the prerequisite for an intensive exchange of ideas. "Since France helped to secure America's liberty, since all writing against despotism by liberal spirits was applauded and approved in France, since France's warriors inhaled the spirit of liberty in North America and there came to know the difference between a free man and a slave of a despot or of his favorites, everything was prepared for France's great revolution."[16]

13. "Auf Deine Weisheit trotze nicht; / Tu' lieber, was Du kannst, das, was Du bist, zu bleiben! / Ein guter Genius trieb liebend Dich zum Licht; / Aus Licht in Finsternis kann Dich ein böser treiben!": Apr. 1790, in Wilhelm Körte, ed., *Vater Gleim's Zeitgedichte, von 1789–1803* (Leipzig, 1841), 10.

14. E.g., Jean André de Luc to Johann Georg Zimmermann, July 27, 1789 (HptStA, Hanover); Karl von Zinzendorf, Tagebuch, Aug. 3, 1789 (XXXIV, fol. 136v, HHStA, Vienna); broadside of the Jacobin Club of True Republicans at Altona, reprinted in Walter Grab, *Norddeutsche Jakobiner. Demokratische Bestrebungen zur Zeit der Französischen Revolution* (Frankfurt, 1967), esp. 108–109.

15. "Diese Verbindung Frankreichs und Amerikas verbreitete den Geist der Freiheit noch mehr": *Neues Deutsches Museum*, Dec. 1789, 636. See also *Politisches Journal*, Dec. 1789, 1494; Karl Ehregott Mangelsdorf, *Über den Geist der Revolutionen* (Königsberg, 1790), 2.

16. "Da Frankreich die Freiheit Amerikas erfechten half, da alle Schriften, welche der Freiheitsgeist dem Despotismus entgegenstellte, in Frankreich gelobt und gebilliget wurden, da Frankreichs Krieger den Geist der Freiheit in Nordamerika einhauchten, in diesem Lande den Unterschied zwischen den freien Menschen und dem Sklaven eines Despoten oder seiner Günstlinge bemerketen, so wurde die große Revolution Frankreichs dadurch allerdings verbreitet": *Der Neue Deutsche Zuschauer*, July 5, 1790, 9–10. See also [Adolf Freiherr von Knigge], *Joseph von Wurmbrand . . . politisches Glaubensbekenntniß, mit Hinsicht auf die französische Revolution und deren Folgen* (Frankfurt and Leipzig, 1792), 44; Theodor Gottlieb von Hippel, "Ueber die bürgerliche Verbesserung der Weiber" (1792), in his *Sämmtliche Werke*, 14 vols. (Berlin, 1828–1839), VI, 257; Paine, *Rechte des Menschen*, I, 104; Girtanner, *Ludwig der Sechszehnte*, 85; *Lebensgeschichte Ludwig XVI. Königs von Frankreich* (Vienna, 1793), 38; [Karl August Lebrecht Bischof], *Tabellarisch-historisches Handbuch der Kirchen- und Staatengeschichte bis auf die neuesten und gegenwärtigen Zeiten* (Nuremberg,

The participation of French soldiers in the American War of Independence took on much significance in the eyes of many, especially among the antagonists of the French Revolution. Yet, before 1789 this fact had hardly been considered. Now it was believed that in America, Frenchmen, from simple peasants to members of the high nobility, first came into contact with the revolutionary ideals of the Americans and the structure of their society and governments. In the New World the French soldiers for the first time stepped out of their own sociopolitical context and came to know a completely different situation, which was as real, however, as the *ancien régime*. Moreover, to a detached observer the connection between the French experience in America, on the one hand, and the later challenge of the French Revolution to absolutist Europe, on the other, appeared to be manifest. "There our countrymen learn that every common soldier may become a general if he has the capabilities of a general, and they learn that a state can exist where all men are equal and there are no differences of estates. They will not easily forget that, and they will tell their relatives and friends about it on their return. They are learning now, so they can teach later."[17]

The veterans' influence was justly emphasized,[18] but it alone did not account for all of the consequences of French participation in the American war or fully explain the importance of this participation in relation to the French Revolution. Militarily, France had been on the side of the victors, but the war in the end had brought few benefits. The state's finances had been so disrupted that they could not be straightened out before 1789, and the anticipated economic advantages did not materialize. France did not succeed in displacing Great Britain in the lucrative trade with North America, and its load of debts became more and more oppressive. Like a number of other, often much weightier, aspects of internal politics, all of these factors pertaining to

---

1793), 351; Woltmann, *Geschichte der Europäischen Staaten*, I, 296, 310; La Roche, *Erscheinungen am See Oneida*, I, 118–119; *Entwurf der neuesten Culturgeschichte*, 22; Steffens, *Was ich erlebte*, I, 79–80.

17. "Unsre Landsleute lernen dort, daß jeder gemeine Soldat General werden kann, wenn er die Fähigkeiten eines Generals besitzet, und finden, daß ein Staat bestehen kann, wo alle Menschen gleich sind und kein Unterschied der Stände angenommen wird. Das werden sie sobald nicht vergessen; das werden sie bei ihrer Zurückkunft ihren Verwandten und Bekannten erzählen. Sie lernen jetzt, um zu lehren!": *Fliegende Blätter*, Nov. 1794, 983. See also *Kurze Lebens- und Regierungsgeschichte Ludwig des Sechszehnten* (Stuttgart, 1793), 50, 54–55.

18. See Forrest McDonald, "The Relation of the French Peasant Veterans of the American Revolution to the Fall of Feudalism in France, 1789–1792," *Agricultural History*, XXV (1951), 151–161. On the influence of American constitutionalism in France, 1788–1789, compared with the English influence, see Joyce Appleby, "America as a Model for the Radical French Reformers of 1789," *WMQ*, 3d Ser., XXVIII (1971), 267–286.

the relationship of the French to the American Revolution were largely ignored by German contemporaries.

The German bourgeoisie were not the only ones who often overrated the influence of the American Revolution on the outbreak of the French Revolution and saw a causal relationship between the two, believing that the latter depended directly on the former.[19] As late as the end of the century one could read in Robert Bisset's biography of Edmund Burke: "If there had been no American Revolution, the French Revolution would not have broken out so soon or would not have taken such a democratic turn."[20]

Statements like these lead us directly to the problems surrounding the understanding and reception of the French Revolution by the German bourgeoisie in the 1790s. A noteworthy change in the bourgeoisie's attitude toward the French Revolution occurred during 1791–1792, a change immediately related to the sequence of developments in France during this period after Mirabeau's death and the king's attempted escape. The start of the Austro-Prussian war against France, the storming of the Tuileries, the September massacres, and the sentencing and execution of the king all influenced and contributed to this evolving attitude. Moreover, the revolution had meanwhile spread to Germany, where it led to uprisings of the oppressed and underprivileged against the authorities in the southwestern region and in other areas.[21]

Georg Forster clearly saw this change of opinion in 1793. From Paris he addressed his fellow German citizens: "When our constitution of 1791 was adopted, who would have doubted the return of the Golden Age? But, with the change of things later on, those utopian dreams had to take an extremely disadvantageous turn; we were held responsible for the miscalculation in their hopes. When on August 10 the dethronement of the king caused blood to be shed, your revolutionary friends renounced everything, and soon they compared our fatal September nights to the St. Bartholomew's Night of

19. E.g., *Deutsche Monatsschrift*, Sept. 1790, 7–8; Julius August Remer's note to his translation of Stedman, *Amerikanischer Krieg*, I, 239.

20. "Hätte die amerikanische Revolution nicht statt gehabt, so würde auch die Französische Revolution nicht so bald ausgebrochen sein oder keine so demokratische Wendung genommen haben": Bisset, *Edmund Burke's Leben in historisch-literarisch-politischer Hinsicht*, trans. from the English by Johann Georg Christian Fick (Leipzig and Gera, 1799), 206.

21. For examples see among others the file, Französische Revolution, 1788–1792 (GLA, Karlsruhe); Gross, "Trierer Geistesleben," 21–22; Vierhaus, "Deutschland vor der Französischen Revolution," 532–547; and in greater depth, Heinrich Scheel, *Süddeutsche Jakobiner. Klassenkämpfe und republikanische Bestrebungen im deutschen Süden des 18. Jahrhunderts* (Berlin, 1962), 56, and *passim*.

Charles IX and his mother. Our activities since then have been so revolutionary that people finally abandoned their initial high hopes."[22]

New developments in France increased the emotional withdrawal from the revolutionary upheaval, and sometimes led to uncompromising condemnation, hitherto unparalleled except in aristocratic circles.[23] What was now happening in Paris and in the provinces no longer seemed to the bourgeoisie to be the realization of the ideals they had so long believed in. Many saw the revolution no longer as a striving for liberty, tolerance, equality of economic opportunities, and abolition of privileges, but as outright violence and absolute rule by those lower classes they derogatorily called the mob.

Such views, as well as the social unrest in large parts of Germany directly after the storming of the Bastille, seem to have inspired large parts of the bourgeoisie with a constantly mounting fear of the petite bourgeoisie and the lower classes.[24] In 1791, for instance, the *Neuer Teutscher Merkur* declared

22. "Als nun gar unsre Verfassung von 1791 zustande kam: wer hätte da noch an der Wiederkehr des goldnen Zeitalters gezweifelt? Diese utopischen Träume mußten bei der Wendung, die hernach die Sachen nahmen, eine höchst nachteilige Wirkung tun; man ließ es uns entgelten, daß man sich in seinen Hoffnungen so verrechnet hatte. Als am 10. August die Absetzung des Königs Blut kostete, da kündigten uns Eure Revolutionsfreunde schon Hut und Weide auf; und bald verglichen sie unsre unseligen Septembernächte mit Karls IX. und seiner Mutter Bartholomäusnacht. Seitdem ist es so revolutionsmäßig bei uns hergegangen, daß man von dem ersten Vorurteil endlich zurückgekommen ist": Forster, "Parisische Umrisse," in his *Über die Beziehung der Staatskunst auf das Glück der Menschheit und andere Schriften*, ed. Wolfgang Rödel (Frankfurt, 1966), 116.

23. E.g., August Freiherr von der Horst to J. G. Zimmermann, Jan. 9, 1791 (Nachlaß Zimmermann, A II, no. 45, fol. 270v, LB, Hanover); Wilhelm von Edelsheim to Johann Eustach Graf von Schlitz (von Görtz), Aug. 24, 1792 (Abt. 48, no. 566, GLA, Karlsruhe); Wilhelm von Humboldt to Friedrich Schiller, Dec. 7, 1792, in Franz Muncker, ed., *Briefwechsel zwischen Schiller und W. v. Humboldt in den Jahren 1792 bis 1805* (Stuttgart, 1893), 60–61; Schiller to Christian Gottfried Körner, Dec. 21, 1792, in Ludwig Geiger, ed., *Briefwechsel zwischen Schiller und Körner, von 1784 bis zum Tode Schillers*, 4 vols. (Stuttgart, n.d.), II, 266; Johann Traugott Fischer, *Preußens und Frankreichs Revolution* . . . (Halberstadt, 1794); also Otto Tschirch, *Geschichte der öffentlichen Meinung in Preußen vom Baseler Frieden bis zum Zusammenbruch des Staates (1795–1806)*, 2 vols. (Weimar, 1933–1934), I, 29–30; Klothilde Kirschbaum, "Deutsche Zeitgenossen zu den Gewalttaten der Französischen Revolution. Meinungsbildung, Erlebnisweise, Urteilsbegründung in der Sicht der deutschen Gebildeten" (unpubl. Ph.D. diss., University of Göttingen, 1951), 56–59; Palmer, *Age of the Democratic Revolution*, II, 35–44; Jacques Droz, "La Légende du complot illuministe et les origines du romantisme politique en Allemagne," *Revue historique*, CCXXVI (1961), 321–322.

24. See Wenck, *Deutschland vor hundert Jahren*, II, 71–73; Rudolf Stadelmann and Wolfram Fischer, *Die Bildungswelt des deutschen Handwerkers um 1800. Studien zur Soziologie des Kleinbürgers im Zeitalter Goethes* (Berlin, 1955), 43, 61–62; Walter Grab, *Demokratische Strömungen in Hamburg und Schleswig-Holstein zur Zeit der ersten französischen Republik* (Hamburg, 1966), 29–30; Grab, "Die Revolutionspropaganda der deutschen Ja-

the "rabble" to be "as thoughtless as a donkey," unable to differentiate between lawful and arbitrary power and therefore incapable of sensibly par-
taking in government.[25] A pamphlet of about the same date painted the
danger in even more violent colors. The uneducated German petite bourgeoisie and the peasants were, according to this pamphlet, "much too backward
to have ideas on constitutional matters." They were "semi-savages. Like a
tiger they will kill everything in their path. As far as French weapons will
reach, the houses of princes, aristocrats, and their servants will go up in
flames, and the smoking Rhine provinces will herald to the rest of Germany a
devastation far more horrible than the scenes of the Thirty Years' War."[26]

It is worth noting that the author of this pamphlet, like Johann Wilhelm
von Archenholtz, was by no means opposed to all revolutions as a matter of
principle. But even Archenholtz, who in the past had often made it clear that
he completely shared the bourgeoisie's political ideals, drew a sharp line of
demarcation between himself and the petite bourgeoisie and lower classes. In
a foreword to an article he published on the Mitau uprising of December
1792 he wrote: "The lower classes, that is artisans and peasants, are, as a
whole, only half human at best. . . . What sets this kind of people apart from
savages is very trifling in the eyes of a philosopher. Proof for this assertion is
furnished by the recent history of France and England."[27]

Thus, fear of the lower classes was felt not only by professed antirevolutionaries, but also by those who shared the bourgeoisie's political ideals. Out
of fear of an upsurging petite bourgeoisie, the upper middle classes now
preferred to see political and social matters in Germany remain unchanged,
and they abandoned altogether the idea of a revolution. Even Georg Forster,
that uncompromising supporter of the French Revolution, wanted the prime

---

kobiner 1792/93," *Archiv für Sozialgeschichte*, IX (1969), 145; also Möller, *Kleinbürgerliche Familie*, 7.

25. "Pöbel. . . . Gedankenlosigkeit eines Lasttiers": *Neuer Teutscher Merkur*, Sept. 1791, 4–5.

26. "viel zu weit zurück, um Begriffe von Staatsverfassung zu haben. . . . ein Halbwilder. Wie Tiger wird er ohne Unterschied alles erwürgen, was ihm in den Weg kommen wird. So weit die Waffen der Franken reichen, so werden die Häuser der Fürsten, des Adels und ihrer Diener in Flammen stehen, und die rauchenden Provinzen am Rhein werden gar bald dem üb-rigen Deutschland eine Verheerung ankündigen, die weit schrecklicher sein wird, als es die Szenen des Dreißigjährigen Krieges gewesen sind": [Eduard von Clauer], *Der Kreuzzug gegen die Franken. Eine patriotische Rede welche in der deutschen Reichs–versammlung gehalten – werden könnte* (Germanien [i.e., Brunswick], [1791]), 53, 56.

27. "Die niedern Klassen, d.h. der Handwerker, der Landmann, sind, im ganzen genom-men, allenthalben nur Halbmenschen. . . . Das, was diese Art Menschen von den Wilden un-terscheidet, ist wahrlich in dem Auge eines Philosophen sehr unbeträchtlich. Die Belege zu dieser Behauptung liefert die neue Geschichte von Frankreich und England": *Minerva*, Mar. 1793, 379.

moving force of any German revolution to be the educated bourgeoisie; he was against a revolution in Germany at this time, partly because the "people . . . this unmeasured and uncalculated power," were too uneducated, in the bourgeois sense of the word.[28]

The Jacobins' decision to purge the Girondists in France served to confirm the fears of large sectors of the German bourgeoisie, and probably contributed more toward a reversal of German opinion than the reception of Burke's ideas. Burke's influence was, in any case, limited to the higher social classes, whereas his great counterpart, Paine, obviously had greater effect among the lower classes.[29] The bourgeoisie increasingly began to doubt that a revolution like the one in France was really advantageous to their interests, and, in the process of reorientation, they drew closer ideologically to the ruling classes in Germany. In the course of the year 1792 the majority of the German bourgeoisie abandoned their formerly overwhelming enthusiasm for the French Revolution and turned toward distinct opposition to it, a turnabout that markedly reinforced the position of the German nobility.[30] This

28. "Volk . . . diese ungemessene, unberechnete Kraft": Forster, "Parisische Umrisse," in his *Über die Beziehung der Staatskunst*, ed. Rödel, 92, cf. 93–95. German history during the 19th and 20th centuries gives ample proof that in times of pressing political and social changes overwhelming feelings of status insecurity spread among large parts of the bourgeoisie and ultimately among the petite bourgeoisie; cf. Edward Shorter, "Middle-Class Anxiety in the German Revolution of 1848," *Journal of Social History*, II (1968–1969), esp. 196, 200–205, 210–211, and, for more recent times, see generally the history of the Weimar Republic from 1918 to 1933.

29. For laudatory opinions of Burke see among others J. G. Zimmermann to Nikolaus Anton Kirchberger, Feb. 4, and to G. A. von Steinberg, June 20, 1791 (Nachlaß Zimmermann, A II, nos. 51, 91, fols. 19v, 16, LB, Hanover); Karl Freiherr von Bühler to Wassili Stephanowitsch Popoff, May 14, 1791 (LB, Stuttgart); Friedrich Heinrich Jacobi to August Wilhelm Rehberg, Nov. 28, 1791, in Jacobi, *Auserlesener Briefwechsel*, 2 vols. (Leipzig, 1825–1827), II, 68–69; also Bisset, *Burke's Leben*, ix (preface by Johann Georg Christian Fick); Frieda Braune, *Edmund Burke in Deutschland. Ein Beitrag zur Geschichte des historisch-politischen Denkens* (Heidelberg, 1917), 19–26. On the considerable influence of Paine among the petite bourgeoisie, compared with that of Burke, see, e.g., J. G. Zimmermann to de Luc, May 24–27, 1791 (StA, Aarau); letter by Herzogin Auguste von Braunschweig, June 15, 1791 (GLA, Karlsruhe); see also R. R. Fennessy, *Burke, Paine and the Rights of Man: A Difference of Political Opinion* (The Hague, 1963), 251–254. As an example of the admiration for Paine as opposed to Burke see G. Forster to Christian Friedrich Voss, June 4, 1791, in Forster, *Briefe an Voß*, ed. Zincke, 68.

30. E.g., Georg Christoph Lichtenberg to Georg August Ebell, Feb. 26, 1795, in Lichtenberg, *Briefe*, ed. Leitzmann and Schüddekopf, III, 146; Christoph Martin Wieland to Heinrich Geßner and wife, Feb. 26, Mar. 18, 1798, in Wieland, *Ausgewählte Briefe von C. M. Wieland an verschiedene Freunde . . .*, 4 vols. (Zurich, 1815–1816), IV, 210, 217; see also La Rochefoucauld Liancourt, *Reisen durch die Nordamerikanische Republik*, I, 41, 496. Kirschbaum, "Deutsche Zeitgenossen zu den Gewalttaten," 72–94, 146, makes this change in attitude clear, but without giving exact dates; she is, however, of the opinion that it was settled by 1792. For a general sociological outline of this very specific historical process see among others Pierre Laroque, *Les Classes sociales*, 4th ed. (Paris, 1968), 62.

climate of fierce opposition brought up all-too-familiar arguments. Indeed, the great educator Johann Heinrich Pestalozzi asserted around 1793–1794 that "nearly everything said now against the French was said against the Americans ten years ago."[31]

To be sure, the French Revolution did not lose all of its followers in Germany; quite the contrary. Many continued to side with the Jacobins, or at least limited their criticism essentially to those events they thought to be deviations from the basic developments. But approval among the bourgeoisie, who once had celebrated the Revolution as the implementation of their own cherished ideals, had clearly decreased. Opposing the Jacobin sympathizers were those who positively rejected any form of revolutionary change, who were prepared to join with others in defending the existing order, and who shared Christoph Ludwig Meiners' fears, expressed in a letter to Franz Oberthür: "Never have I feared violent revolutions so much or believed them to be so near as I do now."[32]

The logical consequence of this development was an increasing ideological isolation of the French Revolution—and at the same time, its detachment from the American Revolution. Many of the bourgeoisie became increasingly dubious about the developments west of the Rhine. Could the two revolutions still be compared? Their origins, it was believed, had been the same or similar, and the first had contributed to the outbreak of the second, but the progress of each had been radically different. In one case they saw the orderly, disciplined, and moderate proceedings of the Americans; in the other, the apparently unbridled and reckless conduct of the Jacobins, whose raucous and repulsive actions seemed to afford no parallels to the wise and exemplary behavior of Washington and Franklin.

The same circles of the bourgeoisie that avoided categorical condemnation of the events in France emphasized also the need to stress the distinctive as well as the common elements of each revolution.[33] Many sectors of the

31. "Fast alles, was man jetzt gegen die Franzosen sagt, sagte man vor zehn Jahren gegen die Amerikaner": Pestalozzi, note on reading Knigge, *Joseph von Wurmbrand* (c. 1793–1794), in Pestalozzi, *Sämtliche Werke*, ed. Arthur Buchenau *et al.* (Berlin, 1927–), X, 235.

32. "Noch nie habe ich gewaltsame Revolutionen so sehr gefürchtet oder so nahe geglaubt als jetzt": Meiners to Oberthür, July 24, 1794 (Nachlaß Oberthür, letter no. 132, UB, Würzburg).

33. E.g., Karl Friedrich Reinhard to Karl Friedrich Stäudlin, Sept. 20, 1789 (Schiller-Nationalmuseum, Marbach); [Johann Gottfried Dyck], "Franklin," in Louis Sébastien Mercier, *Erscheinungen und Träume von Mercier und einigen deutschen Gelehrten*, trans. from the French and ed. Georg Schatz, 2 vols. (Leipzig, 1791), II, 367; Sprengel and G. Forster, eds., *Neue Beiträge zur Völker und Länderkunde*, XII, 101–102; Carl August Böttiger, in *Neuer Teutscher Merkur*, Nov. 1793, 219–220; Ramsay, *Amerikanische Revolution*, I, iii–viii (preface by Günther Karl Friedrich Seidel); [Joel Barlow], *Guter Rath an die Völker Europens bei der Nothwendigkeit, die Regierungsgrundsätze überall zu verändern*, trans. from the En-

bourgeoisie, especially those who summarily rejected the French Revolution, were not satisfied with this kind of careful differentiation. Because of the events in France and because of the great distance between America and Europe, new as well as old adversaries of revolution, among them such men as von Schirach who had condemned the American Revolution before 1789, now denied any revolutionary, that is, subversive, importance to America. What was happening in Europe was incomparably more important and dangerous, so that condemnation of the American Revolution seemed no longer necessary or opportune. These antirevolutionaries thought it neither advisable nor feasible to compare the two events, and they vehemently rejected the interpretations of the French Revolution and the comparisons with the American made by their more open-minded contemporaries. They were convinced that it was necessary to separate good from evil. Putting the two events on the same level would mean "putting side by side reason and madness, wisdom and nonsense, morality and animal instincts, patriotism and wild fanaticism, heroism and recklessness, dignity and depravity, public spirit and roguery, and generous sacrifice and murderous lust."[34]

To be sure, this interpretation does not present a well-founded analysis of the two revolutions, but it shows that the position of the American Revolution in the German bourgeoisie's mental world of politics changed in the years of the French Revolution. On the one side, the moderate, virtuous American Revolution—isolated in a faraway part of the world and an already established fact—found more general approval; on the other side, the French Revolution came to exemplify wild fanaticism and imminent danger to the old society and all its adherents. For tradition-minded contemporaries, only consent to the American Revolution could provide a reasonable position from which to attack events in France.

The Importance of the American Revolution to the German Bourgeoisie in the 1790s

Looking back over the previous ten years, observers saw at the beginning of the 1790s a basic change in world politics that had left distinct traces on European consciousness. It was not only a matter of the American and the

---

glish by Johann Anton Fahrenkrüger, 2 vols. (London [i.e., Hamburg], 1792–1795), II, 57–58; *Europäische Annalen*, Jan. 1796, 15.

34. "das hieße, Vernunft mit Raserei, Weisheit mit Unsinn, Moralität mit Tierheit, Vaterlandsliebe mit wildem Fanatismus, Heldenmut mit Tollkühnheit, Würde mit Verworfenheit,

French revolutions but also of the latter's influence on the bourgeoisie's basic attitude toward the problem of revolution, which now seemed much more complex and difficult than past events in faraway America had made it appear to be. The attitude of bourgeois circles in Germany toward revolution grew more differentiated and encompassed the whole spectrum from enthusiastic approval to unqualified rejection.[35] Moreover, the increasing aversion to the events in France had aftereffects that were felt in Germany well beyond the middle of the nineteenth century.[36] For the first time, the German bourgeoisie seriously questioned their own ideals of liberty and equality, and began to doubt the very principles previously considered unconditionally true.[37]

As at the time of the American Revolution, contemporaries now tried in many ways to explain the events in France to themselves and to others, often by means of historical parallels. Recent events in America seemed more suitable for comparison with the French Revolution than any previous earth-shaking occurrence. A new set of questions completely changed the meaning of the American Revolution, partly because it now appeared as "the beginning of an anti-despotic trend,"[38] and partly because of the actual course of the French Revolution. Thus, there was established a renewed and lasting impetus among the German bourgeoisie to analyze the problems of the American Revolution specifically in relation to the French. It is not strange

---

Gemeingeist mit Beutelschneiderei und großmütige Aufopferung mit Mordlust zusammenstellen": "Untersuchung der Frage: Ob die Aufklärung Revolutionen befördere," *Deutsche Monatsschrift*, Jan. 1794, 30–31 (possibly by Friedrich von Gentz). See also *Politisches Journal*, May 1792, 496–497.

35. E.g., the opinions in Erhard to Karl Leonhard Reinhold, Jan. 16, 1792, in Karl August Varnhagen von Ense, ed., *Denkwürdigkeiten des Philosophen und Arztes Johann Benjamin Erhard* (Stuttgart, 1830), 338–339; Körner to Schiller, Nov. 4, 1794, in Schiller, *Werke*, National ed., XXXV, 87–88 (both laudatory); Jacobi to Zerleder, June 13, 1794, in Jacobi, *Auserlesener Briefwechsel*, II, 171 (rather cool); Friedrich Ludwig Wilhelm Meyer to Bürger, July 9, 1793, in Adolf Strodtmann, ed., *Briefe von und an Gottfried August Bürger...*, 4 vols. (Berlin, 1874), IV, 225–226 (strongly disapproving).

36. See Theodor Schieder, "Das Problem der Revolution im 19. Jahrhundert," in his *Staat und Gesellschaft im Wandel unserer Zeit* (Munich, 1958), 12, 14. For two individual views see Barthold Georg Niebuhr's preface, dated Oct. 5, 1830, to the second edition of Part II of his *Römische Geschichte*, I (Berlin, 1853), xx, and Jakob Burckhardt's introduction to his "Geschichte des Revolutionszeitalters" (1867–1871), in his "Weltgeschichtliche Betrachtungen: Historische Fragmente aus dem Nachlaß," in his *Gesamtausgabe*, ed. Albert Oeri and Emil Dürr, VII (Stuttgart, 1929), 420–437, 474–481.

37. E.g., Bürger's political prophecy, Jan. 24, 1793, in Strodtmann, ed., *Briefe von und an Bürger*, IV, 219; see also Moritz Friedrich to Albrecht von Münchhausen, Oct. 15, 1792 (StA, Wolfenbüttel) (both applauding); Christian Friedrich Fleischer to Friedrich Johann Justin Bertuch, Sept. 18, 1790 (Nachlaß Bertuch, I, 804, GSA, Weimar) (condemning).

38. "als der Anfang einer antidespotischen Progression der Dinge": Bülow, *Freistaat von Nordamerika*, II, 273.

that this reconsideration of the American Revolution in the 1790s brought to the fore many points of view different from those of the previous decade and a half. Thus, 1789 did not mark the end of German consideration of the origin of the United States but rather gave it an important new turn.

Christoph Daniel Ebeling decisively influenced this new phase of the encounter with the American Revolution and the United States. Like many of his fellow citizens, he took a lively, even passionate, interest in the French Revolution. Neither a Freemason nor a member of the Illuminati, though he boasted of friendships with many members of both groups in later years,[39] his attitude toward the French Revolution was very strained in the 1790s. In principle he welcomed it as warmly as he thought the entire German bourgeoisie did. "Even during the terrible catastrophe of the French Revolution the people in Germany were for the revolution itself and distinguished very well the transient accidental enormities from the goodness of the cause, and the blameful influence of aristocrats and English bribery from the furies of factions."[40] He was fully aware of the positive changes in Europe brought about by the French Revolution and therefore warmly approved of the revolution in Switzerland, stressing his personal acquaintance with Peter Ochs.[41] He was convinced that in France, too, the advantages of the revolution by far outweighed its disadvantages, and he firmly hoped for its successful conclusion.[42] Nevertheless, his approval of the course of events was not unqualified, and this, he knew, set him apart from the Jacobins,[43] since he was not willing to condone the cankers of the revolution, as he saw them, such as libertinism and bloody terror.[44]

Ebeling's convictions were deeply rooted in the bourgeois ideas of liberty and an orderly state, both of which he saw partly endangered by the course of events in France. His foremost aim, therefore, was to present his leading principles free of the historical distortion represented by French excesses, which

39. Cf. Ebeling to William Bentley, Mar. 13, 1799, in Lane, ed., *Letters of Ebeling*, 41–42, and to Jedidiah Morse, Mar. 20, 1799 (Morse Family Papers, YUL, New Haven, Conn.).

40. To Noah Webster, May 1, 1795 (Noah Webster Papers, NYPL, New York).

41. See Ebeling to Bentley, Feb. 13, 1798, in William C. Lane, ed., "Glimpses of European Conditions from the Ebeling Letters," Massachusetts Historical Society, *Proceedings*, LIX (1926), 328.

42. See Ebeling to Mathew Carey, Apr. 12, 1795 (Lea and Febiger Coll., PHi, Philadelphia); to Jeremy Belknap, Aug. 24, 1797, and to Bentley, Apr. 28, 1798, in Lane, ed., "Glimpses of European Conditions," Massachusetts Historical Society, *Proceedings*, LIX (1926), 328, 329; to Webster, Sept. 15, 1798 (Noah Webster Papers, NYPL, New York).

43. See Ebeling to Bentley, July 28, 1800, in Lane, ed., *Letters of Ebeling*, 79.

44. See Ebeling to Ezra Stiles, June 26, 1794, in Massachusetts Historical Society, *Collections*, 2d Ser., VIII (1826), 273; to Carey, Feb. 26, 1795 (Lea and Febiger Coll., PHi, Philadelphia).

meant using the United States as an example, for "is it not there that the terrible riddle presented by the French Revolution to a Europe still largely uninformed about North America was solved years since far more clearly and happily than here?"[45] In his own trouble-ridden times, the United States, thanks to its revolution, seemed to him far more happy than Europe, because its people were enjoying a wise constitution and the blessings of liberty and affluence in quiet and peace.[46] He wanted to exhibit in Europe this picture of a truly happy condition, for in the light of events in France, the German bourgeoisie needed an ideal to guide developments in their own country. He consequently interpreted his description of America as "a necessary one considering the great desire of my countrymen for being better acquainted with your happy country."[47] His basic intention, he said, was "to promote human happiness in my country by a faithful picture of your constitutions, laws, and Government."[48] This image of the United States as a happy country, quietly enjoying the blessings of liberty and its constitution, had arisen in Germany at the time of the American Revolution and was by no means original with Ebeling.[49] But the events in France and Ebeling's personality unmistakably contributed toward making this idea highly popular among the German bourgeoisie.[50]

Publications in those years clearly were influenced by these circumstances. Georg Forster, of all the German followers of the French Revolution, was most often occupied at this time with the United States and the history of

45. "Wird nicht dort das fürchterliche Rätsel, das die Französische Revolution dem mit Nordamerika noch immer so unbekannten Europa aufgegeben hat, nicht schon seit Jahren immer deutlicher und weit glücklicher aufgelöst als hier?": Ebeling, *Erdbeschreibung*, I, viii. See also Ebeling to Washington, Oct. 10, 1793 (Miscellaneous Letters Received by the Department of State, Record Group 59, NA, Washington, D.C.).

46. Cf. Ebeling, *Erdbeschreibung*, I, 246–247, and his letters to Carey, Mar. 15, 1793 (Lea and Febiger Coll., PHi, Philadelphia), and to Washington, Oct. 10, 1793 (Record Group 59, NA, Washington, D.C.).

47. Ebeling to Webster, May 1, 1795 (Noah Webster Papers, NYPL, New York); see also Ebeling to the American Philosophical Society, Oct. 14, 1793 (American Philosophical Society Archives [hereafter cited as APSA], Philadelphia), and to Belknap, Oct. 1, 1796, in "The Belknap Papers: Part III," Massachusetts Historical Society, *Collections*, 6th Ser., IV (1891), 609.

48. Ebeling to Jefferson, July 30, 1795 (Thomas Jefferson Papers, XCVIII, 16900, cf. 16898, LC, Washington, D.C.).

49. E.g., Friedrich Leopold to Christian Stolberg, Dec. 23, 1777, in F. L. Stolberg, *Briefe*, ed. Behrens, 99; Isaak Iselin to Franklin, July 28, 1778 (Franklin Papers, X, 154, APSL, Philadelphia).

50. For these views see among others *Vaterländische Chronik*, June 18, 1790, 422; Brissot de Warville, *Neue Reise*, Bayreuth ed., I, 35; Cooper, *Renseignemens sur l'Amerique*, vii, 86; Daniel Jenisch, *Geist und Charakter des achtzehnten Jahrhunderts, politisch, moralisch, ästhetisch und wissenschaftlich betrachtet*, 3 vols. (Berlin, 1800–1801), I, 213; Schilderung des gesellschaftlichen Lebens (c. 1800), fol. 53v (LB, Gotha).

its origin. Between 1790 and 1792 he was determined to translate David Ramsay's *History of the American Revolution* into German,[51] mainly because he was convinced that the American Constitution is "the most liberal one known to us for a large state."[52] Andreas Georg Friedrich von Rebmann, another member of the German Jacobins, thought that the political and social structure of the United States was exemplary.[53] The same predilection for America can be found in those bourgeois circles that had a more distant attitude toward the French Revolution. Günther Karl Friedrich Seidel, for example, the young Berlin professor who had succeeded Forster as the editor of the translation of Ramsay's history, also took it as his purpose—with an eye to France, of course—of drawing a picture of a country quietly enjoying liberty.[54] Paine's writings from the years of the American Revolution, now published in German, and Julius August Remer's and Joseph Milbiller's studies on the United States reveal the same intention. Thus, as late as 1800, countless Germans were attracted by this country, described to them as "the happiest country, a worldly paradise."[55]

Eberhard August Wilhelm Zimmermann

Ebeling's assessment of the American Revolution, most effectively displayed against the backdrop of the French Revolution, could not but affect the German bourgeoisie. Eberhard August Wilhelm Zimmermann, the Brunswick botanist, was most exhaustive in his research on the subject. Apart from his long-standing scientific interest in America, his concern with the United States had been clearly stimulated by the revolutionary developments in France. His work on comparing the two countries can be dated back to the collecting and translating phase, which must have started around 1791.[56] Zimmermann's political convictions, it appears, were behind his profound deliberations on the two revolutions. Doubtless, Enlightenment ideals had influenced him deeply, and he profoundly detested any form of despotism.[57]

51. Forster to Voss, Dec. 18, 1790, Mar. 27, 1792, in Forster, *Briefe an Voß*, ed. Zincke, 15, 134.

52. "die freieste, die wir in einem großen Staate kennen": Forster to his wife, Aug. 21, 1793, in Forster, *Briefwechsel*, ed. Huber, II, 551.

53. Cf. Rebmann, *Hans Kiekindiewelts Reisen*, 437–445.

54. See Seidel's notes to Ramsay, *Amerikanische Revolution*, I, iii–v, vi–viii, x, IV, iv–v, 58.

55. "als das glücklichste Land, als das irdische Paradies": *Reise von Hamburg nach Philadelphia*, 3, cf. 99. Also, Paine, *Gesunder Menschenverstand*, and his *Sammlung verschiedener Schriften*.

56. Zimmermann to David Rittenhouse, June 10, 1793 (APSA, Philadelphia).

57. E.A.W. Zimmermann, *Geographische Geschichte*, I, 24.

His ideal was a "rational liberty" which corresponded to bourgeois values and which, in his opinion, had been implemented only in the United States.[58] To be sure, the character of events in France had raised some doubts in his mind as to whether the recent developments in America could be called a revolution at all, or whether the American example was not rather a "so-called" revolution that was not and could never be a useful model for Europe.[59] However, when in the mid-1790s he meditated on the American model, it seemed to him that, compared to France and his own country, it was so excellent and so inspiring that he would like to have a similar transformation occur in Germany. He expressed himself very cautiously when he said: "As a true and honest patriot one can give expression to this wish without the least ill will toward one's own country."[60]

With these mental reservations Zimmermann set out to compare the American and French republics and their revolutions, "so far as light and shadow may be compared."[61] In a two-volume treatise, the first part of which he also translated into French,[62] Zimmermann related in great detail the concrete facts as seen from his point of view. The fundamental difference between the American and French revolutions, he thought, was that the former had positively protected private property, whereas the French revolutionaries had purposely attacked it and tried to destroy it. This, in his opinion, constituted the "glaring contrast" between the creative and constructive character of the American events and the inherent destructiveness of the French Revolution.[63]

This interpretation of the two revolutions in terms of attitudes toward private property was as erroneous as it was common among the German observers who watched the confiscation of property in France and the fate of the émigrés. Their almost complete disregard for the question of the loyalists and private property in their earlier discussions of the American Revolution had been a grave omission and was responsible for this evaluation. For neither of the revolutions systematically attacked private property, aside from a few

58. Zimmermann to Rittenhouse, June 10, 1793 (APSA, Philadelphia).

59. "sogenannte": Zimmermann's preface to his translation of Imlay, *Westliche Lande der Nordamerikanischen Freistaaten*, xv.

60. "Man kann daher jenen Wunsch als wahrer, redlicher Patriot äußern, ohne im mindesten etwas dem Vaterlande Widriges dabei zu ahnden": E.A.W. Zimmermann, *Frankreich und die Freistaaten*, I, 6.

61. Zimmermann to Rittenhouse, June 10, 1793 (APSA, Philadelphia); see also Zimmermann to Carey, June 12, 1794 (Lea and Febiger Coll., PHi, Philadelphia).

62. See Zimmermann to Bertuch, Oct. 1, 4, 1795, Jan. 25, 1798 (Nachlaß Bertuch, I, 3813, GSA, Weimar).

63. "grelle Kontrast": E.A.W. Zimmermann, *Frankreich und die Freistaaten*, esp. II, 593–594. See also the review of Vol. II in the *Politisches Journal*, June 1800, 581–585.

particular instances in both America and France;[64] on the contrary, they usually meticulously respected it.[65] In both revolutions, however, antirevolutionaries were persecuted and their property confiscated. Zimmermann, like many of his fellow citizens, ignored these facts in his investigation and went on to condemn severely the French Revolution, which to him seemed a "monstrous" occurrence. "Irrationality and malice were its parents; impotence, ignorance, and frivolity its godfathers!"[66]

On the other hand, he saw in the American Revolution an event of paradigmatic character. Its results, from his point of view, differed from the occurrences in France as day differed from night. "In America the (so-called) revolution was bound to effect peace with everybody, an increase in population, and a further improvement in all peaceful activities of life."[67] In contrast, the French Revolution had been nothing but destructive from the very start. Given his convictions, Zimmermann's purpose in contrasting the two revolutions could only have been to stress the exemplary, almost consummate bourgeois ideal of the United States. It was only logical, therefore, that he concluded his ambitious comparison with the wish: "May America continue to be a safe haven for the oppressed for a long time to come!"[68]

Friedrich von Gentz

Another, more famous, attempt to compare the American and French revolutions was that of Friedrich von Gentz. A writer and publicist employed in the Prussian Generaldirektorium in Berlin, and a follower of Kant and Rousseau, he welcomed the events in France from the start. A comment he made to his friend Christian Garve shows how firm a position he had taken by December 1790: "The failure of this revolution would in my view be one of the greatest disasters mankind has ever suffered. It is the first practical

64. See Arthur M. Schlesinger, Sr., "Political Mobs and the American Revolution, 1765–1776," in his *Nothing Stands Still*, ed. Schlesinger, Jr., 91; Palmer, *Age of the Democratic Revolution*, I, 188.

65. See John to Abigail Adams, Apr. 28, 1777, in Butterfield *et al.*, eds., *Adams Family Correspondence*, II, 227, in which John attributed "a violent attachment to property" to the Pennsylvania-Germans, which would cause them to take sides with the Revolution if the British troops were so ill-advised as to plunder just one of their farms.

66. "Ungeheuer. . . . Unvernunft und Bosheit waren ihre Eltern; Kraftlosigkeit, Unkunde und Leichtsinn ihre Paten!" E.A.W. Zimmermann, *Frankreich und die Freistaaten*, II, 583.

67. "In Amerika mußte die (sogenannte) Revolution den Frieden mit jedermann, eine größere Bevölkerung und weitere Vervollkommnung in allen ruhigen Geschäften des Lebens zu Wege bringen": *ibid.*, 598.

68. "Möge Amerika noch lange dem Unterdrückten ein sicheres Asyl sein!": *ibid.*, 612.

triumph of philosophy, the first example of a form of government founded on principles and on a coherent and consistent system. It offers hope and solace against so many old evils that oppress mankind."[69] And in the spring of 1791 he publicly mourned Mirabeau's death, praising him as a "benefactor of mankind."[70]

But in the following months of 1791–1792 Gentz, like many in bourgeois circles, completely reversed his attitude. He no longer believed that his own ideas could be reconciled with those manifested by the French Revolution, and he became convinced that the revolution was leading to destruction. He concluded that the existing political order would have to be defended by all possible means. Unlike Ebeling or E.A.W. Zimmermann, Gentz now became an evermore determined and uncompromising antirevolutionary.[71] It seems that Edmund Burke, who was to influence him greatly later on and whose writings he had first read while he still supported the revolution, was not alone responsible for this change, but Burke undoubtedly made it more decisive.[72]

In 1793, after undergoing this personal change, Gentz presented his first comparison of the American and French revolutions in his essay, "Über die Moralität in den Staatsrevolutionen," an appendix to his translation of Burke's *Reflections on the Revolution in France*. He started with the concept of a total revolution, which so far had occurred only in America and France. In analyzing both events, he isolated five fundamental conditions that must be present for a revolution to be justified. The crucial condition, in his view, was that there must be no appreciable resistance to the revolution from any social class; the revolution must progress as it did in America, where only a handful of royal officials actively resisted it. "A total revolution can be a com-

69. "Das Scheitern dieser Revolution würde ich für einen der härtesten Unfälle halten, die je das menschliche Geschlecht betroffen haben. Sie ist der erste praktische Triumph der Philosophie, das erste Beispiel einer Regierungsform, die auf Prinzipien und auf ein zusammenhängendes System gegründet wird. Sie ist die Hoffnung und der Trost für so viele alte Übel, unter denen die Menchheit seufzt": Dec. 5, 1790, in Wittichen and Salzer, eds., *Briefe von und an Gentz*, I, 178–179.

70. "Wohltäter der Menschheit": to Garve, Apr. 19, 1791, *ibid.*, 205.

71. Besides his correspondence with Garve, see Gentz to Johannes von Müller, May 8, 1799, in Gentz, *Staatsschriften und Briefe*, ed. Hans von Eckardt, 2 vols. (Munich, 1921), I, 270–271; Gentz, ed., *Historisches Journal*, I/1 (1799), 281; also Tschirch, *Öffentliche Meinung in Preußen*, I, 20.

72. Adrien Robinet de Clery, *Les Idées politiques de Frédéric de Gentz* (Lausanne, 1917), 84, 112–113, Paul R. Sweet, *Friedrich von Gentz, Defender of the Old Order* (Madison, Wis., 1941), 20–23, and M. A. Bond, "The Political Conversion of Friedrich von Gentz," *European Studies Review*, III (1973), esp. 6–11, all believe that Burke had little direct influence on Gentz's change of mind. Golo Mann, *Friedrich von Gentz. Geschichte eines europäischen*

pletely legitimate enterprise only if the entire nation concerned approves it unanimously and without the slightest internal resistance."[73]

The tenor of these statements leaves no doubt as to the writer's intentions: Gentz's only concern was a complete condemnation of the French Revolution. His knowledge of American history may indeed have been as meager as is indicated here, particularly since the loyalist problem had never commanded much attention in Germany. But it is incredible that Gentz, who a few years before had extolled the achievements of bourgeois ideals against the inherited monarchical and aristocratic system of government, was really convinced that a revolution could be the common accomplishment of all social classes, with almost no opposition, instead of a struggle of the oppressed against the privileged.

Gentz's second, better-known, and far lengthier comparison of the two revolutions was published in 1800 in his *Historisches Journal*.[74] The concept of total revolution was no longer a factor, and there was no mention of a lack of resistance in America; in fact, Gentz frankly admitted that there indeed had been a small measure of opposition.[75] This formerly essential criterion for legitimacy was replaced in the second treatise by a distinction between defensive and offensive revolutions. England, Gentz maintained, had used violent measures against which the Americans were compelled to defend themselves; thus, their revolution was a defensive one. In addition, the Americans always had been wisely self-restrained and had never lost sight of their limited aims. This, he believed, was the abiding merit of the American patriots as compared to the French revolutionaries.[76]

Gentz considered the French Revolution to have been offensive in character, nothing more than senseless upheaval and complete anarchy. "The American Revolution was founded partly on principles whose legality was evident, partly on those whose illegality at least was very doubtful, and not at

---

Staatsmannes (Zurich and Vienna, 1947), 38, gives far greater emphasis to Burke's influence; similarly, Godechot, *Contre-Révolution*, 127.

73. "Eine Totalrevolution ist nur in dem einzigen Fall ein vollkommen rechtmäßiges Unternehmen, wenn die ganze Nation, die sie trifft, einmütig und ohne den geringsten innern Widerspruch dafür stimmt": Gentz, "Über die Moralität in den Staatsrevolutionen," in his *Betrachtungen über die französische Revolution*, II, 144–174, esp. 172–173, cf. his introduction, I, xxxiv–xxxv.

74. "Der Ursprung und die Grundsätze der Amerikanischen Revoluzion, verglichen mit dem Ursprunge und den Grundsätzen der Französischen," *Historisches Journal*, II/2 (1800), 3–140. John Quincy Adams translated this essay into English; cf. Adams to Gentz, June 16, 1800, in W. C. Ford, ed., *Writings of John Quincy Adams*, II, 463–464.

75. Gentz, "Ursprung und Grundsätze," *Historisches Journal*, II/2 (1800), 126.

76. *Ibid.*, 64–65, 74, 89–90, 97–98, 101–102.

all, from beginning to end, on principles that were definitely illegal. The French Revolution was an uninterrupted sequence of actions whose illegality, strictly speaking, could not even be doubted."[77] Only seven years earlier this same author had asserted that it was the American example "that the French legislators . . . imitated; the maxims of the Americans protected the growth and flowering of this new free state."[78]

As these contradictions show, Gentz had by now completely abandoned the basis of his first comparison and was fitting his argumentation entirely to the circumstances of the long wars of coalition. By using the American Revolution primarily as a foil for condemnation of the French Revolution, and by altering his interpretation of it as necessity dictated, Gentz revealed that the event itself meant very little to him. He used it simply as an instrument in the present dispute and referred only to men like John Dickinson, John Jay, Franklin, and John Adams, whom he thought were relatively harmless, while he completely rejected Paine.[79]

Gentz was unquestionably a political thinker of exceptional gifts, and his statements show that he was reasonably well acquainted with the American scene. Therefore, it seems doubtful that he would be unaware of the deep rift between his own political views and those that found expression in the American Revolution. But since he merely wanted to condemn the French Revolution and the danger it presented to the existing European system of government, these differences were of minor importance to him. By contrasting events in France with those in America, he endeavored to deprive the former of even a shadow of legitimacy, as he had already attempted in 1793, although at that time with less vehemence and aggressiveness. "The French Revolution started as an infringement of laws. Each of its phases has been an infringement of laws; and it did not stop until it had succeeded in establishing absolute lawlessness as the supreme and recognized maxim of a completely disintegrated state existing only in bloody ruins."[80] This position sets him

77. "Die amerikanische Revolution gründete sich zum Teil auf Prinzipien, deren Rechtmäßigkeit evident, zum Teil auf solche, deren Unrechtmäßigkeit wenigstens sehr zweifelhaft, und von Anfang bis zu Ende auf keins, dessen Rechtswidrigkeit klar entschieden war. Die Französische war eine ununterbrochene Folge von Schritten, deren Rechtswidrigkeit sich nach strengen Grundsätzen nicht einmal bezweifeln ließ": *ibid.*, II/2, 48; cf. Gentz, "General Washington," *ibid.*, II/1 (1800), 303–304.

78. "was die französischen Gesetzgeber . . . nachahmten; es waren die Maxime, unter deren Schutz dieser neue Freistaat aufgewachsen war und blühte": Gentz, "Moralität in den Staatsrevolutionen," in his *Betrachtungen über die französische Revolution*, II, 163.

79. Gentz, "Ursprung und Grundsätze," *Historisches Journal*, II/2 (1800), 105–108. Consequently, he saw in the American Revolution no example that could be applied to Europe; Gentz, *Betrachtungen über die französische Revolution*, II, 321.

80. "Die Französische Revolution hat also mit Übertretung der Rechte angefangen. Jeder ihrer Schritte ist Übertretung der Rechte gewesen; und sie hat nicht eher geruht, als bis es ihr

distinctly apart from E.A.W. Zimmermann. Under the impact of the French Revolution, and against the background of the American, Gentz constructed the philosophy of reaction that was to become so powerful in the nineteenth century, a philosophy that rejected on principle any change of governmental structure that would give more political influence to the liberal bourgeoisie and tried to perpetuate the world of the *ancien régime* as it was before 1789 or 1776.

Other Comparisons

Zimmermann and Gentz were not the only German observers who contrasted the American and French revolutions, though these two men published the most detailed and important comparisons of the 1790s. Other contemporaries also deserve mention, even if their thoughts were not published in coherent form or explicitly formulated. One of these is Friedrich Leopold Graf zu Stolberg. In the 1770s and 1780s he was a confirmed follower of the bourgeois ideal of liberty[81] and so utterly convinced of the righteousness of the American Revolution and its blessed character that he seriously asked himself: "What can God do about a man who declares himself against the Americans?"[82]

This statement points to the two criteria Stolberg later used in judging the French Revolution: his ideal of liberty, which prompted him at first to welcome the French Revolution, just as he had welcomed the American;[83] and his basic religious and moral convictions, which caused him to detach himself from the French revolutionaries in the following years and to characterize the events west of the Rhine as ungodly and depraved.[84] At first he excluded the American Revolution from this later judgment and did not interpret it as a detestable event. But this distinction was no more than a

---

gelungen war, die absolute Rechtlosigkeit zur obersten und anerkannten Maxime eines gänzlich aufgelöseten und nur noch in blutigen Ruinen existierenden Staates zu erheben": Gentz, "Ursprung und Grundsätze," *Historisches Journal*, II/2 (1800), 73–74.

81. See Stolberg, "Die Freiheit," in *Musenalmanach für das Jahr 1775* (Göttingen, n.d.), 221. On Stolberg see King, "Echoes of the American Revolution," *PMP*, XIV (1930), 32.

82. "Was könnte Gott anfangen mit einem Menschen, der sich gegen die Amerikaner... erklärt?": to Emilia Schimmelmann, Sept. 25, 1776, in Stolberg, *Briefe*, ed. Behrens, 84. Cf. Stolberg to Luise von Gramm, Oct. 22, 1776, and to Christian Stolberg, Dec. 23, 1777, *ibid.*, 86, 99; also F. L. Stolberg, "Die Zukunft," ed. Hartwig, *ALG*, XIII (1885), 269–270.

83. See Stolberg to Voss, July 21, 1789, in Otto Hellinghaus, ed., *Briefe Friedrich Leopolds Grafen zu Stolberg und der Seinigen an Johann Heinrich Voss* (Münster, 1891), 225, and Stolberg to Gerhard Anton von Halem, Jan. 4, 1790, in Stolberg, *Briefe*, ed. Behrens, 252.

84. Stolberg to Friedrich Heinrich Jacobi, Jan. 13, Feb. 17, 1793, and to Christian Stolberg, Nov. 1, 1797, in F. L. Stolberg, *Briefe*, ed. Behrens, 297, 345–346.

postponement, for eventually Jeffersonian democracy and the long wars of coalition against France made him include the American Revolution and the United States as well; by 1810 he viewed both in an almost completely negative light.[85]

Josef von Sartori, a scholar and librarian from southern Germany who had lived in Vienna since the early 1790s, took a somewhat different view of these events. At the time of the Treaty of Paris we find him expressing sympathy with the American colonies.[86] A scant ten years later he commented in a similarly positive way on the French Revolution, of which, referring to Paine, he thought the events in America were a forerunner.[87] But he soon saw some differences. True, "the French Revolution originated in North America," and "both revolutions had the same motives," but "the North American Revolution was carried out under the rule of the closest unity, without a constitution, and always with moderation against a recognized enemy, whereas the French Revolution was marked by the most horrible cruelties under the shield of the constitutions."[88]

Sartori expressed in these passages the idea of the artificiality and unnaturalness of written constitutions as compared to the rule of ancient customs and privileges, a belief held by many tradition-minded contemporaries in the 1790s and later. In 1798 he wrote: "The motives, the means, and the course of these two revolutions differed as much as did their respective consequences." While he believed the Frenchman was criminal and devilish in his revolution, he admitted about the American that "the state of his own happiness was his only intention, purpose, and aim."[89] Sartori was not opposed, as Gentz was, to revolutions in principle; his reasoning was more in line with Zimmermann's discriminating approach. But like Stolberg, by the

---

85. F. L. to Luise Stolberg, Oct. 29, 1810, *ibid.*, 415; as an example of an earlier, much more moderate, critique, see his letter to Voss, Apr. 18, 1786, in Hellinghaus, ed., *Briefe Stolbergs an Voss*, 154.

86. Sartori, "Bemerkungen der englischen Staatsfehler" (Cod. ser. nov. 1642, NB, Vienna).

87. Sartori, "Nord-Amerika" (c. 1792), esp. fol. 68v (*ibid.*, 1640).

88. "Die Französische Revolution hat in Nordamerika ihren Ursprung erhalten.... Beide Revolutionen hatten ebendieselben Bewegungsgründe. . . . Die Revolution in Nordamerika wurde durch das Gesetz der engsten Vereinigung, ohne Konstitution, mit aller Mäßigung gegen ihren anerkannten Feind durchgesetzt; die Französische zeichnete sich aber unter dem Schild der Konstitutionen durch die abscheulichsten Grausamkeiten aus": Sartori, "Verhältnisse in Nordamerika in Bezug auf die französische Revolution" (c. 1795–1796), esp. fols. 2v, 3r–v (*ibid.*, 1653).

89. "Die Bewegungsgründe, die Mittel und der Gang dieser beiden Revolutionen waren so verschieden als der Kontrast von den Folgen, welche die Revolutionen erzeugten.... Der Zustand seiner eigenen Glückseligkeit war seine einzige Absicht, Endzweck und Bestreben": Sartori, "Betrachtungen über die Verhältnisse Frankreichs mit den nordamerikanischen Staaten" (1798), fols. 26, 28 (*ibid.*, 1655).

beginning of the nineteenth century he had struck a very detached attitude toward the American Revolution.[90]

An analysis of the various comparisons of the American and French revolutions makes it clear that after the initial euphoria following 1789, the interpretation of the French Revolution became frozen into a stereotype in the minds of many of the German bourgeoisie. The two revolutions, it was agreed, had some more or less common elements, chiefly in their original principles, but the differences were widely recognized to be preponderant, and German sympathies generally favored the Americans. This differentiated evaluation was to be found throughout the German bourgeoisie, including both avowed antirevolutionaries and German Jacobins such as Georg Forster and Rebmann.[91] The Jacobins believed that the differences were not a matter of principle but only of details and methods, while the antirevolutionaries placed more emphasis on the differences in principle as well as in substance.

This situation was of far-reaching importance. In the 1770s and 1780s the implementation of bourgeois ideals in America was cause for enthusiasm, but not idolatry. The French Revolution, however, influenced this appreciation to such an extent that, by 1793, the majority of the bourgeoisie no longer viewed the American Revolution merely as a welcome realization of their own opinions. The events in the New World were now so much lauded and exalted that they became the ideal of political action, and, in a way, the prototype of any possible good and justifiable revolution.[92] This idealization of the American Revolution and the conception of its exemplary character reveals once more the German bourgeoisie's political wishes and dreams, as well as their faulty interpretation of events during the last quarter of the century.

90. Sartori, "Neueste Memoiren über die wichtigsten Europäischen Staatsbegebenheiten unserer Zeit" (1806–1807), I, 73–74 (*ibid.*, 12724).

91. See Forster to his wife, Aug. 21, 1793, in Forster, *Briefwechsel*, ed. Huber, II, 551; Rebmann, *Hans Kiekindiewelts Reisen*, 437–445.

92. See Vossler, *Amerikanische Revolutionsideale*, 64–65; also Waldeck, *Diary of the American Revolution*, ed. Learned, 75 (entry of July 15, 1778); Rush to the ministers of the gospel, June 21, 1788, in Butterfield, ed., *Letters of Benjamin Rush*, I, 466.

The Influence of the French Revolution on German Appraisal of the American Revolution

The preceding deliberations have already hinted at the problem of interpreting the German reaction to the French Revolution insofar as it influenced German appraisal of the American Revolution. But it is necessary to enter more deeply into these questions and investigate the various political views of the German bourgeoisie, especially since scholarly conclusions on these matters have, in my opinion, sometimes been incorrect. Some investigators, starting with the known fact that large sectors of the bourgeoisie turned away from the French Revolution in the 1790s, have concluded that this step equaled a rejection of every kind of revolution and that the detachment from the French Revolution necessitated a similar detachment from the American.[93] The examples of Stolberg and Sartori do indicate that such a change may have occurred in Napoleonic times; but it seems to me to be very debatable whether a reaction, such as is claimed to have taken place in the 1790s as a direct consequence of the change in attitude toward the French Revolution, actually occurred.

We must first of all keep in mind a point confirmed by modern historical research as well as by German opinion at the time, that there is a connection between the two revolutions based on more or less distinct elements common to each. Both were movements aimed at implementing certain bourgeois political ideas. But they differed decidedly as to their antecedent situation, their course, and their immediate effects in Germany, and both were multifaceted and highly complex events. We shall see how the spectrum of opinion that had developed within the bourgeoisie compared and appraised the two revolutions in the 1790s.

Looking first at the antirevolutionaries, we are not surprised to find that those who had rejected the events in America in 1776 took the same position toward France in 1789, for they spurned the bourgeois ideas that underlay these cataclysms. Yet the French Revolution did influence their attitudes toward the American somewhat; a change in their opinions can be seen in 1791–1792, at the same time that their condemnation of the French Revolution was finding more and more adherents among the bourgeoisie. Together

93. E.g., Wehe, "Amerika-Erlebnis," *Geist der Zeit*, XVII (1939), 99; Desczyk, "Amerika in der Phantasie deutscher Dichter," *Deutsch-Amerikanische Geschichtsblätter*, XXIV/XXV (1925), 46–47; Jantz, "Amerika im deutschen Dichten und Denken," in Stammler, ed., *Deutsche Philologie*, III, 332–333; also Palmer, *Age of the Democratic Revolution*, I, 240; Fraenkel, *Amerika im Spiegel des deutschen politischen Denkens*, 24.

with their new allies, they viewed America and its revolution, which had run such a harmless course when compared with the events in France, in a much more favorable light.[94] For the United States of America did not threaten the existing political order in Germany, but the French Revolution did. This "detestable matter about the Jacobins revolutionizing the whole world" excited fear and horror.[95] The American Revolution, on the other hand, seemed to be "an example of moderation," limited to its own, faraway country, with no effort to export its political ideas by force or to endanger directly the existing order in other states.[96]

Throughout the 1790s the antirevolutionaries, old or recent, adhered to their relatively benevolent opinion of the American Revolution. But their favorable comparison of the past events in America with the current turmoil in France was not an indication that they had suddenly come to like American implementation of bourgeois revolutionary ideas, as the example of Gentz's comparisons makes clear. They believed that the American Revolution was exemplary only because it was a remote, quasi-internal event that had not threatened Germany's political order. In later years the antirevolutionaries, prompted by political and military developments in Europe and by Jeffersonian democracy,[97] again expressed some coolness toward America's recent history.[98]

Thus, the experience of the French Revolution did not negatively influence the antirevolutionaries' judgment of the American Revolution. Rather, in the 1790s, for the reasons we have seen, it produced the opposite results. It is not surprising, then, that those sectors of the bourgeoisie that exalted

94. See, e.g., Schirach's *Politisches Journal* during these years; also J. G. Zimmermann to Christoph Girtanner, Nov. 18, 1791 (GSA, Weimar); Heinrich Martin Gottfried Köster to de Luc, Dec. 10, 1796 (Jean André de Luc Collection, YUL, New Haven, Conn.).

95. "abscheuliche Sache um dieses jakobinische Revolutionieren der ganzen Welt": Christoph Martin Wieland to Frau Geßner, Feb. 26, 1798. Cf. Wieland to Heinrich Geßner, Mar. 18, 1798, both in Wieland, *Ausgewählte Briefe*, IV, 210, 217. Also, Heinrich August Ottokar Reichard to J. G. Zimmermann, Jan. 1, 1793 (Nachlaß Zimmermann, A II, no. 75, fol. 19, LB, Hanover); *Geist des achtzehnten Jahrhunderts . . .* (Augsburg, 1793), 21, 29; Köster to de Luc, Dec. 10, 1796 (Jean André de Luc Collection, YUL, New Haven, Conn.); see also the poem by Johann Kaspar Lavater on the beginning of the 19th century (copy in Nachlaß Israel Hartmann, Büschel 67, StA, Ludwigsburg).

96. "ein Muster der Mäßigung": Gentz, "Ursprung und Grundsätze," *Historisches Journal*, II/2 (1800), 89, cf. 97–98, 101–102. Also, Sartori, "Verhältnisse in Nordamerika," fol. 4, and his "Betrachtungen über die Verhältnisse Frankreichs," fols. 26–27 (Cod. ser. nov. 1653, 1655, NB, Vienna).

97. See Merrill D. Peterson, *The Jefferson Image in the American Mind* (New York, 1960), 67–111; Max Beloff, *Thomas Jefferson and American Democracy* (New York, 1962), 152–183, 198–207.

98. E.g., Sartori, "Neueste Memoiren," I, § 15 (Cod. 12724, NB, Vienna); Friedrich Leopold to Luise Stolberg, Oct. 29, 1810, in F. L. Stolberg, *Briefe*, ed. Behrens, 415.

America as the realization of their own ideals would continue to hold such positive opinions, even though they turned against France after 1791–1792. E.A.W. Zimmermann and numerous others stated their convictions with full particulars. In the light of their idealism, the United States was a genuine model, that had nothing in common with the detestable spectacle of revolutionary France. "Surely, this miraculously emerging republic looks completely different. Everybody there also speaks of liberty, but it is not spoken with murder and robbery in mind. They are peaceful and quiet citizens; . . . good, gentle people imbued with all the virtues of a respectable middle class."[99]

Since these bourgeoisie were already convinced of the righteousness and moderation of the American Revolution, their retrospective appraisal of it could not be negatively influenced by the French Revolution. Instead, their clear condemnation of events in France threw into stark relief the exemplary character of the American Revolution and the present United States. If the developments in the French republic affected these sectors of the German bourgeoisie at all, it was generally to influence them in favor of America.

Let us turn to the sympathizers of the French Revolution, who may be distinguished from the more radical German Jacobins by a certain reservedness in their attitudes. The best example among the better-known personalities is the poet Friedrich Gottlieb Klopstock. At first he spoke of his enthusiasm for the French Revolution with the same emphasis he had employed when pleading the American patriots' cause,[100] and many of his contemporaries criticized him severely for it.[101] Some investigators have maintained that Klopstock, later disappointed by the course of the French Revolution, was compelled to be less sympathetic toward America.[102] In this context his ode "Zwei Nordamerikaner," written in 1795, is often cited as proof. But if we look at it more closely, we see that the poet presented America and the American Revolution as a paradigm and prototype for France. To be sure,

99. "Freilich ist es ein ganz anderer Anblick, welchen dieser mit Wunderkraft aufstrebende Freistaat gewährt. Auch dort tönet das Wort Freiheit auf allen Lippen; aber die es aussprechen, nähren nicht Mordlust und Raubgier im Herzen. Es sind friedliche stille Bürger . . .; es sind gute sanfte Menschen mit allen Tugenden des achtungswürdigen Mittelstandes": *Berlinische Monatsschrift*, May 1793, 400.

100. E.g., Klopstock to François Alexandre Frédéric, duc de la Rochefoucauld Liancourt, June 25, 1790, and Lavater to Klopstock, Jan. 30, 1793, both in Johann Martin Lappenberg, ed., *Briefe von und an Klopstock* (Brunswick, 1867), 332, 351.

101. E.g., Johann Wilhelm Ludwig Gleim to Bürger, Nov. 15, 1789, in Strodtmann, ed., *Briefe von und an Bürger*, III, 293 (rather critical); J. G. Zimmermann to Girtanner, Nov. 18, 1791 (GSA, Weimar) (sharply condemning).

102. See Wehe, "Amerika-Erlebnis," *Geist der Zeit*, XVII (1939), 99; Desczyk, "Amerika in der Phantasie deutscher Dichter," *Deutsch-Amerikanische Geschichtsblätter*, XXIV/XXV (1925), 46–47.

Klopstock was most unhappy about the bloody course of the French Revolution, but unlike many of his fellow citizens, he never let these developments lead him to break with it entirely.[103] As for the American Revolution, there was nothing to prompt him to turn away, and he continued to regard it as exemplary.

Klopstock's friend Christoph Daniel Ebeling had similar ideas about the great drama in France and is an even better example of this moderate attitude. At the end of 1793 Ebeling wrote to Mathew Carey: "The conflict of aristocracy and the people is terrible in France, but perhaps unavoidable, and is kept up alive as well by Robespierre's faction as by English bribering [*sic*] and secret connections in France."[104] While this remained his attitude toward the French Revolution during the following years, he took a more lively interest in the United States than any of his German contemporaries, drawing a detailed picture of the land of his desires, whose past revolution and present Constitution seemed to him to be equally exemplary. In view of the respect Ebeling enjoyed among his fellow citizens in the 1790s, he probably found followers, at least among those who shared his basic political convictions.

The German Jacobins' attitudes toward the American Revolution were very similar. Georg Forster had reduced their conceptions to the formula: "One is either for absolute liberty or for absolute tyranny. There is no middle way."[105] They thought of both America and France as experiments in implementing bourgeois rule. America's Revolution, in their opinion, had allowed that nation to put this ideal into practice, whereas France was still striving for success. They approved of America without qualification. Men like Adolf Freiherr von Knigge and Rebmann exemplified this view, and Georg Forster, for one, as late as the 1790s made an intensive study of the United States, seeing in Franklin a veritable idol.[106] Like many German Jacobins, they were convinced that the Americans had preceded them on their way to liberty and that the principles realized in the New World constituted the goals of their own political actions.[107]

103. Klopstock, *Sämmtliche Werke*, VI, 175–176; see also Goebel, "Amerika in der deutschen Dichtung," in *Forschungen zur deutschen Philologie*, 105.

104. Ebeling to Carey, Nov. 30, 1793; cf. Ebeling to Carey, Mar. 12, 1794, Feb. 26, Apr. 12, 1795 (all in Lea and Febiger Coll., PHi, Philadelphia).

105. "Man ist entweder für absolute Freiheit oder für absolute Tyrannei. Ein Mittelding gibt es nicht": Forster to his wife, Feb. 4, 1793, in Forster, *Briefwechsel*, ed. Huber, II, 411.

106. Knigge, *Joseph von Wurmbrand*, 44, 46; Rebmann, *Hans Kiekindiewelts Reisen*, 437–445. See Forster's considerations on Franklin in his *Erinnerungen aus dem Jahr 1790*.

107. See the broadside published by Grab, *Norddeutsche Jakobiner*, 107–109. See also among others Johann Kaspar Hirzel to his son Johann Jakob, Oct. 30, 1791 (Familienarchiv Hirzel, CCLXXVIII, 70, ZB, Zurich); Gerning, *Das achtzehnte Jahrhundert*.

This brief survey of the major groupings of political opinion among the German bourgeoisie in the 1790s shows that the French Revolution could appreciably influence popular judgment about America but that it obviously did not necessarily bring about emotional or intellectual detachment from the American Revolution.[108] As late as the 1780s the United States represented an ideal, the country in which bourgeois thinking had been transmuted from theory to practice. Ten years later, the United States was no longer the only ideal, for a similar experiment had been tried elsewhere. But by then both anti- and prorevolutionists agreed that the United States had become an example. To the former, this meant that the American Revolution was an isolated, moderate affair and would not spread to their country and endanger its political order. To the latter, imitation of America seemed a sure way to success, even if the differing prerequisites in each country permitted only vague feelings of hope rather than knowledge of how this model was to be made generally practicable.

One thing is clear. The American Revolution was no longer a controversial subject among the German bourgeoisie as the century ended. Even its former antagonists had come to accept as final a political entity they could not change anyway. This concluded the German bourgeoisie's direct political discussion about the American Revolution for the time being. The French cataclysm was clearly more important in the 1790s, but the very discussion of those events showed that even in this period the American Revolution was still an important factor in the German bourgeoisie's political consciousness.

108. See also Meyer, *Nordamerika im Urteil des Deutschen Schrifttums*, 10; Wertheim, "Amerikanische Unabhängigkeitskampf," *Weimarer Beiträge*, III (1957), 469; Skard, *American Studies in Europe*, I, 220.

II. *The United States and Europe in the 1790s*

America as a Bourgeois Utopia

Throughout the 1790s, despite the establishment of the new republic of the United States, Germans continued to be impressed principally by the American Revolution and its ideals. Nevertheless, there was some interest shown in the young American state under the presidencies of George Washington and John Adams.

The German bourgeoisie's appreciation of the young republic was directly related to their comparison of it with the French Revolution. They liked to see the United States as a sort of ideal. "Among all states there is perhaps no other like the new North American republic, which took into consideration at its very beginning both economic and philosophical principles."[1] It was a virtuous republic of free citizens. "Everything indicates that America's government is powerful and active, that justice is impartial and vigilant, and that men whose reason, knowledge, and virtue merit the respect of all who know them have the greatest influence on public affairs. All this must convince any reasonable and knowledgeable man."[2] To the educated German bourgeoisie this American state, striving for liberty, the abolition of privileges, and the rationalization of political power, was exemplary, especially since its citizens enjoyed at the same time appreciable material affluence.[3] "All this they owe not only to their fertile soil but mainly to their

1. "Unter allen Staaten ist vielleicht nicht einer, der so wie der neue nordamerikanische Freistaat sogleich in der Wiege teils auf kaufmännische, teils auf philosophische Grundsätze Rücksicht genommen": *Historische Uebersicht von Europens Entwicklung seit dem sechzehnten Jahrhundert bis gegen Ende des achtzehnten* ([Leipzig], 1795), 48.

2. "Alles beweist, daß die Regierung von Amerika mächtig und tätig, daß die Gerechtigkeit unparteiisch und wachsam ist und daß solche Männer auf die öffentlichen Angelegenheiten den größten Einfluß haben, deren Verstand, Kenntnisse und Tugend sie der Achtung aller, die sie kennen, würdig machen. Dies alles muß den vernünftigen und unterrichteten Mann überzeugen": Bericht über die politischen und wirtschaftlichen Verhältnisse in Nordamerika (1790) (HptStA, Hanover).

3. See *ibid.*; Lutyens, *Zustand der Auswanderung*, 5; and the same in Hegewisch and Ebeling, eds., *Amerikanisches Magazin*, II, 25.

moderate and rational liberty, their low taxes, and their complete tolerance of all religions."[4]

Indeed, the idea of general religious tolerance, revived by the Revolution, was a major part of the German picture of America. The Virginia Statute for Religious Freedom of 1786 had a lasting influence on German thinking and was one of the few American laws of the time to arouse considerable interest in Germany.[5] True, there continued to be some religious discrimination in the United States,[6] but as a rule it went unnoticed. Throughout the eighteenth century the German public believed that the exercise of religion was generally unfettered in America, and when the prevailing practice became an article of constitutional law, it unquestionably influenced the German bourgeoisie's appreciation of the United States.[7]

As a result of these ideas, the picture of a typical American was one of a man educated, industrious, tolerant, benevolent, and virtuous,[8] in short, the ideal republican. The most eminent, and yet still typical, examples were, of course, Franklin and Washington. Also, the Quakers were generally thought of as the embodiment of this social type,[9] for they represented the ideals of the age more than any other religious group, and Germans usually were sympathetic and open-minded toward them.[10] In view of the popularity of

4. "Und dies alles verdanken sie nicht etwa bloß ihrem fruchtbaren Boden, sondern hauptsächlich ihrer gemäßigten, vernünftigen Freiheit, ihren geringen Abgaben und ihrer vollkommenen Toleranz gegen jede Religion": E.A.W. Zimmermann, in his preface to Imlay, *Westliche Lande der Nordamerikanischen Freistaaten*, xii.

5. For its publication see among others *Neue Litteratur und Völkerkunde*, Jan. 1787, 85–89; a transcript of the statute is in Nachlaß Johann Kaspar Ruef (UB, Freiburg, Germany).

6. See Alvin W. Johnson and Frank H. Yost, *Separation of Church and State in the United States* (Minneapolis, 1948), 3; R. E. Brown, *Middle-Class Democracy*, 108–109; Clifton E. Olmstead, *History of Religion in the United States* (Englewood Cliffs, N.J., 1960), 43–45, 54–56, 88, 97; see also John W. Platner et al., *The Religious History of New England* (Cambridge, Mass., 1917), 54–55.

7. See Jedidiah Morse, "Über die verschiedenen vornehmsten Religionspartheyen in den nordamerikanischen Freystaaten," in Sprengel, ed., *Ausländische geographische und statistische Nachrichten*, V (1796), 243–288. See also the letter to Congress dated Dec. 2, 1783, from Leer, Eastern Frisia, communicated by an H. Dulheuer (or Dulhire), in which is mentioned the plan to settle 4,500 families of Mennonites from Eastern Frisia, Holland, Krefeld, the Palatinate, and Switzerland on the mouth of the Ohio River (Papers of the Continental Congress, 78, VIII, 77–80, NA, Washington, D.C.). I am indebted to Dr. Gerhard Kollmann, Cologne, for bringing this letter to my attention.

8. See *Schilderung des gesellschaftlichen Lebens* (c. 1800) (LB, Gotha).

9. Note the character of the Quaker in the following plays: Johann Christoph von Zabuesnig, *Lucy Hopeleß, oder der Quäker in Amerika* (Augsburg, 1783); Johann Heinrich Bösenberg, "Die amerikanische Waise," in his *Dramatischer Beytrag für das Hoftheater in Dresden* (Dresden and Leipzig, 1791), 289–336; Wilhelm Vogel, *Der Amerikaner* (Hamburg and Altona, 1798); see also the novel *Die Freundschaft im Kloster oder der Amerikanische Flüchtling* (Leipzig, 1781).

10. See [Jacques Pierre Brissot de Warville], *Karakteristik der Quäker*, trans. from the French by Karl Julius Friedrich (Bad Dürkheim, 1792); William Penn, *Kurze Nachricht von*

this sect and the low level of knowledge of the real denominational structure of the United States, it is not altogether surprising that this picture of the good Quaker was very soon enlarged to cover all Americans.

Franklin's reception in Paris shows how much the picture of the virtuous Quaker simply overshadowed all other German images of the American. Franklin's relatively unostentatious conduct in an environment supersaturated with prodigal pomp, and his humane, modest, likeable, and simple appearance made him into an exemplary Quaker in the eyes of a European bourgeoisie dependent on secondhand reports, even though this most outstanding representative of the American Enlightenment was not a member of the sect.[11] This estimation, which was as prevalent in France as in Germany and was even met with in persons who had had direct contact with Franklin,[12] shows the degree to which the picture of the good and virtuous American had been idealized by the German bourgeoisie during the 1780s and 1790s, reflecting as it did their own wishes.

In view of such conceptions, which were contradicted only by a few skeptics or anti-Americans,[13] the United States presented a tremendous lure to large sectors of the German population. At a later date Goethe remembered this as a time when America was Eldorado to those oppressed by circumstances.[14] The marquis de Chastellux joyfully expressed his feelings for this country "from which the first rays of the happiest government have emanated."[15] And Brissot de Warville perceived in America "the miraculous influence of liberty on mankind."[16] Many Germans were no less effusive than Chastellux and Brissot. "Is it not the safest haven from religious as well as political despotism?"[17] For the German bourgeoisie America was unequaled

---

der Entstehung und dem Fortgang der christlichen Gesellschaft der Freunde, trans. from the English (Pyrmont and Hanover, 1792); Jean Marsillac, *Leben Wilhelm Penns des Stifters von Pennsylvanien*, trans. from the French (Strasbourg, 1793).

11. See Alfred Owen Aldridge, *Benjamin Franklin and Nature's God* (Durham, N.C., 1967), 8, and *passim*.

12. See Claude Anne Lopez, *Mon Cher Papa, Franklin and the Ladies of Paris* (New Haven, Conn., 1966), 131, 195.

13. E.g., Schlözer, ed., *Stats-Anzeigen*, 1783, IV, 140–144; Wansey, *Tagebuch einer Reise*, xxvi–xxvii (preface by Karl August Böttiger); also Johann Wilhelm Ludwig Gleim, *Sämmtliche Werke*, ed. Wilhelm Körte, 7 vols. (Halberstadt, 1811–1813), II, 69.

14. Goethe, "Dichtung und Wahrheit," bk. XIX, in his *Werke*, Weimar ed., 1/XXIX, 156; see p. 239 n. 123 above. Goethe wrote this part of his autobiography mostly in the 1820s, up to 1830–1831.

15. "wo die ersten Strahlen der glücklichsten Regierung hervorgegangen sind": Chastellux, *Vortheile und Nachtheile*, 84.

16. "dem wundertätigen Einflusse der Freiheit auf die Menschen": Brissot de Warville, *Neue Reise*, Bayreuth ed., I, 173.

17. "Ist's nicht der sicherste Zufluchtsort gegen religiösen sowohl als bürgerlichen Despotismus?": Meister, *Historische Unterhaltungen*, 230. See also Jean Rodolphe Vautravers to Washington, Dec. 10, 1792 (Washington Papers, reel 102, LC, Washington, D.C.).

as an enlightened state, and its superiority was beyond doubt. "This wonderfully organized state," as Christian Friedrich Daniel Schubart had enthusiastically called it,[18] was a bourgeois utopia, where the inhabitants' affluence continuously increased, according to Georg Heinrich Sieveking, who had been active there as a land speculator.[19]

Indeed, these notions of a bourgeois paradise on the other side of the Atlantic prompted many to go there and settle, even though some returned to Germany later, including Dietrich Heinrich Freiherr von Bülow, and Johann Heinrich Ferdinand von Autenrieth, who later became chancellor of the University of Tübingen.[20] Others had concrete, if never realized, plans to emigrate,[21] and rumor had it at one time that Johann Wilhelm von Archenholtz had fled to America.[22]

The ideals incorporated in the German image of America were significant also to other sectors of the population, especially the lower bourgeoisie of northern Germany. In 1791–1792 the last great appeal of the eighteenth century for emigrants, especially tradesmen and farmers, was made to the inhabitants of Hamburg and the surrounding area by the London Genesee Association to effect the settlement of the Genesee District in the state of New York. William Berczy was in charge in northern Germany. Begun with much propaganda, the undertaking was too successful not to arouse annoyance. While the Danish government remained calm, Prussia became concerned and, in its capacity as co-director of the Circle of Lower Saxony, exerted increasing pressure on the magistrates of Hamburg, who had to give in by forbidding the appeal in the early summer of 1792.[23]

Other members of the bourgeoisie, however, had a different conception of the importance of the United States for Europe. Rather than as a refuge for oppressed humanity, they were convinced that the example of the United States could have a positive effect on Europe. The striking contrast between

18. "Dieser herrlich organisierte Staat . . .": Schubart, ed., *Chronik*, Oct. 21, 1791, 693.

19. Cf. [Georg Heinrich Sieveking], *Verkauf von Ländereyen in Amerika* (Hamburg, 1793), esp. 8; also H. Sieveking, *Georg Heinrich Sieveking*, 365–367.

20. Cf. Eberhard Stübler, *Johann Heinrich Ferdinand von Autenrieth 1772–1835. Professor der Medizin und Kanzler der Universität Tübingen* (Stuttgart, 1948), 29–35.

21. See Christian Rudolf Boie to Ernestine and Johann Heinrich Voss, Oct. 4, 1794 (Nachlaß Boie-Voss, Kasten Boie Flensburg III, 10, LB, Kiel).

22. Cf. the rejection of this report in Johann Joachim Eschenburg to Johann Wilhelm Ludwig Gleim, Aug. 22, 1793 (MS Collection, CVII, 12a, GH, Halberstadt).

23. Files on these events are presently in the Staatsarchive, Hamburg and Wolfenbüttel, the Landesarchiv, Schleswig, Rigsarkivet, Copenhagen, and the Deutsches Zentralarchiv, Merseburg. These records and others make clear that in this period the duke of Brunswick-Wolfenbüttel, together with the elector of Brandenburg, presided over the Lower Saxon Circle, and not the elector of Hanover, as is maintained by some, including Walther Schmidt, "Geschichte des niedersächsischen Kreises von Jahre 1673 bis zum Zusammenbruch der Kreisverfassung," *Niedersächsisches Jahrbuch für Landesgeschichte*, VII (1930), 131–132;

ascending America as a moral and political model, and declining Europe, abandoned to despotism, captured their imagination. Even during the War of Independence this thought had developed among the German bourgeoisie, and Johann Christian Schmohl and others tried to rationalize it: "Europe on its own does not have enough strength to reform itself. But examples and help from others may yet effect something. It is America that will be Europe's savior. America will nobly repay the tyranny and devastation it suffered at Europe's hands with liberty and affluence instead."[24]

According to the bourgeois interpretation, this hope came nearer to realization with the outbreak of the French Revolution. But increasing disappointment with the course of events in France blotted out the idea of a renewal starting there, and many once again turned to the exemplary character of America as the ideal for the long-desired improvement in Europe. "The United States of America first broke the yoke of serfdom, proclaiming liberty and human rights to men and nations. It will be the free states of the New World that will engender the present and future happiness of the peoples of the Old World."[25] This again surrounded North America with the aura of being "the hope of the world."[26]

The United States as a Future World Power

Directly associated with these ideas about America as an example and an inspiration were widespread predictions of America's future greatness and discussion of the consequences of this development for Europe. August

---

Aretin, *Heiliges Römisches Reich*, I, 71. On the emigration projects see also *Berichte über den Genesee-Distrikt*; Franklin, *Auszug der Anmerkungen*; also Paul D. Evans, "The Frontier Pushed Westward," in Alexander C. Flick, ed., *History of the State of New York*, V (1934), 148–167; Ellis *et al.*, *History of New York State*, 153–158.

24. "Aus sich selbst hat Europa nicht mehr Stärke genug, sich zu reformieren. Aber Beispiele, fremde Hülfe vermögen noch etwas. Amerika ist's, aus dem es seine Rettung empfangen wird. Es wird die Tyranneien und Verwüstungen, die es von Europa erlitten, edel vergelten, wird ihm dafür Freiheit und Wohlstand schenken": Schmohl, *Über Nordamerika und Demokratie*, 189. See also Johann Georg Schulthess to Johann Jakob Bodmer, Aug. 13, 1778 (MS Bodmer, 4c. XIX, 46, ZB, Zurich).

25. "Die Vereinigten Staaten von Amerika haben zuerst das Joch der Knechtschaft zerbrochen, und sie haben zugleich Freiheit und Menschenrechte den Menschen und Völkern verkündigt. Diese freien Staaten der Neuen Welt sind es, von denen die jetzige und künftige Freiheit und Glückseligkeit der Völker der Alten Welt sich herschreibt": Bernhard Christoph Faust to Washington, June 18, 1794 (Washington Papers, Reel 105, LC, Washington, D.C.).

26. "der Welten Hoffnung": Johann Gottfried Hagemeister, "An Christoph Colon," *Berlinisches Archiv der Zeit*, July 1799, 10.

von Hennings, in a very general way, had maintained as early as 1782 that "America will rise gradually, and with its rise will go Europe's decline."[27] His statement was an echo of an even more general prognosis made by Christoph Daniel Ebeling in the mid-1760s, but this time tailored to fit the new republic.[28] Though there were political observers in Germany quite prepared to fall in line with Elbridge Gerry's conjecture that the future America might surpass the power and affluence of all other lands on earth,[29] the conclusions they drew were mostly vague and limited to those states of western Europe directly engaged in the American War of Independence.[30]

In the 1790s these ideas gained influence in Germany. Bishop George Berkeley's view, voiced in the first half of the century, that mankind's center of culture would move westward, making America some day dominant in the arts and sciences as well as in material affluence and wealth, gained followers among bourgeois observers other than Ebeling and Hennings.[31] Many claimed to foresee "the approaching heyday of the American republic,"[32] never doubting its future greatness.[33]

It was occasionally questioned, however, whether the great distance separating America from the Old World would in fact permit the young republic to play an appreciable role in the European system of power.[34] In view of the great natural barrier, some observers thought it more likely that a

27. "Nach und nach wird sich Amerika erheben, und so wie es steigt, wird Europa sinken": Hennings, in *Politisches Journal*, 1782, II, 406.

28. Ebeling, "Fragen, welche erst nach einigen Jahrhunderten können aufgelöst werden," *Hannoverisches Magazin*, Nov. 15, 1765, 1447–1448.

29. See Gerry to James Warren, Nov. 8, 1778, in *Warren-Adams Letters*, II, 65; Vautravers to Franklin, Apr. 14, 1778 (Franklin Papers, IX, 40, APSL, Philadelphia). Also, Erwin Hölzle, *Russland und Amerika. Aufbruch und Begegnung zweier Weltmächte* (Munich, 1953), 27.

30. E.g., Gleim to Johannes von Müller, Sept. 8, 1782 (Msc. Mü. LXI/5, 84, StadtB, Schaffhausen); *Beschreibung der dreizehn unabhängigen Nordamerikanischen Staaten*, 55–56; Sprengel, *Allgemeines historisches Taschenbuch*, 149.

31. E.g., Meister, *Historische Unterhaltungen*, 229–230; but see also the remarks by John Quincy Adams on a conversation with Prince Heinrich of Prussia, Dec. 8, 1797, in C. F. Adams, ed., *Memoirs of John Quincy Adams*, I, 210.

32. "die herannahende Blütezeit des amerikanischen Freistaates": Georg Forster, "Ansichten vom Niederrhein" (1791), in his *Werke*, ed. Akademie der Wissenschaften, IX, 104.

33. E.g., E.A.W. Zimmermann, in Bruns and Zimmermann, eds., *Repositorium für die neueste Geographie*, III, 235; *La Fayette als Staatsmann*, [13–14] (preface by Johann Reinhold Forster); also Georg Christoph Lichtenberg to Christoph Heinrich Pfaff, Oct. 16, 1794, in Lichtenberg, *Briefe*, ed. Leitzmann and Schüddekopf, III, 137; La Rochefoucauld Liancourt, *Reisen durch die Nordamerikanische Republik*, III, 784; more skeptical, Bülow, *Freistaat von Nordamerika*, II, 174–230.

34. E.g., Jan Ingenhousz to Franklin, Dec. 14, 1777 (Franklin Papers, I, 41, University of Pennsylvania Library, Philadelphia); *Historisches Portefeuille*, June 1784, 789–790; *Fliegende Blätter*, Aug.–Sept. 1794, 798–799; C. F. Adams, ed., *Memoirs of John Quincy Adams*, I, 210.

relatively powerless though great state would arise across the ocean, without any possibility of direct interference in European political and military matters.[35] Thus, numerous contemporaries thought it probable that far-reaching changes would occur in the world in the long run as a result of American growth. But it is noteworthy that in the era of James Watt and the Montgolfier brothers other observers were unable to imagine the decisive changes in the fields of transportation and communications that in the future would remove the "huge remoteness of the ocean" as a barrier impeding all relations.[36]

These views, partly incorrect, partly contradictory, concerning the future relationship between the United States and Europe were also reflected in one very special case, namely, the question of the real or imaginary effects of the American Revolution on Ireland. At the time of the War of Independence, Germans were not aware that the Americans themselves had made some isolated efforts to exploit Irish dissatisfaction with the London government in order to increase Britain's difficulties.[37] Around 1780 the Irish situation came to a critical point, partly under the influence of the American Revolution.[38] But the German bourgeoisie seem to have disregarded this development, just as they had disregarded Ireland's noteworthy sympathies toward the American Revolution,[39] which probably surpassed the extent of sympathies in Germany. Not until the 1790s do we find some scattered hints of a

35. E.g., Bülow, *Freistaat von Nordamerika*, II, 177. For some opposing, non-German views see Geoffrey Barraclough, "Europa, Amerika und Rußland in Vorstellung und Denken des 19. Jahrhunderts," *HZ*, CCIII (1966), 282–286.

36. "ungeheuren Abgelegenheit über das Weltmeer hinüber": *Fliegende Blätter*, Aug.– Sept. 1794, 798. Jefferson, however, sensed a time when the balloon might be rendered useful on a large scale for communication and transportation; cf. Jefferson to Philip Turpin, Apr. 28, 1784, in Boyd *et al.*, eds., *Jefferson Papers*, VII, 134–137.

37. As early as 1775 the Continental Congress addressed the inhabitants of Ireland; in that same year the address was translated into German and published at Philadelphia as a pamphlet, *An die Einwohner von Irland, von den Abgeordneten der Vereinigten Colonien*. See Owen Dudley Edwards, "The American Image of Ireland: A Study of its Early Phases," *Perspectives in American History*, IV (1970), 200–201. On Mar. 5, 1784, Samuel Hardy wrote to Benjamin Harrison that Ireland was "ripe for a revolution" (Boyd *et al.*, eds., *Jefferson Papers*, VII, 12).

38. See Michael Kraus, "America and the Irish Revolutionary Movement in the Eighteenth Century," in Richard B. Morris, ed., *The Era of the American Revolution* (1939; repr. New York, 1965), 332–348. In more recent research this influence appears considerably reduced; cf. Herbert Butterfield, *George III, Lord North, and the People, 1779–1780* (1949; repr. New York, 1968), 172; Palmer, *Age of the Democratic Revolution*, I, 287–292; Maurice Richard O'Connell, *Irish Politics and Social Conflict in the Age of the American Revolution* (Philadelphia, 1965), 25–35, 394–396; James Camlin Beckett, *The Making of Modern Ireland 1603–1923* (London, 1966), 206–207.

39. Gipson, *British Empire*, XIII, 3.

German awareness of this relationship between Irish and American affairs.[40] These later statements, some of them published in the year of the Irish rebellion of 1798, overrated the actual influence of the American Revolution at a time when the influence of the French Revolution had already become much more decisive.[41]

In addition to this special, concrete example of the repercussions of the American Revolution on the European states, there is need to mention two visionary observations that far outrank everything said up to now. Shortly before his death Schubart wrote: "If America continues on this high, self-blazed trail, it will in all probability in the nineteenth century, together with Russia, be the first power in the world!"[42] This prediction immediately reminds us of Alexis de Tocqueville's famous dictum, pronounced nearly half a century later, on the future, bipolar world dominance of Russia and the United States.[43] Without detracting from the praise due de Tocqueville for his prophetic vision, it is well to remember that this idea can be traced back to the time of Washington and Catherine II, as Schubart's perceptive assertion proves. Moreover, Schubart was not the only one who had such visions. Thoughts of similar import were voiced in the 1790s by Friedrich Melchior Freiherr von Grimm, Johann Gottfried Herder, and others.[44] This remarkable premonition of a global political constellation still one and a half centuries distant also reveals considerable admiration for Russia's breathtaking rise since the reign of Peter the Great. Within a few decades the Tsarist empire had outgrown its peripheral position and become a decisive factor in European politics, yet without apparently having reached its zenith.[45]

40. Meister, *Historische Unterhaltungen*, 227; Milbiller, *Allgemeine Geschichte: Engelland*, III, 362.

41. See Homer L. Calkin, "La propagation en Irlande des idées de la Révolution française," *Annales historiques de la Révolution française*, XXVII (1955), 143–160; Beckett, *Making of Modern Ireland*, 246–267; Thomas Pakenham, *The Year of Liberty: The Story of the Great Irish Rebellion of 1798* (London, 1969), esp. 27–31; Edwards, "American Image of Ireland," *Perspectives in American History*, IV (1970), 241–242.

42. "Schreitet Amerika auf dieser hohen selbstgebrochenen Bahn fort, so wird es im 19. Jahrhundert allem Ansehen nach mit Rußland—die erste Rolle in der Welt spielen!": *Chronik*, Oct. 21, 1791, 693, cf. Jan. 8, 1788, 21.

43. Tocqueville, "De la Démocratie en Amérique," conclusion, in his *Oeuvres complètes*, ed. Mayer, I/1, 430–431. On comparable prophecies during the first decades of the 19th century see Bernhard Fabian, *Alexis de Tocquevilles Amerikabild. Genetische Untersuchungen über Zusammenhänge mit der zeitgenössischen, insbesondere der englischen Amerika-Interpretation* (Heidelberg, 1957), 80–108.

44. Paul Dukes, *The Emergence of the Super-Powers: A Short Comparative History of the USA and the USSR* (London, 1970), 9, 33; Dieter Groh, *Russland und das Selbstverständnis Europas. Ein Beitrag zur europäischen Geistesgeschichte* (Neuwied, 1961), 76; incorrect, however, is Barraclough, "Europa, Amerika und Rußland," *HZ*, CCIII (1966), 284–285.

45. See Hölzle, *Rußland und Amerika*, 26–27; Dukes, *Emergence of the Super-Powers*, 32–37; also Dietrich Gerhard, *England und der Aufstieg Rußlands. Zur Frage des Zusam-*

The second supposition, likewise outstanding for its anticipation of a distant reality, orginated at about the same time and was also voiced by several authors. It did not encompass Russia, but it is distinguished by more detailed reasoning, mostly of an economic nature. In 1787 a professor of history in Königsberg, Karl Ehregott Mangelsdorf, commented on the future relationship between the United States and Europe: "It requires no gift of prophecy to predict that a country that is capable of having the largest population, that is a safe haven from the despotism growing everywhere, and that can make itself independent of European products and European artifacts, must in the end predominate over a continent whose needs have made this country indispensable."[46]

Eleven years later historian Joseph Milbiller, who was born in Munich but was living in Vienna at the time, expressed essentially similar thoughts. His opinion, reinforced by a thorough study of the history of the United States, was also based on the assumption that the New World's raw materials would be indispensable to the Old World, whereas America could make itself independent of Europe in the field of finished products. "By a thoroughly one-sided commerce it can gradually attract all of Europe's money; the enticing advantages of religious toleration and political freedom beckoning every oppressed European can increase its population beyond expectation. Hardly any other state has ever had so many opportunities to make all Europe dependent, or even to bring Europe under its sway, as the united North American provinces will have."[47]

These two forecasts of American power are suggestive of Alexander Hamilton's policy of finance and industrialization as well as of the thesis of the American challenge promoted by Jean-Jacques Servan-Schreiber in the

---

menhanges der europäischen Staaten und ihres Ausgreifens in die außereuropäische Welt in Politik und Wirtschaft des 18. Jahrhunderts (Munich and Berlin, 1933), passim.

46. "Ohne die Gabe der Wahrsagung zu haben, läßt sich vorhersagen, daß ein Land, welches der stärksten Bevölkerung fähig ist, welches einen sichern Zufluchtsort gegen den hier und da immer mehr und mehr wachsenden Despotismus darbietet und welches von europäischen Erzeugnissen und europäischem Kunstfleiße sich unabhängig machen kann, am Ende die Übermacht über einen Erdteil erhalten muß, dessen Bedürfnisse ihm Amerika unentbehrlich gemacht haben": Mangelsdorf, Geschichte der europäischen Staaten, V (1787), 248.

47. "Durch einen ausschließlichen Aktivhandel kann es allmählich alles Geld aus Europa an sich ziehen; durch die anlockenden Vorteile der Religionsduldung und politischen Freiheit, die jedem gekränkten Europäer zu dieser Freistätte heranwinken, seine Volkszahl außerordentlich vermehren. Kaum hatte daher jemals in Staat so viel Anlage, ganz Europa von sich abhängig zu machen oder wohl gar unter seine Herrschaft zu beugen, als die vereinigten nordamerikanischen Provinzen": Milbiller, Allgemeine Geschichte: Vereinigte nordamerikanische Provinzen, I, 5.

Figure 16. Balthasar Friedrich Leizelt, View of Salem (Augsburg, c. 1794). "Salem: A town in English America, in the county of Essex, which was erected by the English in 1629 and has two harbors, one for summer, and one for winter."

Courtesy John Carter Brown Library, Brown University, Providence, R.I.

late 1960s.[48] Without entering into the question of originality, it is obvious that Mangelsdorf could not then have known anything of Hamilton's policy, and presumably he had no knowledge whatsoever of Robert Morris. In order to grasp the sources of Mangelsdorf's thinking, we must keep in mind the historical position of the European bourgeoisie, who for the preceding century had known the Western Hemisphere as primarily an exporter of raw materials. Moreover, England's tremendous headstart in the fields of manufacture and finance had probably never been properly appreciated by the majority of the German bourgeoisie. Regardless of these qualifications, the two prophetic statements are doubtlessly among the most articulate made by members of the German bourgeoisie about the still-young United States at the end of the eighteenth century.

The United States during the Federalist Era

Leaving aside speculations about the future of European-American relations, we have yet to consider the German response to specific conditions in America in the 1790s. Questions such as the following come to the foreground: Did the United States political scene in those years influence German comprehension of the American Revolution? Did it affect the utopian conception of America or the idea of America as a future world power? How did political developments under George Washington and John Adams change bourgeois German thinking?

Washington's inauguration introduced a new chapter of American history. In many spheres of national life the next decade, known as the Federalist era, set the pattern to be followed by the country in the nineteenth century. The existing problems often called for basic decisions that marked United States policy for decades to come. The new constitution had to prove its viability in practice. The individual functions and mutual relationships of the parts of the national government needed to be clarified and formulated by political action. The executive, legislative, and judicial branches could understand their proper roles only after some development, which was not always free of friction. A federal bureaucracy had to be established to ensure communication between the governing and the governed.

48. See Hamilton, *Papers on Public Credit, Commerce, and Finance*, ed. Samuel McKee, Jr. (New York, 1957); Servan-Schreiber, *Die amerikanische Herausforderung*, trans. from the French (Hamburg, 1969), 21–23, 27, and *passim*.

Other fields also presented great problems that were waiting for conclusive solutions. Financial and economic policy had to be entirely reconsidered and set in order. The national debt continued to weigh heavily on the young state. Was America to remain basically an agricultural state or was it to force industrialization? The West had to be opened up and settled. And what was to be the republic's attitude toward the world and especially toward Europe? The problem of isolation versus intervention, familiar in twentieth-century American politics, was already a clamorous issue in the eighteenth century.[49] An abundance of unanswered questions surrounded the birth and the first few years of the American federal state. Not all could be solved at once and without effort, but in many fields the pattern for future developments was determined in the 1790s.[50]

In light of the bourgeoisie's past reactions to events in America, it is not surprising that they rarely paid appropriate attention to these problems. Moreover, Germans were much too captivated by the French Revolution and the issues it raised to give much attention to political disputes in a faraway state which, apparently, were of no direct importance to them. Thus, especially in the early 1790s, German contemporaries devoted little attention to United States external and internal politics. They were, instead, content to talk in general terms about the free, happy, and exemplary young republic.[51] The information on which these ideas were based was not drawn from the immediate American present but rather from inherited ideas about the American Revolution and from some of the typical presuppositions of the German bourgeoisie. This knowledge seemed to them to be more meaningful than, let us say, a discussion of Hamilton's "Report on Public Credit" or the problem of an American national bank.

The unrealistic aura with which the German bourgeoisie surrounded the United States originated to a large extent from their glorification of George Washington. He was not only the republic's president; he was also considered to be the embodiment of its native virtues. As a president, how-

---

49. On the importance of this issue in the 19th century see Günter Moltmann, "Isolation oder Intervention: Ein Prinzipienkonflikt amerikanischer Europapolitik im 19. Jahrhundert," *HZ*, CCVIII (1969), 24–51.

50. See among others E. Wright, *Fabric of Freedom*, 188–236; Alexander DeConde, *Entangling Alliance: Politics and Diplomacy under George Washington* (Durham, N.C., 1958); Marcus Cunliffe, *The Nation Takes Shape 1789–1837* (Chicago, 1959), esp. 1–10; John C. Miller, *The Federalist Era, 1789–1801* (New York, 1960); Helene J. Looze, *Alexander Hamilton and the British Orientation of American Foreign Policy, 1783–1803* (The Hague, 1969).

51. See *Vaterländische Chronik*, June 18, 1790, 422; Georg Forster to his wife, Aug. 21, 1793, in Forster, *Briefwechsel*, ed. Huber, II, 551; *Historische Übersicht von Europens Entwicklung*, 48; Jenisch, *Geist und Charakter*, I, 213; Schilderung des gesellschaftlichen Lebens (LB, Gotha).

ever, Washington failed to receive equal appreciation.[52] To his faraway contemporaries he remained only "the immortal fighter for American liberty," the true, virtuous republican whose fame and glory were reflected on the republic he headed.[53] His political activities as president went virtually unnoticed, and it is significant that the only political action of Washington's that aroused appreciable interest among the German contemporaries was his Farewell Address.[54] The respect for this address in Germany confirms John Quincy Adams's observation that "the address of the president declaring his intention to retire from public service has been republished, translated, and admired all over Europe."[55] The document seemed to represent anew the noble and wise character of the American leader, erecting another monument to his fame.

It was not, therefore, the address's basic remarks on the future foreign policy of the United States that claimed German attention, for diplomatic relations between the young republic and the European states had hardly been of note up to then. The United States's relations with Britain and Spain, neighboring powers on the North American continent, were hampered by unsolved border problems and other questions that could be only partly cleared up in the mid-1790s by two bilateral treaties;[56] but this too aroused little comment in Germany.[57]

52. In lieu of a discussion of his presidency, Washington's letters to Congress during the war were published in a German translation, *George Washington's beständigen Präsidenten und Protektors, officielle und eigenhändige Briefe und Berichte, welche er während des ganzen Krieges zwischen den Amerikanischen Freystaaten und England als Generalissimus an den Congreß geschrieben, nebst andern, welche er von diesem und andern Hauptpersonen erhalten hat* (Leipzig, 1796–1797), 2 vols. Also, a revised German translation of the *U.S. Register for the Year 1795* appeared as Johann Jakob Karl Timaeus, *Nordamerikanischer Staats-Kalender, oder Statistisches Hand- und Addressbuch der Vereinigten Staaten von Nordamerika* (Hamburg, 1796).

53. "der unsterbliche Verfechter der amerikanischen Freiheit": *Europäische Annalen*, Nov. 1796, 161.

54. For its publication see *Europäische Annalen*, Nov. 1796, 156–180; *Minerva*, Dec. 1796, 489–525; *Deutsches Magazin*, Feb. 1797, 174–206. Also Pettenegg, ed., *Ludwig und Karl von Zinzendorf*, 244. Friedrich August Köhler, who in his diaries took no notice whatsoever of America, thought Washington's death important enough to rank among the outstanding events of the year; cf. his Tagebücher, vol. 1800, 209 (LB, Stuttgart).

55. To Abigail Adams, Feb. 8, 1797, in W. C. Ford, ed., *Writings of John Quincy Adams*, II, 109. See generally Felix Gilbert, *The Beginnings of American Foreign Policy: To the Farewell Address* (1961; repr. New York, 1965).

56. On the treaty of 1794 with Great Britain see among others Samuel Flagg Bemis, *Jay's Treaty: A Study in Commerce and Diplomacy*, 2d ed. (New Haven, Conn., and London, 1962); Charles R. Ritcheson, *Aftermath of Revolution: British Policy Toward the United States, 1783–1795* (Dallas, 1969), esp. 317–359; Jerald A. Combs, *The Jay Treaty: Political Battleground of the Founding Fathers* (Berkeley, Calif., 1970). On the treaty of 1795 with Spain see among others Bemis, *Pinckney's Treaty: America's Advantage from Europe's Distress, 1783–1800*, 2d ed. (New Haven, Conn., 1960).

57. Ebeling's vehement attacks on the Jay Treaty are singular; see his letters to Joel Bar-

French-American relations, which had steadily worsened in the 1790s, met with a similar fate. The situation grew more critical in 1798 with the so-called X YZ Affair, in which three obscure French agents, called X, Y, and Z, demanded bribes and tried to force three American emissaries to accept discreditable conditions before the French government would enter into diplomatic negotiations for the purpose of improving relations. The subsequent propagandistic blowup of the matter brought both nations to the brink of war, which large portions of the American Federalist party would have been only too willing to engage in.[58] The propaganda debate also spread to Germany, leading to the publication of some documents, mostly translations of corresponding American documents.[59] But the attention given to such publications was as cursory as the events themselves were spectacular, and those of the German bourgeoisie who meanwhile had rejected the French Revolution now praised the United States for its wise and moderate conduct in the affair. As John Quincy Adams reported: "Out of France and the circle of French fanaticism, the clear and unequivocal voice of Europe declares that in this contest we are right and France is wrong."[60]

It was not only in foreign policy that the United States seemed to compare favorably with France. For quite some time the German bourgeoisie had drawn a clearer line of demarcation between the United States and revolutionary France with regard to internal politics as well. Since the early 1790s, confirmed antagonists of the French Revolution had been trying to make the idea of equality, promulgated by the revolution, into a political bugbear; this idea was responsible, in their opinion, for all the terror and the atrocities that had followed.[61]

As a result of these changed points of view, the protagonists of the new

low, Sept. 15, 1795 (in Lane, ed., *Letters of Ebeling*, 16), and Mar. 16, 1796 (in Harvard College Library, Cambridge, Mass.).

58. See Alexander DeConde, *The Quasi-War: The Politics and Diplomacy of the Undeclared War with France, 1797–1801* (New York, 1966); Henry Blumenthal, *France and the United States: Their Diplomatic Relations, 1789–1914* (Chapel Hill, N.C., 1970), 15–16.

59. *Amerikanische Staats-Papiere. Wichtige Documente und Depeschen . . .*, trans. from the English (n.p., 1798); *Frankreichs Verfahren gegen Amerika*, trans. from the English by J.F.W. Möller (Hamburg, 1798). For the opposite view see *Vertheidigung der französischen Regierung gegen gewisse Beschuldigungen in den Berichten der amerikanischen Gesandten . . .*, trans. from the French (Hamburg, 1798).

60. To Abigail Adams, Sept. 14, 1798, in W. C. Ford, ed., *Writings of John Quincy Adams*, II, 360. See also Ebeling to Timothy Pickering, May 24, 1798 (Timothy Pickering Papers, XXII, 175–176, MHi, Boston), and Ebeling to William Bentley, Sept. 16, 1798, in Lane, ed., "Glimpses of European Conditions," Massachusetts Historical Society, *Proceedings*, LIX (1926), 331.

61. E.g., Christian Adam Horn, *Uiber Gleichheit und Ungleichheit aus dem Gesichtspunkt gegenwärtiger Zeiten* (Hildburghausen, 1792), 99, 111, 153–154, 368–371; Jung-Stilling, *Über den Revolutions-Geist*, 31.

United States, who often condemned the French Revolution, grew more reluctant to emphasize equality as an ideal of the American Revolution. They still spoke of "equality and liberty" in connection with the United States,[62] but more qualifiedly as rejection of the French Revolution grew. Count Luigi Castiglioni wrote about the American people that "although the new legislation denies all differences of rank, one can well divide them into four classes."[63] Günther Karl Friedrich Seidel spoke of a "natural aristocracy" anchored in the Constitution,[64] and Julius August Remer came up with similar findings: "In all states the privileges of birth have been abolished, but wealth and inherited property still give lasting advantages to some families."[65] Others merely mentioned the "greatest possible equality," which was said to be prevalent in the United States, but they did not offer further explanation.[66] It was clear, in any case, that many now thought that only America, and not France, had implemented their ideals, for it was in America that strong barriers existed to help secure the bourgeoisie's claim to power against the lower social classes, thus definitely limiting the possibility of real equality.

The contradictions between the political reality of the Federalist era and the German bourgeoisie's greatly idealized views of it were exposed the moment someone published a more realistic picture of the United States. More than anyone else, Dietrich Heinrich Freiherr von Bülow, known mainly as a writer on military matters, must be given credit for this. In the last years of the century he systematically attacked the bourgeois idealization of the United States in a two-volume work and in numerous essays.[67] Archenholtz called it a "terrible artillery" that Bülow was mounting against the wishful thinking

62. "Gleichheit und Freiheit": G. Forster, *Kleine Schriften*, III (1794), 155 (written after 1790). See also *Entwurf der neuesten Culturgeschichte*, 13.

63. "Obschon der neuen Gesetzgebung zufolge kein Unterschied des Ranges stattfindet, so kann man sie doch füglich in vier Klassen einteilen": Castiglioni, *Reise durch die vereinigten Staaten*, 222. He identified large landowners and wealthy merchants as the new aristocracy of New York; theirs were the families that had been settled for generations in the province, and they had developed a deeply rooted feeling of distinction above the other classes of society (*ibid.*, 222–223).

64. "natürlichen Aristokratismus": Seidel, "Staatsverfassung," in his translation of Ramsay, *Amerikanische Revolution*, IV, 14, cf. generally 11–14.

65. "In allen Staaten ist jeder Unterschied, den Geburt gibt, aufgehoben, wenn auch gleich Reichtum und langer Besitz einigen Familien einen bleibenden Vorzug erteilt": Remer, *Handbuch der neuern Geschichte*, 567 (the same in his *Handbuch der Geschichte unsrer Zeiten*, 39).

66. "größtmögliche Gleichheit": *Berlinische Monatsschrift*, Nov. 1796, 464.

67. Bülow, *Freistaat von Nordamerika*; see also his 15 letters in *Minerva*, Apr., June, Dec. 1796, 73–103, 486–517, 385–424, and Jan., Dec. 1797, 105–113, 540–551; also his "Betrachtung über die politische Lage der Vereinigten Staaten," *ibid.*, Sept. 1798, 536–547, and his "Ueber Washington's Briefe und N. Amerika," *Neuer Teutscher Merkur*, June 1798, 129–136.

of the German bourgeoisie.[68] But Bülow, who had once shared these ideals and had spent years of disappointment and economic failure in the United States as a result, did not rage blindly against the Americans. His position was determined instead by very different factors, and formed not by resentment but by serious political considerations: "I am by no means an enemy of the Americans. I am neutral. I wish that they might improve, reform their customs, and become true republicans, which they certainly are not now."[69] Bülow's political orientation was represented above all by Jefferson and his party.

The writings of Bülow and of the other critics of the United States are worthy of notice because they show the lack of thoroughness with which the German bourgeoisie studied the political development of the United States. Uncritical enthusiasm and idealization had largely characterized their thinking, and when someone who had been in direct contact with the situation and was politically competent to analyze it began to explore the American present, the rift between ideal and reality was clearly demonstrated.

Of course, not everyone in bourgeois circles appreciated such perceptions, which undermined their idols and wishful thinking. Ebeling, for one, misunderstood Bülow completely, and took it to be his duty to defend summarily his beloved Americans against the heretic.[70] But there were others who did not think that the basis of Bülow's book was libelous and who found his assertions to be useful and helpful. "The author's judgment is somewhat harsh, but his book is well worth reading. It rids us at once of many empty rumors and prejudices."[71] Even John Quincy Adams, though he was a Federalist, could not but remark that the book was "written with considerable ingenuity. It contains beyond all doubt a vast deal of falsehood, but every American who feels for the honor of his country must confess with shame that it also contains too much of truth."[72]

---

68. "fürchterl. Artillerie": to Johann Wilhelm Ludwig Gleim, Mar. 25, 1797 (MS Collection, LXXXIV/7, 20, GH, Halberstadt).

69. "Ich bin nämlich im geringsten kein Feind der Amerikaner. Ich bin neutral. Ich wünsche, daß sie sich bessern, ihre Sitten reformieren und wahre Republikaner werden mögen, welches sie jetzt gewiß nicht sind": *Minerva*, Dec. 1797, 551.

70. Ebeling to Henry E. Mühlenberg, Aug. 24, 1797, Mar. 6, 1798 (Henry E. Mühlenberg Papers, Lutheran Theological Seminary, Philadelphia).

71. "Der Verfasser urteilt etwas scharf, aber das Buch ist durchaus lesenswert. Es befreit uns auf einmal von so manchen großen leeren Vorurteilen und Gerüchten": Karl Ludwig von Knebel to Johann Gottfried Herder, Mar. 9, 1798, in Heinrich Düntzer and Ferdinand Gottfried von Herder, eds., *Von und an Herder. Ungedruckte Briefe aus Herders Nachlaß*, 3 vols. (Leipzig, 1856–1862), III, 119.

72. To Abigail Adams, May 7, 1799, in W. C. Ford, ed., *Writings of John Quincy Adams*, II, 418.

The German Amerikabild and the
Alien and Sedition Acts of 1798

The increased attention to the political and social development of the United States that Bülow had encouraged soon centered on a special phase of America's political history. In defiance of Madison's urgent warning against factionalism,[73] political parties had formed in the United States by the 1790s. Governmental measures, especially the economic and financial policies advocated by Hamilton, met with increasing resistance after 1790, above all from the southern states. The government, made up mainly of Federalists, was also increasingly criticized for its preferential foreign policy toward England as compared to revolutionary France, with matters coming to a head in 1795 in the dispute over the Jay Treaty. The Republican opposition, led by Jefferson, who had withdrawn from the cabinet in 1793 because of his disapproval of Hamilton's policy,[74] firmly resisted the government's apparent aristocratic and pro-British inclinations.

In those years the German bourgeoisie, as a rule, had no knowledge of the formation of political parties in America.[75] It was not until the end of the century that they began to pay attention to this development, for which, in any case, they had no sympathy and less understanding. At that same time, some well-informed authors tried to familiarize Germany with one of America's most violent political controversies, the Alien and Sedition Acts of 1798 and the disputes these acts engendered between the Federalists and the Republicans.

The Alien and Sedition Acts were directly connected with the formation of American parties and with the tension between the American and French governments after the XYZ Affair. Officially, the acts were intended to stop the allegedly seditious activities of the too-vociferous disciples of the French Revolution and to defer the naturalization of foreigners, particularly since

73. Madison, Federalist No. 10, in *The Federalist*, ed. Cooke, 56–58.
74. See William Nisbet Chambers, *Political Parties in a New Nation: The American Experience, 1776–1809* (New York, 1963); Noble E. Cunningham, Jr., *The Jeffersonian Republicans*, Vol. I, *The Formation of Party Organization, 1789–1801* (Chapel Hill, N.C., 1957). Joseph Charles, *The Origins of the American Party System: Three Essays* (Williamsburg, Va., 1956), gives stronger emphasis to the importance of the Jay Treaty in the origins of the party system than does Chambers. See also Richard Hofstadter, *The Idea of a Party System: The Rise of Legitimate Opposition in the United States, 1780–1840* (Berkeley and Los Angeles, 1969), 1–39, 86–90, and Richard Buel, Jr., *Securing the Revolution: Ideology in American Politics, 1789–1815* (Ithaca, N.Y., 1972).
75. See, however, the remarks by Wansey, *Tagebuch einer Reise*, 111–112.

many Frenchmen who had immigrated in recent years were distrusted by the anti-Jacobin Federalists. It cannot be denied that these laws and their concomitant provisions severely curtailed civil liberties, seriously endangering, above all, the freedoms of speech and of the press, as the Republicans charged.[76] Jefferson and his followers fought with determination against this policy, accusing the government of unconstitutional usurpation of powers. The fierce resistance of the Republicans becomes understandable when one considers that some Federalists had hinted that the acts were meant to be used mainly to silence the Republicans. What was paraded as a patriotic policy was thus suddenly suspect of being an unscrupulous effort to exercise unchallenged political power.[77]

The controversy over these acts was the culmination of American political disputes in the 1790s, surpassing even the controversy over the Jay Treaty. Although the practical application of the acts did not confirm all of the Republicans' fears, it is nevertheless true that the spirit of the acts deviated from the principles of the American Revolution in essential points.[78]

The Alien and Sedition Acts did not remain completely unknown in Germany; in fact, they provoked some acid criticism. It is significant that this criticism came from men who knew the United States from personal experience and thought of themselves as dedicated followers of Jefferson. If they expressed their opinion of the threatening "despotism in the North American republic,"[79] they did so within the framework of United States party politics, sharply condemning the Federalists, and in a few cases even criticizing Washington himself.[80] They shared the conviction of the Jeffersonians in

76. See Donald H. Stewart, *The Opposition Press of the Federalist Period* (Albany, N.Y., 1969), 464–474.

77. See Frank M. Anderson, "The Enforcement of the Alien and Sedition Laws," American Historical Association, *Annual Report for the Year 1912* (Washington, D.C., 1914), 113–126; Adrienne Koch and Harry Ammon, "The Virginia and Kentucky Resolutions: An Episode in Jefferson's and Madison's Defense of Civil Liberties," *WMQ*, 3d Ser., V (1948), 145–176; John C. Miller, *Crisis in Freedom: The Alien and Sedition Acts* (Boston, 1951), 74–85; James Morton Smith, "The Sedition Law, Free Speech, and the American Political Process," *WMQ*, 3d Ser., IX (1952), 497–511; Smith, "The Enforcement of the Alien Friends Act of 1798," *Mississippi Valley Historical Review*, XLI (1954–1955), 85–104; Smith, *Freedom's Fetters: The Alien and Sedition Laws and American Civil Liberties* (Ithaca, N.Y., 1956), 21.

78. See the First Amendment, enacted in 1791: "Congress shall make no law . . . abridging the freedom of speech, or of the press."

79. This is the title of an article by Karl von Bülow in the periodical, *Geschichte und Politik*, 1800, I, 181–207.

80. In the United States, too, Washington met with growing opposition because of his signing of the Jay Treaty and his defense of the controversial acts; see Marshall Smelser, "George Washington and the Alien and Sedition Acts," *AHR*, LIX (1953–1954), 322–334, and Buel, *Securing the Revolution*, 105–112.

America that the odious acts were "unrepublican and despotic" and expressed "the government's striving for unconstitutional rule."[81] These and similar statements implied that the Federalist-supported administrations of Presidents Washington and Adams threatened to deprave the principles of the Revolution and to cause the republic to abandon its former lofty civic ideals and become a despotic state of the European variety instead.[82]

These attacks, launched entirely by followers of the Republican party's viewpoint, were rebutted by America's staunchest adherents. Even Ebeling, increasingly worried about recent developments in international affairs and the possibility that the United States would enter the anti-French war coalition,[83] thought that these attacks on the Federalist administration went too far.[84] The German bourgeoisie at the time could hardly imagine the sharpness of the party dispute in the United States and comprehended very little of it.

The Jeffersonians in Germany had made it clear that their reaction was not simply a question of anti-Americanism. They all clearly differentiated between the Revolution and the present. At the same time that they severely condemned the Federalists and their policy, they also approved of the American Revolution's ideals and bourgeois principles without reservation. More than fifteen years after the end of the War of Independence, the time had finally come when it was possible for Germans to judge the present condition of America without distorting reality by looking at the republic exclusively through the halo of its Revolution. America had formerly been condemned mainly by the adversaries of bourgeois ideals, who had rejected the new nation for its Revolution. Now some of the advocates of the American Revolution were also condemning the new nation, but in this case for its failure to live up to the revolutionary ideals it had fought for. This easily misinterpreted situation rendered America's image more complex and its contours more fluid. "To some, not unjustifiably called Americomaniacs, the North American republic is a golden country and the ideal among all state structures. Others, having seen and investigated with their own eyes and

81. "unrepublikanischen und despotischen . . . Streben der Regierung nach einer konstitutionswidrigen Herrschaft": Bülow, "Despotismus im Freistaat Nordamerikas," *Geschichte und Politik*, 1800, I, 200, 207.
82. See K. A. Kierulf, "Bemerkungen über die berühmtesten Männer des Freistaates in Nordamerika," *Geschichte und Politik*, 1800, I, 112–124, 232–236, 272–286; "Authentische Nachrichten über den Aufruhr in einigen Gegenden der vereinigten Staaten von Amerika im Jahre 1799," *Genius der Zeit*, June 1800, 183–249. The latter article, written by a supporter of Jefferson, reports on the resistance of the Republicans, and especially of Pennsylvania-Germans, to the Alien and Sedition Acts.
83. See Ebeling to William Bentley, Sept. 7, 1799, in Lane, ed., *Letters of Ebeling*, 73.
84. See Ebeling to John Eliot, July 26, 1800, *ibid.*, 77–78.

judging from their own experience, draw such a derogatory picture of this country and its inhabitants that a comparison of the results shows glaring contrasts. The truth, as always, lies in the middle."[85] It was this differentiated and controversial appreciation of the United States that gained significance in Germany during the nineteenth century.[86]

In Germany the dispute about the Alien and Sedition Acts ended an epoch of bourgeois ideas about America. For the preceding quarter of a century this part of the Western Hemisphere had been commonly looked upon only from the enthusiastic standpoint of the American Revolution. Any other picture of America simply did not exist. Now, at the end of the century, the German bourgeoisie saw the United States emancipating itself, in a sense, from its own Revolution. The result of this development was not condemnation of the American Revolution in favor of the present situation, but a critical balancing of the present against the background of the Revolution. In both America and Germany the Revolution itself retained its semi-mythical and glorified aura, and the will and intentions of the Founding Fathers continued to be held sacrosanct.

Doubtless, this process of realization had social causes, for the distance in time back to the Revolution was continuously increasing, and the number of living participants and contemporaries decreasing. But the immediate occasion of this change in perceptions, which clearly set apart the German from the French understanding of America,[87] was that moment when for the first time America was criticized, not by anti-Americans, but by staunch adherents of the American Revolution. It was this situation that gave birth to an *Amerikabild* independent of the judgment of the Revolution itself, and which, subject to historical change, became the basis of the German assessment of America in future decades and centuries.

---

85. "Für die einen, die man nicht mit Unrecht Amerikomanen genannt hat, ist der Freistaat von Nordamerika ein goldnes Land und das Ideal aller Staatenordnungen. Andre, die mit eignen Augen gesehen und untersucht haben und durch Erfahrungen zu Urteilen und Vorstellungen veranlaßt werden, entwerfen von diesem Lande und seinen Bewohnern ein so nachteiliges Bild, daß die Prüfung der Resultate zu grellen Kontrasten führt. Die Wahrheit liegt, wie immer, auch hier in der Mitte": *Politisches Journal*, Sept. 1800, 873–874.

86. See also Friedrich Brie, "Die Anfänge des Amerikanismus," *Historisches Jahrbuch*, LIX (1939), 352–387.

87. Echeverria, *Mirage in the West*, 175–224.

PART IV

The American Revolution and the German Bourgeoisie at the End of the Eighteenth Century

12. *The Effects of the American Revolution in Germany*

The Widening of the Bourgeoisie's Horizon

The influence of the American Revolution on German contemporaries was profound as well as persistent, and was exceeded during these years only by the impression left by the French Revolution.[1] Accordingly, the events in the Western Hemisphere are extremely useful as a focal point for study of the German bourgeoisie's self-awareness and of the process by which they formed opinions on public issues. The American Revolution found the German bourgeoisie at an early stage of their increased interest in events beyond the individual's own limited sphere of existence, before the French Revolution broke through German provincialism more catastrophically, which makes the exploration of German responses to America all the more interesting. The general widening of horizons in this period is unmistakably indicated by the noticeable increase in the number of books, newspapers, and periodicals that were marketed. The growing importance of the written word expressed by this development was logically supplemented by a marked increase in the size of the reading public.[2]

In the eighteenth century Europe reached far out into the world, as is exemplified by the numerous journeys of discovery from Bering to Cook, and by scientific expeditions to faraway parts of the world. At the same time, Newton's achievements, and later Linnaeus's in botany and zoology, decisively and permanently stimulated the sciences. Geographical expansion and advances in the physical sciences were a background to the evident European interest in new lands and new ways of life. The predilection for the simplicity

---

1. Though not always correct in details, see Palmer, *Age of the Democratic Revolution*, I, 282; Hertz, *German Public Mind*, II, 417–419; Klaus Epstein, *The Genesis of German Conservatism* (Princeton, N.J., 1966), 293–295. For an opposing view see Fay, *L'Esprit révolutionnaire*, 68.
2. See Jentsch, "Zur Geschichte des Zeitungslesens," 14.

of foreign countries was also an expression of the cultural fatigue arising in Europe. As a consequence of these bourgeois inclinations, travel books became a separate and flourishing branch of literature. Among others, the scientist Georg Forster, who participated in Cook's second journey around the world, played an outstanding part in promoting such literature in Germany.[3]

A very fertile field of enterprise for this kind of systematic scientific penetration of the world was America, "where everything is new and important," as Friedrich Maximilian Klinger said in a different context.[4] The Western Hemisphere attracted discoverers and scientists throughout the eighteenth century, of whom the most prominent in Europe was Peter Kalm.[5] Exploration in the New World by many others increased the volume of information on America's fauna and flora.[6] In the field of botany this expansion of interest to regions outside Europe and especially to North America was closely connected with the horticultural fad of the era, which manifested itself in such countries as Germany and Spain.[7] Horticulture offered the most opportunities to cater to the taste for the exotic, for a number of North American plants were successfully cultivated in German landscaped gardens, many of which originated in the latter half of the eighteenth century. With all their apparent naturalness, these plants gave a distinctly foreign touch to European gardens, as the park of Wilhelmshöhe in Kassel shows even today.

In the latter third of the eighteenth century German scientific interest in America concerned not only botany but also other sciences, including medicine.[8] The international reputation of personalities like Benjamin Franklin

3. See Ludwig Uhlig, *Georg Forster. Einheit und Mannigfaltigkeit in seiner geistigen Welt* (Tübingen, 1965), 227–237.

4. "wo alles neu, alles bedeutend ist": Klinger, "Sturm und Drang" (1776), in his *Theater*, 4 vols. (Riga, 1786–1787), II, 268.

5. See Martti Kerkkonen, *Peter Kalm's North American Journey: Its Ideological Background and Results* (Helsinki, 1959), 235–237.

6. See among others the books by Jean Bernard Bossu, Marc Catesby, Pieter Cramer, Nikolaus Joseph Freiherr von Jacquin, Georg Wolfgang Franz Panzer, and Andreas Gotthelf Schütz, as compiled in Dippel, *Americana Germanica*, esp. nos. 2, 17, 65, 85, 128, 297, 379, 398, 554, 662, 691.

7. The botanical gardens on Tenerife, Canary Islands, were founded in 1788 to acclimatize plants, mostly from tropical America, to the Royal Gardens in Spain.

8. See the German publications on forestry that bear directly on North America, by Gottlob Börner, Johann Philipp Du Roi, Humphry Marshall (trans. from the English), Friedrich Kasimir Medicus, Heinrich Christoph Moser, August Christian Heinrich Niemann, and Friedrich Adam Julius von Wangenheim, in Dippel, *Americana Germanica*, nos. 21, 257, 397, 447, 463, 546, 557, 588, 589, 658, 681, 693. Medical treatises include those by Johann David Schoepf, *Materia Medica Americana potissimum Regni Vegetabilis* (Erlangen, 1787); Lionel Chalmers, *Nachrichten über die Witterung and Krankheiten in Südcarolina . . .*, trans. from the English, 2 vols. (Stendal, 1788–1792); Benjamin Smith Barton, *Abhandlung über die vermeinte Zauberkraft der Klapperschlange und anderer amerikanischen Schlangen . . .*, trans. from the English by E.A.W. Zimmermann (Leipzig, 1798). For other sciences see works by

and Benjamin Rush contributed to this interest, especially Franklin's invention of the lightning rod and Rush's discussion of the yellow fever epidemics that occurred in Philadelphia and its environs in the 1790s.[9] There was, in general, increasing esteem for the United States in the world of scholarship,[10] stimulated in part by the founding of the American Philosophical Society and its publications. In the last three decades of the eighteenth century many German scholars were members of that society, among them renowned scientists like Johann Reinhold Forster, Jan Ingenhousz, Johann Friedrich Blumenbach, the anatomist and naturalist from Göttingen, and Eberhard August Wilhelm Zimmermann. German participants in the war, on one side or the other, were members as well, including Christian Friedrich Michaelis, a Hessian field surgeon and son of the famous orientalist, and Major Friedrich von Brahm of Koblenz.[11]

The Enlightenment urge toward rational penetration and comprehension of the world led to a broadening of intellectual interests within the German bourgeoisie, with consequent attention to America. The simultaneous extension of the bourgeoisie's interests to include public life, however, was even more important for their confrontation with the American Revolution and for their political self-understanding. The increased awareness of alien modes of life and foreign societies caused the bourgeoisie to think more about their own situation and the relationship between bourgeois society and the absolutist state.[12] Parallel with this intellectual concern was an expanded interest and participation in public life in Germany.

William Bailey, Johan Daniel Herholdt, Joseph Priestley, and Joseph von Weber, in Dippel, nos. 82, 563, 706, 769, 774.

9. See the numerous German translations of works by Franklin (Dippel, *Americana Germanica*, nos. 22, 40, 121, 135, 223, 388, 405, 427, 454, 508, 539, 579, 635, 649, 650, 680, 714, 816) and by Rush (*ibid.*, nos. 318, 441, 596, 597, 732, 757, 829). Besides Rush's *Beschreibung des gelben Fiebers*, see the treatises by Robert Robertson, *Abhandlung über das Fieber dessen eigenthümliches Wesen, und vernunftmäßige Heilart, als Resultat in Europa, Afrika und Amerika angestellter Bemerkungen*, trans. from the English (Liegnitz and Leipzig, 1796), and Constantine Didier, *Commentatio medica de Febre Flava Americana . . .* (Göttingen, 1800). See also Johann Ferdinand Heinrich Autenrieth's report on his travels through the United States, in Hegewisch and Ebeling, eds., *Amerikanisches Magazin*, I, 131–159; and on these travels see Stübler, *Autenrieth*, 29–35.

10. Cf. E. B. Greene, "Educational Values," *APSP*, LXVIII (1929), 185–194; Hindle, *Pursuit of Science*, 382–385.

11. Chinard, "American Philosophical Society," *APSP*, LXXXVII (1943–1944), 2, 3–5. For example, the Cologne scientist Johann Wilhelm Karl Adolf Freiherr von Hüpsch von Lontzen was a member of several academies and was deeply interested in contact with American scientists; see his letters to Franklin, June 7, 1778 (Franklin Papers, X, 22, APSL, Philadelphia), and to the American Philosophical Society, Apr. 23, 1789, Apr. 15, 1802 (APSA, Philadelphia).

12. See Erich Angermann, "Das 'Auseinandertreten von Staat und Gesellschaft' im Denken des 18. Jahrhunderts," *Zeitschrift für Politik*, N.S., X (1963), 89–101.

Innumerable examples are available to illustrate this awakening interest of the German bourgeoisie in public affairs. Two outstanding works are Friedrich Christoph Jonathan Fischer's *Ueber die Geschichte des Despotismus in Teutschland*,[13] and the German edition of Montesquieu's *Esprit des lois*.[14] Other indications are August Ludwig von Schlözer's Göttingen lectures on politics and forms of government, and the increasing number of political journals and newspapers. For it was in this period, as we have noted, that German newspapers took the first steps toward abandoning the domain of exclusively moral and scholarly journals and advancing into the new field of political journalism. The year 1773, in which Christoph Martin Wieland's *Teutscher Merkur* was founded, is usually considered the beginning of this long-term development, the initial phase of which did not come to a conclusion until the time of the French Revolution.[15]

The American Revolution and the spread of political journalism within Germany were inseparably linked. The Revolution aroused the popular interest; newspapers and periodicals were full of American events and covered them more extensively than any other foreign news. This situation doubtlessly contributed toward making newspapers and periodicals generally more popular. Their number increased, and so did their circulation. Naturally this development did not remain confined to American affairs; the tendency continued into the 1780s, when publications increasingly dealt with topics from German public and political life.

Although the American Revolution did not have effects as profound as the French, the period between 1770 and 1790 does show a great increase in the German bourgeoisie's interest in public life, a development that was directly influenced by the American Revolution. The events in the Western Hemisphere directed the bourgeoisie's attention for the first time in an enduring way to concrete questions of political sovereignty and to the fundamental principles of governmental organization.[16]

13. (Halle, 1780).

14. Charles de Secondat, baron La Brède et de Montesquieu, *Werk vom Geist der Gesetze*, trans. from the French by Karl Gottfried Schreiter and August Wilhelm Hauswald (Altenburg, 1782). Schreiter also translated the first edition (of Crèvecoeur's *Letters from an American Farmer*, which appeared as *Sittliche Schilderung von Amerika* 1784).

15. See Valjavec, *Politische Strömungen*, 95; Vierhaus, "Deutschland vor der Französischen Revolution," 423–426.

16. See Doll, "American History," *APST*, N.S., XXXVIII (1948), 439; Fraenkel, *Amerika im Spiegel des deutschen politischen Denkens*, 20; Schneider, *Pressefreiheit*, 81–100; also Constantin Breffka, *Amerika in der deutschen Literatur* (Cologne, 1917), 3–4.

The Development of Political Divisions

The stimulating effects of the American Revolution on the German bourgeoisie's political thinking are best elucidated by a discussion of the political divisions that were forming in Germany at the time. As Fritz Valjavec has shown in a fundamental study, these undercurrents started to develop in the 1770s and 1780s, enlivened by the unsettling influence of the Enlightenment.[17] Basically, three loose groupings developed, which may be characterized by their differing attitudes toward the Enlightenment. One group approved of the Enlightenment's ideal of liberty and of the rationalization of government in favor of an aspiring bourgeoisie, and urged the necessary political changes. A second faction rejected these enlightened bourgeois ideas because it was, on principle, opposed to the abolition of privileges and to any changes whatsoever. Finally, a third group thought that the Enlightenment's reform impetus did not go far enough in demanding changes in the existing conditions.[18] The terms liberal, conservative, and radical come to mind to describe these groupings, but we must remember that in the 1770s and 1780s there existed only the crude beginnings of such political alignments in Germany. They were still in the developmental stage and had not yet taken definite shape.

Not surprisingly, there is a close correspondence between these divisions over the Enlightenment and the German response to the American Revolution. Let us deal first with the large group of "liberals" (designated as such only for simplicity's sake), those who evidently shared the Enlightenment's liberal bourgeois ideals and approved of the appropriate changes in the structure of the state. During the 1770s and 1780s nearly all of these men were enthusiastic adherents of the American Revolution—Johann Jakob Bodmer, Christoph Daniel Ebeling, Georg and Johann Reinhold Forster, Friedrich and Ludwig Gedike, Isaak Iselin, Friedrich Gottlieb Klopstock, Jakob Mauvillon, Johann Heinrich Pestalozzi, Christian Friedrich Daniel Schubart, Matthias Christian Sprengel, Friedrich Leopold Graf zu Stolberg, Karl von Zinzendorf, and many others. Even if we cannot conclude that every "liberal" in Germany supported the American Revolution, we may safely say that those who ap-

17. Valjavec, *Politische Strömungen*.
18. See Schnabel, *Deutsche Geschichte*, II, 18–19; Valjavec, *Politische Strömungen*, 5, 11, 15–17, 25–26, 77; Heinz Gollwitzer, "Ideologische Blockbildung als Bestandteil internationaler Politik im 19. Jahrhundert," *HZ*, CCI (1965), 308; Epstein, *German Conservatism*, 3, 5, 7–22, 76.

proved were generally proponents of the Enlightenment and its ideals of liberty and reason.

The attitudes of the antagonists of the American Revolution were also molded by general criteria. This again points up that, apart from a few exceptions, responses toward the Revolution were not subjective but were mostly part of a larger complex of ideas on general political order. The political convictions of men basically opposed to the American Revolution—men like Georg Friedrich Brandes, Christian Gottlob Heyne, Heinrich Martin Gottfried Köster, Christoph Heinrich Korn, Christian Leiste, Rochus Friedrich Graf von Lynar, Justus Möser, Gottlob Benedikt von Schirach, Martin Ernst von Schlieffen, Woldemar Friedrich Graf von Schmettau, Johann Matthias Schroeckh, Helferich Peter Sturz, and Johann Georg Zimmermann—were in agreement on fundamental questions of governmental structure. Most of them rejected the ideals of liberty and equality held by large numbers of the bourgeoisie. As a rule, these men also had a predilection for monarchist and aristocratic structures of state and rejected the idea of a bourgeois republic. Lynar, Möser, Schmettau, Zimmermann, and others emphatically stated this conviction, and many showed a distinct antipathy toward the Enlightenment, or at least to all kinds of social and governmental changes nourished by it, as Albrecht von Haller did in his comment on the Wilkes affair in England. Other persons also held these views of course, but in the 1770s and 1780s the bourgeoisie apparently did not give nearly as much approval to these "conservative" attitudes as they did to liberal Enlightenment thought.

The number of those who did not fit into either of these groups is much smaller. Some of them were "liberals" from Hanover, Georg Christoph Lichtenberg for one, who were very much influenced by England and therefore condemned the American Revolution in spite of their assent to the ideal of liberty. Also, the "radicals," though few in number in those years, deserve mention. Like the liberals, they were enthusiastic about the American Revolution, but their basic political convictions went beyond the typical political ideals of the Enlightenment. In print, this attitude was propounded only by Johann Christian Schmohl.[19]

The structure of German bourgeois political ideas in 1789 and during the two following years was substantially the same. At first the French Revolution did not effect a decisive change in bourgeois thinking on the basic problems of revolution. Liberals and radicals like Ebeling, the Forsters, Klopstock, Mauvillon, Peter Ochs, Schubart, Stolberg, Zinzendorf, and many others approved of events in France just as openly as they had the American

19. Schmohl, *Über Nordamerika und Demokratie*; see also Rahmel, *Über den Dienst* (1783), 2d ed. (1784).

Revolution. Those whose conservative attitudes had prompted them to reject the American Revolution now also rejected the French Revolution—Heyne, Schirach, Schmettau, and J. G. Zimmermann among them.

This continuity of political interpretation was possible because the German bourgeoisie at first had no doubt that the French Revolution was the result of the same political principles that had determined their attitudes toward events in America in the years before. Only this background can explain the seemingly fatuous comments made to the French revolutionaries by Germans innocent of their own vanity and completely ignorant of the facts: "Oh Gaul, great and beautiful and honorable is your undertaking. But do act carefully and thoughtfully; . . . then, friend, we shall clasp your hand, rejoicing in our common happiness!"[20] Most such statements originated in countries where the state had taken on a veneer of Enlightenment, Prussia especially. Certainly, the political situation in several German states in the 1780s was much better than in absolutist France,[21] but even an enlightened absolutist Prussia was hardly the pinnacle of liberal state structures, as many of the German bourgeoisie recognized. By this time the American Revolution had permanently influenced the German ideal of a political commonwealth, which enabled some observers to look beyond enlightened despotism, though the German bourgeoisie's reflections on basic political questions in 1789 had by no means reached the stage of thought in France.[22]

As the French Revolution progressed, its German supporters, the liberal bourgeoisie, saw their ideals increasingly challenged. Liberty, property, and social order were threatened by revolutionary terror and the claim to power

20. "O Gallier, groß und schön und ehrenvoll ist dein Unternehmen. Aber gehe mit Vorsicht und Überlegung zu Werke . . . dann, Freund, reichen wir dir traulich die Hand und freuen uns, daß auch du glücklich bist!": Friedrich Leopold Brunn, "Der preußische Staat, der Glücklichste unter allen in Europa," *Berlinisches Journal für Aufklärung*, Oct. 1789, 124–125. See also Johann Traugott Fischer, "Ueber das Eigenthümliche der Preussischen Monarchie," *ibid.*, Jan., May, July 1789, 54–75, 148–161, 43–49. Numerous similar tracts were published during these years; see Karl Biedermann, *Deutschland im achtzehnten Jahrhundert*, 2 vols. (Leipzig, 1854–1880), II/2/3, 1191, and Tschirch, *Öffentliche Meinung in Preußen*, I, 11.

21. See Aris, *Political Thought in Germany*, 25; Fritz Hartung, "Der aufgeklärte Absolutismus," *HZ*, CLXXX (1955), 30–31. For similar contemporary remarks see [Anton Cyriacus Karl Bansen], *Neuere Geschichte der beiden letzten Jahrhunderte zum Nutzen und Vergnügen beschrieben*, 2 vols. (Hanover, 1775–1777), I, 43–44; Fischer, *Despotismus in Teutschland*, 104.

22. See Weber, *America in Imaginative German Literature*, 41; Aris, *Political Thought in Germany*, 31; Droz, *L'Allemagne et la Révolution française*, 22, 26; Valjavec, *Politische Strömungen*, 142, 144; D. W. Brogan, *The Price of Revolution* (New York, 1951), 4–5; Hertz, *German Public Mind*, II, 354; Rudolf Vierhaus, "Montesquieu in Deutschland. Zur Geschichte seiner Wirkung als politischer Schriftsteller im 18. Jahrhundert," in *Collegium Philosophicum. Studien Joachim Ritter zum 60. Geburtstag* (Basel, 1965), 413–414; see also Girod-Chantrans, *Reisen eines Schweizers*, 275.

of the lower classes. The French Revolution thus confronted the German bourgeoisie with questions about their political maxims much more forcefully than the American Revolution had done. It became impossible to hold on to equivocal attitudes. The process of clarification brought on by the French Revolution not only led to the well-known rejection of the revolution by many of the bourgeoisie; it also brought about an intensive review of the substance of bourgeois political beliefs. The political divisions in Germany that emerged during the years of the American Revolution were not destroyed by the complex response to the French Revolution, but a redistribution within the membership of these groups occurred, as well as deeper qualitative distinctions.

During the following years, up to the turn of the century, radical, liberal, conservative liberal, and conservative groups can be clearly distinguished. Their political convictions and their composition do not make them basically new groups. What set them apart from the situation in the 1770s and 1780s was their relative distinction from one another, brought about by an inner process of sharper definition and the clarification of lines of demarcation between the groups.[23] Among the radicals, the German Jacobins, we find Georg Forster, Andreas Georg Friedrich von Rebmann, Adolf Freiherr von Knigge, Ochs, and many others who approved of the American and French Revolutions on principle, just as the late Schmohl had earlier lauded events in the New World. Many, like Ochs and Forster, who can be interpreted as liberals before 1789 now joined the radicals, a development that appreciably increased the number of this group in Germany.[24]

During this period those who can justifiably be called liberals—that is, those who, notwithstanding their basic approval of the American and the French revolutions, outspokenly criticized the latter's violence and its alleged infringements on property rights—had visibly decreased in number as compared to the 1770s and 1780s. Yet among the older liberals were some whom we have come to know as confirmed liberals before 1789, such as Klopstock, Ebeling, Pestalozzi, and Zinzendorf. Thus, the substance of political convictions appears to have been remarkably stable within the bourgeoisie. It is this stability that permits us to trace these political divisions to their beginnings at the time of the American Revolution.

It seems appropriate to set apart from the others a group that may be called, in the sense of the period, "conservative liberals": liberals because the adherents of this group did indeed approve of the bourgeois ideal of liberty as

23. See also generally Hedwig Voegt, *Die deutsche jakobinische Literatur und Publizistik* (Berlin, 1955).
24. See Grab, *Norddeutsche Jakobiner*, 9–10, 30–31, 51, and *passim*.

derived from the Enlightenment, and they unflaggingly admired the American Revolution, even in the 1790s. But unlike Ebeling or Klopstock, men such as Julius August Remer, Sprengel, and E.A.W. Zimmermann sharply condemned the French Revolution for the disregard shown to personal property and for the resort to senseless violence. By attaching more importance to these problems than did the liberals, they demonstrated traits that brought them quite close to the conservatives. It cannot be denied that these views helped to perpetuate Germany's system of government, even if the conservative liberals were not as aware of the consequences of their opinions, as the more ardent conservatives must have been.

The conservative faction, no less than the liberal, had begun before 1789. It was represented by such men as Heyne, Köster, Schirach, Schroeckh, and J. G. Zimmermann. After 1791–1792 they were joined by many former adherents of the bourgeois ideal of liberty, of whom Stolberg is the most famous example. By this time it was clear to these men that the American Revolution would be no danger to the existing order in Germany, unlike the French Revolution, which appeared to the conservatives like a monster from hell. Consequently, they were able to reconcile themselves to American events. Although this change in attitude may have been something more than merely a political maneuver to gain greater support from those circles of the bourgeoisie that were enthusiastic about America, it was by no means the result of hidden sympathies for a bourgeois revolution, as Friedrich von Gentz demonstrated beyond any doubt in his translation of Burke's *Reflections on the Revolution in France*.[25] To the conservatives, America was no more than an argument in their confrontation with the French Revolution.

In sum, it would be a mistake to underestimate the influence of the American Revolution on the development of political groupings within the German bourgeoisie. To be sure, these undercurrents had begun before the inception of the German controversy about the events in America. Yet, more than any other event before 1789, the American Revolution stimulated the first efforts at political clarification. Whereas formerly England had been the political prototype for the liberal bourgeoisie, after 1776 the American Revolution largely supplanted the British image, except in Hanover. The French Revolution built upon, substantiated, and further refined the political divisions originally enhanced by the American Revolution; it did not destroy them. However, it should be noted that the American Revolution, unlike the French, did not produce any sizable radical political group among the bourgeoisie in Germany.

25. Gentz, *Betrachtungen über die französische Revolution*.

Reform or Revolution in Germany?

Given the enthusiasm in Germany for the American Revolution, one question remains: Does the criticism leveled by a liberal and enlightened bourgeoisie against the situation in their own country indicate that they were working toward, or even focusing on, a comparable political overthrow in Germany? True, they would have welcomed changes in accord with their own political principles. But was revolution the inexorable prerequisite? Or did they believe that their social ideals could be attained by reform of existing conditions?

Investigators have often maintained that during the two decades prior to the French Revolution a mood prevailed among the German bourgeoisie that could properly be termed "readiness for revolution."[26] If this is true, why then was there no revolution in Germany? In fact, there is no real evidence to show that such a frame of mind did prevail in the 1770s and 1780s. Even men like Peter Ochs and Georg Forster, who were in the revolutionary vanguard in the 1790s, can hardly be called "radicals," but only "liberals," before 1789.

Numerous local disturbances and crises occurred throughout the German-speaking countries before 1789, but the bourgeoisie as a rule played only a minor part in them. Moreover, it seems very doubtful that these localized phenomena were sufficiently influenced by political maxims to permit us to refer to them as revolutionary incidents. These events were most likely rooted in immediate economic and social grievances without being influenced, in general, by revolutionary ideas or, specifically, by the American Revolution. Neither before nor after 1789 were past events in the New World considered of such importance in Germany that they could stimulate direct political activity. We do know that north German Jacobins explicitly cited the American happenings in their argumentation,[27] and radicals like Forster and Rebmann kept an eye on America even during the French Revolution. But the incentive to revolutionary movements in Germany in the 1790s was doubtlessly furnished by France.

As far as we know, this applies also to the major uprising in Switzerland in the decade before the 1798 revolution, the Stäfa Dispute. In the mid-1790s there was revolutionary unrest, directed against the Zurich canton govern-

---

26. See among others Leo Balet, *Die Verbürgerlichung der deutschen Kunst, Literatur und Musik im 18. Jahrhundert* (Strasbourg, 1936), 164; Werner Krauss, *Studien zur deutschen und französischen Aufklärung* (Berlin, 1963), 331; Krauss, *Die französische Aufklärung im Spiegel der deutschen Literatur des 18. Jahrhunderts* (Berlin, 1963), xxxix.

27. See Grab, *Norddeutsche Jakobiner*, 108, 109.

ment, at Stäfa on Lake Zurich. Even though the uprising was strictly localized and did not endure for long, it was enough to excite the Zurich bourgeoisie. Some investigators have maintained that the American Revolution influenced this event.[28] But the date alone makes that doubtful, and the available sources clearly refer to France. Paine's *Rights of Man* is often mentioned; several copies of the German translation of this pamphlet made the rounds among the insurgents. But the pamphlet, though referring occasionally to the American Revolution, is primarily concerned with the French Revolution. Thus, the sources indicate no direct link to the American Revolution.[29]

In view of these facts and the very small number of radicals, the theory of the German bourgeoisie's "readiness for revolution" seems hardly tenable. If radical thinking had been more widespread in Germany before 1789, undoubtedly reactions to the American Revolution would have been more extensive than they were. True, the majority of the bourgeoisie did not flatly reject the idea of a revolution, but they do not seem to have thought of it yet as their own problem. Thus, it appears that the bourgeoisie before 1789 were not even faced with the alternatives of revolution or reform.[30] In 1783, for example, Sprengel casually remarked that a revolution like the one in America was unthinkable in Europe.[31]

Even after 1789 one cannot generally speak of a readiness to revolt on the part of the German bourgeoisie. E.A.W. Zimmermann, a conservative liberal, was not at all sure in the mid-1790s that the American Revolution, as much as he was in sympathy with it, could be a model for similar change in Germany, the French Revolution being altogether out of the question. In July 1793 the liberal *Schleswigsches Journal* published a treatise "On the Reasons Why, for the Time Being, there will be no Dangerous Major Political Revolution in Germany." It stated that the decisive consideration was the bourgeoisie's social structure, which in Germany consisted primarily of "servants to princes, councillors, secretaries, civil servants, officials, court administrators, suppliers, lawyers, doctors, etc., all living more or less off the crumbs from the princes' tables." How different was the situation, the article

28. See William E. Rappard, *Notre Grande République Soeur. Aperçu sur l'Evolution des Etats-Unis et sur les Rapports Suisses-Américains* (Geneva, 1916), 27–28.

29. See Johann Kaspar Hirzel, "Geschichte der Unruhen im Kanton Zürich 1794/95," 5, 6 (Familienarchiv Hirzel, CCXCV, ZB, Zurich). See also the further files and documents concerning the riots at Stäfa ("Stäfner Handel") which have been consulted in the Zentralbibliothek, Zurich, as well as Otto Hunziker, ed., *Zeitgenössische Darstellungen der Unruhen in der Landschaft Zürich 1794–1798* (Basel, 1897), and Wolfgang von Wartburg, *Zürich und die französische Revolution* (Basel, 1956), 207–362.

30. E.g., Rudolf Vierhaus, "Politisches Bewußtsein in Deutschland vor 1789," *Der Staat*, VI (1967), 184.

31. Sprengel, *Allgemeines historisches Taschenbuch*, 28.

concluded, in a state "where the *tiers-état* consists of, for example, rich businessmen, capitalists, and manufacturers."[32]

Another liberal, Ebeling, who had taken such a lively interest in the American Revolution and who surely was not, on principle, opposed to the French Revolution, welcomed the revolt in Switzerland in 1798 but summarily rejected a similar occurrence in Germany at the end of the century: "As to political revolution, no man of sense wishes (at least now) for a sudden one, nor intruded [*sic*] upon us by others with [*sic*] force of arms. We wish for reforms of abuses where they are." Moreover, he was proud of living in the small, happy republic of Hamburg.[33] An even more outstanding example is Georg Forster, a radical, who played a leading role in the short-lived revolutionary republic of Mainz but who nevertheless was very skeptical, even disapproving, of the idea of a revolution east of the Rhine.[34]

Large numbers of the German bourgeoisie rejected violent revolution as a mode of political change, believing that it was highly dangerous to life and property and did not necessarily have a happy ending, as the developments in France showed. If there was no inclination to revolt among the German bourgeoisie[35]—leaving aside some radicals—it was doubtlessly due in part to their accommodation to "enlightened despotism," which vaguely reflected some of their bourgeois ideals.[36] But we must not disregard the role that the

32. "Fürstendienern, Räten, Sekretarien, Beamten, Offizianten, Hoffaktoren, Liefranten, Advokaten, Ärzten u. dgl., die alle mehr oder weniger von den Brosamen leben, welche von der Herren Tische fallen . . . wo zum Beispiel reiche Negoziaten, Kapitalisten und Fabrikanten den Tiers-état ausmachen": *Schleswigsches Journal*, July 1793, 284, cf. the whole article, 273–290, which was written by Adolph Freiherr von Knigge.

33. Ebeling to William Bentley, Mar. 13, 1799 (Harvard College Library, Cambridge, Mass.). See also Ebeling to Mathew Carey, Feb. 26, 1795 (Lea and Febiger Coll., PHi, Philadelphia), to Noah Webster, May 1, 1795 (Noah Webster Papers, NYPL, New York), and to the American Philosophical Society, Oct. 14, 1793 (APSA, Philadelphia).

34. See G. Forster, *Über die Beziehung der Staatskunst*, ed. Rödel, 92–95; J. Hansen, ed., *Quellen zur Geschichte des Rheinlandes*, II, 468–470; Grab, "Revolutionspropaganda," *Archiv für Sozialgeschichte*, IX (1969), 125; Gordon A. Craig, "Engagement and Neutrality in Germany: The Case of Georg Forster, 1754–1794," *Journal of Modern History*, XLI (1969), 9–10.

35. See among others Johannes Schultze, *Die Auseinandersetzung zwischen Adel und Bürgertum in den deutschen Zeitschriften der letzten drei Jahrzehnte des 18. Jahrhunderts* (Berlin, 1925), 163–165; Droz, *L'Allemagne et la Révolution française*, 26; Droz, *Histoire des doctrines politiques en Allemagne* (Paris, 1968), 47; Horst Rieber, "Liberaler Gedanke und Französische Revolution im Spiegel der Publizistik der Reichsstadt Ulm," *Ulm und Oberschwaben*, XXXIX (1970), 138–148; more general, Franco Venturi, *Utopia and Reform in the Enlightenment* (Cambridge, 1971), esp. 129–136.

36. See Leo Kofler, *Zur Geschichte der bürgerlichen Gesellschaft. Versuch einer verstehenden Deutung der Neuzeit*, 3d ed. (Neuwied and Berlin, 1966), 432; Reinhard Kühnl, *Formen bürgerlicher Herrschaft. Liberalismus–Faschismus* (Reinbek, 1971), 12; see also Ingrid Mittenzwei, "Über das Problem des aufgeklärten Absolutismus," *Zeitschrift für Geschichtswissenschaft*, XVIII (1970), 1165.

American Revolution and the United States played in this context as a kind of fantasy escape from the political realities in Europe. After the Revolution, at the latest, this "land of earthly happiness" had some irresistible attraction,[37] which transformed it into an asylum for oppressed mankind, mainly because it corresponded completely to the bourgeois concept of the ideal state. Instead of actively pursuing political change, both liberals and radicals within the German bourgeoisie longed for the American utopia. Ebeling merely echoed many other German liberals when he wrote to Friedrich Nicolai in 1792: "Meanwhile my consolation is America, whose blissful flourishing is of much solace to me in this time when misfortune is threatening Europe, for I read nothing but American laws, newspapers, and periodicals. If I were in good health I would be living there now."[38] In the 1790s even the German adherents of the French Revolution, of whom Forster and Rebmann were the spokesmen, often cast yearning glances toward America.[39]

These ideas were actively nourished by those who had succeeded in starting a new life in America without entirely losing touch with the Old World. Unfortunately, we do not have many documents from this period concerning emigrants to America. But existing contemporary comments express the fundamental political and social differences between Germany and America with all the clarity we could desire. One war veteran from Hesse-Kassel exclaimed in a letter to his former superior: "How happy I and others are who have left the slavish spirit for republican and democratic angels!"[40] Another contented new citizen of the young republic summed up his changed feelings with the words: "Happy is the man that is not liable to the pryed [*sic*] or condemned by the mere option of a despotic monarch."[41] These and other remarks express the same profound contempt for the European *ancien régime* that we find in the statements of Americans traveling in Europe at this

37. "Land der irdischen Glückseligkeit": Buchenröder, *Nord-Amerika*, IV, 51.
38. "Indeß ich tröste mich mit Amerika, dessen glückseliges Aufblühen mich jetzt, da ich nichts als seine Gesetze, Zeitungen, Journale lese, wegen des Unglücks, das Europa droht, ungemein tröstet. Wäre ich gesund, ich lebte schon dort": July 13, 1792 (Nachlaß Nicolai, XVI, 35, Staatsbibliothek der Stiftung Preußischer Kulturbesitz, Berlin). See also Varnhagen von Ense, ed., *Denkwürdigkeiten Erhards*, 378–379.
39. In addition to the works already mentioned see Trenck, *Merkwürdige Lebensgeschichte*, 278.
40. "Wie glücklich ich und andere geworden bin, die nach republikanisch-demokratischen Engeln den Sklavengeist verlassen haben": Justus Hartmann Scheuber to Friedrich von der Malsburg, Savannah, Ga., Feb. 12, 1796 (340 von der Malsburg, Escheberg, StA, Marburg).
41. A. von Bardeleben to Malsburg, Dec. 12, 1802 (*ibid.*). Malsburg participated in the American war as an officer with the troops of Hesse-Kassel. His sympathies for the American cause and the esteem in which he was still held by many of his former soldiers who stayed in America led to his honorary membership in the German Society of New York, whose president was General Steuben; cf. Murrarius to Malsburg, Mar. 31, 1788 (*ibid.*).

time, a keen satisfaction at the knowledge that one belongs to a better world than the European.

In Germany the events in America did not inspire the wish for an independent bourgeois revolution; rather, they increased the hopes for reforms such as those that were characteristic of the Austrian variant of enlightened despotism, Josephinism. But even in this area the influence of the American Revolution remained very limited. What influence the Revolution did have was most conspicuous in the constitution project in Tuscany. Initiated around 1780 by the grand duke and later emperor, Leopold, it was unmistakably based on American concepts of political structure. Like no other reform project of the era, it shows direct spiritual and personal—Filippo Mazzei played a part—ties with America. That the project was never implemented does not minimize its importance.[42]

American influence on the discussion concerning the Swiss constitution during the Helvetian period was much less pronounced. The 1798 revolution had transformed the old confederacy into the Helvetian Republic, which was dependent on France. Around 1800 a vehement controversy arose over the country's future constitution. The argument centered on the question of whether the centralist state structure in existence since 1798 should continue or whether a federalist organization would be more appropriate for the Swiss people. It would seem reasonable to presume that in all questions concerning federalism the United States would be an obvious example, since it was the only nation organized on this basis. Indeed, many spoke affectionately of the American constitutional structure and its usefulness as an example for Switzerland.[43] But we find, to our astonishment, that there was very little actual analysis and evaluation of the American constitutions. Obviously, there was no clear idea of the 1787 federal Constitution, and the *Federalist* was virtually left unnoticed. It seems that during the discussion about the future constitutional structure of Switzerland there was no clear conception of the Americans' new start; indeed, hardly anyone knew that a confederation and a federation were two different systems, to be kept rigorously distinct. In view of these failures, it is not surprising that the American Constitution did

42. See Palmer, *Age of the Democratic Revolution*, I, 386.
43. E.g., Johann Rudolf Tschiffeli to Franklin, Aug. 1, 1778 (Franklin Papers, XI, 9, APSL, Philadelphia); Johann Georg Müller to his brother Johannes von Müller, May c. 15, 25, July 6, 1799, in Eduard Haug, ed., *Der Briefwechsel der Brüder J. Georg Müller und Joh. v. Müller, 1789–1809* (Frauenfeld, 1893), 175, 177, 185; and J. von Müller to J. G. Müller, May 29, 1799, in J. von Müller, *Sämmtliche Werke*, ed. J. G. Müller, XXXII, 53. Johannes persuaded his brother that the American example was not adaptable to their native Switzerland. See also Philipp Albert Stapfer to Louis Begos, Oct. 8, 1800, Feb. 23, 1801, in Johannes Strickler, ed., *Amtliche Sammlung der Acten aus der Zeit der Helvetischen Republik (1798–1803)*, VI (Bern, 1897), 260, 721 (according to these letters, Napoleon favored the idea of an American-like federation as the basis for the new Swiss constitution).

not have a lasting influence on Switzerland, especially since the discussion there did not have any direct results.[44] America's influence in this matter was much less than its influence on French constitutional thinking before 1792.[45]

It seems possible, however, that the American example had some influence in another field where reform thought in Germany was noticeable at that time. These decades witnessed in theory and practice an ascendancy of the country estates in political affairs. As yet, we know very little about this development and its fundamental causes. However, we can by no means exclude the possibility that the experience of the American Revolution and the resultant increased confrontation with problems of governmental structure and power had some influence.[46]

However, another fairly well-known reform of the late eighteenth century was almost certainly not influenced directly by events in America, namely, the Prussian General Code, which went into effect in 1794. This important work of legal codification united in one essential point the demands of the moment and the ideals associated with America: complete freedom of creed and conscience for all citizens.[47] This provision satisfied a central demand of the German Enlightenment and at the same time paralleled an American development that had contributed largely to making America the promised land in the eyes of the bourgeoisie.[48]

It might be supposed that the American Revolution would have stimulated nationalist sentiments in Europe, since in some respects the war had the character of a struggle for liberation from foreign control. But this aspect of the faraway events in America had no immediate political or practical consequences in Germany, and could not arouse a wave of nationalist enthusiasm. True, in Switzerland some kind of national consciousness had developed after 1760, when the Helvetian Society was founded.[49] But the bourgeoisie in

44. See the tracts by Bieler, Bernhard Friedrich Kuhn, Franz Rudolf Lerber, and Louis Secrétan listed in Dippel, *Americana Germanica*, nos. 768, 819–822, 830. Except for Secrétan's *Réflexions sur le Fédéralisme en Helvétie* (Bern, 1800), all the others spoke favorably, though rather vaguely, about the U.S. Constitution as a model for Switzerland.

45. Cf. Echeverria, *Mirage in the West*, 163–164.

46. Aretin, *Heiliges Römisches Reich*, I, 32, 34, makes the same assumption; see also, more generally, Vierhaus, "Deutschland vor der Französischen Revolution," 124–125.

47. See among others Hermann Conrad, *Die geistigen Grundlagen des Allgemeinen Landrechts für die preußischen Staaten von 1794* (Cologne and Opladen, 1958), 11; Lothar Weber, "Die Parität der Konfessionen in der Reichsverfassung von den Anfängen der Reformation bis zum Untergang des alten Reichs im Jahre 1806"(publ. Ph.D. diss., University of Bonn, 1961), 245–246; Aretin, *Heiliges Römisches Reich*, I, 39.

48. See, e.g., Franz Rudolph von Grossinger, *Allgemeines Toleranz und Religions System für alle Staaten und Völker der Welt* (Leipzig, 1784), 20–22; Jäger, *Zeitungs-Lexicon*, 2d ed., II, 261b.

49. See among others Wartburg, *Zürich und die französische Revolution*, 39–43; Ulrich Im Hof, *Aufklärung in der Schweiz* (Bern, 1970), 81–86.

the Holy Roman Empire were still largely cosmopolitan and preferred to think of themselves as members of a worldwide *république des lettres* rather than to find their destiny in the formation of an independent national state. Their political consciousness had not yet reached the level necessary for such a process, which occurred only after they had gone through the long experience of the French Revolution and the subsequent Napoleonic era.[50]

Undoubtedly, there are other examples of real or possible American influences. But after this brief survey it seems safe to conclude that only in exceptional cases did the American Revolution directly influence concrete national reform projects, which as a rule were neither initiated nor instituted by the bourgeoisie.[51] On the other hand, bourgeois *ideas* of reform seem to have been influenced quite often by the experience of the American Revolution. This becomes more clear if we consider that German confrontation with the American Revolution was mainly a concern of the bourgeoisie. It was their political consciousness more than governmental reforms that reflected the enduring effects of the American Revolution in Germany.

50. See Friedrich Meinecke, "Weltbürgertum und Nationalstaat," in his *Werke*, ed. Hans Herzfeld, V (Munich, 1962); Alfred Luz, "Das deutsche Nationalgefühl im Zeitalter der Französischen Revolution" (unpubl. Ph.D. diss., University of Tübingen, 1941); Wolfgang von Groote, *Die Entstehung des Nationalbewußtseins in Nordwestdeutschland 1790–1830* (Göttingen, 1955); Vierhaus, "Deutschland vor der Französischen Revolution," 48–55; Ritter, "Neudeutscher Nationalismus," in his *Das deutsche Problem*, 55–146.

51. Palmer, *Age of the Democratic Revolution*, I, 265–266, comes to a similar conclusion.

13. The Political Thinking of the German Bourgeoisie

The German Bourgeoisie's Evaluation of the American Revolution

To assess properly the influence of the American Revolution on the formation of German bourgeois political consciousness in the last third of the eighteenth century, it is imperative to see clearly the origins of bourgeois judgment of the events in the New World. But before this can be attempted, we must visualize the conditions that underlay the formation of political judgment, both as to the process itself and its results.

Numerous investigations have shown that the American Revolution commanded intense attention virtually everywhere in Europe. Both the nobility and the bourgeoisie, whether in countries directly involved in the war or in noncombatant countries, were strongly interested, though, of course, there were important differences from place to place.[1] The German-speaking

---

1. On the impact of the American Revolution in different non-German countries in general, see among others, Samuel Flagg Bemis, *Diplomacy of the American Revolution* (Bloomington, Ind., 1957), 113–114; Palmer, *Age of the Democratic Revolution*, I, 239–282. From the mass of literature bearing on Canada, I need only cite Gustave Lanctot, *Canada and the American Revolution 1774–1783*, trans. from the French (Cambridge, Mass., 1967). On Great Britain see William John Potts, "British Views of American Trade and Manufactures During the Revolution," *PMHB*, VII (1883), 194–199; Fred J. Hinkhouse, *The Preliminaries of the American Revolution as Seen in the English Press 1763–1775* (New York, 1926); Eunice Wead, "British Public Opinion of the Peace with America 1782," *AHR*, XXXIV (1928–1929), 513–531; Dora Mae Clark, *British Opinion and the American Revolution* (New Haven, Conn., and London, 1930); Robert B. Heilman, *America in English Fiction 1760–1800: The Influences of the American Revolution* (Baton Rouge, La., 1937); Charles R. Ritcheson, *British Politics and the American Revolution* (Norman, Okla., 1954); Ritcheson, "The London Press and the First Decade of American Independence, 1783–1793," *Journal of British Studies*, II (1963), 88–109; Ritcheson, *Aftermath of Revolution*; Martin Kallich and Andrew MacLeish, eds., *The American Revolution Through British Eyes* (Evanston, Ill., 1962); Bernard Donoughue, *British Politics and the American Revolution: The Path to War, 1773–1775* (London, 1964); Richard W. Van Alstyne, "Great Britain, the War for Independence and the 'Gathering Storm' in Europe, 1775–1778," *Huntington Library Quarterly*, XXVII (1963–1964), 311–346; Van Alstyne, *Empire and Independence: The International*

countries were no exception. No happening in world politics in the 1770s and 1780s captivated those classes of society as completely as events in distant America. Many contemporary statements verify this fact. Lafayette, whose popularity in Germany and in America in the 1770s and 1780s is attributable only to his participation in the War of Independence, summed up for John Jay his impression of a tour of Germany: "Wherever I went, America was naturally the subject of conversation."[2] He undoubtedly voiced the thoughts of many others.

The events in the New World were not the special concern of any individual government or of only certain commercial groups. As the bourgeoisie saw things, the American Revolution concerned society in general. This explains the overwhelming interest that the American Revolution, as compared to other contemporary events, aroused in Germany. It also seems to justify linking these events and their interpretation to the bourgeoisie's political consciousness.

The bourgeoisie had at their disposal, no doubt, an immense quantity of informative material about America. Translations of foreign publications were much more in evidence than was usually the case. Yet numerous impor-

History of the American Revolution (New York, 1965); Solomon Lutnick, The American Revolution and the British Press 1775–1783 (Columbia, Mo., 1967); Dalphy I. Fagerstrom, "Scottish Opinion and the American Revolution," WMQ, 3d Ser., XI (1954), 252–275. On France see Henri Doniol, Histoire de la participation de la France à l'établissement des Etats-Unis d'Amérique. Correspondance diplomatique et documents, 5 vols. (Paris, 1886–1892); Paul Leicester Ford, "Affaires de l'Angleterre et de l'Amérique," PMHB, XIII (1889), 222–226; Fay, L'Esprit révolutionnaire; Frank Monaghan, French Travellers in the United States, 1765–1932 (New York, 1933), viii; Sagnac, Fin de l'Ancien Régime, 335; Echeverria, Mirage in the West. On the Netherlands see Herman Theodor Colenbrander, De Patriottentijd. Hoofdzakelijk naar buitenland bescheiden, 3 vols. (The Hague, 1897–1899); Friedrich Edler, The Dutch Republic and the American Revolution (Baltimore, 1911); Francis Paul Renault, Les Provinces-Unies et la Guerre d'Amérique (1775–1784), I–V (Paris, 1924–1932). On Belgium see Thomas Kieley Gorman, America and Belgium: A Study of the Influence of the United States upon the Belgian Revolution of 1789–1790 (London, 1925). On Italy see Emilio Goggio, "Italy and the American War of Independence," Romanic Review, XX (1929), 25–34; Dante Visconti, Le origini degli Stati Uniti d'America e l'Italia (Rome, 1940). On Sweden see Adolph Burnett Benson, Sweden and the American Revolution (New Haven, Conn., 1926); Elovson, Amerika i svensk litteratur; H. A. Barton, "Sweden and the War of American Independence," WMQ, 3d Ser., XXIII (1966), 408–430. On Poland see Miecislaus Haiman, Poland and the American Revolutionary War (Chicago, 1932); Zofia Libiszowska, Opinia polska wobec rewolucji amerykańskiej w XVIII wieku (Lodz, 1962) (with English summary, pp. 146–147); Libiszowska, "L'Opinion polonaise et la révolution américaine au XVIIIᵉ siècle," Revue d'histoire moderne et contemporaine, XVII (1970), 984–998. On Russia see Francis Paul Renault, Les Relations Diplomatiques entre la Russie et les Etats-Unis (1776–1825) (Paris, 1923); Dieter Boden, Das Amerikabild im russischen Schrifttum bis zum Ende des 19. Jahrhunderts (Hamburg, 1968), 31–48.
2. "Partout où j'allais, l'Amérique était naturellement l'objet de la conversation": Feb. 11, 1786, in Mémoires du général Lafayette, II, 144.

tant publications, especially from England and France, were overlooked and remained untranslated or were never printed in Germany in a foreign language. This selectivity was not based on technical communications problems. It seems rather that certain aspects of events in America did not arouse appreciable interest, particularly the internal and constitutional development of the United States. Significant documents, such as the Declaration of Independence, the Articles of Confederation, the Northwest Ordinance, and the *Federalist* were not taken into account sufficiently, if at all. Not until the end of the eighteenth century was there even slight interest in the federal Constitution of 1787. Basic questions of economy and finance, foreign relations, internal distribution of political power, and formation and rivalry of political parties were likewise almost wholly neglected.[3]

Like their counterparts in France,[4] the German bourgeoisie combined excessive enthusiasm and sympathy for America and its revolution with a very low level of factual knowledge. The enthusiasm often led them to forget the deficiencies in their knowledge, but an informed American could hardly overlook them. Thus, in spite of his warm reception in the Palatinate, Jakob Rieger, an officer in the American service, said at the end of 1778: "In general the Germans have had but a faint idea of the strength of our country and what our glorious opposition was for."[5] Whereas Rieger referred mainly to the bourgeoisie and lower strata, Lafayette in the 1780s observed the same of the highest social classes, calling them generally "ill informed."[6] And at the end of the century John Quincy Adams noted that the men he talked to in Prussia had only "a few general ideas" about America.[7] But these three witnesses from three different decades shared positive as well as negative impressions: they found that the level of interest in America was high everywhere.

We might well refer here to John Locke, who in his *Essay Concerning Human Understanding* differentiated between two faculties for determining true from false: "knowledge," which is *certain*, on the one hand, and "judgment," which is *probable*, on the other, the latter being able to qualify as a

3. For a less critical view, however, see Friedrich Kapp, "Zur deutschen wissenschaftlichen Literatur über die Vereinigten Staaten von Amerika," *HZ*, XXXI (1874), 241–242.

4. See Fay, *L'Esprit révolutionnaire*, 102; Echeverria, *Mirage in the West*, 43.

5. To Franklin, Oct. 10, 1778 (Franklin Papers, XII, 40, APSL, Philadelphia).

6. To Washington, Feb. 6, 1786, in Gottschalk, ed., *Letters of Lafayette to Washington*, 306; similarly, Lafayette to Franklin, Feb. 10, 1786, in John Bigelow, ed., *The Works of Benjamin Franklin*, 12 vols. (New York, 1904), XI, 228–229; Gottschalk, *Lafayette between the Revolutions*, 189.

7. Entry of Dec. 7, 1797, in C. F. Adams, ed., *Memoirs of John Quincy Adams*, I, 210; see also the following entry.

right judgment only by being in agreement with reality.[8] If we transfer this distinction to the German bourgeoisie's appraisal of the American Revolution and the United States, we can easily see that as a rule bourgeois opinions about America belong not in the category of reliable knowledge, but in the Lockean category of judgment; that is, bourgeois opinions were a strange but characteristic mixture of foregone conclusions and prevailing ideas, supplemented and interwoven with partial information. This obvious lack of solid data was only to a small degree due to communications difficulties, and it was not due to a general lack of interest. It seems that the cause of these shortcomings lies primarily with the German bourgeoisie's historical situation and the interests shaped by it. In this regard Jürgen Habermas has spoken of "the interest that guides knowledge."[9] If one accepts that the bourgeoisie's situation and their resulting "interests" had indeed profoundly influenced their insight,[10] then we must begin with that premise if we want to understand their confrontation with the American Revolution and the United States in the last third of the eighteenth century.

The aspiring bourgeoisie thought it desirable, above all, to have more unobstructed latitude for economic and cultural activities and to have equal status with the privileged social classes. Given their immediate situation, they focused mainly on these questions and on the basic goals of general civil and legal parity, equality of economic opportunity, religious toleration, and security before the law.[11] Detailed constitutional questions such as the problems of federalism, political representation and responsibility, and the delegation of governmental power, which were being discussed in America, hardly aroused interest at first, since these questions were of no practical importance in Germany until after an extensive change of the existing political and social situation of the bourgeoisie. When the French Revolution brought such a change potentially closer, these questions were likely to receive more attention. It thus becomes understandable that the German bourgeoisie of the last three decades of the eighteenth century, limited by the boundaries of their immediate practical interests, had little concern for the detailed consti-

8. John Locke, *An Essay Concerning Human Understanding*, ed. John W. Yolton (London, 1961), II, 248–249 (bk. IV, chap. 14, §4).

9. Habermas, "Erkenntnis und Interesse," in his *Technik und Wissenschaft als "Ideologie,"* 159.

10. See *ibid.*, 159–164; Habermas, *Erkenntnis und Interesse*, 59–87; Vojin Milić, "Das Verhältnis von Gesellschaft und Erkenntnis in Marx' Werk," in Kurt Lenk, ed., *Ideologie. Ideologiekritik und Wissenssoziologie*, 4th ed. (Neuwied, 1970), esp. 178–179.

11. See Kühnl, *Formen bürgerlicher Herrschaft*, 12; Albrecht Wellmer, *Kritische Gesellschaftstheorie und Positivismus*, 3d ed. (Frankfurt, 1971), 48; also Karl Marx, :"Die Bourgeoisie und die Konterrevolution," *Neue Rheinische Zeitung*, Dec. 10, 15, 1848, reprinted in Marx and Friedrich Engels, *Werke*, ed. Institut für Marxismus-Leninismus beim ZK der SED, 39 vols. (Berlin, 1958–1968), VI, 104–105, 107–108.

tutional and internal problems of a faraway country. With regard to their own political situation, these problems had comparatively low informational value.

On the other hand, the situation was very different with respect to American revolutionary ideals, especially the ideals of liberty and equality. More than any other concepts, these corresponded to the bourgeois intellectual world of the Enlightenment, and they were of resounding importance within the framework of existing political and social realities. Both liberty and equality had been effectively realized in the New World, or so it appeared in Germany. During the entire length of the discussion on America and its Revolution, the apparent implementation of these ideals into political and social reality was much more important to the German bourgeoisie than any detailed questions of constitutional structure.

Only the German bourgeoisie's historically conditioned special interests can explain the peculiar slant of these convictions. For their stated views on revolutionary ideals are more of a comment on their own situation than an analysis of the American reality, which they bypassed only too often. The distortion inherent in their interpretation is best revealed by their belief that the ideal of equality expressed during the American Revolution applied to internal politics and directly affected the social structure. Yet no principle with this consequence was either a theoretical or a practical aim of the American Revolution. The German bourgeoisie, however, striving for civil and legal equality and the abolition of privileges within their own social and political realm, thought of equality as one of the foremost goals of the American Revolution.

A similar distortion, but this time the other way around, applies to the ideal of human rights, which was a vital element in the American Revolution but was hardly noted in Germany before 1789. Fritz Hartung has suggested that the "restrained character" of the American declarations in this area explains the weak echo they got from Germany.[12] But this cannot be the definitive cause. Compared to the ideal of equality, which was not an original aim of the American Revolution, the safeguarding of the human rights of man can be interpreted as one of the Revolution's major goals, in spite of the deficiencies of the early constitutions in implementing these rights. But in Germany, equality was a much more popular topic of conversation. Therefore, the reasons for the German neglect of the rights of man issue must be found elsewhere.

In contrast to the ideals of liberty and equality, the Enlightenment had in no comparable way prepared the German-speaking countries to receive the

12. Hartung, *Die Entwicklung der Menschen- und Bürgerrechte von 1776 bis zur Gegenwart*, 3d ed. (Göttingen, 1964), 12.

idea of human rights that was coming from America. The German bourgeoisie did not yet consider the establishment of human rights as one of their main political objectives, and they therefore paid scarcely any attention to its emergence as a fundamental principle of politics in the New World. This initial indifference to certain far-reaching problems of politics and to practical politics in general (essentially an attempt to retain a sphere of privacy in defiance or denial of the public sphere) is graphically illustrated by a remark made by Christian Friedrich Michaelis, the field surgeon from Hesse-Kassel and son of the orientalist at the University of Göttingen, when he visited Benjamin Rush before returning to Germany with the auxiliary troops. Michaelis thanked Rush for his great hospitality, although he was "a man of so different a creed in politics." But, Michaelis continued, "what are politics to us? Or what has the republic of letters to do with taxation?"[13]

The Enlightenment as a Bourgeois Ideology

In addition to the immediate political and social situation of the German bourgeoisie as a factor influencing their response to the American Revolution, it is also necessary to consider the philosophy of the Enlightenment, which provided the intellectual context for the expression of bourgeois political ideas.[14] Though the Enlightenment was a phenomenon of the entire European world, with certain common characteristics, it would nevertheless be a mistake to overlook the differences between what was called variously

13. Michaelis to Rush, July 22, 1783 (Rush Collection, MSS Correspondence, X, 24, Library Company of Philadelphia).

14. See among others Cassirer, *Philosophie der Aufklärung*; Fritz Valjavec, *Geschichte der abendländischen Aufklärung* (Vienna and Munich, 1961); Vierhaus, "Deutschland vor der Französischen Revolution," 302–366; Isidor Schneider, ed., *The Enlightenment: The Culture of the Eighteenth Century* (New York, 1965); Peter Gay, *The Enlightenment: An Interpretation*, 2 vols. (New York, 1966–1969); Norman Hampson, *The Enlightenment* (Harmondsworth, 1968); Lester G. Crocker, ed., *The Age of Enlightenment* (New York, 1969); Im Hof, *Aufklärung in der Schweiz*; Venturi, *Italy and the Enlightenment*, trans. and ed. Woolf, esp. 1–32; also Max Horkheimer and Theodor W. Adorno, *Dialektik der Aufklärung. Philosophische Fragmente*, 2d ed. (Frankfurt, 1969), esp. 50–127. On America, and notably on John Adams, see Zoltán Haraszti, *John Adams and the Prophets of Progress* (Cambridge, Mass., 1952); Edward Handler, *America and Europe in the Political Thought of John Adams* (Cambridge, Mass., 1964), 34; Loren Baritz, *City on a Hill: A History of Ideas and Myths in America* (New York, 1964), 146; see, however, Daniel J. Boorstin, *America and the Image of Europe: Reflections on American Thought* (New York, 1960), 63–78. Also see Adams to Jefferson, Nov. 13, 1815, in Cappon, ed., *Adams-Jefferson Letters*, II, 456.

die Aufklärung, the Enlightenment, *les Lumieres*, and *l'Illuminismo*.[15] The differences are evident in the different characteristics of the leading personalities of each country as well as in the leading periodicals, which in Germany were the *Berlinische Monatsschrift* and the *Allgemeine deutsche Bibliothek*. As opposed to the French Enlightenment, the German movement seems to have been much more static in its consciousness of history and its interpretation of contemporary events. Also, enlightened thought in Germany reflected the peculiarly German situation of religious particularism and heterogeneity by making the goal of religious toleration one of its foremost demands.[16] But we would not do justice to the German Enlightenment if we interpreted it merely as a movement to procure religious toleration from the state. It was in its aims the expression of the whole reform sentiment of the bourgeoisie.[17]

It has been repeatedly stated that the Aufklärung in Germany was essentially an unpolitical, spiritual movement,[18] an interpretation that has met with little contradiction up to now.[19] There were indeed contemporary voices who agreed with Mauvillon when in the mid-1770s he deplored that "our nation is extremely unpolitical." He was convinced that the bourgeoisie's interest in political problems was not intense enough.[20]

---

15. See Gay, *Enlightenment*, I, 4–8; Gay, "The Enlightenment," in Woodward, ed., *Comparative Approach to American History*, 34–46.

16. See, e.g., Gotthold Ephraim Lessing's *Erziehung des Menschengeschlechts*, and his drama, *Nathan der Weise*, both in his *Werke*, ed. Herbert G. Göpfert (Munich, 1970–); also Kant, "Beantwortung der Frage: Was ist Aufklärung?" in his *Werke*, ed. Weischedel, VI, esp. 60; Gay, *Enlightenment*, I, 328–335; Droz, *Doctrines politiques*, 34–35; Im Hof, *Aufklärung in der Schweiz*, 61–63; Epstein, *German Conservatism*, 34; Werner August Mühl, *Die Aufklärung an der Universität Fulda mit besonderer Berücksichtigung der philosophischen und juristischen Fakultät (1734–1805)* (Fulda, 1961).

17. See generally Lucien Goldmann, *Der christliche Bürger und die Aufklärung* (Neuwied and Berlin, 1968), 38–43, 91, 93; also Kühnl, *Formen bürgerlicher Herrschaft*, 13.

18. E.g., Wilhelm Dilthey, "Friedrich der Große und die deutsche Aufklärung," in his *Gesammelte Schriften*, ed. Bernhard Groethuysen, 3d ed., III (Stuttgart and Göttingen, 1962), 133; Hermann August Korff, *Voltaire im literarischen Deutschland des XVIII. Jahrhunderts* (Heidelberg, 1917–1918), I, 337–340; Valjavec, *Aufklärung*, 91, and *passim*; Hans Matthias Wolff, *Die Weltanschauung der deutschen Aufklärung in geschichtlicher Entwicklung*, 2d ed. (Bern, 1963), 10; Wilhelm Mommsen, *Größe und Versagen des deutschen Bürgertums*, 2d ed. (Munich, 1964), 20–21; Kurt Klotzbach, *Das Eliteproblem im politischen Liberalismus. Ein Beitrag zum Staats- und Gesellschaftsbild des 19. Jahrhunderts* (Cologne, 1966), 13; Klaus Scholder, "Grundzüge der theologischen Aufklärung in Deutschland," in *Geist und Geschichte der Reformation. Festschrift für Hanns Rückert* (Berlin, 1966), 484; Gay, *Enlightenment*, I, 4; see also Krieger, *German Idea of Freedom*, 43; Im Hof, *Aufklärung in der Schweiz*, 5.

19. E.g., Krauss, *Studien zur deutschen und französischen Aufklärung*, 309–399; Gerhard Schulz, *Das Zeitalter der Gesellschaft* (Munich, 1969), 81.

20. "Unsre Nation ist im höchsten Grade unpolitisch": Mauvillon, *Sammlung von Aufsätzen*, I, [8].

A few months before the outbreak of the French Revolution Gottlob Nathanael Fischer, a noted pedagogue and writer, remarked that the Aufklärung had two basic aims, "political and religious enlightenment," the former being nothing but the postulation of the "proper concepts of the essential needs of man in society." This, according to Fischer, meant both theoretical and practical knowledge of the relationship between citizen, state, and society.[21] Such an aim can hardly be called unpolitical, especially since it gives us a wider framework in which to understand the German bourgeoisie's interest in the American Revolution. The confrontation with the American Revolution, therefore, necessarily led to discussion in a very general way of the basic principles of politics.

If we inquire into the German bourgeoisie's conceptions of their essential social and political needs, the first in order of importance would be liberty, which they saw as a political goal directly related to society's material welfare. Liberty in this sense also implied civil and legal equality, for the material well-being that was sought through liberty was attainable only when special privilege was abolished and all citizens were allowed to develop freely from the same starting point.[22] It is not hard to see that Enlightenment concepts of liberty and equality—the "true and genuine liberty" that was declared to be an absolute prerequisite for a "society's welfare"[23]—were in fact inherent in the political notion of liberty.

The Aufklärung indeed had political overtones that help to explain the character of the German bourgeois response to the American Revolution. There were definite limitations during the 1770s and 1780s on the scope of bourgeois interest in the material problems of politics; but under the influence of the French Revolution, German thought expanded to include previously disregarded constitutional and other questions. On the other hand, some of these limitations on German interest in politics, induced partly by the character of the Enlightenment in Germany, undeniably remained even into a much later period.[24] Nevertheless, I do not believe that the Aufklärung

---

21. "politische und religiöse Aufklärung . . . als richtige Begriffe von den wesentlichen Bedürfnissen des gesellschaftlichen Menschen": Fischer, "Ueber politische Aufklärung," *Berlinisches Journal für Aufklärung*, Jan. 1789, 1–2, cf. 3–5, 9–10.

22. See Isaak Iselin in his *Ephemeriden der Menschheit*, Jan. 1776, 116–117, and Eberhard August Wilhelm Zimmermann in Imlay, *Westliche Lande der Nordamerikanischen Freistaaten*, xii.

23. "wahre und echte Freiheit. . . . Wohlstand einer Gesellschaft": *Ephemeriden der Menschheit*, Oct. 1776, 107.

24. See "Warum haben die Teutschen keinen politischen Charakter?" *Minerva*, 1813, I, 100–105; Helmuth Plessner, *Die verspätete Nation. Über die politische Verführbarkeit bürgerlichen Geistes* (Stuttgart, 1959); Carlo Schmid, "Die deutschen Bildungsschichten und die Politik," in his *Politik und Geist* (Stuttgart, 1961), 51–81. In this context it may be noted that in recent times sociologists have given convincing proof that even an apolitical attitude has

is fairly characterized as "unpolitical." Contemporaries were keenly aware of its political components, even if the movement did not produce a Montesquieu, Rousseau, Jefferson, or Franklin. Justus Möser was often compared to the latter, and many German antagonists of the French Revolution were convinced that Enlightenment philosophers, writers, Freemasons, and illuminati were mainly responsible for the French cataclysm.[25]

If the Aufklärung, in agreement with both contemporary and present-day interpretations, is understood to include a political dimension as an essential element, however limited it may have been, this realization sheds an entirely different light on the innumerable statements expressing contemporary pride in belonging to an enlightened philosophical age.[26] The same Jakob Mauvillon who reproached his fellow citizens for their lack of concern about politics considered himself happy "if our efforts contribute a little toward spreading liberal thought among our fellow countrymen,"[27] the term "liberal" probably being a mere synonym for enlightened. This understanding of the Aufklärung explains also a retrospective statement made by an observer in the early 1790s: "It was fortunate for mankind that when the American republic was formed, Europe's spirit was enlivened by philosophy, the latter, in turn, giving the former a more rational direction."[28]

The philosophical link between the European Enlightenment and the American Revolution was pointed out by Isaak Iselin: "I am strongly inclined to believe that North America is the country where reason and humanity will develop much more rapidly than anywhere else."[29] If there was such a cogent link between reason and humanity and the American Revolution,

---

far-reaching political implications; see Theodor W. Adorno, "Einleitung," in Adorno *et al.*, *Positivismusstreit*, 71–72, and Kurt Lenk, "Werturteilsfreiheit als Fiktion," in Adorno *et al.*, *Soziologie zwischen Theorie und Empirie*, ed. Willy Hochkeppel (Munich, 1970), 145–149.

25. E.g., *Geist des achtzehnten Jahrhunderts*, 5, 21, 29; Heinrich August Ottokar Reichard to Johann Georg Zimmermann, Jan. 1, 1793 (Nachlaß Zimmermann, A II, no. 75, fol. 19, LB, Hanover); Heinrich Martin Gottfried Köster to Jean André de Luc, Dec. 10, 1796 (de Luc Collection, YUL, New Haven, Conn.); Heinrich Scheel, "Die Mainzer Republik im Spiegel der deutschen Geschichtsschreibung," *Jahrbuch für Geschichte*, IV (1969), 15; Droz, "La Légende du complot illuministe," *Revue historique*, CCXXVI (1961), 313–338.

26. See among others Pezzl, *Faustin*, 331; Christoph Daniel Ebeling to Joel Barlow, Mar. 16, 1796, in Lane, ed., *Letters of Ebeling*, 18.

27. "wenn unsere Bemühungen etwas zur Ausbreitung einer liberalen Denkungsart unter unsern Landsleuten beiträgt": Mauvillon, in his translation of Raynal, *Besitzung und Handel der Europäer in beiden Indien*, III (1775), [17].

28. "Zum Glück für die Menschheit belebte damals, als der amerikanische Freistaat sich bildete, die Philosophie den Geist von Europa, und dieser erhielt von ihr eine vernünftigere Richtung": Imlay, *Westliche Lande der Nordamerikanischen Freistaaten*, 1.

29. "Je suis fort tenté de croire que l'Amérique septentrionale est le pays où la raison et l'humanité se développeront beaucoup plus rapidement que partout ailleurs": to Peter Ochs, June 17, 1777, in Steiner, ed., *Korrespondenz des Peter Ochs*, I, 104.

between the Enlightenment and America, then we can feel confident that the German reaction to the revolution in the New World is in itself an important disclosure of the dissemination of Enlightenment ideas, including their political implications.

If we distinguish the German antagonists of the American Revolution from its supporters according to social criteria, we find that the Revolution's sympathizers, who as a rule were equally in favor of the Enlightenment, were largely of the bourgeoisie, whereas most of its antagonists belonged to the nobility. Thus, it was mainly members of the bourgeoisie who were more than usually affected by the political dimensions of the Aufklärung, just as the Enlightenment as a whole seems to have been a concern primarily of the bourgeoisie, notwithstanding the approval it found among the nobility.

If the Enlightenment was mostly a bourgeois affair, then it may also be interpreted as an "ideology,"[30] meaning, in this case, not a false consciousness,[31] but used as "a collective term denoting the social consciousness of any one class."[32] In this sense the Enlightenment appears to be the theoretical expression of the political aims of the bourgeoisie, especially with respect to their striving for equality with the privileged classes and their desire to be unfettered in seizing economic opportunities. The intellectual leaders of the Enlightenment did not present these ideals of liberty and equality as the expression of a particular social class, with specific class interests in mind. Instead, wittingly or unwittingly, they universalized these claims and ideals by calling them the natural product of reason, or the expression of universal humanity, and thus gave the Enlightenment an appeal to followers beyond the bourgeoisie.[33] But it was the very controversy over the American Revolution, and over the French even more so, that made clear how much the

30. On the term *ideology* see among others Hans Barth, *Wahrheit und Ideologie* (Zurich, 1945); Theodor Geiger, *Ideologie und Wahrheit. Eine soziologische Kritik des Denkens*, 2d ed. (Neuwied, 1968); Kurt Lenk, ed., *Ideologie*, 4th ed. (Neuwied, 1970); Hermann Zeltner, *Ideologie und Wahrheit. Zur Kritik der politischen Vernunft* (Stuttgart, 1966); *Akten des XIV. Internationalen Kongresses für Philosophie, Vienna, Sept. 2–9, 1968*, I (Vienna, 1968), 381–509.

31. Compare the term as used by Marx in his *Deutsche Ideologie* and in other writings. See also Max Horkheimer, *Anfänge der bürgerlichen Geschichtsphilosophie* (Frankfurt, 1971), 56–57.

32. Erich Hahn, "Zur Kritik des bürgerlichen Bewußtseins," in Lenk, ed., *Ideologie*, 155; see also Henri Lefebvre, "Soziologie der Erkenntnis und Ideologie," in *Folgen einer Theorie. Essays über "Das Kapital" von Karl Marx*, 4th ed. (Frankfurt, 1971), 135–136; and Georg Mende, "Philosophie und Ideologie," in *Akten des XIV. Internationalen Kongresses für Philosophie*, I, 394–395; Walter Hollitscher, "Der Ideologiebegriff in marxistischer Sicht," *ibid.*, 506.

33. See Lefebvre, "Soziologie der Erkenntnis," in *Folgen einer Theorie*, 140.

concepts of the Enlightenment were aimed at the realization of a bourgeois social order.[34]

The American Revolution, the Enlightenment, and the Political Thinking of the German Bourgeoisie

With the above considerations in mind, we are in a better position to appraise the German bourgeoisie's response to the events in the New World. For we find that their reception of those events can be comprehended only if we take into account their own sphere of interests as expressed in theoretical terms by the Enlightenment. This relationship is manifest in a letter written to Franklin by Johann Karl von Zinner, from Budapest, late in October 1778: "I was born a subject of a great monarchy under a mild government; yet I cannot explain the transports of joy that I experience on hearing or reading of progress on your side."[35] The reasons for this joy were inexplicable because they were all too obvious. Robert R. Palmer, arguing with the advantage of scholarly distance, has made them explicit: "The American Revolution coincided with the climax of the Age of Enlightenment. It was itself, in some degree, the product of this age. . . . It proved that the liberal ideas of the Enlightenment might be put into practice."[36] Numerous German and other contemporaries expressed much more clearly what Zinner hinted at. Charles Stedman observed in his *Geschichte des Americanischen Krieges*: "Philosophy had predicted the American Revolution."[37]

This relationship between abstract philosophy and practical politics

34. See also Geiger, *Ideologie und Wahrheit*, 12; Zeltner, *Ideologie und Wahrheit*, 17; Horkheimer, *Bürgerliche Geschichtsphilosophie*, 58, 66–67. Venturi, *Utopia and Reform in the Enlightenment*, 10–16, opposes this view. The concept of bourgeois ideology has relevance for the American Revolution as well; see Willi Paul Adams, "Das Gleichheitspostulat in der amerikanischen Revolution," *HZ*, CCXII (1971), 59–99. In the early years of the growing conflict with Britain, the intellectual leaders of the American Revolution propagated the idea of equality. However, when mob actions and other internal controversies during the second half of the 1770s made the ideological character and possible consequences of this idea apparent, the leaders of the Revolution avoided further use of the term. W.P. Adams, however, does not make this context quite clear.

35. "Je suis né sujet d'un grand monarchie sous un gouvernement doux; mais je ne sais pas, dans quel transport de joie je deviens, en cas, que j'entende ou que je lise de vos progrès": Zinner to Franklin, Oct. 26, 1778 (Franklin Papers, XII, 84, APSL, Philadelphia).

36. Palmer, *Age of the Democratic Revolution*, I, 239.

37. "Die Philosophie hatte die Revolution von Amerika vorausgesagt": Stedman, *Americanischer Krieg*, II, 554.

goes far toward explaining German enthusiasm for events in the Western Hemisphere. In the American Revolution, as seen through German eyes, bourgeois aspirations and ideals were fought for and implemented. The new United States embodied the principles and theories developed in the European Enlightenment; the practical applicability of these ideals was now proven.[38] American political success secured for the young republic a place in the circle of the truly enlightened nations.[39]

As Stedman, Gilbert Imlay, and others had indicated, these ideas were not confined to Germany. They were widespread also in France during the War of Independence. Like the majority of the German officers who offered their services to the Americans, Lafayette, Chastellux, and other distinguished French volunteers had gone to America compelled by the basic principles of the Enlightenment and not as professional revolutionaries, a notion that was alien to them, in any case.[40]

Because of his long stay first in England and then in France, Franklin was well informed of the importance of the ideas of the Enlightenment for the European bourgeoisie. In a letter to Chastellux, then an officer in the American war and author of the enlightened publication, *De la Félicité publique*, Franklin spoke of the link between the Enlightenment and the American Revolution as seen from the Old World:

I congratulate you on the success of your last glorious campaign. Establishing the liberties of America will not only make that people happy, but will have some effect in diminishing the misery of those, who in other parts of the world groan under despotism, by rendering it more circumspect, and inducing it to govern with a lighter hand. A philosopher, endowed with those strong sentiments of humanity, that are manifested in your excellent writings, must enjoy great satisfaction in having contributed so extensively by his sword, as well as by his pen, to the *félicité publique*.[41]

The German bourgeoisie saw eye to eye with him in this matter. In this sense, the American Revolution was truly "the alarm bell for the European

38. See Vossler, *Amerikanische Revolutionsideale*, 34; Palmer, *Age of the Democratic Revolution*, I, 242; Douglass, "German Intellectuals," *WMQ*, 3d Ser., XVII (1960), 201, 215.

39. See Johann Philipp Breidenstein to Franklin, Feb. 1, 1783: "Americae qua est vera Philosophiae pars . . ." (pamphlets from the Franklin Papers, APSL, Philadelphia). See also Maj. von Wolff, who proclaimed to Franklin, Mar. 4, 1784: "J'abandonne sans regret mes titres de noblesse pour acquerir celui de citoyen utile de votre république" (Franklin Papers, XXXI, 103, *ibid.*).

40. Echeverria, *Mirage in the West*, 114–115; see also Echeverria's introduction to his edition of Jacques Pierre Brissot de Warville, *New Travels in the United States of America 1788*, trans. Mara Soceanu Vamos and Durand Echeverria (Cambridge, Mass., 1964), x–xi; Louis Gottschalk, *Lafayette Comes to America* (Chicago and London, 1965), 135–137; Howard C. Rice, Jr., in his edition of François Jean, marquis de Chastellux, *Travels in North America in the Years 1780, 1781 and 1782*, 2 vols. (Chapel Hill, N.C., 1963), I, 14–16.

41. Franklin to Chastellux, Apr. 6, 1782, in Smyth, ed., *Writings of Franklin*, VIII, 416.

bourgeoisie," as Karl Marx put it,[42] because it appeared to implement the ideals of the Enlightenment visibly and convincingly, particularly the principle of civil and legal equality and the idea of liberty. Liberty was the motto of an enlightened bourgeoisie who were bound to welcome any event that seemed to work toward this ideal.[43] Franklin could not but notice how the idea of liberty gave wings to the imagination of European spectators, so that, without exaggerating, he could write home to his fellow countrymen: "Hence 'tis a Common Observation here, that our Cause is the Cause of all Mankind, and that we are fighting for their Liberty in defending our own."[44]

Since the German bourgeoisie interpreted the American Revolution as the implementation of the ideals of the Enlightenment, and thus their own ideals, and since it was mainly because of this connection that they considered the Revolution to be of the greatest importance, the reasons for their virtual disregard of the problems of the United States with respect to internal politics, society, and economy become clear. They made a spiritual event out of a revolution that could be understood only through an analysis of the concrete political interests that supported it.[45]

Franklin himself indirectly contributed to this interpretation. As early as the second half of the 1760s he had presented himself to the continental European public as a scientist and moral philosopher, and had consciously encouraged the impression that he represented an enlightened people. Eventually he was able to exchange the intellectual and moral credit thus accumulated for political capital.[46] Franklin established himself not only as the undisputed spokesman of the American Enlightenment but also as a very wise statesman, politician, and diplomat, whom the German bourgeoisie looked upon as the leading exponent of the American Revolution. In reality, Franklin's role was not nearly as central as was believed in Europe. The overrating of his share in the American Revolution can be explained only as a function of the spiritual and moral authority that he enjoyed in enlightened European circles. When he embraced Voltaire in Paris, it was more than the pathetic, theatrical gesture of two old men; it was the embrace, to the applause of all Europe, of the Enlightenment in the Old and the New World.[47]

42. Marx, "Das Kapital," preface to the first edition, in Marx and Engels, *Werke*, ed. Institut für Marxismus-Leninismus, XXIII, 15.

43. See also F. Schneider, *Pressefreiheit*, 87.

44. Franklin to Samuel Cooper, May 1, 1777, in Smyth, ed., *Writings of Franklin*, VII, 56.

45. See Vossler, *Amerikanische Revolutionsideale*, 8.

46. See among others Alfred Owen Aldridge, *Franklin and his French Contemporaries* (New York, 1957), 21–73; Echeverria, *Mirage in the West*, 24, 26, 29–30.

47. See Vossler, *Amerikanische Revolutionsideale*, 56; Gerald Stourzh, *Benjamin Franklin and American Foreign Policy*, 2d ed. (Chicago, 1969), 3–4; Hartz, *Liberal Tradition*, 51; Gay, *Enlightenment*, II, 555, 557–558.

There is no doubt that under such circumstances Franklin's image developed into a myth, with hardly any reference to reality. But this mythification is what explains his influence on the German bourgeoisie's evaluation of the American Revolution. As the most eminent exponent of enlightened thought in America and as the Revolution's alleged driving force, he was also the perfect embodiment of the connection between the Revolution and the Enlightenment. To put it another way: that a person of Franklin's stature took part in the American Revolution was not only undeniable proof that its aims were justified but also that these aims were in complete agreement with the ideas of the Enlightenment. Thus, the fight in the Western Hemisphere was not for purely American aims but for popular bourgeois ideals. A mediator of these ideas and a leader of the Revolution, Franklin was to an enthusiastic bourgeoisie the patron saint of American politics.[48]

The glorification of Franklin's image in Germany received new impetus in 1790 when he died. All Europe mourned the old man, whose death was announced by Mirabeau to the National Assembly with the simple and touching words, "Franklin est mort!"[49] The Enlightenment had lost one of its last great idols, for none had equaled Franklin as an apparently perfect embodiment of his century's bourgeois principles. All that remained was, in a way, "a precious relic."[50]

By interpreting the Revolution as a victory for philosophy rather than as an expression of concrete interests, Germany hid from itself the radical implications of the event. The bourgeoisie extolled America because it had fought for liberty and civil and legal equality; they rejoiced over an event that would have been very revolutionary indeed had it occurred in Germany in the same measure. But apart from Johann Christian Schmohl's *Über Nordamerika und Demokratie*, there were no truly radical statements made in the numerous essays and books written on the subject. "Their dreams were of liberty."[51] But they were only dreams, not a realistic program of political and social change, and entirely inarticulate. Christian Friedrich Daniel Schubart, one of Germany's first pronounced liberals, who in spite of his ambivalent attitudes toward authority had a better understanding of his times than most of his fellow citizens,[52] was completely justified in saying, though with bitter

---

48. Schmohl, *Über Nordamerika und Demokratie*, 204.

49. Grimm, *Correspondance*, ed. Tourneux, XVI, 30.

50. "eine köstliche Reliquie": *Genius der Zeit*, May 1794, 72. See also *Deutsche Monatsschrift*, Sept. 1790, 7; Lebrecht Johann von Knebel to his brother Karl Ludwig, Feb. 28, 1793 (Nachlaß Karl Ludwig von Knebel, VI/7, fol. 149v, GSA, Weimar); *Berlinisches Archiv*, June 1797, 566.

51. "Man träumte jetzt Freiheit": Sartori, "Nord-Amerika" (c. 1792), fol. 68v (Cod. ser. nov. 1640, NB, Vienna).

52. See Schubart's letter to his wife, Sept. 5, 1783, calling the duke of Württemberg a

irony: "It's true, the taste for liberty is nearly dead in Germany. But one thing is certain: It is neither stupidity nor apathy that makes us so docile to subordination, but mature reflection, and love of order."[53]

Many of the bourgeoisie had probably ceased to believe that "nature has created three or four races of men, with one of them destined to work much and eat little."[54] But only a few saw the import of the inherent contradiction between the widespread enthusiasm aroused by the American events, on the one hand, and their own political and social reality, on the other.[55] Thus, "in politics the Germans thought out what other nations did,"[56] or, as Carlo Schmid has said with some justification: "The German bourgeoisie received the ideas of the French Revolution mainly through the instrumentality of German idealistic philosophy. Kant, Fichte, and Hegel translated into philosophical systems the political energies and the revolutionary pathos of the French Revolution, thus divorcing material political interests and facts from their theoretical expressions. A life of action in the West was transformed into a life of contemplation in Germany."[57]

We have contemporary statements from France and England that refer to the connection between the American Revolution and the Enlightenment in a fashion similar to that found in Germany. For example, Guillaume-Thomas-François Raynal noted that "these principles had originated in Europe, especially in England, and were propagated in America by philosophy."[58] But the German bourgeoisie took longer than their French or English contemporaries to realize that the American Revolution was a complex of concrete political interests. Therefore, the influence of the American Revolution in Germany remained mostly intellectual and did not stimulate questioning of the wide-

---

"Peiniger" and a "Schöpfer der Knechtschaft," but at the same time praying "aufrichtig für seine glückliche Rückkunft"; cf. Schubart, *Leben in seinen Briefen*, ed. Strauss, II, 88–89.

53. "Wahr ist's, 's Gefühl der Freiheit ist unter uns Deutschen ziemlich erstorben. Aber es ist gewiß: weder Dummheit noch Phlegma, sondern reife Überlegung und Ordnungsliebe ist's die uns zur Subordination so geschmeidig macht": *Deutsche Chronik*, Jan. 1, 1776, 6.

54. "daß die Natur drei oder vier Menschenrassen geschaffen habe, von denen eine bestimmt sei, viel zu arbeiten und wenig zu essen": Mazzei, *Geschichte und Staatsverfassung*, II, 227. The phrase is, of course, Condorcet's.

55. See, e.g., [Honoré Gabriel Riquetti, comte de Mirabeau], *Des Lettres de cachet et des prisons d'Etat*, 2 vols. (Hamburg, 1782), I, 284–285; Pestalozzi, ed., *Ein Schweizer-Blatt*, Jan. 24, 1782, reprinted in Pestalozzi, *Sämtliche Werke*, ed. Buchenau *et al.*, VIII, 23–30.

56. Karl Marx, "Kritik der Hegelschen Rechtsphilosophie," introduction, in Marx and Engels, *Werke*, ed. Institut für Marxismus-Leninismus, I, 385, cf. 386–387.

57. Schmid, *Politik und Geist*, 67.

58. "Diese Grundsätze waren in Europa und vornehmlich in England entstanden und durch die Philosophie in Amerika fortgepflanzt worden": Raynal, *Staatsveränderung von Amerika*, 23–24. See also John Philip Agnew, "Richard Price and the American Revolution" (unpubl. Ph.D. diss., University of Illinois, Urbana, 1949), 221.

spread enlightened bourgeois ideology as the French Revolution did later. In the 1790s conservatives considered this survival of the ideals of the Enlightenment into the era of the French Revolution to be one of the basic ills of their epoch. Ernst Brandes put it this way: "Exaggerated ideas of the possible perfectibility of man by the enlightenment of his intellect have led to exaggerated ideas on the perfection of a civil constitution."[59] Years later, he was of the opinion that "the misconception endured much longer than one should have imagined, until, at last, great world events tore up the fabric of the treacherous veil. The philosophical century, a term invented in scorn but later adopted by the era itself in rank usurpation and extreme narrow-mindedness, simply disappeared. From several sides, observers in Germany began to see that there might also be a progression toward wretchedness."[60]

The most intelligent among the political opponents eventually became aware of the limitations of bourgeois political thinking, as illustrated, for example, by the sizable difference between the conception of a state such as was realized in America and the cautious political formulations of a few figures in Germany.[61] Anticipating Hegel, who said at a later time that the Enlightenment was not "enlightened about itself,"[62] Schubart scoffed: "They called it the Enlightenment, but it was a darkening; they boasted of light, but it was only an artificial glow, which blinded the eyes as in an optical device, so that the people could not see naturally anymore."[63] With this remark we reach the end of the German bourgeoisie's political thinking as it was prepared and expanded by the ideology of the Enlightenment and profoundly stimulated by the American Revolution.

The French bourgeoisie, in contrast, began in the 1780s to look beyond

59. "Übertriebene Begriffe von der möglichen Perfektibilität der Menschen durch die Aufklärung des Verstandes haben auf übertriebene Begriffe von der Vervollkommnung der bürgerlichen Verfassung geführt": Ernst Brandes, *Über einige bisherige Folgen der Französischen Revolution, in Rücksicht auf Deutschland*, 2d ed. (Hanover, 1793), 40.

60. "Viel länger, wie man glauben sollte, dauerte die Täuschung, bis endlich die Hand der großen Weltbegebenheiten das trügerische Gewebe des Schleiers zerriß. Das philosophische Jahrhundert, ein Wort, das die ersten Urheber spottweise erfanden, dessen Name sich hernach das Zeitalter in der gröbsten Anmaßung und einseitigsten Beschränktheit selbst beilegte, verschwand. Von mehreren Seiten fing man an, in Deutschland einzusehen, daß es auch ein Fortschreiten im Erbärmlichen gebe": Ernst Brandes, *Betrachtungen über den Zeitgeist in Deutschland in den letzten Decennien des vorigen Jahrhunderts* (Hanover, 1808), 251.

61. See, e.g., Jefferson to Edward Carrington, Jan. 16, 1787, in Boyd *et al.*, eds., *Jefferson Papers*, XI, 48–49; and for an opposing German view, Meyen, *Franklin der Philosoph und Staatsmann*, 35–38.

62. Georg Wilhelm Friedrich Hegel, "Phänomenologie des Geistes," in his *Werke in 20 Bänden*, ed. Eva Moldenhauer and Karl Markus Michel (Frankfurt, 1969–1971), III, 418.

63. "Man nannte es Aufklärung, es war aber Verfinsterung; man prahlte mit Licht, es war aber nur ein künstlicher Schein, der wie in einer Optica die Augen blendete, daß die Leute gar nichts natürlich mehr sehen konnten": Schubart, *Wetterleuchten über Europa*, 65.

the general principles of the Enlightenment and toward the concrete political problems that were confronting them.[64] The vistas thus opened appreciably transcended all former ones. When Brissot de Warville went to America in 1788, he had in mind questions far different from those considered important by Lafayette or Chastellux earlier. He described his American experiences in a book significantly and programmatically entitled *Nouveau voyage dans les Etat-Unis*; someone else might have called it *De la liberté en Amérique*.[65] When he and others spoke of America, they really meant France.[66]

The German bourgeoisie's political comprehension failed to develop quite as far. As Rudolf Vierhaus has asserted, "philosophy's share in events was grossly overrated."[67] This remark pinpoints the central issue: the bourgeoisie's consistent overrating of the connection between revolution and enlightenment was precisely the problem with German political analysis up to the early 1790s. Moreover, this interpretation of the American Revolution was now transferred in the same measure to the French Revolution. The bourgeoisie still understood the Enlightenment to be "the German theory of the French Revolution,"[68] and they saw that revolution as the implementation of the ideals of the Enlightenment. (It is significant that the first German translation of Aristotle's *Politics* did not appear until the very end of the century, whereas an English translation had appeared more than twenty years earlier.)[69] But once it became obvious that more was at stake in France than a mere realization of the general principles of the Enlightenment, the situation began to change decisively. Both enemies and supporters of the French Revolution began to perceive concrete political facts and conflicts behind the events and to change or modify their political attitudes appropriately. By the 1790s the formerly exalted "noble and true spirit of liberty"[70] appeared to an increasing number of the bourgeoisie to be a destructive phantom.[71]

64. See Eberhard Naujoks, *Die Französische Revolution und Europa 1789–1799* (Stuttgart, 1969), 49–51.

65. See Echeverria's edition of Brissot de Warville, *New Travels*, x.

66. See Vossler, *Amerikanische Revolutionsideale*, 62, 64; Echeverria, *Mirage in the West*, 42, 78.

67. Vierhaus, "Politisches Bewußtsein," *Der Staat*, VI (1967), 193; see, however, Hegel, "Philosophie der Geschichte," in his *Werke*, ed. Moldenhauer and Michel, XII, 527–528.

68. Karl Marx, "Das philosophische Manifest der historischen Rechtsschule," in Marx and Engels, *Werke*, ed. Institut für Marxismus-Leninismus, I, 80.

69. Manfred Riedel, "Aristoteles-Tradition am Ausgange des 18. Jahrhunderts. Zur ersten deutschen Übersetzung der *Politik* durch Johann Georg Schlosser," in *Alteuropa und die moderne Gesellschaft. Festschrift für Otto Brunner* (Göttingen, 1963), 278–315.

70. "edlen wahren Freiheitsgeist": E.A.W. Zimmermann, in Imlay, *Westliche Lande der Nordamerikanischen Freistaaten*, xv.

71. See de Luc to J. G. Zimmermann, July 27, 1789 (HptStA, Hanover).

Consequently, the German appraisal of the French Revolution as a political phenomenon underwent a significant change. Observers now began to
take into account the complex origins of the revolution, without tracing all
factors ultimately to the Enlightenment, or even assuming that the Enlightenment was closely linked with the revolution or legitimated it.[72] For the first
time, the German bourgeoisie came face to face with revolutionaries, many
of whom had come from their midst. The question of whether someone was
or was not a revolutionary became a decisive consideration in government
and conservative circles. Students at the University of Göttingen, for example,
were watched with increasing concern from Hanover, for a split into French
and English factions had occurred there involving even the professors.[73]

To this day Georg Forster has been the best-known representative of the
era's German revolutionaries. Like nearly all of his political associates, his
early thinking was in close accordance with the liberal philosophy of the
Enlightenment. But in the early 1790s he began to side with the revolutionaries because he believed that liberalism could no longer meet the present
situation and was unable to solve the new problems. He therefore changed
his creed to political radicalism and suffered all the concomitant difficulties
and personal disappointments and disadvantages that flowed from this decision. But he held to it inexorably to his death.

Many tried to guess why Forster took this step.[74] A persuasive answer to
this question can only be given if we include in our discussion the bourgeoisie's general attitude toward "the people," that is, the petite bourgeoisie
and the preindustrial proletariat, and all the ramifications of this attitude.
Notwithstanding some obvious reservations, Forster's feeling toward the

72. See Knigge, *Joseph von Wurmbrand*, 46.

73. E.g., Christoph Ludwig Meiners to Franz Oberthür, July 24, 1794 (Nachlaß Oberthür, letter no. 132, UB, Würzburg); Georg Christoph Lichtenberg to Georg August Ebell,
Feb. 26, 1795, in Lichtenberg, *Briefe*, ed. Leitzmann and Schüddekopf, III, 146. See also the
characterizations used by Ernst Brandes, "der Herr Revolutionsrat Campe und der Herr Re-
bellionsrat Mauvillon . . .," which would have been unthinkable during the time of the American Revolution (Brandes to J. G. Zimmermann, Dec. 23, 1791 [Nachlaß Zimmermann, A II,
no. 10, LB, Hanover]).

74. Though they are generally not satifying, see Jakob Venedey, *Die deutschen Republikaner unter der französischen Republik* (Leipzig, 1870), 87–157; Wilhelm Langewiesche,
*Georg Forster. Das Abenteuer seines Lebens. Unter Wiedergabe vieler Briefe und Tagebuch-
eintragungen* (Ebenhausen and Leipzig, 1923), 192–215; Kurt Kersten, *Der Weltumsegler
Johann Georg Adam Forster 1754–1794* (Bern, 1957), 193–297; Rödel, *Forster und
Lichtenberg*, 127–137; Uhlig, *Georg Forster*, 166, 197, 219; Craig, "Engagement and Neutrality," *Journal of Modern History*, XLI (1969), 1–16; also Scheel, "Mainzer Republik,"
Jahrbuch für Geschichte, IV (1969), 9–72. See also Forster's *Briefwechsel*, ed. Huber, published by his wife, which contains additional valuable information, though it is often distorted
and abridged by biased editing. Of supreme importance are Forster's writings during the time
of the French Revolution, now reliably accessible as Vols. IX and X of the Deutsche Akademie
der Wissenschaften edition of Forster's *Werke*.

people was considerably more positive than that of large portions of the liberal bourgeoisie. The question remains: How serious were the bulk of the liberals and radicals about the idea of equality in the 1790s?[75] Forster interpreted this idea much more comprehensively than did the majority of his liberal contemporaries, as is demonstrated, for example, by his discussion of the social conditions of the Rhenish winegrowers.[76] And when the French revolutionary army arrived in Mainz, he acted according to his political convictions and joined the revolution.

Although the seeds of a new and more accurate interpretation of the American Revolution were present in the 1790s, no widespread change in German thinking took place. True, the excesses of the French Revolution and, by contrast, the apparent harmlessness of America caused even conservative circles to give up their antagonism toward the American Revolution—in some cases not without ridicule from liberals and radicals.[77] Moreover, the bourgeoisie were increasingly prepared to deal with concrete political questions, as exemplified by discussion of the 1787 federal Constitution in the second half of the 1790s. But in spite of this expanding horizon, America and the American Revolution retained the characteristics attributed to them by the bourgeoisie who had lived through two decades of the Enlightenment; that is, their interpretation was still largely based on all-encompassing ideals and not on concrete political facts.[78]

Thus, the United States, primarily because of its resplendent and glorious Revolution, still remained an Eldorado and a shining example to the bourgeoisie who were looking for escape fantasies from a confined and unsatisfactory situation. The United States was the image of hope for a better future, or, as Robert R. Palmer has put it, the success of the American Revolution "made a good many Europeans feel sorry for themselves, and induced a kind of spiritual flight from the Old Régime."[79]

To the German bourgeoisie the United States represented a genuine utopia, one of the many and varied utopias encountered in Europe in the age of Enlightenment, spawned by the wish for social change without a program

75. See also Bloch, *Naturrecht und menschliche Würde*, 188–190.

76. Forster, "Ansichten vom Niederrhein," in his *Werke*, ed. Deutsche Akademie der Wissenschaften, IX, esp. 5–6.

77. See Knigge, *Joseph von Wurmbrand*, 13–14.

78. See Vossler, *Amerikanische Revolutionsideale*, 52–53; also Wertheim, "Amerikanische Unabhängigkeitskampf," *Weimarer Beiträge*, III (1957), 430–431; Engelsing, "Deutschland und die Vereinigten Staaten," *Welt als Geschichte*, XVIII (1958), 139; Joachim Streisand, *Geschichtliches Denken von der deutschen Frühaufklärung bis zur Klassik* (Berlin, 1964), 75.

79. Palmer, *Age of the Democratic Revolution*, I, 282.

for political action.[80] This longing for a utopia occupied radical as well as liberal German bourgeoisie and was reinforced by the experience of the French Revolution, for the bourgeois dream of liberty leading to material welfare had been realized, they believed, only in America; France had not, or not yet, found the way. This interpretation agrees with Marx's later description of the United States as the "most perfect example of a modern state," because it had completely implemented the rule of a bourgeoisie based on private property.[81] Many Germans held the faraway country "dearer than the mother country,"[82] admiring in it "the beginning and progress of the structure of reason" at a time when Europe was undergoing one of its worst crises. [83] To quote Palmer once more: "The American Revolution dethroned England, and set up America, as a model for those seeking a better world."[84]

The bourgeoisie in the Age of Enlightenment had formed a comprehensive ideology that supplied the basis for elevating the American Revolution and the United States to the status of a perfect ideal. Unlike the case in France, where this utopian image of America had foundered along with the failure of the Jacobins' rule,[85] among the German bourgeoisie it thrived well beyond the 1790s.[86] Not until the very last years of the century did German ideas about the contemporary United States even begin to shed the preconceptions of the Enlightenment, though the Revolution retained still its original glory. America's development in internal politics was the immediate stimulus, but the genuine causes lay in the changed political consciousness of the German bourgeoisie, which was about to modify profoundly its earlier Enlightenment-based ideology.

80. On this point see especially Bronislaw Baczko, "Lumières et utopie. Problème des recherches," *Annales. Économies, Sociétés, Civilisations*, XXVI (1971), 357, 363, 366–371, 382.

81. Marx and Engels, "Deutsche Ideologie," in their *Werke*, ed. Institut für Marxismus-Leninismus, III, 62.

82. "teurer als Vaterland": "Die Freiheit Amerika's," *Berlinische Monatsschrift*, Apr. 1783, 390.

83. "Anfang und Fortgang des Anbaues der Vernunft": La Roche, *Erscheinungen am See Oneida*, I, 4. See also [Christian Adam Müller], *Das achtzehnte Jahrhundert. Eine Skizze* (Hof, 1801); Gerning, *Das achtzehnte Jahrhundert*, 11–12; also Raynal, *Staatsveränderung von Amerika*, 56; *Politisches Journal*, 1782, II, 405; Hennings, *Geschichte der Freyheit in Engeland*, 365; *Vaterländische Chronik*, July 1787, 10–11; *Berlinisches Journal für Aufklärung*, 1789, III, 266–289, IV, 13–32.

84. Palmer, *Age of the Democratic Revolution*, I, 282. In general see also Gay, *Enlightenment*, II, 555–568.

85. Echeverria, *Mirage in the West*, 175–224.

86. Epstein, *German Conservatism*, 293, makes a similar point; Hertz, *German Public Mind*, II, 418, is not quite correct; Fay, *L'Esprit révolutionnaire*, 68, completely distorts the picture.

Bibliography
and Index

Bibliography

Primary Sources

Manuscripts

AARAU

Kantonsbibliothek

August Ludwig Schlözer, Vorlesungen über die Politik. Gehalten im Winterhalbjahr 1787, and, Vorlesungen über die Regierungsformen. Gehalten im Winterhalbjahr (1787?) (transcript by Karl Friedrich Rudolf May): Ms. B.N. 62q.

Staatsarchiv

Johann Georg Zimmermann, 246 Briefe an Jean André de Luc, 1777 bis 1795: Abt. Nachlässe: J. G. Zimmermann, Briefe I–II.

ANSBACH

Historischer Verein für Mittelfranken

Acta die verschiedene Gnaden Ertheilungen, an die in Königl. Großbrittanni. Sold nach America abgegangene hiesige Hochfürstl. Trouppes betr. 1779–1784: Ms. hist. 487.

Heinrich Büttner, Nachlaß: Ms. hist. 660–661.

Gesang bey dem Abmarsch der Hochfürstlich Brandenburg Anspach-Baireuthischen Auxiliar-Truppen nach Amerika, Anno 1777: Ms. hist. 485a.

March Ruthen für Georg Adam Stang Haudtboist. Bayreuth den 19ᵗ Januar 1784: Ms. hist. 482.

Wortgetreue Abschrift des Tagebuchs eines Markgräflichen Soldaten über den Aufenthalt in Amerika, 1777–1781: Ms. hist. 485.

Stadtarchiv

Enrollement, Anwerbung und Desertion Ansbacher Soldaten, 1742–1787: AM 994–998.

Soldaten Marsch- und Quartiersachen 1676–1783: AM 990.

Werbungen und Desertiones fremder Soldaten, 1715–1784: AM 992.

BAMBERG

Staatsarchiv
Collectanea Spiess. Die in kgl. Großbrittannischen Sold nach Amerika über-
lassenen hochfürstl. Brandenburgischen Kriegsvölker betr. 1777ff.: C 18, 1
No. 26.

Staatsbibliothek
Bernhard Gottfried von Haupt, Tagebuch, Bd. 1: Msc. Hist. 173^t.

BASEL

Staatsarchiv
Isaak Iselin, Nachlaß: Privatarchiv 98.

Peter Ochs, Action d'Amérique, 1798–1818: PA 633 FA His "Action d'Amérique."

Universitätsbibliothek
Fremden-Buch 1664–1822: Mscr. AN II 30.

BAYREUTH

Historischer Verein für Oberfranken
Tagebuch des markgräflichen Jäger-Leutnants Carl Philipp von Feilitzsch,
März 1777 bis Juni 1780: Ms. 100.

BERLIN

Staatsbibliothek der Stiftung Preußischer Kulturbesitz
Autographensammlung Darmstaedter.

August Hermann Francke, Nachlaß.

Philipp Krug, Nachlaß.

Friedrich Nicolai, Nachlaß.

BERN

Burgerbibliothek
Albrecht von Hallers Korrespondenz: Mss. H. H. XVIII. 1–68.

Erasmus Ritter, Nachlaßpapiere: Mss. H. H. XXV. 71.

Staatsarchiv
England. Erskinisches Werbungsgeschäft, 1781–1782: Fremde Kriegsdienste,
Verschiedene Staaten, No. 2.

Englische Werbungen durch Landmajor Müller: Fremde Kriegsdienste, Generalia, No. 35.

Englische Werbungen durch Landmajor Müller: Ratsmanuale 359, 360.

BOSTON

Massachusetts Historical Society
James Otis Papers.

Robert Treat Paine Papers.

Timothy Pickering Papers.

Theodore Sedgwick Papers.

BRUNSWICK

Stadtarchiv
Briefe von meinem Bruder J. C. J. Dehn und zwar von der Abfahrt von Portsmouth und seinen Aufenthalt in Nord America bis den Jahren 1782: H VI 6 No. 26.

Journal der Seereise nach Nord America, wie auch von denen darin gemachten Campagnen gehet an von den 15ten May 1776 bis zu den 10ten October 1783 und ist der Warheit gemäß zu seinen eigenen Vergnügen aufgezeichnet von Friedrich Julius von Papet jun: Premier Lieutenant . . . : H VI 6 No. 25.

Notizen den Feldzug der Br. Truppen nach Amerika in den Jahren 1776 bis 1783 betr.: H VI 6 No. 22.

Tagebuch des in Herzogl. Brschw. Diensten stehenden Lieutenants und Adjudanten [August Wilhelm] du Roi des älteren. 1776–1777: H VI 6 No. 80.

Tagebuch über den Feldzug der Braunschw. Troupen in America vom 29. Aug. 1777. bis zum 15. Jan. 1779. von dem Hauptmann (nachmals Generalmajor) Cleve: H VI 6 No. 78.

Tagebuch von Braunschweig bis America von Johann Conrad Ruff, 2 vols. 1777–1781: H VI 6 No. 74.

CAMBRIDGE, MASS.

Harvard University Library
Christoph Daniel Ebeling Papers, 26 vols.: MS Ger I.

Christoph Daniel Ebeling, Bibliotheca Americana quinquaginta Annorum indefessu opera, summo studio, maximumque impendio collecta a Chr. Dan. Ebeling . . . (Copy made for Dr. G. Cogswell): US 56.5.4F.

Christoph Daniel Ebeling, "Description of South Carolina," 1778: Ms Am 627.

Christoph Daniel Ebeling, "Ueber das gelbe Fieber in Philadelphia," 1793: Autograph File.

Christoph Daniel Ebeling, 4 letters to Joel Barlow, 1795–1812: bMS Am 1448.

Christoph Daniel Ebeling, 42 letters to William Bentley: Ms Am 576.

Arthur Lee Papers, 8 vols.: bMS Am 811.

COBURG

Staatsarchiv
Acta die von dem Churhannöverischen Obristen von Schleicher [*sic*] gesuchte Errichtung eines Bataillons von 1000. Mann in den hiesigen herzogl. Landen zum Dienste der Krone Engelland betr. 1781: LAF 4300.

Blätter, Braunschweigische Werbungen betr. 1776, 1777: LAF 4283.

Kaiserliche Verordnung vom 10. Okt. 1769: LReg 3487.

Tagebücher des Prinz Friedrich Josias von Sachsen-Coburg-Saalfeld, 1770–1800: A.I.28.b.11.a.1. Nos. 18, 19, 22–25, 28, 30, 32–36, 38, 45, 46, 51, 54, 55, 63.

COPENHAGEN

Rigsarkivet
Auswanderung von Holstein nach Nordamerika, 1792: Dept. f.u.A., Alm. korr. 5, litr. U, Udvandring 1783–1843, Nos. 1–15.

DARMSTADT

Staatsarchiv
Auswanderungskartei.

DRESDEN

Landesbibliothek
Carl August Böttiger, Nachlaß: Msc. Dresd. h 37, quarto vol. 4, 76, 84, 101, 157, 187, 196, 210, 224, 225; folio vol. 4; Vermischtes quarto vols. 3, 5; Sammlungen zur Zeitgeschichte.

Staatsarchiv
Acta den Französisch Amerikanischen Handel betr. Anno 1779. Item den mit den NordAmerikanischen Staaten zu schließenden Handels-Tractat betr.—1785: Locat 5366.

Acta den Nordamerikanischen Handel betr., 2 vols. 1778–1801: Locat 2610.

Acta die Eröffnung eines unmittelbaren Handels nach Nord-Amerika und die Errichtung einer diesfalsigen Handlungs-Societät betr. 1783–1803; Locat 2420.

Acta Die zu einen unmittelbaren Handel mit denen Americanischen Colonien durch die Dänische Insul St. Thomas beschehenen Vorschläge betr. 1768–1770: Locat 5291.

Chambellan Cte. Maurice de Brühl de Martinskirch, envoyé extraordinaire à la Cour de Londres, [Diplomatic dispatches], 1771–1784: Locat 2685–2686.

Correspondance de Mr. Du Bois à la Haye, 1776–1778: Locat 2862, vols. 33–35.

Correspondance politique, litteraire et secrète de Paris, 1775–1779: Locat 2790.

Des geheimen Raths Grafens Loss bzw. Cammerherrn von Schönfeld Abschikkung an den Koenigl. franzoesischen Hof und dessen sowie des Legationsraths Rivière daselbst geführte Negotiationen betr. 1775–1783: Locat 2747–2748.

EBERSTADT

Privatbesitz Juliana Gräfin von Gatterburg
August du Roi, 7 Briefe an seine Schwester Cornelia, 1776–1782.

ERLANGEN

Universitätsbibliothek
Briefe an J. Ch. D. Schreber: Ms 1918–1924.

FRANKFURT

Stadtarchiv
Betr. heimliche Auswanderung aus Hessen-Hanau 1785: Ugb. A 9 No. 7.

Chronik des Lorenz Friedrich Finger, 1776–1782: S 5/62.

Verhinderte Auswanderung von wertheim'schen Untertanen nach Amerika, 1773: Ugb. A 9 No. 4.

Versuchte Werbung von Auswanderern nach Süd-Carolina durch den Frankfurter Bürger B.W. Stöcken 1773: Ugb. A 9 No. 3. (There is also a xerox copy of nos. 3, 4, and 7 in S4d/28, vol. 1.)

Stadt- und Universitätsbibliothek
Wilhelms Heinse, Nachlaß.

FREIBURG, GERMANY

Militärgeschichtliches Forschungsamt
Graf Neithard von Gneisenau, Nachlaß: A 10, A 23, A 25.

Universitätsbibliothek
Nachlaß Friedrich Dominikus Ring, Briefe von Christian von Mechel: Hs. 484.

Johann Caspar Ruef, Nachlaß: Hs. 433.

GOTHA

Landesbibliothek
Briefe des Herrn Palairet aus London an Herzog Friedrich III. (betr. engl. Politik), 1759–1772: Chart. A 1052.

Schilderung des gesellschaftlichen Lebens u.s.w. in den vereinigten Staaten von Amerika, aus einem französischen Briefe (ca. 1800): In: Nachlaß Hg. Ernst II., Chart. A 1275.

GÖTTINGEN

Archiv der Akademie der Wissenschaften
Ausscheiden von Mitgliedern, 1793ff.: Pers. 66, Nos. 1, 2.

Briefe vermischten Inhalts zur Geschichte der Akademie, 1753–1857: Chron. 23.

Herausgabe der Periodischen Druckschriften: Gött. Gel. Anz.: Briefe an Heyne zur Zeit seiner Redaktion, 5 vols., 1770–1812: Scient. 47, 3.

Staats- und Universitätsbibliothek
American Colony, Göttingen: Cod. Ms. Hist. lit. 108.

Briefwechsel Heinrich Christian Boie—Louise Mejer, 1777–1785: Cod. Ms. philos. 167ᵐ Cim.

Christian Gottlob Heyne, Nachlaß: Cod. Ms. Heyne 112–120, 124–132, 134, 135.

Georg Christoph Lichtenberg, Nachlaß: Cod. Ms. Lichtenberg.

Johann David Michaelis, Nachlaß: Cod. Ms. Michaelis, vols. 320–331.

Jeremias David Reuss, Nachlaß: Cod. Ms. Philos. 169, vols. 1, 4, 5.

HALBERSTADT

Gleimhaus
Johann Wilhelm Ludwig Gleim, Nachlaß.

HAMBURG

Kommerzbibliothek
Protocollum Deputationis Commercii, 1775–1783.

Staatsarchiv
Acta betr. das Hambg. GeneralConsulat zu Philadelphia, errichtet 1794: Senatsakten Cl. VI No. 16p, vol. 4ᵃ, Fasc. 1.

Acta, betr. eine von dem Obersten Scheiter angeblich hieselbst angestellte heimliche Werbung für die nach America bestimmten Englischen Truppen 1775/1776: Senatsakten Cl. VII Lit. Gᵍ Pars 1 No. 7, vol. 4.

Acta betr. eine von Hessen-Cassel hieselbst nachgesuchte aber declinirte Werbung, 1778: Senatsakten Cl. VII Lit. Gᵍ Pars 1 No. 9a, vol. 1.

Acta betr. Schreiben der Landgräfl. Hessen-Kasselschen Regierung betr. Werbung für America 1795: Senatsakten Cl. VII Lit. Gᵍ Pars 1 No. 1, vol. 18.

Acta pto. der Hessen-Casselschen Requisition, betreffend, diejenigen der in Königl. Großbritannischen Sold tretenden Hochfürstl. Hessischen Truppen, welche etwa im Marsche desertiren sollten und sich hier betreten liessen, arretiren und ausliefern zu lassen 1776: Senatsakten Cl. VII Lit. Gᵍ Pars 2 No. 7a, vol. 1.

Akta betr. den amerikanischen Konsul John Parish bzw. Joseph Pitcairn in Hamburg 1793–1800: Senatsakten Cl. VII Lit. J^b No. 20, vol. 18$^{al-6, b-e}$.

Akta betr. die von William Berczy als Generalbevollmächtigten der Genesee-Association mit Beyhülfe des hiesigen Bürgers Lemmen, hier vorgenommenen Colonisten Werbung für den Genesee District in Nordamerika, 1792: Senatsakten Cl. VII Lit. G^g Pars 1 No. 1, vol. 17.

Akte wegen einer hier ohne Erlaubnis entstandenen Werbung für die Englische Kolonien, 1778: Senatsakten Cl. VII Lit. G^g Pars 1 No. 7, vol. 5.

Rathsprotokoll-Extrakte und Aktenstücke betr. Senatus Glückwunschschreiben an den Kongreß der Nordamerik. Staaten zur erworbenen Unabhängigkeit mit Empfehlung zur Begünstigung wechselseitiger Handelsbeziehungen, 1783: Senatsakten Cl. VI No. 16p, vol. 1, Fasc. 1a.

Staats- und Universitätsbibliothek
August von Hennings, Nachlaß.

HANOVER

Hauptstaatsarchiv
Acta aus dem Nachlaß des Obersten Georg Heinrich Albrecht von Scheither (gest. 1789) betr. seine Werbungen für die Krone England 1775–1782: Hann. Des. 47, II, No. 114.

Acta betr. zwei zu Hamburg arretirte Schiffe der Americanischen Rebellen, 1776: Hann. Des. 92, XXX, III, No. 11.

Bericht über die politischen und wirtschaftlichen Verhältnisse in Nordamerika, 1790: Dep. 52, II, e, No. 14.

Diarium (Briefe) des als Adjudant des englischen Generals Sir William Howe am Nordamerikanischen Freiheits-Kriege teilnehmenden Hauptmanns Friedrich v. Münchhausen übersandt an seinen Bruder Wilhelm v. M., Geh. Kriegsrat in Hannover, 1776–1778: Dep. 52, III, No. 29.

Die muthmaßlich für die Americanischen Rebellen im Hannoverschen und in den benachbarten Gegenden verfertigten Kriegsbedürfnisse betr. 1775–1777: Hann. Des. 92, XXX, III, No. 10.

Überlassung diesseitiger Off. und Mannschaften an das nach Amerika bestimmte Hanauische Jäger-corps betr. 1777: Hann. Des. 41, V, No. 36.

Werbungen des Oberst v. Scheither u. anderen Personen für die Krone v. England, 1775–1776: Hann. Des. 41, V, No. 4.

Johann Georg Zimmermann, Briefe von Jean André de Luc 1789–1795: Hann. Des. 91 J. G. Zimmermann, No. 1.

Landesbibliothek
Johann Georg Zimmermann, Nachlaß: XLII, 1933–1985.

KARLSRUHE

Generallandesarchiv

Briefe der Herzogin Auguste von Braunschweig, Princess Royal von Großbritannien und Irland 1782–1806 (copy): Abt. 65, No. 2559.

Diplomatische Korrespondenz: Frankreich: Berichte des Hessen-Kasselschen Gesandten beim französischen Hof von Boden an Markgraf Karl Friedrich 1775–1778: Abt. 48, No. 1966.

Diplomatische Korrespondenz: Niederlande: Korrespondenz des Gesandten Bosset de la Rochelle im Haag mit Markgraf Karl Friedrich, 1782–1784: Abt. 48, No. 2193–2194.

Diplomatische Korrespondenz: Niederlande: Korrespondenz des Residenten von Treuer im Haag mit Markgraf Karl Friedrich 1769–1782: Abt. 48, No. 2180–2192.

Französische Revolution, 1788–1792: Abt. 50, Fasc. 736–738.

Korrespondenz Wilhelm und Georg Ludwig von Edelsheim: Abt. 48, No. 563–595.

Korrespondenz des Legationsrats von Schmidt zu Rossau, 1770–1787: Abt. 46, No. 6867.

Landesbibliothek

Anleitung zur Geschichte der Friedensschlüsse (1797): K. 755.

"Beschreibung der Reise von Stade nach Quebeck aufgesetzt zum Besten der Nachfolger von J. F. C. E. Frhr. von Linsingen Lieut. bei dem Regiment Ew. Durch. der Fürstin von Anhalt-Zerbst, Quebeck d. 24. Sept. 1778": K. 84.

Friedrich Peter Wundt, Beyträge zur Geschichte und Geographie, 1782: K. 566.

KASSEL

Murhard'sche Bibliothek der Stadt- und Landesbibliothek

Actenstücke, Correspondenzen und Aufzeichnungen den amerikanischen Feldzug und die Theilnahme der Brigade von Mirbach an demselben betreffend. Enthält u.A. die Correspondenz des Landgrafen Friedrich II. von Hessen mit v. Mirbach, die Tagebücher von dessen Adjudanten, Premierlieutenant (Friedrich Andreas Hermann) Schotten: 2° Ms. hass. 247.

Amerikanische Miscellanien gesammlet von Johann Christoph Grau (?). 2ter Theil. Cassell, 1777: 8° Ms. hass. 126.

Valentin Asteroth, Erinnerungen aus dem nordamerikanischen Krieg 1776–1784: 8° Ms. hass. 127.

Bopp, 1. Fehler, 2. Mißbräuche, und 3. Verbesserungen in Heßen! (ca. 1778): 8° Ms. hass. 16.

Brief des Soldaten Martin Appell an seinen Vater Johann Christoph Appell, 1777 (copy): 4° Ms. hass. 293/3.

Eine Chronik der Stadt Cassel aus den Jahren 1734 bis 1779 geschrieben von einem unter dem Weinberge ansäßigen Einwohner Joh. Ernst Graßmeder (copy): 2° Ms. hass. 427.

Diarium aller Mir Ernst Philipp Theobald bey dem Hochfürstl. Hessen Hanau-ischen Infanterie Regiment ErbPrinz, Feldprediger, vom 15ten Mertz bis den 10ten Aug. 1776 auf meiner americanischen Reiße vorgefallenen, und von mir beobachteten merkwürdigkeiten (copy): 2° Ms. hass. 314.

General von Langenschwarz, "Meine militär Laufbahn und Erlebniße vom Jahr 1776 an": 8° Ms. hass. 123, H. 1.

Tagebuch des Obrist-Lieutenants von Dincklage 1776–1784 (copy): 4° Ms. hass. 186.

Verschiedene Berichte über den Feldzug der Hessen in America, 1777–1783 (copy): 4° Ms. hass. 204.

Privatbesitz Fritz Koch
"Kurze Kriegsgeschichte des siebenjährigen deutschen, des achtjährigen Englisch-amerikanischen, der Begebenheiten zwischen Hessen und Bückeburg, nebst anderen Vorfällen in Hessen und zuletzt des französisch-deutsch-russischen Krieges. Aufgestellt und geführt von dem Sergeanten Barthold Koch damals noch gemeiner Soldat jetzt pensionirter Capitain" (copy).

KIEL

Landesbibliothek
Nachlaß Boie-Voß.

Universitätsbibliothek
Carl Friedrich Cramer, Tagebuch: Cod. MS. S. H. 406[J].

Ludwig Timotheus Spittler, Geschichte der Friedensschlüsse und der Hauptrevolutionen des 16., 17. und 18. Jahrhunderts. Göttingen WS 1782/1783, Vorlesungsnachschrift: Cod. MS. K. B. 282.

KOBLENZ

Staatsarchiv
Grafschaft Sayn-Altenkirchen, Abt. A Abzugsachen. Generalia, 1784: Abt. 30, No. 44.

Verordnung die Auswanderung der Untertanen betr. 1764–1784: Abt. 22, No. 4064.

Verordnungen über die Auswanderung: Abt. I c, No. 1208.

KORBACH

Stadtarchiv
Werbungen für das Battl. Waldeck für Holland oder England 1776, 1785: A
IV 46.

LEIPZIG

Universitätsbibliothek
Autographensammlung Kestner.

LONDON

Public Record Office
Correspondence with the ambassadors in Berlin, James Harris *et al.*, 1773–
1780: S.P. 90/93–104.

Correspondence with the envoys in Bern, Jean Gabriel Catt *et al.*, 1773–1780:
S.P. 96/47–48.

Correspondence with the ambassadors in Dresden, John Osborn *et al.*, 1773–
1779: S.P. 88/105, 109, 112, 113, 115.

Correspondence with the ambassador to the Hanseatic cities, Emanuel Mathias, 1773–1780: S.P. 82/92–98.

Correspondence with the ambassadors in Munich, L. de Visme *et al.*, 1773–
1780: S.P. 81/110–116.

Correspondence with the ambassador at the Rhenish Catholic electorates,
George Cressener, 1773–1780: S.P. 81/152–157.

Correspondence with the ambassador in Vienna, Sir Robert Murray Keith,
1773–1780: S.P. 80/213–223.

LÜBECK

Archiv der Hansestadt
Acta und Correspondenz unter den Hansestädten den Abschluß eines Handels-
Traktates mit den Nordamerikanischen Freistaaten betr. 1782–1784: Altes
Senatsarchiv: Externa, Generalia und außerdeutsche Staaten I: Amerika: Ve-
reinigte Staaten von Amerika und Texas, vol. A, Fasc. 1 (Microfilm, original at
Potsdam).

LUDWIGSBURG

Staatsarchiv
Abzug nach Pennsylvanien 1770: A 213, Oberrat, Spezialia, No. 24.

Israel Hartmann, Nachlaß: J 4.

Wegzug 1781–1785: A 212, Oberrat, Generalia, No. 674.

LÜNEBURG

Museumsverein
Tagebuch eines Teilnehmers am Feldzug des General Bourgoyne in Albany 1776: Handschrift Hd 3.

MAINZ

Stadtarchiv
Kurmainzische Verordnungen, I. Sammlung, vols. 7, 9, 10, II. Sammlung, vol. I.

MARBACH

Schiller-Nationalmuseum
Ludwig Ferdinand Huber, 62 Briefe an Christian Gottlob Heyne, 1795–1800.

Karl Friedrich Graf Reinhard, 13 Briefe an Carl Friedrich Stäudlin, 1789–1797.

MARBURG

Staatsarchiv
Acta betr. Gesetze gegen die Auswanderungen aus hiesigen Lande, 1718–1787: 98 d X No. 1.

Acta die Auswanderung der Unterthanen und dahin einschlagende Sachen betr. 1785–1786: 17 b Gef. 97ª No. 6.

Amerikanischer Krieg 1776–1783, Aushebung, Werbung etc. Berichte der Commissaren und der Landräthe auch über Lage der zurückgelassenen Soldaten-Frauen und Kinder: 11 F 1 d.

Anwerbung von Soldaten für das dritte englisch-waldeckisch Regiment in Amerika durch den Leutnant Heus in Pyrmont 1780–1782: 118 No. 1017.

Auswärtige Werbungen für das dritte englisch-waldeckische Soldregiment 1776, 1777: 118 No. 1009.

Berichte des Gesandten von Boden in Paris 1773–1783: 4 f Frankreich No. 1703, 1716–1718, 1725.

Berichte des Kommandeurs des dritten englisch-waldeckischen Söldnerregiments in Amerika, Oberstleutnants v. Hanxleden an den Fürsten und an Frensdorff 1776–1780: 118 No. 974.

Briefe an Friedrich v. d. Malsburg betr. seine Dienstzeit in Amerika sowie sein Gefängnis auf der Festung Spangenberg 1784 bis 1823: 340 v. d. Malsburg, Escheberg.

Die dem königl. Französischen Gesandten M. le Comte de Grais geschehene Eröffnung, wegen des von Ser^mo an die Crone Engelland überlaßenen Corps Trouppen gegen die revoltirenden Colonien in America betr. 1776: 4 h Frankreich No. 1712.

Emigration oder Auswanderung der Hanauischen Unterthanen nach America und sonstigen außer dem teutschen Reich gelegenen Ländern betr. 1785: 98 d X No. 9.

Das Emigriren derer Unterthanen und die deswegen getroffenen Vorkehrungen betr. 1764–1795: 86 No. ∝2812.

Joseph Friedrich Engelschall, Briefe und Manuskripte 1767–1797: 340 Justi No. 11.

Journal des Hochfürstl.-Hessischen Grenadier-Regiments von Bischhausen vom 4. Martius 1776 bis den 1. November 1783: 12 b I Ba 3.

Journal des Hochlöblichen Fuselier Regiments von Alt-Lossberg. Geführt durch den RegimentsQuartierMeister Heusser, vom AusMarch aus der Garnison Rinteln an, bis zur Zurückkunft des gedachten hochlöblichen Regimentes aus America. Vom 10ten Merz 1776 bis den 5ten Octobr. 1783: 12 b I Ba 2.

Journal über die merkwürdigsten Vorfälle bey dem Hochloeblichen Leib Infanterie-Regiment modo Erb Prinz angefangen im Februario 1776, da solches nach America marchirte, geendigt Ende Maji 1784, da solches nach der Retour von America in die bestimmte Garnison zu Marburg in Oberheßen einrückte. Geführt von Staabs-Auditeur und RegimentsQuartierMeister Lotheissen: 12 b I Ba 10.

Journal vom Hochfürstlich-Hessischen Grenadier-Bataillon Platte vom 16ten Februar 1776 bis den 24ten May 1784. Geführt durch den RegimentsQuartier-Meister Carl Bauer: 12 b I Ba 16.

Journal von dem Hochlobl. Heßischen GrenadierBataillon olim von Minnigerode modo von Loewenstein vom 20ten januarii 1776 bis den 17ten May 1784: 12 b I Ba 15.

Journal von Sr. Hochfürstl. Durchlaucht Prinz Friedrichs Hochlöblichen Infanterie Regiment von 1776 bis Ende 1783. Vom RegimentsQuartierMeister Ludewig: 12 b I Ba 11.

Korrespondenz des Fürsten und Frensdorffs mit dem Oberstleutnant v. Horn vom III. englisch-waldeckischen Soldregiment in Amerika 1776–1784: 118 No. 975.

Korrespondenz mit Capitain von Kutzleben in London. 1775–1783, vols. I–VIII: 300 Philippsruhe E 11/6.

Korrespondenz mit dem Geheimen Rat von Gemmingen wegen Gestellung von Hilfstruppen 1775–1781: 13 Generalstab Acc. 1930/5 No. 239.

Soldatenwerbungen in Wetzlar, auf dem Eichsfeld, in Waldeck und in Friedberg 1777–1783: 118 No. 1015.

Tagebuch meines Vaters des damaligen Capitains, späterhin Obristlieutenant und ritterschaftlichen OberEinnehmers des adeligen Stiftes Kaufungen Friedrich von der Malsburg aus dem Hause Escheberg: 12 b I Ba 18½.

Werbung des Hauptmanns v. d. Osten-Sacken in Friedberg und Wetzlar 1781–1782: 118 No. 1019.

Werbung des Leutnants Becker in Wittgenstein und Erbach 1777: 118 No. 1023.

Werbungen des Hauptmanns v. Romrodt im Solmsischen 1776–1778: 118 No. 1020.

Werbungen des Leutnants Becker in Wetzlar (und Friedberg) 1776–1777: 118 No. 1022.

Werbungen des Leutnants Noezel in Franken 1777–1778 (1781): 118 No. 1021.

Werbungen des Sergeanten Gerle 1776–1783: 118 No. 1018.

Werbungen des Sergeanten Göbel in Friedberg, Wetzlar, Worms und Speyer 1777–1783: 118 No. 1016.

Werbungen in Hamburg 1776. 1781: 118 No. 1010.

Werbungen in Lippe-Detmold, Ysenburg und Frankfurt für die in Amerika stehenden hess. Truppen. Angelegenheiten des hess. Truppendepots in Ziegenhain. 1782–1783: 4 h 328 No. 158.

MERSEBURG

Deutsches Zentralarchiv

Acta betr. dasjenige was mit dem Englischen Gesandten Elliot und den Amerikanischen Deputirten . . . vorgefallen. 1777: Rep. 75 d England, Hofsachen 1760–1780, fols. 276–299.

Acta betr. den Americanischen Handel und Krieg, 2 vols.: (Rep.) General-Direktorium. General-Finanz-Kontrolle. Tit. LVIII, No. 7.

Acta betr. die Schickung und Zurückberufung der Englischen Gesandten an dem hiesigen Hofe, 1772–1802: Rep. XI. 73 (B). Conv. 176A.

Acta der Gesandtschaft zu Hamburg betr. die reichsgesetzwidrige Anwerbung reichsständischer Unterthanen zur Bevölkerung des Genesee-Districts in America, 1792: Rep. 81 Hamburg A 149.

Acta des Kabinetts Friedrich Wilhelms II. Consulats- und Schiffahrts-Sachen, 1787–1795: Rep. 96. 224C.

Acta des Kabinetts Friedrich Wilhelms II. Handels- und Zollsachen, 1786–1797: Rep. 96. 224A.

Akten des Auswärtigen Departements: Amerika: Vereinigte Staaten. 1778–1804: Rep. XI. 21a, Conv. 1 and 2.

Anno 1784 im July entworfene Übersicht des Nord-Amerikanischen Handels: Rep. 96. 424K.

Graf Heinrich Adrian von Borcke, Nachlaß: Rep. 92 v. Borcke III, No. 53, vols. II–XI.

England. Hofsachen, 1761–1780: Rep. XI. 75 and 75e. Conv. 138.

England. Hofsachen, 1780–1800: Rep. XI. 75. Conv. 174.

England. Privata et Intercessionales, 1780–1786: Rep. XI. 73^{IV}. Conv. 5.

Friedrich II., Nachlaß: Rep. 92 Preußen, Kg. Friedrich II., A 13.

Prinz Heinrich, Nachlaß: Rep. 92 Preußen, Pr. Heinrich, A I 13–21.

Korrespondenz mit Goltz, Paris, 1775–1783: Rep. XI. 89. Fasc. 244–255, 258–261, 263–265, 267–271.

Der politische Schriftwechsel des Grafen von Maltzan bzw. von Lusi, London, 1775–1783: Rep. XI. 73. Conv. 129, 131, 133–135, 137, 140, 142, 143.

Des preuß. Gen. Maj. W. v. Anhalt geheime Aufträge für den Kumpel u. den Herzer, 1776–1777: Rep. 96. 73C.

Des preußischen Gesandten Barons von Goltz Depeschen, 1775–1783: Rep. 96. Nos. 28A–I, 29A–F.

Des preußischen Gesandten Grafen von Lusi Depeschen, 1781–1783: Rep. 96. Nos. 36A–D.

Des preußischen Gesandten Grafen von Maltzan Depeschen, 1770–1781: Rep. 96. Nos. 34E–H, 35A–H.

Des preußischen Gesandten von Thulemeier Depeschen, 1775–1783: Rep. 96. Nos. 41B–I, 42A–D.

Wilhelm von Thulemeier, Nachlaß: Rep. 92 Thulemeier, Nos. 3, 8, 10, 12, 15.

MUNICH

Geheimes Staatsarchiv

Die Abstellung fremder Werbungen im Reich betr. 1772–1785: Kasten blau. 139/16.

Les affaires de Prusse 1777: Kasten schwarz 1443.

Briefe betr. die militärischen Operationen in Amerika: Kasten schwarz 15379.

Briefe der bayer. u. pfälz. Minister an auswärtigen Höfen an Anton Frhr. v. Cornet 1770–1776, 1777–1783: Kasten blau 354/10. 354/12.

Correspondance avec le Baron de Reichlin à Vienne, 1776–1786: Kasten schwarz 15373.

Gesandtschaft zu London. Politische Korrespondenz mit den Höfen zu München und Mannheim 1770–1783: Bayer. Gesandtschaft. London. Nos. 248–260.

Joseph Xaver Graf von Haslang, Briefwechsel mit dem kurbayrischen Minister Joseph Franz Graf von Seinsheim in München 1778–1783: Bayer. Gesandtschaft. London. No. 434.

Korrespondenz des Grafen von Haslang, London, 1778–1798: Kasten schwarz 15380–15397.

Korrespondenz von Hermant mit Baron Vieregg, 1777–1779: Kasten schwarz 16096.

Korrespondenz zwischen der Regierung in Mannheim und der pfalz-bayerischen Gesandtschaft in Berlin: Bayer. Gesandtschaft. Berlin. No. 156.

Korrespondenz zwischen der Regierung in München und der bayerischen Gesandtschaft in Berlin: Bayer. Gesandtschaft. Berlin. No. 28.

Joseph Franz Maria Ignaz Graf von Seinsheim, Politischer Briefwechsel mit Maximilian Emanuel Franz Graf von Eyck: Bayer. Gesandtschaft. Paris. No. 36.

Kriegsarchiv
Beschreibung, derer vom 7. Mart. 1777 bis 9. Decembr. 1783 in Nord-America mitgemachten Feld-Züge. Von Johann Ernst Prechtel, Premier-Lieutenant bei dem hochfürstl.: Brandenburg: Obrist von Voitil: Infant: Regiment: HS IV n. 2.

Staatsarchiv für Oberbayern
Acta Emigrations Wesen vom Unterdonaukreise, namentlich von Passau betr. 1764–1806: GR Fasc. 431 No. 60.

MÜNSTER

Staatsarchiv
Goswin Anton von Spiegel Nachlaß, No. 32: Herrschaft Desenberg.

NEW HAVEN, CONN.

Yale University Library
Jean André de Luc Collection.

Benjamin Franklin Collection.

Jedidiah Morse, Morse Family Papers.

Roger Sherman Collection.

Ezra Stiles, Copy of Letter to Christoph Daniel Ebeling, Feb. 20, 1795: MS Vault, Stiles, Letters, Vol. VII, 196–280.

Benjamin Trumbull Collection.

John Trumbull Collection.

NEW YORK

New York Public Library
Samuel Adams Papers.

Boston Committee of Correspondence, General Correspondence, Case 4, Box 1.

Benjamin Franklin Papers.

Harkness Collection.

Hessian Mss.

South Carolina—Loyalists: S.C. Box, Subject.

Noah Webster Papers.

NUREMBERG

Germanisches Nationalmuseum
Samuel Wilhelm Oetter, Nachlaß: Autogr. Oetter.

Staatsarchiv
Ansbacher Ausschreibung vom 17. Sept. 1778: Ansbacher Ausschreibungen, Tit. 29, tom. 2, 109.

Faucitts Auftrag, Vertrag und Ratifikation mit Markgraf Alexander von Ansbach-Bayreuth über ansbachische Söldnertruppen, 1777: Rep. 105, Nos. 1–3.

Karl Friedrich Reinhard Frhr. v. Gemmingen, Nachlaß: Rep. 314 A.

OLDENBURG

Landesbibliothek
Gerhard Anton von Halem, Nachlaß.

Helferich Peter Sturz, Nachlaß.

Staatsarchiv
Graf Rochus Friedrich von Lynar, Briefe an den Kanzleirat Zacharießen zu Oldenburg von 1766 bis 1781 (copy): Best. 270, 3: Nachlaß Lynar.

Peter Friedrich Ludwig, Prinz von Holstein-Gottorp, Briefwechsel mit Hg. Friedrich August von Oldenburg, 1772–1785: Best. 6 D, No. 19.

PHILADELPHIA

American Philosophical Society
Benjamin Franklin Papers.

Jan Ingenhousz, Letterbook: Film 615.

Pamphlets from the Franklin Papers, 608 P19. Archives.

Baron von Welffen to Franklin, May 30, 1778: B F85.BA.

Historical Society of Pennsylvania
John Adams, Letters to Francis Adrian van der Kemp, 1781–1825: Am. 006.

John and William Bartram Papers.

Benjamin Franklin Collection.

Benjamin Franklin Papers.

Gratz Collection.

Peter A. Grotjan, Memoirs, 1774–1850, 2 vols.: AM. 0708.

Lea and Febiger Collection.

Muhlenberg Collection.

Munstering Book of the Brittannia of James Peters from Rotterdam to Philadelphia, July 1, 1773: Am. 209.

Shippen Papers.

Society Collection.

John Warder, Letterbook, 1776–1778: Am. 179.

Library Company of Philadelphia
Benjamin Rush Collection.

Lutheran Theological Seminary
Henry Ernst Muhlenberg Papers: PM 94. Z4.

University of Pennsylvania Library
Benjamin Franklin Papers.

POTSDAM

Staatsarchiv
W. von Freytag, Briefe aus London an den hann.-engl. Generalfeldmarschall Christian Ludwig von Hardenberg: Pr. Br. Rep. 37 (Herrschaft Neuhardenberg) No. 1608.

SCHAFFHAUSEN

Stadtbibliothek
Johannes von Müller, Nachlaß: Msc. Mü.

SCHLESWIG

Landesarchiv
Betr. Auswanderung nach dem Genesee-District in Nordamerika, 1792: Abt. 65.2, No. 4860.

SIGMARINGEN

Staatsarchiv
Auswanderung Fürstl. Hohenzoll. Sigmar. Unterthanen in benachbarte Staaten und bezieh. nach Amerika und die Erhebung des Vermögens Abzugs betr. 1785–1834: C. I. 2. d. 7.

Auswanderung. Oberamt Haigerloch 1640–1851: II 1158.

SPEYER

Staatsarchiv

Akt, betr. Auswanderung, 1778, 1785: Abt. Kurpfalz, No. 37 1/2.

Akt, betr. Ein- und Auswanderung, auch Bürger-Annahme, 1685–1779: Abt. Kurpfalz, No. 35[1].

Auswanderung 1784: Abt. Grafschaft Hanau-Lichtenberg, Akt No. 3492.

Herzogtum Pfalz-Zweibrücken, Cabinetsprotokolle, 1781.

STUTTGART

Hauptstaatsarchiv

Friedrich Ferdinand Drück, Personalakte: A 272, Hohe Carlsschule, Bü. 126.

Generalrescripte: A 39.

Relationen des Correspondenten Römer von London 1776–1783: A 74, Bü. 178–180.

Relationen des herzoglichen Gesandten am königl. franz. Hof Geh. Rats Baron von Thun 1770–1783: A 74, Bü. 124–137.

Ludwig Timotheus von Spittler, Nachlaß: Q 3/6.

Landesbibliothek

18 Briefe von Frhr. Carl von Bühler, kaiserl. russischer Geheimer Rat, Gesandter an verschiedenen deutschen Höfen an Wassili Stephanowitsch Popoff, russ. General, aus den Jahren 1788–1796: Cod. Hist. 4° 639.

Friedrich Ferdinand Drück, Professor an der Hohen Karlsschule, Stuttgart, Vorlesungsmanuskripte, vol. III: Geographie von Asien, Afrika und Amerika, 1780: Cod. Hist. 4° 384.

Franziska von Hohenheim, 7 Briefe an den Prälaten und Hofprediger Georg Heinrich Müller: Cod. Hist. 4° 422.

Briefe der Familie des Pfarrers Friedrich August Köhler: Cod. Hist. 4° 459.

Tagebücher des Friedrich August Köhler, 1792–1800: Cod. Hist. 8° 140a.

Tabellen über die Volkszahl in Württemberg 1767, 1769, 1797: Cod. Hist. 2° 456.

TÜBINGEN

Universitätsbibliothek

Eberhard Hehl, Tagebuch von 1778–1785: Md. 311.

Anton Christian Ludwig König, Index aus der Lektüre: Stiftung Preuß. Kulturbesitz, Depot der Staatsbibliothek Tübingen, Ms. Germ. Fol. 233.

VIENNA

Haus-, Hof- und Staatsarchiv

Berichte Beelen-Bertholffs an die Regierung in Brüssel 1784–1789: Belgien DDB 182a–e.

Berichte des österreichischen Gesandten in Berlin an Fürst Kaunitz, 28. Juni–2. Aug. 1777: Staatskanzlei: Staatenabteilung, Preußen, Fasc. 53.

Berichte und Weisungen, österreichische Botschaft Paris, 1775–1783: Staatskanzlei: Staatenabteilung, Frankreich, K. 150, 153, 155–168.

Berichte und Weisungen, österreichische Gesandtschaft Den Haag, 1773–1783: Staatskanzlei: Staatenabteilung, Holland, K. 67–72.

Berichte und Weisungen, österreichische Gesandtschaft Lissabon, 1777–1784: Staatskanzlei: Staatenabteilung, Portugal, K. 21–22.

Berichte und Weisungen, österreichische Gesandtschaft London, 1770–1783: Staatskanzlei: Staatenabteilung, England, K. 115–122, 128.

Berichte und Weisungen, österreichische Gesandtschaft Madrid, 1776–1783: Staatskanzlei: Staatenabteilung, Spanien, K. 132–145.

Jan Ingenhousz, "Remarques sur les affaires presente de l'Amerique septentrionale" [c. late 1777] and: Extrait des deux lettres de Benjamin Franklin [i.e. those of Feb. 12 and Mar. 6, 1777]: Handschrift W 443.

Quelques Reflexions sur la politique de l'Angleterre (1778): Staatskanzlei: Staatenabteilung, England, Varia, K. 12.

Georg Frhr. v. Vega, Korrespondenz: Wissenschaft und Kunst, 6. Naturwiss. u. Mathematik.

Karl Johann Christian Graf von Zinzendorf, Tagebuch 1770–1800: Nachlaß Zinzendorf, Tagebuch, vols. 15–45.

Hofkammerarchiv

Consuln in verschiedenen Ländern item in den vereinigt Nord Amerikanischen Staaten 1754–1800: Abt. Kommerz Rote No. 651.

Kommerz nach Ost- und Westindien 1763–1809: Abt. Kommerz Rote No. 616.

Kriegsarchiv

Hessische, Hanauische, Ansbachische, Waldeckische, Braunschweigische, Hannoversche, Englische Werbungen im Reich betr.: Hofkriegsrat, Protokolle 1780–1783.

Nationalbibliothek

"Discours sur la Grandeur et importance de la dernière Révolution de l'Amérique septentrionale: Sur les causes principales qui l'ont déterminée: et sur son influence vraisemblable sur l'Etat Politique et sur le commerce des Puissances Européennes" (Milan, 1783): Bibl. Pal. Vind. Cod. 12613.

Jan Ingenhousz, Bericht an Maria Theresia über zwei Briefe Franklins, 18. Mai 1777 [with a French translation of Franklin's *Comparison of Great Britain and the United States in Regard to the Basis of Credit in the Two Countries* (1777)]: 6/97.

Joseph von Sartori, Collectio manuscriptorum, Anglia, vols. 2, 4, Europa, vol. 2, Gallia, vols., 2, 4: Cod. ser. nos. 1640, 1642, 1649, 1653, 1655.

Joseph von Sartori, Neueste Memoiren über die wichtigsten Europäischen Staatsbegebenheiten unserer Zeit, 4 vols.: Cod. 12724–12727.

WASHINGTON, D.C.

Library of Congress
Benjamin Franklin Papers.

Thomas Jefferson Papers.

George Washington Papers.

Copies from German archives:
Acta Camera Daß wegen des abgebrochenen Commercii zwischen Engelland und America ratione des Krieges zubefürchtenden starcken Banquerouts in Engelland, Holland und Hamburg, und daß die pommersche Kaufleute dabei alle Vorsicht gebrauchen möchten, 1777: Staatsarchiv, Stettin, Tit. 12, Sekt. 1 Commercien-Sachen, No. 171.

Acta vom mutuellen Commercio zwischen Schlesien und America, vol. 1: 1779 bis Xber 1801: Staatsarchiv, Breslau, Rep. 199, M. R. VI, No. 14, vol. 1.

Aufbringung von zwei amerikanischen Rebellen-Schiffen auf der Elbe, 1776: Hauptstaatsarchiv, Hanover: Hann. Des. 9 E. England, No. 35a.

Betr. Bestellung von Kriegsbedürfnissen für die rebellischen Colonien in Amerika, 1775–1777: Hauptstaatsarchiv, Hanover, Hann. Des. 9 E. England, No. 34.

Betr. den Marsch ansbachischer Truppen nach Amerika, 1777–1782: Staatsarchiv, Würzburg: Militärsachen, No. 95.

Briefe der Sophie Charlotte, Gemahlin Georgs III. von England an ihren Bruder 1775–1785: Hauptarchiv, Neustrelitz: Briefe der Sophie Charlotte.

Correspondenz mit dem Herrn Grafen von Schwerin während der Campagne in Bretagne und America, 1779–1782: Fürstlich Wiedisches Archiv, Neuwied: Schrank 2, Gef. 13, Fasc. 2.

Journal vom 15ten Mertz 1776 an, da das Heßen Hanauische Regim. 1ten Batallions Nach America marschiret ist. von mir F. G.: Geschichtsverein, Hanau: Ms. No. 1640.

Nachrichten von den Unruhen in N. Amerika, 1764–1781: Archiv der Brüder-Unität Herrnhut: Archiv der Unitäts-Ältesten-Conferenz, Rubr. 14.A, No. 46.

7 Briefe des Regiments Auditeurs Paul Wilhelm Schaeffer, 1776: Geschichtsverein, Hanau: Mss. Nos. 559, 559a–f.

Varia betr. die Hanauischen Truppen in America, 1776–1782: Geschichtsverein, Hanau: Mss. Nos. 505, 561, 561a, 1608, 1608a, 2189, 2189a.

National Archives

Despatches from John Quincy Adams, U.S. Minister to Prussia, 1799–1801: M 44, Roll 1–2.

Despatches from the U.S. Consuls in Bremen, 1794–1906: T-184, T 1.

Despatches from the U.S. Consuls in Hamburg, 1790–1906: T-211, T 1.

Miscellaneous Letters Received by the Department of State, Record Group 59.

Miscellaneous Papers of the Continental Congress, 1774–1789: M 332, Roll 3: Papers Relating to Foreign Affairs.

Papers of the Continental Congress, 1774–1789: M 247.

WEIMAR

Goethe- und Schiller-Archiv

Friedrich Johann Justin Bertuch, Nachlaß.

Karl Ludwig von Knebel, Nachlaß.

Johann Georg Zimmermann, 63 Briefe an Christoph Girtanner: Abt. II: 44, 9.

WIESBADEN

Haupstaatsarchiv

Emigration 1697–1805: Abt. 300 Gen. XIV^c, No. 1.

Emigrationes nach Pennsylvanien, Ungarn, und Litthauen 1709–1787: Abt. 300 Gen. XIV^c, No. 2.

Englische Werbungen 1776–1797: Abt. 150, No. 2664.

Englische Werbungen 1776ff.: Abt. 150, No. 2665.

Regierungsacta über die Emigration nach fremden Colonien 1766–1787: Abt. 172, No. 2664$^{2-5}$.

Reichs-Kriegs-Acten insbesondere den Zurückmarsche 250 Mann Hessen-Hanauischer nach America bestimmter Recruten von Bendorf nach Hessen betr. 1777: Abt. 150, No. 2666.

Rekruten Auszug und Verbot fremder Kriegsdienste und Werbungen in den Ämtern Nassau und Miehlen 1771–1783: Abt. 350, No. VII^a 9.

Verordnungen die Emigration betr. 1699–1792: Abt. 150, No. 4493.

WOLFENBÜTTEL

Herzog August Bibliothek
Heinrich Philipp Konrad Henke, Briefe: Cod. Guelf. 623. 1–25 Novi.

Staatsarchiv
Acta die in Hamburg pp. vorgewesene Anwerbung teutscher Unterthanen zur Bevölkerung des Geneser Districts in America betr. 1792: 2 Alt 1382.

Affaires du temps, 37 vols. 1775–1782: 1 Alt 22, Nos. 826–862.

Akten und Briefschaften Riedesels aus dem amerikanischen Kriege, 1776–1783: 237 N 47–96.

Americanische Briefe an des Herrn Erbprinzen Hochfürstl. Durchl. 1776–1777: 38 B Alt 236.

Amerikanischer Feldzug, 1776–1779: Landschaftl. Bibl. Braunschweig, No. 3152.

Aufsätze von Gottfried C. Querner, Lehrer in Helmstedt: VI Hs 6 No. 32.

Aufzeichnungen des Feldschers Julius Friedrich Wasmus, 3 vols. 1757–1800: VI Hs 11 No. 248.

Briefe des Auditeur, Kriegsrat und Kanonikus Friedr. Otto Wilh. Gärtner an die Töchter des Akademiedirektors Adam Friedr. Oeser in Leipzig, besonders an Friederike Oeser über allerlei persönliche Angelegenheiten und Tagesereignisse in Braunschweig: 298 N, vorl. No. 203, vols. 1–2.

Briefe und Geldabrechnungen des Börries Hilmar v. Münchhausen, zuletzt landgräfl. hess. Obrist u. Kommandant v. Rinteln an seinen Bruder Geh. Rat u. Hofmarschall Albrecht v. Münchhausen in Braunschweig, 1757–1794: 7 N 1 No. 155.

Briefe und Zinsquittungen des landgräfl. hessischen Staatsminister Moritz Friedrich v. Münchhausen in Rinteln, später Kassel, an seinen Bruder Geh. Rat u. Hofmarschall Albrecht von Münchhausen in Braunschweig, 2 vols.: 1756–1794: 7 N 1 No. 154.

Fragment eines Tagebuchs über die Braunschweigischen Truppen im Amerikanischen Feldzuge. 2. Jul.–26. Okt. 1777: VI Hs 5 No. 23.

Journal des Herzogs Ludwig Ernst, 30 vols. 1774–1780: 1 Alt 22, Nos. 871–900.

Lettres (Bulletin) de Mr. S . . . de Paris, d.h. Berichte eines nicht Genannten [M. Schulz?] in franz. Sprache, an den Sekretär Haenichen des Herzogs Ludwig Ernst, vols. 13–19, 1775–1781: 1 Alt 22, Nos. 1504–1510.

March Route von Braunschweig bis America. Nebst den vornehmsten Gegebenheiten der Herzoglichen Braunschweigischen Trouppen. Die 1te Division. Von Johann Bense: VI Hs 18 No. 7.

Nachrichten und Tagebuch des Regiments-Adjudanten und Lieutenant Anton Adolf Heinrich Du Roi, 1776: VI Hs 11 No. 76.

Georg Septimus Andreas von Praun, Materialien zur außerdeutschen Geschichte: IX Hs 11.

Serenissimi Edict, gegen das Auswandern der Unterthanen in fremde Lande, und insonderheit nach Amerika. d.d. Braunschweig, den 29. März 1784 [printed]: 40 Slg 12497.

Werbungen für die amerik. Truppen, 1775–1783: 38 B Alt 233.

WÜRZBURG

Staatsarchiv
Die von denen Hanauischen Werbern zum Dienst deren Königl. Englischen Hilfsvölkern in Amerika mit List und Gewalt theils angeworbene, theils entführte dienststrithige Unterthanen betr. 1777–1778: M.R.A. 359/Hess.-K. 966.

Die von einem Grafen v. Wertheim hieher geschickte Closter-Kleydungen zur debauchirung hiesiger Leuten betr. 1782: Gebr. Amt VII H 39/174.

Verordnungen und überhaupt die Auswanderungen aus dem deutschen Reich betr. 1754–1766, 1803–1805: Mainzer Polizeiakten 352.

Die Werbung des Hl. Grafen Friedrich Ludwig von Wertheim für die Crone Engelland betr. 1781/1782: Gebr. Amt VII H 39/171.

Universitätsbibliothek
Franz Oberthür, Nachlaß.

ZURICH

Zentralbibliothek
Acta den Revolutions-Handel zu Stein am Rhein betr. 1781–1784: G 249–250.

Johann Jakob Bodmer, Nachlaß: Ms. Bodmer, vols. 2–19.

Johann Caspar Hirzel, u.a., Nachlaß: F. A. Hirzel, vols. 240, 278–279, 295, 310–311, 315.

Johann Kaspar Lavater, Nachlaß: FA Lav. Ms. 502–587.

Heinrich von Moos, Merkwürdigkeiten des Jahres 1795: J 331a.

Sammelband zum Stäfner Handel: V 813.

Stäfner Handel 1795: J 312.

Paul Usteri, Schriftstücke und Drucke zur französischen Revolution 1792–1800: H 504.

Printed Sources

Letters

Adams, John. *The Adams-Jefferson Letters: The Complete Correspondence Between Thomas Jefferson and Abigail and John Adams*. Edited by Lester J. Cappon. 2 vols. Chapel Hill, N.C., 1959.

────── . *The Works of John Adams, Second President of the United States. With a Life of the Author, Notes and Illustrations*. Edited by Charles Francis Adams. 10 vols. Boston, 1850–1856.

Adams, John Quincy. *The Writings of John Quincy Adams*. Edited by Worthington Chauncey Ford. 7 vols. New York, 1913–1917.

Adams, Samuel. *The Writings of Samuel Adams*. Edited by Harry Alonzo Cushing. 4 vols. 1904–1908. Reprint. New York, 1968.

Adams Family Correspondence. Edited by L. H. Butterfield *et al*. Cambridge, Mass., 1963– .

American Independence through Prussian Eyes: A Neutral View of the Peace Negotiations of 1782–1783; Selections from the Prussian Diplomatic Correspondence. Edited by Marvin L. Brown, Jr. Durham, N.C., 1959.

Baurmeister, Carl Leopold von. *Revolution in America: Confidential Letters and Journals, 1776–1784*. Translated and edited by Bernhard A. Uhlendorf. New Brunswick, N.J., 1957.

Beelen-Bertholff, Baron de. "Die Berichte des ersten Agenten Österreichs in den Vereinigten Staaten von Amerika Baron de Beelen-Bertholff an die Regierung der österreichischen Niederlande in Brüssel 1784 bis 1789." Edited by Hanns Schlitter. *Fontes Rerum Austriacarum*, 2d Ser., XLV, no. 2 (1891), 225–892.

Boie, Heinrich Christian. *Ich war wohl klug, dass ich dich fand. Heinrich Christian Boies Briefwechsel mit Luise Mejer 1777–1785*. Edited by Ilse Schreiber. With a foreword by Joachim Kaiser. Munich, 1961.

Bürger, Gottfried August. *Briefe von und an Gottfried August Bürger. Ein Beitrag zur Literaturgeschichte seiner Zeit. Aus dem Nachlasse Bürgers und anderen, meist handschriftlichen Quellen*. Edited by Adolf Strodtmann. 4 vols. Berlin, 1874.

Ebeling, Christoph Daniel. "Glimpses of European Conditions from the Ebeling Letters." Edited by William Coolidge Lane. Massachusetts Historical Society, *Proceedings*, LIX (1926), 324–376.

────── . "Letter of Professor Ebeling to President Stiles" [June 26, 1794]. [With an introductory letter by Barlow to Stiles, May 27, 1794.] Massachusetts Historical Society, *Collections*, 2d Ser., VIII (1826), 267–275.

────── . *Letters of Christoph Daniel Ebeling to Rev. Dr. William Bentley of Salem, Mass., and to Other American Correspondents*. Edited by William Coolidge Lane. Worcester, Mass., 1926.

────── . Letters of Christopher D. Ebeling to Jeremy Belknap. In "The Belknap Papers: Part III." Massachusetts Historical Society, *Collections*, 6th Ser., IV (1891), 579–584, 594–601, 607–609, 620–627.

Forster, Georg. *Briefe an Christian Friedrich Voß*. Edited by Paul Zincke. Dortmund, 1915.

———. *Johann Georg Forster's Briefwechsel. Nebst einigen Nachrichten von seinem Leben*. Edited by Therese Huber, née Heyne. 2 vols. Leipzig, 1829.

Franklin, Benjamin. *Calendar of the Papers of Benjamin Franklin in the Library of the American Philosophical Society*. Edited by I. Minis Hays. 5 vols. Philadelphia, 1908.

———. *The Papers of Benjamin Franklin*. Edited by Leonard W. Labaree *et al*. New Haven, Conn., 1959– .

———. *The Works of Benjamin Franklin, Including the Private as well as the Official and Scientific Correspondence together with the Unmutilated and Correct Version of the Autobiography*. Compiled and edited by John Bigelow. 12 vols. New York, 1904.

———. *The Writings of Benjamin Franklin*. Compiled and edited by Albert H. Smyth. New York, 1905–1907.

Friedrich II. *Politische Correspondenz Friedrichs des Grossen*. Compiled by Gustav Berthold Volz. Edited by the Preußische Akademie der Wissenschaften. Vols. XXVII–XLVI. Berlin, 1902–1939.

Garve, Christian. *Briefe von Christian Garve an Christian Felix Weiße und einige andere Freunde*. Edited by Manso and Schneider. 2 vols. Breslau, 1803.

Gentz, Friedrich von. *Briefe von und an Friedrich von Gentz*. Edited by Friedrich Carl Wittichen and Ernst Salzer. 3 vols. Munich and Berlin, 1909–1913.

Grimm, Friedrich Melchior. *Correspondance littéraire, philosophique et critique par Grimm, Diderot, Raynal, Meister, etc.* Edited by Maurice Tourneux. 16 vols. Paris, 1877–1882.

Haller, Albrecht von. *Briefwechsel zwischen Albrecht von Haller und Eberhard Friedrich von Gemmingen. Nebst dem Briefwechsel zwischen Gemmingen und Bodmer*. Edited by Hermann Fischer. Tübingen, 1899.

Hamann, Johann Georg. *Briefwechsel*. Edited by Walther Ziesemer and Arthur Henkel. Wiesbaden and Frankfurt, 1955– .

Hasenclever, Peter. *Peter Hasenclever aus Remscheid-Ehringhausen ein deutscher Kaufmann des 18. Jahrhunderts. Seine Biographie, Briefe und Denkschriften (mit 3 Abbildungen)*. Edited by Adolf Hasenclever. Gotha, 1922.

———. "Zwei Briefe von Peter Hasenclever an Benjamin Franklin." Edited by Adolf Hasenclever. *Zeitschrift des Bergischen Geschichtsvereins*, LX (1931), 10–27.

Heim, Johann Ernst. *Schreiben eines Geistlichen, an sein gewesenes Beicht-Kind, einen in das Feld gehenden Soldaten*. N.p., 1777.

Heinrichs, Johann. "Extracts from the Letter-Book of Captain Johann Heinrichs of the Hessian Jäger Corps, 1778–1780." *Pennsylvania Magazine of History and Biography*, XXII (1898), 137–170.

Henry, Patrick. *Patrick Henry: Life, Correspondence, and Speeches*. Edited by William Wirt Henry. 3 vols. New York, 1891.

Herder, Johann Gottfried. *Von und an Herder. Ungedruckte Briefe aus Herders*

Nachlaß. Edited by Heinrich Düntzer and Ferdinand Gottfried von Herder. 3 vols. Leipzig, 1856–1862.

Jacobi, Friedrich Heinrich. *Auserlesener Briefwechsel.* 2 vols. Leipzig, 1825–1827.

Jefferson, Thomas. *The Papers of Thomas Jefferson.* Edited by Julian P. Boyd *et al.* Princeton, N.J., 1950– .

———. *The Writings of Thomas Jefferson.* Edited by H. A. Washington. 9 vols. New York and Washington, D.C., 1853–1854.

Joseph II. und Katharina von Russland. Ihr Briefwechsel. Edited by Alfred Ritter von Arneth. Vienna, 1869.

Kinloch, Francis. *Letters from Geneva and France Written During a Residence of Between Two and Three Years, in Different Parts of Those Countries and Addressed to a Lady in Virginia.* Boston, 1819.

Klopstock, Friedrich Gottlieb. *Briefe von und an Klopstock.* Edited by Johann Martin Lappenberg. Brunswick, 1867.

———. *Briefwechsel zwischen Klopstock und den Grafen Christian und Friedrich Leopold zu Stolberg.* Edited by Jürgen Behrens. Neumünster, 1964.

Lafayette, Marie Joseph, marquis de. *The Letters of Lafayette to Washington, 1777–1799.* Edited by Louis Gottschalk. New York, 1944.

———. *Mémoires, correspondance et manuscrits du général Lafayette, publiés par sa famille.* 6 vols. Paris, 1837–1838.

Lee, Richard Henry. *The Letters of Richard Henry Lee.* Compiled and edited by James Curtis Ballagh. 2 vols. New York, 1911–1914.

Lenz, Jakob Michael Reinhold. *Briefe von und an J.M.R. Lenz.* Edited by Karl Freye and Wolfgang Stammler. 2 vols. Leipzig, 1918.

Letters from America 1776–1779: Being Letters of Brunswick, Hessian, and Waldeck Officers with the British Armies During the Revolution. Translated by Ray W. Pettengill. Boston and New York, 1924.

Letters of Brunswick and Hessian Officers During the American Revolution. Translated by William L. Stone. Albany, N.Y., 1891.

Lichtenberg, Georg Christoph. *Briefe.* Edited by Albert Leitzmann and Carl Schüddekopf. 3 vols. Leipzig, 1901–1904.

———. "Neues von Lichtenberg." Edited by Albert Leitzmann. *Zeitschrift für Bücherfreunde,* N.S., IV, no. 1 (1912), 75–91, 123–132, 172–180.

Madison, James. *Letters and other Writings of James Madison, Fourth President of the United States.* 4 vols. Philadelphia, 1865.

Maria Theresa. *Correspondance secrète entre Marie-Thérèse et le Cte de Mercy-Argenteau avec les lettres de Marie-Thérèse et de Marie Antoinette.* Edited by Alfred Ritter von Arneth and M. A. Geffroy. 3 vols. Paris, 1875.

Mason, George. *The Papers of George Mason, 1725–1792.* Edited by Robert A. Rutland. 3 vols. Chapel Hill, N.C., 1970.

Matthisson, Friedrich von. *Briefe.* 2d ed. Zurich, 1802.

Michaelis, Johann David. *Literarischer Briefwechsel.* Edited by Johann Gottlieb Buhle. Vols. II and III. Leipzig, 1795–1796.

Möser, Justus. *Briefe*. Edited by Ernst Beins and Werner Pleister. Hanover and Osnabrück, 1939.

Müller, Johann Georg. *Der Briefwechsel der Brüder J. Georg Müller und Joh. v. Müller, 1789–1809*. Edited by Eduard Haug. Frauenfeld, 1893.

Ochs, Peter. *Korrespondenz des Peter Ochs (1752–1821)*. Edited by Gustav Steiner. 3 vols. Basel, 1927–1937.

Rainsford, Charles. "Transactions as Commissary for Embarking Foreign Troops in the English Service from Germany. With Copies of Letters Relative to it. For the Years 1776–1777." New-York Historical Society, *Collections*, XII (1879), 313–543.

The Revolutionary Diplomatic Correspondence of the United States. Edited by Francis Wharton. 6 vols. Washington, D.C., 1889.

Rush, Benjamin. *Letters of Benjamin Rush*. Edited by L. H. Butterfield. 2 vols. Princeton, N.J., 1951.

Schiller, Friedrich von. *Briefe. Kritische Gesamtausgabe*. Edited by Fritz Jonas. 7 vols. Stuttgart, 1892.

––––––––. *Briefwechsel zwischen Schiller und Körner, von 1784 bis zum Tode Schillers*. With a foreword by L. Geiger. 4 vols. Stuttgart, n.d.

––––––––. *Briefwechsel zwischen Schiller und W. v. Humboldt in den Jahren 1792 bis 1805*. Edited by Franz Muncker. Stuttgart and Berlin, 1893.

Schubart, Christian Friedrich Daniel. *Leben in seinen Briefen*. Edited by David Friedrich Strauß. 2 vols. Berlin, 1849.

Stein, Heinrich Friedrich Karl Reichsfreiherr vom und zum. *Briefe und Amtliche Schriften*. Compiled by Erich Botzenhart. Newly edited by Walter Hubatsch. Vol. I. Stuttgart, 1957.

Stolberg, Friedrich Leopold Graf zu. *Briefe*. Edited by Jürgen Behrens. Neumünster, 1966.

––––––––. *Briefe Friedrich Leopolds Grafen zu Stolberg und der Seinigen an Johann Heinrich Voß*. Edited by Otto Hellinghaus. Münster, 1891.

––––––––. *Friedrich Leopold Graf zu Stolberg und Herzog Peter Friedrich Ludwig von Oldenburg. Aus ihren Briefen und andern archivalischen Quellen*. Edited by Johann Heinrich Hennes. Mainz, 1870.

Warren, James. *The Warren-Adams Letters: Being Chiefly a Correspondence among John Adams, Samuel Adams, and James Warren*. Massachusetts Historical Society, *Collections*, LXXII–LXXIII. Boston, 1917–1925.

Washington, George. *The Writings of George Washington from the Original Manuscript Sources, 1745–1799*. Edited by John C. Fitzpatrick. 39 vols. Washington, D.C., 1931–1944.

Wieland, Christoph Martin. *Ausgewählte Briefe von C. M. Wieland an verschiedene Freunde in den Jahren 1751. bis 1810. geschrieben, und nach der Zeitfolge geordnet*. 4 vols. Zurich, 1815–1816.

––––––––. *Briefe an Sophie von La Roche, nebst einem Schreiben von Gellert und Lavater*. Edited by Franz Horn. Berlin, 1820.

Zimmermann, Johann Georg. *Briefe an einige seiner Freunde in der Schweiz*. Edited by Albrecht Rengger. Aarau, 1830.

————. *Sein Leben und bisher ungedruckte Briefe an denselben von Bodmer, Breitinger, Geßner, Sulzer, Moses Mendelssohn, Nicolai, der Karschin, Herder und G. Forster*. Edited by Eduard Bodemann. Hanover, 1878.

Diaries, Autobiographies, Memoirs

Adams, John Quincy. *Memoirs of John Quincy Adams, Comprising Portions of his Diary from 1795–1848*. Edited by Charles Francis Adams. 12 vols. Philadelphia, 1874–1877.

Allen, James. "Diary of James Allen, Esq., of Philadelphia, Counsellor-at-Law, 1770–1778." *Pennsylvania Magazine of History and Biography*, IX (1885), 278–295, 424–441.

Büttner, Johann Carl. *Büttner, der Amerikaner. Eine Selbstbiographie*. 2d ed. Camenz, 1828.

Closen, Ludwig von. *The Revolutionary Journal of Baron Ludwig von Closen 1780–1783*. Translated and edited by Evelyn M. Acomb. Chapel Hill, N.C., 1958.

Döhla, Johann Konrad. "Tagebuch eines Bayreuther Soldaten aus dem Nordamerikanischen Freiheitskrieg 1777–1783." *Archiv für Geschichte und Altertunskunde von Oberfranken*, XXV (1912–1914), no. 1, 81–201, no. 2, 107–224.

Dohm, Christian Wilhelm von. *Denkwürdigkeiten meiner Zeit oder Beiträge zur Geschichte vom lezten Viertel des achtzehnten und vom Anfang des neunzehnten Jahrhunderts 1778 bis 1806*. 5 vols. Lemgo and Hanover, 1814–1819.

Dörnberg, Karl Ludwig Freiherr von. *Tagebuchblätter eines hessischen Offiziers aus der Zeit des nordamerikanischen Unabhängigkeitskrieges*. Edited by Gotthold Marseille. 2 vols. Pyritz, 1899–1900.

Du Roi, August Wilhelm. *Journal of Du Roi the Elder, Lieutenant and Adjutant, in the Service of the Duke of Brunswick, 1776–1778*. Translated by Charlotte S. J. Epping. Philadelphia and New York, 1911.

Erhard, Johann Benjamin. *Denkwürdigkeiten des Philosophen und Arztes Johann Benjamin Erhard*. Edited by Karl August Varnhagen von Ense. Stuttgart and Tübingen, 1830.

Forbach, Wilhelm Graf von. *My Campaigns in America: A Journal kept by Count William de Deux-Ponts, 1780–81*. Translated and edited by Samuel Abbott Green. Boston, 1868.

Forster, Georg. *Tagebücher*. Edited by Paul Zincke and Albert Leitzmann. Berlin, 1914.

Heeren, Arnold Hermann Ludwig. "Schreiben an einen Freund, biographische Nachrichten enthaltend." In Heeren, *Vermischte historische Schriften*, Pt. I, pp. xi-lxxviii. Göttingen, 1821.

Heister, Lieutenant von. "Auszüge aus dem Tagebuche eines vormaligen kurhessischen Offiziers über den Nordamerikanischen Freiheitskrieg 1776 und 1777.

Mitgetheilt durch den Lieut. von Heister." *Zeitschrift für Kunst, Wissenschaft und Geschichte des Krieges*, XII, no. 3 (1828), 223–270.

Krafft, Johann Karl Philipp von. "Journal of Lt. John Charles Philip von Krafft, 1776–1784." Edited by Thomas Henry Edsall. New-York Historical Society, *Collections*, XV (1882), 1–202.

Matthisson, Friedrich von. *Erinnerungen.* 3 vols. Zurich, 1810–1816.

Meyer von Knonau, Ludwig. *Lebenserinnerungen.* Edited by Gerold Meyer von Knonau. Frauenfeld, 1883.

Michaelis, Johann David. *Lebensbeschreibung von ihm selbst abgefaßt, mit Anmerkungen von Johann Matthäus Hassencamp.* Rinteln and Leipzig, 1793.

Morris, Gouverneur. *The Diary and Letters of Gouverneur Morris, Minister of the United States to France.* Edited by Anne Cary Morris. 2 vols. New York, 1888.

Päusch, Georg. *Journal of Captain Pausch, Chief of the Hanau Artillery during the Burgoyne Campaign.* Translated and edited by William L. Stone. With an introduction by Edward J. Lowell. Albany, N.Y., 1886.

Popp, Stephan. "Popp's Journal, 1777–1783." Edited by Joseph G. Rosengarten. *Pennsylvania Magazine of History and Biography*, XXVI (1902), 25–41, 245–254.

Pütter, Johann Stephan. *Selbstbiographie.* 2 vols. Göttingen, 1798.

Riedesel, Friederike Charlotte Luise. *Baroness von Riedesel and the American Revolution: Journal and Correspondence of a Tour of Duty 1776–1783.* Newly translated and edited by Marvin L. Brown, Jr. Chapel Hill, N.C., 1965.

Schlieffen, Martin Ernst von. *Einige Betreffnisse und Erlebungen.* Berlin, 1830.

Schüler von Senden, Ernst Johann Friedrich. "Denkwürdigkeiten." *Zeitschrift für Kunst, Wissenschaft und Geschichte des Krieges*, XLVII (1839), no. 8, 137–189, no. 9, 257–286.

The Siege of Charleston, With an Account of the Province of South Carolina: Diaries and Letters of Hessian Officers from the von Jungkenn Papers in the William L. Clements Library. Translated and edited by Bernhard A. Uhlendorf. Ann Arbor, Mich., 1938.

Steffens, Henrich. *Was ich erlebte.* 10 vols. Breslau, 1840–1844.

Trenck, Friedrich Freiherr von der. *Merkwürdige Lebensgeschichte.* Stuttgart, 1883.

Trumbull, John. *Autobiography, Reminiscences and Letters of John Trumbull, from 1756 to 1841.* London, New York, and New Haven, Conn., 1841.

Waldeck, Philipp. *Diary of the American Revolution, Printed from the Original Manuscript with Introduction and Photographic Reproduction of the List of Officers.* Edited by Marion Dexter Learned. Philadelphia, 1907.

Wiederhold, Bernhard Wilhelm. "Tagebuch des Capt. Wiederholdt vom 7 October 1776 bis 7 December 1780." Edited by Marion Dexter Learned and C. Grosse. *Americana Germanica*, IV (1902), 1–93.

Zinzendorf, Karl Graf von. *Ludwig und Karl Grafen und Herren von Zinzendorf, Minister unter Maria Theresia, Josef II., Leopold II. und Franz I. Ihre Selbstbiographien nebst einer kurzen Geschichte des Hauses Zinzendorf.* Edited by Eduard Gaston Graf von Pettenegg. Vienna, 1879.

Newspapers, Periodicals

Allerneueste Mannigfaltigkeiten. Berlin, 1781–1782.

Allgemeine deutsche Bibliothek. Edited by Friedrich Nicolai. Berlin and Stettin, 1770–1796.

Allgemeine geographische Ephemeriden. Edited by F. von Zach. Weimar, 1798–1800.

Annalen der Brittischen Literatur, vom ganzen Jahre 1780. Edited by Johann Joachim Escheburg. Leipzig, 1781.

Berlinische Monatsschrift. Edited by Friedrich Gedike and Johann Erich Biester. 1783–1796.

Berlinische Nachrichten von Staats- und Gelehrten Sachen (Haude- und Spenersche Zeitung). 1777.

Berlinische privilegirte Zeitung (Vossische Zeitung). 1777.

Berlinisches Archiv der Zeit und ihres Geschmacks. Edited by F. E. Rambach and I. A. Feßler. 1795–1800.

Berlinisches Journal für Aufklärung. Edited by G. N. Fischer and A. Riem. 1788–1790.

Bibliothek für Denker und Männer von Geschmak. Edited by Peter Adolf Winkopp. Gera, 1783–1786.

Braunschweigisches Journal philosophischen, philologischen und pädagogischen Inhalts. Edited by E. C. Trapp *et al.* 1788–1790.

Briefwechsel meist historischen und politischen Inhalts. Edited by August Ludwig Schlözer. Göttingen, 1777–1782.

Briefwechsel meist statistischen Inhalts. Edited by August Ludwig Schlözer. Göttingen, 1775.

Bunzlauische Monatsschrift zum Nutzen und Vergnügen. 1774–1783.

Chronik. Edited by Christian Friedrich Daniel Schubart. Stuttgart, 1790–1791.

Chronologen. Edited by Wilhelm Ludwig Wekhrlin. Frankfurt, 1779–1781.

Deutsche Chronik. Edited by Christian Friedrich Daniel Schubart. Augsburg and Ulm, 1774–1777.

Deutsche Monatsschrift. Edited by F. von Kleist *et al.* Berlin, 1790–1794, 1795–1799.

Der Deutsche Zuschauer. Edited by Peter Adolf Winkopp. Zurich, 1785–1789.

Deutsches Magazin. Edited by C.U.D. von Eggers. Hamburg, 1791–1799.

Deutsches Museum. Edited by Heinrich Christian Boie (and, until 1778, Christian Wilhelm von Dohm). Leipzig, 1776–1788.

Englische allgemeine Bibliothek. Translated by J.C.F. Schulz. Leipzig, 1775.

The English Lyceum, or, Choice of Pieces in Prose and in Verse, Selected from the Best Periodical Papers. . . . Edited by Johann Wilhelm von Archenholtz. Hamburg, 1787–1788.

Ephemeriden der Menschheit oder Bibliothek der Sittenlehre und der Politik. Edited by Isaak Iselin. Basel, 1776–1782.

Ephemeriden über Aufklärung, Litteratur und Kunst. Edited by J. F. Engelschall. Marburg, 1785.

Europäische Annalen. Edited by Ernst Ludwig Posselt. Tübingen, 1795–1800.

Fliegende Blätter dem französischen Krieg und dem Revolutionswesen unsrer Zeiten gewidmet. Hanover, 1794.

Frankfurter gelehrte Anzeigen. 1774, 1776–1779, 1781–1784.

Frankfurter Kayserl. Reichs-Ober-Post-Amts-Zeitung. 1773–1777, 1779–1783.

Freytags-Zeitung. Zurich, 1770–1783.

Der Genius der Zeit. Edited by August Hennings. Altona, 1794–1800.

Geschichte und Politik. Edited by Karl Ludwig Woltmann. Berlin, 1800.

Göttingische Anzeigen von gelehrten Sachen. 1770–1800.

Göttingisches Historisches Magazin. Edited by Christoph Meiners and Ludwig Timotheus Spittler. Hanover, 1787–1791.

Göttingisches Magazin der Wissenschaften und Litteratur. Edited by Georg Christoph Lichtenberg and Georg Forster. 1780–1785.

Das graue Ungeheuer. Edited by Wilhelm Ludwig Wekhrlin. Nuremberg, 1784–1787.

Hamburgischer Correspondent, i.e., *Staats- und Gelehrten Zeitung des Hamburgischen unpartheyischen Correspondenten.* 1770–1783.

Hannoverisches Magazin. 1765, 1770–1790.

Historische Litteratur. Edited by Johann Georg Meusel. Erlangen, 1781–1784.

Historisches Journal. Edited by Johann Christoph Gatterer. Göttingen, 1772–1781.

Historisches Journal. Edited by Friedrich Gentz. Berlin, 1799–1800.

Historisches Portefeuille. Edited by Karl Renatus Hausen and August Ferdinand Lueder. Vienna, 1782–1788.

Historisch-Litterarisch-Biographisches Magazin. Edited by Johann Georg Meusel. Zurich and Chemnitz, 1788–1792.

Hurtersche Zeitung. Schaffhausen, 1777.

Hyperboreische Briefe. Edited by Wilhelm Ludwig Wekhrlin. Nuremberg, 1788–1790.

Iris. Edited by Johann Georg Jacobi. Düsseldorf, 1775–1776.

Journal von und für Deutschland. Edited by Leopold Friedrich Günther von Goeckingk and Heinrich Freiherr von Bibra. Ellrich, 1784–1792.

Leipziger Zeitung. 1770–1783.

Litteratur und Völkerkunde. Edited by Johann Wilhelm von Archenholtz. Dessau, 1782–1786.

Magazin für die Geographie, Staatenkunde und Geschichte. Edited by Johann Ernst Fabri. Nuremberg, 1797.

Magazin für die neue Historie und Geographie. Edited by Anton Friedrich Büsching. Halle, 1770–1788.

Minerva. Edited by Johann Wilhelm von Archenholtz. Berlin, 1792–1800.

Nachrichten zum Nuzen und Vergnügen. Edited by Friedrich Schiller. Stuttgart, 1781.

Neue allgemeine deutsche Bibliothek. Edited by Friedrich Nicolai. Kiel, 1793–1800.

Neue Deutsche Monatsschrift. Edited by Friedrich Gentz. Berlin, 1795.

Der neue Deutsche Zuschauer. Zurich, 1789–1791.

Neue Litteratur und Völkerkunde. Edited by Johann Wilhelm von Archenholtz. Dessau and Leipzig, 1787–1791.

Neuer Teutscher Merkur. Edited by Christoph Martin Wieland. Weimar and Leipzig, 1790–1800.

Neues Deutsches Museum. Edited by Heinrich Christian Boie. Leipzig, 1789–1791.

Neues Göttingisches historisches Magazin. Edited by Christoph Meiners and Ludwig Timotheus Spittler. Hanover, 1792–1794.

Neueste Geschichte der Welt oder das Denkwürdigste aus allen vier Welttheilen. . . . Ulm and Augsburg, 1774–1776.

Neueste Litteratur der Geschichtkunde. Edited by Johann Georg Meusel. Erfurt, 1778–1780.

Neueste Mannigfaltigkeiten. Berlin, 1777–1780.

Die neuesten Staatsbegebenheiten mit historischen und politischen Anmerkungen. Edited by Heinrich Martin Gottfried Köster. Frankfurt and Mainz, 1776–1784.

Nichts Neues, aber doch manches Brauchbare. Dresden, 1778–1779.

Osnabrückische Intelligenzblätter, i.e., *Wöchentliche Osnabrückische Anzeigen nebst Nützlichen Beylagen zum Osnabrückischen Intelligenz-Blate*. 1770–1782.

Patriotisches Archiv für Deutschland. Edited by Friedrich Karl Freiherr von Moser. Frankfurt and Leipzig, 1785–1790.

Politisches Journal, nebst Anzeige von gelehrten und andern Sachen. Edited by Gottlob Benedikt von Schirach. Hamburg, 1781–1800.

Schleswigsches ehemals Braunschweigisches Journal. Altona, 1792.

Schleswigsches Journal. Edited by August Hennings. Altona, 1793.

Stats-Anzeigen. Edited by August Ludwig Schlözer. Göttingen, 1782–1793.

Teutscher Merkur. Edited by Christoph Martin Wieland. Weimar, 1773–1789.

Unächter Acacien-Baum. Zur Ermunterung des allgemeinen Anbaues dieser in ihrer Art einzigen Holzart. Edited by Friedrich Kasimir Medicus. Leipzig, 1796–1802.

Vaterländische Chronik. Edited by Christian Friedrich Daniel Schubart. Stuttgart, 1787.

Vaterlandschronik. Edited by Christian Friedrich Daniel Schubart. Stuttgart, 1788–1789.

Wiener Realzeitung, i.e., *Kaiserlich Königliche allergnädigst privilegierte Realzeitung der Wissenschaften, Künste und der Kommerzien*. 1770–1783.

Wienerisches Diarium oder Nachrichten von Staats, vermischten, und gelehrten Neuigkeiten. 1770–1776.

Wöchentliche Nachrichten von neuen Landcharten, geographischen, statistischen und historischen Büchern und Sachen. Edited by Anton Friedrich Büsching. Berlin, 1773–1787.

Americana Germanica, 1770–1800

[Accarias de Sérionne, Jacques]. *Situation Politique Actuelle de l'Europe, considérée relativement à l'ordre moral, pour servir de supplément à l'ordre moral*. Augsburg, 1781.

Achenwall, Gottfried. *Einige Anmerkungen über Nord-Amerika und über dasige Grosbrittannische Colonien. Aus mündlichen Nachrichten des Herrn D. Frank-*

lins verfaßt von Hrn. D. Gottfried Achenwall. Nebst Herrn John Wesleys Schrift von den Streitigkeiten mit den Colonien in Amerika. 2d ed. Helmstedt, 1777.

Adair, James. *Geschichte der Amerikanischen Indianer; besonders der am Mississippi, an Ost- und Westflorida, Georgien, Süd- und Nord-Karolina und Virginien angrenzenden Nationen, nebst einem Anhange.* Translated from the English [by Hermann Ewald Schatz]. Breslau, 1782.

Adams, John Quincy. *Beantwortung der Paineschen Schrift von den Rechten der Menschen.* Translated from the English [by W.H.F. Abrahamson]. Copenhagen, 1793.

Alfieri, Vittorio. *L'America Libera odi di Vittorio Alfieri da Asti.* Kehl, 1784.

Amerikanische Staats-Papiere. Wichtige Documente und Depeschen, begleitet von der Bothschaft des Präsidenten der vereinigten Staaten von Amerika an die beiden Häuser des Congresses am 3. April 1798, in Hinsicht auf die Mißhelligkeiten zwischen Amerika und Frankreich enthaltend die Instruktionen der amerikanischen Gesandten und ihre ganze Correspondenz mit dem executiven Direktorium von Frankreich, nebst des Präsidenten Bothschaft an den Congreß, den 19. März 1798. Translated from the English. N.p., 1798.

Anburey, Thomas. *Reisen im Innern von Nordamerika, welche eine Schilderung der Sitten und Eigenthümlichkeiten des Landes Kanada, Neu-England und Virginien, imgleichen die Geschichte des Feldzuges, der Uebergabe und der ferneren Schicksale der Armee unter dem General Bourgoyne enthalten.* Translated from the English by Georg Forster. Berlin, 1792.

Anmerkungen aus der neuen und alten Welt bey Gelegenheit der Beschreibung des Siebenjährigen Seekrieges zwischen England und den amerikanischen Staaten, in Briefen abgefaßt, für Leser, die darüber denken wollen. Berlin, 1786. Reprint. Berlin, 1788.

Arnould, Ambroise Marie. *System der Seehandlung und Politik der Europäer während dem Achtzehnten und als Einleitung in das Neunzehnte Jahrhundert. Ein Handbuch für den Staats- und Kaufmann, für den Statistiker und Geschichtsschreiber mit Hinsicht auf die Ruhe, Sicherheit und Freiheit aller europäischen Staaten nach ihren Friedens- Kommerz- und Schiffahrtstraktaten und andern öffentlichen Urkunden.* Translated from the French [by J. Dominkus]. Erfurt, 1798.

Auszug der allgemeinen Weltgeschichte, mit einer Einleitung. 3 pts. Amberg, 1776.

[Barlow, Joel.] *Guter Rath an die Völker Europens bei der Nothwendigkeit, die Regierungsgrundsätze überall zu verändern.* Translated from the English [by Johann Anton Fahrenkrüger]. 2 vols. London, [i.e., Hamburg], 1792–1795.

[Barron, William]. *Geschichte der Kolonisirung der freien Staaten des Alterthums, angewandt auf den gegenwärtigen Streit zwischen Großbritannien und seinen amerikanischen Kolonien, nebst Betrachtungen über die künftige Einrichtung dieser Kolonien.* Translated from the English. Leipzig, 1778.

[Bartholomäi, Christian Friedrich von]. *Die Eroberung von Charlestown Poetisch beschrieben von einem Anspachischen Jäger in America.* N.p., 1785.

Barton, Benjamin Smith. *Benjamin Smith Barton's . . . Abhandlung über die ver-*

meinte Zauberkraft der Klapperschlange und anderer amerikanischen Schlangen; und über die wirksamsten Mittel gegen den Biss der Klapperschlange. Translated from the English by E[berhard] A[ugust] W[ilhelm] von Zimmermann. Leipzig, 1798.

Bartram, William. *William Bartram's Reisen durch Nord- und Süd-Karolina, Georgien, Ost- und West-Florida, das Gebiet der Tscherokesen, Krihks und Tschaktahs, nebst umständlichen Nachrichten von den Einwohnern, dem Boden und den Naturprodukten dieser wenig bekannten großen Länder.* Translated from the English by Eberhard August Wilhelm Zimmermann. Berlin, 1793.

[Bauer, Georg Lorenz]. *Neuestes Lehrbuch der Erdbeschreibung vornehmlich über den Homännischen Schulatlas von sechs und dreyßig Karten.* Nuremberg, 1787.

Baumann, Ludwig Adolph. *L. A. Baumanns . . . Abriß der Staatsverfassung der vornehmsten Länder in Amerika. Nebst einem Anhange von den nordlichen Polarländern.* Brandenburg, 1776.

[Baur, Samuel]. *Geschichtserzählungen großer und seltener Menschen unsers Zeitalters, aus den ersten und richtigsten Quellen genommen.* 2 vols. Leipzig, 1798.

Bayer, Johann Georg. *Die Geographie im Kleinen, in deutsche Verse gebracht.* Breslau, 1777.

Bayer, Joseph Wilhelm. *Historisch-summarische Darstellung der vorzüglichsten Staatsveränderungen, die sich in den verschiedenen Völkerbeherrschungen, so weit die Geschichte reichet, eräugnet haben. Als eine Nachlese zu der Historisch-chronologischen und Geographischen Weltkarte aller Reiche und Freystaaten, die nach der berühmten englischen Karte des Doctor Priestley bearbeitet und zum Behuf derjenigen herausgegeben ist, welche mittelst derselben ohne Anstrengung des Gedächtnisses die allgemeine Weltgeschichte studiren, und von der alten und neuen Geographie eine richtige Kenntniss erlangen wollen.* Vienna, 1796.

Bericht eines Englischen Amerikaners von Philadelphia an seinen Freund in Engelland über den dermahligen Krieg Groß-Brittaniens mit seinen Amerikanischen Colonien vom 15 December 1776. Translated from the English. Frankfurt and Leipzig, 1777.

Berichte über den Genesee-Distrikt in dem Staate von Neu-York der vereinigten Staaten von Nord-Amerika nach der im Jahr 1791 Englischen herausgegebenen Ausgabe übersetzt. N.p., 1791.

Beschreibung aller Länder und Völker der Erde, zur Belehrung und Unterhaltung. Halle, [1796].

Beschreibung der dreizehn unabhängigen Nordamerikanischen Staaten, aus den bäßten änglischen Quellen. Translated from the French. Cologne, 1783.

Betrachtungen über den Feldzug des Generals Bourgoyne in Canada und Neu-York. Translated from the English. Brunswick, 1780.

[Bischof, Karl August Lebrecht]. *Tabellarisch-historisches Handbuch der Kirchen- und Staatengeschichte bis auf die neuesten und gegenwärtigen Zeiten.* Nuremberg, 1793.

Bisset, Robert. *Edmund Burke's Leben in historisch-literarisch-politischer Hinsicht unpartheiisch dargestellt.* Translated from the English by Joh[ann] Christian Fick. Leipzig and Gera, 1799.

Bösenberg, Johann Heinrich. *Dramatischer Beytrag für das Hoftheater in Dresden.* Dresden and Leipzig, 1791.

Brandes, Ernst. *Ueber einige bisherige Folgen der Französischen Revolution, in Rücksicht auf Deutschland.* Hanover, 1792. 2d ed., Hanover and Osnabrück, 1793.

Bretzner, Christoph Friedrich. *Das Räuschgen. Ein Lustspiel in vier Akten.* Leipzig, 1786.

Briefe über den gegenwärtigen Zustand von England, besonders in Ansehung der Politik der Künste, der Sitten und der schönen Wissenschaften. Translated from the English. 2 pts. Leipzig, 1777.

Briefe über die jetzige Uneinigkeit zwischen den Amerikanischen Colonien und dem Englischen Parlament. Translated from the English. Hanover, 1776.

Brissot de Warville, Jacques Pierre. *J. P. Brissot's (Warville), Französischen Bürgers, neue Reise durch die Nordamerikanischen Freistaaten im Jahr 1788.* Translated from the French by Johann Reinhold Forster. Berlin, 1792.

[_____]. *Karakteristik der Quäker.* Translated from the French [by Karl Julius Friedrich]. Boston [i.e.,Bad Dürkheim], 1792.

_____ . *Neue Reise durch die Vereinigten Staaten von Nord-Amerika im Jahre 1788.* Translated from the French by Albrecht Christoph Kayser. 3 vols. Bayreuth, 1792–1793.

Bruns, Paul Jakob, and Zimmermann, Eberhard August Wilhelm. *Repositorium für die neueste Geographie, Statistik und Geschichte.* 3 vols. Tübingen, 1792–1793.

[Buchenröder, Johann Nickolaus Karl]. *Gesammlete Nachrichten von den Englischen Kolonien in Nord-Amerika bis auf jetzige Zeiten.* Hamburg and Schwerin, 1776.

[_____]. *Grundriß von Nordamerika.* Hamburg, 1778.

[_____]. *Kurzgefaßte Historisch-geographische Nachrichten von den Englischen Kolonien in Nord-Amerika bis auf jetzige Zeiten.* 2d ed., Hamburg, 1778.

[_____]. *Das Nord-Amerika Historisch und Geographisch beschrieben.* 4 vols. Hamburg, 1777–1778. 2d ed., Hamburg, 1778.

Bülow, Dietrich Heinrich Freiherr von. *Der Freistaat von Nordamerika in seinem neuesten Zustand.* 2 vols. Berlin, 1797.

Burke, Edmund. *Jahrbücher der neuern Geschichte der Englischen Pflanzungen in Nord-Amerika Seit dem Jahr 1755. bis auf itzige Zeiten. Zur Fortsetzung der Geschichte der Englischen Kolonien in Nordamerika seit der Entdeckung dieser Länder bis 1763.* Translated from the English [by Samuel Wilhelm Truner]. 4 vols. Danzig, 1777–1781.

Burnaby, Andrew. *Reisen durch die Mittlern Kolonien der Engländer in Nord-Amerika, nebst Anmerkungen über den Zustand der Kolonien.* Translated from the English [by Christoph Daniel Ebeling]. Hamburg and Kiel, 1776.

Büsch, Johann Georg. *Grundriß einer Geschichte der merkwürdigsten Welthändel neuerer Zeit in einem erzählenden Vortrage.* Hamburg, 1781. 2d ed., Hamburg, 1783. 3d ed., Hamburg, 1796.

_____ . *Versuch einer Geschichte der Hamburgischen Handlung, nebst zwei kleineren Schriften eines verwandten Inhalts.* Hamburg, 1797.

————, and Ebeling, Christoph Daniel. *Handlungsbibliothek.* 3 vols. Hamburg, 1785–1797.

Carli, Gian Rinaldo. *Briefe über Amerika nach der neusten, verbeßerten und mit dem dritten Theile vermehrten Ausgabe.* Translated from the Italian by Christian Gottfried Hennig. 3 vols. Gera, 1785.

Carver, Jonathan. *Johann Carvers Reisen durch die innern Gegenden von Nord-Amerika in den Jahren 1766, 1767 und 1768, mit einer Landkarte.* Translated from the English. Hamburg, 1780.

Castiglioni, Luigi Conte. *Luigi Castiglioni's . . . Reise durch die vereinigten Staaten von Nord-Amerika, in den Jahren 1785, 1786 und 1787. Nebst Bemerkungen über die nützlichsten Gewächse dieses Landes.* Translated from the Italian by Magnus Petersen. Memmingen, 1793.

Chalmers, Lionel. *Lionel Chalmer's Nachrichten über die Witterung und Krankheiten in Südcarolina. Nebst John Linings Tabelle über die Aus- und Absonderungen des Körpers im dortigen Klima.* Translated from the English. 2 vols. Stendal, 1788–1792.

[Chastellux, François Jean, marquis de]. *Abhandlung über die Vortheile und Nachtheile die für Europa aus der Entdeckung von America entstehen. Auf Veranlassung eines von dem Herrn Abt Raynal ausgesetzten Preises.* Translated from the French [by Johann August Eberhard]. Halle, 1788.

————. *Des Ritters von Chastellux Reisebeobachtungen über Amerika.* Translated from the French. Hamburg, 1785.

Christiani, Wilhelm Ernst. *Geschichte der neuesten Weltbegebenheiten, von 1748 oder von dem Aachner Frieden an, bis auf die gegenwärtige Zeit.* 3 vols. Leipzig, 1788–1793.

[Cluny, Alexander]. *Reisen durch Amerika, oder Beobachtungen über den gegenwärtigen Zustand, Cultur und Handel der brittischen Colonien in Amerika, deren Aus- und Einfuhr mit Großbrittannien, und Uebersicht der Einkünfte, welche letzteres daraus zieht.* Translated from the English. *Nebst einem Abriß von Nord-Amerika, und der Republik der dreyzehn vereinigten Staaten* [by Joseph Mandrillon]. Translated from the French. Leipzig, 1783.

Contant d'Orville, André Guillaume. *Geschichte der verschiedenen Völcker des Erdbodens, deren gottesdienstliche und bürgerliche Gebräuche, Ursprung der Religionen, Secten, Aberglauben, Sitten und Gewohnheiten enthaltend, nebst einer genauen geographischen Beschreibung der Kaiserthümer, Königreiche und freyen Staaten in allen vier Theilen der Welt.* Translated from the French. 6 vols. Hof and Leipzig, 1773–1778.

Cooper, Thomas. *Renseignemens sur l'Amérique.* Translated from the English. Hamburg, 1795.

[Crèvecoeur, Hector St. John de]. *Briefe eines Amerikanischen Landmanns an den Ritter W. S. in den Jahren 1770 bis 1781.* Translated from the French by Johann August Ephraim Goeze. 3 vols. Leipzig, 1788–1789.

————. *Sittliche Schilderung von Amerika, in Briefen eines Amerikanischen*

Guthsbesitzers an einen Freund in England. Translated from the English [by Karl Gottfried Schreiter]. Liegnitz and Leipzig, 1784.

Crome, August Friedrich Wilhelm. *Über die Größe, Volksmenge, Clima und Fruchtbarkeit des Nordamerikanischen Freystaats.* Dessau and Leipzig, 1783.

Curtius, Michael Konrad. *Grundriß der Universal Historie.* Marburg, 1790.

Delacroix, Jacques Vincent. *Verfassung der vornehmsten europäischen und der vereinigten amerikanischen Staaten.* Translated from the French. 6 vols. Leipzig, 1792–1803.

Deslandes, [Pierre Delaunay?], Chevalier. *Discours sur la grandeur et l'importance de la révolution qui vient de s'opérer dans l'Amérique Septentrionale; Sujet proposé par l'Académie des Jeux Floraux.* Frankfurt and Paris, 1785.

Deutsche Encyclopädie oder Allgemeines Real-Wörterbuch aller Künste und Wissenschaften von einer Gesellschaft Gelehrten. [Edited by Heinrich Martin Gottfried Köster and Johann Friedrich Roos]. 23 vols. Frankfurt, 1778–1804.

Didier, Constantine. *Constantinii Didier Gallo-Belgici Commentatio medica de Febre Flava Americana.* Göttingen, [1800].

[Dillinger, Georg Adam]. *Nach dem jetzigen Staat eingerichtete Bilder-Geographie, darinnen von den vier Hauptheilen des Erdbodens Europas, Asia, Afrika und Amerika Nachricht gegeben, alle Nationen nach ihrer Kleidung in saubern Figuren vorgestellet, und die Länder nach ihrer Lage, Flüssen, Clima, Fruchtbarkeit, Einwohnern, Handlung, Macht, Regierungsform, vornehmsten Städten und Merkwürdigkeiten beschrieben werden; als ein bequemes Handbuch zum Gebrauch der neuesten geographischen Charten eingerichtet und mit doppeltem Register versehen.* Nuremberg, 1770. 2d ed., Nuremberg, 1773. 3d ed., Nuremberg, 1781.

Dohm, Christian Wilhelm. *Materialien für die Statistick und neuere Staatengeschichte.* 5 vols. Lemgo, 1777–1785.

Die drey vollständigen Subsidien-Tractaten, welche zwischen Sr. Großbritannischen Majestät einer Seits, und dem Durchlauchtigsten Landgrafen von Hessen-Cassel, dem Durchlauchtigsten Herzoge von Braunschweig und Lüneburg, und dem Durchlauchtigsten Erb-Prinzen von Hessen-Cassel, als regierenden Grafen von Hanau, andrer Seits, geschlossen sind. English and German texts. Frankfurt and Leipzig, 1776.

[Du Buisson, Pierre Ulric]. *Historischer Abriß der in Nord-Amerika vorgefallenen Staats-Veränderung. Vom Anfange des Jahrs 1774. bis den ersten Jenner 1778.* Translated from the French. Bern, 1779. 2d ed. as *Vorstellung der Staatsveränderung in Nordamerika, von den ersten Unruhen im Jahr 1774 bis zu dem Bündniß der Krone Frankreichs mit den Kolonien.* Bern, 1784.

[Duché, Jacob]. *Briefe des Herrn T. Caspipina, welche Beobachtungen über verschiedene Gegenstände aus der Litteratur, Moral und Religion enthalten. Nebst dem Leben und Charakter des Herrn Penn ersten Eigenthümers von Pensylvanien.* Translated from the English. Leipzig, 1778.

Ebeling, Christoph Daniel. *Amerikanische Bibliothek.* 4 pts. Leipzig, 1777.

_____ . *Christoph Daniel Ebelings . . . Erdbeschreibung und Geschichte von Amerika. Die vereinten Staaten von Nordamerika.* 7 vols. Hamburg, 1793–1816.

Entwurf der neuesten Culturgeschichte seit der Ideenwanderung über Freiheit und Rechte der Menschheit. Ein Anhang zu Adelungs Versuch einer Geschichte der Cultur. Leipzig, 1800.

Erklärung der Repräsentanten der vereinigten Colonien in Nord-Amerika abgefaßt auf dem General-Congreß zu Philadelphia, enthalten die Ursachen und Bewegungsgründe zur Ergreifung der Waffen, nebst angehängten Kriegs-Reglement der vereinigten Truppen. Translated from the English. Frankfurt and Leipzig, 1775.

Essich, Johann Georg. *Johann Georg Essigs Einleitung zu der allgemeinen und besondern Welthistorie, aufs neue übersehen, vermehrt, und bis auf gegenwärtige Zeit fortgesetzet.* Edited by Johann Christian Volz. 10th ed., Stuttgart, 1773.

Ewald, Johann von. *Abhandlung über den kleinen Krieg von Joh. Ewald. . . .* Kassel, 1785.

Examen impartial de la vie privée et publique de Louis XVI, Roi de France. Hamburg and Paris, 1797.

Fabri, Johann Ernst. *J. E. Fabri . . . Handbuch der neuesten Geographie für Akademien und Gymnasien.* 2 vols. Halle, 1784–1785. 2d ed., Halle, 1787. 3d ed., Halle, 1790. 4th ed., Halle, 1793. 5th ed., Halle, 1795. 6th ed., Halle, 1797. 7th ed., Halle, 1800.

Falconbridge, Alexander, and Clarkson, Thomas. *Alex. Falconbridges und Thomas Clarksons Bemerkungen über die gegenwärtige Beschaffenheit des Sclavenhandels und dessen politische Nachtheile für England.* Translated from the English and edited by Matthias Christian Sprengel. Leipzig, 1790.

[Fenning, Daniel]. *Neue Erdbeschreibung von ganz Amerika.* Translated from the English. Edited by August Ludwig Schlözer. 6 vols. Göttingen and Leipzig, 1777.

Filson, John. *Reise nach Kentucke und Nachrichten von dieser neu angebaueten Landschaft in Nordamerika.* Translated from the English. Leipzig, 1790.

Forster, Georg. *Erinnerungen aus dem Jahr 1790 in historischen Gemälden und Bildnissen von D. Chodowiecki, D. Berger, Cl. Kohl, J. F. Bolt und J. S. Ringck.* Berlin, 1793.

_____ . *Geschichte der Reisen, die seit Cook an der Nordwest- und Nordost-Küste von Amerika und in dem nördlichsten Amerika selbst von Meares, Dixon, Portlock, Coxe, Long u.a.m. unternommen worden sind.* Translated from the English by Georg Forster. 3 vols. Berlin, 1791. Vol. III also appeared as *Nathaniel Portlocks und Georg Mortimers Reisen an die Nordwestküste von Amerika; nebst den Reisen eines Amerikanischen Dolmetschers und Pelzhändlers, welche eine Beschreibung der Sitten und Gebräuche der Nordamerikanischen Wilden enthalten, herausgegeben von John Long.* Translated from the English by Georg Forster. Berlin, 1796.

_____ . *Kleine Schriften. Ein Beytrag zur Völker- und Länderkunde, Naturgeschichte und Philosophie des Lebens.* 6 vols. Leipzig and Berlin, 1789–1797.

Forster, Johann Reinhold, and Sprengel, Matthias Christian, eds. *Beiträge zur Völker und Länderkunde.* 14 vols. Leipzig, 1781–1790.

Fortgesetztes Schreiben eines Hessischen Officiers aus Amerika, welches die weiter vorgefallenen Attaquen und gemachten Eroberungen enthält. N.p., 1776.

[Francis, Philip]. *Briefe über den jetzigen Zustand von Großbritannien. Erster Band welcher die Briefe des Junius enthält.* Translated from the English. Frankfurt and Leipzig, 1776.

Franklin, Benjamin. *Auszug der Anmerkungen zum Unterricht derjenigen Europäer, die sich in Amerika niederzulassen gesonnen sind, von dem letztlich verstorbenen berühmten Dr. Franklin.* N.p., [1791].

———. *Benjamin Franklins Kleine Schriften meist in der Manier des Zuschauers, nebst seinem Leben.* Translated from the English by Georg Schatz. 2 vols. Weimar, 1794.

———. *Bericht für diejenigen, welche nach Nord-Amerika sich begeben, und alldort ansiedeln wollen.* Translated from the English [by Jean Rodolphe Vautravers]. Hamburg, 1786.

[———]. *Merkwürdiger Americanischer Haushaltungs Calender, eingerichtet auf die itzige Zeiten.* Translated from the English. Boston [i.e., Germany], 1771.

Frankreichs Verfahren gegen Amerika. Oder vollständige Actenstücke über die nun abgebrochenen Negociationen zwischen den vereinigten Staaten und der französischen Republik. Translated from the English [by J.F.W. Möller]. Hamburg, 1798.

Franz, Friedrich Christian. *Lehrbuch der Länder- und Völkerkunde in zween Theilen.* 2 vols. Stuttgart, 1788–1790.

———. *Ueber die Kultur der Amerikaner. Eine Rede am Geburtsfeste Seiner Durchlaucht des regierenden Herrn Herzogs zu Wirtemberg den 11. Febr. 1788.* Stuttgart, 1788.

Die Freundschaft im Kloster oder der Amerikanische Flüchtling. enthaltend eine vollständige Beschreibung der Erziehung in Klöstern in hoher und niedrer Kost; der Sitten und Karaktere der Nonnen; den Künsten, deren man sich bedient junge Personen zu dieser Lebensart anzulocken und ihrer traurigen Wirkung auf die menschliche Gesellschaft. Leipzig, 1781.

Galloway, Joseph. *Briefe an einen vornehmen Herrn und Pair von Groß-Britannien über den in den Mittlern Colonien in America geführten Krieg so wol als über den Anfang und Fortgang der daselbst entsponnenen Unruhen, nebst einem Anhange, und einem in Kupfer gestochenen Operations-Plan der gegenseitigen Kriegs-Heere.* Translated from the English. Hamburg, 1780.

Gaspari, Adam Christian. *Lehrbuch der Erdbeschreibung zur Erläuterung des neuen methodischen Schul-Atlasses.* 2 vols. Weimar, 1792–1793. 2d ed., Vol. I, Weimar, 1795. 3d ed., Vol. II, Weimar, 1799. 4th ed., Vols. I–II, Weimar, 1799–1801.

Gatterer, Johann Christoph. *Johann Christoph Gatterers Abriß der Geographie.* Göttingen, 1775 [i.e., 1778].

———. *Johann Christoph Gatterers Kurzer Begriff der Geographie.* 2 vols. Göttingen, 1789.

Gedancken eines Land-Geistlichen über eine an dem Ohio-Fluß in America entdeckte Juden-Kolonie besonders vernünftigen Israeliten zum Nachdencken geschrieben. Frankfurt and Leipzig, 1774.

Gedanken über den Aufstand der englischen Colonien in dem nördlichen Amerika. Göttingen, 1776.

Geisler, Adam Friedrich. *Geschichte und Zustand der Königlich Grosbrittannischen Kriegsmacht zu Wasser und zu Lande von den frühesten Zeiten bis an's Jahr 1784. Nebst einem Abris des lezten amerikanischen Krieges, und anhangweise: Schilderungen einiger in diesem Kriege sich vorzüglich ausgezeichneter Brittischer Offiziere, wie auch Verzeichnisse einiger deutscher in diesem Kriege rühmlichst zur Hülfe gewesener Offiziere.* Dessau and Leipzig, 1784.

Geographische Belustigungen zur Erläuterung der neuesten Weltgeschichte. 2 pts. Leipzig, 1776.

Gercken, Wilhelm Friedrich. *Periodisch-synchronistische Tabellen zur Universal-Geschichte, eingerichtet nach des Herrn Joh. Matth. Schröck fürtrefl. Lehrbuch der allgemeinen Weltgeschichte, nebst einem kurzen Abriß der Geschichte, zum Gebrauch für die Jugend.* Hamburg, 1792.

Geschichte der Englischen Kolonien in Nord-Amerika von der ersten Entdeckung dieser Länder durch Sebastian Cabot bis auf den Frieden 1763. Translated from the English [by Anton Ernst Klausing]. 2 vols. Leipzig, 1775–1776. 2d ed., Leipzig, 1777.

Geschichte der zweyten Decade der Regierung Georgs des Dritten, Königs von Grosbritannien, Irland, u.s.w. von dem Schlusse der dritten Session des dreyzehnten Parlements im Jahre 1770 an, bis zum Ende der letzten Session des vierzehnten Parlements von Grosbritannien im Jahre 1780. Translated from the English by Albrecht Wittenberg. Hamburg, 1784.

[Girod-Chantrans, Justin]. *Reisen eines Schweizers in verschiedene Kolonien von Amerika während dem letztern Krieg. Nebst einer kurzen Relation von dem Seetreffen vom 12. April 1782. und einer Beschreibung von den Inseln Martinique, Curaçao und Saint Domingue, ihrer Produkten, Regierungsverfassung, Zustand der Sklaven, Handel u.s.w.* Translated from the French. Leipzig, 1786.

Girtanner, Christoph. *Schilderung des häuslichen Lebens, des Karakters und der Regierung Ludwigs des Sechszehnten Königs von Frankreich und Navarra.* Frankfurt and Leipzig, 1793.

[Glauber, Christian Gottlieb]. *Peter Hasenclever.* Landeshut, 1794.

Grohmann, Johann Gottfried. *Neues Historisch-biographisches Handwörterbuch, oder kurzgefaßte Geschichte aller Personen, welche sich durch Talente, Tugenden, Erfindungen, Irrthümer, Verbrechen oder irgend eine merkwürdige Handlung von der Erschaffung der Welt bis auf gegenwärtige Zeiten einen ausgezeichneten Namen machten.* 10 vols. Leipzig, 1796–1808.

Hammerdörfer, Karl. *Allgemeine Weltgeschichte von den ältesten bis auf die neuesten Zeiten. Ein Lesebuch, auch für Nichtgelehrte.* 4 vols. Halle, 1789–1791.

————, and Kosche, Christian Traugott. *Amerika ein geographisch-historisches Lesebuch zum Nutzen der Jugend und ihrer Erzieher.* 2 vols. Leipzig, 1788.

Hausleutner, Philipp Wilhelm Gottlieb. *Gallerie der Nationen.* 4 vols. Stuttgart and Ulm, [1792–1800].

[Heeringen, von]. *Auszug eines Schreibens aus Amerika an Sr. Exzellenz den Herrn Generallieutenant von ****. [Darmstadt?], 1776.

Hegewisch, Dietrich Hermann, and Ebeling, Christoph Daniel. *Amerikanisches Magazin oder authentische Beiträge zur Erdbeschreibung, Staatskunde und Geschichte von Amerika, besonders aber der vereinten Staaten.* 4 vols. Hamburg, 1797 [i.e., 1795–1797].

[Heinzmann, Johann Georg]. *Gemälde aus dem aufgeklärten achtzehenden Jahrhundert.* 2 pts. Bern and Leipzig, 1786.

[Hempel, Christian Gottlob]. *Kurzer Abriß der neuesten europäischen Denkwürdigkeiten, Politick, Religion, Sitten, Geschmack und Litteratur betreffend.* 2 vols. Berlin, 1788–1789.

Hennicke, Johann August Philipp. *Synchronistische Tabellen über Schröckhs Lehrbuch der allgemeinen Weltgeschichte, zum Gebrauch der niedern Classen in den Schulen.* Leipzig, 1797.

Hennings, August. *Philosophische und Statistische Geschichte des Ursprungs und des Fortgangs der Freyheit in Engeland.* Copenhagen, 1783.

————. *Sammlung von Staatsschriften, die, während des Seekrieges von 1776 bis 1783, sowol von den kriegführenden, als auch von den neutralen Mächten, öffentlich bekannt gemacht worden sind; in so weit solche die Freiheit des Handels und der Schiffahrt betreffen.* 2 vols. Altona, 1784–1785.

Herder, Johann Gottfried. *Briefe zu Beförderung der Humanität.* 10 vols. Riga, 1793–1797.

[Hereford, Charles John Ann]. *Frankreichs Geschichte von der ersten Gründung der Monarchie, bis zu der gegenwärtigen Umänderung.* Translated from the English. 3 vols. Frankfurt and Leipzig, 1792.

Hervey, Frederick. *Geschichte der Schiffahrt und Seemacht Groß-Britanniens von den frühesten Zeiten an bis auf das Jahr 1779. von Friedrich Hervey Esq. und andern.* Translated from the English. 3 vols. Leipzig, 1779–1781.

Heyne, Christian Gottlob. *Chr. G. Heynii . . . opuscula academica collecta et animadversionibus locupletata.* 6 vols. Göttingen, 1785–1812.

Hilliard d'Aubertueil, Michel René. *Historischer und politischer Versuch über die Anglo-Amerikaner und die Staats-Veränderung in Nord-Amerika.* Translated from the French [by Albrecht Wittenberg]. 2 vols. Hamburg and Kiel, 1783.

Historisch-geographische Unterhaltungen oder Reisen des Herrn *** durch alle vier Welttheile. Ein unterrichtendes Lesebuch für die Jugend. Translated from the French. 2 pts. Brunswick, 1790.

Historisch moralisch und politisch abgefaßte Belustigungen für alle Stände. 2 vols. Leipzig, 1780–1782.

Historische Uebersicht von Europens Entwicklung seit dem sechszehnten Jahrhundert bis gegen Ende des achtzehnten. [Leipzig], 1795.

Hoff, Heinrich Georg. *Kurze Biographien oder Lebensabrisse merkwürdiger und berühmter Personen neuerer Zeiten von unterschiedlichen Nazionen und allerley Ständen.* 4 vols. Brünn, 1782. Vol. III reprinted as *Kurze Biographien berühmter Staatsmänner, Helden, Künstler und Frauenzimmer.* Frankfurt and Leipzig, 1783.

Hübner, Johann. *Johann Hübners reales Staats- Zeitungs- und Conversations-Lexicon, darinn so wohl die Religionen, die Reiche und Staaten, Meere, Seen, Inseln, Flüsse, Städte, Festungen, Schlösser, Häfen, Berge, Vorgebirge, Pässe und Wälder . . . Als auch andere in Zeitungen und täglichem Umgang vorkommende, ingleichen juristische und Kunstwörter beschrieben werden.* Leipzig, 1777, 1782, 1789, 1795. Vienna, 1780.

Ildebald, J. C. *J. C. Ildebald's Reise nach dem Lande der Freiheit, in den Jahren 1780 bis 1790.* Translated from the English. Berlin, 1793.

Imlay, Gilbert. *G. Imlay's . . . Nachrichten von dem westlichen Lande der Nordamerikanischen Freistaaten, von dem Klima, den Naturprodukten, der Volksmenge, den Sitten und Gebräuchen desselben, nebst einer Angabe der Indianischen Völkerstämme, die an den Gränzen wohnen, und einer Schilderung von den Gesetzen und der Regierung des Staates Kentucky. In Briefen an einen Freund in England.* Translated from the English by Eberhard August Wilhelm Zimmermann. Berlin, 1793.

Jäger, Wolfgang. *Geographisch-Historisch-Statistisches Zeitungs-Lexicon.* 2 vols. Nuremberg, 1782–1784. 2d ed., Nuremberg, 1791–1793.

[Kleinsorg, Raphael]. *Abriß der Geographie, zum Gebrauche in und ausser Schulen, nebst der besondern Geographie des Erzstifts Salzburg, und einem Unterricht vom Weltgebäude und vom Gebrauche der Globen.* Salzburg, 1782. 2d ed., Salzburg, 1787. 3d ed., 2 vols., Salzburg, 1797.

Klinger, Friedrich Maximilian. *F. M. Klinger's Theater.* 4 vols. Riga, 1786–1787.

[Kloppenburg, Jakob]. *Geographie für Jedermann, insonderheit für die Jugend.* 2 vols. Schleswig, 1785–1786.

Koch, Christophe Guillaume. *Abrégé de l'Histoire des traités de paix entre les puissances de l'Europe depuis la paix de Westphalie.* 4 vols. Basel, Paris, Strasbourg, Leipzig, 1796–1797.

Koch, Johann Gottlieb Franz Friedrich. *Versuch eines Kriegs-Rechts der Negern in Afrika und Indianer in Amerika.* Compiled and edited by J.G.F. Koch. Tübingen, 1781.

[Kolb, Johann Ernst]. *Erzählungen von den Sitten und Schiksalen der Negersklaven.* Bern, 1789.

[Korn, Christoph Heinrich]. *Geschichte der Kriege in und ausser Europa Vom Anfange des Aufstandes der Brittischen Kolonien in Nordamerika an.* 30 vols. Nuremberg, 1776–1784.

[———]. *Kurzgefaßte Geschichte des englisch-französisch-spanischen Krieges, aus Veranlassung des Aufstandes der englischen Kolonien in Nordamerika.* Salzburg, 1780.

[Krauseneck, Johann Christoph]. *Feldgesang eines teutschen Grenadiers in Nordamerika.* Bayreuth, 1778.

———. *Gedichte.* 2 vols. Bayreuth, 1776–1783.

———. *Die Werbung für England. Ein ländliches Lustspiel in einem Aufzuge.* Bayreuth, 1776.

Kurze Geographie von Asia, Afrika, Amerika und den Südländern. Versuch einer Fortsetzung von Raffs Geographie für Kinder. Nuremberg, 1790.

Kurze Vorstellung der ganzen Welt oder Atlas cosmographiae portatilis. Zum Unterricht der Jugend in ein und dreyßig Landkarten beschrieben. Nuremberg, 1780.

La Fayette als Staatsmann als Krieger und als Mensch. Translated from the French [by Heinrich Julius Ludwig von Rohr]. With an introduction by Johann Reinhold Forster. Magdeburg, 1794.

La Roche, Sophie von. *Erscheinungen am See Oneida.* 3 vols. Leipzig, 1798.

La Rochefoucauld Liancourt, François Alexandre Frédéric, duc de. *De la Rochefoucauld Liancourt Reisen in den Jahren 1795, 1796 und 1797 durch alle an der See belegenen Staaten der Nordamerikanischen Republik; imgleichen durch Ober-Canada und das Land der Irokesen. Nebst zuverläßigen Nachrichten von Unter-Canada.* Translated from the French. 3 vols. Hamburg, 1799.

Lebensgeschichte Ludwig XVI. Königs von Frankreich. Vienna, 1793.

Lehrbuch der neuesten Erdbeschreibung für öffentliche und Privat-Schulen, nach Wilhelm Guthrie frey bearbeitet. 3 vols. Berlin, 1794–1796.

Leiste, Christian. *Beschreibung des Brittischen Amerika zur Ersparung der englischen Karten. Nebst einer Special-Karte der mittlern Brittischen Colonien.* [Wolfenbüttel], 1778.

Lessing, Karl Gotthelf. *Die Mätresse. Ein Lustspiel in fünf Aufzügen.* Berlin, 1780.

Lidner, Bengt. *Dissertatio Academica De Iure revolutionis Americanorum. . . .* Greifswald, 1777.

[Lindemann, Johann Gottlieb]. *Geschichte der Meinungen älterer und neuerer Völker, im Stande der Roheit und Cultur, von Gott, Religion, und Priesterthum. . . .* 7 vols. Stendal, 1784–1795. Vol. VII also appeared as *Die Moral älterer kultivierter und neuerer wilder Völker, historisch und philosophisch bearbeitet.* Stendal, 1795.

Lobethan, Friedrich Georg August. *Schauplatz der merkwürdigsten Kriege und der übrigen politischen Hauptbegebenheiten des achtzehnten Jahrhunderts. Zum Gebrauche für alle Klassen der Leser.* 4 vols. Leipzig, 1793–1796.

Long, John. *J. Long's westindischen Dollmetschers und Kaufmanns See- und Land-Reisen, enthaltend: eine Beschreibung der Sitten und Gewohnheiten der Nordamerikanischen Wilden; der Englischen Forts oder Schanzen längs dem St. Lorenz-Flusse, dem See Ontario u.s.w.; ferner ein umständliches Wörterbuch der Chippewäischen und anderer Nordamerikanischen Sprachen.* Translated from the English and edited by Eberhard August Wilhelm Zimmermann. Hamburg, 1791.

————. *Reisen eines Amerikanischen Dolmetschers und Pelzhändlers, welche eine Beschreibung der Sitten und Gebräuche der Nordamerikanischen Eingebornen, und einige Nachrichten von den Posten am St. Lorenz-Flusse, dem See Ontario u.s.w. enthalten.* Translated from the English by Georg Forster. Berlin, 1792.

[Loewe, Andreas Friedrich]. *Historische und geographische Beschreibung der zwölf Vereinigten Kolonien von Nord-Amerika. Nebst einer Abschilderung des gegenwärtigen Zustandes von Großbrittannien.* Bunzlau, [1777].

Lutyens, Gotthilf Nicolas. *Etwas über den gegenwärtigen Zustand der Auswande rungen und Ansiedlungen im Staate von Pennsylvanien in Nord-Amerika, beson- ders in Ansehung der Deutschen.* Hamburg, 1796.

Mably, Gabriel Bonnot de. *Observations sur le gouvernement des États-Unis d'Amé- rique.* Hamburg, 1784.

Maison, Johann Georg. *Das den 24 Junii 1777 von neuem feyerlich zu begehende höchst erwünschte Geburts-Fest der Durchlauchtigsten Fürstin und Frauen Frauen Friderica Carolina Marggräfin zu Brandenb . . . nebst vorausgeschichter Allusion auf die Worte Cäsars Transivimus Rubiconem bey Gelegenheit der den Ocean paßirten teutschen Truppen.* Kulmbach, [1777].

Mangelsdorf, Karl Ehregott. *Allgemeine Geschichte der europäischen Staaten ein durchaus verständliches Lesebuch zur nüzlichen Unterhaltung.* 12 vols. Halle, 1784–1794.

Marsillac, Jean. *Leben Wilhelm Penns des Stifters von Pensylvanien.* Translated from the French by [Karl Julius] Friedrich. Strasbourg, 1793.

[Marsy, François Marie de, and Richer, Adrien]. *Neuere Geschichte der Chineser, Japaner, Indianer, Persianer, Türken, Russen und Amerikaner etc. als eine Fort- setzung von Rollins ältern Geschichte.* Translated from the French [by Friedrich Wilhelm Zachariä]. Vols. XIX–XXVI. Berlin, 1775–1777.

Martens, Georg Friedrich von. *Receuil des principaux traités d'Alliance, de Paix, de Neutralité, de commerce, de limites, d'échange etc. conclus par les Puissances de l'Europe tant entre elles qu'avec les puissances et Etats dans d'autres parties du monde Depuis 1761 jusqu'à présent. Tiré des copies publiées par autorité, des meilleures collections particulières de traités, & des auteurs les plus estimés.* 7 vols. Göttingen, 1791–1801.

Mauvillon, Jakob. *J. Mauvillon's . . . Sammlung von Aufsätzen über Gegenstände aus der Staatskunst, Staatswirthschaft und neuesten Staaten Geschichte.* 2 vols. Leipzig, 1776–1777.

[Mazzei, Filippo]. *Geschichte und Staatsverfassung der vereinigten Staaten von Nordamerika. Von einem virginischen Bürger.* Translated from the French. 2 vols. Leipzig, 1789. Vol. II also appeared as *Amerikanische Anekdoten aus den neue- sten Zeiten.* Leipzig, 1789.

Meister, Leonhard. *Leonhard Meisters vermischte Historische Unterhaltungen, über Europens Umbildung während der letzten Hälfte des XVIII^{ten}. Jahrhunderts.* 2 vols. St. Gallen, 1790.

Melzheimer, Friedrich Valentin. *Tagebuch von der Reise der Braunschweigischen Auxiliär Truppen von Wolfenbüttel nach Quebec.* Minden, 1776. Another edi- tion, Frankfurt and Leipzig, 1776.

Mercier, Louis Sébastien. *Erscheinungen und Träume von Mercier und einigen deutschen Gelehrten.* Translated from the French by G[eorg] Scha[t]z. 2 pts. Leip- zig, 1791.

Meyen, Johann Jakob. *Franklin der Philosoph und Staatsmann. In fünf Gesängen.* Alt-Stettin, 1787.

[Milbiller, Joseph]. *Allgemeine Geschichte der berühmtesten Königreiche und Freistaaten in und ausserhalb Europa.* Pt. I, *Engelland.* 3 vols. Leipzig, 1797–1798. Pt. II, *Die vereinigten nordamerikanischen Provinzen.* 2 vols. Leipzig, 1798–1799.

Militärischer Almanach auf das Jahr 1780. Leipzig, n.d.

Milke, Christian Benedikt. *M. Christian Benedikt Milkens . . . Geographie, tabellarisch eingekleidet zum Schul-Gebrauch.* Leipzig and Altona, 1792.

Milon, C. *Denkwürdigkeiten zur Geschichte Benjamin Franklins.* St. Petersburg, 1793.

[Mirabeau, Honoré Gabriel Riquetti, comte de]. *Avis aux Hessois et autres peuples de l'Allemagne Vendus par leurs Princes à l'Angleterre.* Kleve, 1777. Translated into German as *Nachrichten und Erinnerungen an verschiedene teutsche Völker, die von ihren Fürsten nach America geschickt worden sind.* N.p., 1778.

———. *Des Grafen von Mirabeau Sammlung einiger philosophischen und politischen Schriften, die vereinigten Staaten von Nordamerika betreffend.* Translated from the French [by Johann Brahl]. Berlin and Libau, 1787.

Moser, Johann Jakob. *Nord-America nach den Friedensschlüssen vom Jahr 1783.* 3 vols. Leipzig, 1784–1785.

Müller, Georg. *Der Englische Friedensplan wurde bey der höchsterfreulichen Zurückkunft der Hochfürstl. Brandenb. Onolz-Culmbachischen Kriegstruppen aus Amerika, im Monat November 1783. abgehandelt.* Bayreuth, 1784.

[Mursinna, Friedrich Samuel]. *Leben und Charaktere berühmter und edler im Jahr 1790 verstorbener Männer.* Halle, 1792.

Neues geographisches Zeitungslexicon, oder kurzgefaßte Beschreibung der Länder, Städte, Oerter, Meere, Flüsse und Berge in allen vier Theilen der Welt, und ihren besondern Merkwürdigkeiten. . . . Augsburg, 1790.

Neusinger, Johann Leonhard. *Johann Leonhard Neusingers . . . kurze Geschichte von der Erschaffung der Welt bis auf unsre Zeiten für die Jugend.* 4 vols. Nuremberg, [1786–1788].

[Oldmixon, John]. *Das Britische Reich in America Worinnen enthalten Die Geschichte der Entdeckung, der Aufrichtung, des Anwachses und Zustandes der Englischen Colonien Auf dem festen Lande und den Insuln von America.* 2 vols. Lemgo, 1776–[1744].

Osterwald, Friedrich. *Herrn Friedrich Osterwalds Historische Erdbeschreibung zum Nutzen deutscher Jugend eingerichtet. . . .* 5th ed. 2 pts. Strasbourg, 1791.

Paine, Thomas. *Gesunder Menschenverstand. An die Einwohner von America gerichtet.* Translated from the English. Copenhagen, 1794.

———. *Kurzer Abriß der Entstehung der französischen Revolution.* Translated from the French [by Johann Gottfried Dyck]. Leipzig, 1791.

———. *Payne's kurze Darstellung der Begebenheiten aller bisherigen Staaten in der Welt.* 2 vols. Leipzig, 1797. Presumably not by Paine.

———. *Die Rechte des Menschen. Eine Antwort auf Herrn Burke's Angriff gegen die französische Revolution.* Translated from the English [by Dorothea Margarete

Liebeskind]. With an introduction [by Georg Forster]. 3 vols. Berlin and Copenhagen, 1792–1793. 2d ed. 2 vols. Copenhagen, 1793.

———. *Sammlung verschiedener Schriften über Politik und Gesetzgebung.* Translated from the English. Copenhagen, 1794.

———. *Untersuchungen über wahre und fabelhafte Theologie.* Translated from
the English. 2 vols. Germany [i.e., Lübeck], 1794–1797.

Palm, Georg Friedrich. *Adel der Menschheit in biographischen Schilderungen Edler
Menschen.* Leipzig, 1798.

*Paul-Jones, ou prophéties sur l'Amérique, l'Angleterre, la France, l'Espagne, la Hol-
lande, etc. par Paul-Jones Corsaire, Prophéte et sorcier comme il n'en fût jamais. Y
joint Le Réve d'un Suisse sur la révolution de l'Amérique, Dédié à Son Excellence
Mgneur l'Ambassadeur Franklin, & à leurs Nobles & Hautes Puissances Messeig-
neurs du Congres* [by Jérome Helvetius]. [Basel, 1781].

Penn, William. *Wilhelm Penn's kurze Nachricht von der Entstehung und dem Fortgang der christlichen Gesellschaft der Freunde die man Quaker nennt.* . . . Translated from the English by Ludwig Seebohm. Pyrmont and Hanover, 1792.

[Pezzl, Johann]. *Faustin oder das philosophische Jahrhundert 1780.* N.p., 1783.
Another edition, [Frankfurt?], 1784. 2d ed., n.p., 1783. 3d ed., n.p., 1783,
[Zurich], 1785. 4th ed., n.p., 1788.

Pföter, A. J. *Betrachtungen über die Quellen und Folgen der merkwürdigsten Revolutionen unseres Jahrhunderts, über die Entstehung der Staaten, und die verschiedenen Verfassungen derselben; nebst einer gelegentlichen Untersuchung,
welchen Einfluß die Aufklärung auf das Wohl der bürgerlichen Gesellschaft habe.*
Vienna, 1794.

Poppe, Johann Friedrich. *Geschichte der Europäischen Staaten.* 2 vols. Halle, 1783–
1784.

[Purmann, Johann Georg]. *Sitten und Meinungen der Wilden in America.* 4 vols.
Frankfurt, 1777–1781. 2d ed., Vienna, 1790.

Raff, Georg Christian. *Geographie für Kinder.* 5th ed. 3 vols. Göttingen, 1786–
1791. [Vols. II and III are by Christian Carl Andre, 1st ed.; 2d ed., Göttingen,
1792–1794].

[Rahmel, August Wilhelm Leopold von]. *Ueber den Dienst, von einem, ehemals
unter der preußischen Armee gestandenen, und jetzt unter den Amerikanern
dienenden Offizier. Entworfen noch eh' derselbe seinen ersten Dienst verließ.* Boston [i.e., Breslau], 1783. 2d ed., Boston [i.e., Breslau], 1784.

Ramsay, David. *Geschichte der Amerikanischen Revolution aus den Acten des Congresses der vereinigten Staaten.* Translated from the English [by Günther Karl
Friedrich Seidel]. 4 vols. Berlin, 1794–1795.

Raynal, Guillaume-Thomas-François. *Considérations sur la paix de 1783. Envoyées
par l'Abbé Raynal au Prince Frédéric Henri de Prusse. Qui lui avoit demandé ce
qu'il pensoit de cette Paix.* Berlin, 1783.

———. *Geschichte der Revolution von Nord-America vom Abt. Raynal. Nebst
Anmerkungen über diese Geschichte von Thomas Payne, Staats-Secretair des*

americanischen Congresses in dem Departement der auswärtigen Affairen. Translated from the French [by F. H. Wernitz]. Berlin, 1786.

————. *Philosophische und Politische Geschichte der Besitzungen und des Handels der Europäer in beiden Indien.* Translated from the French by J[akob] Mauvillon. 7 vols. Hanover, 1774–1778.

————. *Staatsveränderung von Amerika.* Translated from the French. Frankfurt and Leipzig, 1782.

[Rebmann, Andreas Georg Friedrich von]. *Hans Kiekindiewelts Reisen in alle vier Welttheile und den Mond.* Leipzig and Gera, 1794.

[Reccard, Gotthilf Christian]. *Lehr-Buch darin ein kurzegefaßter Unterricht aus verschiedenen philosophischen und mathematischen Wissenschaften, der Historie und Geographie gegeben wird.* Edited by [P. J. Hecker]. 6th ed. 2 vols. Berlin, 1782–1783.

Reise von Hamburg nach Philadelphia. Hanover, 1800.

Remer, Julius August, ed. *Amerikanisches Archiv.* 3 vols. Brunswick, 1777–1778.

————. *Darstellung der Gestalt der historischen Welt in jedem Zeitraume.* Berlin and Stettin, 1794. Reprint, Frankfurt and Leipzig, 1794.

[————]. *Geschichte des Krieges zwischen Großbritannien und den vereinigten Bourbonischen Mächten und Nordamerikanischen Kolonien.* Leipzig, 1780.

————. *Handbuch der allgemeinen Geschichte.* 3 vols. Brunswick, 1783–1784. A third edition of Vol. III also appeared as *Handbuch der neuern Geschichte. Von der Kirchenverfassung bis auf das Jahr 1799.* Brunswick, 1799.

————. *Handbuch der Geschichte neuerer Zeiten von der grossen Völkerwanderung bis auf den Hubertusburger-Frieden.* Brunswick, [1771].

————. *Handbuch der Geschichte unsrer Zeiten vom Jahre 1740 bis zum Jahre 1799.* Brunswick, 1799.

————. *Lehrbuch der allgemeinen Geschichte für Akademien und Gymnasien.* Halle, 1800.

Reuss, Jeremias David. *Das Gelehrte England oder Lexikon der jeztlebenden Schriftsteller in Grosbritannien, Irland und Nord-Amerika nebst einem Verzeichnis ihrer Schriften. Vom Jahr 1770 bis 1790.* 2 vols. Berlin and Stettin, 1791.

[Richer, Adrien]. *Neuere Geschichte von Amerika.* Translated from the French [by Friedrich Wilhelm Zachariä]. 8 vols. Berlin, 1778.

Riedesel, Friederike Charlotte Luise Freifrau zu Eisenbach. *Die Berufs-Reise nach America. Briefe der Generalin von Riedesel auf dieser Reise und während ihres sechsjährigen Aufenthalts in America zur Zeit des dortigen Krieges in den Jahren 1776 bis 1783 nach Deutschland geschrieben.* Berlin, 1800.

Robertson, Robert. *Robert Robertson's . . . Abhandlung über das Fieber, dessen eigenthümliches Wesen, und vernunftmäßige Heilart, als Resultat in Europa, Afrika und Amerika angestellter Bemerkungen.* Translated from the English. Liegnitz and Leipzig, 1796.

Robertson, William. *Wilhelm Robertson's . . . Geschichte von Amerika.* Translated from the English by Johann Friedrich Schiller. 2 vols. Leipzig, 1777.

Robin, Abbé. *Neue Reise durch Nordamerika, in dem Jahr 1781, nebst dem Feld-*

zuge der Armee des Herrn Grafen von Rochambeau. Translated from the French. Nuremberg, 1783.

Rush, Benjamin. *Benjamin Rush, Doctor der Heilkunde, und Lehrer der Anfangs-gründe der Arzneiwissenschaft und der Klinik auf der Universität zu Philadelphia, über die Vortheile, welche das Aderlassen in vielen wichtigen Krankheiten gewährt*. Translated from the English by Dr. Christian Friedrich Michaelis. Leipzig, 1800.

————. *Benjamin Rush; D. der Medicin u. Prof. der Chemie auf der Universität in Pensilvanien, Untersuchung über den Einfluß körperlicher Ursachen auf die Moralität. Eine Vorlesung vor der Amerikanischen philosophischen Societät in Philadelphia den 27sten Hornung 1786 gehalten*. Translated from the second English edition by D. A[ugust] F[riedrich] A[drian] D[iel]. Offenbach, 1787.

————. *Beschreibung des gelben Fiebers, welches im Jahre 1793 in Philadelphia herschte*. Translated from the English by P[hilipp] Fr[iedrich] Hopfengärtner and J[ohann] F[erdinand] H[einrich] Autenrieth. Tübingen, 1796.

Russell, William. *Geschichte von Amerika von dessen Entdeckung an bis auf das Ende des vorigen Krieges. Nebst einem Anhange, welcher eine Geschichte des Ursprunges und des Fortganges des gegenwärtigen unglücklichen Streites zwischen Groß-Britannien und seinen Colonien enthält*. Translated from the English. 4 vols. Leipzig, 1779–1780. Vol. IV also appeared as *Geschichte des Ursprunges und des Fortganges des gegenwärtigen Streites zwischen England und seinen Colonien*. Leipzig, 1780.

Sackville, George, Lord Germain. *Correspondance du Lord G. Germain, avec Les Généraux Clinton, Cornwallis & les Amiraux dans la station de l'Amérique, avec plusieurs lettres interceptées du Général Washington, du Marquis de la Fayette & de M. de Barras, chef d'Escadre*. Translated from the English. Bern, 1782.

Schenk, Johann Gottfried. *M. Johann Gottfried Schenkens Geographische Tabellen zum Gebrauche der Anfänger*. 2d ed. Dresden and Leipzig, [1775].

Schiller, Karl August. *Gallerie interessanter Personen. Oder Schilderung des Lebens und Charakters der Thaten und Schicksale berühmter und berüchtigter Menschen der ältern und neuern Zeit*. Berlin and Vienna, 1798.

[Schirach, Gottlob Benedikt von]. *Historisch-statistische Notiz der Großbrittannischen Colonien in America, mit politischen Anmerkungen, die gegenwärtigen Americanischen Unruhen betreffend*. Frankfurt and Leipzig, 1776.

Schlichtegroll, Adolf Heinrich Friedrich von. *Nekrolog auf das Jahr 1790. Enthaltend Nachrichten von dem Leben merkwürdiger in diesem Jahr verstorbener Personen*. Vol. I. Gotha, 1791.

[Schlieffen, Martin Ernst von]. *Des Hessois en Amerique, de leur Souverain et des declamateurs*. N.p., 1782. Translated into German as *Von den Hessen in Amerika, Ihrem Fürsten und den Schreyern*. [Dessau], 1782.

Schlözer, August Ludwig. *Vertrauliche Briefe aus Kanada und NeuEngland vom J. 1777. und 1778*. Göttingen, 1779.

Schmettau, Woldemar Friedrich Graf von. *Des Grafen Woldemar Friederich von Schmettow Kleine Schriften*. 2 pts. Altona, 1795.

[Schmohl, Johann Christian]. *Über Nordamerika und Demokratie. Ein Brief aus England.* Copenhagen [i.e., Königsberg], 1782.

Schoepf, Johann David. *Materia Medica Americana potissimum Regni Vegetabilis.* Erlangen, 1787.

_____ . *Reise durch einige der mittlern und südlichen vereinigten nordamerikanischen Staaten nach Ost-Florida und den Bahama-Inseln unternommen in den Jahren 1783 und 1784.* 2 pts. Erlangen, 1788.

_____ . *Von der Wirkung des Mohnsafts in der Lustseuche. Nebst andern zur Arzneygelahrtheit und Naturlehre gehörigen Beobachtungen Nord Amerika betreffend.* Edited by [Heinrich Friedrich von] Delius. Erlangen, 1781.

Schroeckh, Johann Matthias. *Allgemeine Weltgeschichte für Kinder.* 4 vols. Leipzig, 1779–1784. Translated into French as *Histoire universelle à l'usage de la jeunesse.* 4 vols. Leipzig, 1784–1791.

_____ . *Johann Matthias Schröckhs . . . Lehrbuch der allgemeinen Weltgeschichte zum Gebrauche bey dem ersten Unterrichte der Jugend.* Berlin and Stettin, 1774.

[Sebaldt, Georg Friedrich]. *Kurzes Lehrbuch der Historie und Geographie, zum nützlichen Gebrauch niederer Schulen für die allerersten Anfänger auf die leichteste Art.* Nuremberg, 1775.

Seidel, Günther Karl Friedrich. *Neueste Geschichte von Europa seit dem Ende des siebenjährigen Krieges.* 2 vols. Berlin, 1798–1799.

_____ . *Die Staatsverfassung der Vereinigten Staaten von Nordamerika und historische Beiträge und Belege zu der Geschichte ihrer Revolution.* Berlin, 1795. [Appeared as Vol. IV of Ramsay, *Geschichte der Amerikanischen Revolution.*]

Sell, Johann Jakob. *Versuch einer Geschichte des Negersclavenhandels.* Halle, 1791.

[Sieveking, Georg Heinrich]. *Verkauf von Ländereyen in Amerika.* Hamburg, 1793.

[Smith, Adam]. *Abhandlung über die Colonien überhaupt und die Amerikanischen besonders.* [Translated from the French?] Bern, 1779.

_____ . *Untersuchung der Natur und Ursachen von Nationalreichthümern.* Translated from the English [by Johann Friedrich Schiller]. 2 vols. Leipzig, 1776–1778.

Snell, Karl Philipp Michael. *Von den Handlungsvortheilen, welche aus der Unabhängigkeit der vereinigten Staaten von Nord-Amerika für das russische Reich entspringen.* Riga, 1783.

Some Short and Impartial Enquiries into the Propriety and Equity of the Present War in America, with Regard to the British Arms. [Göttingen], 1778.

Soulès, François. *Vollständige Geschichte der Revolution in Nord-Amerika.* Translated from the French by Karl Hammerdörfer. 2 vols. Zurich, 1788.

Sprengel, Matthias Christian. *Allgemeines historisches Taschenbuch oder Abriß der merkwürdigsten neuen Welt-Begebenheiten enthaltend für 1784 die Geschichte der Revolution von Nord-America.* Berlin, [1783]. Reprint, Berlin, [1784]. Reprinted as *Geschichte der Revolution von Nord-America. Mit einer illuminirten accuraten Charte von diesem neuen Freystaate.* Frankenthal, 1785, Speyer, 1785, Frankenthal, 1788.

_____ . *Auswahl der besten ausländischen geographischen und statistischen Nachrichten zur Aufklärung der Völker und Länderkunde.* 14 vols. Halle, 1794–1800.

[————]. *Briefe den gegenwärtigen Zustand von Nord America betreffend.* Göttingen, 1777.

————. *Geschichte der Europäer in Nordamerika.* Leipzig, 1782.

[————]. *Kurze Schilderung der Grosbrittannischen Kolonien in Nord-America.* Göttingen, [1776]. Reprint and 2d ed., Göttingen, 1777.

————. *Über den jetzigen Nordamericanischen Krieg und dessen Folgen für England und Frankreich.* Leipzig, 1782.

————. *Vom Ursprung des Negerhandels. Ein Antrittsprogramm.* Halle, 1779.

————, and Forster, Georg, eds. *Neue Beiträge zur Völker- und Länderkunde.* 13 vols. Leipzig, 1790–1793.

Staatsgesetze der dreyzehn vereinigten amerikanischen Staaten. Translated from the French. Dessau and Leipzig, 1785.

Stedman, Charles. *Carl Stedman's Geschichte des Ursprungs, des Fortgangs und der Beendigung des Americanischen Kriegs.* Translated from the English by Julius August Remer. 2 vols. Berlin, 1795.

Stöver, Dietrich Johann Heinrich. *Historisch-statistische Beyträge zur nähern Kenntniß der Staaten und der neuern Weltbegebenheiten.* Hamburg, 1789.

————. *Unser Jahrhundert. Oder Darstellung der interessantesten Merkwürdigkeiten und Begebenheiten und der größten Männer desselben. Ein Handbuch der neuern Geschichte.* 8 vols. Altona, 1791–1800. Vols. I and II appeared in a second edition, Altona, 1795–1796.

[Struensee, Karl August]. *Kurzgefaßte Beschreibung der Handlung der vornehmsten europäischen Staaten.* 2 vols. Liegnitz and Leipzig, 1778–1782.

Sturz, Helferich Peter. *Schriften von Helfrich Peter Sturz.* 2 vols. Leipzig, 1779–1782.

Taube, Friedrich Wilhelm. *Geschichte der Engländischen Handelschaft, Manufacturen, Colonien und Schiffahrt in den alten, mittlern und neuern Zeiten, bis auf das laufende Jahr 1776.* Leipzig, 1776.

————. *Historische und Politische Abschilderung der Engländischen Manufacturen, Handlung, Schiffahrt und Colonien, nach ihrer jetzigen Einrichtung und Beschaffenheit, Theils aus eigener Erfahrung, theils aus zuverläßigen und glaubwürdigen, sowohl schriftlichen als mündlichen Nachrichten.* Vienna, 1774. A second edition appeared as *Abschilderung der Engländischen Manufacturen, Handlung, Schiffahrt und Colonien, nach ihrer jetzigen Einrichtung und Beschaffenheit.* 2 vols. Vienna, 1777–1778.

Timaeus, Johann Jakob Karl. *Nordamerikanischer Staats-Kalender, oder Statistisches Hand- und Addressbuch der Vereinigten Staaten von Nordamerika.* Translated from the English. Hamburg and Leipzig, 1796.

Torén, Olof. *Reise des Herrn Olof Toree nach Surate und China, nebst einer kurzen Beschreibung von der Chinesischen Feldökonomie, und einer Nachricht von dem gegenwärtigen Zustande der engländischen Colonien in dem nördlichen Amerika.* Edited by [Carl von Linné]. Leipzig, 1772.

Über den Aufstand der englischen Colonien in Amerika. Frankfurt and Leipzig, 1776.

Umfreville, Edward. *Über den gegenwärtigen Zustand der Hudsonsbay, der dortigen Etablissements und ihres Handels, nebst einer Beschreibung des Innern von Neu Wallis, und einer Reise von Montreal nach Neu York.* Translated from the English and edited by E[berhard] A[ugust] W[ilhelm] Zimmermann. Helmstedt, 1791.

Der Unglickliche Walter oder Leiden und Verfolgungen eines Deutschen in Americka. Vienna and Prague, 1798.

Vertheidigung der französischen Regierung gegen gewisse Beschuldigungen in den Berichten der amerikanischen Gesandten, nebst der dadurch veranlaßten Correspondenz zwischen dem französischen Minister Talleyrand und Herrn Gerry, dem noch in Paris gebliebenen amerikanischen Minister. Hamburg, 1798.

[Vogel, Daniel]. *Neues Geographisches Handbuch zum Unterricht der Jugend eingerichtet.* Breslau, 1775. 4th ed., Breslau, 1792.

Vogel, Wilhelm. *Der Amerikaner. Ein Lustspiel in fünf Aufzügen nach dem italiänischen von Federici.* Edited by N. H. Brämer. Hamburg and Altona, [1798?].

Volckmann, Johann Jakob. *Neues geographisches Handlexicon, oder alphabethisches Verzeichniß der vornehmsten Länder, Städte, Oerter und Flüße in allen vier Theilen der Welt, nebst einer kurzen Anzeige der vornehmsten Merkwürdigkeiten eines jeden Ortes, und warum er in der Geschichte zu merken ist.* Leipzig, 1778.

Volkelt, Johann Gottlieb. *M. Johann Gottlieb Volkelts . . . kurze Erdbeschreibung zum Gebrauch der Landcharten für die Jugend, nebst einer vorangesetzten Einleitung für die Anfänger.* 2d ed. Breslau, 1791.

Vorläufige Nachricht und Beschreibung von dem großen siebenjährigen Kalbskopf, welcher in Engelland bei dem angestellten Freudenfest wegen des Anno 1783. mit denen Amerikanern geschlossenen Friedens, auf eine bisher noch niemal erhörte kostbare Art zubereitet, und bei demselben mit einem großen Pracht verzehret werden soll. Edited by Fabian Sebastian Wilkes. Translated from the English. N.p., [1783].

[Walther, Friedrich Ludwig]. *Neueste Erdkunde welche Asien, Afrika, Europa, Amerika, die Südländer oder den fünften Welttheil, und die Polarländer nebst einem Anhange von der natürlichen und wissenschaftlichen Erdkunde, aus den neuesten und zuverläßigsten Reisebeschreibungen, historischen Zeit- und andern Schriften, enthält.* Nuremberg and Altdorf, 1785.

Wansey, Henry. *Heinrich Wansey's . . . Tagebuch einer Reise durch die vereinigten Staaten von Nord-Amerika, im Sommer des Jahres 1794.* Translated from the English and with an introduction by C[arl] A[ugust] Böttiger. Berlin, 1797.

Washington, George. *George Washington's beständigen Präsidenten und Protektors, officielle und eigenhändige Briefe und Berichte, welche er während des ganzen Krieges zwischen den Amerikanischen Freystaaten und England als Generalissimus an den Congreß geschrieben, nebst andern, welche er von diesem und andern Hauptpersonen erhalten hat.* Translated from the English. 2 vols. Leipzig, 1796–1797.

Weld, Isaac. *Isaac Weld's des Jüngeren Reisen durch die Staaten von Nordamerika, und die Provinzen Ober- und Nieder-Canada, während den Jahren 1795, 1796 und 1797*. Translated from the English. Berlin, 1800. Three different editions by the publishers Voss, Öhmigke, and Haude und Spener.

Wendeborn, Gebhard Friedrich August. *Der Zustand des Staats, der Religion, der Gelehrsamkeit und der Kunst in Grosbritannien gegen das Ende des achtzehnten Jahrhunderts*. 4 vols. Berlin, 1785–1788.

Weppen, Johann August. *Gedichte*. 2 pts. Leipzig, 1783. Reprint, Karlsruhe, 1783.

[Westenrieder, Lorenz von]. *Erdbeschreibung für die churbaierischen Realschulen*. 2 pts. Munich, 1776.

Woltmann, Karl Ludwig. *Geschichte der Europäischen Staaten*. 2 vols. Berlin, 1797–1799.

Zabuesnig, Johann Christoph von. *Lucy Hopeleß, oder der Quäker aus Amerika: Trauerspiel, oder Lustspiel; in fünf Aufzügen*. Augsburg, 1783.

[Zahn, Christian Jakob]. *D. B. Franklins Leben*. Tübingen, 1795.

[Zeplichal, Anton Michael]. *Neueste Geographie zum Gebrauche der Jugend*. 2 pts. Breslau, 1774.

Zimmermann, Eberhard August Wilhelm. *Frankreich und die Freistaaten von Nordamerika*. 2 vols. Berlin, 1795–1799. Zimmermann translated Vol. I into French as *Essai de Comparaison entre la France et les Etats-Unis de l'Amérique Septentrionale, par rapport à leur sol, à leur climat, à leurs productions, à leurs habitans, à leur constitution, et à leur formation progressive*. 2 vols. Leipzig, 1797.

————. *Geographische Geschichte des Menschen und der allgemein verbreiteten vierfüßigenThiere, nebst einer hieher gehörigen Weltcharte*. 3 vols. Leipzig, 1778–1783.

Zinner, Johann. *Merkwürdige Briefe und Schriften der berühmtesten Generäle in Amerika, nebst derselben beygefügten Lebensbeschreibungen*. Augsburg, 1782.

Zopf, Johann Heinrich. *Johann Heinrich Zopfens . . . Neueste Geographie nach allen vier Theilen der Welt. . . .* New ed. 2 vols. Leipzig, 1770.

Other Primary Sources

Die Abmarsch-Arie des Herzoglichen Braunschweigischen neuen Leib-Regiments-Marsch. N.p., 1776.

Abmarsch-Lied der Herzoglichen Braunschweigischen Krieges-Völker im Monate Februar 1776. N.p., n.d.

Achenwall, Gottfried. *Anmerkungen über Nordamerika und über dasige Grosbritannische Colonien aus mündlichen Nachrichten des Herrn Dr. Franklins*. Frankfurt and Leipzig, 1769.

American Archives. Edited by Peter Force. 4th Ser., 6 vols. 5th Ser., 3 vols. Washington, D.C., 1837–1846, 1848–1853.

The American Revolution Through British Eyes. Edited by Martin Kallich and Andrew MacLeish. Evanston, Ill., 1962.

Amtliche Sammlung der Acten aus der Zeit der Helvetischen Republik (1798–1803). Compiled by Johannes Strickler. Vol. VI. Bern, 1897.

Archenholtz, Johann Wilhelm von. *Geschichte des siebenjährigen Krieges in Deutschland von 1756 bis 1763*. Mannheim, 1788. Reprinted in 2 vols., Berlin, 1793.

[Bansen, Anton Cyriacus Karl]. *Neuere Geschichte der beiden letzten Jahrhunderte zum Nutzen und Vergnügen beschrieben*. 2 vols. Hanover, 1775–1777.

Bauer, Johann Christian August. *Franklin und Washington oder Sammlung der merkwürdigsten bekannten Züge aus dem Leben dieser um Amerika verdienten Männer. (Unterhaltende Anekdoten aus dem achtzehnten Jahrhundert*, vol. XVIII). Berlin, 1806.

Bilder zur Frankfurter Geschichte. Compiled by Franz Lerner. Edited by Waldemar Kramer. Frankfurt, 1950.

[Bodmer, Johann Jakob]. *Cajus Gracchus. Ein politisches Schauspiel*. Zurich, 1773.

[_____]. *Die Cherusken. Ein politisches Schauspiel*. Augsburg, 1778.

[_____]. *Der Haß der Tyranney und nicht der Person, Oder: Sarne durch List eingenommen*. N.p., 1775.

Briefe eines reisenden Punditen über Sclaverei, Möncherei, und Tyrannei der Europäer. An seinen Freund in U-pang. Leipzig, 1787.

Brissot de Warville, Jacques Pierre. *New Travels in the United States of America 1788*. Translated by Mara Soceanu Vamos and Durand Echeverria. Edited by Echeverria. Cambridge, Mass., 1964.

Chastellux, François Jean, marquis de. *Travels in North America in the Years 1780, 1781 and 1782*. Translated and edited by Howard C. Rice, Jr. 2 vols. Chapel Hill, N.C., 1963.

Claudius, Matthias. *Werke. Asmus omnia sua secum portans oder Sämtliche Werke des Wandsbecker Boten*. 6th ed. Stuttgart, 1965.

[Clauer, Eduard von]. *Der Kreuzzug gegen die Franken. Eine patriotische Rede welche in der deutschen Reichs–versammlung gehalten–werden könnte*. Germanien [i.e., Brunswick], [1791].

Dankgebet so nach der im Monat November 1783 erfolgten glücklichen Zurückkunft der von Ihro hochfürstl. Durchlaucht zu Brandenburg-Onolz-Culmbach nach Amerika zum Dienste Ihro Königl. Majestät von Großbrittanien abgesandten Kriegstruppen auf Verordnung des hochfürstl. Consistorii zu Bayreuth von allen Canzeln in dem Culmbachischen Fürstenthum abgelesen wurde. Bayreuth, 1783.

Documents Illustrative of the Formation of the Union of the American States. Compiled and edited by Charles C. Tansill. Washington, D.C., 1927.

[Du Buisson, Pierre Ulric]. *Abrégé de la révolution de l'Amérique Angloise. Depuis le commencement de l'année 1774, jusqu'au premier Janvier 1778. Par M. ***, Americain*. Paris, 1778.

Ehlers, Martin. *Ueber die Lehre von der menschlichen Freyheit und über die Mittel, zu einer hohen Stufe moralischer Freyheit zu gelangen*. Dessau, 1782. Translated into French, *Discours sur la liberté*. Dessau and Leipzig, 1783.

[Embser, Johann Valentin]. *Die Abgötterei unsers philosophischen Jahrhunderts. Erster Abgott. Ewiger Friede*. Mannheim, 1779.

English Historical Documents. Edited by David C. Douglas. Vol. IX, *American Colonial Documents to 1776*, edited by Merrill Jensen. London, 1955.

Entretiens de Guillaume de Nassau, Prince d'Orange, et du Général Montgomery, sur la Révolution ancienne des Pays-Bas, et les Affaires actuelles d'Amérique. London and Paris, 1776.

European Treaties bearing on the History of the United States and its Dependencies. Edited by Frances Gardiner Davenport. Vol. IV, *1716–1815*, edited by Charles O. Paullin. Washington, D.C., 1937.

Ewald, Johann Ludwig. *Über Revolutionen, ihre Quellen und die Mittel dagegen.* Berlin, 1792.

Facsimiles of Manuscripts in European Archives Relating to America, 1773–1783. With Descriptions, Editorial Notes, Collations, References and Translations. Edited by Benjamin Franklin Stevens. 4 vols. London, 1889–1895.

Fäsi, Johann Konrad. *Unterredungen verstorbener Personen über wichtige Begebenheiten der ältern, mittlern und neuern Geschichte.* Halle, 1777.

The Federal and State Constitutions, Colonial Charters, and Other Organic Laws of the States, Territories, and Colonies Now or Heretofore Forming the United States of America. Compiled and edited by Francis Newton Thorpe. 7 vols. Washington, D.C., 1909.

The Federalist. Edited by Jacob E. Cooke. Middletown, Conn., 1961.

Fischer, Friedrich Christoph Jonathan. *Ueber die Geschichte des Despotismus in Teutschland.* Halle, 1780.

Fischer, Johann Traugott. *Preußens und Frankreichs Revolution. Eine Vorlesung in der Litterarischen Gesellschaft zu Halberstadt zu der jährigen Feyer des Geburtstags Friedrichs des Einzigen den 24. Januar 1793.* Halberstadt, 1794.

Forster, Georg. *Sämmtliche Schriften.* Edited by his daughter. With a characterization of Forster by G. G. Gervinus. 9 vols. Leipzig, 1843.

―――. *Über die Beziehung der Staatskunst auf das Glück der Menschheit und andere Schriften.* Edited by Wolfgang Rödel. Frankfurt, 1966.

―――. *Werke.* Edited by the Deutsche Akademie der Wissenschaften. Vol. IX, *Ansichten vom Niederrhein*, compiled by Gerhard Steiner. Berlin, 1958.

Friedrich II. *Oeuvres de Frédéric le Grand.* Edited by Johann David Erdmann Preuss. 30 vols. Berlin, 1846–1856.

Gebet für die in Königl. Groß-Britannische Kriegs-Dienste überlassene Hochfürstl. Brandenburgische Kriegs-Völcker, Welches auf höchsten Befehl Ihro des glorwürdigst-regierenden Herrn Marggrafen zu Brandenburg-Onolz und Culmbach, Hochfürstl. Durchlaucht, nach dem gewöhnlichen Kirchen-Gebet in allen Sonn- und Feyertäglichen, auch wochentlichen Gottes-Diensten zu sprechen ist. N.p., 1777.

Gebetsformel um glückliche Rückreise der nach erfolgten Frieden aus America zurückgehenden Hochfürstlich Brandenburgischen Truppen welche auf immediaten Befehl Ihro Hochfürstlichen Durchlaucht vom Hochfürstl. Consistorio zu Bayreuth den Geistlichen des Obergebürgischen Fürstentums, bey dem öffentlichen Gottesdienst abzulesen vorgeschrieben worden. N.p., 1783.

Geist des achtzehnten Jahrhunderts, den Unbehutsamen aufgedekt, zu ihrem Verwahrungs- oder Heilungsmittel wider die gegenwärtige Verführung. Augsburg, 1793.

Gentz, Friedrich von. *Schriften.* Edited by Gustav Schlesier. 5 vols. Mannheim, 1838–1840.

————. *Staatsschriften und Briefe.* Edited by Hans von Eckardt. 2 vols. Munich, 1921.

Gerning, Johann Isaak von. *Das achtzehnte Jahrhundert. Saecularischer Gesang.* Gotha, 1802.

Gesang bey dem Abmarsch der hochfürstlich Brandenburg-Anspach-Baireuthischen Auxiliar-Truppen nach Amerika. Ansbach, 1777.

Gleim, Johann Wilhelm Ludwig. *Sämmtliche Werke.* Edited by Wilhelm Körte. 7 vols. Halberstadt, 1811–1813.

————. *Vater Gleim's Zeitgedichte, von 1789–1803.* Edited by Wilhelm Körte. Leipzig, 1841.

Goeckingk, Leopold Friedrich Günther von. *Gedichte.* 3 vols. Leipzig, 1780–1782.

Goethe, Johann Wolfgang von. *Werke.* 143 vols. Weimar, 1887–1912.

[Günderode, Friedrich Justinian Freiherr von]. *Briefe eines Reisenden über den gegenwärtigen Zustand von Cassel mit aller Freiheit geschildert.* Frankfurt and Leipzig, 1781.

Hamilton, Alexander. *Papers on Public Credit, Commerce, and Finance.* Edited by Samuel McKee, Jr. With an introduction by J. Harvie Williams. New York, 1957.

Hertzberg, Ewald Friedrich Graf von. *Huit Dissertations que M. le Comte de Hertzberg . . . a lues dans les assemblées publiques de l'Académie Royale des Sciences & Belles-Lettres de Berlin, Tenues pour l'anniversaire du Roi Frédéric II dans les années 1780–1787.* Berlin, 1787.

Hippel, Theodor Gottlieb von. *Sämmtliche Werke.* 14 vols. Berlin, 1828–1839.

Horn, Christian Adam. *Uiber Gleichheit und Ungleichheit aus dem Gesichtspunkt gegenwärtiger Zeiten.* Hildburghausen, 1792.

[Iselin, Isaak]. *Über die Geschichte der Menschheit.* 2 vols. Frankfurt and Leipzig, 1764. 2d ed., Zurich, 1768. 3d ed., Zurich, 1770. 4th ed., Basel, 1779. Reprint, Karlsruhe, 1784. 5th ed., Basel, 1786.

Jenisch, Daniel. *Geist und Charakter des achtzehnten Jahrhunderts, politisch, moralisch, ästhetisch und wissenschaftlich betrachtet.* 3 vols. Berlin, 1800–1801.

Jung-Stilling, Johann Heinrich. *Über den Revolutions-Geist unserer Zeit zur Belehrung der bürgerlichen Stände.* Marburg, 1793.

Kalm, Peter. *The America of 1750: Peter Kalm's Travels in North America; The English Version of 1770* [by Johann Reinhold Forster]. Newly translated by Edith M. L. Carlborg and Adolph B. Benson. Edited by Adolph B. Benson. 2 vols. 1937. Reprint, New York, 1966.

Kant, Immanuel. *Werke.* Edited by Wilhelm Weischedel. 6 vols. Wiesbaden and Darmstadt, 1960–1964.

Klopstock, Friedrich Gottlieb. *Sämmtliche Werke.* 12 vols. Karlsruhe, 1818–1822.

[Knigge, Adolf Freiherr von]. *Joseph von Wurmbrand . . . politisches Glaubensbekenntniß, mit Hinsicht auf die französische Revolution und deren Folgen.* Frankfurt and Leipzig, 1792.

Knüppeln, Julius Friedrich. *Die Rechte der Natur und Menschheit, entweiht durch*

Menschen. Szenen aus der heutigen Welt, für den Menschen, Bürger und Richter. Berlin, 1784.

Kröger, Alfred. *Geburt der USA: German Newspaper Accounts of the American Revolution, 1763–1783.* Madison, Wis., 1962.

Lessing, Gotthold Ephraim. *Werke.* Edited by Herbert G. Göpfert. Munich, 1970–.

Lichtenberg, Georg Christoph. *Aphorismen.* Edited by Albert Leitzmann. 5 vols. Berlin, 1902–1908.

———. *Gedanken, Satiren, Fragmente.* Edited by Wilhelm Herzog. 2 vols. Jena, 1907.

Lied eines deutschen Kriegers in Amerika. Bayreuth, 1778.

Mangelsdorf, Karl Ehregott. *Ueber den Geist der Revolutionen. Eine Rede am Stiftungstage der Preußischen Königswürde im akademischen Hörsaale gehalten.* Königsberg, 1790.

Mauchart, Gottfried Heinrich. *Ueber die Rechte des Menschen vor seiner Geburt.* Frankfurt and Leipzig, 1782.

Mayer, Charles Joseph. *Les Ligues achéenne, suisse et hollandoise; et révolution des Etats Unis de l'Amérique, comparées ensemble.* 2 vols. Geneva and Paris, 1787.

[Mazzei, Filippo]. *Recherches historiques et politiques sur les États-Unis de l'Amérique Septentrionale . . . Par un citoyen de Virginie.* 4 vols. Colle and Paris, 1788.

[Mirabeau, Honoré Gabriel Riquetti, comte de]. *Des Lettres de cachet et des prisons d'Etat.* 2 vols. Hamburg, 1782.

Mohr, Johann Melchior. *Analytischer Versuch zu einer Modification der Einheit im Staat, mit Hinsicht auf die Schweiz.* Lucerne, 1800.

Monneron, Frédéric. *Essai sur les nouveaux principes politiques.* Lausanne, 1800.

Montesquieu, Charles de Secondat, baron de La Brède et de. *Des Herrn von Montesquieu Werk vom Geist der Gesetze.* Translated from the French by Karl Gottfried Schreiter and August Wilhelm Hauswald. 2 vols. Altenburg, 1782.

———. *Oeuvres complètes.* Edited by Roger Caillois. 2 vols. Paris, 1949–1951.

[Moser, Friedrich Karl Freiherr von]. *Ueber Regenten, Regierung und Ministers. Schutt zur Wege-Besserung des kommenden Jahrhunderts.* Frankfurt, 1784.

Möser, Justus. *Sämmtliche Werke.* Edited by B. R. Abeken. 10 vols. Berlin, 1842–1843.

———. *Sämtliche Werke.* Historical-critical edition. Edited by the Akademie der Wissenschaften zu Göttingen. Oldenburg and Berlin, 1944–.

[Müller, Christian Adam]. *Das achtzehnte Jahrhundert. Eine Skizze.* Hof, 1801.

Müller, Johannes von. *Sämmtliche Werke.* Edited by Johann Georg Müller. 40 vols. Stuttgart and Tübingen, 1831–1835.

Musenalmanach für das Jahr 1775. Göttingen and Gotha, n.d.

Musenalmanach für das Jahr 1776. Edited by Johann Heinrich Voss and Leopold Friedrich Günther von Goeckingk. Lauenburg, 1775.

Musenalmanach für das Jahr 1783. Edited by Johann Heinrich Voss and Leopold Friedrich Günther von Goeckingk. Hamburg, n.d.

Niemeyer, August Hermann. *Gedichte.* Leipzig, 1778.

Pamphlets of the American Revolution, 1750–1776. Edited by Bernard Bailyn. Cambridge, Mass., 1965–.

[Pauw, Corneille de]. *Recherches philosophiques sur les Américains, ou Mémoires intéressants pour servir à l'Histoire de l'Espèce humaine. Par Mr. de P * * *.* 2 vols. Berlin, 1768–1769.

Pestalozzi, Johann Heinrich. *Sämtliche Werke*. Edited by Arthur Buchenau *et al*. Berlin and Leipzig, 1927– .

Pfeffel, Gottlieb Conrad. *Poetische Versuche*. 4th ed. 10 vols. Tübingen, 1802–1820.

Poncelin de la Roche-Tilhac, Jean Charles. *Philosophische Beschreibung des Handels, und der Besitzungen der Europäer in Asien und Afrika*. Translated from the French. 2 vols. Strasbourg, 1783–1784.

Prologue to Revolution: Sources and Documents on the Stamp Act Crisis, 1764–1766. Edited by Edmund S. Morgan. Chapel Hill, N.C., 1959.

Quellen zur Geschichte des Rheinlandes im Zeitalter der französischen Revolution 1780–1801. Edited by Joseph Hansen. 4 vols. Bonn, 1931–1938.

[Raynal, Guillaume-Thomas-François]. *Histoire philosophique et politique des établissements et du commerce des Européens dans les deux Indes.* 7 vols. The Hague, 1774.

————. *Révolution de l'Amérique*. London and The Hague, 1781.

[Rebmann, Andreas Georg Friedrich]. *Der politische Thierkreis oder die Zeichen unserer Zeit.* 2d ed. 2 vols. Strasbourg, 1800.

Reitzenstein, Friedrich Wilhelm Philipp Ernst Freiherr von. *An die aus America zurückgekommenen Ruhmvollen Bayreuthischen Krieger und Freunde. Gesprochen bey Ihrem Einzug in Culmbach, den 16. Nov. 1783.* Kulmbach, 1783.

Remer, Julius August. *Lehrbuch der Staatskunde der vornehmsten europäischen Staaten.* Brunswick, 1786.

Rousseau, Jean-Jacques. *Oeuvres complètes.* Edited by Bernard Gagnebin and Marcel Raymond. Vol. III. Paris, 1964.

Rush, Benjamin. *The Selected Writings of Benjamin Rush.* Edited by Dagobert D. Runes. New York, 1947.

[Sack, Friedrich Samuel Gottfried]. *Briefe über den Krieg*. Berlin, 1778.

Scherber, Johann Heinrich. *Gemeinnütziges Lesebuch für die Bayreuthische Vaterlandsgeschichte.* 2 vols. Hof, 1796–1797.

Schiller, Friedrich von. *Werke*. National edition. Edited by Julius Peterson *et al*. Weimar, 1943– .

"Schillers Bibliothek." In *Zum 9. Mai 1905. Schiller-Ausstellung im Goethe- und Schiller-Archiv* (Weimar, 1905), 47–83.

Schlegel, Friedrich. *Kritische Ausgabe.* Edited by Ernst Behler *et al*. Munich, Paderborn, Vienna, and Zurich, 1958– .

Schubart, Christian Friedrich Daniel. *Gesammelte Schriften und Schicksale.* 8 vols. Stuttgart, 1839–1840.

[————]. *Das Wetterleuchten über Europa am Ende des Jahrhunderts gesehen im Jahr 1788.* Malta and Cairo [i.e., Düsseldorf], 1799.

Seume, Johann Gottfried. *Sämmtliche Werke.* 4th ed. 8 vols. Leipzig, 1839.

Sr. Excellenz, dem Herrn Geheim Rath von Keller widmet nach erhaltener Nachricht von der glorreichen Eroberung des Forts Klinton durch Dero Herrn Sohn diese wenigen Zeilen E. v. Z. Heiligenstadt, 1778.

Stettler, Rudolf. *Ueber Einheit und Föderalism, oder Plan zu einer neuen Staatsverfassung für die Schweiz.* Bern, 1800.

Stolberg, Friedrich Leopold Graf zu. *Jamben.* Leipzig, 1784.

_____ . "Die Zukunft. Ein bisher ungedrucktes Gedicht des Grafen Friedrich Leopold zu Stolberg aus den Jahren 1779–1782." Edited by Otto Hartwig. *Archiv für Litteraturgeschichte*, XIII (1885), 83–115, 251–272.

[Stöver, Johann Hermann]. *Niedersachsen.* 3 vols. Rome [i.e., Berlin], 1789.

Vattel, Emer de. *Le Droit des gens ou principes de la loi naturelle appliqués à la conduite et aux affaires des nations et des souverains* (1758). Translated from the French by Wilhelm Euler. With an introduction by Paul Guggenheim. Tübingen, 1959.

Verhandlungen der Helvetischen Gesellschaft d. J. 1776–83. N.p., 1776–1783.

Vier neue Arien. N.p., [1777].

Voltaire, François Marie Arouet de. *Oeuvres complètes.* 46 vols. Paris, 1875–1891.

Washington, George. *George Washington as the French Knew Him: A Collection of Texts.* Translated and edited by Gilbert Chinard. Princeton, N.J., 1940.

Watson, Richard. *Les Principes de la Révolution, Justifiés dans un sermon prêché devant l'Université de Cambridge, le Mécredi 29 Mai 1776.* London, 1777.

[Weikard, Melchior Adam]. *Der philosophische Arzt.* 3d ed. 4 vols. Linz, 1787.

Wieland, Christoph Martin. *Werke.* Edited by Gustav Hempel. Vol. XXXV. Berlin, 1879.

Wolff, Christian. *Ius naturae methodo scientifica pertractatum.* Edited by Marcel Thomann. 8 vols. Halle, 1740–1748. Reprinted in Wolff, *Gesammelte Werke*, Pt. II, Vols. XVII–XXIV. Hildesheim, 1968–1972.

Zeitgenössische Darstellungen der Unruhen in der Landschaft Zürich 1794–1798. Edited by Otto Hunziker. *Quellen zur Schweizer Geschichte*, vol. XVII. Basel, 1897.

[Ziehen, Conrad Siegismund]. *Nachricht von einer bevorstehenden großen Revolution der Erde, die insonderheit das südliche Europa und einen Theil Deutschlands treffen.* Frankfurt and Leipzig, 1783.

[Zubly, John Joachim]. *Eine Kurzgefaßte Historische Nachricht von den Kämpfen der Schweitzer für die Freyheit.* Translated from the English. Philadelphia, 1775.

Selected Secondary Sources

Acomb, Evelyn M. "The Journal of Baron Von Closen." *William and Mary Quarterly*, 3d Ser., X (1953), 196–236.

Adamietz, Horst. "Christian Friedrich Daniel Schubarts Volksblatt *Deutsche Chronik*." Published Ph.D. dissertation, University of Berlin, 1941.

Adams, Henry Nason. *Prussian-American Relations, 1775–1871*. Cleveland, 1960.

Arendt, Hannah. *On Revolution*. New York, 1963.

Aretin, Karl Otmar Freiherr von. *Heiliges Römisches Reich 1776–1806. Reichsverfassung und Staatssouveränität*. 2 vols. Wiesbaden, 1967.

Aris, Reinhold. *History of Political Thought in Germany from 1789 to 1815*. With a foreword by G. P. Gooch. 1936. Reprint. London, 1965.

Baasch, Ernst. *Beiträge zur Geschichte der Handelsbeziehungen zwischen Hamburg und Amerika*. Hamburg, 1892.

————. *Geschichte des Hamburgischen Zeitungswesens von den Anfängen bis 1914*. Hamburg, 1930.

[Bauer, Edgar]. *Die politische Literatur der Deutschen im achtzehnten Jahrhundert*. Edited by Martin von Geismar. Vol. I. *Politische Aufklärer aus der Zeit der Französischen Revolution*. Leipzig, 1847.

Berney, Arnold. "August Ludwig von Schölzers Staatsauffassung." *Historische Zeitschrift*, CXXXII (1925), 43–67.

Beutin, Ludwig. *Bremen und Amerika. Zur Geschichte der Weltwirtschaft und den Beziehungen Deutschlands zu den Vereinigten Staaten*. Bremen, 1953.

Beutler, Ernst. "Von der Ilm zum Susquehanna. Goethe und Amerika in ihren Wechselbeziehungen." In his *Essays um Goethe*, 5th ed. Bremen, 1957, 580–629.

Bezzel, Oskar. "Ansbach-Bayreuther Miettruppen im Nordamerikanischen Freiheitskrieg 1777–1783." *Zeitschrift für bayerische Landesgeschichte*, VIII (1935), 185–214, 377–424.

Biedermann, Karl. "Die nordamerikanische und die französische Revolution in ihren Rückwirkungen auf Deutschland." *Zeitschrift für deutsche Kulturgeschichte*, III (1858), 483–495, 562–576, 654–668, 723–727.

Bloch, Ernst. *Naturrecht und menschliche Würde*. Frankfurt, 1961.

Böhm, Gottfried. *Ludwig Wekhrlin (1739–1792). Ein Publizistenleben des achtzehnten Jahrhunderts*. Munich, 1893.

Bond, M. A. "The Political Conversion of Friedrich von Gentz." *European Studies Review*, III (1973), 1–12.

Bossenbrook, William John. "Justus Möser as a Historian." Unpublished Ph.D. dissertation, University of Chicago, 1932.

————. *Justus Möser's Approach to History*. Chicago, 1938.

Brandes, Ernst. *Betrachtungen über den Zeitgeist in Deutschland in den letzten Decennien des vorigen Jahrhunderts*. Hanover, 1808.

Brandt, Otto. *Geistesleben und Politik in Schleswig-Holstein um die Wende des 18. Jahrhunderts*. Stuttgart, Berlin, and Leipzig, 1925.

Braubach, Max. "Die kirchliche Aufklärung im katholischen Deutschland im Spiegel des *Journal von und für Deutschland* (1784–1792)." *Historisches Jahrbuch*, LIV (1934), 1–63, 178–220.

Braune, Frieda. *Edmund Burke in Deutschland. Ein Beitrag zur Geschichte des historisch-politischen Denkens*. Heidelberg, 1917.

Breffka, Constantin. *Amerika in der deutschen Literatur*. Cologne, 1917.

Breunig, Juliane. "Das *Journal von und für Deutschland* 1784–1792. Eine deutsche

Zeitenwende im Spiegel einer deutschen Zeitung." Published Ph.D. dissertation, University of Munich, 1941.

Brie, Friedrich. "Die Anfänge des Amerikanismus." *Historisches Jahrbuch*, LIX (1939), 352–387.

Brite, John Duncan. "The Attitude of European States toward Emigration to the American Colonies and the United States, 1607–1820." Unpublished Ph.D. dissertation, University of Chicago, 1937.

Brown, Marvin Luther, Jr. "American Independence Through Prussian Eyes: A Neutral View of the Negotiations of 1782–1783." *Historian*, XVIII (1956), 189–201.

Bruford, Walter Horace. *Culture and Society in Classical Weimar 1775–1806.* Cambridge, 1962.

Buchwald, Reinhard. *Schiller.* 2d ed. 2 vols. Wiesbaden, 1953–1954.

Butterfield, Lyman H. "Psychological Warfare in 1776: The Jefferson-Franklin Plan to Cause Hessian Desertions." American Philosophical Society, *Proceedings*, XCIV (1950), 233–241.

Carruth, William H. "Schiller and America: An Address at the Schillerfeier of the University of Wisconsin, May 9, 1905." *German American Annals*, N.S., IV (1906), 131–146.

Carus, Paul. "Goethe on America." *Open Court*, XXIII (1909), 502–503.

Chinard, Gilbert. "The American Philosophical Society and the World of Science (1768–1800)." American Philosophical Society, *Proceedings*, LXXXVII (1943–1944), 1–11.

Craig, Gordon A. "Engagement and Neutrality in Germany: The Case of Georg Forster, 1754–1794." *Journal of Modern History*, XLI (1969), 1–16.

Curti, Merle. "The Reputation of America Overseas (1776–1860)." *American Quarterly*, I (1949), 58–82.

Desczyk, Gerhard. "Amerika in der Phantasie deutscher Dichter." *Deutsch-Amerikanische Geschichtsblätter*, XXIV/XXV (1925), 7–142.

Dippel, Horst. "The American Revolution and the Modern Concept of *Revolution*." In Erich Angermann *et al.*, eds., *New Wine in Old Skins: A Comparative View of Socio-Political Structures and Values Affecting the American Revolution* (Stuttgart, 1976), 115–134.

———. *Americana Germanica 1770–1800. Bibliographie deutscher Amerikaliteratur.* Stuttgart, 1976.

———. "Prussia's English Policy after the Seven Years' War." *Central European History*, IV (1971), 195–214.

———. "Sources in Germany for the Study of the American Revolution." *Quarterly Journal of the Library of Congress*, XXXIII (1976), 199–217.

———. "Die Wirkung der amerikanischen Revolution auf Deutschland und Frankreich." *200 Jahre amerikanische Revolution und moderne Revolutionsforschung. Geschichte und Gesellschaft, Sonderheft*, II (1976), 101–121.

Doll, Eugene Edgar. "American History as Interpreted by German Historians from 1770 to 1815." American Philosophical Society, *Transactions*, N.S., XXXVIII (1948), 421–534.

Döllner, Max. *Erlebnisse der ansbach-bayreuthischen Hilfstruppen im Kriege Großbritanniens gegen die Vereinigten Staaten von Nordamerika (1777–1783).* Neustadt an der Aisch, 1933.

Douglass, Elisha P. "German Intellectuals and the American Revolution." *William and Mary Quarterly,* 3d Ser., XVII (1960), 200–218.

Droz, Jacques. *L'Allemagne et la Révolution française.* Paris, 1949.

————. "La Légende du complot illuministe et les origines du romantisme politique en Allemagne." *Revue historique,* CCXXVI (1961), 313–338.

Drumm, Ernst. *Das Regiment Royal Deuxponts. Deutsches Blut auf fürstlichen Befehl in fremden Dienst und Sold.* Zweibrücken, 1936.

Düring, Kurt von. "Der angebliche Verkauf von Landeskindern durch Reichsfürsten im 17. und 18. Jahrhundert." *Hanauisches Magazin,* XII (1933), 87–93.

Ebeling, Friedrich Wilhelm. *Wilhelm Ludwig Wekhrlin. Leben und Auswahl seiner Schriften. Zur Culturgeschichte des achtzehnten Jahrhunderts.* Berlin, 1869.

Eelking, Max von. *Die deutschen Hülfstruppen im nordamerikanischen Befreiungskriege, 1776 bis 1783.* 2 vols. Hanover, 1863.

————. *Leben und Wirken des Herzoglichen Braunschweig'schen General-Lieutenants Friedrich Adolph Riedesel Freiherrn zu Eisenbach. Nebst vielen Original-Correspondenzen und historischen Aktenstücken aus dem siebenjährigen Kriege, dem nordamerikanischen Freiheits-Kampfe und dem französischen Revolutions-Kriege.* 3 vols. Leipzig, 1856.

Ehlers, Karl. "Der Soldatenhandel Karl Wilhelm Ferdinands von Braunschweig während des nordamerikanischen Freiheitskrieges." *Niedersachsen,* XXXI (1926), 601–604.

Elovson, Harald. *Bengt Lidners Greifswalder Dissertation "De iure revolutionis Americanorum".* Jena, 1928.

Elsasser, Robert. *Über die politischen Bildungsreisen der Deutschen nach England (vom achtzehnten Jahrhundert bis 1815).* Heidelberg, 1917.

Engelsing, Rolf. "Deutschland und die Vereinigten Staaten im 19. Jahrhundert." *Die Welt als Geschichte,* XVIII (1958), 138–156.

————. "England und die USA in der bremischen Sicht des 19. Jahrhunderts." *Jahrbuch der Wittheit zu Bremen,* I (1957), 33–65.

————. "Geschäftsformen in den Anfängen des deutschen Nordamerikaverkehrs (1783)." In *Tradition,* 5. Beiheft. *Beiträge zur bremischen Firmengeschichte,* (Munich, 1966), 20–32.

————. "Schlesien und der bremische Leinenhandel bis zur Kontinentalsperre." *Jahrbuch der schlesischen Friedrich-Wilhelms-Universität zu Breslau,* III (1958), 155–181.

Epstein, Klaus. *The Genesis of German Conservatism.* Princeton, N.J., 1966.

Faust, Albert B. "Swiss Emigration to the American Colonies in the Eighteenth Century." *American Historical Review,* XXII (1916–1917), 21–44.

Florer, W. W. "Schiller's Conception of Liberty and the Spirit of '76." *German American Annals,* N.S., IV (1906), 99–115.

Ford, Guy Stanton. "Two German Publicists on the American Revolution." *Journal of English and Germanic Philology,* VIII (1909), 144–176.

Fraenkel, Ernst. *Amerika im Spiegel des deutschen politischen Denkens. Äuße-rungen deutscher Staatsmänner und Staatsdenker über Staat und Gesellschaft in den Vereinigten Staaten.* Cologne and Opladen, 1959.

Frey, John R. "George Washington in German Fiction." *American-German Review,* XII, no. 5 (1946), 25–26, 37.

Friedenthal, Richard. *Goethe. Sein Leben und seine Zeit.* Munich, 1963.

Friedrich, Carl Joachim. *The Impact of American Constitutionalism Abroad.* Boston, 1967.

Fritsch, W. A. "Stimmen deutscher Zeitgenossen über den Soldatenhandel deutscher Fürsten nach Amerika." *Deutsch-Amerikanisches Magazin,* I (1887), 589–593.

Fürst, Friederike. *August Ludwig von Schlözer, ein deutscher Aufklärer im 18. Jahrhundert.* Heidelberg, 1928.

Gaiser, Konrad. *Christian Friedrich Daniel Schubart, Schicksal/Zeitbild. Ausgewählte Schriften.* Stuttgart, 1929.

Gallinger, Herbert Percival. "Die Haltung der deutschen Publizistik zu dem amerikanischen Unabhängigkeitskriege, 1775–1783." Published Ph.D. dissertation, University of Leipzig, 1900.

Gay, Peter. *The Enlightenment: An Interpretation.* 2 vols. New York, 1966–1969.

Gerber, Adolf. *Die Nassau-Dillenburger Auswanderung nach Amerika im 18. Jahrhundert. Das Verhalten der Regierungen dazu und die späteren Schicksale der Auswanderer.* Flensburg, 1930.

Ghelfi, Gerald John. "European Opinions of American Republicanism During the 'Critical Period' 1781–1789." Unpublished Ph.D. dissertation, Claremont Graduate School, 1968.

Giddey, Ernest. "Quelques aspects des relations anglo-suisses à la fin du XVIIIe siècle: Louis Braun et Hugh Cleghorn." *Zeitschrift für Schweizerische Geschichte,* XXIX (1949), 47–64.

Godechot, Jacques. *La Contre-Révolution: Doctrine et action 1789–1804.* Paris, 1861.

───── . *La Pensée révolutionnaire en France et en Europe 1780–1799: Textes choisis et presentées par Jacques Godechot.* Paris, 1964.

───── . *Les Révolutions (1770–1799).* Paris, 1963.

Goebel, Julius. "Amerika in der deutschen Dichtung." In *Forschungen zur deutschen Philologie. Festgabe für Rudolf Hildebrand* (Leipzig, 1894), 102–127.

Goldfriedrich, Johann. *Geschichte des deutschen Buchhandels vom Beginn der klassischen Litteraturperiode bis zum Beginn der Fremdherrschaft (1740–1804).* Vol. III. Leipzig, 1909.

Gottschalk, Louis. *Lafayette between the American and the French Revolution (1783–1789).* Chicago, 1950.

Grab, Walter. *Norddeutsche Jakobiner. Demokratische Bestrebungen zur Zeit der Französischen Revolution.* Frankfurt, 1967.

Graewe, Richard. "The American Revolution Comes to Hannover." *William and Mary Quarterly,* 3d Ser., XX (1963), 246–250.

Griewank, Karl. *Der neuzeitliche Revolutionsbegriff, Entstehung und Entwicklung.* Edited by Ingeborg Horn. With an epilogue by Hermann Heimpel. Weimar, 1955.

Haacke, Wilmot. *Die politische Zeitschrift, 1665–1965*. Vol. I. Stuttgart, 1968.

Habermas, Jürgen. *Strukturwandel der Öffentlichkeit. Untersuchungen zu einer Kategorie der bürgerlichen Gesellschaft*. 4th ed. Neuwied and Berlin, 1969.

Hanfstaengl, Ernst Franz Sedgwick. *Amerika und Europa von Marlborough bis Mirabeau*. Edited by Adolf Dresler. Munich, 1930.

Hänsch, Bruno Felix. "Matthias Christian Sprengel, ein geographischer Publizist am Ausgange des 18. Jahrhunderts." Published Ph.D. dissertation, University of Leipzig, 1902.

Hansen, Marcus Lee. *The Atlantic Migration 1607–1860: A History of the Continuing Settlement of the United States*. Edited by Arthur M. Schlesinger, Sr. Cambridge, Mass., 1940.

Hartnack, Karl. "Ein Beitrag zur Geschichte der waldeckischen Auswanderung nach Nordamerika." *Geschichtsblätter für Waldeck und Pyrmont*, XXIX/XXX (1931), 133–139.

Hatfield, James Taft, and Hochbaum, Elfrieda. "The Influence of the American Revolution upon German Literature." *Americana Germanica*, III (1899–1900), 338–385.

Hauff, Gustav. *Christian Friedrich Daniel Schubart in seinem Leben und seinen Werken*. Stuttgart, 1885.

Haworth, Paul Leland. "Frederick the Great and the American Revolution." *American Historical Review*, IX (1904), 460–478.

Hay, Joseph. "Staat, Volk und Weltbürgertum in der *Berlinischen Monatsschrift* von Friedrich Gedike und Johann Erich Biester (1783–1796)." Published Ph.D. dissertation, University of Breslau, 1913.

Hegeman, Daniel V. "Franklin and Germany: Further Evidence of His Reputation in the Eighteenth Century." *German Quarterly*, XXVI (1953), 187–194.

Heigel, Karl Theodor von. "Die Beteiligung des Hauses Zweibrücken am nordamerikanischen Befreiungskrieg." Bayerische Akademie des Wissenschaften, Philosophisch-philologische und historische Klasse, *Sitzungsberichte*, 6th transaction (Munich, 1912).

Heineken, Philipp. "Bremens Handelsbeziehungen zu den Vereinigten Staaten in ihrer 140jähr. Entwicklung." *Jahrbuch des Norddeutschen Lloyd Bremen, 1922/1923* (Bremen, 1924).65–76.

Hellersburg-Wendriner, Anna. "America in the World View of the Aged Goethe." *Germanic Review*, XIV (1939), 270–276.

Hertz, Friedrich. *The Development of the German Public Mind: A Social History of German Political Sentiments, Aspirations and Ideas*. 2 vols. London, 1957–1962.

Hofstaetter, Walther. *Das "Deutsche Museum" (1776–1788) und das "Neue Deutsche Museum" (1789–1791). Ein Beitrag zur Geschichte der deutschen Zeitschriften im 18. Jahrhundert*. Leipzig, 1908.

Hölzle, Erwin. "Bruch und Kontinuität im Werden der deutschen modernen Freiheit." In Theodor Mayer, ed., *Das Problem der Freiheit in der deutschen und schweizerischen Geschichte (Vorträge und Forschungen, II)* (Lindau and Constance, 1955), 159–177.

——— . "Justus Möser über Staat und Freiheit." In *Aus Politik und Geschichte. Gedächtnisschrift für Georg von Below* (Berlin, 1928), pp. 167–181.

——— . "Naturrecht, Staatsrecht und Historisches Recht im Zeitalter der englischen und amerikanischen Revolution." *Vierteljahrsschrift für Sozial- und Wirtschaftsgeschichte*, XXIV (1931), 452–465.

Horkheimer, Max, and Adorno, Theodor W. *Dialektik der Aufklärung. Philosophische Fragmente.* 2d ed. Frankfurt, 1969.

Houtte, Hubert van, and Burnett, Edmund C. "American Commercial Conditions, and Negotiations with Austria, 1783–1786." *American Historical Review*, XVI (1910–1911), 567–587.

Huth, Hans. "Letters from a Hessian Mercenary." *Pennsylvania Magazine of History and Biography*, LXII (1938), 488–501.

Im Hof, Ulrich. *Aufklärung in der Schweiz.* Bern, 1970.

——— . *Isaak Iselin und die Spätaufklärung.* Bern and Munich, 1967.

Jacob, Adolf. "Die Zürcherische Presse bis zur Helvetik." In *Beiträge zur Geschichte des Zürcherischen Zeitungswesens* (Zurich, 1908), 1–73.

Jaggi-Wildbolz, Hanni. "Der Widerhall des amerikanischen Unabhängigkeitskrieges in der Schweiz." Unpublished paper, Historisches Seminar, University of Bern, 1960.

Janssen-Sillenstede, Georg. "Eine Verlustliste verkaufter deutscher Soldaten während des nordamerikanischen Freiheitskrieges (1778–1783)." *Oldenburger Jahrbuch*, XLIV/XLV (1940–1941), 102–114.

Jantz, Harold. "Amerika im deutschen Dichten und Denken." In *Deutsche Philologie im Aufriß*, ed. Wolfgang Stammler, 2d ed., III (Berlin, 1962), 309–372.

——— . "The Myths About America: Origins and Extensions." *Jahrbuch für Amerikastudien*, VII (1962), 6–18.

Jentsch, Irene. "Zur Geschichte des Zeitungslesens in Deutschland am Ende des 18. Jahrhunderts. Mit besonderer Berücksichtigung der gesellschaftlichen Formen des Zeitungslesens." Published Ph.D. dissertation, University of Leipzig, 1937.

Julku, Kyösti. *Die revolutionäre Bewegung im Rheinland am Ende des achtzehnten Jahrhunderts.* 2 vols. Helsinki, 1965–1969.

Kahn, Robert L. "George Forster and Benjamin Franklin." American Philosophical Society, *Proceedings*, CII (1958), 1–6.

——— . "Franklin, Grimm, and J. H. Landolt." American Philosophical Society, *Proceedings*, XCIX (1955), 401–404.

Kapp, Friedrich. *Friedrich der Grosse und die Vereinigten Staaten von Amerika. Mit einem Anhang: Die Vereinigten Staaten und das Seekriegsrecht.* Leipzig, 1871.

——— . *Leben des Amerikanischen Generals Friedrich Wilhelm von Steuben.* Berlin, 1858.

——— . *Der Soldatenhandel deutscher Fürsten nach Amerika. Ein Beitrag zur Kulturgeschichte des achtzehnten Jahrhunderts.* 2d ed. Berlin, 1874.

——— . "Zur deutschen wissenschaftlichen Literatur über die Vereinigten Staaten von Amerika." *Historische Zeitschrift*, XXXI (1874), 241–288.

Kellenbenz, Hermann. "Peter Hasenclever (1716–1793)." In *Rheinische Lebensbilder*, IV (Düsseldorf, 1970), 79–99.

Kelly, John Alexander. *England and the Englishman in German Literature of the Eighteenth Century*. New York, 1921.

Kersten, Kurt. *Der Weltumsegler Johann Georg Adam Forster 1754–1794*. Bern, 1957.

King, Henry Safford. "Echoes of the American Revolution in German Literature." University of California, *Publications in Modern Philology*, XIV (Berkeley, 1930), 23–193.

Kipping, Ernst. *Die Truppen von Hessen-Kassel im amerikanischen Unabhängigkeitskrieg 1776–1783*. Darmstadt, 1965.

Kirchner, Joachim. *Das deutsche Zeitschriftenwesen, seine Geschichte und seine Probleme*. 2d ed. 2 vols. Wiesbaden, 1958–1962.

_____. *Die Grundlagen des deutschen Zeitschriftenwesens. Mit einer Gesamtbibliographie der deutschen Zeitschriften bis zum Jahre 1790*. 2 vols. Leipzig, 1928–1931.

Kofler, Leo. *Zur Geschichte der bürgerlichen Gesellschaft. Versuch einer verstehenden Deutung der Neuzeit*. 3d ed. Neuwied and Berlin, 1966.

Koselleck, Reinhart. *Kritik und Krise. Ein Beitrag zur Pathogenese der bürgerlichen Welt*. Freiburg and Munich, 1959.

Kraus, Michael. "America and the Utopian Ideal in the Eighteenth Century." *Mississippi Valley Historical Review*, XXII (1935–1936), 487–504.

_____. "Literary Relations Between Europe and America in the Eighteenth Century." *William and Mary Quarterly*, 3d Ser., I (1944), 210–234.

Krauss, Werner. *Die französische Aufklärung im Spiegel der deutschen Literatur des 18. Jahrhunderts*. Berlin, 1963.

_____. *Studien zur deutschen und französischen Aufklärung*. Berlin, 1963.

Krieger, Leonard. *The German Idea of Freedom: History of a Political Tradition*. Boston, 1957.

Landis, Charles I. *Charles [i.e., Christoph] Daniel Ebeling, Who from 1793 to 1816 Published in Germany a Geography and History of the United States in Seven Volumes*. Lancaster, Pa., 1929.

Langewiesche, Wilhelm. *Georg Forster: Das Abenteuer seines Lebens. Unter Wiedergabe vieler Briefe und Tagebucheintragungen*. Ebenhausen and Leipzig, 1923.

Learned, Marion Dexter. "Gesang nach Amerika Anno 1777." *Americana Germanica*, I (1897), 84–89.

_____. "Herder and America." *German American Annals*, N.S., II (1904), 531–570.

Liedtke, Kurt. "Die Darstellung Amerikas durch den Abbé Raynal und damit verbundene Zeitprobleme des 18. Jahrhunderts." Unpublished Ph.D. dissertation, University of Erlangen, 1954.

Lindemann, Margot. *Deutsche Presse bis 1815. Geschichte der deutschen Presse*. Vol. I. Berlin, 1969.

Losch, Philipp. *Soldatenhandel. Mit einem Verzeichnis der Hessen-Kasselischen Subsidienverträge und einer Bibliographie*. Kassel, 1933.

Lübbing, Hermann. "Deutsche Soldaten unter anhalt-zerbstischer Fahne im englischen Solde." *Oldenburger Jahrbuch*, XLIV/XLV (1940–1941), 82–101.

Lutz, Henry F. "The Germans, Hessians and Pennsylvania Germans." *Pennsylvania-German*, X (1909), 435–443.

Mackall, Leonard L. "Briefwechsel zwischen Goethe und Amerikanern." *Goethe-Jahrbuch*, XXV (1904), 3–37.

Maenner, Ludwig. *Bayern vor und in der Französischen Revolution.* Stuttgart, 1927.

Mann, Golo. *Friedrich von Gentz. Geschichte eines europäischen Staatsmannes.* Zurich and Vienna, 1947.

————. *Vom Geist Amerikas. Eine Einführung in amerikanisches Denken und Handeln im zwanzigsten Jahrhundert.* 3d ed. Stuttgart, 1961.

Matheson, P. E. *German Visitors to England 1770–1795, and Their Impressions.* Oxford, 1930.

Max, Hubert. *Wesen und Gestalt der politischen Zeitschrift. Ein Beitrag zur Geschichte des politischen Erziehungsprozesses des deutschen Volkes bis zu den Karlsbader Beschlüssen.* Essen, 1942.

Meinhardt, Günther. "Gottfried Achenwall und Benjamin Franklin. Beziehungen des Elbinger Gelehrten zu dem amerikanischen Staatsmann." *Westpreußen-Jahrbuch*, XXII (1972), 83–86.

Merlan, Philip. "Parva Hamanniana (II): Hamann and Schmohl." *Journal of the History of Ideas*, X (1949), 567–574.

Merzdorf, J.F.L. Theodor. "Helferich Peter Sturz." *Archiv für Litteraturgeschichte*, VII (1878), 33–92.

Meyen, E. "Die Berliner Monatsschrift von Gedike und Biester. Ein Beitrag zur Geschichte des deutschen Journalismus." *Literarhistorisches Taschenbuch*, V (1847), 151–222.

Meyer, Christian. "Soldatenhandel deutscher Fürsten nach Amerika." In Meyer, *Biographische und kulturgeschichtliche Essays.* Leipzig, 1901, 381–394.

Meyer, Hildegard. *Nord-Amerika im Urteil des Deutschen Schrifttums bis zur Mitte des 19. Jahrhunderts. Eine Untersuchung über Kürnbergers "Amerika-Müden."* Hamburg, 1929.

Miller, Max. "Ursachen und Ziele der schwäbischen Auswanderung." *Württembergische Vierteljahrshefte für Landesgeschichte*, XLII (1936), 184–218.

Mohl, Robert von. *Die Geschichte und Literatur der Staatswissenschaften.* 3 vols. Erlangen, 1855–1858.

Morrison, Alfred J. "Doctor Johann David Schoepf." *German American Annals*, N.S., VIII (1910), 255–264.

Müller, Bruno Albin. *Hamburger Beiträge zur Amerikanistik. Beschreibung und Würdigung ausgewählter Schaustücke aus der zum 24. Internationalen Amerikanisten-Kongreß in Hamburg von der Staats- und Universitäts-Bibliothek veranstalteten Ausstellung.* Hamburg, 1933.

Neu, Heinrich. "Die rheinische Auswanderung nach Amerika, bis zum Beginn des 19. Jahrhunderts." *Annalen des Historischen Vereins für den Niederrhein*, CXLIV/CXLV (1946–1947), 103–140.

Neukam, Wilhelm Georg. "Brandenburgisch-Ansbachisch-Bayreuthische Kriegs-dichtung aus den Jahren 1776–1783. Zugleich ein Beitrag der Beziehungen Frankens zu Nordamerika im 18. Jahrhundert." *Fränkisches Land*, I (1953–1954), 65–67, 69–70.

Palmer, Robert R. *The Age of the Democratic Revolution: A Political History of Europe and America, 1760–1800.* 2 vols. Princeton, N. J., 1959–1964.

Paschke, Max, and Rath, Philipp. *Lehrbuch des Deutschen Buchhandels.* 5th ed. 2 vols. Leipzig, 1920.

Peyer, Hans Conrad. "Zürich und Übersee um die Wende vom 18. zum 19. Jahrhundert." In *Beiträge zur Wirtschafts- und Stadtgeschichte. Festschrift für Hektor Ammann* (Wiesbaden, 1965), 205–219.

Pfeiffer, Albert. "Die Grafen Christian und Wilhelm von Forbach und ihre Beteiligung am nordamerikanischen Freiheitskriege." *Pfälzisches Museum*, XXXIX (1922), 275–277.

Pfund, Harry W. "*Amerika, du hast es besser*: The Main Aspects of Goethe's Interest in America." German Society of Pennsylvania, *Yearbook*, I (1950), 33–43.

Price, Lawrence Marsden. *English Literature in Germany.* Berkeley and Los Angeles, 1953.

Rappard, William E. *Notre Grande République Soeur. Aperçu sur l'Evolution des Etats-Unis et sur les Rapports Suisses-Américains.* Geneva, 1916.

Raumer, Kurt von. "Absoluter Staat, korporative Libertät, persönliche Freiheit." *Historische Zeitschrift*, CLXXXIII (1957), 55–96.

Reeves, Jesse S. "The Prussian-American Treaties." *American Journal of International Law*, XI (1917), 475–510.

Reichardt, Carl. "Ein waldeckischer Feldprediger im amerikanischen Freiheitskriege. Seinem Tagebuch nacherzählt." *Geschichtsblätter für Waldeck*, XLI (1949), 44–64, XLII (1950), 5–30.

Reinsch, Frank H. "Goethe's Political Interests Prior to 1787." University of California, *Publications in Modern Philology*, X (Berkeley, 1923), 183–278.

Riedel, Manfred. "Aristoteles-Tradition am Ausgange des 18. Jahrhunderts. Zur ersten deutschen Übersetzung der *Politik* durch Johann Georg Schlosser." In *Alteuropa und die moderne Gesellschaft. Festschrift für Otto Brunner* (Göttingen, 1963), 278–315.

Robinet de Clery, Adrien. *Les Idées politiques de Frédéric de Gentz.* Lausanne, 1917.

Rödel, Wolfgang. *Forster und Lichtenberg. Ein Beitrag zum Problem deutsche Intelligenz und Französische Revolution.* Berlin, 1960.

Rosengarten, Joseph G. "A Defense of the Hessians." *Pennsylvania Magazine of History and Biography*, XXIII (1899), 157–183.

———. *Der Deutsche Soldat in den Kriegen der Vereinigten Staaten von Nordamerika.* Translated from the English. Kassel, 1890.

———. *Frederick the Great and the United States.* Lancaster, Pa., 1906.

Rosenstock, Eugen. "Revolution als politischer Begriff in der Neuzeit." In *Festgabe für Paul Heilborn zum 70. Geburtstag* (Breslau, 1931), 83–124.

Rosenstock-Huessy, Eugen. *Die europäischen Revolutionen und der Charakter der Nationen.* 2d ed. Stuttgart and Cologne, 1951.

Ruof, Friedrich. *Johann Wilhelm von Archenholtz. Ein deutscher Schriftsteller zur*

Zeit der Französischen Revolution und Napoleons (1741–1812). Berlin, 1915.

Rupp, August. *Pfälzische Kolonisation in Nordamerika*. 2d ed. Stuttgart, 1938.

Salomon, Ludwig. *Geschichte des deutschen Zeitungswesens, von den ersten Anfängen bis zur Wiederaufrichtung des Deutschen Reiches*. 2d ed. Vol. I. Oldenburg and Leipzig, 1906.

Schairer, Erich. "Christian Friedrich Daniel Schubart als politischer Journalist." Published Ph.D. dissertation, University of Tübingen, 1914.

Scheel, Heinrich. *Süddeutsche Jakobiner. Klassenkämpfe und republikanische Bestrebungen im deutschen Süden des 18. Jahrhunderts*. Berlin, 1962.

Schib, Karl. *Johannes von Müller, 1752–1809*. Thayngen and Schaffhausen, 1967.

Schlitter, Hanns. "Die Beziehungen Österreichs zu Amerika." Vol. I. "Die Beziehungen Österreichs zu den Vereinigten Staaten von Amerika." Published Ph.D. dissertation, University of Innsbruck, 1885.

Schlözer, Christian von. *August Ludwig von Schlözer. Öffentliches und Privatleben aus Originalurkunden und mit wörtlicher Beifügung mehrer dieser letzteren*. 2 vols. Leipzig, 1828.

Schlumbohm, Jürgen. *Freiheit. Die Anfänge der bürgerlichen Emanzipationsbewegung in Deutschland im Spiegel ihres Leitwortes (ca. 1760–ca. 1800)*. Düsseldorf, 1975.

Schmidt, Adalbert. *Helferich Peter Sturz. Ein Kapitel aus der Schrifttumsgeschichte zwischen Aufklärung und Sturm und Drang*. Reichenberg, 1939.

Schmidt, H. D. "The Hessian Mercenaries: The Career of a Political Cliché." *History*, LVIII (1958), 207–212.

Schmitt, Albert R. *Herder und Amerika*. The Hague and Paris, 1967.

Schneider, Franz. *Pressefreiheit und politische Öffentlichkeit. Studien zur politischen Geschichte Deutschlands bis 1848*. Neuwied and Berlin, 1966.

Schulte, Albert. *Ein englischer Gesandter am Rhein. George Cressener als Bevollmächtiger Gesandter an den Höfen der geistlichen Kurfürsten und beim Niederrheinisch-Westfälischen Kreis 1763–1781*. Bonn, 1971.

Schünzel, Eva. "Die deutsche Auswanderung nach Nordamerika im 17. and 18. Jahrhundert." Unpublished Ph.D. dissertation, University of Würzburg, 1959.

Sell, Friedrich C. "American Influences Upon Goethe." *American-German Review*, IX, no. 4 (1943), 15–17.

Sieveking, Heinrich. "Das Handlungshaus Voght und Sieveking." *Zeitschrift des Vereins für Hamburgische Geschichte*, XVII (1912), 54–128.

———. *Georg Heinrich Sieveking. Lebensbild eines Hamburgischen Kaufmanns aus dem Zeitalter der französischen Revolution*. Berlin, 1913.

Singer, Ernst. "Der Soldatenhandel deutscher Fürsten im 18. Jahrhundert in der schönen Literatur." Unpublished Ph.D. dissertation, Univerity of Vienna, 1935.

Skard, Sigmund. *The American Myth and the European Mind: American Studies in Europe, 1776–1960*. Philadelphia, 1961.

———. *American Studies in Europe: Their History and Present Organization*. Vol. I. Philadelphia, 1958.

Stadelmann, Rudolf. *Deutschland und Westeuropa. Drei Aufsätze*. Schloß Laupheim, 1948.

Städtler, Erhard. "Die Ansbach-Bayreuther Truppen im Amerikanischen Unabhängigkeitskrieg 1777–1783." Published Ph.D. dissertation, University of Erlangen, 1955.

Stammler, Wolfgang. "Politische Schlagworte in der Zeit der Aufklärung." In *Lebenskräfte der abendländischen Geistesgeschichte. Dank- und Erinnerungsgabe an Walter Goetz zum 80. Geburtstag* (Marburg, 1948), 199–259.

Stern, Alfred. "Jakob Mauvillon als Dichter und Publizist." *Preußische Jahrbücher*, CCXXX (1932), 239–252.

Strassburger, Ralph Beaver. *Pennsylvania German Pioneers: A Publication of the Original Lists of Arrivals in the Port of Philadelphia from 1727 to 1808.* Edited by William John Hinke. 3 vols. Norristown, Pa., 1934.

Streisand, Joachim. *Geschichtliches Denken von der deutschen Frühaufklärung bis zur Klassik.* Berlin, 1964.

Stübler, Eberhard. *Johann Heinrich Ferdinand v. Autenrieth 1772–1835. Professor der Medizin und Kanzler der Universität Tübingen.* Stuttgart, 1948.

Sweet, Paul R. *Friedrich von Gentz, Defender of the Old Order.* Madison, Wis., 1941.

Tiemann, Hermann. "Christoph Daniel Ebeling. Hamburger Amerikanist, Bibliothekar und Herausgeber Klopstocks." *Zeitschrift des Vereins für Hamburgische Geschichte*, XLI (1951), 352–374.

Trautz, Fritz. *Die Pfälzische Auswanderung nach Nordamerika im 18. Jahrhundert.* Heidelberg, 1959.

Tschirch, Otto. *Geschichte der öffentlichen Meinung in Preußen vom Baseler Frieden bis zum Zusammenbruch des Staates (1795–1806).* 2 vols. Weimar, 1933–1934.

Uhlig, Ludwig. *Georg Forster. Einheit und Mannigfaltigkeit in seiner geistigen Welt.* Tübingen, 1965.

Urzidill, Johannes. *Das Glück der Gegenwart. Goethes Amerikabild.* Zurich and Stuttgart, 1958.

Valjavec, Fritz. *Die Entstehung der politischen Strömungen in Deutschland, 1770–1815.* Munich. 1951.

Victory, Beatrice Marguerite. *Benjamin Franklin and Germany.* New York, 1915.

Vierhaus, Rudolf. "Deutschland vor der Französischen Revolution." Unpublished Habilitationsschrift, University of Münster, 1961.

———. "Politisches Bewußtsein in Deutschland vor 1789." *Der Staat*, VI (1967), 175–196.

Vossler, Otto. *Die amerikanischen Revolutionsideale in ihrem Verhältnis zu den europäischen. Untersucht an Thomas Jefferson.* Munich and Berlin, 1929.

Wadepuhl, Walter. "Goethe and America." *Deutsch-Amerikanische Geschichtsblätter*, XXII/XXIII (1924), 77–108.

———. *Goethe's Interest in the New World.* Jena, 1934.

Wagner, W. "Erlebnisse eines Braunschweigers im nordamerikanischen Freiheitskriege." *Braunschweigisches Magazin*, XIII (1907), 49–55, 61–66.

Wahl, Hans. *Geschichte des Teutschen Merkur. Ein Beitrag zur Geschichte des Journalismus im achtzehnten Jahrhundert.* Berlin, 1914.

Walz, Hans. "Benjamin Franklin in Hannover 1766." *Hannoversche Geschichts-blätter*, N.S., XXI (1967), 59–65.

Walz, John A. "The American Revolution and German Literature." *Modern Language Notes*, XVI (1901), 336–351, 411–418, 449–462.

————. "Three Swabian Journalists and the American Revolution." *Americana Germanica*, IV (1902), 95–129, 267–291, *German American Annals*, I (1903), 209–224, 257–274, 347–356, 406–419, 593–600.

Wätjen, Hermann. *Aus der Frühzeit des Nordatlantikverkehrs. Studien zur Geschichte der deutschen Schiffahrt und deutschen Auswanderung nach den Vereinigten Staaten bis zum Ende des amerikanischen Bürgerkrieges*. Leipzig, 1932.

Weber, Paul Carl. *America in Imaginative German Literature in the First Half of the Nineteenth Century*. New York, 1926.

Wehe, Walter. "Das Amerika-Erlebnis in der deutschen Literatur." *Geist der Zeit*, XVII (1939), 96–104.

Weinhold, Karl. *Heinrich Christian Boie. Beitrag zur Geschichte der deutschen Literatur im achtzehnten Jahrhundert*. Halle, 1868.

Weissel, Bernhard. *Von wem die Gewalt in den Staaten herrührt. Beiträge zu den Auswirkungen der Staats- und Gesellschaftsauffassungen Rousseaus auf Deutschland im letzten Viertel des 18. Jahrhunderts*. Berlin, 1963.

Wenck, Woldemar. *Deutschland vor hundert Jahren. Politische Meinung und Stimmungen bei Anbruch der Revolutionszeit*. 2 vols. Leipzig, 1887–1890.

Wertheim, Ursula. "Der amerikanische Unabhängigkeitskampf im Spiegel der zeitgenössischen deutschen Literatur." *Weimarer Beiträge*, III (1957), 429–470.

Wittke, Carl. "The America Theme in Continental European Literatures." *Mississippi Valley Historical Review*, XXVIII (1941–1942), 3–26.

Witzleben, Cäsar Dietrich von. *Geschichte der Leipziger Zeitung. Zur Erinnerung an das zweihundertjährige Bestehen der Zeitung*. Leipzig, 1860.

Wolzendorff, Kurt. *Staatsrecht und Naturrecht in der Lehre vom Widerstandsrecht des Volkes gegen rechtswidrige Ausübung der Staatsgewalt. Zugleich ein Beitrag zur Entwicklungsgeschichte des modernen Staatsgedankens*. 1916. Reprint. Aalen, 1961.

Zelger, Renate. "Der Historisch-Politische Briefwechsel und die Staatsanzeigen August Ludwig von Schlözers als Zeitschrift und Zeitbild." Unpublished Ph.D. dissertation, University of Munich, 1953.

Zenker, Ernst Victor. *Geschichte der Wiener Journalistik von den Anfängen bis zum Jahre 1848. Ein Beitrag zur deutschen Culturgeschichte. Mit einem bibliographischen Anhang*. Vienna and Leipzig, 1892.

Zermelo, Theodor. "August Ludwig Schlözer, ein Publizist im alten Reich." In *Jahresbericht über die Friedrichs-Werdersche Gewerbeschule in Berlin* (Berlin, 1875).

Zimmermann, Paul. "Beiträge zum Verständnis des zwischen Braunschweig und England am 9. Januar 1776 geschlossenen Subsidienvertrages." *Jahrbuch des Geschichtsvereins für das Herzogtum Braunschweig*, XIII (1914), 160–176.

Index

A

Accarias de Sérionne, Jacques, 223
Achenwall, Gottfried, 218
Adair, James, 135
Adams, John, 70, 91, 97, 186, 188, 298, 307, 317, 325; on literature concerning American Revolution, 35, 242, 244, 253; his *Defense of the Constitutions* unknown in Germany, 37
Adams, John Quincy, 319, 320, 322, 347; traveled in Germany, 40; American emissary at Berlin, 271
Adams, Samuel, 70, 97, 131, 186, 188
Ahlwardt, Peter, 215, 229
Alfieri, Conte Vittorio: on Franklin, 252
Alien and Sedition Acts, 323–326 *passim*
Alleghenies, 65
Allgemeine deutsche Bibliothek, 351
Altona, 234
Altstetten, 47, 147, 227
America: as utopian ideal, 307–311 *passim*, 341 (*see also* Ebeling, Christoph Daniel; Forster, Georg; Jacobins, German; Iselin, Isaak; Knigge, Adolph Freiherr von; Rebmann, Andreas Georg Friedrich von; Schmohl, Johann Christian; Schubart, Christian Friedrich Daniel); future greatness of, 199–205 *passim*, 311–317 *passim* (*see also* Bülow, Dietrich Heinrich Freiherr von; Crome, August Friedrich Wilhelm; Hennings, August von; Lynar, Rochus Friedrich Graf von; Mangelsdorf, Karl Ehregott; Milbiller, Joseph; Schubart, Christian Friedrich Daniel; Snell, Karl Philipp Michael; Sprengel, Matthias Christian)
Americana Germanica: compared with total book production, 14; characteristics of, 30–37 *passim*, 212–213, 215, 222
American Revolution, xi, xvii, xviii, xix, xx, xxii, xxiii, 32, 49, 51, 63, 66, 89, 90, 99, 131, 145, 152; impact of, xi, xx–xxi, xxii–xxiii, 172–173, 203, 204, 207, 210–211, 237, 247, 261, 262, 307, 308, 313–314, 329–346 *passim*, 350, 352, 354; considered as globally important, xii, xvii, 131–141 *passim*, 289–293 *passim*; considered as "revolution," xii, xxi–xxii,

134–138 *passim*; German interest in, 8, 39, 40, 56; expected consequences of, 11, 194–205 *passim*, 314; inadequately dealt with by newspapers, 24, 40; dealt with in periodicals, 25, 29, 40; German books on, 32–35 *passim*; history of, written by Sprengel, 52; omitted in Ebeling's *Erdbeschreibung*, 56; Schlözer's concern with, 56; Remer's concern with, 57; compared with French Revolution, 68, 279–289 *passim*, 293–301 *passim*; inadequate information on, 70; fundamental principles of, 73, 131–180 *passim*, 186, 188, 190, 191, 239, 248, 277, 318, 321, 324, 349; reasons for, 78, 80, 81, 94; legality of, 81–95 *passim*, 99; as expression of natural rights doctrine, 83, 92, 93; opponents of, 87, 89, 90, 93, 94, 146, 147, 148, 156, 158, 172, 173, 189, 198, 202, 217, 218, 225, 226, 228, 229, 230, 234, 238, 243, 253, 254, 266, 334, 335, 354; advocates of, 89, 90, 91, 103, 104, 105, 147, 148, 171, 172–173, 195, 199, 204, 221, 225–226, 227, 228, 229, 231, 232, 233, 234, 252, 265, 267, 325, 326, 333–337 *passim*; and subsidiary treaties, 118, 130; popularizes idea of liberty, 144–145; and equality, 152–156 *passim*, 162; achievements of, 160, 170, 171, 177–179, 190, 191, 192, 198, 231; historical parallels to, 181–193 *passim*; judgment on, 206–256 *passim*, 317, 326, 345–350 *passim*, 352, 363; personified by Franklin, 249–256 *passim*, 357, 358; as political model, 292, 293, 301, 303, 304, 364; set apart from American present, 327–328; as expression of Enlightenment ideals, 353, 355–364 *passim*. *See also* Frederick II of Prussia; French Revolution; War of Independence
Amerikabild: emergence of, xxii, 323–326
Anburey, Thomas, 65
André, Christian Carl, 64
Anger, 230
Anhalt-Zerbst, 90, 118, 216
Ansbach, 235
Ansbach-Bayreuth, 47, 48, 160, 219, 238;